—— CHRISTIANITY IN ——

East and Southeast Asia

Editorial Team

Editors
Kenneth R. Ross
Francis D. Alvarez SJ
Todd M. Johnson

Associate Editor
Albert W. Hickman

Managing Editor
Julia Kim

Editorial Advisory Board
Alexander Chow
José Mario C. Francisco SJ
Septemmy Lakawa
Julie Ma
Peter C. Phan
Kang-San Tan

Demographic Profile
Editor: Gina A. Zurlo
Data Analyst: Peter F. Crossing
Layout and Design: Justin Long
Cartography: Bryan Nicholson

9. Christianity in Eastern and Southern Europe
10. Compact Atlas of Global Christianity

As series editors, we rely heavily on the regional expertise of the dedicated third editor who joins us for each volume. Furthermore, each volume has its own editorial advisory board, made up of senior scholars with authoritative knowledge of the field in question. We work together to define the essay topics for the volume, arrange for compilation of the required demographic data, recruit the authors of the essays and edit their work. Statistical and demographic information is drawn from the highly regarded *World Christian Database* maintained by the Center for the Study of Global Christianity at Gordon-Conwell Theological Seminary (South Hamilton, MA, USA) and published by Brill. For each volume, 35–40 authors are recruited to write the essays, and it is ultimately upon their scholarship and commitment that we depend in order to create an original and authoritative work of reference.

Each volume in the series will be, we hope, a significant book in its own right and a contribution to the study of Christianity in the region in question. At the same time, each is a constituent part of a greater whole – the 10-volume series, which aims to provide a comprehensive analysis of global Christianity that will be groundbreaking in its demographic quality and analytical range. Our hope is that the Companions will be of service to anyone seeking a fuller understanding of the worldwide presence of the Christian faith.

Kenneth R. Ross and Todd M. Johnson
Series Editors

Volume Preface

This volume combines two United Nations regions, Eastern and Southeastern Asia. Together these span more than 16 million square kilometres. This is only 11% of the total land area of the planet, yet it is home to more than 2.3 billion people, almost one-third of the world's population. Within this terrain are found breath-taking contrasts in such matters as wealth and poverty or war and peace. In East Asia, we have the economic juggernaut that is China. Japan has been a member of the Group of 7, the countries with the most advanced economies, since it was known as the Group of 5 in 1973. Yet right beside South Korea, the world's eleventh largest economy by nominal gross domestic product (GDP) (as of 2018), is North Korea, where, according to a 2017 United Nations study, more than half of children under two years old and half of pregnant and breastfeeding women are malnourished. In Southeast Asia, the Credit Suisse Research Institute reports that in 2018 Singapore was home to more than 180,000 millionaires. According to *US News and World Report*, as of 2018, Hong Kong had 93 billionaires, ranking it seventh in the world. By contrast, in 2017, the entire GPD of Timor-Leste was less than US$3 billion.

In the 2018 Global Peace Index, this part of the world had two countries in the top 10 (Singapore at number 8 and Japan at number 9). By contrast, the Philippines ranked 137th out of 163. Security analysts predict that in this and nearby countries, fundamentalist violence will increase before the situation gets better. Yet the Philippines also ranks in the upper half of all countries in the UN's 2018 World Happiness Report. More than 1,800 languages are spoken in these regions, by adherents of Buddhism, Chinese folk religion, Islam and the fastest-growing belief system in the region, Christianity. The Christian faith itself is far from monolithic in East and Southeast Asia. Rather, it comes to expression in many different ways. How does one present the many facets of Christianity in a diverse expanse of ethnicities, histories, cultures and sensitivities?

He Qi's *Adoration of the Magi* has two versions: one in crayon and gouache, as reproduced on the cover of this volume; and the other in silk, the painstaking work of Chinese artisans who dyed individual silk strands and then wove them following He Qi's design. Depending on where the viewer stands, the different hues in the tapestry take on a myriad of tones, tints and shades. Each viewpoint reveals a subtly different art piece. This volume presents Christianity in East and Southeast Asia from many points of view, from the diverse perspectives of our authors, and from a great variety of disciplinary, cultural and confessional standpoints. It is the fruit of a collaborative effort that has spanned every country in the two regions.

In pursuit of understanding, the volume offers four angles of analysis. The first is demographic, using the methodology of the highly successful *Atlas of Global Christianity* (Edinburgh University Press, 2009) to present reliable statistical information in an attractive, user-friendly format. Maps and charts depict the status of Christianity regionally and in terms of the principal church traditions. This ranges from countries where Christians form a majority of the population to others where the Christian presence is marginal. It also varies from Christian communities that have been established for many generations to those formed by new movements of faith in the twenty-first century.

The second angle of analysis is at the country level. Account is taken of the presence and influence of Christianity in each of the 19 countries and regions in East and Southeast Asia. Scholars who are either indigenous or have long experience of the region have contributed interpretative essays that offer a 'critical insider' perspective on the way in which Christianity is finding expression in their context. Most countries are the subject of a dedicated essay, while China, in view of its size and population, is considered in three essays that examine each of its three main forms of Christianity, with a further two essays devoted to the Special Administrative Regions of Hong Kong and Macau.

Thirdly, Christianity in East and Southeast Asia is considered in terms of its principal ecclesial forms or traditions. Four types of church are considered: Anglican, Orthodox, Protestant and Catholic. It is a distinctive feature of this volume that it does not include an essay on Independent churches. This respects the problematic nature of this category in the two regions, while an editorial note points to essays elsewhere in the volume that include consideration of this ecclesial type. In addition, the Evangelical and Pentecostal/Charismatic movements, which cut across ecclesial affiliation, are examined.

Fourthly, selected themes are considered. Eight of these run right through the entire Edinburgh Companions series: faith and culture; worship and spirituality; theology; social and political context; mission and evangelism; gender; religious freedom; and inter-religious relations. A further two have been selected by the editorial board specifically for this volume on account of their salience in the context of East and Southeast Asia: migration; and colonial and post-colonial context. Each of these themes is examined on a region-wide basis, deepening our understanding of features that are definitive for Christianity in this part of the world.

As is evident from the short bibliography offered at the end of each essay, this book rests on the body of scholarship that has illumined our understanding of East and Southeast Asian Christianity, particularly the burgeoning literature of the early twenty-first century. Besides many detailed local studies, much insight has been derived from *The Oxford Handbook of Christianity in Asia*, edited by Felix Wilfred (Oxford University Press, 2014), which has become the standard reference work on Asian Christianity. An earlier valuable but now dated work is *A Dictionary of Asian Christianity*, edited by Scott Sunquist and David Wu Chu Sing (Eerdmans, 2001). A magisterial historical study is Samuel Hugh Moffett's two-volume *History of Christianity in Asia* (Orbis, 1998, 2005). Robbie B. H. Goh's *Christianity in Southeast Asia* (Institute of Southeast Asia Studies, 2005) offers a concise and helpful introduction. The three-volume *Asian Christian Theologies: A Research Guide to Authors, Movements, Sources* by John C. England, Jose Kuttianimattathil, John M. Prior, Lily A. Quintos, David Suh Kwang-sun and Janice Wickeri (Orbis, 2002, 2003, 2004) is comprehensive in its coverage and well geared to be a resource for theological research.

While resting on the preceding scholarship, this volume breaks new ground through its reliable demographic analysis, its contemporary focus, the indigenous authorship of its essays and the originality of the analyses. The essay authors employ a variety of disciplinary approaches – historical, theological, sociological, missiological, anthropological – as appropriate to their topics. Taken together, the volume offers a deeply textured and highly nuanced account of Christianity in East and Southeast Asia, one that will reward the attention of any who wish to deepen their knowledge of this subject.

Kenneth R. Ross
Francis D. Alvarez sj
Todd M. Johnson

May 2019

Contributors

Francis D. Alvarez SJ, a Filipino Jesuit priest, is Assistant Professor of Biblical Theology and Religious Education at Loyola School of Theology in Quezon City, the Philippines. He also teaches theology at the Ateneo de Manila University.
Christianity in East and Southeast Asia; Brunei

David Andrianoff was raised in Laos by missionary parents and served there himself with World Concern from 1983 to 1992. He continues to visit Laos and church leaders there at least once each year.
Laos

Maruja M. B. Asis is Director of Research and Publications of the Scalabrini Migration Center, based in Manila, the Philippines. She is a sociologist who has been researching migration and social change in Asia.
Migration

Sharon A. Bong is Associate Professor in Gender and Religious Studies at Monash University, Malaysia. She is author of *The Tension Between Women's Rights and Religions* (Edwin Mellen Press, 2006) and co-editor (with Pushpa Joseph) of *Re-imagining Marriage and Family in Asia: Asian Christian Women's Perspectives* (Strategic Information and Research Development Centre, 2008).
Gender

Yang-en Cheng is Professor of Church History at the Taiwan Graduate School of Theology. A long-term participant in the ecumenical movement, he is currently a Central Committee member of the World Council of Churches, representing the Presbyterian Church in Taiwan.
Taiwan

Alexander Chow is Senior Lecturer in Theology and World Christianity at the School of Divinity, University of Edinburgh. He has written two books, most recently *Chinese Public Theology: Generational Shifts and Confucian Imagination in Chinese Christianity* (Oxford University Press, 2018), and is an editor of the academic journal *Studies in World Christianity* (Edinburgh University Press).
Theology

Meehyun Chung is an ordained minister of the Presbyterian Church in the Republic of Korea (PROK), Professor of Systematic Theology at the United

Graduate School of Theology of Yonsei University, Seoul, South Korea, and Chaplain to Yonsei University. She has served as Vice-President of the Ecumenical Association of Third World Theologians (EATWOT) and as head of the Women and Gender Desk at Mission 21, Switzerland (2005–13).
South Korea

Jayeel Cornelio is Associate Professor of Developmental Studies and Director of the Development Studies Program at the Ateneo de Manila University, the Philippines. A sociologist of religion, he is the author of *Being Catholic in the Contemporary Philippines: Young People Reinterpreting Religion* (Routledge, 2016) and the associate editor of the journal *Social Sciences and Missions* (Brill).
The Philippines

Sanurak Fongvarin is Director of the Research Institute for Thai Church Development and full-time Lecturer in Research Methods for Ministries at Bangkok Institute of Theology, Christian University of Thailand.
Thailand

José Mario C. Francisco SJ, a Filipino Jesuit professor at the Ateneo de Manila University and Pontifical Gregorian University, explores the interface between cultural studies and theology in Asian and Philippine contexts. He is a member of the editorial boards of the *International Journal of Asian Christianity* and *Asia Pacific Mission Studies*.
Faith and Culture

Bayarjargal Garamtseren is Mongolian Standard Version project manager in the Mongolian Union Bible Society and a board member and Academic Committee Chair of the Mongolian Research Institute for Christianity. He pastors the Life Community Church in Ulaanbaatar, Mongolia, and is married with four children.
Mongolia

Louis Ha is Director of the Centre for Catholic Studies, Chinese University of Hong Kong. A Catholic diocesan priest, he is author of *Foundation of the Catholic Mission in Hong Kong, 1841–1894* (Open Dissertation Press, 1998) and editor of the *Hong Kong Journal of Catholic Studies* (published by the Centre for Catholic Studies).
Macau

Hrang Hlei is Director of Christian Education and a pastor at Indiana Chin Baptist Church, Indianapolis, Indiana, USA. An ordained American Baptist minister, he is the author of *The Formation of Chin Immigrant Congregations in the United States: Discovering Their Ecclesiological Identities* (Luther Seminary, 2015) and a former faculty member of the Myanmar Institute of Theology, Yangon, Myanmar.
Myanmar

Mary Ho is International Executive Leader of All Nations Family, a global missions organisation focused on igniting church-planting movements in more than 40 countries. She received her Doctor of Strategic Leadership degree from Regent University in 2016.
The Future of Christianity in East and Southeast Asia

Hwa Yung is Bishop Emeritus of the Methodist Church in Malaysia and taught theology for many years in Malaysia and Singapore. He has served on the Lausanne Board and on the Council for the Oxford Centre for Mission Studies.
Malaysia

Sulistyowati Irianto is Professor of Legal Anthropology at the Faculty of Law, University of Indonesia. She publishes books and articles focused on law, society and gender justice.
Indonesia

Filomeno Jacob SJ is Associate Professor of Sociology and Cultural Anthropology at the Faculty of Social Sciences of the Pontifical Gregorian University. He was a cabinet member for the United Nations Transitional Administration in East Timor (UNTAET) in 2001.
Timor-Leste

Violet James is chaplain at the Singapore Bible College, where she formerly served as Professor of Church History for more than 35 years, teaching Asian church history and Asian religions.
Singapore

Todd M. Johnson is Paul E. and Eva B. Toms Distinguished Professor of Mission and Global Christianity and co-Director of the Center for the Study of Global Christianity at Gordon-Conwell Theological Seminary in South Hamilton, Massachusetts, USA. His most recent book is the *World Christian Encyclopedia*, 3rd edition (Edinburgh University Press, 2019). He also serves as a Series Editor for the Edinburgh Companions to Global Christianity (Edinburgh University Press).
Methodology and Sources of Christian and Religious Affiliation

Philo Kim is Associate Professor at the Institute for Peace and Unification Studies (IPUS), Seoul National University, South Korea.
North Korea

Sebastian C. H. Kim is Director of the Korean Studies Center and Professor of Theology and Public Life at Fuller Theological Seminary, California, USA. Previously, he held the Chair in Theology and Public Life in the Faculty of Education and Theology at York St John University, UK. He is the co-author (with Kirsteen Kim) of *Christianity as a World Religion: An Introduction* (Bloomsbury Academic, 2nd revised edition 2016).
Social and Political Context

Sivin Kit is Lecturer in Christian Theology and Religious Studies at the Malaysia Theological Seminary. He also serves as Director of the Centre for Religion and Society and is an ordained Lutheran pastor.
Inter-Religious Relations

Akemi Kugimiya is Professor at the Center for Catholic Education of Shirayuri University in Japan. She is the co-author of *The Aspects of Christianity in Modern Japan* (Oriens Institute for Religious Research, 2008), co-editor (with Masayuki Shimizu, Yoshio Tsuruoka and Naoki Kuwabara) of *The Meaning of Life* (Oriens Institute for Religious Research, 2017) and the editor of *The Collected Works of Klaus Riesenhuber* (Chisenshyokan, 2015).
Japan

Septemmy E. Lakawa is President of the Jakarta Theological Seminary, Indonesia (2019–23). Her research interests are in the areas of mission theology, trauma and theology, and feminist theology.
Mission and Evangelism

Timothy T. N. Lim is a Visiting Lecturer with the London School of Theology. Formerly, he was the Director of Chinese Research and Training at the Carey Baptist College (Auckland, New Zealand). He has published on ecclesiology, ecumenism and theological trajectories in Asia in addition to *Ecclesial Recognition with Hegelian Philosophy, Social Psychology, and Continental Political Theory* (Brill, 2017).
Protestants

Manhong Melissa Lin is Associate General Secretary of the China Christian Council and Academic Dean and Associate Professor of Christian Ethics at Nanjing Union Theological Seminary. She is ordained and the first woman PhD holder in the Protestant Church in Mainland China.
Mainland China (Protestant)

Seree Lorgunpai is General Secretary of the Thailand Bible Society and a member of the Committee on Translation Policy of the United Bible Societies.
Thailand

Julie Ma is Associate Professor of Intercultural Studies at Oral Roberts University, Tulsa, Oklahoma, USA. She is the author of *When the Spirit Meets the Spirits: Pentecostal Ministry Among the Kankana-ey Tribe in the Philippines* (Peter Lang, 2000).
Pentecostals/Charismatics

Wonsuk Ma, a Korean Pentecostal, serves as Dean and Distinguished Professor of Global Christianity at Oral Roberts University, Tulsa, Oklahoma, USA. He is the author of many publications and is series editor and publisher of the 35-volume Regnum Edinburgh Centenary Series (2009–17).
Worship and Spirituality

Barnabas Mam is Asia Ministry Advisor of Ambassadors for Christ International. He is a gospel songwriter and the author of *Church Behind the Wire: A Story of Faith in the Killing Fields* (Moody, 2012).
Cambodia

Paul Marshall is Wilson Professor of Religious Freedom and Research Professor of Political Science at Baylor University, Senior Fellow at the Hudson Institute's Center for Religious Freedom, and Senior Fellow of the Religious Freedom Institute and member of its South and Southeast Asia Action Team.
Religious Freedom

Ken Christoph Miyamoto is Professor of Christian Studies at Kobe Shoin Women's University in Kobe, Japan. He received his PhD in Mission and Ecumenics from Princeton Theological Seminary, USA, and is the author of *God's Mission in Asia* (Pickwick, 2007).
Anglicans

Peter C. Phan is the inaugural holder of the Ignacio Ellacuria Chair of Catholic Social Thought at Georgetown University, Washington, DC. A native of Vietnam, he has obtained three doctorates and authored and edited some 30 books and 300 essays on theology and the history of missions.
Vietnam

Daniel Franklin E. Pilario CM is Professor at St Vincent School of Theology – Adamson University, Quezon City, the Philippines. He is the author of *Back to the Rough Grounds of Praxis: Exploring Theological Method with Pierre Bourdieu* (Peeters, 2005). He belongs to the editorial board of *Concilium* and other philosophical and theological journals. As a member of the Congregation of the Mission, he ministers in a garbage dump parish in Manila.
Catholics

David Ro is Director of the J. Christy Wilson Center for World Missions at Gordon-Conwell Theological Seminary, South Hamilton, Massachusetts, USA, and serves as Regional Director for the Lausanne Movement in East Asia.
Mainland China (House Churches)

Kenneth R. Ross is Professor of Theology at Zomba Theological College, Malawi. His most recent book is *Mission as God's Spiral of Renewal* (Mzuni Press, 2019) and he serves as a Series Editor for the Edinburgh Companions to Global Christianity (Edinburgh University Press).
Brunei

Nikolay Samoylov is Professor and Head of the Department of Theory of Asian and African Social Development at Saint Petersburg State University, Russia, where he also serves as Director of the Center for Chinese Studies. He has published extensively on Russian interactions with China and Japan.
Orthodox

Kang-San Tan serves as General Director of BMS World Mission – the Baptist Missionary Society. Previously he was Director for Mission Research at Overseas Missionary Fellowship, Head of Mission Studies at Redcliffe College, UK, and Executive Director of AsiaCMS, a network for Asian mission movements based in Kuala Lumpur, Malaysia.
Evangelicals

Edmond Tang was Director of East Asian Christian Studies at the University of Birmingham, UK, before his retirement. He researched extensively on Asian theology and Chinese Christianity and was editor of the *China Study Journal* from 1990 to 2011.
Mainland China (Catholic)

Wai Ching Angela Wong is Vice President for Programs at the United Board for Christian Higher Education in Asia, having earlier served as Professor in the Department of Cultural and Religious Studies, the Chinese University of Hong Kong. Her latest works include *Gender and Family in East Asia* (Routledge, 2014), *Sex/Gender Politics and the Local Movements* (Commercial, 2015) and *Christian Women in Chinese Society: The Anglican Story* (HKU Press, 2018).
Colonial and Post-Colonial Context

Fuk-tsang Ying is Professor and Director of the Divinity School of Chung Chi College, the Chinese University of Hong Kong. His research focuses on state–church relations in China and the history of Protestant Christianity in China and Hong Kong.
Hong Kong

Ambrose-Aristotle Zographos (Song-Am Cho) is Metropolitan of the Orthodox Metropolis of Korea and Professor in Hankuk University of Foreign Studies, Seoul, South Korea. His publications include *Gabriel of Thessalonica and the Unpublished Homiliarion Attributed to Him* (in Greek; Kéntro Byzantinon Ereunon, 2007).
Orthodox

Gina A. Zurlo is co-Director of the Center for the Study of Global Christianity at Gordon-Conwell Theological Seminary, South Hamilton, Massachusetts, USA. She is co-editor of the *World Christian Database* and Associate Editor of the *World Religion Database*.
A Demographic Profile of Christianity in East and Southeast Asia; Methodology and Sources of Christian and Religious Affiliation

Introduction

A Demographic Profile of Christianity in East and Southeast Asia

Gina A. Zurlo

Majority Religion by Province, 2020

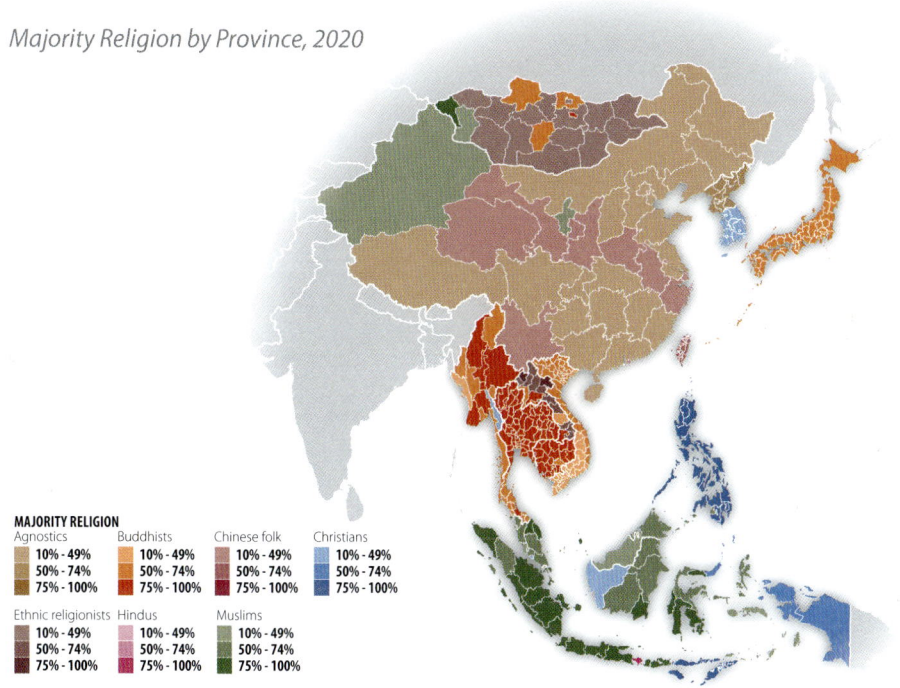

East and Southeast Asia are two of the most religiously diverse regions in the world. In 2020, they were home to significant percentages of Buddhists (22%), agnostics (22%), Chinese folk-religionists (20%), Christians (12%) and Muslims (12%). Of these large religions, Christianity experienced the fastest growth between 1970 and 2020 (3.1% per year).

Religions in East and Southeast Asia, 1970 and 2020

	1970		2020	
Religion	Adherents	%	Adherents	%
Buddhists	219,502,000	17.2	505,021,000	21.7
Agnostics	423,480,000	33.2	503,423,000	21.6
Chinese folk-religionists	237,681,000	18.6	465,951,000	20.0
Christians	62,196,000	4.9	281,889,000	12.1
Muslims	108,894,000	8.5	275,008,000	11.8
Atheists	100,445,000	7.9	111,072,000	4.8
Other	124,834,480	9.8	190,271,600	8.2
Total	1,277,032,000	100.0	2,332,635,000	100.0

Source: Todd M. Johnson and Gina A. Zurlo (eds), *World Christian Database* (Leiden/Boston: Brill), accessed July 2019. Figures do not add to 100% due to rounding.

Christianity in East and Southeast Asia, 1970–2020

Christians by Country, 2020
282 Million Christians, 12.1% of Population

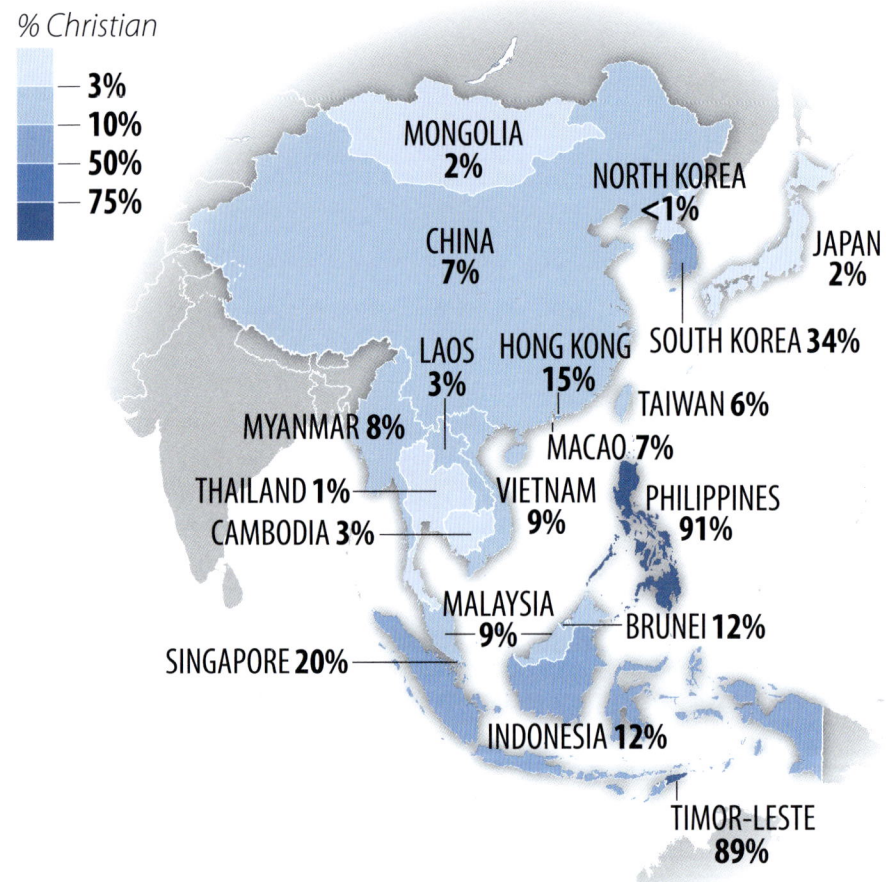

Christianity (282 million, 12% of region) in East and Southeast Asia has a long history that has reflected the religious, cultural, political and socio-economic diversity of the region. Churches in the region have experienced the political challenges of colonialism, conflict, communism and religious fundamentalism. Despite this, Christianity has grown in the region in recent decades, although in many countries still remains a small proportion of the population, most under 10%. Much of the growth has been in Pentecostal/Charismatic churches, and often among poor and marginalised people. China is, by far, home to the largest number of Christians (106 million), who are found in both government-sanctioned and 'underground' churches. The region is also home to Asia's only two Christian-majority countries: the Philippines and Timor-Leste, both with long Catholic histories.

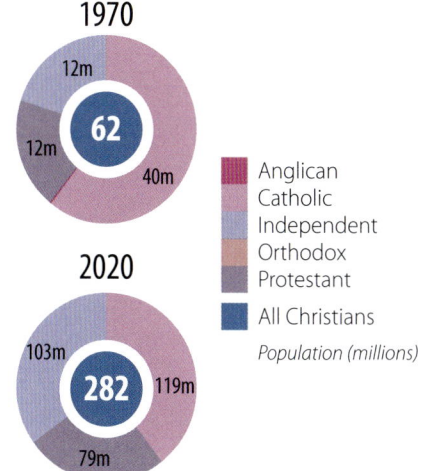

Major Christian traditions, 1970 and 2020
East and Southeast Asia is home to historic Catholic populations, such as in the Philippines and Vietnam, both with Christian populations that are more than 80% Catholic. The region is also home to newer Protestant and Independent churches. Independents grew the fastest between 1970 and 2020, from 12 million to 103 million.

Christians, 1970–2020
Christianity in East and Southeast Asia has been on a gradual increase since 1970, from 5% of the population then to 12% in 2020. Countries with the most significant growth include Brunei (6% to 12%), China (<1% to 7%) and Singapore (8% to 20%).

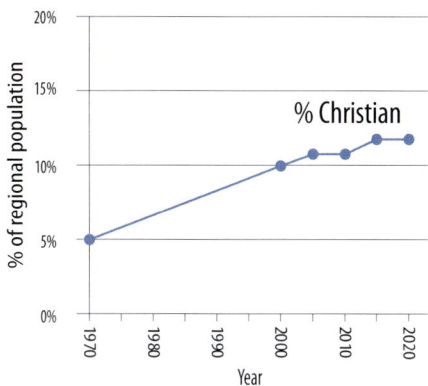

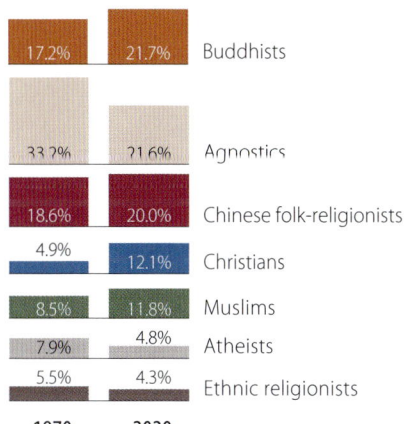

Religious affiliation, 1970 and 2020
Asia is the most religiously diverse continent as the historic home to many of the world's religions, including Christianity, Islam, Judaism, Sikhism and Jainism. The region experienced significant change in the twentieth century due to the rise of communism and state-imposed atheism in China.

Note: Throughout this profile, traditions will not add up to total Christians in each region because of double-affiliation and the unaffiliated. Only the religions over 1% are identified.

Major Christian Traditions, 1970 and 2020

Christians

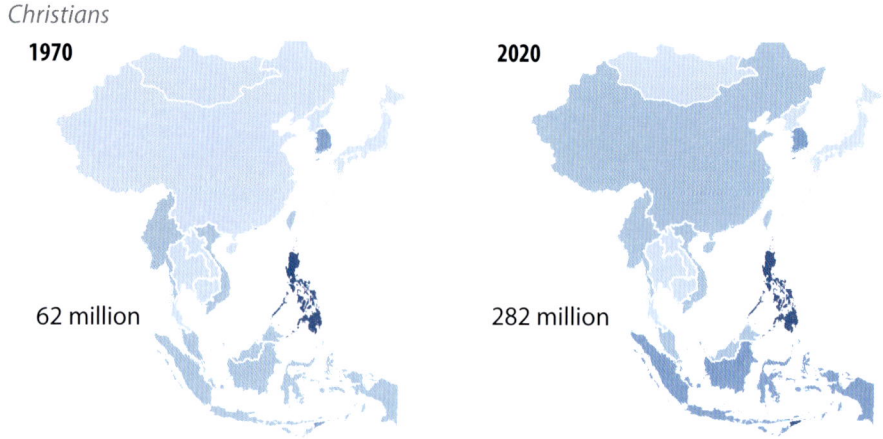

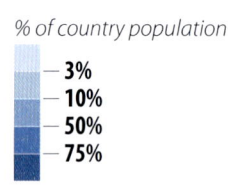

Overall, Christianity has grown in the region, although some countries experienced decline in their Christian populations from 1970 to 2020, such as Macao (13% to 7%) and North Korea (1% to 0.4%). The largest Christian populations are found in China (106 million), the Philippines (100 million) and Indonesia (33 million), the last of which is also the country with the most Muslims.

Anglicans

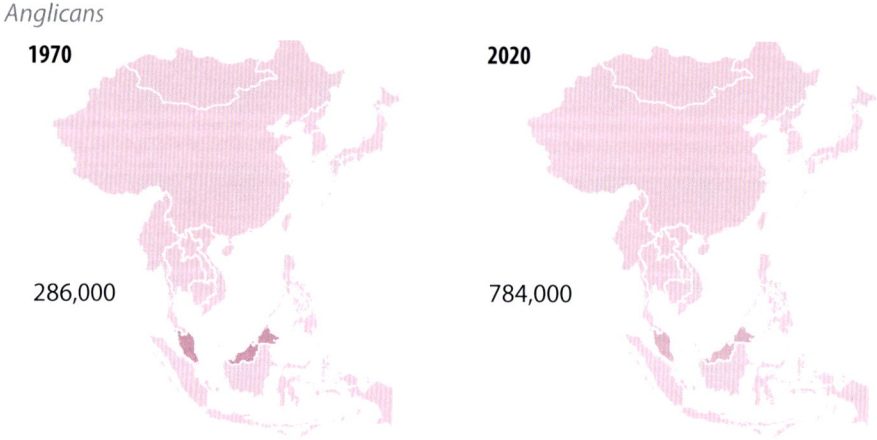

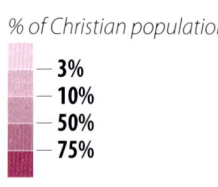

Anglicans in East and Southeast Asia represent a minority tradition, with less than 1 million adherents in 2020. Most countries in the region were not impacted by British colonisation, which decreased the tradition's influence. The highest percentages of Anglicans (among all Christians) are found in Malaysia (9%), Brunei (7%) and Hong Kong (3%).

Catholics

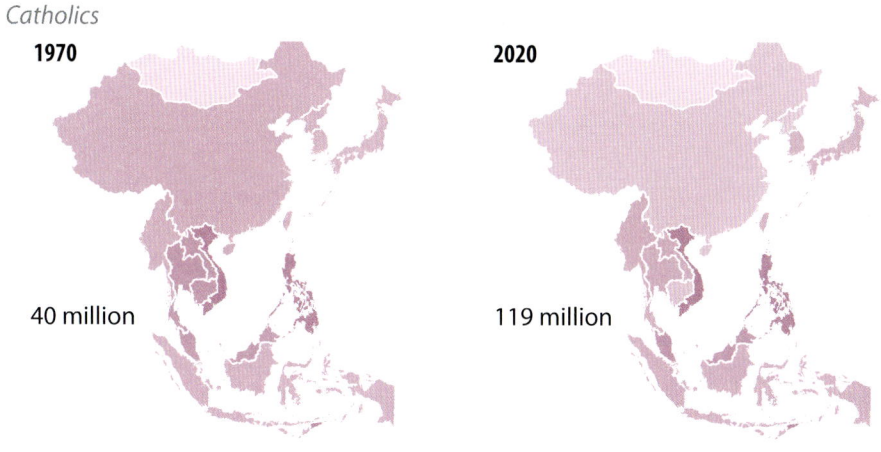

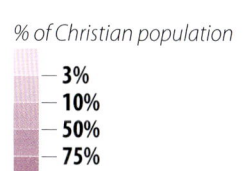

The number of Catholics has grown slightly in proportional terms (3% in 1970 to 5% in 2020) but substantially in absolute terms, from 40 million to 119 million. Between 1970 and 2020 the proportion of Catholics among Christians grew substantially in some countries, such as Brunei (1% to 39%) and South Korea (15% to 32%). In other countries, it dropped substantially, such as Cambodia (60% to 5%) and Laos (67% to 24%).

Independents

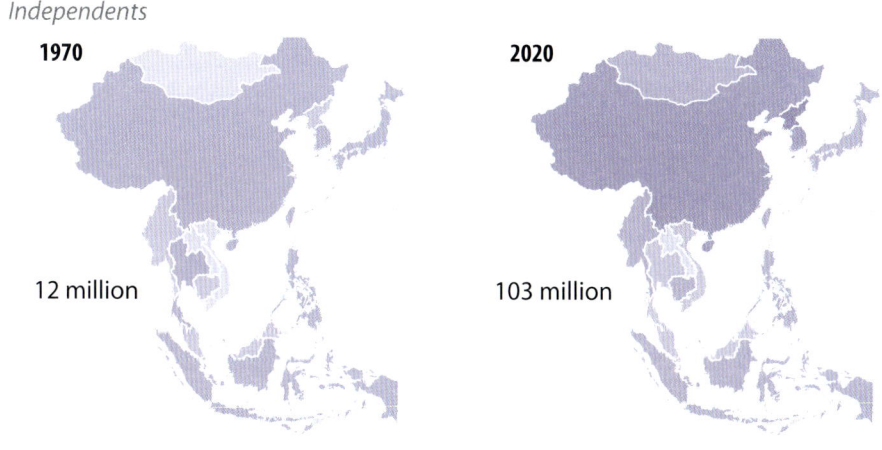

Independent Christianity grew the second fastest (after Pentecostals/Charismatics, although there is overlap between the two) regionally between 1970 and 2020, averaging over 4.3% per year. Thirty-seven per cent of all Christians in the region are Independents, due mainly to the large numbers of house churches in China, both rural and urban. The region is also home to large Independent churches such as the Philippine Independent Church.

Major Christian Traditions, 1970 and 2020

Orthodox

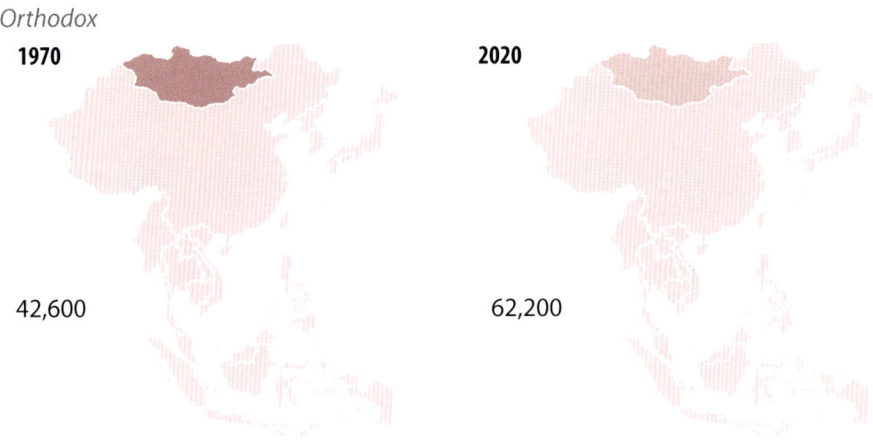

% of Christian population
- 3%
- 10%
- 50%
- 75%

Orthodox Christianity is a minority tradition in East and Southeast Asia, with fewer than 100,000 members in the region. Mongolia is the only country with any indication of a robust Orthodox community (4% of all Christians), due to historical Russian influence. Japan also has a historical Orthodox population, at 1% of all Christians.

Protestants

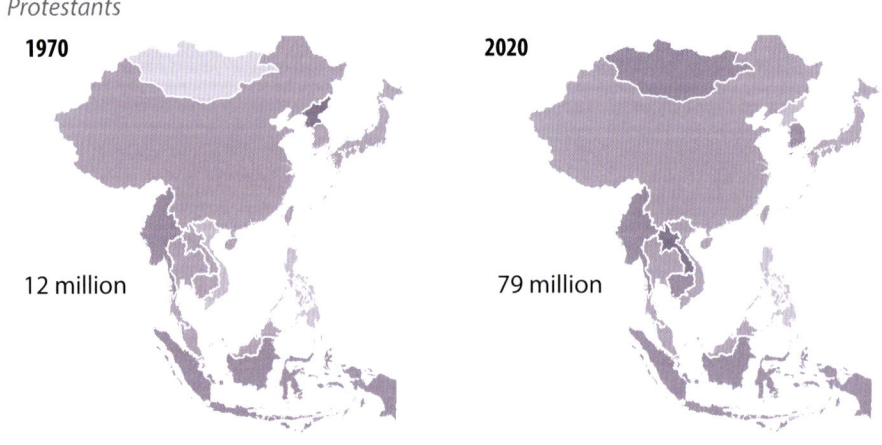

% of Christian population
- 3%
- 10%
- 50%
- 75%

Protestantism grew to 79 million adherents by 2020, up from 12 million in 1970. East Asia is home to a greater proportion of Protestants than Southeast Asia (36% of all Christians versus 21%). This is due mostly to large Protestant denominations in China (where 32% of all Christians are Protestants) and South Korea (where 60% of all Christians are Protestants).

Movements Within Christianity, 1970 and 2020

Evangelicals

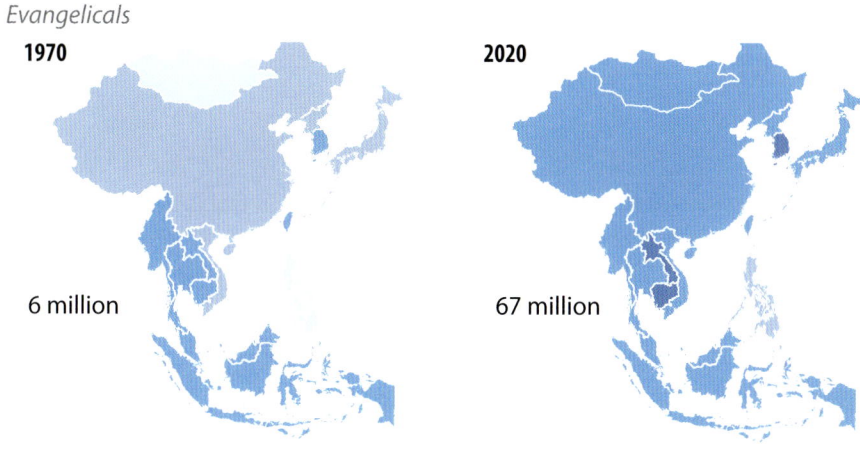

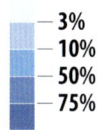

% of Christian population
- 3%
- 10%
- 50%
- 75%

Evangelicalism – historically a white, Western tradition – is a minority movement in East and Southeast Asia but grew from 0.5% of the region's population in 1970 to nearly 4% in 2020. South Korea has the highest Evangelical percentage (74% of all Christians), followed by Laos (73%) and Thailand (45%).

Pentecostals/Charismatics

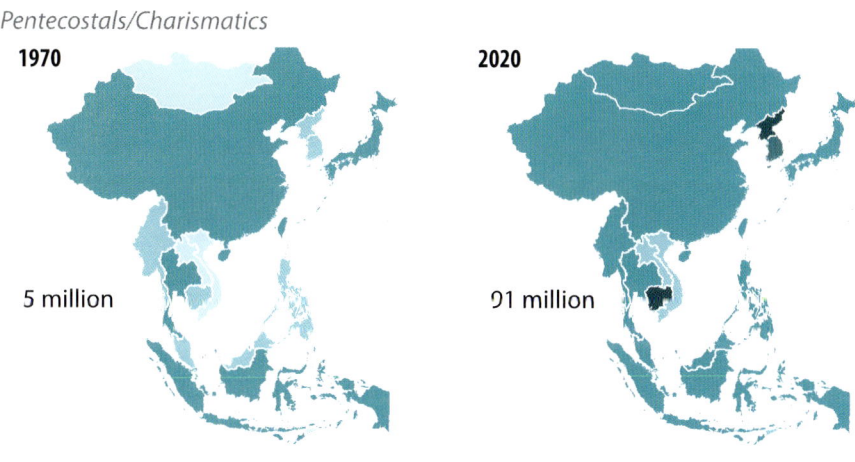

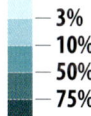

% of Christian population
- 3%
- 10%
- 50%
- 75%

Pentecostal/Charismatic Christianity was the fastest-growing tradition in East and Southeast Asia from 1970 to 2020 and now represents more than 32% of the region's Christian population. In many countries, Christians are more than 30% Pentecostal/Charismatic: Cambodia (78%), South Korea (53%), the Philippines (38%) and Indonesia (33%).

Christianity in East Asia, 1970–2020

Christians by Country, 2020
129 Million Christians, 7.7% of Population

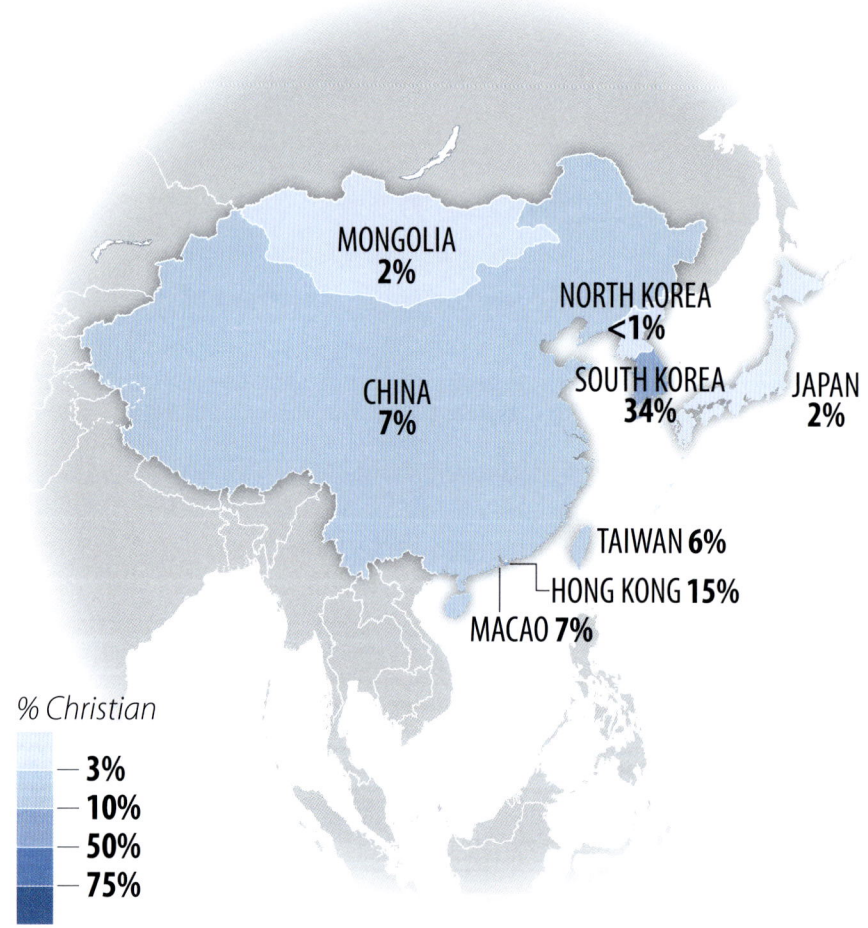

East Asian Christianity exhibits a significant amount of diversity. In China, Christianity is split into both 'official' and 'unofficial' churches and thus difficult to enumerate. Japanese Christianity was driven underground in the seventeenth century and has remained a minority tradition. South Korea is, in many ways, the 'success story' of twentieth-century world Christianity, growing from less than 1% in 1900 to 34% in 2020, and now sends the third-largest number of foreign missionaries worldwide (after the USA and Brazil). The hermit kingdom of North Korea is notorious for persecution of Christians under successive dictatorships, despite the impact of a prominent Pentecostal revival in Pyongyang in 1907. Mongolia is home to one of the world's newest Christian communities, since only 1991, and is in the process of discerning how to create authentic, indigenous expressions of the faith.

A Demographic Profile of Christianity in East and Southeast Asia

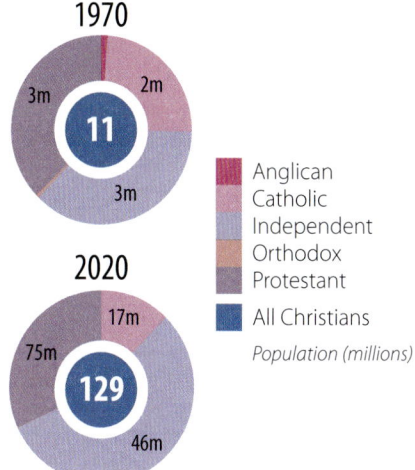

Major Christian traditions, 1970 and 2020
In 2020, Christianity in East Asia was largely Independent (58% of all Christians) and Protestant (36% of all Christians). Independents had the fastest growth rate between 1970 and 2020, averaging nearly 7% per year, though Protestants and Catholics also experienced high growth rates, at 5% and 4%, respectively.

Christians, 1970–2020
Christianity in East Asia increased from 1% of the population in 1970 to 8% in 2020, an average of 5% growth per year. Some of the most significant growth in the region was in China (10% growth per year) and Mongolia (6% per year).

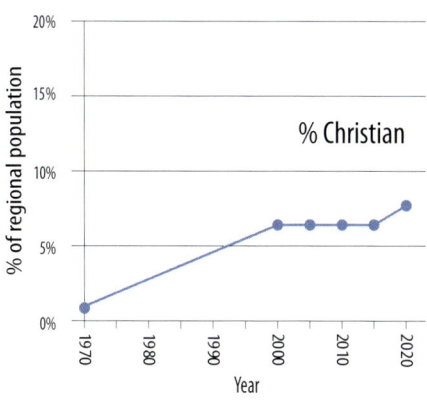

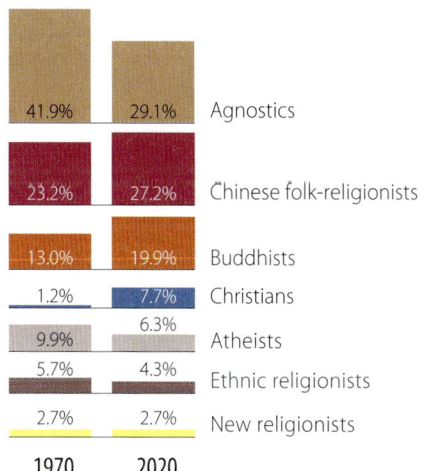

Religious affiliation, 1970 and 2020
Atheists' and agnostics' share of the region's population dropped dramatically, from a combined 52% in 1970 to 35% in 2020, largely due to relaxed restrictions in China. Gains were made by Chinese folk-religionists (453 million in 2020) and Buddhists (331 million).

Christianity in Southeast Asia, 1970–2020

Christians by Country, 2020

153 Million Christians, 22.9% of Population

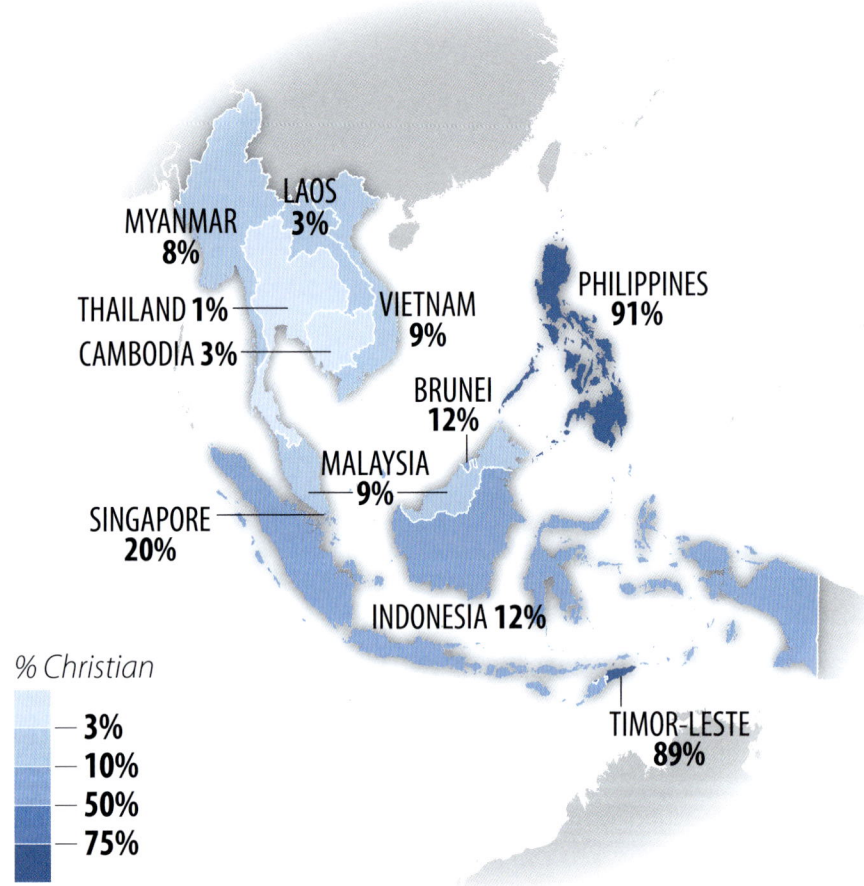

Southeast Asia has been heavily influenced by outside powers, from Muslim Arabs in the thirteenth century (Indonesia, the Philippines) to Portuguese, Spanish, Dutch, French and British imperialists beginning in the sixteenth century. As a result, Christianity took root in the region as a minority tradition. Today's exceptions are the Philippines and Timor-Leste, the only Christian-majority countries in Asia. While Western missionaries contributed to positive transformation of societies in this region, many simply transplanted Western Christian expressions. Many Southeast Asians rejected Christianity from deeply held anti-colonial sentiments.

In 2020, Southeast Asia was 23% Christian (153 million) and home to both historic Catholic populations as well as newer Pentecostal/Charismatic expressions of the faith. Many young churches throughout the region are active in developing indigenous theologies and expressions of the faith. At the same time, persecution is on the rise and proselytisation is prohibited in Brunei, Cambodia, Laos and Vietnam.

A Demographic Profile of Christianity in East and Southeast Asia

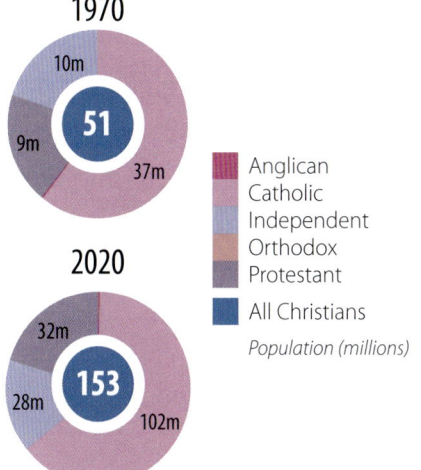

Major Christian traditions, 1970 and 2020
Most Christians in Southeast Asia are Catholic (67% of all Christians), largely due to the weight of the Philippines. All Christian traditions experienced growth between 1970 and 2020, with the largest denominations found in Indonesia: Batak Christian Protestant Church and Bethel Church Indonesia.

Christians, 1970–2020
Christianity's share of the population in Southeast Asia remained mostly steady between 1970 and 2020, rising four percentage points (to 23% in 2020). Every country in the region (except the Philippines) experienced an increase in its Christian proportion, including Timor-Leste (35% to 89%) and Brunei (6% to 12%).

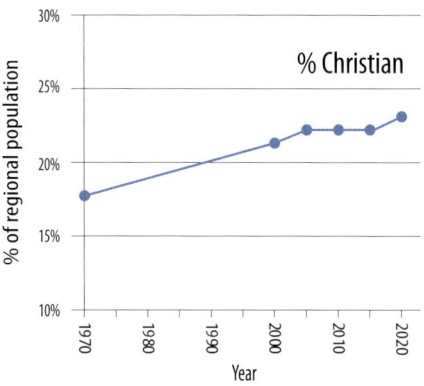

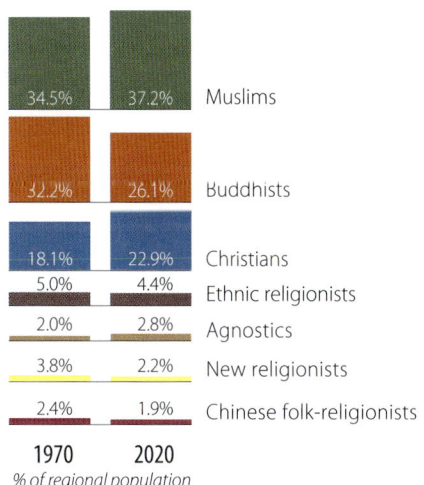

Religious affiliation, 1970 and 2020
Islam in Southeast Asia is the largest religion, with only a slight proportional increase from 1970 to 2020 (35% to 37%). The region is home to some large Muslim populations, including Indonesia (217 million) and Malaysia (18 million). Christianity grew the fastest of any major religion over the 50-year period, at an average of 2.2% per year.

Future of Christianity in East and Southeast Asia, 2020–2050

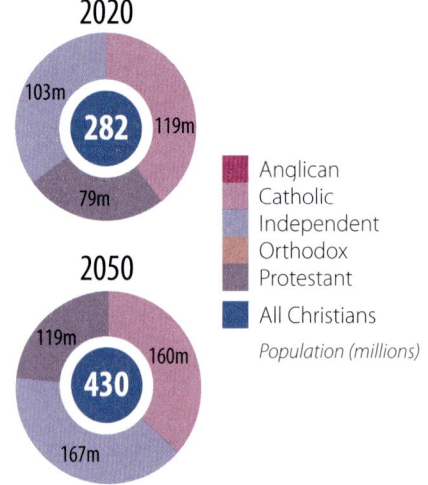

Major Christian traditions, 2020 and 2050
Looking forwards, Independents are likely to outpace Protestants and Catholics in Southeast Asia by 2050 as Christianity becomes far more indigenised in the region. Many of these Independent churches are also Pentecostal/Charismatic in nature.

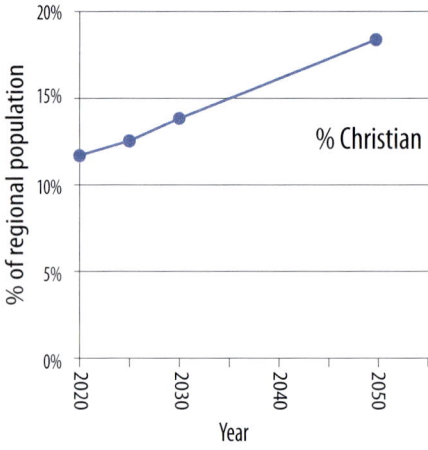

Christians, 2020–2050
By 2050, Christians will likely number 431 million in the region, 18% of the population. Future growth of Christianity in the region is uncertain given social and governmental restrictions in many countries, in particular China.

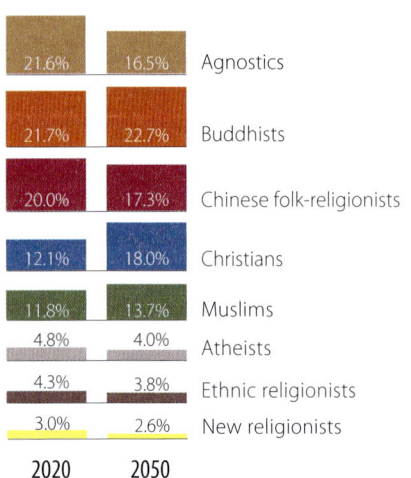

Religious affiliation, 2020 and 2050
Christians are projected to grow faster than any other religious group (1.4% per year); in fact, the percentages of non-religious and Chinese folk-religionists are expected to decline slightly by 2050, and Buddhists and Muslims are projected to keep pace with general population growth.

Christianity in East and Southeast Asia

Francis D. Alvarez SJ

Chuang Tzu's (莊子) parable of the first look between a disfigured parent and child plays out in a number of slightly different versions. In Burton Watson's translation, the drama unfolds moments after the mother's labour. The joy of her delivery is marred by the fear of discovery: 'When the leper woman gives birth to a child in the dead of the night, she rushes to fetch a torch and examine it, trembling with terror lest it look like herself.' Angus Charles Graham recasts the mother into a man, still leprous and still anxious to see what his son looks like. These variations can already serve as a metaphor for the multiplicity of Christianities in East and Southeast Asia. They can further make one wonder, 'If the protagonist changes in gender, is it still the same story?' In the same vein, we risk drawing blood with the question 'How much can you change in Christianity and still call it Christianity?'

Thomas Merton, a Trappist monk and student of Zen Buddhism and Taoism, expands and pushes Chuang Tzu's tale further:

> When a hideous man becomes a father
> And a son is born to him
> In the middle of the night
> He trembles and lights a lamp
> And runs to look in anguish
> On that child's face
> To see whom he resembles.

We can debate whether or not Merton's extension is already overreaching, but I do not think we can deny that as Chuang Tzu's parable wades into poetic lines and then goes further into ambiguities, one is drawn to dive deeper into complexity. The hideous man could have been made ugly because of leprosy, or, heartbreakingly, he could have just been born that way. Leprosy, as we now know, cannot be transmitted from a pregnant mother to her unborn child, and definitely not from a father to the child in his wife's womb. But hideousness can. Changing the sex of the parent adds a twist of uncertainty. A mother can be sure that the child to whom she has just given birth is hers. Her husband cannot rest assured of the same. The father is afraid that his son will be ugly like him. If the boy is, the father blames himself. But if the boy is handsome, then pounces the doubt – is this really his son? The parable unfolds in the dark of the night. But was the boy born in the middle of the night? Or did the man wait until the middle of the night to look at the boy? Is the man so ugly that it is only during the night that he can venture to see the child? This adds to the darkness, too.

As a Filipino Christian, I tremble as I open this volume on Christianity in East and Southeast Asia. What Christianity will I see lying before me? If it is depicted unflatteringly, will I have only myself to blame? If the portrayal is too complimentary, can I still call it my own?

'To See Whom He Resembles'

Since the late 1990s, church weddings have challenged and even outnumbered traditional Shinto nuptial rites as the ceremony of choice for young couples in Japan. These church weddings are patterned after Protestant rites even if the couples are not Christian. The entourage marches down the aisle, the men in suits and the women in dresses like those worn in the fairy-tale wedding of Prince Charles and Lady Diana; Joseph Scriven's 'What a Friend We Have in Jesus' (the most widely known Christian hymn in Japan) is sung in Nihongo using Charles Crozat Converse's melody; the great ode to love in 1 Corinthians 13 is read; and a Caucasian man officiates the service in a mix of English and Japanese. Having a white minister is important because it is easier to believe he is Christian, and to have a Christian officiant is the finishing touch on the bride and groom's dream of a Western wedding.

This reveals how Christianity has been and still is seen in many parts of Asia – it is the religion of the West. In the Vietnam of 1615, an Italian missionary tried to correct the translation of the key question in the baptismal rite to 'Do you want to enter the Christian religion?' Before his intervention, it was 'Do you want to become a Portuguese?' But as late as the eighteenth century, Vietnamese court documents still referred to Catholic Christianity as *Đạo Hoa Lang*, 'the way of the Portuguese'. In Malaysia, Christianity is still sometimes referred to as *agama orang putih*, 'the white man's religion'. In Myanmar, some Buddhist monks still call Christianity a 'guest religion' without affording it even perfunctory hospitality.

Geographically, the case can be made that Christianity is Asian in its origins. Jesus did walk the roads of Palestine in Western Asia, and it was in Antioch, whose ruins lie near present-day Antakya in south-central Turkey, where followers of the Way were first known as Christians.

Culturally, we can point out that life as pictured in the Bible is closer to Asian ways than Western ways today. The scene in Mark 3: 31–5, when Jesus's mother and brothers call for him and seemingly are rejected, would be particularly striking and puzzling for many Asians. It can be argued that this is exactly Mark's intention, and this is also what fuels the Thai and Cambodian apprehension that Christianity separates its converts from family and community. Earlier in the same chapter in Mark, the detail of Jesus not having the opportunity to eat would not escape the eye of many Asians, especially Filipinos, who greet each other not only with a 'How are you?' or '*Kumusta*?' but with a 'Have you eaten?' or '*Kumain ka na ba*?' For us, Jesus's relatives would be justified in seizing him and asking if he was still in his right mind.

Historically, we can cite the coming of the Syriac monk Alopen to China in the seventh century. Many scholars still refer to him and his followers as 'Nestorian' Christians, though this term has been challenged and 'Church of the East', this group's self-description, has been proffered instead. Whatever designation is used, the eighth-century 'Nestorian' stele, inscribed with Chinese and Syriac text memorialising the propagation of the 'luminous' religion in the Middle Kingdom, is proof that our first encounter with Christianity in East and Southeast Asia was Eastern. However, this mission lasted only 150 years. Today, we cannot deny that the Christianity thriving in Asia is from the West.

While Christianity in East and Southeast Asia definitely manifests Western influence, this does not mean that Christianity remains foreign to East and Southeast Asians today. Many church buildings have taken on the aesthetics of local architecture. Phát Diệm Cathedral in Vietnam, built by Father Tran Luc in 1892, features upturned pagoda roofs crowning Gothic towers. In Thailand, some Catholic churches follow the style of Buddhist temples. Like Buddhist temples, they are called *wats*, and have murals telling the story of Jesus just as the walls of Buddhist *wats* depict scenes from the life of the Buddha. But this does not mean that Baroque churches in the Philippines are less Asian. Looking more closely at these churches, one will notice that they are squat rather than towering, a necessary modification because of the earthquakes that shake the Pacific Ring of Fire. They are also constructed of local materials like adobe and coral stone. The Church of Saints Peter and Paul in Singapore (characterised not only as neo-Gothic but tropical Gothic) is adorned with lotus motifs. Similarly, many Philippine colonial churches are decorated with bananas and papayas, mirroring the flora around – the local artisans stamping their signature on their work.

Local touches, though, are not always welcomed by Asians. While some Thai Catholics feel at home in church-*wats*, others cannot pray in them. When a Protestant missionary in the 1960s first introduced the use of the xylophone-like *ranat ek* into worship, Thai congregants objected because these percussion instruments reminded them of the cult of the *phii* (spirits). Nods to local culture also court controversy in Korean representations of the Holy Family. The faithful are divided on whether, in such images, Joseph, Mary and the boy Jesus in churches should be dressed in *hanbok*s made of ramie and silk like royalty, or dressed instead in hemp and cotton, as peasants were attired.

Church buildings do not have to be made of *nipa* (palm leaves) for them to be Asian. Our Christianity does not have to be expressed with joss sticks for us to call it our own. Christianity does not always need to shed its Western-ness to become Asian. In Mongolia, original Christian music pieces with a distinct Mongol flavour have been composed. In the Philippines also, religious hymns that resonate with the traditional *kundiman*s, courtship songs pledging devotion, are popular. But when we choose to sing in the melodies and words of the St Louis Jesuits from Missouri, USA, and Hillsong worship from Sydney, Australia, we still celebrate as Asians. Even when rites are most Western, they do not remain alien. Catholics in rural China felt a strong connection to the Mass when it was in Latin – strong enough that they resisted when Second Vatican Council (1962–5) pushed for the use of the vernacular. There must have been something in the Latin to which they related. Perhaps it was the strangeness of the language that allowed them to express that what they were doing and believing was something strange, something different from what they had known – and the mystery was part of their faith. Or perhaps the connection was simply that their great-grandparents and grandparents prayed in this way, and continuing this paid them honour and made them present.

In Korea, it was a conscious choice by Koreans in the past not to indigenise church architecture, so that Christianity would be seen as distinct from Shamanism. Today, Korean mega-churches are often compared to their American counterparts. But as Western as these might seem, the Asian-ness creeps in. Mega-churches in the USA and Korea risk becoming personality cults. In Korea, this can be partly explained by the Shamanism in the background. As a shaman's followers become increasingly dependent on the shaman's powers, so too the members of a mega-church can become inordinately attached to a pastor's charisma.

When something is transmitted, it is received in the mode of the receiver rather than that of the transmitter. Thus, what was transmitted as Western we have received as Asian. And our ownership of the tradition that has been shared with us is made stronger when we in turn pass it on.

Japanese weddings in the Protestant style reflect the aspirations of the young to be modern. They are actually cheaper as well. But most importantly, these rites, more than the traditional Shinto proceedings, allow the couples to be more 'romantic' and to express themselves more. Many couples are brought to silence and moved by the Western ceremony. They are able to connect to it, and so these rites are no longer just Western. Romance and self-expression might not fit the Japanese stereotype, but the popularity of these weddings tells us that they have also become part of what it means to be Japanese.

In a similar way, Korean pop music (or K-pop) has been criticised for being nothing but copycat music. Songs sample American popular music and are riddled with English words that are meaninglessly repeated. Yet not only has K-pop connected in Korea, it also has become a very successful export to other East and Southeast Asian countries. Why? In these songs, Koreans can feel *han*, an untranslatable combination of sorrow, anger, pain and the hope to struggle through these – a concept also used in Minjung theology. In the case of BTS (Bangtan Sonyeondan), one of Korea's most successful boy bands and the first to crack the Billboard 200 at number 1, the story of the group's struggles to reach the top of the charts is also full of *han*. This might be another reason why K-pop has resonated with the Chinese, Japanese, Taiwanese, Filipino, Indonesian, Singaporean, Malaysian, Cambodian and Thai psyches.

It is important to stress how Christianity is not foreign to Asian Christians any more. This recognises the agency of the faithful in East and Southeast Asia. We do not merely receive passively; we make Christianity our own, and this volume can be read as an account of how we are continuing to make Christianity Asian.

If what is transmitted is received in the mode of the receiver, if what is transmitted to us as Western is received by us as Asian, what happens to the call for inculturation? Theologians and missionaries still need to look for the best ways to translate Christianity for other cultures, but at the same time they cannot ignore the inculturation that is always and already happening from below.

We return to Chuang Tzu's parable as expanded by Thomas Merton. Fatherhood is not limited to biological or genetic parentage. One can be a parent by accepting another's child and nurturing it. Though with Western features, Asian Christianity need not be ashamed of the faith we have fathered or mothered.

To say that Asian Christianity is still foreign to us is to belittle and even betray the sacrifice of the many Asian Christians who have given their lives for their faith. The Catholic Church counts almost 500 saints and blesseds from all over Asia, most of whom were killed for witnessing to the gospel. The Eastern Orthodox Church recognises as saints more than 200 Chinese Christians who were martyred during the Boxer Rebellion. More recently, we have the examples of Lisi Meng and Xinheng Li, missionaries in their twenties from China's house churches, who were killed by ISIS radicals in Pakistan in May 2017. We must recognise not only those who have died but also those who continue to live in persecution and whose fervour also continues to increase. How can we say that their Christianity is foreign to them? (Here, and in the 'Minority' section below, I am indebted to José Mario C. Francisco, a contributor to and a member of the editorial advisory board of this volume, for helping me flesh out my thoughts.) Despite the persecution, Christianity in the region has seen and is projected to have more growth than any other religion. This is another sign that East and Southeast Asians have truly made Christianity our own.

History can be instructive, as it also underlines the need to break through the barrier of the foreignness of Christianity. The Church of the East, Christianity's initial foray into this region, lasted only 150 years in China because it fell victim to the systematic oppression of all foreign religions during the latter half of the Tang dynasty. Threatened by the growing influence of Buddhism – then also considered foreign – Emperor Wuzong (840–6) started demolishing Buddhist temples and monasteries. Followers of Zoroastrianism, Manichaeism and 'Nestorian' Christianity were not spared. Again, this persecution was not anti-Christian but anti-foreign. Sadly, while Buddhism was later considered one of the Three Doctrines of China, alongside the indigenous ways of Confucianism and Taoism, Christianity continues to be seen as foreign. As it did from the late Qing dynasty to the Nationalist period, so this stigma persists today. In 2014, in the eastern coastal province and Christian stronghold of Zhejiang, where Wenzhou, a city dubbed China's Jerusalem, is located, officials ordered the removal of hundreds of crosses and the demolition of dozens of churches. Their reason was simply expressed: 'To stave off the penetration of hostile foreign forces'. In this conflict, Communist Party members used the expression *yáng jiào* (洋教), translated as 'foreign teaching' and meant to be derogatory, to designate Christianity.

It is not just in China but also in Vietnam, Cambodia, Laos, Myanmar, Malaysia, Indonesia and Japan that being considered foreign has created problems for Christianity. This was well expressed by one nationalist, Kanzō Uchimura (1861–1930), who proclaimed (in parallel English and Japanese lines):

> I love two J's and no third; one is Jesus, and the other is Japan. I do not know which I love more, Jesus or Japan. I am hated by my countrymen for Jesus' sake as *yaso* [Christian], and I am disliked by foreign missionaries for Japan's sake as national and narrow. Even if I lose all my friends, I cannot lose Jesus and Japan . . . my faith is not a circle with one center; it is an ellipse with two centers. My heart and mind revolve around the two dear names. And I know that one strengthens the other; Jesus strengthens and purifies my love for Japan; and Japan clarifies and objectives my love for Jesus. Were it not for the two, I would become a mere dreamer, a fanatic, an amorphous universal man.

In a similar vein, Archbishop Albertus Soegijapranata (1896–1963), the first native Indonesian bishop, is well known for the slogan '100% Catholic and 100% Indonesian', which Indonesian Catholics often feel the need to repeat to this day.

How a Western religion can be seen as not foreign is complicated enough without it being compounded by the experience of colonialism. But we must confront the fact that the Christianity that came to our shores after our first contact with Alopen and the Church of the East not only rode on ships but on the coat-tails of imperialist governments wanting to expand their reach. Christian missionaries took advantage of their governments' resources to spread the gospel (even as they were also used by their governments), and this compromised their message. Colonial Christianity has a chequered past. With it came oppression and exploitation but also modernisation and education – and special mention must be made of the educational opportunities given to women. Friars were used to pacify the locals, but they also sometimes took the side of their charges and protected them against the conquerors. The white man looked down on the abilities of the natives, but Westerners also helped heighten our self-awareness. In the Philippines, for example, colonisers spurred on our national awakening by sharing with us the idiom to understand ourselves in the Christ story. The experience of being colonised has already shaped us, and we cannot go back to a pre-colonial identity. This is also the child to whom we must accept our role as parent.

If we are able to shed the perceived foreignness of Christianity and unload the baggage of colonisation, will Christianity be more easily welcomed? Will it encounter less resistance, at least from the state?

The image of the Catholic Church leading the fight against the Marcos dictatorship in the Philippines in 1986 can be a threatening reminder or a beacon of hope, depending on which side of the conflict you find yourself. In Vietnam, perceptions of Catholics as more loyal to the Vatican and of Protestants as colluding with the USA are slowly changing, but the Vietnamese government is still wary that Christian conversions among the Hmong people will trigger an independence movement.

An encouraging sign is the 2016 election of Henry Van Thio, a Chin Christian, as vice president of Myanmar. Also in 2016, Taiwan elected as vice president Dr Chen Chien-Jen, a Catholic who is still very much active in his parish. Tarō Asō, also a Catholic, rose from the ranks to serve as prime minister of Japan from September 2008 to September 2009 and as of 2019 was deputy prime minister and minister of finance.

In Indonesia's fight for independence from Dutch colonisation, Christians battled alongside Muslims, and this watered the seed of what was to become the philosophy of Pancasila. In Korea, Protestantism has always been seen as part of the nationalist struggle. Enshrined in the constitution of Timor-Leste is the invaluable contribution of the Catholic Church to its independence. This, though, might not be viewed in a favourable light in Indonesia.

In 1982, with the issuance of Document 19, *The Basic Viewpoint and Policy on the Religious Question During Our Country's Socialist Period*, the Chinese Communist Party finally came to terms with the impossibility of eradicating religion, but it still insisted that the state should be prioritised above all. This is where the fundamental difference with Christianity lies. In the wake of an increasing number of worship spaces being shut down and an increasing number of leading Christians being jailed, more than 400 pastors of Chinese house churches (which consider themselves self-governing, self-supporting, self-propagating and patriotic, but not members of the Three-Self Patriotic Movement) issued a strongly worded statement in September 2018. Here, the fundamental difference is underscored:

> Christian churches in China believe unconditionally that the Bible is the Word and Revelation of God. It is the source and final authority of all righteousness, ethics, and salvation. If the will of any political party, the laws of any government, or the commands of any man directly violate the teachings of the Bible, harming men's souls and opposing the gospel proclaimed by the church, we are obligated to obey God rather than men, and we are obligated to teach all members of the church to do the same. (From 'A Joint Statement by Pastors: A Declaration for the Sake of the Christian Faith')

The document went on to stress that Chinese Christians 'are willing to obey authorities in China whom God has appointed and to respect the government's authority to govern society and human conduct' as long as the state 'does not overstep the boundaries of secular power laid out in the Bible and does not interfere with or violate anything related to faith or the soul'. Christians will fervently pray for the government and society, but they are also 'eager and determined to walk the path of the cross of Christ and are more than willing to imitate the older generation of saints who suffered and were martyred for their faith'. The document ended strongly: 'For the sake of the gospel, we are prepared to bear all losses – even the loss of our freedom and our lives.'

The perceived foreignness of Christianity arises not only from Christianity's Western connection but also from its relativisation of the loyalty due to government and state. Catholics have been stigmatised as 'Romanists' and 'papists', but even with efforts to clarify that their connections to the Vatican are not political, there is no going around their conviction that ultimate loyalty belongs to God. Beyond competition, can there be another way to approach the relationship between churches and states?

Aside from the spectre of foreignness arising from Christianity's Western influence and its subordination of all loyalties to the Divine, there is another foreignness that haunts East and Southeast Asian Christianity: ethnicity. As an example, in Japan, migrant Catholics (mostly Filipinos and Brazilians) already outnumber native Japanese Catholics. Ethnic (non-Japanese) Pentecostal churches are also increasing, as evidenced by the many old warehouses being converted into worship spaces. But as Japanese Catholic bishops themselves admit, living with people from a different race, culture or religion can be threatening to many Japanese people. There is an insider–outsider dynamic in Japan that, while not yet devolving into persecutions similar to those in the country's isolationist and even xenophobic past, has resulted in micro-aggression and discrimination. The Catholic Church in Cambodia is blessed with Vietnamese immigrants who either have established families there already or are just settling down, but many Cambodians do not consider them a blessing. In Malaysia, most Christians are members of indigenous tribes, or are of Indian or Chinese descent. These Christians endure a double marginalisation, stemming from their religion and their race. For politicians looking for a rallying point to garner support, it is easy to drum this up into an insidious narrative of us versus them. Beyond ethnicity and faith, can there be other ways of conceiving nationhood?

'Hideous Man Becomes a Father'

In December 2013, after almost six years of construction and at a cost of some ¥20–30 million (US$3–5 million), local Christians in Yongjia County near Wenzhou, China, finally saw the fruit of their pooled resources with the completion of Sanjiang Church. Just four months later, on 28 April 2014, despite thousands of Chinese Christians camping out to protect the 2,000-seat church, it was demolished by the government. It stood on 100,000 square feet of land, when approval had been given for only 20,000. But skirting around regulations is not uncommon in Zhejiang Province. The authorities claimed that the building was structurally unsound, but they had also earlier cited it as a model project. Local faithful allege it was toppled because a Communist Party official objected to the number of crosses going up in that area. While there are definitely political motives behind the tearing down of Sanjiang Church, it is worth noting that a pretext used for the demolition was a complaint by local practitioners of Chinese geomancy that the building disrupted the area's *feng shui* (referring to the balance of *chi* or energy).

Chinese Christians, including those in the Philippines, Singapore and other Southeast Asian countries, would not find this objection too strange to understand. After all, though some of them have MBAs, though they are able to crunch the numbers needed to run financial projections and though they know how to assess the stock market using advanced metrics, they are still afraid to invest during August, the Hungry Ghost Month. *Feng shui* governs on what date and at what time a deceased loved one should be buried and when the next wedding can be auspiciously celebrated. When many Chinese Christians choose the officiants who will solemnise their marriages, they avoid pastors who were born in the year of the tiger.

Quiapo Church in the Philippines attracts millions of devotees of the Black Nazarene. With the image, they march barefoot on hot Manila roads for 6.5 kilometres every year on 9 January. But every day, right outside the basilica, *anting-anting* (native amulets and talismans) are sold that are supposed to grant success in business, love and other areas of life. To guarantee their effectiveness, these magical artefacts must be charged with prayers on Good Friday.

As a priest, I have been invited to bless construction sites and newly built houses with holy water, but I am not surprised when the owners tell me that they had slaughtered chickens and sprinkled their blood before I came. As a hospital chaplain, I have also been called by doctors, nurses and medical technicians to light candles in wards, rooms and laboratories to dispel the strange feelings these scientifically trained personnel have experienced in them.

The disenchanted world described by Charles Taylor in *A Secular Age*, where the environment is evacuated of spirits, ghosts and demons, is still far from being the reality in East and Southeast Asia. Here, it is not just the human mind that imbues meaning. Meaning and power are inherent in the world, and things that we cannot see are at work.

The still-palpable magic in the Asian world can be advantageous to Christianity. It brings Christians closer to the experience of the Bible, with its legion of demonic possessions. In Laos, ethnic minorities are able to find liberation from the animistic fear of evil spirits in the power of Jesus Christ. Our belief in spirits can also open us up to the mighty workings of the Holy Spirit and a more vibrant pneumatology. The surging growth of Pentecostalism in East and Southeast Asia may be partly attributed to practices that highlight the activity of the Spirit.

But our belief in spirits might also stoke the accusation that East and Southeast Asian Christians are nothing but syncretists. If the accuser is kinder and wants to be more politically correct, we can be more gently criticised for our multiple religious belonging. This can be one explanation for how in Japan the reported membership of religious groups is larger than the total population. Respondents must be self-identifying with more than one religion. Syncretism and the phenomenon of multiple religious belonging assume the definition of religion as a clearly articulated system of dogma, ethical norms and liturgical rubrics embraced by a defined and delineated community. But this is far from the Asian experience. As a combination of historians and philosophers have pointed out, in Asia we do not really have a pre-modern word for religion. In the Tagalog language, we settled on the loanword *relihiyon*, which was how we heard the Castilians say *religión*. *Zōngjiào*, a compound consisting of *zōng*, derived from a pictogram of an ancestral altar, and *jiào*, meaning 'teaching', appeared in the Chinese lexicon only in the late nineteenth century.

The European experience has promoted a division between the secular and the sacred, but the Asian experience has proved that boundaries between the realm of social life – which includes worldview, ethos and ethics – and the realms of politics and economics are porous. The teachings of the Buddha presupposed social and political transformation, not just individual enlightenment and psychological satisfaction. Muhammad saw Islam not just in the narrow definition of religion but in the larger context of nation. Western categories have been used to try to understand Asian realties, and they have been found wanting.

The history of Christianity in East and Southeast Asia must always include a discussion of the Rites Controversy, which was not only a clanging cymbal in China but also resounding gongs in Taiwan (with Shinto rites during the Japanese occupation) and in rural villages in Thailand, where Christians and Muslims are expected to *wai* (show reverence) to the Buddha. The easy solution to these controversies is to make a distinction between civil rites and religious rites. But can we easily separate the civil and the religious? When politicians in the Philippines visit the worship gatherings of the Iglesia ni Kristo or the Jesus Is Lord Church to ask for the leaders' endorsement and blessing, when the flocks pray over these politicians and vote as blocs, are we in the realm of the civil or the religious? It has been proclaimed many times that to be Thai is to be Buddhist. If this is so, then there can be no Thai Christians – unless we change our ways of distinguishing religion and culture, and, as we saw in the previous section, church and state.

It has been observed that Christianity has had difficulty securing a foothold where world religions are already planted. But is this just about religious beliefs, or is it also about culture, a way of seeing, hearing, smelling, tasting and feeling things? Is this not also about having a strong leadership that pushes for the continuation of the status quo? Religion and culture, church and state, the spirit world and the secular, faith and economics and politics are not easily separable spheres. After their conversion, new Evangelicals are told to break radically from their previous beliefs and past lives. Might this imposed hard boundary be a contributing factor to why Evangelicalism is growing only modestly in East and Southeast Asia?

> Once, Chuang Tzu dreamt he was a butterfly, a butterfly flitting and fluttering around, happy with himself and doing as he pleased. He didn't know he was Chuang Tzu. Suddenly he woke up and there he was, solid and unmistakable Chuang Tzu. But he didn't know if he was Chuang Tzu who had dreamt he was a butterfly, or a butterfly dreaming he was Chuang Tzu. Between Chuang Tzu and a butterfly there must be some distinction!

Can the key to this conundrum be in transcending distinctions? This is one of the central ideas of Taoism and the key also to Chuang Tzu's parable of the hideous man. From the first line, we learn that the hideous man has already accepted being the father of the child, whether it is his or not. The question that remains is, will he be a happy father? As long as he sees himself as hideous, he will be miserable and will only make his son miserable, whatever the son looks like. The father must transcend the distinction of beauty and ugliness and relish the gift of being a father and having a child. Can Asian Christianity learn from Chuang Tzu?

A challenge that Christianity has faced in Timor-Leste is how to deal with practices involving *lulik*. One manifestation of the *lulik* culture is the storing in sacred houses of objects that are charged with power. These objects can be heirlooms passed down from ancestors or symbolic artefacts that link the Timorese to their origins and their past. Foreigners – and anything foreign – are prohibited from entering these sacred houses lest death come to the family who cares for the sacred house. Catholic missionaries once engaged in the iconoclastic practice of burning these sacred houses but are now more open to this ancestral custom. But long before Catholic thought became open to *lulik*, Timorese people opened their sacred houses to statues of Saint Anthony and other Catholic images. The Timorese faithful had transcended the distinction between foreign and local before their pastors.

Taoists might disagree, but I side with philosophers who have studied Taoism and opine that it is impossible to live totally without distinctions or categories. This is why I emphasise that the key is in transcending distinctions and categories, not eliminating them. I think that when Chuang Tzu tells us to forget distinctions, he is telling us first and foremost not to be fixated on them. After all, distinctions are never fixed. Distinctions can be helpful for analysis, but after the unravelling and the dissection, there must be a synthesis or a putting together again – and not always in the same way.

There is a need to go beyond distinctions and categories, but distinctions and categories need also to be made so they can make our thoughts clearer. When we have enough light then we can, as Chuang Tzu challenges us, 'leap into the boundless'. Distinctions of ethnicity and categories of civil and religious, of state and church, of the realms of politics and economics and the world of the spirit can help us think, but in everyday life these all blend and flow as one. To transcend distinctions and categories is to imagine new ways of conceiving them and then living in them.

Kintsugi (金継ぎ; literally, gold joining technique; or more poetically, golden joinery) is the Japanese art of piecing together broken pottery using, as an adhesive agent, lacquer mixed with gold, silver or platinum. The repaired vessel is then considered more valuable than the original, as it has become unique, and the seams strengthened with precious metals create patterns that add to its aesthetic appeal. Some Japanese people even break expensive bowls and dishes intentionally so that they can be beautified through *kintsugi*. Similarly, we now break existing distinctions and categories – vessels of our thoughts and understanding. We break them by questioning their validity, and then we challenge the reader to put these distinctions and categories back together again, hopefully in a way that sheds more light on our reality.

Minority

Christians are viewed as a minority in East and Southeast Asia. While percentages of the total population will bear this out for many years in the future, it might now be time to start nuancing this statement. Since 1970, Christianity has been the fastest-growing religion in the region, and until 2050 it is expected to grow faster than any other religious group. By 2030, it is projected that, in terms of absolute numbers, China might have more churchgoers than the USA. The idea of the white missionary is also being challenged by South Korea, which is now second only to the USA in the number of missionaries it sends abroad. Filipino migrant workers can also be counted as informal missionaries, bringing their faith to other parts of Asia and the Middle East by their life witness and recharging the churches in Europe and the USA with their lively worship.

Can we really say that Christians are a minority if we factor in the impact Christian institutions have had in East and Southeast Asian countries? In Vietnam, for example, many people have acknowledged that the best schools are those run by the Saint Jean-Baptiste de La Salle Brothers and other Christians. Catholic groups also run hospitals, leprosaria and other social service centres that are open to people of all faiths. Christian NGOs serve Christians and non-Christians, locals and migrants, in Taiwan, Hong Kong, Cambodia, Myanmar, Japan, Korea and many other places. Christian schools with a tradition of excellence have contributed to nation-building by providing the basic instruction and advanced scholarship that a number of governments have not been able to achieve. These schools have also produced outstanding graduates who are not just competent in their fields but also compassionate and passionate about serving others. As young countries slowly entered modernisation, as newly established governments groped their way towards legitimacy, Christian institutions were there to help set solid foundations. In Mongolia, for example, where Christian communities began only in 1991, shortly after the end of the communist regime, Christianity has affected significant portions of the population through ministries in the areas of health, education, family life, children's welfare, care for the disabled and the dying, outreach to the poor and the imprisoned, support for alcoholics and drug addicts, small business and agriculture, mass communication and even the arts. And Christians make up only around 2% of the Mongolian population! Institutions like these, though, have also prompted many Asians to ask whether Christianity is nothing more than social service and education.

Inter-religious conversations with Muslim intellectuals in Indonesia have revealed that the rise of Muslim fundamentalism among ordinary people is fed by Muslims feeling threatened by Christians. But Indonesia is the most populous Muslim country in the world, with Muslims numbering more than 200 million and Christians only around 20 million. How could a minority be perceived as threatening? What ordinary Muslims pick up from media – traditional and, increasingly, social – is the cultural, political and economic domination of the West, identified as mostly Christian. This not only challenges seeing Christianity as a minority but also underlines how boundaries between religion, culture, politics and economics are blurred.

Community
East and Southeast Asian Christians are seen as more communal than individual. The theory that this comes from our rice culture has been proposed. No one person or even family can plant, cultivate and harvest rice: it takes a village. But what happens to our community orientation as we move from rural to urban centres and as agriculture becomes industrialised?

One insight comes from the experience of helping edit this volume: our contributors know much about their own traditions but are challenged when asked about other Christian groups. If we are communal, why is the value of community not expressed more in ecumenism? Formally, in the state documents of countries like China, Vietnam and Indonesia, Catholicism and Protestantism are seen as different religions. Informally, in people's eyes, this is also the case. In South Korea, the *Gidokgyo* (Protestant Christians) do not treat the *Chonjugyo* or the *Gatolic* (Catholic Christians) as their brothers and sisters in the faith. There are some exceptions and pockets of hope, as in Christianity in Brunei, but, overall, there seems to be more competition than cooperation among different Christian groups. In some instances we might actually be doing better at relating with Buddhists and Muslims than with other followers of Christ.

In the Philippines, two different Independent groups have set up rival television stations. A significant portion of the programming on each is devoted to criticising the other. Disgruntled members of one group are often featured on the opposing channel as whistleblowers. There is televised worship music, but there is also much airing of dirty laundry. Pentecostals and Charismatics have touched more than 40% of the region's population, and this has pushed other groups onto the defensive. They put down these movements as attracting only the naïve and the gullible. Some Pentecostals and Charismatics then go on the offensive by proclaiming how they are enlivened by the Spirit while the other groups are just dry bones in the desert.

We can critique each other more kindly, and our differences can help us open our eyes to more ways of encountering God. Ecumenism can lead us to healthy self-reflection, but though our leaders always tout it, those on the ground have not given it much of a chance. Two areas often seen as needing more resources are the education and formation of leaders. While we do have different traditions, we have not exerted enough effort to explore ways for our seminaries, Bible schools and theological institutes to collaborate.

Even when we are communal, our communities do not really cross national boundaries. The Association of Southeast Asian Nations (ASEAN) has been criticised for not doing more to correct Myanmar, one of its member countries, with regard to the 2017 Rohingya crisis that is still burning. Non-interference might be the ASEAN way, but in 1999 Aung San Suu Kyi herself decried this policy as being just an excuse for not helping.

When Christians in East and Southeast Asia think about building ties with others, it is most of the time from the point of view of what we can do for others. But others have also done much for us. In January 2019, shortly after terrorists bombed Our Lady of Mount Carmel Cathedral in Muslim-populated Sulu Province in the southern Philippines, Muslim professionals formed a human barricade around Santa Isabel Cathedral in Basilan, the largest island in Sulu. They said they did this so that their Christian brothers and sisters could worship in less fear. Similarly, moderate Muslims from Nahdlatul Ulama and Muhammadiyah, the two largest socio-religious organisations in Indonesia, guard their Christian neighbours from attacks by militant groups. They support Christians in their celebration of Christmas and allow them to join in the festivities of the Great Ramadan. These are a few examples of 'neighbourology', which

Kosuke Koyama, the Japanese Protestant missionary in Thailand who is also known for his 'water buffalo theology', explains simply as stepping into the lives of our neighbours. In China, not only Christians but also Xinjiang Muslims and Tibetan Buddhists are harassed. Can the common experience of persecution also make our neighbourology stronger?

Connected with neighbourology is inter-religious dialogue. It is almost a slogan that to be religious in Asia is to be inter-religious. Moreover, there is not just one Christianity, not just one Islam, not just one Buddhism, but many Christianities, many Islams, many Buddhisms, and so on. Catholicism is highly centralised, with a clear hierarchy, but the other religious groups are not as clearly defined. Which Protestantism, which Islam and which Buddhism are we talking about? And who will assign their representatives? Is it, then, really a dialogue between religions or a dialogue between believers that we should be aiming for? And what will the goal of this dialogue be? Some strains of East and Southeast Asian Christianity still look to convert others to accept Christ; some Christians seek, in the ensuing dialogue, only to convert themselves to Jesus more. Is there another way of building community with other religions beyond the exclusivist, inclusivist and pluralist paradigms we now have?

Rationality

The West is usually characterised as being more inclined towards rationality than the East. This does not mean that we Asians are irrational, but we do pay more attention to extra-rational sources of knowledge and wisdom, sources that go beyond mathematical logic but are still full of reason. Lü Xiaomin's formal education might have gone only as far as elementary school, but her more than 1,600 religious songs about pain and suffering are theology. They touch on themes of Pentecostal Christology, pneumatology and eschatology without ignoring present Chinese political reality. East and Southeast Asian theology also draws from paintings and other art forms, as this introduction will also venture to do below. Alongside the inspired words of the Bible, we have the wisdom of the sages – and so this introduction has turned to Chuang Tzu for inspiration. East and Southeast Asian Christianity is inter-scriptural.

Another extra-rational source is our bodies. Pentecostal and Charismatic worship is quite physical, with raising of hands, speaking in tongues and being slain in the Spirit. Catholic sacraments, too, engage the body: visits to churches are not really complete without dipping your fingers in holy water and touching the feet of the statues of the saints. Cambodian Christians kneel in worship with hands above their heads. Japanese Catholics, on the other hand, rarely genuflect but execute a profound bow. If given a choice, they would receive Communion by the hand rather than stick out their tongue to the priest. These are not just practices that have been 'socialised' into us; our bodies are actually expressing something deep within.

It is tempting to fall into dichotomising between the Western predilection for clear and distinct ideas and Eastern ambiguity and fluidity, but humans are never static. Intellectual Christian humanism is on the rise in China as the urban intelligentsia explore faith. Modernisation and globalisation in Singapore have introduced Christians to the beauty of logic and systematisation in faith. Now, they are attracted to how religion 'makes sense'. Some might argue that Singapore has become too Western, but can we say that this is now also part of their way of being Asian?

Poverty

East Asia is home to the world's second-largest economy: China, which might overtake the USA by 2030. Japan remains the third-largest economy. The tiger economies of South Korea, Taiwan, Hong Kong and Singapore, and the tiger cubs that are Indonesia, Malaysia, the Philippines, Thailand and Vietnam, are ready to pounce. But according to a 2018 World Bank report, 9% of the 783 million people globally who are considered extremely poor are in Asia and the Pacific region. Less than 10% might not seem many, but this still means an estimated 70 million are living below the poverty line of US$1.90 a day. Justifiably, the Federation of Asian Bishops' Conferences (FABC) emphasises dialogue with the poor.

There has already been great progress. Again, according to the World Bank, from 1990 to 2015, the world's poverty rate fell from almost 36% to 10%, with all regions except the Middle East and North Africa gaining ground in the fight against poverty. Still, great inequality exists. ASEAN reports that in 2018, Thailand's and Indonesia's richest 1% controlled around half of their countries' wealth.

A significant number of conversions to Christianity in East and Southeast Asia have come from the sector of the marginalised, like the ethnic peoples of Myanmar. In Singapore, members of mega-churches tend to come from less-privileged, non-English-speaking families. But growth has also come from the affluent, the urban middle class, as well as the working classes who have aspirations to climb the social ladder. The growth of Christianity in China has been accompanied by Christians improving their economic status. But the dialogue with poverty must include reflection on wealth and its purpose.

The message of prosperity theology has attracted many. In the Philippines, followers of Mike Velarde's Catholic Charismatic group El Shaddai are told to open their umbrellas and hold them upside down to catch blessings from God. A similar trend has been observed in Malaysia, Laos and the house churches in China, where there seems to be a preoccupation with blessings and miraculous healings. While the gospel of prayers answered and favours granted has dangers, this is where people are. And there are signs of maturing faith. Many devotees of the Black Nazarene join the long and physically challenging procession every 9 January because of petitions for themselves or for family. But when they do not receive what they ask for, they turn to the image of Jesus bearing his cross and say, 'We are assured we are not alone in our suffering'.

Youth

Despite the ageing populations and the negative growth rates of Japan and Korea, despite also the slowing down of the birth rate in China, United Nations figures show that the majority of the world's youth live in the Asia Pacific region. In East Asia, 30% of the population is in the 0–24-year age bracket; in Southeast Asia, 44.2%.

Any projection of the growth of Christianity has to take into account the youth population. The great potential of Christian youth goes hand in hand with the possibility of unpredictable change. Are our young people getting sufficiently formed to have the torch of faith passed on to them? It is still the family that is most formative for Asians, but what happens now that the traditional family setup has been challenged by migration and other factors? We want to give the young the best opportunities for economic development, but greater wealth has also been shown to lead to greater individualism. Where will the youth take us?

In China, Catholic youth attend the services of both the patriotic and the underground churches. Convenience is the deciding factor for where they go to Mass. They say they are not affected by the baggage of their elders and that involvement in politics is only for a few. Is this a ray of hope for the unification of the patriotic and underground churches? Can the wounds of division be healed by those who do not know the past? An enduring source of hope for unity comes from the old friendships formed before the separation of the churches. What happens when that generation passes away?

The youth value authenticity. Christianity has suffered from sex scandals, association with politicians who have questionable ethics, lack of financial transparency, and corruption. How will all of these affect the youth, especially in South Korea, Macau and Taiwan, where it is already a challenge to attract them?

In spite of this ominous picture, growth is still projected for Christianity. Perhaps this is a sign that communist ideals and capitalist promises are not really able to quench a deepening spiritual thirst. If the youth are not as present in religious gatherings as before, maybe it is because religiosity is really something for those who are older. Studies have shown that millennials have a different view of commitment. They sow many seeds, wait for what bears the most fruit for them and only then invest themselves. Maybe we just have to give them the space and time to explore.

Christianity still has much to learn with regard to women. Chinese academics estimate that 72% of Christians in China are women, but this is not reflected in the leadership positions given to them. The same is true in other East and Southeast Asian countries. In Asia, also, more and more women are joining the labour force, but expectations of what they are supposed to do at home – cook, clean, wash clothes and so on – are not lessened. They are also given much of the menial work in churches. Will young women be drawn to be active in religious activities? Will they have time to form the next generation – another responsibility that more often than not we pass on to women?

These are but five examples of distinctions that can be confirmed or challenged in this volume. We invite the reader to join in confirming or challenging them. This, too, is part of nurturing the child we have chosen to parent. It is also worth noting that though we started talking about definite categories, we always ended up going beyond them and touched on other themes – proof that categories are indeed porous and connected.

'The Middle of the Night'

What can unite East and Southeast Asia beyond the boundaries of longitude and latitude? We are multicultural, multi-ethnic and multi-religious. Though its neighbours were colonised by either the British or the French, Thailand was never colonised. The Philippines was under Spain for 300 years and under the USA after that; Indonesia, under the Dutch; Malaysia, under the British. But it was Japan that colonised Korea. Western Christianity was brought by the colonisers in the former countries, but Koreans brought Christianity to Korea. Our histories are as varied as the tonal and non-tonal languages that are spoken in the region. Our theologies occupy the whole spectrum – from conservative pietism to fundamentalism to liberal strains that emphasise social action. We are Independents, Catholics, Protestants, Pentecostals, Charismatics, Evangelicals, Anglicans and Orthodox. We come to the faith because we seek blessings and miracles, because of the personal witness of others, because of family, because of a spiritual thirst or because of intellectual curiosity. In terms of mission, we have groups centred on strengthening hierarchy and internal organisation, and we have groups who are ready to branch out, plant churches and evangelise even outside their countries. We have churches that work with their governments and churches that have gone underground. Religious freedom is challenged in communist China, Laos, North Korea and Vietnam and in the authoritarian states of Cambodia and Myanmar. In the Muslim-majority countries of Brunei, Indonesia and Malaysia, Christianity faces difficulties. But in Japan, Mongolia, the Philippines, Singapore, South Korea, Thailand and Timor-Leste, a greater degree of freedom is accorded to us. China is the most populous country in the world, while Brunei has fewer than half a million people in an area of 5,765 square kilometres. But Brunei has been ranked as high as fourth in the world by gross domestic product per capita at purchasing power parity. Singapore hosts the highest percentage of millionaires in the world; the portrayal of 'crazy rich Asians' in the groundbreaking Hollywood film of that title (2018) is not really hyperbole. But in Myanmar, unemployment rates hover around 30%, and in Timor-Leste half the population lives below the poverty line.

If the contributors to and editors of this volume were gathered in one room, would we be able to agree about East and Southeast Asia? Trying to characterise this region at times seemed like working in the dark. Categories that worked for other regions in this series did not really fit us. And it is not just the famous Asian false modesty that makes me say the portrait that we have painted here is still far from complete. After all, who can really say what is Asian and what is Christian? Cultures are always fluid and changing. The Asians the colonisers met in the sixteenth century are not the Asians of today.

To say this has repercussions for how we see the work of inculturation. If no one fully knows what is Asian and what is Christian, how can we translate between the two? Perhaps all we can say is that we are trying to pass on only what we understand of Asia and Christianity today while humbly admitting that Asia and Christianity can be something more tomorrow. Perhaps, then, the work of inculturation starts with striving to answer these two key questions: Who are Asians today? Who are Christians today? These are the questions we have tried to answer in the next pages – not just for us, but for other Christians and for other peoples from other regions too. Our hope is that in our wrestling with who we are, in our trembling in the dark, in our acceptance of how we have made something foreign our own, in our confirming and challenging distinctions, and in our putting it all back together, lamps will be lit and readers will have a better understanding not only of us but of themselves.

We began our introduction with Chuang Tzu's parable of the first look between a disfigured parent and child. We end our introduction with the story of another first look – the first gaze strange men cast on the newborn baby Jesus as depicted in *Adoration of the Magi*, He Qi's artwork featured on the cover of this volume. In this painting, Jesus is rightfully one of the foci. The donkey's and the horse's eyes are directed towards the infant Saviour. Mary's eyes are closed as she holds her child. She does not need to see Jesus's face. Whatever he looks like, he is her son. Fast forward this scene 33 years and pause to consider Michelangelo's *Pietà*. Mary is still cradling Jesus. Her eyes are still closed. Whatever has happened, however he looks, he is still her son.

Returning to He Qi, two of the magi are facing Jesus, but, curiously, the third – the one dressed in a Chinese *chángshān* (literally, long shirt) – is looking straight at the viewer of the painting, as Jesus also does. In Chuang Tzu's parable, the emphasis is on the look the parent gives the child. Nothing is said about the child looking at the parent. In He Qi's art, the baby Jesus looks back at those beholding him. I interpret this as a challenge for the reader of this volume. After finishing all the essays, contemplate the painting on the front cover. How do you now see East and Southeast Asian Christianity? Whether or not you are Asian, has anything changed about how you view Asia? Whether or not you are Christian, has anything changed about how you view Christianity? The Roman dramatist Terence once wrote, '*Homo sum, humani nihil a me alienum puto*' ('I am human, and nothing human is alien to me'). After reading about East and Southeast Asian Christianity, has anything been touched in your own humanity?

One focus of the painting is Jesus; the other is the blue and white vase He Qi places in the centre of his artwork. Judging by its colours, one can say the vase was fired in a Chinese kiln. The crane on it can be a symbol of nobility – the perfect gift for a child of the Divine. Taking this blue and white vase in the context of this book, one can see it as a metaphor for the gift of East and Southeast Asian Christianity.

To see that East and Southeast Asian Christianity is indeed a gift, four hermeneutics are crucial. First, a hermeneutic of openness: our Christianity might be Western in influence, but it is no longer foreign to us. It might still look Western in some areas, but it is already our own child. And where it looks non-Western, it still is Christian. Acceptance of our Christianity, though, does not mean that it cannot be critiqued. There is still much we can learn, and we have plenty of room to grow. For example, the 2006 crisis in Timor-Leste, which continued to rumble even in 2008, saw violence gripping the young Catholic nation. Rampaging mobs burned houses – but only after 'evacuating' statues of saints and images of the Virgin Mary from the homes. Our popular religiosity still needs to be wedded to our ethical practice.

This and similar critiques can lead us to the second hermeneutic, of constant questioning and healthy doubt. Are we still who we say we are, or have we changed? Are the categories and distinctions we and others have used to characterise us still valid? The first hermeneutic needs to be balanced by the second.

Reflection on the second can open us up to the third – the hermeneutic of distance. Is there anyone who has grasped what 'Asian' really means and what 'Christian' really means? No one person, and no one culture even, possesses the final definition of what is Asian and what is Christian. It is not already written somewhere and just waiting to be applied. What is Asian and what is Christian are still being both constructed and discovered. Quite a distance still must be travelled, but we are on the way.

What is Asian and what is Christian will always be a few steps ahead of us. But we are not aimlessly wandering. We are going deeper. The fourth hermeneutic, of depth, can give us hope. Our running after what is Asian and what is Christian is not a futile pursuit. Though it does not come easily, we are growing in understanding.

As the magi gift Jesus with the blue and white vase that can stand for Asia, Jesus also has a gift, though it is not for the magi but for the viewer of the painting: an apple. Is this apple supposed to remind us of the fruit in Genesis that led to our sin, which Jesus now takes away? Or is it something else? In *feng shui*, a red apple symbolises peace, because in Mandarin the word for apple (苹果, *píngguǒ*) sounds like the word for peace (平安, *píng'ān*). The apple Jesus gives to us, in my interpretation, is a wish and another set of challenges for the reader: may you come to peace with the East and Southeast Asian Christianity you find. Amid many disagreements, persecution, violence stemming from fundamentalism, amid great difference, there can still be peace. Find the peace in openness and acceptance. Find the peace by questioning and doubting. Find the peace even if there is distance. The waters might seem turbulent on the surface, but find the peace by going deeper.

Bibliography

Federation of Asian Bishops' Conferences (FABC) Papers available online at <http://www.fabc.org/fabc%20papers>; indexes by James H. Kroeger MM (see FABC Papers 100, 125 and 150).

Frankopan, Peter, *The New Silk Roads: The Present and Future of the World* (London: Bloomsbury, 2018).

Hayes, Peter, and Chung-In Moon (eds), *The Future of East Asia* (London: Palgrave Macmillan, 2017).

Phan, Peter, *Asian Christianities: History, Theology and Practice* (Maryknoll, NY: Orbis Books, 2018).

Wilfred, Felix (ed.), *The Oxford Handbook of Christianity in Asia* (Oxford: Oxford University Press, 2014).

Countries

Mainland China (Protestant)

Manhong Melissa Lin

Beginning in the early nineteenth century, Protestant missionaries of different denominations came to mainland China one after another. Based on their efforts in areas ranging from evangelism to education, medicine and translation work, they can be viewed as bearers of the gospel of Jesus Christ and contributors to modern China's development. Nevertheless, due to their relation to imperialist and colonial powers and their failure to root Christianity in Chinese culture and society, Christianity was regarded as a tool used for aggression and cultural invasion and was largely resisted by common Chinese people.

As a result, building a Chinese Christian church became imperative. The idea was first officially brought to the table by Chinese church leaders at the National Christian Conference in 1922. The method proposed was the Three-Self Movement – self-governing (rather than being governed by missionary societies or personnel), self-supporting (rather than relying on foreign resources) and self-propagating (rather than being a dot on missionary maps). In the following decades, however, China was caught up in battles among warlords, the war of resistance against Japan and the war of liberation, and Chinese people, including Christians, struggled for survival in the subsequent disasters. Thus, the course of promoting a Chinese church through the Three-Self Movement did not proceed much further in that period.

Because of the needs of the church and the political climate, the task of building a Chinese Protestant church through the Three-Self Movement was again placed on the agenda of the Chinese Christian leadership after the establishment of the People's Republic of China in 1949. In 1950, 'The Christian Manifesto', a key document advocating for the Three-Self Movement and signed by 1,527 church leaders, was released; by 1954 it was actively supported by more than 400,000 Christians. The Committee of the Three-Self Patriotic Movement (TSPM) was officially established in 1954 to safeguard the achievements of the churches in China, including eliminating the control of administration, finance and personnel by Western mission boards, uniting the majority of church leaders from all denominations and theological backgrounds to build up an independent church, and responding to the national mandate for anti-imperialism, patriotism and the construction of a new China. From then on, the Protestant church in China was no longer a branch or sub-branch of Western churches but gained its sovereignty on an equal footing with other churches in the world.

In 1958, almost all congregations belonging to the more than 70 Protestant denominations and over 120 missionary societies present in China started to hold joint worship and became a post-denominational church based upon the spirit of mutual respect and seeking common ground while preserving the differences. Unfortunately, due to political movements that came one after another and to the influence of ultra-leftism, religion came to be considered a negative social element, even to the point of being attacked and nearly exterminated. Therefore, the process of building a post-denominational Chinese church did not go any further at that time.

In the four decades since the reform and opening up of China in 1979, however, the Chinese Protestant church has progressed in all areas. Not only have the churches made exciting progress, but the whole nation has also developed tremendously. Two among many significant changes will be briefly highlighted here. Beginning from the early 1980s, steady economic growth in China has enabled Chinese people to experience the transformation to a better life through the alleviation of poverty. In 1978, the gross domestic product per capita of China was US$156; by 2017 it had grown to US$8,583. Over the same period, the Engel's coefficient – the proportion of income spent on food purchases – of rural households dropped from 67.7% in 1978 to 33% in 2017, and that of city households dropped from 57.8% in 1978 to 29.3% in 2017. The consistent policy of reform and opening up has not only led to an improved standard of living but also granted much greater freedom for Chinese people. Such freedom is reflected in the change of attitude and the tolerance of the Chinese government towards religion.

Christianity in China, 1970 and 2020

Tradition	1970 Population	%	2020 Population	%	Average annual growth rate (%), 1970–2020
Christians	876,000	0.1%	106,030,000	7.4%	10.1%
Anglicans	100	0.0%	950	0.0%	4.6%
Independents	183,000	0.0%	62,000,000	4.4%	12.4%
Orthodox	5,000	0.0%	10,000	0.0%	1.4%
Protestants	254,000	0.0%	33,999,000	2.4%	10.3%
Catholics	400,000	0.0%	10,000,000	0.7%	6.6%
Evangelicals	59,300	0.0%	35,000,000	2.5%	13.6%
Pentecostal/Charismatics	93,400	0.0%	28,000,000	2.0%	12.1%
Total population	**824,788,000**	**100.0%**	**1,424,548,000**	**100.0%**	**1.1%**

Source: Todd M. Johnson and Gina A. Zurlo (eds), *World Christian Database* (Leiden/Boston: Brill), accessed March 2018.

In 1982, the Communist Party of China issued its landmark Document 19, *The Basic Viewpoint and Policy on the Religious Question During Our Country's Socialist Period*, which acknowledged that it is impossible to use political orders or coercive measures to eliminate religion and which ensured that the freedom of religious belief would be a fundamental and long-term policy. Document 19 expressed the desire of the Party to unite believers and non-believers and to enable them to centre all their will and strength on the common goal of building a modernised and strong socialist state. Since then, religion has gradually been regarded as encompassing social, historical and cultural phenomena and as deserving a place in the development of human society. Religious believers have come to enjoy the same political, economic, social and cultural rights as non-believers, for they have been deemed a part of the common Chinese people and must not be treated unequally due to a difference in belief. Religious believers are also encouraged to play a positive role in the reform and opening up, in the construction of a harmonious society and in the realisation of the Chinese dream of national rejuvenation.

Major Features and Church Ministries

Benefiting from the friendly environment and the church's own sense of spiritual empowerment, the Protestant church in mainland China has grown rapidly. If the TSPM was established in 1954 to unite all Chinese Christians to work for the complete independence of the Chinese church and to take an active part in socialist reconstruction, the China Christian Council (CCC) was formed in 1980 at the Third National Christian Conference to run the church well by attending to the pastoral needs of Chinese Christians, including: to print the Bible, hymnals and Christian literature; to reopen the seminary; to strengthen the pastoral work of local Christian communities; and to do the work of evangelism. Following the model of the CCC and national TSPM, Christian councils at the provincial and local levels were launched during provincial or local Christian conferences, and local TSPMs were either re-established or established at the same time. They are called the Christian *lianghui* (two organisations) in Chinese.

Nowadays, both parts of the Christian *lianghui* at all levels aim to run the church well based upon the Three-Self principle as stated in their constitutions, but with a division of labour. Generally speaking, the TSPM deals more with the church's relationship to public affairs, while the CCC has its focus more on internal church affairs. Though each organisation has its own constitution, leadership and standing committee, the *lianghui* always work together, sharing the same office and jointly holding their assembly every five years to elect new leadership. The leadership of the *lianghui* usually serves no more than two consecutive terms.

Each local and provincial *lianghui* is independent in administration and finance, while the CCC and national TSPM also serve as the umbrella organisations for the provincial *lianghui*, providing guidance and various services to them; the provincial *lianghui* play the same role for the local *lianghui*. The CCC and national TSPM represent Protestantism in mainland China, while the provincial and local *lianghui* represent Protestantism in their respective provinces, cities or counties. The Christian *lianghui* can be seen as a typical church structure in mainland China.

Different kinds of ministry are carried out by the *lianghui* at different levels. Bible publication is under the CCC and national TSPM. By 2017, more than 80 million copies of the Bible in Mandarin, 11 ethnic minority languages and Braille had been printed and distributed for churches in mainland China. Ordination is conducted by the provincial *lianghui*; theological schools are run by the national or provincial *lianghui*. The rest of the church ministries, including Christian publications, lay leadership training, social service and ecumenical fellowship, are carried out by the *lianghui* at all levels and even by local congregations.

Pastoral work is taken care of by the local churches. The more than 60,000 churches and affiliated congregations are led by around 4,000 ordained pastors, 6,000 full-time elders, 50,000 evangelists (some of whom are theologically trained but not yet ordained) and over 190,000 lay leaders. Churches in urban areas usually have full-time pastors, while in rural areas many congregations are led by elders, evangelists or lay leaders. Many congregations have multiple services on both Sunday and Saturday to ensure that every church member has a place to worship, but still the churches are usually full for each service. Church life is active and lively. Bible study, testimony sharing, prayer meetings, choir rehearsals, fellowships for various age groups and professions, and other church activities are offered throughout the week. Baptism is usually conducted twice a year, at Easter and Christmas, and may take the form of sprinkling or immersion. Most churches have Holy Communion once a month, while a small number of congregations hold it once a week or once every quarter.

Different practices of baptism and forms of celebrating Holy Communion exist due to the post-denominational feature of the Chinese church. The unity, holiness, catholicity and apostolicity of the post-denominational church are understood to be derived from the authority of the Bible, the proper preaching of the Word and the apt administration of the sacraments. This unity is more radical than that in reconciled diversity because the church has abolished denominational organisations. Nevertheless, it is not coercive but tolerates differences, partly owing to the influence of the traditional Chinese cultural value of 'Great Harmony'. The churches still exhibit some of their previous denominational elements, reflected in liturgy, worship style, spirituality, sacraments and architecture. Local churches are rather independent, and the pastors, elders, evangelists and leading lay workers join in decision-making. Some congregations have more autonomy in church operation and personnel allocation, while others are more under the leadership of the local *lianghui*.

Despite all the differences, a significant commonality in the Chinese church is that it is a church of the Word and proclamation. Chinese Christians treasure the Bible and respect it as the true authority for their life and faith. Almost every Christian carries the Bible – at least a digital Bible on their mobile phones, if not a print copy – to the Sunday worship services and other weekly church activities. In interpreting the Bible and applying biblical teachings to their actual lives, they focus more on the 'hermeneutics of faith' rather than the 'hermeneutics of doubt'.

Christians are constantly reminded that conversion is a transformation in all aspects of life. To follow Jesus is to demonstrate good works that bear fruit so as to glorify God's name. Such important teaching contributes significantly to the growth of the church. This growth relies not on door-to-door evangelism or popular evangelists conducting massive outdoor revival meetings, but on the personal witness of each individual Christian.

In 1949, the number of Protestant Christians was around 700,000; it had reached 3 million by the early 1980s and 38 million in 2017. In the early 1980s, 80% of Christians lived in rural areas, but with urbanisation that percentage has now been reduced to 50%. The average age of Christians is 51, and women make up around 72%, according to a recent survey conducted by Chinese academics.

While most rejoiced in the reopening of the churches, a small number of Chinese Christians continued worshipping in homes and, for their own reasons, did not want to associate with the *lianghui*. They have become a part of the private home gatherings, the so-called 'house churches'. The private home gatherings also include Christians who live too far away to go to a church building to worship, those who prefer worshipping with fewer people or in their own circles, and those who are influenced, supported and often manipulated by overseas groups. Some home gatherings belong to the *lianghui* and some do not. For the latter, as long as they are faithful to biblical truth, not averse to the Three-Self principles and law abiding, they are also considered by the *lianghui* to be a part of the Chinese church.

Theological Reconstruction and Christianity That Is *Zhongguohua*

During the first two decades after China's reform and opening up, the church put its priority on the return of church properties, the re-establishment of church institutions, the training of clergy, the printing of the Bible and the establishment of ecumenical relations. Nevertheless, to maintain unity, the theology taught by fundamentalist missionaries in the late nineteenth and early twentieth centuries that shaped the Chinese church was neither criticised in the 1950s nor challenged when the church was reopened in the early 1980s. Such theology can be criticised as negative and otherworldly in its thinking because it deemed that humanity and human society were totally depraved and therefore worthless and hopeless. In this theology, Christian hope basically lay in the other world, and the most important earthly obligation for Christians was to convert people in order to gain heavenly reward and personal salvation. God was portrayed as a divine punisher who was hard to please and in favour only of the select few. It also taught that Christians and Christian nations were blessed and the rest were condemned; thus, a distinct line had to be drawn between believers and non-believers. Such theological thinking aroused concern that it might hinder the development of the Chinese church.

Bishop K. H. Ting (丁光訓), the most important Chinese Christian leader of the twentieth century, whose role in the Chinese church is unparalleled, initiated the process of Theological Reconstruction for the Chinese church in 1998. He deemed it was time to bring Chinese Christians back to the essence of Christian teaching by challenging and decolonising the Western theological discourse taught by the fundamentalist missionaries, so that the Christian message could be properly preached and understood in the Chinese context. His hope was that through Theological Reconstruction, a Chinese Christianity that was faithful to biblical teachings, that highlighted God's inclusive love and that focused on Christians' ethical and moral responsibilities could emerge. Ting made great efforts to promote Theological Reconstruction by widely discussing and sharing his theological reflections with church leaders and theological educators at all levels in China, as well as with his ecumenical friends. He reflected on a wide range of theological themes, but here only his most well known and important arguments will be briefly rehearsed.

Ting asserted that a negative or pessimistic worldview was not the gospel, and an overemphasis on sin or the human fall would not be compatible with the God whose name is love. Ting stressed that God's grace far surpasses human sin, just as the impact of Christ on humanity is infinitely greater than that of Adam. With God's grace and love, Christians will have the strength and courage to carry out their social and ethical responsibilities in the world as an embodiment of their Christian faith.

Ting emphasised that God's love is God's most important and most fundamental attribute. God's love is the love reflected in the cosmic nature of Christ, who gave up his life for all and whose domain, concern and care are universal. The love of the Cosmic Christ is God's all-inclusive love, which extends all over the world, to all of God's people. To help rid Chinese Christians of an image of God as a divine punisher, Ting pointed to the mother image used to describe God and God's love (such as in Isaiah 66: 13 and 49: 15, and in Psalm 131: 2). By using the mother image, Ting demonstrated that God's love does not coerce but works through education, persuasion, transformation and sanctification.

Ting criticised the overly simplistic and even distorted interpretation of justification by faith leading to spiritual pride and antinomianism. Ting claimed that believing in God and converting people are not the only dimensions of Christian faith. Justification cannot be used as an excuse for Christians to escape their social responsibilities and to avoid integrating into the whole community. Christians' good works do not merely aim to expand the church but, more importantly, to follow the Cosmic Christ's example of serving others. Ting strongly argued for a doctrine of sanctification alongside the doctrine of justification.

The Theological Reconstruction advocated by Bishop Ting aroused some debate at the beginning due to the response of the fundamentalist wing in the church. After two decades, however, through thousands of conferences, essay presentations and sermons, more and more clergy and Christians have come to appreciate the significance of Theological Reconstruction and to support the positive changes and healthy development it has brought to the Chinese church.

To deepen Theological Reconstruction and to make Christianity more relevant to the Chinese cultural, social and political context, the Ninth National Chinese Christian Conference in 2013 proposed the promotion of Christianity that is *Zhongguohua* (Christianity in China must be Chinese in orientation – that is, further contextualised). A Five-Year Outline Plan to Promote Protestant Christianity's *Zhongguohua* was released by the CCC and TSPM in March 2018. The goal of further contextualisation is to develop a Chinese church that exalts Christ and that maintains unity, that is faithful to biblical truth and rooted in Chinese culture, that has a contextualised theology relevant to the Chinese social as well as political context, and that is courageous in taking up social responsibilities. It aims to realise the transformation from 'Christianity in China' to 'Chinese Christianity'. Some of the major tasks of this further contextualisation include building a solid theological foundation for it by deepening Theological Reconstruction, continuing to standardise theological education and accelerate the pace of personnel training, using Chinese cultural forms to express faith, engaging in social service and practising the core values of Chinese socialism, which are prosperity, democracy, civility, harmony, freedom, equality, justice, the rule of law, patriotism, dedication, integrity and friendship.

Theological Education

Since 1981, 22 seminaries and Bible schools have been either reopened or opened in China. From the perspective of enrolment, these theological institutes are divided into three levels: Nanjing Union Theological Seminary (NJUTS), which enrols students nationwide; five regional seminaries, each of which enrols students from its own region; and the rest of the provincial seminaries and Bible schools, each of which enrols students from its particular province. Some specialised courses, such as the sacred music programme and the programme for the deaf run by certain seminaries, have started to enrol students nationwide as well.

According to the design, these 22 schools are divided into two categories. Nine seminaries and Bible schools run a three-year or two-year programme, while the rest of the seminaries offer a full undergraduate programme, including NJUTS, which also grants master's and doctoral degrees. NJUTS is run by the CCC and TSPM, while the provincial theological institutes are led by the provincial *lianghui*, and the regional ones by the *lianghui* in their respective regions.

Nearly 3,800 students attend these theological schools. Baptised Christians with high-school diplomas who have been church members for at least one year and are called to serve the church full time, and who have the recommendation of the local church and the endorsement of the local or provincial *lianghui*, are eligible to apply for the undergraduate programme or lower. To be admitted, applicants need to pass the entrance examinations in four or five subjects (depending on the theological school), an interview and a physical examination. With the same requirements, those who apply for the master's programme at NJUTS should also have either a four-year seminary or secular university education, and those who apply for the doctoral programme should have a master's degree in either theology or another subject in the liberal arts. There is no age limit for admission to NJUTS, while other schools generally do not enrol students over 35, making the average age of all theological students under 30.

The curriculum of these schools covers biblical, theological, historical and practical theological studies and some liberal arts courses, but the number and level of the courses offered vary from school to school. There are more than 280 faculty members, most of whom have master's degrees, with a dozen also holding doctoral degrees.

More than 23,500 students have graduated from the 22 seminaries and Bible schools since 1985. Most of those from the provincial and regional theological schools, together with those who have attended the undergraduate programme in NJUTS, have returned to their home churches to serve. Many graduates of NJUTS with a Master of Theology (MTh) degree have become faculty members in various theological institutes.

NJUTS, with nationwide enrolment, is the model for many other seminaries and Bible schools in China in terms of curriculum plan, faculty development, library development and so forth. NJUTS started to run both the four-year undergraduate and the three-year graduate programme in 1981, the Doctor of Theology (ThD) programme in 2016 and the Doctor of Ministry programme in 2017. It began to confer bachelor's and master's degrees in 1995. Due to the separation between education and religion, no degree from a religious institute in China is accredited by the Ministry of Education, but they are recognised in religious circles.

NJUTS joined the Association for Theological Education in South East Asia (ATESEA) in 2015 and is in the process of being accredited by ATESEA. It has 21 full-time faculty members and a handful of visiting professors teaching over 450 students. By 2020, the number of students will exceed 500, including 90 students in the MTh programme and around 10 doctoral students. Currently, three faculty members have either PhD or ThD degrees, while another three are pursuing their doctoral studies overseas; the rest hold master's degrees. The doctoral programme at NJUTS depends heavily on visiting professors who are well established scholars in their fields. The library has a collection of more than 60,000 volumes, not including digital resources such as ATLAS and CNKI. NJUTS also runs a three-year correspondence course to train lay leaders, with an enrolment of nearly 3,000.

During the second half of the 1980s, the CCC and TSPM started to send seminary graduates abroad for advanced degree programmes as a supplement to Chinese theological education. Since 2008, more than 130 people have been sent to seminaries in North America, Europe, Australia and the Chinese territories of Hong Kong and Taiwan.

Church and Society

Christian personal witness contributes not only to the growth of the Chinese Protestant church but also to its good reputation in society. With the understanding that 'a good Christian should be a good citizen' in mind, Christians in all walks of life endeavour to achieve professional success and good working relationships with peers. In recent years, the stories of the achievement in career and in Christian witness of some renowned painters, artists, singers, musicians, dancers, athletes, coaches, writers, educators, entrepreneurs, philanthropists, physicians and many others, including some model workers or advanced workers, have been shared in almost every issue of the church monthly magazine *Tian Feng*, which is publicly distributed and has more than 57,000 subscriptions. Christians in rural areas are also active in promoting the common good of their villages. There are Christians among the deputies to the People's Congress (PC) and the members of the Chinese People's Political Consultative Conference (CPPCC) at all levels. The churches can raise any concerns on religious freedom, social issues, social conditions and public opinions to government at all levels through the bills and proposals forwarded by Christians in the PC and CPPCC. The restoration of church property in many places in the 1980s and the policy concerning social and medical insurance enacted for religious workers in recent years are two examples among many that are indebted to the bills and proposals from these Christians.

Another way for the church to participate in society has been to offer social service, especially after the release of *Opinions on Encouraging and Regulating Religious Circles' Participation in Public Welfare Charitable Activities* by six government departments at the national level in 2012, which has granted religious circles more space and policies favourable to engaging in charity. In 2003, the CCC and TSPM had already established a Social Service Department (SSD) to foster the work of Christian social service. The SSD has worked with local churches all over the country to carry out various kinds of ministry in social service, including education support and child care, medical and health care, service to the elderly, community development, social welfare, disaster relief, capacity building and poverty alleviation. Annually, it has operated around 40 projects with local churches. The funds raised over the years have totalled around ¥119 million (around US$19.8 million).

Every September, during Religious Charity Week, many local churches together with the SSD conduct programmes to help people in need near and far. The SSD also works with other religious groups, for example inviting Muslim participation in training projects and visiting overseas Buddhist care homes for the elderly. Local churches also have joint social service programmes with other religious groups from time to time.

Apart from social service, Protestant churches have interactions with other faith groups in different ways. For instance, conferences on religious dialogue and religious harmony have often been held at the international, national and local levels among the five major religions in China, namely Buddhism, Taoism, Islam, Catholicism and Protestantism. Leaders of religious groups at all levels maintain good relationships, and some are PC deputies or CPPCC members. Theological institutes of different religions arrange visits to one another from time to time. A course on religious dialogue is offered in some seminaries and Bible schools, and representatives of other religions are often invited to introduce their own religion.

Relations with Churches Worldwide

Since China's reform and opening up, the Chinese churches have either resumed or newly established friendship with churches overseas. In the past 20 years, apart from the provincial *lianghui*, the CCC and TSPM alone have received more than 1,600 delegations of over 13,000 people representing Protestant churches on all continents. Some significant groups and individuals included leaders from the World Council of Churches, the World Evangelical Alliance, the World Communion of Reformed Churches, the Baptist World Alliance, the Lutheran World Federation and the Christian Conference of Asia, as well as the Archbishop of Canterbury and the Patriarch of the Russian Orthodox Church. During the same period, the CCC and TSPM organised about 500 delegations of around 1,600 people, including church leaders, theological educators, lay people and youth. Overseas exchanges included mutual sharing on the whole range of church ministries, theological education, social service, church media, inter-faith dialogue and Christian music and arts. The Protestant church in mainland China also has close contacts and cooperation with churches and seminaries in Hong Kong, Macau and Taiwan. The CCC is the largest Protestant member of the World Council of Churches.

Challenges and Prospects
What the Chinese church has achieved has gone far beyond what Chinese Christians could ever have predicted 40 years ago. In the meantime, however, it also faces unprecedented challenges. For instance, the churches have been challenged in various ways by a lack of well trained clergy. Because many rural congregations are led by lay leaders, elders or evangelists without theological training, proper teaching of the Bible and pastoral care are inadequately provided, so some misguided individuals can take advantage and lead some Christians astray. In some rural areas, tensions between Christianity and Chinese folk religions remain, and the distinction between inculturation and syncretism is sometimes hard for some Christians to make. Due to urbanisation, members of city churches often come from all walks of life, ranging from rural migrant workers to well established white-collar staff, from illiterate grannies to college students and well educated elite, from the jobless to the entrepreneur. It is truly challenging to prepare one Sunday sermon that will speak well to the spiritual needs of thousands of Christians with different backgrounds and to provide apt pastoral care to them with a limited number of clergy serving each church. Though affected less by heretical teachings, urban churches also face the negative influence of the theology of prosperity and of Charismatic trends brought from overseas.

The *lianghui* at all levels are fully aware of these challenges. In order to create a wide variety of personnel who can properly address the issues of the church, a more effective mechanism of training is being established to study and analyse training needs; to define training objectives; to design training programmes; and to expand training channels, including continuing education and overseas study. The seminary curriculum is also being revised in response to the new challenges to the churches.

A concern to many Chinese Christians is the divisive influence of forces from abroad. With the opening up of China, some overseas Christian groups have either publicly or secretly flocked into China with their own agendas. They raise funds by misinforming people outside mainland China about the situation of the Chinese churches and society. They claim that the 'real churches' that they want to establish or support in China should be 'underground' and 'opposing the Chinese government'. Their common teaching is to stay away from churches that do not fit their standard and from society as well unless it can be used to convert people to the churches they accept. In the eyes of many Chinese Christians, such groups from overseas have created confusion, division and chaos in the Chinese churches, a situation that the whole church needs to resist.

To safeguard the post-denominational unity, the Protestant church in China also needs to develop its own ecclesiology as a solid foundation for continuing to form a uniting church. A revised set of *Church Regulations* is expected to be released once it receives the approval of Tenth National Christian Conference as a step forward in building up the ecclesiology of the Chinese church.

The future of the Chinese church will be shaped by the extent to which it is able to renew itself in a changing society by putting the calls for Theological Reconstruction and further contextualisation of Christianity into practice. For Protestantism in mainland China to become more relevant to its Chinese context, it will be important for Chinese Christians to embrace a theology emphasising God's all-inclusive love and its ethical implications. In this way the Chinese church will be able to address the issues and common concerns of the time more effectively, and Chinese Christians will be equipped to follow the example of Jesus Christ more closely.

Bibliography

Chinese Theological Review (1985–2018).
Lin, Manhong Melissa, *Ethical Reorientation for Christianity in China: Individual Community, and Society* (Hong Kong: Christian Study Centre on Chinese Religion and Culture, 2010).
Luo, Weihong (罗伟) (ed.), *Zhongguo jidujiao(xinjiao)shi* [中国基督教] [The History of Christianity (Protestantism) in China] (Shanghai: Shanghai renmin chubanshe [上海人民出版社], 2014).
Tian Feng [天] [*The Magazine of the Protestant Churches in China*], 1981–2019.
Wickeri, Philip L., *Reconstructing Christianity in China: K. H. Ting and the Chinese Church* (Maryknoll, NY: Orbis Books, 2007).

Mainland China (Catholic)

Edmond Tang

On 22 September 2018, the Vatican signed a provisional agreement with the Chinese government regarding the selection of bishops in the Chinese Catholic Church. According to the agreement, the government will have a role in the selection process but concedes the final veto to the Vatican, thus ensuring that all future candidates will be acceptable to Rome. In return, the Vatican has moved to recognise the eight remaining Chinese bishops who were not yet in communion with the Holy See, including one posthumously. As Bishop Michael Yang Ming-cheung of Hong Kong commented before his untimely death in November 2018, the present arrangement is far from perfect and important issues remain to be resolved, including the release of clergy and laity who are in prison or in detention. It is also not clear whether underground Catholics can still worship separately. Cardinal Joseph Zen Ze-kiun, Bishop Emeritus of Hong Kong, however, is more critical of the Vatican, believing the agreement will bring serious harm to the underground communities without any benefit to the church as a whole. Nevertheless, it is a step forward towards healing the division within the Catholic community. In his message to Chinese Catholics, Pope Francis also reiterated that the agreement was made for pastoral reasons and wished the Catholic Church would heal and then move forwards together in the task of evangelisation, an important theme in his pontificate.

The last time the Catholic faith came close to being accepted into Chinese culture was during the sixteenth and seventeenth centuries, when Jesuit missionaries were allowed into the imperial court and when officials of the state became prominent Christians. This 'golden age' ended with the so-called Rites Controversy, which mainly concerned the practice of ancestor worship. In reality, the Controversy covered a range of unavoidable conflicts in the encounter between two major cultural systems, including different understandings of human nature, morality and the ultimate authority of the emperor. Nevertheless, the Jesuits' approach to mission in China, as in India at that time, has been upheld in more recent decades as a model of mission to another culture. This defining experience, called 'inculturation' in more recent theology, has been written into the DNA of the Catholic Church in China. Since the 1980s, the term has frequently appeared in Chinese Catholic discourse as well as in papal pronouncements regarding China. This approach also distinguishes the evangelism of the Catholic Church from that of Protestant groups in the country. However, the challenges of inculturation in seventeenth-century China are very different from those of the twentieth and twenty-first centuries, and we shall return to this later in the essay.

The second defining experience in the history of the Catholic Church in China is the colonial missions of the nineteenth and twentieth centuries that marked the church out to be both foreign and imperialistic. Very few of the Christian missions were not guilty of association with colonial powers, but this was even more true of the Catholic Church, because its faith requires the acceptance of a foreign authority. In the eyes of the government, and to the majority of the Chinese population, the Vatican is not only a foreign religious authority but a political one as well.

The nineteenth-century missions, both Catholic and Protestant, used and abused the power of their respective governments to open missionary routes beyond the trading ports and into the Chinese hinterland. Of course, the missions made contributions to the development of modern China with the introduction of modern health care, education and, above all, new social and political ideas. Modern Chinese people can appreciate the role of the West in hastening the end of the old imperial order but still resent the imposition of a foreign religion. This has played well into the propaganda of the communist government since the 1950s.

It is worth noting that a resentment of Christianity is not exclusive to the communist period in China. There is a continuum of anti-foreign and anti-Christian movements from the late Qing dynasty (the Boxer Uprising of 1900), through the Nationalist period (the May Fourth Movement of 1919) to the present day. The communist government has effectively channelled these popular feelings into its official narrative despite numerous protestations that times have changed and Christianity is no longer a political threat to Chinese society or culture. However, the idea of Christianity as a foreign and aggressively hostile religion has entered into the popular consciousness. These sentiments can still be detected among the general populace; even intellectuals and academics who are critical of the communist government share the same point of view.

The challenges to Christianity, and to the Catholic Church in particular, are twofold. On the one hand, the Catholic Church has to change fundamentally its image in Chinese society by shedding its 'foreign character', but more crucially it has to discover its role in the evolving Chinese culture through an in-depth inculturation. On both counts, it is interesting to see how the Jesuit missions of the sixteenth century have been constructed as an exemplary model of mission, and how their most prominent representative, Matteo Ricci, has acquired iconic status in Catholic discourse in both China and the Vatican. Before the Catholic Church in China can respond effectively to the twofold challenge above, however, it must come to terms with the third defining experience, of separation and division, that is as intense today as when it began in the 1950s.

When the communist government in China came to power in 1949 it began to bring all non-communist organisations under the United Front. For the religions, it established 'patriotic associations' as a tool of management and control. Through these patriotic associations, the government has direct control of institutions, clergy and places of worship. Because of their foreign connections, the principles of self-finance, self-government and self-propagation were imposed on Christians. The Protestant Three-Self Patriotic Movement was established in 1952 with some support from more progressive leaders among their ranks, but the similar effort among Catholics encountered fierce resistance. For the latter, communion with the Holy See is not only a question of organisational links but part of their belief. Foreign priests and nuns were expelled and indigenous leaders were put in prison. Not until 1957 was the Chinese Catholic Patriotic Association (CCPA) finally established. In the same year the CCPA proceeded to consecrate the first new bishops to fill the vacancies of the departed bishops. The Vatican condemned this act as schismatic. Those who followed the Vatican and opposed the Patriotic Association went underground. For more than 30 years the 'underground church' was persecuted by the government, and many accused the CCPA of taking an active part in that persecution. The Cultural Revolution (officially 1966–76) drove the church further into the shadows. The churches under the CCPA were also closed and their clergy disbanded or forced to marry. The 1980s saw a general liberalisation in China, however, and the religions were allowed to resurface.

Churches under the Chinese Catholic Patriotic Association

A document released by the CCPA in 1987 stated:

> The Chinese Catholic Church affirms that on the basis of independence and autonomy, the self-management of the Church is a response to the will of God and the interests of the country. This is our position which will not change: a Chinese Catholic religion on Chinese soil.

It is worth pointing out the nuance in the use of the phrase 'independence and autonomy'. 'Autonomy' means running the church's affairs according to local circumstances, which is acceptable according to the theology of the local church since the Second Vatican Council, but 'independence' amounts to rejecting allegiance to Rome or jurisdiction under the Pope and therefore is not acceptable.

The 1987 document also gave an analysis of the Vatican's *Ostpolitik*, successfully applied in Eastern Europe in the 1980s, which saw the resurgence of the Catholic Church as a formidable political force in such countries as Poland and Yugoslavia. The fear of the CCPA is that the Vatican's call for dialogue is a cover for subversion and infiltration. It also accuses the Vatican of sending secret missions into China to recruit agents (the underground church) in order to organise a reactionary force against the independent church and further the downfall of the government, just as it had done in former Soviet satellites. The overall tone is one of suspicion and hostility.

Opinions in China differ regarding the CCPA. Those who oppose it believe it is the work of the devil, an instrument of the government to destroy the church. They blame the CCPA for creating division in the church and attempting to separate it from the seat of Peter. They also think that politically motivated persons and priests of doubtful reputation have taken control of its leadership.

On the other hand, some are sympathetic to the historical injustices of colonialism that underpin its foundation. As the communist government took over in the 1950s and political purges began, many in the church believed that to accept an independent administration was the only way to safeguard the continued existence of the church under the new regime.

It is possible to find evidence to support either view. At present, it is difficult to say with confidence that the CCPA is working to eliminate the church. Government policy has definitely changed; it now accepts that religion will be a permanent feature of Chinese society, and a more effective policy is to bring the various groups into the mainstream. Since the 1980s, the CCPA has assisted in the return of 6,000 places of worship and has opened eight major seminaries for the training of priests and 10 minor seminaries for younger vocations. It has printed Bibles, liturgical texts and prayer books for the use of the faithful. In fact, many Catholics, like the majority of Chinese citizens, believe that politics is only for the elite. If they are resigned to government control then they can go to Mass, confess their sins, receive the sacraments of healing and even baptise their children. Perhaps this explains why the 'patriotic' churches are generally well attended, especially on major feast days. It is estimated that half of the Catholic population in China come under the CCPA.

This is not to say, however, that the CCPA is loved and supported. Most of its bishops and priests resent its presence. The organisation's power is strong nationally and in large cities, while in many areas the local branches of the CCPA are often ignored until they are needed to negotiate with the government. Sometimes the clergy can be creative in their passive resistance. In a few churches, the local clergy took the initiative to join the CCPA in order to become officials in the organisation while quietly working for the pastoral benefits of the faithful. In other cases, the local bishop, supported by his priests, has stood up against the CCPA and wrested back a certain amount of authority in the running of the church. In short, the picture is quite complicated. As the rapprochement with the Vatican appeared on the horizon, many bishops consecrated under the CCPA have reconciled with the Holy See. Before the rapprochement between the Vatican and Chinese authorities in 2018, only eight of the 60 or so 'patriotic bishops' were not yet regularised, and they have since been accepted by the Vatican in the provisional agreement.

The 'Underground Church'
Those who opposed the CCPA went underground in the 1950s; this underground church was sometimes called the 'faithful church' because of its loyalty to the Pope. It was a difficult existence and there were heroic stories, recounted in letters smuggled out of China, of how priests moved about from one home to another, sometimes in the middle of the night, to avoid arrest. Local Catholics lived in fear of detention, discrimination in employment and disadvantages in the educational opportunities for their children. Sometimes underground communities could operate in a semi-open environment, tolerated by local officials as long as they did not create any trouble. As the political atmosphere eased after the Cultural Revolution, some underground priests could 'hide' in plain sight in official churches but still minister to a non-official congregation.

The formation of a more structured underground community began in the 1980s, when China embarked on its drive for modernisation. In 1979 the Congregation for the Evangelization of Peoples sent a document to China giving the underground community certain concessions regarding the administration of sacraments outside of the framework of the CCPA. At roughly the same time, the Vatican also gave permission to set up unofficial seminaries, even though they could not fulfil the requirements of canon law, and most importantly for bishops to ordain other bishops and priests. Some in the underground church considered this a green light to organise a parallel church. The number of 'clandestine' bishops suddenly increased at an alarming rate. Many priests were ordained secretly, sometimes with only a few months of doctrinal instruction. They were then sent around the country to warn Catholics away from the official churches, and claimed they had a mandate from Rome. They warned that the sacraments administered by CCPA priests were invalid, and those who received sacraments from these priests were committing a sin instead of receiving grace from God. As a result, the number of Catholics going to official churches declined and many of the faithful were confused.

Some seminarians left the official church because they began to doubt the validity of their ordinations.

The so-called underground church found its leadership among bishops coalesced around a leader, Bishop Fan Xueyuan of Baoding in Hebei province, who spent more than 30 years in prison. In 1988 Bishop Fan, in between prison or detention, gave an interview that was subsequently summarised in a circular known as the 'Thirteen Points'. The document repeated the attack on the 'patriotic church', as mentioned, and called on Catholics to boycott the churches under the CCPA.

Rome was alarmed, as the prospect of a permanent schism was on the horizon. In a series of programmes broadcast to China from Manila, the Vatican's Radio Veritas toned down the claims of the Thirteen Points. Radio Veritas stated firmly that only the Pope had the power of excommunication, and some bishops, priests and even lay people overstepped their authority when they excommunicated others on behalf of the Pope. It recognised that CCPA membership did not necessarily mean the person in question was anti-Vatican, and some actually were secretly loyal to Rome. It stressed that according to canon law the sacraments administered by priests of the CCPA were still valid and receiving them would not be considered a sin.

In September 1988 the Congregation for the Evangelization of Peoples sent a letter to the bishops of the world giving the Vatican's evaluation of the situation in China and its view of the CCPA, namely that within the organisation there were members of an intermediate way, those who 'conserve in their hearts as unrelinquishable their bonds of communion with the Holy Father, as well as accepting the religious policy imposed by the [Chinese] Authorities'.

The letter also referred to a confidential document circulated in China, *Directives on Some of the Problems of the Church in Continental China*, that had been prepared at the request of Pope John Paul II and approved by him. The *Directives* more or less repeated the same clarifications on excommunications, validity of ordinations and the 'presumed' validity of sacraments administered by priests not in communion with Rome. Nevertheless, the *Directives* advised that the faithful should still seek out priests who remained loyal to Rome.

The intervention from Rome halted the schism, but the two communities were still running parallel to each other. Many areas have overlapping communities, each with its own bishop, group of priests and religious sisters, including the religious orders that have resurfaced since the 1980s. In 1989 the underground church consolidated its structures by creating its own bishops' conference, with Bishop Fan elected as chairman, although he was still in prison. The government's crackdown was fierce. Bishop Fan died in custody in 1992, his body dumped by the authorities in front of the rural church where he served, showing signs of torture and broken ribs.

Towards Reconciliation

After the Tiananmen incident in 1989, the atmosphere in the country changed. In Eastern Europe, the former communist regimes collapsed one after another. The role played by the churches in their demise, as in Poland, East Germany, Yugoslavia and Romania, was not unnoticed. Consequently, the Chinese government imposed tighter control on the religions, but at the same time set out a new policy to bring the religions more tightly into the mainstream. Resources were provided to improve local religious infrastructure and for the training of religious leaders.

The Vatican, alarmed by the danger of schism, took a series of measures to minimise further divisions and left open opportunities for future reconciliation. Despite its support for the 'faithful church', it did not give recognition to the underground bishops' conference, and from 1993 onwards refused permission for the underground church to ordain bishops without prior Vatican agreement. It also opened more communication with the priests and bishops of the official church, allowing bishops under the CCPA to secretly reconcile with the Holy See.

Under Pope John Paul II (1978–2005) the church in China became a priority. In his early statements he praised China as a great nation (1979) and sought to reassure the Chinese government that it had nothing to fear from the Catholic Church, for 'a good Catholic is also a good citizen' who would treat the authorities with filial piety (1981). The Catholic Church would be a Chinese church through inculturation. In 2001 he acknowledged that mistakes had been made in the past by some in the church and apologised for them. He repeatedly made clear his desire for dialogue in public statements as well as through diplomatic channels, including an undisclosed letter that he sent to Deng Xiaoping personally in 1982.

As for the divided Catholic community, there is no doubt that his sympathies lay with the suffering faithful, but he also showed understanding that many followed the CCPA against their will. Above all, he called for the church to seek unity. In January 1995, from the World Youth Day in Manila, he sent an open message to China calling for the church to unite, first of all among themselves and with the successor of Peter in Rome.

Pope Benedict XVI (2005–13) followed with a similar call for unity in an open letter to Chinese Catholics in June 2007. He acknowledged the suffering of Catholics under the rule of the Chinese Communist Party but said it was time to forgive past wrongdoings and for the underground and official communities to reconcile. To the CCPA, however, he made it clear that it was not possible for the church to operate independently of the Vatican. He also advised Catholics to worship with priests who are faithful to Rome, although he added that sacraments performed by the official church were still valid.

It is left to Pope Francis (2013–) to continue the negotiations with the Chinese authorities. He elevated Cardinal Pietro Parolin, until then the chair of the Vatican's China committee, to secretary of state. This was a sign that dialogue with Chinese authorities would intensify. On 22 September 2018 the dialogue led to a provisional agreement on the appointment of bishops, the main issue dividing the Catholic communities in China. Aware of the strong feelings inside and outside China about the agreement, Pope Francis explained the reasons in a message to Chinese Catholics on 26 September. The purpose of the accord is to provide a stable relationship between the Vatican and the Chinese authorities so that they can cooperate in the selection of shepherds for the flock. The agreement is provisional and needs improvement; above all, it is only 'an instrument, and not of itself capable of resolving all existing problems'. He asks for a 'deep commitment' by all, especially bishops, priests and consecrated persons, to leave behind past conflicts and personal interest to work for the common good of the church and to advance the task of evangelisation. He recognises the suffering of many Catholics but deems the rise of the underground church 'abnormal' and asks all Chinese Catholics to work towards reconciliation.

The agreement will not produce the expected reconciliation if there is no grassroots desire for unity. The conflict between the two communities is well documented, but less so the instances of local reconciliation. At present, this information is anecdotal and fragmentary, in some cases to avoid outside intervention. Nevertheless, they are not uncommon, suggesting a changing atmosphere since the early 1990s. We can cite with confidence two such examples.

In 1995 someone paid a visit to Jin Peixian, the official Bishop of Shenyang diocese in north-east China. Jin is well respected for his pastoral oversight of the diocese and had brought the local CCPA under his control. After attending morning Mass the visitor left the cathedral and was surprised to hear another Mass being celebrated in the old refectory within the cathedral compound. He asked Bishop Jin what was going on, and the old bishop said matter-of-factly, 'It's the underground church having Mass there'. When the visitor joined the bishop and his priests for breakfast in his residence, the bishop introduced him to an old priest sitting at the table: 'This is Father [X], the underground priest who was saying Mass in the refectory'.

Earlier, in 1994, another visitor was in the city of Wuhan. The Bishop of Wuhan, Dong Guangqing, was the first bishop to be consecrated in

China without the approval of Rome. The episcopal seat had been vacant for more than five years after the departure of the previous bishop, who was Italian. The diocese sent a message to the Pope asking for permission to consecrate a new bishop to fill the vacancy, but it was firmly rejected. It was said that the bishop cried for three days and three nights before he succumbed to government pressure to proceed with the ordination. Late in the evening Bishop Dong brought the visitor to another wing of his residence, where he introduced the visitor to an old friend. This turned out to be the underground bishop of the neighbouring diocese, Bishop Liu Hede, who had been jailed for 22 years for his opposition to the CCPA. Then the two old friends, both in their 80s, recounted how they reconciled with each other through a common friend and now worked together, with the local government's tacit understanding, for the pastoral care of the diocese and the seminary.

Since the older generation knew each other personally before the split in the 1950s, it was perhaps easier to re-establish communications and understanding. This cannot be said of the younger generation of priests. Some of those from the underground church did not know any form of community but their own and have become fiercely militant against the official church. There are signs, though, that contact and communication channels are opening, and with the agreement clearly directed by the Pope himself, many from the underground church are willing to explore reconciliation with the official church.

Second Vatican Council and Renewal

It will not do justice to the story of the Catholic Church in China if we attend only to its division and the task of reconciliation, important as they are. The four decades or more since the end of the Cultural Revolution have also been a time of rebuilding and renewal. In the 40 years since its return to public worship, the church has grown steadily to about 10 million members, from less than 3 million just before the Cultural Revolution. As of 2017 some 6,000 churches are open, divided between 96 dioceses (144 in the old boundaries of 1951). There are 101 bishops (though not all are active), with 65 in the official church and 36 belonging to the underground church. The numbers of priests have gone up to 2,550 and 1,320 respectively. There are also 3,170 sisters in official convents and 1,400 underground. The number of priests is dwarfed by the much larger number of pastors in the Protestant churches. Reasons for this include the requirement that Catholic priests be celibate, which is an obstacle to vocations under the one-child policy, and the fact that the training of Catholic priests usually takes two to three times longer than that for Protestant clergy.

Very often the growth of the Catholic Church is compared unfavourably to the exponential expansion of Protestants. Indeed, many Catholic leaders in China are worried about the slow speed of evangelisation, although the number of annual baptisms is quite steady. Specific reasons include greater government control, the more institutionalised approach to mission and the curse of division. Perhaps it is also worth considering that Catholicism is a different way of 'being church' – that is, the Catholic Church takes a different trajectory, giving more emphasis to rebuilding its hierarchy and pastoral infrastructure before branching out from the centre. On the other hand, compared with Protestantism there is greater coherence in doctrine (aside from the 'political' question of allegiance to Rome), fewer 'heresies and cults', more institutional identity, a greater sense of belonging, an educated clergy and greater theological openness to cultural changes in society.

If asked to identify the most important change in the Catholic Church in China, many would not hesitate to mention the Second Vatican Council. First and foremost is the introduction of the new liturgy, particularly saying Mass in the vernacular. For more than a century, Chinese Catholics were used to Mass in Latin, with the priest facing away from a passive congregation, performing obscure rituals in an obscure language. This was considered the height of Catholic worship and identity. Even the powerful CCPA dared not tamper with it. Slowly, with help from the churches in Hong Kong and Taiwan, the new liturgy was introduced in a few places, then gradually to the whole country. In short, the changes, introduced with patience and accompanied by a good educational programme, were well received, and the whole style of worship was transformed. The Mass has become more lively and the sermons more meaningful and relevant, and the congregation is more active in its participation. The new liturgy was a test case of whether the faithful were open to adopting a new way of practising their religious life. The Chinese texts, with minor changes, are now the same as the ones used in overseas Chinese communities, re-establishing the common bond with the universal church. If even the Eucharist can be changed, what cannot be improved in other areas of Catholic life? Social responsibility, culture and spirituality are good examples.

The most prominent Catholic development agency in China is the Beifang Jinde Social Service Centre in Shijiazhuang, an industrial city not far from Beijing. It is special because it was not established by the church's central authority, but by a priest in the Shijiazhuang diocese, Father John-Baptist Zhang. He started a local Catholic newspaper in 1991 that grew into a regional and then national publication. The government almost closed it at one point because of its independence. The social service side grew out of the newspaper, from the stories about small church projects in disaster relief and help to the poor. Now it is staffed by several priests, sisters and lay professionals and its work has gone national. In the 2000s, the newspaper started a publishing house with a series of books on Catholic doctrine, spirituality and ethics.

Similarly, the Institute for the Study of Christianity and Culture was started by a priest in the Beijing diocese. Father Peter Zhao obtained his doctorate in canon law from the University of Leuven in Belgium in 2002. Upon his return to China he devoted his ministry to forwarding the dialogue between Catholicism and Chinese culture. The small initiative is now an established academic platform that organises national conferences with Chinese universities and publishes a journal in cultural dialogue as well as books in academic theology. The only other comparable Catholic publishing house is the Guangqi Press in Shanghai, which was revived after the Cultural Revolution.

Another important development since the first decade of the 2000s is the increase in the number of centres of spirituality around the country. Several spiritual traditions, including Benedictine, Franciscan and Augustinian, have been revived through the re-establishment of religious orders and houses. In seminaries and churches, training workshops are organised in Catholic social teaching, pastoral counselling and eco-theology.

The significance of these and similar initiatives is that they were taken by a new generation of leaders who are academically competent and who embraced wholeheartedly the spirit of the Second Vatican Council. These are the elements of a modern Chinese church.

The Politics of Inculturation

In the introduction to this essay we outlined the three defining experiences of the Catholic Church in China that are also its main challenges: from foreign to Chinese; from colonial to national; from division to unity. With the agreement reached between the Vatican and China, and the clear appeal from the Pope for unity, we can expect that reconciliation will gradually take place, especially with the passing of the older generation. As for its colonial image, it remains for the church to demonstrate that it can emerge from the past stigma, by actively serving the Chinese people through service to society, a strong Chinese leadership and building up national institutions with a clear cultural identity. The danger of external intervention, except in narrow areas of doctrine, is likely to subside; the statements of recent Popes have conceded as much.

As China's economy develops at an unprecedented speed, Chinese society has become more materialistic and secular, while social relations, which broke down through 70 years of tumultuous political campaigns, are still to be healed or even reinvented. There is a thirst for values and spirituality. Christianity – in many different forms, from fundamentalism through Pentecostalism to an intellectual Christian humanism – is finding echoes from different sectors of Chinese society. However, will Christianity be just another form of the religious escapism that was so despised in the past, or will it be a positive contributor to a new system of values and a new cultural identity?

The greatest barrier to inculturation today comes from a new nationalism emerging in China that appears in both cultural and political forms. The government version is the most political. In trying to forge a new political and cultural cohesion in society, and to consolidate its control over all spheres of social life, the government has launched a campaign of 'Sinicisation', including the Sinicisation of Marxism and Sinicisation of religions. President Xi Jinping explained the meaning of that in a speech to the United Front in 2015: follow the party, adapt to socialist society, support economic progress and maintain ethnic unity.

Inculturation requires immersion and commitment in order to belong and to be part of a community or culture. At the same time, there must also be discernment guided by faith and knowledge. How to be 'in the world and not of the world' and to discern what role the Catholic Church can play in President Xi's vision of the 'Chinese dream' will be a daunting task.

Bibliography

Chu, Cindy Yik-yi, *The Catholic Church in China: 1978 to the Present* (New York: Palgrave Macmillan, 2012).
Lam, Anthony Sui-ki, *The Catholic Church in Present-Day China* (Hong Kong: Holy Spirit Study Centre, 1997).
Madsen, Richard, *China's Catholics: Tragedy and Hope in an Emerging Civil Society* (Berkeley, CA: University of California Press, 1998).
Tiedemann, Gary, *Handbook of Christianity in China, Vol. II: 1800–Present* (Leiden: Brill, 2009).
Yan, Chiaretto Kin Sheung, *Evangelization in China* (Maryknoll, NY: Orbis Books, 2014).

Mainland China (House Churches)

David Ro

The house-church movement in China comprises millions of Christians who worship without legal status. Around the time China opened its door to the world in 1979, a house-church movement grew rapidly: first in the countryside among semi-literate peasants, followed by another church movement in the cities, among intellectuals. On the surface, the political reforms provided more freedoms and saw the release of pastors from prison. More influential, however, was a movement of spiritual renewal that resulted in the emergence of a house-church movement, marked by many of the characteristics of the early church, as described in the Book of Acts.

This movement quickly attracted millions of people in rural China, with little outside influence. After an intense period of suffering, a house-church movement grew explosively, without foreign seminaries, denominations, mission agencies or para-church organisations. Miraculous healings were one of the primary reasons the gospel spread like wildfire in the countryside. Chinese evangelists with only elementary- or middle-school education had nothing but the Bible and their conversion testimonies, yet they made a profound impact. Several large networks representing millions of rural Christians spread across China in the 1980s and 1990s. Evangelists from Henan and Anhui travelled from village to village and to cities throughout China to preach the gospel and plant churches. Entrepreneurs from Wenzhou started churches as they launched their businesses across China. However, millions of rural young people migrated to the cities due to China's urbanisation, resulting in a decline of Christianity in the countryside and the growth of the urban church in the cities.

In the 1990s and 2000s, a church movement emerged in the cities among a new group of urban intellectuals. A generation of young people came to faith after the Tiananmen Square incident in 1989, resulting in the emergence of a 'newly formed emerging urban church' (新兴型城市教会). This 'new wineskin' urban church consists of mainstream white-collar professionals and intellectuals. It surfaced independently in cities all across China, 'newly formed and emerging' as opposed to the existing traditional urban house churches. Many of these urban churches are generally theologically Reformed and have developed new alliances and denominational affiliations. Christianity continues to experience steady growth in the cities through both urban intellectuals who are coming to faith and the rural church in its migration to the cities.

Another type of house church is the 'traditional house church', which persevered through an experience of suffering during the Cultural Revolution. Christians belonging to this kind of house church endured persecution for refusing to compromise their faith by joining the official Three-Self Patriotic Movement (TSPM), which they consider to be under the control of an atheistic government. Theologically conservative and deeply pietistic, these house-church Christians endured and kept the faith. The traditional house church exists in the coastal regions of Shandong, Zhejiang, Wenzhou, Fujian and Guangzhou and in the large cities of Shanghai and Beijing. Several patriarchs of this movement, including Wang Mingdao, Allen Yuan, Moses Xie, Samuel Lamb and Li Tianen, who suffered 20 or more years in prison, have already passed away. However, their legacy continues to inspire today's house-church Christians who remember their persevering spirituality and sacrificial faith.

House Church and Official Church

China's Protestant church was estimated in 2015 to comprise some 55 million members in the unregistered house churches and about 30 million in the official Three-Self Patriotic Movement church. House churches are Evangelical in theology and have no formal membership in any foreign organisations. The official China Christian Council has been a member of the World Council of Churches since 1991 and is aligned theologically with the liberal mainline denominations. At the grassroots, however, both TSPM pastors and house-church leaders tend to align with Evangelical doctrine and practice unless prevented by the authorities. Typically, they regard the Bible as central to their faith, believe in a conversion born-again experience by grace through faith in Jesus Christ to be saved, accept in literal terms the biblical accounts of the miracles and the virgin birth, and are evangelistic within their limitations.

Why doesn't the house church submit to the authorities and join the official TSPM? In general, house-church Christians are patriotic Chinese citizens and do not hold animosity towards the Communist Party. At the same time, house-church believers as a matter of conscience have decided not to compromise with an atheistic government on faith- and church-related matters. The 'A Joint Statement by Pastors' explains this position:

> Christian churches in China are willing to obey authorities in China whom God has appointed and to respect the government's authority to govern

society and human conduct. We believe and are obligated to teach all believers in the church that the authority of the government is from God and that as long as the government does not overstep the boundaries of secular power laid out in the Bible and does not interfere with or violate anything related to faith or the soul, Christians are obligated to respect the authorities, to pray fervently for their benefit, and to pray earnestly for Chinese society.

House-church leaders often look to Wang Mingdao, who suffered 26 years in prison (1955–80) for his uncompromising stance. Wang's famous quote, 'it is because of our faith [我们是为了信仰]', implied that his persecution was not because of politics but because of his refusal to compromise by joining the TSPM. Wang viewed the TSPM as being under the control of an atheistic Communist Party that became the final authority on church-related matters, especially the appointment of pastors.

The Chinese house-church position is the historic Evangelical Protestant theology of suffering and martyrdom sometimes called 'cooperative resistance'. This involves cooperating with the authorities unless under attack for faith-related matters, when believers appeal to a transcendent standard above the law. The house churches' uncompromising cooperative resistance does not preclude the desire to be a legally recognised entity outside of the control of the TSPM. In 2005, a prominent urban house church, Beijing Shouwang Church, attempted to register with the government when a new regulation allowed for legal registration apart from the TSPM. This Beijing house church submitted all the required documents, but the government rejected the application on the basis that the TSPM did not ordain or recognise any of the pastors.

If a future legal registration process for house churches does not provide a satisfactory answer to the question of who the head of the church is, we can expect a return to the same problem seen in the previous generation. The 2018 decision by the Vatican to enter into an agreement with the Chinese government is viewed with anxiety by some house-church leaders, who fear that it will 'keep China in charge of the church', with priest appointments decided by the Chinese government and only veto power given to the Pope. The house churches might soon divide over this issue of the separation of church and state. The more conservative house-church leaders would consider those who sign away part of their autonomy as compromisers, calling them 'a new TSPM'. More than 400 pastors and elders who have signed the non-compromising Joint Statement represent millions of house-church Christians. They are ready to be the new generation of torchbearers for the principle of freedom from state control, repeating Chinese church history by suffering in prison for this conviction like Wang Mingdao.

The essential difference between the TSPM and the house church is not necessarily legal status but overall direction. While the TSPM church is focused on a Five-Year Plan for Sinicisation (2018–22) and works closely with the governing Communist Party, the house church is in preparation to impact the world through urban church planting and global missions. The house-church movement is now expanding globally by sending cross-cultural missionaries overseas. Rural house-church networks have already been sending hundreds of missionaries to serve in many difficult regions of the world through the Back to Jerusalem Movement. Urban house-church leaders are planting churches in the cities as well as preparing for a Mission China 2030 vision to send 20,000 missionaries by the year 2030.

House-church attitudes to the official TSPM church vary, ranging from compassion to indifference to strong negativity. The younger urban house churches that have not experienced persecution have less animosity to the TSPM than the traditional house-church generation. Their attitude is often indifference, as they worship in an unregistered house church due to practicality and expediency. Other house-church leaders feel compassion for their TSPM counterparts, as they consider them to be under the 'bondage' of an atheistic ruler. For example, urban house-church leaders travelled to Wenzhou at considerable risk to show support for the Wenzhou TSPM when crosses were removed from some churches. Among the traditional house churches, a strong negative feeling to the TSPM persists as they remember the persecution that resulted from their refusal to join.

Nevertheless, the existence of both the TSPM and the house churches can be mutually beneficial. TSPM churches can benefit from the house churches, as the authorities often give them a freer hand when the house churches are under attack. For example, a Beijing TSPM church was permitted to plant new church meeting points when a nearby house church was under attack in order to encourage house-church members to join the Three-Self church. At the same time, the house churches benefit from the TSPM, as many house-church believers' first exposures to Christianity were through TSPM churches. The TSPM's legal status also allows for the printing of millions of Bibles through Amity Press. On occasion, TSPM leaders have provided legal protection for house-church religious activity.

Worship, Spirituality and Pastoral Life

Spirituality and worship styles vary according to the different kind of churches. The traditional house-church worship is conservative, fundamentalist and pietistic, usually done in smaller groups in private homes. The rural house church closely aligns with Pentecostal/Charismatic spirituality, emphasising the experiential in worship, prayer, Bible study, simple faith and evangelistic fervour. Hundreds of indigenous worship songs have been written by a rural middle-school-educated hymn writer called Lü Xiaomin, drawing on experiences of hardship and suffering. The urban house church is usually led by a full-time pastor focused on preaching of the Word and is usually more Reformed and theologically grounded, with an orderly congregational worship and governing structure. Urban house churches have moved from homes to office complexes but still call themselves 'house churches' since they originally started in homes, as opposed to the church buildings of the official TSPM. Some 'house churches' in Wenzhou have cathedral-style buildings like the TSPM. In the earlier days, worship in homes would involve 20–60 worshippers crowded together under tight security. Only the faithful believers would be invited, as government infiltrators were considered a real threat.

The overall house-church spirituality springs from the historic Evangelical pietism of the earlier missionaries such as Hudson Taylor and the China Inland Mission. It is marked by prayer, Bible study, deep affection for God, repentance, evangelism, simple living and a deep faith in God under extreme circumstances. Chinese characteristics have included courage, sacrifice, perseverance and suffering, developed from the way of the cross through persecution and the example of patriarchs like Wang Mingdao. John Sung made a mark on the house church through his evangelistic revivals, which stressed repentance, being filled with the Holy Spirit and personal holiness. Watchman Nee and the Brethren Movement influenced house-church ecclesiology and its emphasis on the laity. Other indigenous influences include the Jesus Family, with its emphasis on communal living, simple lifestyle and brokenness. More recently, Koreans have influenced the urban house church with prayer, the ordination of pastors, larger church buildings, shepherding the congregation, discipleship, tithing and overseas cross-cultural missions.

Theological Fault Lines

The house church has split into two major camps: the Charismatic-leaning rural and the urban Reformed. The majority of the rural church networks are shaped by Charismatic and Holiness influences from Arminian theology. The newly formed emerging urban churches and the traditional house church in the coastal cities have generally adopted Reformed theology. This summary is, however, an oversimplification, as these divisions are also caused by historical lineage, rural and urban differences, younger and older generations, power struggles and personalities.

The large rural networks from Henan, Wenzhou and Anhui have Pietistic, Holiness and Pentecostal Charismatic leanings. Though Pietism, the Holiness Movement and Pentecostalism influenced the church even before the communist takeover, it was after the opening up of China in the 1980s that Pentecostal missionary Dennis Balcombe introduced the baptism of the Holy Spirit. However, the term 'Charismatic' has negative connotations for some. The two largest networks, Yinshang from Anhui and the China Gospel Fellowship from Henan, would not call themselves Charismatic. Some urban church pastors influenced by the third-wave Charismatics are largely rejected by the Reformed urban churches. More recently, Charismatic influences have come through the 'Coming Home' conferences led by Egyptian-Canadian elder David Damien from Vancouver. Overseas Chinese Charismatic pastors invited Damien to hold a Coming Home conference in Hong Kong in 2010, and 5,000 supporters attended. The following year, 12,000 believers came together, two-thirds of them from mainland China. In 2012, the number increased to 15,000, and in 2016 the total attending the conference reached 30,000, probably the largest-ever gathering of mainland Chinese Christians outside of China.

Reformed theology has also experienced a resurgence. Overseas Chinese Reverend Stephen Tong and Dr Jonathan Chao along with Korean Presbyterians had an earlier impact with the introduction of Reformed theology. More recently, a Reformed church-planting ministry called Grace to City was launched in 2012 with a vision to see churches planted in the cities of China. Some 50–70 urban churches were planted between 2012 and 2018, and there are plans to launch more. A younger generation of house-church participants has attended large conferences in Hong Kong and Taiwan. In 2014 in Hong Kong, 1,500 met. In 2017, the 500th anniversary of the Reformation was celebrated by 2,700. In August 2018, around 800 participants met in Kinmen, Taiwan, for the conference Gospel-Centred Discipleship.

The gospel-centred church-planting city movement has fostered a resurgence of Reformed theology and a return to denominations. However, more significant is a return of the doctrine of grace and the centrality of Christ's work on the cross. For a younger generation, the gospel-centred grace has been a breath of fresh air against the traditional legalistic house-church culture. During a period of persecution, faithful obedience in the midst of suffering became the dominant theme.

Another reason for the popularity of Reformed theology among urban intellectuals is a doctrinal foundation along with organisational structure. An anti-intellectualism from fundamentalism influenced the traditional urban churches and rural networks. These older churches viewed theological education with scepticism. For the more-educated Christian urbanites and even some traditional churches, the Reformed faith provided an all-inclusive system of doctrine and practice that made sense.

Reformed denominations have returned to China. Reformed pastors have been forming alliances and creating new associations and denominations. Critics have alleged that some of these Reformed pastors with

Presbyterian denominational alliances have become 'hyper-Calvinist' as they now no longer associate with non-Reformed pastors and churches. Several younger pastors who studied in seminaries abroad have returned to China to establish a network of 'Returnee Seminarians'. Many of these overseas-educated younger pastors have decided to align themselves with the Reformed Baptists and are less exclusive than the Presbyterians.

China's Reformed church mission is primarily a gospel-centred church-planting movement in the cities, with a strong emphasis on the distinction and importance of Reformed theology. Reverend Wang Yi, pastor of Early Rain Covenant Church in Chengdu, has been very vocal and courageous in pointing out the injustices of society. He has also been the leading voice defending the churches from recent government attacks and has been attacked by the authorities for conducting memorial services for the victims of the Tiananmen Square incident and the Sichuan earthquake. Reformed churches have little interest in joining the Mission China pastors who are engaged in a global endeavour to send missionaries to the unreached areas of the world.

An Overall Political Tightening

China is undergoing an overall tightening in control of all sectors, including academia, business, entertainment, media and religion. Particular targets include Xinjiang Muslims, Tibetan Buddhists, Catholics and Protestants. President Xi's overall government strategy is the rejuvenation of the nation through a 'Chinese dream', with plans to Sinicise 200 million religious adherents to become more loyal citizens. Chinese characteristics must be incorporated into all activities, beliefs and traditions; chief among them is unwavering loyalty to the Communist Party.

The official Protestant TSPM churches were the first to be targeted for attacks, which from 2014 often took the form of removing the crosses from church buildings. In February 2018, with new regulations governing religious affairs, the government instituted some of the most restrictive policies since the Cultural Revolution. As a result, virtually all religious activity outside the TSPM became illegal, including attendance at events outside China. In the summer and autumn of 2018, reports surfaced of a coordinated all-out attack on the house churches. The attacks targeted regions previously considered quite peaceful in terms of the churches' relations with the government: Lanzhou, Liaoning, Shenyang, Jiangsu, Hunan, Hebei, Guangdong, Guizhou, Guiyang, Taizhou and Anhui. In autumn 2018, the Wenzhou city government issued an order instructing both TSPM and house churches to stop youth and children's ministry, and further warned against church connections overseas. The largest house church in Beijing has been under attack from the authorities after refusing to install surveillance cameras in its sanctuary. The intensity of these attacks has far surpassed anything seen in recent years. Cross removals and church demolitions previously experienced in Wenzhou have now shifted to Henan, and hundreds of churches have suffered persecution.

In response to the wave of attacks in September 2018, 439 house-church pastors and elders signed 'A Joint Statement by Pastors: A Declaration for the Sake of the Christian Faith'. This stressed the following principles: the Bible is the Word of God, carrying final authority over the laws of the government; Christians will be willing to walk the way of the cross of Christ, following the examples of the saints who suffered and were martyred for their faith; the house churches respect and submit to government authority; and under no circumstances will the pastors and elders allow the house churches to be under the control of the government, being willing to pay any price for this principle. Particularly significant is the last statement: 'For the sake of the gospel, we are prepared to bear all losses – even the loss of our freedom and our lives'.

Are we to expect a 'winter season' for Christians for the foreseeable future under President Xi's reign? With the removal of presidential term limits, China experts predict a harsher environment for all religions, including Protestant Christianity, both TSPM and house church. However, some house-church leaders have been informed by officials of a new era to come that will provide a path to legal recognition. It would be highly unlikely for a new path to lead to a complete break from at least some government control. House-church leaders have expressed readiness for either scenario, whether a season of persecution or a more open environment. The churches have weathered far worse in the past. A freer, more open environment would make carrying out evangelism, church planting and missions far easier. However, greater freedom could have a cost. Some have expressed the fear that the greater danger is not a harsher government but a free, materialistic, liberalised world.

An area of concern for the authorities has been religious activities connected to foreign entities, primarily related to the West but also more recently South Korea. In October 2010, more than 200 invited Chinese participants primarily from the house churches were prevented from attending the Third Lausanne Congress on World Evangelisation in Cape Town, South Africa. The risk of international embarrassment was considered too great. Officials imagined 'anti-China' foreign forces infiltrating the Chinese church to use this occasion to embarrass the authorities while the world was watching. Though these fears were unfounded, unfortunately an opportunity was lost, as most were stopped from attending. The chair of the Lausanne Movement, Doug Birdsall, openly apologised to China at the Congress:

We are very sorry that those who received the word of Lausanne's activity in China did not seemingly understand the spirit and intent of our having people here from every stream of the church, but we want them to know, not only those who are our brothers and sisters in Christ but also the leaders of that nation, that we want the best for the church there and we want the best for the nation.

The government sees foreign entities, even those with no ill-will, as a potential threat. Some officials have privately acknowledged that they might have over-reacted, yet this incident reveals the general mistrust of foreign connections among China's authorities. According to hardliners, Western powers were using religion to undermine the Chinese government. A statement from the new TSPM leader Xu Xiaohung at the Chinese People's Political Consultative Conference (CPPCC) in Beijing on 11 March 2019 read: 'Anti-China forces in the West are trying to continue to influence China's social stability and even subvert our country's political power through Christianity'.

A Global Mission Movement

Urban pastors from the 'newly formed emerging urban church' have embraced global missions as their primary focus. As a precursor to global missions, Reverend Tianming Jin, former senior pastor of Beijing Shouwang Church, launched a 'City on a Hill' vision to prompt the urban house-church movement to rise to the surface, changing from an underground church to a visible public witness in society. This paved the way for the urban house church to have a wider operating space for local outreach as well as for the mobilisation of global missions. Even though Tianming Jin has been under house arrest since 8 April 2011, other pastors have taken on the global mission mantle. Pastors from Beijing, Shanghai and Xian have been hosting annual mission conferences to mobilise an indigenous mission-sending movement. Following the Lausanne World Congress at Cape Town in 2010 and a subsequent landmark gathering at the Asia Church Leaders' Forum in Seoul in 2013, Mission China 2030 was launched 'to send 20,000 missionaries by the year 2030'. In 2015, the first in a series of large mission conferences started in Hong Kong, followed by another Mission China 2030 conference in Jeju, South Korea, in 2016. A third conference was held in Chiang Mai, Thailand, in 2017, at which some 200 students and young people made mission commitments. A fourth conference, in Singapore, was held in December 2018 for marketplace ministry and business as mission.

Criticism of Mission China 2030 has been voiced overseas as well as within China. It is suggested that Mission China 2030 is numbers-driven, overly optimistic, triumphalist, nationalistic and even too Korean. Rural house-church leaders have questioned the passion and faith of the urban churches. Others have questioned the wisdom of launching a mission movement at a time with one of the tightest political environments in decades. Is the church in China ready for missions or is this just the wishful thinking of a few high-profile urban pastors? The reality of the challenges and cost of mission-sending has dampened earlier optimism. The recent attacks on the house churches by the Chinese state, martyrdom in the field elsewhere, and division within have slowed the momentum.

On 24 May 2017, two young Chinese missionaries – Ms Meng Lisi (aged 26) and Mr Li Xinheng (aged 24) – were kidnapped and later killed by ISIS radicals in Pakistan. The ISIS radicals were most likely looking for Chinese people to kill as a warning to President Xi's Belt and Road Initiative conference of world leaders on 14–15 May 2017. This tragic loss of two young lives is viewed by the Chinese mission movement as falling within the long Christian tradition of martyrdom and thus as a significant form of witness to the faith. As Meng Lisi herself stated, 'If a life sacrificed can be exchanged for a people's revival, I think it would be worth it'.

The origins of the missionary movement from China can be traced back to the 1940s, when the first wave of Back to Jerusalem (B2J) missionaries arrived in Xinjiang, north-west China. The B2J Chinese missionaries felt a calling from God to head back to Jerusalem with the gospel but were not able to leave China due to persecution. However, their sacrificial lives served as an example for the generation to follow. Christians came into contact with surviving members of the first group of B2J missionaries, who were now in their 80s and 90s. One of the best-known B2J ministers, Simon Zhao, served more than 30 years in prison. Seven of his colleagues died in prison.

A second wave of the B2J movement began around the year 2000, when a team of 39 Chinese missionaries arrived in Thailand. Hundreds of rural-church missionaries were sent out. The failure rate has been high for reasons relating to levels of education, cultural awareness and global sophistication. One of the largest sending networks estimates that it has sent 140 missionaries overseas. Most of these Chinese missionaries in the field still struggle with language, culture and fundamental survival issues. Currently, it is estimated that between 1,000 and 2,000 Chinese missionaries are serving overseas, primarily in the Middle East and Southeast Asia. As China's economic influence and global reach are growing, so too are opportunities for the Chinese Christian missionary movement.

Mission China represents a large-scale mission-sending initiative by a church that is still not legally recognised. All Nations Church, a house church in Shanghai, sent out a team to Thailand less than a year after being attacked. Beijing Shouwang Church sent out missionaries to Africa during a time when their pastor was under house arrest, and Beijing Zion Church commissioned overseas missionaries while the authorities recently closed it down. A sending church has to take into account security concerns both at home and in the field. China's political condition requires its church mission movement to set up low-key, creative sending structures. These challenges, while difficult, are also helpful for work in regions that are hostile to Christianity.

Conclusion

China's house-church movement exploded in growth, with millions becoming Christians in the countryside soon after the end of the Cultural Revolution in 1979, followed by a newly formed emerging urban church of intellectuals in the cities soon after 1989. As the official TSPM church appears to be focused inwardly on Sinicisation, the house church is on an outwardly expanding trajectory, with a global mission vision to plant churches in the cities and to send 20,000 missionaries to the world. The challenges are growing with the increased political tightening, as churches across China are experiencing the harshest attacks since the Cultural Revolution. The cost has been high at home but also in the mission field, with the first two missionary martyrs in Pakistan. The threats of divisions are real between the rural and urban, the traditionalist pietist and grace gospel-centred, the Charismatics and Reformed churches. There seems to be something beyond what meets the eye: a spiritual movement among a persecuted people on a mission with the gospel of grace and ready to take the way of the cross. The house church in China is on a global mission with a desire to reach a suffering world with the hope of the good news of Jesus Christ.

Bibliography

Aikman, David, *Jesus in Beijing: How Christianity Is Transforming China and Changing the Global Balance of Power* (Washington, DC: Regnery, 2003).

Balcome, Dennis, *China's Opening Door: Incredible Stories of the Holy Spirit at Work in One of the Greatest Revivals in Christianity* (Lake Mary, FL: Charisma House, 2014).

Conkling, Timothy Garner, *Mobilized Merchants-Patriotic Martyrs: China's House-Church Protestants and the Politics of Cooperative Resistance* (Scotts Valley, CA: CreateSpace Independent Publishing Platform, 2014).

Fulton, Brent, *China's Urban Christians: A Light That Cannot Be Hidden* (Eugene, OR: Pickwick Publications, 2015).

Hattaway, Paul, *Back to Jerusalem: Three Chinese House Church Leaders Share Their Vision to Complete the Great Commission* (Carlisle: Piquant, 2003).

Hong Kong

Fuk-tsang Ying

In 1807, the British Protestant missionary Robert Morrison (1782–1834) arrived in Canton (now Guangzhou), signifying the advent of the modern Western missionary movement in China. The Chinese Empire had been unwilling to join the international community and the movement of Western powers into the East increased the tension in Sino-foreign relations. The influx of opium, which was auctioned in exchange for silver to redress a trade imbalance between Qing Imperial China and Britain, led to the outbreak of the Anglo-Chinese War (also known as the First Opium War). In 1841, the British army occupied Hong Kong Island. The following year, the Treaty of Nanjing was signed and Hong Kong Island was ceded to the British in perpetuity. The boundary of the Crown Colony extended to the Kowloon peninsula in 1860, and the Qing Empire further leased the New Territories to the British in 1898. Sovereignty over Hong Kong eventually reverted to the People's Republic of China (PRC) from the UK in 1997. This international city of only 1,102 square kilometres was formally changed from a British colony into a Special Administrative Region of the PRC.

Hong Kong Island lacks natural resources. When it was occupied by the British, its population was only a few thousand. Lord Palmerston (1784–1865), the British foreign secretary, mocked Hong Kong as nothing but 'a barren island with hardly a house upon it'. The main focus of the British was cementing Hong Kong's strategic role in its policy towards China, as the island functioned as a stepping stone for the British Empire to enter China. A similar understanding was shared by most of the Christian missionaries to China. The development of Christianity in Hong Kong was built upon a 'go into China' mindset. In the nineteenth century, Hong Kong became a springboard to South China and logistical base for Western missionary societies. To understand the development of Christianity in Hong Kong, one must view it from the setting of South China.

The Roman Catholic Church was established there as an apostolic prefecture in 1841; the prefecture expanded to cover part of Guangdong Province (Xin'an and Huiyang prefectures) and became an apostolic vicariate in 1874. In 1946, the Hong Kong Vicariate was raised to a diocese, with Apostolic Vicar Enrico Valtorta installed as the first bishop on 31

October 1948. The Hong Kong Diocese was under the jurisdiction of the Archdiocese of Guangzhou.

When the Chinese Communist Party (CCP) took power in October 1949, the Western missionary movement in China came to an end. To sever all ties between Christianity (including both Roman Catholicism and Protestantism) and imperialism, churches in China implemented the state-regulated and state-controlled Anti-imperialist Patriotic Movement (Protestant Three-Self Patriotic Movement and Catholic Patriotic Movement), which had self-support, self-governance and self-propagation as its objectives. Against this background, Hong Kong Christianity could not maintain ecclesiastical relations with its South China dioceses and was forced to operate independently. Nevertheless, Hong Kong Christians still felt a strong affinity with churches in their motherland under communist rule and prayed for the reopening of China. After the Cultural Revolution, the CCP allowed Christian churches to reopen. Hong Kong Christianity resumed contact and exchanges with churches in China and advocated 'care for the churches in China' as one of its missions at a Protestant mission consultation held in 1980.

The establishment of Christian churches in Hong Kong depended to a large extent on support from Western missionary societies for personnel and finance. Since the beginning of the twentieth century, how to realise self-governance and self-support had been an important issue for the development of Protestantism in Hong Kong. While different Protestant denominations developed at different paces, by the 1970s most denominations established by Western missionary societies had basically achieved self-support and self-governance. The first local (Chinese) Anglican bishop, Peter Kwong, was installed in 1981. Protestant Christianity became rooted in Hong Kong, achieving financial and administrative independence while maintaining close relationships with ecumenical partner

Christianity in Hong Kong, 1970 and 2020

Tradition	1970 Population	%	2020 Population	%	Average annual growth rate (%), 1970–2020
Christians	623,000	16.1%	1,146,000	15.2%	1.2%
Anglicans	23,200	0.6%	29,200	0.4%	0.5%
Independents	57,200	1.5%	170,000	2.3%	2.2%
Orthodox	50	0.0%	100	0.0%	1.4%
Protestants	193,000	5.0%	411,000	5.4%	1.5%
Catholics	256,000	6.6%	590,000	7.8%	1.7%
Evangelicals	122,000	3.1%	259,000	3.4%	1.5%
Pentecostal/Charismatics	82,300	2.1%	320,000	4.2%	2.8%
Total population	**3,873,000**	**100.0%**	**7,548,000**	**100.0%**	**1.3%**

Source: Todd M. Johnson and Gina A. Zurlo (eds), *World Christian Database* (Leiden/Boston: Brill), accessed March 2018.

churches. The localisation of the Catholic Church was also achieved in the 1970s, as a consequence of the ground-breaking Second Vatican Council (1962–5). Bishop Francis Hsu was appointed as the third bishop in 1969 as the diocese was handed over to local clergy.

After the transfer of sovereignty of Hong Kong to the PRC in 1997, according to the Sino-British Joint Declaration and the Basic Law, Hong Kong Christianity was placed under the new 'One Country, Two Systems' model. The Hong Kong churches have called for both ties between the region's religious groups and the independence and self-management of the Christian church in China to be based on 'non-subordination, non-interference and mutual respect' while maintaining and developing relations with religious organisations and Christians in other regions. The Catholic Church in Hong Kong also sought to play the role of bridge between the Vatican and China, between the underground church and the official church in China.

Protestantism: Denominational Diversity, Church Unity

Hong Kong has a large number of denominations. According to the Hong Kong Church Census of 2014, among the 1,287 local churches, 1,064 were under 71 different denominations. Those denominations with the longest legacies in Hong Kong are identified with the earliest missionary societies that entered the Chinese mainland, particularly South China. The more prominent societies included the American Baptist Mission (1842), the London Missionary Society (1843), the (Anglican) Church Missionary Society (1843), the Basel Mission (1847) and the Rhenish Mission (1847). Towards the end of the nineteenth century, these five denominations, along with the Wesleyan Methodist Mission (1882) and the American Congregational Mission (1883), were considered to be the seven traditional mainline denominations in Hong Kong.

From the late nineteenth to the early twentieth century, the non-mainstream traditions began to send missionaries to China and began missionary work in Hong Kong. These included the Seventh-day Adventist Church (1888), Pentecostal Church (1907), Pentecostal Holiness Church (1907) and Assemblies of God (1928). The footprints of 'faith missionaries' in Hong Kong are also visible from this time. In line with the Independent Movement in China and the development of indigenous churches, independent churches with more local essences were also founded in Hong Kong, including the China Christian Church (1903), Chinese Church of Christ (1926), True Jesus Church (1932) and Christian Assembly (1936?). Early in the Sino-Japanese War (1937–45), certain denominations, such as the Evangelical Free Church (1937) and Bethel Church (1937), moved to South China to escape the war and began ministry in Hong Kong.

The rapid increase in the number of denominations in Hong Kong occurred mainly from the 1950s. Due to the change in the political regime in China, many Western missionaries and Chinese clergy who originally did not have ministries in Hong Kong retreated to the British colony. Witnessing the huge number of refugees flooding into the region, they decided to launch new services there, targeting the diasporic Chinese, to extend their visions of serving China. At the same time, some pastoral workers and Christians also established new denominations in Hong Kong, such as the Church of Brethren in Christ, Charismatic Mission, Lock Tao Christian Association and Chinese Overseas Christian Mission, resulting in a surge of different denominations. By 1956, more than 300 missionaries were working in Hong Kong, and over 50 missionary organisations had offices there.

Denominational diversity in Hong Kong has not resulted in estrangements or sectarianism; on the contrary, it has encouraged cross-denominational cooperation. In 1915, the Hong Kong China Christian Churches Union was established (renamed the Hong Kong Chinese Christian Churches Union in post-war Hong Kong) with the objective of promoting cooperation among churches in evangelistic and other charity works. The Hong Kong Christian Council was founded in 1954, strengthening the linkage between Hong Kong and the ecumenical movement. In 1975, the amalgamation of the British-affiliated Chinese Methodist Church, Hong Kong, and the American-affiliated Methodist Church, Hong Kong, marked a major step towards church unity.

Catholicism: Diverse Individuals, Universal Church

A variety of Catholic religious and missionary institutions arrived in Hong Kong in the nineteenth century: the Order of Friars Minor (1842), Paris Foreign Mission (1847), Sisters of St Paul de Chartres (1848), Pontifical Foreign Missions Institute (1858), Canossian Daughters of Charity (1860) and Order of Preachers (Dominican Fathers, 1861). They started the difficult task of exploring mission in China through the colony. During the twentieth century, Jesuits, Maryknoll sisters, Salesians, Sacred Heart and other religious orders and missionary congregations also arrived to start their missions. Responding to the influx of refugees in turbulent post-war Hong Kong, 27 new religious institutions arrived during the 1950s and 1960s.

Since the reform and opening up of China in 1979, some religious orders have also built connections in mainland China. The Hong Kong Diocese now hosts 47 religious orders and missionary congregations, from Italy, France, Spain, the USA, Canada, Ireland, Mexico, India, Australia and the Philippines. While stressing the universality of the church, the Catholic

Church in Hong Kong manifests great diversity. Some orders, such as the Jesuits, specialise in education, while others, such as the Little Sisters of the Poor, focus on service to the poor and elderly.

Church Growth

The different missionary societies and congregations in Hong Kong had far fewer resources than their counterparts in South China because of the effects of the Conquer China for Christ Movement and the evangelisation of China. The overall development of Christianity during its first 100 years in Hong Kong was slow. Before the outbreak of the Sino-Japanese War in 1937, Protestants in Hong Kong numbered about 10,000, only 0.5% of the total population. According to the statistics of Hong Kong Dioceses, the number of Catholics in 1948 was 33,848.

In contrast, Christianity developed much faster in post-war Hong Kong, particularly after 1949. The 1950s was a golden era for the growth of Christianity there. Between 1955 and 1968, the number of Protestants rose from 53,917 to 159,359 and the number of Catholics from 64,399 to 235,937. The rapid growth was closely related to the influx of Chinese refugees after 1949. Hong Kong was a refugee society in the 1950s, which intensified local social problems. Benefiting from huge overseas missionary and relief resources, as well as colonial government policies, the Christian church responded swiftly to address the physical and spiritual needs of local society. This effort greatly relieved the crisis in Hong Kong society and boosted the growth of Hong Kong Christianity.

From the 1950s, a solid foundation for education and social services had been laid by Hong Kong Protestant churches, and Hong Kong had become a hub of theological education and Christian literature for Chinese-speaking churches in the region and the diasporic Chinese communities overseas. The relocation of some theological seminaries and Christian publishers from the mainland to Hong Kong aided this shift.

After the 1970s, however, the increase in the number of Christians could not match the fast pace of population growth, which resulted in a slowing of church growth rates. The regular census held by Hong Kong Protestant churches showed that the number of Christians in Hong Kong remained at about 4% of the population. Protestant churches had a Sunday-service attendance of 305,097 in 2014. In 1999, a 'negative growth' signal appeared as the number of local churches increased while the number of church attenders declined. In the twenty-first century, a depletion in the number of younger-generation church-goers has been a critical issue. The annual statistics of the Hong Kong Diocese, however, indicate steady Catholic growth. The resident local Catholic population was around 581,000 in 2017.

Social Change and Cultural Exchange

Although evangelism was China's main concern about the influx of Western missionaries, the impact of Christianity's inner-worldly spirit and the effects of Western civilisation on social transformation, as revealed by Christianity, were also significant. During the process of evangelism, Hong Kong churches did not neglect the needs of the marginalised and disabled, and offered them care and services. Protestant organisations such as the Young Men's Christian Association (YMCA, 1901), the Hong Kong Mutual Christian Improvement Society (1903) and the Young Women's Christian Association (YWCA, 1920) offered comprehensive charitable services. The missionaries' emphasis on education rights for girls and care for the disadvantaged in society contributed to improvement and reform in social customs, and missionaries became pioneers of these issues in Hong Kong society. For example, Hong Kong churches and Christians were at the core of the Anti-Mui Tsai (slave girl) Campaign from the 1920s to the 1930s. As Hong Kong was undergoing an industrial boom in the 1960s, the working conditions of factory workers and increasing labour conflicts aroused much public concern. A Catholic priest founded the Industrial Relations Institute in 1968 to encourage labourers to claim their rights. The Hong Kong Christian Industrial Committee and the Industrial Evangelistic Fellowship were established in 1968 and 1975, respectively, to defend labourers' rights and advocate the industrial missions of Hong Kong Christianity. Christianity played a positive role during the rapid changes in Hong Kong society.

Western missionaries were also the intermediaries for cultural exchanges between East and West. The Western-style schools with the longest histories in Hong Kong were established by Western missionaries (such as the Anglo-Chinese College in 1843, St Paul's College in 1851, St Savior's College in 1866, St Francis' Canossian College in 1869 and St Joseph's College in 1875). They contributed greatly to the nourishment of Chinese–English bilingual elites and shaped the bicultural face of Hong Kong Christianity. These elites with proficiency in Western culture not only met the needs in the colonial context: quite a number of them went back to China, contributing to China's intellectual and institutional reform and modernisation by bringing in new values, knowledge and technology.

Furthermore, Protestant Christianity in Hong Kong also played a special role in the revolutionary movement of the late Qing dynasty. Christian civilisation had broadened the visions of many Christians and Chinese intellectuals. The new concepts of Western democracy and liberalism made them realise the deficiencies of monarchy and stimulated revolutionary thinking. Hong Kong enlightened the revolutionary ideas of Dr Sun Yat-sen (1866–1925), with Christianity playing an indispensable role. A considerable number of Protestants also participated in the revolutionary movement.

Social Presence

The number of Christians has always been relatively small. However, the role of Christianity in the public sector is considered indispensable, particularly in the realms of education and social services. Such development not only grew from Christianity's inner-worldly spirit but also was closely related to policies of the colonial government. The unique feature of Hong Kong was the post-war government policies on education and social welfare, which benefited the Christian church (both Catholic and Protestant) as a service provider and partner of the government. During the 1950s, because the social welfare policy of the Hong Kong government was very passive and was not expected to meet the needs of the new immigrants, the relief work for refugees in Hong Kong relied on the financial support of international relief organisations, including contributions from Christian institutions. According to the handbook *Working Together* published by the Hong Kong Council of Social Services in 1958, among more than 70 social services institutions, about 30% were affiliated with Christian organisations, including the Canossian Sisters Foundling Home, Society of St Vincent de Paul, Ebenezer Home and School for the Blind, YMCA, Kwong Yam Home for the Aged, YWCA, Little Sisters of the Poor, Salvation Army, Sisters of the Precious Blood, Church World Services, Catholic Relief Services, Hong Kong Catholic Social Welfare Conference, Maryknoll Sisters Catholic Welfare Centre, Lutheran World Services and Hong Kong Christian Welfare and Relief Council.

Overseas donations began to drop in the mid-1960s, and international relief agencies, having assessed the refugee question in Hong Kong as being no longer urgent, were preparing to retreat. The reorganisation of Caritas–Hong Kong in 1966 and the establishment of the Hong Kong Christian Services in 1967 signified a new chapter of Christian involvement in social welfare. The Hong Kong government also reformulated its social welfare policy. The new measures adopted by the colonial government included cooperation with voluntary/charitable organisations and the adoption of Christian churches as partners.

Under these circumstances, Christian churches, as sponsoring bodies of schools and social services organisations, could receive government subsidies to provide education and social services. Nearly half of all schools and social services agencies in Hong Kong are run by Protestant and Catholic churches, offering various services to different social sectors under the supervision of the education and social services departments of the government. Concurrently, the government allows religious activities to take place within the related premises. In 2014, almost 30% of Hong Kong Protestant churches used the premises of publicly funded schools and subvented social services centres for religious ministry. About 25% of Catholic congregations and parishes also made use of school halls in their charge for their Sunday gatherings. Moreover, the churches were allowed to provide religious education as spiritual cultivation. As a result, the Christian churches became the government's major partners in providing social services, and Christianity was even described as the mainstream of the social and cultural ideology in Hong Kong. In an epoch emphasising the separation of church and state, this was a unique phenomenon in the history of the ecumenical church.

According to the *Hong Kong Annual Report 2016*, Protestant organisations operated 180 high schools, 199 primary schools, 260 kindergartens and 127 nursery schools. They also operated and managed seven hospitals, 17 clinics and many social services organisations, including over 100 special centres for families and teenagers, 11 children's homes, 169 elderly care centres and residential homes, and 59 rehabilitation centres for drug addicts and handicapped persons. For the Roman Catholic community, 252 Catholic schools and kindergartens impart education to about 149,600 pupils. Caritas–Hong Kong is the diocese's official social welfare arm, offering services to Catholics and non-Catholics alike. It provides medical and social services through six hospitals, 13 clinics, 43 social and family services centres, 23 hostels, 16 homes for the aged, 26 rehabilitation service centres and many self-help clubs and associations.

Approaches to Mission

Three main approaches have emerged in the understanding of mission among Hong Kong Protestant churches: the fundamentalist, evangelical and ecumenical approaches. Differences of opinion among these three have resulted in a broad but often tense theological spectrum. The fundamentalists believe that mission is concerned exclusively with preaching the gospel with a view to the salvation of the individual soul and negates any form of social concern and participation. The fundamentalists shaped the theological and spiritual tradition of the Hong Kong churches with evangelistic enthusiasm and revivalist spirit, emphasising the individual's born-again experience, living a holy life, reading the Bible diligently, preaching the gospel enthusiastically and longing for the second coming of Jesus Christ.

During the 1950 and 1960s, the evangelicals' social roles were driven by the urgent needs of the refugees rather than deriving from thorough theological reflection on Christianity's social responsibility. After the Lausanne Congress of 1974, however, the evangelicals began to emphasise social responsibility. This approach considers social services as merely the means to realise the Great Commission of personal conversion. Facing the challenges of the transfer of sovereignty over Hong Kong in 1997, leaders of the evangelical movement encouraged Christians to care about Hong Kong and undertake mission responsibilities. The promulgation of *The Conviction of Hong Kong Christians in Current Social and Political Changes* in 1984 was one of the models.

The ecumenicals interpret the gospel holistically and consider social involvement as an intrinsic part of the witness and realisation of the gospel. Since the 1970s, ecumenicals have been working with other non-governmental groups in fighting for labour rights, pushing forward community development and even democratising the political system.

Having been built by overseas missionaries, Hong Kong churches also put great effort into their own overseas missions. They have set up missionary societies and send out missionaries to different parts of the world to fulfil their responsibility to preach the gospel to the world. According to statistics of 2014, 55.7% of local churches have set up permanent mission/evangelisation ministries.

Catholics, too, believe that Christian faith is relevant to the world. According to the *Pastoral Constitution on the Church in the Modern World* of 1965, a large proportion of the world's population is still struggling in hardship caused by disaster and poverty. To promote world justice and Christian concern and brotherly love for the poor and afflicted, it was urged that a world organisation be set up to assist in the development of the poorer nations. The Vatican officially set up the Pontifical Commission for Justice and Peace in 1967. However, the implementation of these social teachings by the Catholic Church in Hong Kong was far from being fully realised for fear that the social teaching and action might embarrass the colonial government. It was not until 1977, when the Justice and Peace Commission of Hong Kong Catholic Diocese was established, that the local churches became better able to fulfil the role of prophet and advocate for justice and peace in accordance with the social teachings of the Second Vatican Council.

Hong Kong churches have also launched alternative missions and pastoral care initiatives. Besides traditional prison ministry and gospel-based detoxification, churches are caring for homosexuals, sex workers, refugees seeking asylum in Hong Kong and the homeless. They aim to stand with those who are being ignored and marginalised, sharing their burdens and struggles.

Internationally renowned Protestant evangelists (such as Billy Graham) have been invited to conduct large-scale rallies in Hong Kong. One such annual event is the Hong Kong Bible Conference, which dates from 1928.

Nevertheless, the effectiveness of this kind of large-scale evangelistic event has often been debated within church circles. Pope Paul VI made a historic three-hour visit to Hong Kong on 4 December 1970. He said Mass at the Happy Valley Racecourse and preached to the Catholic community. At the end of his sermon, he said, 'Christ is a teacher, a shepherd and a loving redeemer for China too'.

Indigenisation and Religious Dialogue

Hong Kong is a cultural crossroads where East meets West: more than 150 years of British colonial rule enabled the spread of Western culture and religions, while the many Chinese migrants settling there helped sustain and develop traditional culture and customs. Ever since the British settlement in Hong Kong, Eastern and Western religions have coexisted peacefully. Large-scale religious conflicts and disputes are rare. During the missionary process in Hong Kong, many efforts were been made to integrate Western religion into local Chinese culture.

Hong Kong is a typical immigrant society. The development of Christianity reflects this multi-ethnic characteristic. Besides Cantonese churches, there are also churches belonging to different ethnic groups, such as Hakka churches, Chiuchow churches, fisherman churches, Hokkien churches, and Shanghainese, Fuzhou, Hainan and Mandarin churches. These churches, with local dialects as their defining characteristic, reflect the discrete situation of immigrants and how they combine religion with ethnic identity, cohering strength and mutual vigilance, and establishing identity within the South China Cantonese-speaking community. At the same time, Hong Kong, as an international city where Eastern and Western cultures fuse, plays host to English, Filipino, Japanese and Korean churches that enrich the spectrum of internationalisation. Special attention should be paid to the Filipino community, which constitutes the largest ethnic minority in Hong Kong. According to recent Hong Kong Diocese statistics, 171,000 Filipino Catholics live in Hong Kong.

The boat people represent another special ethnic group in Hong Kong. As an ethnic underclass, fishermen were often discriminated against by the land people. The Hong Kong Harbor Mission Church was established by some Chinese Protestant leaders in 1911 for the evangelisation of the fishing communities. Later, several Western missionaries of the China Peniel Missionary Society and Pentecostal Holiness Church also sought to minister to this specific ethnic group. Immediately after the founding of the PRC, the South China Boat Mission transferred its work from Canton to Hong Kong. The integration of the Christian faith with the fishing communities, as exemplified by the distinguished 'Fishermen Church', is a unique example of the practice of indigenised Protestant Christianity in

Hong Kong. Indigenisation is a major concern of Hong Kong Christianity. In 1931, Norwegian missionary Karl L. Reichelt (1877–1952) dedicated a Christian ministry centre in Tao Fong Shan; it is notable for its design in the style of a Buddhist monastery. Reichelt was also the founder of the Christian Mission to Buddhists, which aimed to discover a fulfilment relationship between Mahayana Buddhism and Christianity.

In the mid-1930s, two Anglican churches (Holy Trinity Church and St Mary's Church) were built according to traditional Chinese architectural design, reflecting indigenisation through combining with traditional culture. Another famous church building of Sinicising Christian architecture in Hong Kong is the Regional Seminary for South China (renamed Holy Spirit Seminary in 1964). The design of the building was conceived by the Benedictine father Dom Adelbert Gresnigt. His original intention was that it would have four sides built around an open courtyard. Owing to a shortage of funds, however, only one side of the building was constructed.

The positive and inventive approach of the Catholic Church towards other religions is intimately connected with other new directions resulting from the Second Vatican Council, which spoke clearly about dialogue with other religions. Moreover, liturgy in local dialects and sacred music in Cantonese (instead of Latin) also signalled a significant renewal in the expression of the faith with local forms.

Hong Kong has always been an important platform for religious dialogues. The Christian Study Center on Chinese Religion and Culture, established in 1957 by Sino-foreign church members, is another indigenised organisation supported by ecumenical partners and local churches. In 1978, representatives of Buddhism, Taoism, Islam, Confucianism, Protestantism and Catholicism established the Colloquium of the Six Religious Leaders of Hong Kong to exchange views on different current social issues from their respective positions, seeking common ground while preserving differences between religious faith and social practices. The Colloquium is not just a pioneer in Chinese society: it also embodies mutual respect among different religions and the spirit of inclusiveness.

Facing up to Challenges

Since the advent of British colonisation in 1841, with the exception of a turbulent period during the Japanese occupation (December 1941 to August 1945), Hong Kong Christianity has developed in a relatively stable social environment, resulting in an accumulation of abundant resources and experiences. In the 1980s, shadowed and confronted by the 1997 question, Hong Kong churches worried about their prospects – in particular, whether the original religious freedom could be sustained and whether the communist Beijing government would restrain the churches from participating in education and social services, to reduce their influence in the public domain. In response to the signing of the Sino-British Joint Declaration in September 1984, Bishop John B. Wu of the Hong Kong Diocese made a 'Statement on the Catholic Church and the Future of Hong Kong', which underlined the right to religious freedom as a basic human right and expressed the wish that this right and its free exercise be explicitly expressed and effectively guaranteed in the Joint Declaration and in the Basic Law of the future Hong Kong Special Administrative Region (SAR). A similar statement, signed by the leaders of some 200 Hong Kong Anglican and Protestant churches, was communicated to both the Chinese and the British governments. Eventually, provisions in the Basic Law stipulating that 'the Government of Hong Kong Special Administrative Region shall not restrict the freedom of religious belief' and 'religious organizations may, according to their previous practice, continue to run seminaries and other schools, hospitals, and welfare institutions, and to provide other social services' (article 141) directly addressed the worries felt by members of religious communities.

During the years since the transfer of sovereignty, the Hong Kong churches have faced various challenges. Some Christian leaders, both Catholic and Protestant, have taken a very clear-cut stance in fighting for democracy in Hong Kong. Cardinal Joseph Zen Ze-Kiun, Emeritus Bishop of Hong Kong Catholic Diocese, often voiced his concerns about the critical situation of local society. The Protestant involvement (including clergy, Christian professionals and young Christian students) in the large-scale civil disobedience movement in 2014 was also remarkable. In the rapidly changing social and political environment, tensions among different political stances have also emerged within the Christian community, resulting in a lack of consensus on the role of the Christian church in public affairs.

In recent years, the Beijing government has strengthened its governance and control of Hong Kong, intensifying contradictions between Hong Kong and the mainland. It has also triggered different explorations by the Hong Kong Christian churches of their own identity and how to face up to the Chinese authoritarian regime. As the Hong Kong SAR government pushes forward reforms in education and social services as well as its relations with service providers, the question of how the Hong Kong churches adjust their role is widely debated. Any substantial changes in school and social services policy by an unsympathetic or unfriendly government would present great challenges to the development of the Hong Kong churches. In the development of the worldwide Chinese church, the Hong Kong church, with its special historical background, has enjoyed various opportunities and accumulated many resources. Changing eras and circumstances have required the Hong Kong churches to keep abreast of the times to confront the challenges of fulfilling their mission.

Bibliography

Ha, Louis, 'The Foundation of the Catholic Mission in Hong Kong, 1841–1894', PhD dissertation, University of Hong Kong, 1998.

Leung, Beatrice, and Chan, Shun-hing, *Changing Church and State Relations in Hong Kong, 1950–2000* (Hong Kong: Hong Kong University Press, 2003).

Smith, Carl T., *Chinese Christians: Elites, Middlemen, and the Church in Hong Kong* (Hong Kong: Oxford University Press, 1984).

Ying, Fuk-tsang, and Pan-chiu Lai, 'Diasporic Chinese Communities and Protestant Christianity in Hong Kong during the 1950s', *Studies in World Christianity*, 10:1 (2004), 36–153.

Macau

Louis Ha

As of 2018, Christians in Macau constituted only around 5% of the 660,000 population, with around 30,000 Catholics and about 8,000 Protestants, of whom not more than half were actively attending church services. This Christian presence traces its origins to the arrival of Portuguese traders and Catholic priests in Macau in 1553. The former came to exploit the lucrative silk trade between China and Japan, while the latter had the Catholic mission as their calling, with a papal mandate. At first, the missionaries served only the Portuguese and other foreigners, but before long Macau became a stepping stone for the Jesuits to enter China.

The Catholic hierarchy was set up in Macau when it became a suffragan diocese of Malacca in 1576, covering the whole of the Far East, including Indochina, China, Mongolia, Japan and Korea. The Bishop of Macau started to provide social and medical services to the settlers. In 1594, the Jesuit-run St Paul's College was opened to offer the first university degree in Asia. However, it was closed for more than two decades during the eighteenth century when the Jesuits were banned from Macau.

Macau was given the name 'City of the Name of God' by the King of Portugal in 1654. Despite this high accolade, the city was trapped in the tension between Portugal, Spain and the Holy See in matters relating to the appointment of a bishop. As a result, Macau went without a bishop from 1633 to 1690.

Catholic missionaries expelled from China in 1746 after the Rites Controversy eventually settled in Macau. They suffered a setback in 1834 when Macau, following a policy of the Portuguese monarchy, confiscated all the properties of religious orders. A year later, the church building that was part of St Paul's College was destroyed in a fire. The remaining façade became one of Macau's best-known landmarks. Along with eight other baroque-style church buildings it formed an area that was declared to be a UNESCO World Heritage Site in 2005.

In 1887, the Portuguese signed a treaty with the Qing court and thereby formally obtained the governance of Macau. After this, the Catholic mission started to take the Macau Chinese seriously as a missionary target. During the Cultural Revolution (1966–76), drastic changes occurred in Macau that transformed the pro-Taiwan enclave into a 'patriotic' pro-mainland one.

This put a sudden stop to some traditional pro-Taiwan Catholic schools and created a chilling effect on other church activities. The change was affirmed politically by the Joint Declaration in 1987, which led to the handover of Macau to China in 1999.

During this modern period, Domingos Lam (林家駿, 1928–2009) became the first Chinese bishop of Macau in 1988 and began the localisation of the church. In 2016, Auxiliary Bishop Stephen Lee (李斌生, b. 1956) of Hong Kong was transferred to Macau to replace Bishop José Lai (黎鴻昇, b. 1946), who retired early for health reasons. Under Bishop Lee, the church has undergone a series of reorganisations, with a new emphasis on formation activities, particularly for the youth.

Formerly, Mass in the Catholic Church was offered only in the two official languages – Cantonese and Portuguese. Over the past two decades, Masses in English, Putonghua and Vietnamese also became available in some of the 10 parishes. This reflects changes in the composition of the parishioners, as there are more Filipino workers and new immigrants from mainland China, while at the same time there has been an exodus of Macanese Portuguese and refugees from Timor-Leste since around the time of the 1999 handover.

As is evident from this condensed history, missionary work of the Catholic Church in Macau started very late and the localisation of the church began even later.

Non-Catholic Churches

The first Protestant missionary to China, Robert Morrison (1782–1834) of the London Missionary Society, arrived in Macau in 1807. He translated the entire Bible into Chinese and published the translation in 1823. Morrison carried out most of his missionary work in Macau, making the island the birthplace of Protestant Christianity in China.

Christianity in Macao, 1970 and 2020

Tradition	1970 Population	%	2020 Population	%	Average annual growth rate (%), 1970–2020
Christians	32,600	13.2%	44,600	6.8%	0.6%
Anglicans	200	0.1%	150	0.0%	−0.6%
Independents	50	0.0%	2,800	0.4%	8.4%
Protestants	5,400	2.2%	10,200	1.6%	1.3%
Catholics	27,000	11.0%	31,200	4.8%	0.3%
Evangelicals	3,100	1.2%	6,800	1.0%	1.6%
Pentecostal/Charismatics	1,800	0.7%	2,800	0.4%	0.9%
Total population	**246,000**	**100.0%**	**652,000**	**100.0%**	**2.0%**

Source: Todd M. Johnson and Gina A. Zurlo (eds), *World Christian Database* (Leiden/Boston: Brill), accessed March 2018.

Through the influence of the London Missionary Society small groups of Protestants emerged in Macau during the nineteenth century. This led to the foundation of the Chi Tao Church (志道堂), probably the first Chinese Protestant church in Macau. It opened its first church building in 1906. It has developed significant educational institutions. The early twentieth century also witnessed the establishment of the Macau Baptist Church, which opened its first church building in 1927. The early Anglican Church in Macau was justifiably seen as a 'foreign' church; it was created by Royal Letters Patent in 1849 as the Diocese of Victoria. Though the church has remained small in numbers, it has the distinction of having ordained the first woman in the Anglican communion to become a priest, Florence Li Tim-Oi (李添媛, 1907–92). She was ordained on 25 January 1944 as part of the response of the Anglican Church to the crisis brought about by the Japanese invasion. The Macau Anglican Church is presently only a missionary area of the Hong Kong Sheng Kung Hui (as the Anglican Church is now known in Hong Kong). It has had limited development, with only four churches, seven schools and nine social services centres.

Although the mainline non-Catholic churches, such as the Anglican Church, the Baptists and the Church of Christ in China, started their work in Macau more than a century ago, the fruits are few. During the last 50 years, large numbers of immigrants from mainland China, educated under an atheistic system, have made the development of churches in Macau unpredictable. At the same time, the churches suffer from a 'brain drain' of the younger generation from Macau because of their financial structure and political arguments that are not helping the development of church leadership.

However, a conservative Independent church, the Evangelical Church (宣道堂, Christian Shuen Tao Church of Macau), which is supported mostly by local members, has seen great development in recent years. It started in 1950 and has established 11 local congregations with a membership totalling 6,550, more than half of the Protestants in Macau. The growth might be attributable to its 10-year plans, campus evangelisation, household visits, more than 10 large-scale evangelisation assemblies since 1978 and the passing of leadership from the Reverend Yam-man Lam (藍欽文, b. 1936) to his son, the Reverend Chung-kong Lam (藍中港), which had provided continuity.

A Challenging Context

Protestant denominations in Macau are mostly branches from Hong Kong or vice versa. In either case, they maintain close relations, which find expression in formation, evangelisation and theology exchanges. Christians in Macau maintained relations with the official Chinese Christian Church in mainland China based on the principles of non-subordination, non-interference and mutual respect laid down in the Basic Law of Macau. After their consecrations, both Bishop Lai and Bishop Lee made visits to the official church in China in Beijing. Bishop Lam was also a member of the Basic Law Drafting Committee. At the same time, some individuals or groups also connect with the underground Catholic community or the Protestant house-church movement, both of which are deemed illegal by the Beijing government.

The national security law, which caused a major conflict in Hong Kong, was swiftly passed in 2009 in Macau without much dispute. Moreover, the religious freedom that Christians enjoy was not disturbed by the new law. Pastoral contacts between the Macau Diocese and the Portuguese Bishops' Conference, based on their historical roots, were also unaffected.

After 450 years of Catholic missionary work and 200 years of mission endeavour by the Protestants, the number of Christians in Macau remains small, while the dominant Chinese religion is primarily ancestor worship and a blend of Taoism, Confucianism and Buddhism. Buddhism in Macau started in 1632, during the Ming dynasty. Several monasteries and pagodas were set up in the twentieth century as a sign of redevelopment. Contrarily, there is a decrease in the folk worship of the Goddess of Macau, which has the oldest temple in the territory.

Socially, harmony constitutes one of the outstanding characteristics of Macau. It accepts a plurality of identities. Christianity, especially Catholicism, is regarded as a Macanese cultural institution, as it is closely related to Macau's system of education, particularly through famous and celebrated Catholic schools.

The future of Christianity in Macau is hard to predict, as its membership fluctuates. It is strongly influenced by the contemporary political situation, as has always been the case throughout history. Perhaps the most pressing problem of Christianity in Macau is how to attract the young, as they are immersed in an economy that depends mainly on gambling and they often prefer to work in casinos rather than pursuing other careers. The values of the gambling industry, however, run counter to those of the Christian faith. The temptation to pursue material wealth presented an even greater moral struggle for Christians after the relaxation, in the early twenty-first century, of restrictions that prevented casino employees from gambling in their workplace. A bright future for Christianity in Macau is hardly to be assumed.

Bibliography

Berlie, Jean (ed.), *Macao 2000* (Oxford: Oxford University Press, 1999).

Chan, Chi-hou, *Religion and Culture: Past Approaches, Present Globalisation, Future Challenges* (Macau: Macau Ricci Institute, 2004).

Lam, Domingos, *A Diocese de Macau* (Macau: Publicação do paço Episcopal, 2000).
Latourette, K. S., *A History of Christian Missions in China* (New York: Macmillan, 1929).
Zheng Wei-ming, and Huang Qi-chen, *Ao Men Zong Jiao* [*Macau Religions*] (Macau: Fundação Macau, 1994).

Mongolia

Bayarjargal Garamtseren

Mongolia is a large country, at 1.5 million square kilometres, landlocked between Russia and China. The country has the lowest population density in the world, and almost half of its 3.2 million population (2017) live in the capital, Ulaanbaatar ('Red Hero'). There are over 20 ethnic groups (2010) in Mongolia, the largest of which is the Khalkh (82%). The Khalkh Mongolian dialect is the only official and written language, but 20 other dialects of Mongolian are spoken in different regions. The Kazakh and Tuva, who together comprise about 4% of the population, speak Turkic dialects. Since the 1940s, Cyrillic script has been used in all written communication. The communist regime collapsed in 1990 and the country currently has a single-chamber parliament with 76 members, elected every four years. The president, elected every four years, is the head of state and the prime minister is the head of government. It is estimated that Mongolia has the following religious composition: Buddhism (53%), atheism (39%), shamanism (3%), Islam (3%) and Christianity (2%).

Historical Background

Christianity arrived in the land of today's Mongolia in the sixth and seventh centuries through missionaries and traders from the Church of the East, representing Syriac Christianity. Turkic tribes, ancestors of the Mongols, began to embrace the Christian faith, and by the twelfth and thirteenth centuries Christianity was one of the well known and well established faiths in Mongolia. Four Turkic tribes were Christian, and there was a specific term for a person of Christian faith, *erke'ün*. Markos, from the Turkic Onguud tribe, was the Catholicos of the Church of the East in Baghdad from 1281 until 1317. The Syriac form of Christianity in Mongolia had its connection with the mother church in the Middle East and had its own ecclesiastical structure, with bishops, teachers and disciples. A few archaeological remains – for example, the Runi inscription discovered in Bulgan province, two Syriac rock inscriptions in western Mongolia and Christian gravestones and inscriptions in Inner Mongolia, China – testify to the extent and depth of the Christianity of this period. However, Christianity declined and ceased to exist by the sixteenth century, due to the disintegration of the Mongol Empire, assimilation and relocation of

Christians, the forceful spread of Islam in the Middle East and the instatement of Buddhism as the state religion in Mongolia.

In modern times, Protestants made attempts to preach the gospel and evangelise Mongolians, including that of the famous English missionary James Gilmour in the late 1800s, the American mission in Kalgan among the Mongols in North China, and the Swedish and other Scandinavian missions from the end of the nineteenth century until 1924. Catholic mission experienced sizeable growth in Inner Mongolia from the 1860s until the 1930s, with the development of a few church buildings, a training college and a Mongolian priest. All Protestant and Catholic mission work, though, was forcefully stopped in 1924 in Mongolia and in the 1930s in Inner Mongolia.

Contemporary Christianity

Contemporary Christianity in Mongolia is the result of mission work that began from nothing in 1990, after the country chose democracy and the market economy. Leadership by foreign missionaries in churches and para-church organisations characterised the first 10 years, until about 2000. During that time of economic hardship and social disorientation, foreign missionaries came through NGOs to work with street children, alcoholics, and the poor and needy, as well as to teach English in educational institutions. Teenagers and young adults were the primary regulars in churches that started in the capital and across the countryside. Evangelistic outreach was common in the form of showing the *Jesus* film, distributing tracts, door-to-door encounters, friendship, teaching English and the running of various youth camps.

The next 10 years saw the highest growth rate of Christianity and the advancement of national Christians into the leadership positions of various ministries. Thanks to the advantages of being a largely

Christianity in Mongolia, 1970 and 2020

Tradition	1970 Population	%	2020 Population	%	Average annual growth rate (%), 1970–2020
Christians	3,500	0.3%	62,400	1.9%	5.9%
Independents	100	0.0%	24,000	0.7%	11.6%
Orthodox	3,400	0.3%	2,600	0.1%	−0.5%
Protestants	0	0.0%	34,000	1.1%	17.7%
Catholics	50	0.0%	1,300	0.0%	6.7%
Evangelicals	10	0.0%	9,000	0.3%	14.6%
Pentecostal/Charismatics	100	0.0%	17,000	0.5%	10.8%
Total population	**1,279,000**	**100.0%**	**3,209,000**	**100.0%**	**1.9%**

Source: Todd M. Johnson and Gina A. Zurlo (eds), *World Christian Database* (Leiden/Boston: Brill), accessed March 2018.

monolingual society, of the adaptability of Mongolians to hard physical and climactic conditions, and of the general openness and hospitality of the people, Mongolian Christians endeavoured to travel to distant as well as nearby provinces and rural settlements to start Bible study or home groups and local churches. Foreign missionaries began to leave, and Mongolians started to take over their responsibilities. Various Christian social ministries started in the areas of health, education, family, small business, agriculture, hospice, care for the disabled, prisons, alcoholics and addicts, street children and families, orphanages, child protection, radio and television, arts and sports. Church-planting efforts and movements and the sending of Mongolians to overseas missions – especially to China and Russia, but also to other countries – were most active in this period.

The reasons for the rapid growth of Christianity in Mongolia in this period were the need to fill the spiritual and moral gap left by the communist system, the life-transforming power of the Christian message, the good and sincere spirit of Christian fellowship, the attractiveness to the youth and young adults, and practical help offered to the needy. Many Mongolians became Christians because the gospel genuinely answered their fundamental questions regarding meaning and goals in life. The Christian churches provided a place where people could experience acceptance, concern and love for each other. While, nationally, morality seemed to have been broken on the levels of the individual, family, workplace and society during the communist era, the Christian message and the Bible brought clear lines between right and wrong, moral and immoral. For instance, sexual relations and cohabitation before marriage had become an accepted social phenomenon even for parents of young partners, but now Christians took a stand against such behaviour, demonstrating to society what a holy wedding means. Christians also showed their stance against alcoholism by holding wedding feasts with no alcoholic drinks. Christians are gaining a good reputation in society for being honest, responsible and reliable people. The Bible has become the source of guidance for their personal lives, interpersonal relationships and work ethics.

Today, possibly all leadership and key roles of churches, para-church organisations, Bible schools, the Bible society, mission movements and mercy and outreach ministries are occupied by Mongolian Christians, although the declining number of foreign missionaries still play a supporting role. Mongolian Christians have started churches or fellowship groups among migrant overseas Mongolians, usually affiliated with and supported by local churches in those countries. These small churches and groups, about 100 of them, are located especially in South Korea, the USA and Europe, part of the overall diaspora Mongolian church. Vision 20/10, from the early 2000s, aims to see 10% of the population of Mongolia become disciples of Christ by the year 2020. The National Council of the Mongolian Church, which aims to lead and provide guidelines for Mongolian churches and meet urgent needs, has been seeking to lead this effort. Mongolian Christians have been praying and working for this high calling, but it asks for much more concentrated effort in evangelism, church planting and leadership development. When the name of Jesus is no longer a new phenomenon in the country and many people have become indifferent to religions and more concerned with personal health and financial gain, effective and contextualised methods need to be explored to reach and disciple today's Mongolians.

Christian Denominations

The majority of Mongolian Christians are Protestant Evangelicals (approximately 60,000), while the Catholic and Russian Orthodox churches each have about 1,500 members. There are about 600 Protestant churches in the country, half of which are in the capital city and the rest spread across all 21 provinces. The churches started and led by Mongolians have generally good mutual communication and cooperation. This explains the large percentage (45%) of all churches that claim to be independent and have no strong affiliation with a particular denomination. The biggest denominational affiliation (35%) is Presbyterianism from South Korea. Pentecostal (6%), Baptist (6%), Methodist (4%), Charismatic (2%) and Lutheran (2%) churches make up the rest.

The Catholic Church has one cathedral and six parishes, and over 1,000 national believers. They run the Don Bosco Technical and Industrial Training Center, which has over 300 students, mostly from poor families and school dropouts. The first Mongolian Catholic priest in the modern era, Father Joseph Enkh Baatar, was ordained in 2016.

Government–Church Relations

The government requires all religious groups to register through the city or provincial council of local representatives after having met certain criteria. Buddhism is regarded as the traditional religion and has a preferred and elevated status compared with other faiths. There are no formal relations or discussions between Christianity and Buddhism or shamanism. Registering Christian churches with the government presents difficulties, and one province has not registered a single Christian church. About 30% of all Protestant churches (183 churches in 2016) have registration from the government. The registration gives the opportunity to employ staff legally and invite foreign missionaries on a religious visa. However, because registration needs to be extended every year and the extension process is often delayed by months, there are practical difficulties in registering churches.

Bible Translation

A Franciscan missionary, Giovanni of Montecorvino, ministered in the capital of the Mongol Empire, in today's Beijing, between 1294 and 1328. In 1305, he wrote to Rome that he had translated the whole of the New Testament and the Psalms. The next undertaking of Bible translation came with the effort of I. J. Schmidt, a Moravian missionary working among the Kalmucks, an ethnic Mongol people in the lower Volga area, from 1815. Schmidt translated and published the New Testament in the Kalmuck dialect, while his assistant Badma adapted his translation into the Buryat dialect in 1827. The most important translation came through the great effort and sacrifice of British missionaries, particularly William Swan and Edward Stallybrass, who were stationed in Buryatia between 1817 and 1840. As well as evangelising the people and running an elementary school, they translated the Old Testament (1840) and New Testament (1846) from the biblical languages into the Mongolian language in the traditional vertical script. This literary translation was revised a number of times, and the last revised New Testament was published in 1952 in Hong Kong.

The efforts to translate the Scriptures into the Cyrillic script were started in the 1970s by John Gibbens during the communist era and resulted in the publication in 1990 of the New Testament in contemporary language. The Mongolian Bible Translation Committee, a team of missionaries and Mongolians, produced another translation, the 'Holy Bible' version, in the Cyrillic script in 2000. This word-for-word-style translation is the most commonly used version today. In 2014, the Mongolian Union Bible Society, a member of the United Bible Societies, started the Mongolian Standard Version project, aiming to produce a fresh translation from the biblical languages by a team of Mongolian Christians.

The issue of how to translate the name of God in the Mongolian language has provoked some debate. In most historic and contemporary translations and revisions, the generic traditional term *Burkhan*, meaning 'God, god or deity', was used. But the 1990 New Testament translation used a new term, *Yertuntsiin Ezen*, meaning 'Lord of the universe'. Since the Christian context clarifies the referent (namely, the God of the Bible), and the advantages of the traditional term outweigh any possible disadvantages, almost all Mongolian Christians and churches now use the term *Burkhan*. Today, about 250,000 print copies of the Holy Bible have been sold and the Bible is now available in digital format. Mongolian Christians read their Bibles and many Christian publications.

Developments in Spirituality and Liturgy

Since most of the Protestant churches were planted and led by foreign missionaries, the style of worship and leadership structures are usually carried over from the missionary-denomination style to current Mongolian leaders. Thus, while churches started by Korean missionaries have a Korean style and flavour in prayer and worship, the Western missionary-planted churches have a Western style. Many churches use Western musical instruments such as guitar, keyboard and drums to accompany the singing of translated contemporary Christian songs from English and Korean.

Mongolians are naturally highly gifted in music, dance, art and poetry. The worship songs composed by Mongolians have been particularly effective in expressing natural and genuine worship from the hearts of Mongolians. Therefore, there need to be many more Christian worship songs composed by Mongolians with beautiful poetic lines and Mongolian melodies. Another area waiting for the development of effective and contextualised methods and styles of worship is in reaching out to herders and people in remote regions.

Leadership in Churches and Ministries

While in the 1990s and 2000s many of the leadership positions in churches were filled by untrained lay people, today it is becoming increasingly expected that pastors and leaders will have at least a certificate-level Bible-school training. Union Bible Theological College (UBTC), the only inter-denominational Bible school, with its beginning in the early 1990s, is accredited by the Asian Theological Association and is now largely staffed by Mongolians who have been trained at overseas Bible schools to the master's and doctoral levels. UBTC remains the main school where Mongolian pastors and leaders are trained for church and other ministries. There are other denominational and church- or ministry-affiliated Bible training and discipleship schools, such as those associated with the Assemblies of God, Presbyterians, Methodists, Theological Education by Extension, Youth With A Mission, mobile training schools to remote areas, Langham preaching, and others.

The fact that the majority of Mongolian Christians are women is reflected in the gender ratio of leaders. According to a 2015 survey by Mongolian Evangelical Alliance, 44% of Christian leaders are women, serving in pastoral and ministerial capacities. Generally, women play a much more active role in society and carry more responsibilities than men. Out of all women Christian leaders, 15% are single mothers who are responsible for both their families and their ministries.

The Christian church in Mongolia today is still young and developing; thus, much strategic and theological work is yet to be done. The biggest and most fundamental need is the development and maturity of pastors and leaders. The Association of Mongolian Pastors and Elders recognises ordained Mongolian pastors and aims to encourage fellowship and training and to serve the spiritual and emergency needs of pastors. Now there are more than 400 ordained Mongolian pastors serving throughout the country and overseas. About one-third of these have bachelor-level theological education. Mongolian pastors and leaders need systematic and comprehensive training and coaching that gives not only biblical knowledge but also more support and development in personal character and maturity as well as ministerial training. The needs for such spiritual maturity and character development and striving for unity within the whole Mongolian church are reflected in the Jeju Proclamation of the First Congress of Diaspora Mongolian Pastors and Elders, which convened at Jeju Island, South Korea, in June 2017.

The formation of Mongolian Christian scholars, researchers and Bible teachers is a felt need for the organic growth and long-term sustainability of the church. The Mongolian Research Institute for Christianity was formally established in 2017 to foster the development of the study of Christianity in Mongolia, to accurately inform society about Christianity and to be a centre for research interaction and cooperation. The Institute held its first symposium in December 2017, covering a wide range of topics from the history of Christianity in Mongolia to Bible translation and current issues for pastoral ministry.

Bibliography

Baigalmaa, S. (prep.) and D. Batbayar and J. Olonbayar (eds), *Khristiin mongol chuulgan, baigguullagyn sudalgaanii dun (Mongol ulsiin khemjeend 2015 ony baidlaar)* [*Report of the Survey of Christian Churches and Organizations in Mongolia as of 2015*]. (Ulaanbaatar: Mongolyn Evangeliin Evsel, 2015).

Garamtseren, Bayarjargal, 'Re-establishment of the Christian Church in Mongolia: The Mongolian Standard Version Translation by National Christians', *Unio Cum Christo*, 2:2 (October 2016), 49–66.

Garamtseren, Bayarjargal, 'A History of Bible Translation In Mongolian', *Bible Translator*, 60:4 (2009), 215–23.

Kemp, Hugh, *Steppe by Step: Mongolia's Christians – From Ancient Roots to Vibrant Young Church* (London: Monarch Books, 2000).

Kemp, Hugh, and Bayarjargal Garamtseren, 'Mongolia', in Hope Antone, Wati Longchar, Hyunju Bae, Huang Po Ho and Dietrich Werner (eds), *Asian Handbook for Theological Education and Ecumenism* (Oxford: Regnum, 2013), 565–73.

Taiwan

Yang-en Cheng

The establishment of Christianity in Taiwan (known earlier as Formosa) came about in three separate and distinguishable waves. The first began with the Dutch and Spanish colonial enterprises in the seventeenth century. The second came with the Great Missionary Movement in the latter half of the nineteenth century. The third occurred when, with the defeat of the Nationalist regime by the communists in China, nearly all of the Christian denominations moved their bases to Taiwan in the mid-1950s.

Christianity with a Colonial Face

For thousands of years the aborigines who lived on the island of Taiwan were largely undisturbed by outsiders. Then, in the early sixteenth-century, small unorganised groups of settlers and privateers from China and Japan began to occupy parts of the island. Before the arrival of Dutch and Spanish colonial forces and subsequent Chinese feudalistic regimes, Taiwan was a 'no-man's-land', enjoying a free and unaffiliated status. One scholarly theory is that the Austronesian peoples originated in Taiwan. During the early seventeenth century Taiwan appeared on the world map, when several foreign powers became interested in invading the island.

In August 1624, in order to safeguard their monopoly of trade in the East Indies, Dutch fleets and troops occupied southern Taiwan and became its first sovereign regime. In 1626, Spanish troops despatched from Luzon in the Philippines conquered northern Taiwan, and Catholic missionaries, predominantly Dominicans, briefly established mission posts. The Spaniards were expelled by the Dutch in 1642. Under the chartered system of the Dutch East Indian Company, headquartered in Batavia (now Jakarta), Dutch colonial rule lasted for 37 years. More than 30 Dutch Reformed missionaries, in addition to catechists and schoolmasters, were sent to Formosa during this period.

The Dutch Reformed missionaries came to Taiwan and extended so-called 'international Calvinism' beyond European domains. With military muscle they worked efficiently among the plain aborigines, chiefly the Siraya tribes, by means of itinerant preaching, catechism, schooling and moral enforcement. In order to increase trade for the Company, the church–state policy of Holland was transplanted to this new context.

However, the new faith was not deeply rooted. The translation of the Bible and the setting up of a seminary for aboriginal converts came too late, and the method of 'mass conversion' proved problematic. The expulsion in early 1662 of the Dutch regime by Koxinga, a famous general from the late Ming dynasty, led to two centuries of 'silence' so far as Christian presence is concerned; all traces of the Dutch and Spanish missions had disappeared within half a century.

Christianity and the Modernisation of Taiwan

A second wave of missionary activity in Taiwan began in the late 1850s and 1860s, as part of the Great Missionary Movement of the West. This was facilitated by the Tien Chin Treaty of 1858, contracted between the Ching Empire of China and several Western nations. With the opening of trading seaports, Dominican priests from Manila and Amoy arrived in 1859 and began the so-called Restoration of Mission. The Catholic priests worked mainly among the plain aborigines in the south and maintained a 'qualitative' approach to local converts.

Missionaries from the English Presbyterian Mission, many of Scottish descent, began their work in southern Taiwan in 1865, followed by Canadian Presbyterian missionaries in the north in 1872. The anti-foreign mentality of the Taiwanese people elicited several religion-related incidents, resulting in persecutions of both missionaries and local converts. Under these trying circumstances, the Reformed spirit of *nec tamen consumebatur* ('and yet it was not consumed', a reference to the burning bush of Exodus 3: 2) was upheld. Early missionaries adopted a rather comprehensive approach to mission, engaging in evangelism as well as medical, educational and social services. These efforts marked the beginning of modernisation in Taiwan, which lasted until the onset of Japanese rule in 1895, when the Presbyterian mission had to compete with the new colonial government in the provision of social services.

Christianity in Taiwan, 1970 and 2020

Tradition	1970 Population	%	2020 Population	%	Average annual growth rate (%), 1970–2020
Christians	933,000	6.3%	1,463,000	6.1%	0.9%
Anglicans	2,100	0.0%	1,100	0.0%	−1.2%
Independents	210,000	1.4%	510,000	2.1%	1.8%
Protestants	261,000	1.8%	450,000	1.9%	1.1%
Catholics	305,000	2.1%	240,000	1.0%	−0.5%
Evangelicals	127,000	0.9%	225,000	0.9%	1.1%
Pentecostal/Charismatics	178,000	1.2%	365,000	1.5%	1.4%
Total population	**14,693,000**	**100.0%**	**23,818,000**	**100.0%**	**1.0%**

Source: Todd M. Johnson and Gina A. Zurlo (eds), *World Christian Database* (Leiden/Boston: Brill), accessed March 2018.

In time, medical work became the most efficient means of mission, facilitated by advanced Western surgical skills. Indeed, the spread of the gospel was coupled with the introduction of modern medicine and the scientific worldview. In contrast, non-medical missionaries were concerned more with the enlightening of the mind, conversations on science and religion and the development of a 'theology of creation' based on arguments from design and evidence. This 'enlightened mission' and its educational philosophy can be traced back to the combined impact of the Scottish Enlightenment and subsequent evangelical revivals. However, with the exception of a few individuals who had strong respect for and identification with the local people, most of the missionaries carried with them a sense of superiority and paternalism, as well as a strong prejudice against non-Western culture.

From the 1880s, the Presbyterian missionaries felt pressured to start middle schools as preparatory institutions for theological education. Interestingly and unexpectedly, after having passed through middle schools, a fairly large portion of graduates went into various professions and became leading elites in Taiwanese society under Japanese rule. In fact, during this period, a quarter of all graduates from medical college and two-fifths of all those who studied abroad, in Europe or North America, were children of Christian families. This is noteworthy, given that Christians formed less than 1% of the population.

As was generally true in all Presbyterian missions, the education of women was advocated from an early stage in Taiwan, the pioneers being Hugh Ritchie and his wife Eliza C. Cooke in the south and George L. Mackay in the north. Women's education under the sponsorship of the Presbyterian missions was generally free of charge, the only qualification for entrance being that 'the pupils must not bind their feet'. The women graduates contributed greatly to the life of the church as well as to community cultural life. However, under the influence of the Japanese frame of mind towards women's education, the girls' schools were also courted to perform the function of training capable and obedient housewives.

In 1926, the Holiness Church from Japan and the True Jesus Church from China were introduced to Taiwan and began evangelising among the Taiwanese, thus ending the dominance of the Presbyterian missions and creating new tensions. These two new churches, nonetheless, remained small until the end of the Second World War.

Christianity Tested: War and Militarism
In 1912 the English and Canadian Presbyterian missions merged and formed the Taiwan Synod, the forerunner of the Presbyterian Church

in Taiwan (PCT). From 1915 onwards, when the English Presbyterian Mission celebrated its fiftieth anniversary, some local leaders, notably the Reverend Gou Hi-Eng, began to advance the missionary principle of 'self-support, self-government and self-propagation'. This gradually led to the formation of a native and autonomous church. It was on this foundation that the church in Taiwan endured difficult times under the Japanese colonial regime and its aggressive militarism.

With the outbreak of the war against China in 1937, and particularly of the Pacific War in 1941, the Japanese government accelerated the 'spiritual mobilisation' movement, aiming to foster the national spirit and to enlist all religious bodies in support of the war. This reinforced the Royal Citizen Movement imposed earlier to Japanise the Taiwanese people and their lifestyle and to enforce Shintoism, in association with *tennosei* (the emperor system) and military patriotism, on all families and institutions. The question of shrine attendance brought about a collision between the principle of freedom of religion and the national Shinto system. The Presbyterian schools became major targets.

In Japan itself, as the Far Eastern crisis deepened in the 1930s, Christian views on state Shintoism gradually changed from opposition to accommodation, with the National Council of Churches in Japan and the Christian Educational Association adopting the official interpretation that the shrine ceremonies were 'supra-religious' and the act of obeisance, the bow, was simply meant to indicate patriotism and loyalty. This allowed Japanese Christians to cooperate with the war effort. In Taiwan, under the colonial educational system, with the issuance of private school regulations in 1905, attendance at Shinto shrines was already compulsory. Private schools that refused to take their pupils to shrines were deprived of government recognition, thus blocking the way of their graduates to higher education. In the end, all Presbyterian schools were forced to make the 'expedient decision' to follow the 'non-religious' interpretation and the policy adopted by Christian schools in Japan, namely allowing the pupils to attend shrine ceremonies.

Under the extremely hostile situation and hoping to relieve Taiwanese Christians of the constant suspicion of being associated with foreigners, both British and Canadian missionaries decided to leave in late 1940 and early 1941. Around this juncture, theological colleges, church schools and hospitals, and many churches were either closed or confiscated. In 1944 the two Presbyterian synods, along with Japanese churches, were co-opted into the Taiwan branch of the Kyōdan (United Church of Christ in Japan) for convenient control under the wartime system.

In comparison with their counterparts in Korea, and even in Manchukuo, who chose to resist for their principles, Presbyterian missionaries and Christians in Taiwan seemed timid and acquiescent. The young Presbyterian Church in Taiwan, barely self-sufficient and functional, was caught unprepared. Only a handful of young pastors who were able to study in Japan learned about Karl Barth's 'Theology of Crisis'. There was no genuine theological reflection on the issue at hand, and thus no courage was instilled nor acts of conscience followed. However, it is noteworthy that the small Holiness Church did experience persecution and closure of churches due to the hostile Japanese policy on its 'mother church' in Japan.

Ecclesiological Scene after the Second World War

The third wave of mission to Taiwan began in the late 1940s. After suffering defeat by the Communists, the Nationalist regime in China retreated to Taiwan. The situation gradually stabilised under American military and economic aid after the outbreak of the Korean War in 1950, in particular with the signing of the Sino-American Mutual Defense Treaty in 1954. This led to an influx of missionaries and mission agencies withdrawing from China and relocating to Taiwan. After the mid-1950s, virtually all denominations were represented in Taiwan. Christian churches seized the opportunity to engage in evangelistic work among the numerous refugees whose lives had been greatly disrupted. The PCT also launched a series of evangelising movements, of which the Church Doubling Movement (1955–65) and the New Century Mission Movement (1965–78) were the most significant. Within a short period of time (up to 1960), the number of Christians increased from 51,000 to 220,000, that of seminaries from two to 10, and that of mission-related bodies from four to 33.

The political refugees fleeing from China, soon referred to as 'Mainlanders', numbered around 1.5 million and slowly settled into Taiwanese society among the 6.5 million 'Native Taiwanese'. Under unsettling political circumstances, and influenced by the fact that Chiang Kai-shek and his Methodist-affiliated wife Madame Song openly propagated Christian faith among high-ranking governmental officers, a significant number of Mainlanders became Christians and found solace and hope in their new faith, to a certain degree similar to the situation in South Korea after the Korean War.

Six distinct and emergent Christian groups could be identified in Taiwan by the mid-1960s. The first included those that already existed before the end of the Second World War, including the large and well established Presbyterians and the tiny, late-coming Holiness and True Jesus churches. The second was the oldest Catholic Dominican mission, soon to be overpowered and marginalised by the Chinese Regional Bishops' Conference, which brought abundant human and financial resources to Taiwan. The third was the historic mainstream churches comprising the Lutherans, the Methodists, the Anglicans and the Baptists, all of which paid more attention to the Chinese refugees and thus established mainly Mandarin-speaking churches. The fourth was the minor historical churches, including the Free Methodists, the Mennonites, the Quakers, the Alliance Church and the Seventh-day Adventists, who established Taiwanese-speaking as well as Mandarin-speaking congregations. The fifth was Independent churches, including the Assembly Hall Church (founded by Watchman Nee and later renamed Church of Christ), Evangelize China Fellowship and Ling Liang World-Wide Evangelistic Mission Association (now Bread of Life Christian Church), focusing also more on the Mandarin-speaking congregations. The sixth was newly established churches which called themselves 'Mandarin churches' or 'local churches'.

In general, the Han-Taiwanese Christian groups experienced initial success and growth in the post-war period of the late 1950s and early 1960s, due primarily to the critical political atmosphere of the time. However, after the stabilisation of the political and economic situation, owing largely to American aid and the martial law imposed by the Nationalist regime, and with gradual industrialisation and urbanisation after 1965, the growth of the church became stagnant. The only exceptions were the non-historical Taiwanese-speaking churches such as the Holiness Church, True Jesus Church and Assembly Hall Church, which continued to experience a certain degree of growth. Han-Taiwanese Christians continue to be a minority and a 'community of strangers' in society at large.

On the other hand, after the Second World War, mission work among the aborigines in Taiwan flourished like 'the blossoming of wildflowers'. Growing from around 3,000 Christians belonging to a single tribe, the Truku, in 1945, to more than 100,000 among virtually all of the 10 aboriginal tribes in the 1960s, this mission movement has been termed 'the miracle of the twentieth century'. At the peak of the mission movement in the 1970s, the percentage of Christians among the aboriginal population reached 65%, in some tribes even as high as 85%. George Vicedom, a German missiologist, has identified four factors that led aboriginals to Christianity in large numbers: Christianity helped them in the process of assimilation into Han-Taiwanese society; it helped in their resistance to the Japanese; it would improve the standard of living of the tribes; and it filled the vacuum caused by the failure of the Japanese.

In the midst of this new social and ecclesiastical context, the PCT was formally founded, resulting from the union of the North and South synods in 1951. Immediately, the PCT joined the World Presbyterian Alliance and the World Council of Churches and became an active member of the world ecumenical community. This young indigenous church, both historic and ecumenically minded, soon encountered tremendous challenges, including issues of mission and contextualisation, ethnic tension and national identity, globalisation and economic justice, spiritual renewal and Charismatic movements.

Meanwhile, with the arrival of the Regional Bishops' Conference in the 1960s, the Catholic Church has exhibited a strong presence in Taiwan; it has established hospitals and social services agencies in rural and remote areas, and founded three universities and three professional nursing schools. It has also worked continuously among marginalised communities, in particular the aboriginal tribes, with keen 'inculturating' efforts. During the last two decades, the Catholic Church has also laboured and cared for the many Filipino foreign workers in Taiwan.

In line with the spirit of Second Vatican Council and epitomising a major advance in terms of indigenisation, the Rites of Ancestor Veneration were officially adopted in 1971, with Cardinal Yu-Ping officiating the ceremonies, thus marking a break with the historical legacy of the Rites Controversy. Since the 1960s, the Fu Jen Faculty of Theology of St Robert Bellarmine had engaged compassionately with indigenous Chinese philosophy and culture, exemplified by the innovative work of Aloysius B. Chang, Mark Fang and Luis Gutheinz. In addition, Father Andrew Zhao Yizhou worked diligently over many years on the translation of Latin liturgical texts into Chinese and published *Institutio Generalis Missalis Romani* in 2003.

In 2016, with the re-election of the Democratic Progressive Party (DPP) government, Dr Chen Chien-Jen KSG KHS, a renowned epidemiologist and a Catholic, became vice president. Yet, with the signing of a provisional agreement on the appointment of bishops between the Holy See and China in September 2018, there are concerns that the long-lasting diplomatic relation between Taiwan and the Vatican might be jeopardised, potentially exacerbating Taiwan's international isolation.

Ideological Confrontation and Ecumenical Movement

From 1960s on, the emergent ecumenical movement was threatened by ideological confrontations under the Cold War framework. The Nationalist regime (Kuomintang, KMT), embracing anti-communist ideology and instigated by Carl McIntire of the International Council of Christian Churches, a conservative rival to the World Council of Churches (WCC), put great pressure on the PCT to withdraw from the WCC. With the tacit understanding of ecumenical leaders, the PCT was forced to leave the WCC in 1970; it rejoined in 1985. Other mainline churches, including the Anglicans, Methodists and Lutherans, also left the WCC, but never rejoined.

This tension triggered efforts from Western missionaries for democratic development in Taiwan. New missionaries arriving in Taiwan gradually realised that despite Generalissimo Chiang and Madame Song's claim that the tiny island-state was 'Free China', it was in fact 'neither free nor China'. More than 30 missionaries, mostly from the Reformed family, were politically involved and became 'voices for the voice-less Taiwanese people'; they were either deported or denied re-entry to Taiwan in the late 1960s and 1970s.

Since the 1970s, the democratic development and the political future of Taiwan have become a paramount concern, as well as a divisive issue, for the Taiwanese churches. In 1971 the People's Republic of China was admitted to the United Nations and the membership of the Republic of China was concluded. Taiwan experienced diplomatic setbacks and international isolation. In response, the PCT issued three public statements: 'A Public Statement on Our National Fate' (1971), 'Our Appeal' (1975) and 'A Declaration of Human Rights' (1977). Through these prophetic statements the PCT called for social and political reforms, proclaimed the right of the Taiwanese people to self-determination, and expressed hope for a 'new and independent country'.

During this critical stage, drawing on the pioneering theological work of Shoki Coe and C. S. Song, homegrown theologies were adeptly articulated, including Wang Hsien-Chih's 'Homeland Theology', Chen Nan-Jou's 'Theology of Identification' and Huang Po-Ho's 'Theology of Self-Determination', as well as emergent theologies on gender and ecological justice, aboriginal culture and ethnic identity, contextual liturgies and arts.

On 10 December 1979, World Human Rights Day, the momentous Kao-Hsiong Incident, a crackdown on pro-democracy demonstrators, signalled the dawning of a new era for Taiwanese democratic movements, with the PCT implicated as a civil community. As a result, the PCT was severely persecuted and suppressed by the Nationalist regime, with the Reverend C. M. Kao, its general secretary, imprisoned for more than four years. Intriguingly, the ecumenical bodies and the local Taiwanese churches reacted very differently. On the one hand, the three main ecumenical organisations (the WCC, World Alliance of Reformed Churches and Christian Council of Asia) and more than 30 partner churches all over the world sent representatives or official letters to support the PCT, whereas other Christian churches in Taiwan, both mainstream denominations and independent churches, did not share these same convictions and were critical of the PCT. The grounds for their negative reactions were not theological in nature but rather stemmed largely from ideological and ethnic differences in the Taiwanese context. There was an intermingling of religious faith and anti-communist ideology among the so-called 'party-state Christians' in Taiwan, and this impacted local inter-church relations.

From the 1980s onwards, the longing of the Taiwanese people for *chhut-thâu-thi^n* ('free at last,' Taiwanese slang signifying 'political liberation') and the PCT's advocacy of 'self-determination' were gradually interwoven and profoundly contributed to the formation of a new Taiwanese identity. The Democratic Progressive Party was formed by pro-independence opposition factions in 1986, and martial law, in force for 38 years, was lifted in 1987.

Since the late 1970s, these two 'camps' (PCT and non-PCT) have often divided and split on pro-ecumenical/anti-ecumenical lines. Debates revolving around whether Christians should engage in social and political actions or conflicting political ideologies and contrasting attitudes towards the former Nationalist regime and its China-oriented policy to a certain degree still alienate Christian churches from each other. From the late 1970s, the PCT continued to embrace an ecumenical ethos and joined hands with the democratic movement in Taiwan. This self-understanding is reflected in the section on ecclesiology in its 1985 *Confession of Faith*: 'We believe that the Church is the fellowship of God's people . . . both ecumenical and rooted in this land, identifying with all its inhabitants, and through love and suffering becoming the sign of hope'.

Within this intricate context, the Ecumenical Consultative Committee (ECC) of Taiwan, founded in 1963, was rarely vigorous and responsive in the face of emergent and contentious issues. In 1991 the ECC was succeeded by the National Council of Churches in Taiwan (NCCT), which has never played a prophetic role and continues to serve only inter-church fellowship functions.

The Charismatic Movement

Since the late 1960s, Taiwanese society has experienced rapid social change, resulting in the breakdown of rural and aboriginal communities. The impact of globalisation has been profoundly felt. Prevailing phenomena include the disintegration of traditional ethical values, the emergence of a popular and Westernised 'mono-culture', the dwindling of communal ways of life and ethos, the existence of an individualistic and privatised mentality among the bourgeois class, the unending pursuit of materialism and, most critical of all, the confusion of national identity. Inevitably, Taiwanese Christians have also experienced the challenge and impact of the globalising trends.

Since the 1990s, one response to the new situation has been the emergence and growth of Charismatic groups in urban areas. Of these there are several, variously influenced by Korean, Singaporean and North American trends as well as developing from indigenous church groups. From South Korea, these groups were highly influenced by the Prayer

Mountain revival modelled on the Yoido Full Gospel Church under the leadership of the Reverend David Yonggi Cho; from Singapore, by high-tech mega-churches, the theology of prosperity and market-oriented strategies; from Northern America, by Charismatic leaders exercising healing ministry, 'Power Ministry' and church growth movements.

According to Murray Rubinstein, Charismatic Christians account for roughly one-third of Protestant Christians in Taiwan, with members of mainstream churches such as the Presbyterians and the Baptists also participating in Charismatic activities. He argues that, even as mainstream churches in Taiwan were faltering, this Holy Spirit-centred, experiential form of Christianity continued to grow and to demonstrate dynamism. Charismatic churches include: the Taiwan Assemblies of God, which are linked closely to their Western roots and mission bodies; the Prayer Mountain revival movement, which maintained a careful relationship with its Western 'parent churches' yet existed at the same time as aggressively independent entities; and the True Jesus Church, which represents the indigenised wing of the spectrum and is determinedly 'non-political', thus offering an alternative form of Christianity to the Taiwanese to that of mainstream churches such as the PCT.

In addition to the three types of Charismatic groups presented by Rubinstein, what is noteworthy in the twenty-first century is the emergence of several Independent church groups – such as the Bread of Life Christian Church, the Evangelical Covenant Church and the Truth Lutheran Church – that attempted to combine Charismatic elements, cell-group church growth strategies and the mega-church model. In general, with the onset of Charismatic movements during the early twenty-first century, subjectivist spiritual experiences gradually prevailed among the urban middle-class churches, especially among young professionals.

Intriguingly, aboriginal Christianity in Taiwan, compared with the tiny and marginalised Han Christianity, emerged as a kind of 'new religion' after the Second World War and was embraced by the majority of the aboriginal population. As first-generation Christians, they exhibited great energy and dynamic strength of faith, first in Pentecostal movements and then in missionary activities. Among the various aboriginal Christian communities, the most significant ones are among the Tayal, the Amis, the Paiwan and the Bunun tribes. One episode will be sufficient to illustrate their vitality. In 1972, a few churches of the Tayal tribe began to experience a spiritual revival via itinerant lay preaching and visitations that included some extraordinary manifestations, such as shaking of the body, going into trances, falling like a stick to the floor, seeing visions, prophesying and passing judgements on others (mostly by women). Though controversial and conflictive, the spiritual movement left a powerful and lasting legacy after some 30 years: not only did these 'burnt-over' churches experience renewal and growth, but they are now engaged in overseas mission work in Saipan Island, Thailand and Indonesia.

On the other hand, these spiritual movements were severely criticised as creating and classifying two rival groups of Christians (spiritual and non-spiritual), promoting self-righteousness and pride, causing division and schism, being misled by political ideologies and lacking biblical teaching.

Current and Emergent Issues

Several issues have special relevance for contemporary Taiwan. The first of these is transformative justice. The ethnic relationship in Taiwan has always been sensitive and tense and often tangled with political ideologies. For a long time, the minor ethnic groups were overpowered and marginalised by the dominant groups, especially the so-called 'internal colonialism' that was experienced by the aboriginal peoples. There is a pressing need for transformative justice as well as healing of historical wounds.

In 2016, the DPP government offered a formal apology to all aboriginal peoples in Taiwan, followed by a resolution issued by the PCT to stand in solidarity with the aborigines. The Transitional Justice Commission was formally established in 2017 to deal with major political incidents and grave cases of injustice during the White-Terror Era, that is, the martial law period which began in 1947 and was marked by the suppression of political dissidents. Evidently, however, the old KMT political alignment and associated groups will resist and fight for their vested interests. Will some of the Christian churches still be entangled in the party-state alliance and struggle against structural reform? Should the churches advocate for restorative justice instead of transformative justice?

The second issue is the rise of civil society. Despite the lifting of martial law and the beginning of the end of dictatorial rule in 1987, the building of civil society in Taiwan never truly got underway. In the midst of political reform and social and economic transformations, politics and economics continued to assume command, with the government and big corporations continually manipulating power and resources and the so-called 'third sector' constantly compressed and pushed to the corner. The non-profit and non-governmental organisations, and grassroots and advocacy groups were largely marginalised and not able to facilitate social change or transformation.

After two peaceful yet painful transfers of political regime in 2000 (DDP) and 2008 (KMT), the majority of the Taiwanese people were certainly awakened by the civil movements in 2013 and 2014, especially the Sunflower Movement. This was a protest movement driven by a coalition of students and civic groups against the passing of the Cross-Strait Service Trade Agreement by the ruling KMT party. The Trade Agreement symbolised the younger generation's fear that trade with China would hurt Taiwan's economy and leave it vulnerable to political pressure from Beijing. This movement resulted in the election of a new DPP government and the first woman president, Dr Tsai Ing-wen, in 2016.

Thus, within the first two decades of the third millennium, the pursuit of civil power and the establishment of a robust civil society have become a compelling reality in Taiwan. The younger generations, born and educated after the martial law era, were able to receive better ideas about human rights, democracy and independent thinking, and have a well founded sense of Taiwanese identity. These new energies had triggered greater civil awareness. How are the Christian churches responding to these rising powers?

The Cross-Straits Christian Forum is a third issue of relevance. Taiwan's national identity and the identity of the Taiwanese people continue to occupy the minds of Christians. From the 1990s onwards, after the internal process of gradual indigenisation and democratisation, Taiwan began to face the external threat and hegemonic pressure of China as a 'rising power', with political, diplomatic, military, economic, cultural and even religious measures. The struggle for a 'normalised' national identity and a 'dignified' identity for the Taiwanese people remains a pressing issue.

When the China Christian Council (CCC) joined the WCC in 1991 and became an active player on the ecumenical stage, the relationship between the PCT and the CCC presented itself as a challenging issue for the ecumenical community. Many ecumenical partners even considered the interaction between the two churches as a situation of 'impasse' and urged for open dialogue. From the early 2010s onwards, the CCC created a Cross-Straits Christian Forum and invited representatives of Christian churches in Taiwan to join the gathering, although bypassing the PCT as formal ecumenical partner. The Chinese factor is now a significant influence in the ecclesiastical as well as political Taiwanese scene.

Another critical issue is gender justice and same-sex marriage. The promotion of equal rights and the participation of women had enjoyed modest success among Christian communities until the 1990s. For example, since the 1960s the PCT had adopted the policy of ordaining women pastors and church leaders. Even though the male-dominant and patriarchal culture of Taiwanese society still had strong repercussions within church life, the PCT continued to promote gender justice, following and building upon the completion of the WCC's Ecumenical Decade of the Churches in Solidarity with Women in 1998.

However, conservative Christian groups, nurtured by right-wing ideologies, joined hands with anti-LGBT parties to form the Family Guardian Coalition in 2013 to oppose the legalisation of same-sex marriage in Taiwan. As a result, this critical issue created divisions among the Christian communities and instilled negative impressions of Christian faith in the minds of the Taiwanese public, especially among the younger generations.

Becoming Christians in Taiwanese Society

Campbell N. Moody, the Scottish missionary who worked in Taiwan more than a century ago, paid special attention to the 'reception' of the Christian message and the psychological, spiritual and social aspects of Taiwanese Christians in his famous books *The Heathen Heart* and *The Saints of Formosa*. He noted that, from the dogmatic Christian's viewpoint, the Han Taiwanese were 'disappointedly good' and their realistic mentality (always seeking 'what is useful'), lack of 'sinfulness of sin' and heartlessness towards human sufferings had rendered the gospel 'almost without market'. He nearly concluded that Taiwanese Christians were 'non-ethical' and 'non-religious' and even considered them a sort of 'rice Christian'.

Almost a century later, due to the accumulated efforts of Christian elites working devotedly in the larger society during the Japanese era, of the PCT's struggle during the process of democratisation in the 1970s, and of the social welfare services in needed areas during the past decades, the Christian community in Taiwan, according to surveys conducted in 2012 and 2015, now comprises 5.8% of the population and plays a prominent and collaborative role as it actively participates in the public domain.

Bibliography

Chen, Nan-Jou (ed.), *A Testament to Taiwan Homeland Theology: The Essential Writings of Wang Hsien-Chih* (Taipei: Yeong Wang, 2011).

Cheng, Yang-en, 'Calvinism and Taiwan', *Theology Today*, 66:2 (July 2009), 184–202.

Ion, A. Hamish, *The Cross and the Rising Sun: The British Protestant Missionary Movement in Japan, Korea, and Taiwan, 1865–1945* (Waterloo, ON: Wilfrid Laurier University Press, 1993).

Rubinstein, Murray A., *The Protestant Community of Modern Taiwan: Mission, Seminary, and Church* (Armonk, NY: M. E. Sharpe, 1991).

So, Francis K. H., Beatrice K. F. Leung and Ellen Mary Mylod (eds), *The Catholic Church in Taiwan: Problems and Prospects* (Singapore: Palgrave Macmillan, 2018).

North Korea

Philo Kim

At the time of liberation from Japanese colonial rule in 1945, there are believed to have been around 3,000 churches with 300,000 Christians in the northern half of the Korean peninsula, while there were around 1,000 churches with 120,000 Christians in the southern half. According to the official North Korean Central Yearbook, as of 1950 there were around 200,000 Protestants and 53,000 Catholics in the country. It was recorded that there were 410 pastors, 498 evangelists and 2,142 elders in the North.

The communists began to persecute Christians after taking power in 1945, since Christians were considered to represent the most potent threat to the regime. The government sought to suppress Christians by forcing them either to go to work or to attend schools on Sundays, thus disrupting worship and church attendance. The regime also used physical force to repress those who wished to continue their lives as believers.

The tragic Korean War (1950–3) brought seismic change to the Christian community in the north. During that war, the leadership of the Protestant Church was largely annihilated. According to Protestant Church research, 260 Presbyterian and 50 Methodist ministers in the north either were martyred or fled to the south following the war. Unfortunately, however, records for only around 100 persons can be found. What happened to the remainder cannot be ascertained, although some of them were absorbed into the Korean Christian Federation (KCF), the official Christian organisation in North Korea.

Repression initially was sporadic following the war, but from 1958 surveys to set up the family-background-based system of *Songbun* coincided with far more extreme repression targeting Christians, namely arrests and expulsions. From 1958 to 1960, central party leadership supervised the classification of 'the religious and their families', which numbered around 100,000 households, with a total of 450,000 people. Such data were then used to implement an ongoing policy of mass repression. It is a moderate estimate that about 100,000 Christians survived the war and faced these severe repressions. Families were arrested, imprisoned or expelled to the countryside and remote regions, while some managed to escape surveillance and continue to worship on their own.

Along with the expulsion policy, from the early 1960s the regime initiated a concentrated policy of anti-religious education, making it impossible for religious people to practise their faith in public any longer. Sporadic resistance and underground worship disappeared, and the last vestiges of the community vanished from view. The ruthless punishment and purging of Christian households set members of families against one another, with children encouraged to denounce their parents as part of a society-wide campaign against religion. In such circumstances, worship had to be entirely hidden or carried out in the privacy of individual minds alone.

Emergence of Official Practices

In the late 1960s, the state's 'relaxation policy' was applied to some families previously associated with Kim Il-sung's revolutionary past, but social and policy-based discrimination and oppression did not abate. It is said that 200 household places of worship were legally created in 1968 based on the state policy, but only around 20–40 households actually were functional, with the rest of the household congregations existing only on paper. It appeared that there were 100 household congregations as North–South dialogue was progressing in 1972.

According to North Korean refugee testimony, the sixtieth birthday of Kim Il-sung in 1972 was accompanied by a great amnesty, and as a result a number of Christians returned from exile in remote regions to their original places of residence. Another large number of Christians were reportedly pardoned just before the Sixth Party Congress, in October 1980, and among them were many who returned from internal exile in remote areas. Whether they became part of underground churches or were summoned to congregate in the official church, they became the centre of what could be called church attenders in North Korea.

In 1988, a unique event occurred in North Korean history: the Bongsu Church (for Protestants) and Changchung Cathedral (for Catholics) were

Christianity in North Korea, 1970 and 2020

Tradition	1970 Population	%	2020 Population	%	Average annual growth rate (%), 1970–2020
Christians	142,000	1.0%	99,000	0.4%	−0.7%
Independents	8,000	0.1%	90,000	0.3%	5.0%
Protestants	119,000	0.8%	6,000	0.0%	−5.8%
Catholics	15,000	0.1%	3,000	0.0%	−3.2%
Evangelicals	8,800	0.1%	10,000	0.0%	0.3%
Pentecostal/Charismatics	8,600	0.1%	90,000	0.3%	4.8%
Total population	**14,410,000**	**100.0%**	**25,841,000**	**100.0%**	**1.2%**

Source: Todd M. Johnson and Gina A. Zurlo (eds), *World Christian Database* (Leiden/Boston: Brill), accessed March 2018.

built. It has been alleged that this church construction took place for propaganda purposes, targeting a foreign audience to demonstrate that North Korea had religious freedoms. There are also those who argue that as North Korea began to attempt reform and opening, it sought to gain access to South Korean churches. However, it should not be overlooked that there were a number of other changes that occurred from the early 1980s, both internally and externally. A decisive factor were the frequent visits of overseas Korean Christian leaders. Yet the change also resulted from internal demands.

As the North Korean authorities explain, they had a problem to solve: the higher population concentration that came with high-rise apartment blocks rendered it impractical to conduct worship informally within the household. A large number of people living in a concentrated area wanted to worship together and thus needed a place where such activities could be practically carried out. Hence, the government claims that Bongsu Church was built to provide for religious households in the Kwangbok Street area of Pyongyang. At the same time, household-based worship continued in eastern Pyongyang. While it is undeniably true that religious activities became visible again in part because the authorities wanted to improve North Korea's relations with other countries and also to earn foreign currency, their re-emergence also speaks to a need that the North Korean regime felt in terms of integrating religious families.

Official Churches and Household Congregations

Bongsu has a congregation of 300, while Chilgol Church, the second Protestant church built, has 90 members. Many of these people are descendants of believers, mobilised to participate due to familial relations. Those with duties inside the church in particular are often first-generation believers or their families. An observer estimates that there are around eight or nine elders, 6–14 exhorters and 5–16 deacons at Bongsu Church, and it is likely that they were Protestants prior to the regime's religious repressions or are relatives of those who were. At Chilgol Church, there are three elders, one exhorter (a woman) and three deacons (one man, two women), all thought to be from Christian families; many believers are also thought to be from Christian families. Of course, believers are mobilised by the authorities, but they also have had experience with Christian faith or have a family background of Christian tradition.

Household congregations were the means through which Christian families practised their faith in the 1970s. These congregations became more active in the 1980s. In accordance with changes in North Korean government control policies, household congregations sometimes numbered as many as 100–200 and sometimes as few as 20–40. In the

1980s, their numbers appeared to rise as high as 520 house churches nationwide. Contrary to the assertions of the North Korean authorities, the household congregations located outside the capital appear to be inactive. Visits to household congregations have been allowed only in Pyongyang. No authorisation has yet been given for official visits outside Pyongyang, such as to North Pyongan, a place that has witnessed a large revival of Protestantism.

On the basis of observations from South Korean visitors to 10 household congregations, each was composed of around 12 members, one or two of whom were first-generation believers. The household congregation visited by the present author in Okryu in the District of Taedong River, Pyongyang, had nine members present, with three more not in attendance due to work commitments. Some participants told the author that they had been attending for only two or three years, while others had been coming since 1989. Each had different reasons for joining, but generally they were connected in one way or another to Christian families.

The North Korean authorities assert that household congregations are run by lay people who serve as elders, exhorters and deacons. However, an observer who lived in North Korea for an extended period and frequented the Chilgol Church for a number of years told the author that household congregations do not seem to convene regularly, but only when the need arises. A KCF official stated that among the 12,300 Protestants in the country, around 6,000 are organised into the official household congregations, with the other 6,000 being spread out in the countryside but not members of KCF-organised household congregations.

At present, there are five religious organisations in North Korea: the Korean Christian Federation, the Korean Buddhist Federation, the Korean Catholic Association, the Korean Chondoist Association and the Korean Orthodox Church. The Korean Religionists Council consisting of the aforementioned organisations was formed on 30 May 1989. According to an official explanation given by North Korea, there are 40,000 religious believers in the country, including 12,300 Christians (Protestants), 12,000 Buddhists, 3,000 Catholics and 15,000 Chondoists. There are two Protestant churches, 20 ministers and 520 house churches; one Catholic church and two assembly sites; and about 60 Buddhist temples with some 300 monks, including one central temple, seating 100, at Chundokyo in Pyongyang. There are also an estimated 800 Buddhist house prayer places (this has not been confirmed due to inaccessibility). Each religious organisation has its own educational centres for training religious leaders, such as the Pyongyang Theological Seminary operated by the Central Committee of the KCF and the Buddhist School run by the Korean Buddhist Federation.

'Underground Church'

The 'underground church' refers to religious organisations that exist outside the control of the North Korean government, as 'illegal' organisations. In contrast to the loose organisation of old Christian families into a social community, the underground church is considered to be highly active as a set of Christian organisations. During the famine of the mid-1990s, as many as 300,000 North Koreans escaped to China, where some 80% of them were exposed to the Christian community. Among them, as many as 100,000 returned to North Korea, with a number having become Christians. Some of them created a new, vibrant religious community after coming into contact with Christianity from the outside world. While the old Christian families have sought to maintain their identities within the household or groups of relatives, the typical underground church is composed of 4–10 members who connect and bond through a network in an unofficial faith organisation.

Evidence suggests that the underground church includes several tens of thousands of people newly converted by North Korean refugees. It appears that many believers have come from old Christian families, while some who do not have become connected to these families when they engage in faith activities. They are basically individuals who often form family-based or friend-based groups. These underground churchgoers gather in household congregations in such localities as Chungjin, Musan, Hoeryong, Hyesan and Sinuiju.

The worship activities of the underground church are often connected to old Christian families. This is because while it is likely they will come under the control of North Korea's police, religious families have tacit permission from the authorities to organise networks among family and relatives and/or are able to worship in private. There are numerous cases of converted believers who were from old Christian families. A refugee who became a Protestant while in China returned to North Korea and told his mother about his faith. His mother confessed to him that she had hidden her faith from him. Another refugee remembers how they found out about their father's faith and time at Pyongyang Seminary only after escaping the North. There are also those who, having become Protestants in China, have found out about their families' religious past and returned to the North to proselytise. For example, the mother-in-law of a North Korean refugee lived in Pyongyang as a believer until the age of 23. Underground church activities centre on old Christian families partly because many refugees from the North come from places to which old Christian families were expelled in the past. Such locations formerly were considered distant backwaters, but now they are some of the easiest places from which to escape the country.

The underground church is known to South Korean society largely through Christian missions that seek to spread Protestantism in the North. Each missionary organisation gives different estimates regarding the size of the underground church. This is because there is disagreement as to whether the networks of underground churches are purely Protestant faith communities, whether business activities should be included, and/or whether former Christian families should be included. South Korean missionary groups sometimes include former Christian families in their numbers as well as potential Christians, and thus cite figures as high as 100,000–300,000. However, where the underground church is treated purely as a faith organisation, some estimate such organisations may include as few as several thousands; in other words, when former Christian families and returned refugees who are not religiously active are discounted, the number of people who have actually maintained their faith is small.

Close inspection of the activities of the underground church indicates that reporting might have been distorted significantly. Taking the assertions of South Korean missions at face value raises many issues. North Korean intelligence operatives have infiltrated and are using many of these underground organisations. Furthermore, the activities of the underground church are also used by North Korean refugees to address their own personal needs. Thus, it is possible that the size and reality of the underground church have been exaggerated, and many aspects of what has been reported cannot simply be accepted without independent verification. In this regard, underground church activities centring on North Korean refugees that have begun in recent times would struggle to exist without external support. And while a network of organisations exists, their activities are not just faith-oriented but also business-related.

The format of worship in underground churches is not as highly developed as one might expect. Christians communicate with each other in various ways and on various occasions. They sometimes meet in one place to share biblical texts that they have memorised and to pray together. At other times they conduct business affairs and exchange information. Except for the old Christian families who are not very active in their faith, most Christians have an external connection. This is why the North Korean intelligence agency regards them as spy organisations and tries to catch them.

Interactions with South Korea and China have decreased in recent years, and the crackdown by Chinese authorities on religious activities there has intensified. This situation directly affected the Christian community in North Korea and caused a serious contraction in their activities. Early in 2018, however, inter-Korean dialogue and talks resumed, and a series of summit talks have begun between North Korea and China, South Korea and the USA. Christians inside North Korea expect to gain great help and strength from the diplomatic dialogues. It is expected that as North Korea becomes more open to international society, the Christian community in North Korea might have opportunities to mature in faith.

Bibliography

Baek, Joong Hyun, *Is There a Church in North Korea?* (Seoul: Kookmin Ilbo, 1998).

Kim, Heung-Soo, and Dae-Young Ryu, *A New Understanding of North Korean Religion* (Seoul: Dasan Books, 2002).

Kim, Philo, *Unification Concert of North and South Korean Churches* (Seoul: Christian Mission to North Korea, 2006).

Song, Won-Keun, *Changes of Religious Topography in North Korea* (Seoul: Cheong Media, 2013).

South Korea

Meehyun Chung

Korea's warm and enthusiastic reception of Christianity can be explained in part by the rich multi-religious complexity of Korean culture and tradition. The rich religious background of script religions like Buddhism and Confucianism as well as the ancient indigenous religion of shamanism have informed the development of Christianity on the peninsula. Shamanism is related to the Korean founding myth, which includes the Supreme Deity. For centuries shamanism has influenced the reception of Buddhism, Confucianism and the more recently arrived Christianity. Through this influence Koreans have preserved faith in the heavenly Supreme Being.

Koreans are proud that Christianity was introduced to their country not by foreign missionaries but rather by indigenous Koreans returning from abroad. Lee Seung-hun, who was baptised in Beijing, China, introduced Catholicism to Korea in 1784, while Protestantism was introduced by Seo Sang-ryun in 1884. Seo had met the Scottish missionary John Ross in Manchuria and worked with him on the translation of the Bible into the Korean Hangul language before returning to found the first Protestant church at Solnae, now in North Korea.

During the eighteenth century, the Catholic faith spread as Koreans were eager to learn more of Western science and philosophy in order to renew conventional thinking and customs. However, the new faith, with its doctrine of the equality of all people before God, presented a challenge to the strictly hierarchical order of the Chosun dynasty. As a result, the first Korean Catholics suffered severe persecution, and many were martyred for their faith. Through the work of French priests and German Benedictine missionaries, the Catholic Church gradually took root. Today, around a tenth of the South Korean population are Catholics. The Metropolitan Archdiocese of Seoul also covers North Korea. South Korean dioceses are organised under three ecclesiastical provinces and include a total of 14 suffragan dioceses, the Military Ordinariate of South Korea and the pre-diocesan Territorial Abbey of Tokwon, in North Korea.

The Orthodox Church was introduced in the eighteenth century through contacts with Russia. Partly as a result of changes in Russia, Orthodoxy in Korea has had a chequered history but an unbroken presence. An archdiocese was established in 2004.

Protestantism was a late arrival, first appearing in the late nineteenth century. It proved, however, to be the fastest-growing form of Christianity in Korea. Having begun through Korean initiative, it was significantly influenced by missionaries from the USA such as the first medical missionary, Horace Newton Allen (1858–1932). Especially influential were Horace Grant Underwood (1859–1916), an American of British heritage, whose work from his arrival in 1885 laid the foundation for the Presbyterian churches, and Henry Gerhard Appenzeller (1858–1902), an American of Swiss heritage, whose work was foundational for the Methodist Church.

Through missionary efforts, Protestant churches contributed in a major way to education and health care in Korea. Baejae Hakdang, the Methodist high school for boys; Ewha Hakdang, the Methodist school for girls; the Presbyterian Kuse Hakdang ('Underwood') orphanage school for boys; the Presbyterian Chung-shin school for girls; and Chosen Christian College (which later became Yonsei University) are examples of educational institutions that exercised great influence in Korea.

However, Koreans themselves took initiatives that proved decisive for the Christian faith. The translation of the Bible into the Korean Hangul script grounded the Protestant faith in the consciousness of the ordinary people. While the upper classes had historically used Chinese, the ordinary people preferred Hangul. As Minjung theologians pointed out in the 1970s, opting for Hangul meant that Christianity became a faith that was from 'below'. In contrast to the male-dominated Chinese language, Hangul was considered to be a female language. Indeed, women were educated through the Korean Bible to learn Korean Hangul.

A pivotal moment in the development of Protestantism was the Great Revival of 1907 that took place in Pyongyang (today in North Korea) in the midst of political upheaval. In the face of Japanese oppression, Protestantism became a rallying point for people who felt that traditional religious

Christianity in South Korea, 1970 and 2020

Tradition	1970 Population	%	2020 Population	%	Average annual growth rate (%), 1970–2020
Christians	5,747,000	17.8%	17,277,000	33.5%	2.2%
Anglicans	32,400	0.1%	90,000	0.2%	2.1%
Independents	1,718,000	5.3%	11,330,000	22.0%	3.8%
Orthodox	3,000	0.0%	2,300	0.0%	−0.5%
Protestants	2,117,000	6.6%	10,400,000	20.2%	3.2%
Catholics	838,000	2.6%	5,500,000	10.7%	3.8%
Evangelicals	2,132,000	6.6%	12,855,000	25.0%	3.7%
Pentecostal/Charismatics	324,000	1.0%	9,150,000	17.8%	6.9%
Total population	**32,209,000**	**100.0%**	**51,507,000**	**100.0%**	**0.9%**

Source: Todd M. Johnson and Gina A. Zurlo (eds), *World Christian Database* (Leiden/Boston: Brill), accessed March 2018.

values had failed them and were looking for a new faith that would be transformative. Many became Christians at this time, causing Pyongyang to be called the Jerusalem of East Asia. From then on, Christianity, and Protestantism in particular, became closely identified with Korean nationalism and resistance to Japanese rule. Many Christian leaders, both male and female, such as An Chang-ho, Kim Kyu-sik, Kim Maria and Yu Gwan-sun, participated in the independence movements in various ways.

Another formative period for Korean Protestantism was the 1950s, when people were learning how to live in the aftermath of both Japanese colonial rule and the Korean War. In these difficult times, Korean believers never lost their zeal and their desire for God. Following significant economic growth, the ecclesiastical landscape changed somewhat, but a living relationship with God, even if it is sometimes associated with fear of punishment, remains a point of emphasis in Korean Christianity today. The Pentecostal message found particular resonance at this time. The ideology of the Cold War was incorporated into Pentecostalism's rapidly growing following and found fertile soil among the lower strata of society and a people whose primary concern was material and economic growth. This resulted in a period of rapid numerical growth among marginalised people during the 1960s and 1970s.

Today, the number of Christians is stagnating or decreasing. According to Korean government statistics published in 2015, 43.9% belonged to religious communities, and this percentage is generally decreasing. Women's participation stands at 48.4%, while men's is at 39.4%. Among people in their twenties, 64.9% do not have any religion, whereas 58.2% of people in their seventies profess to belong to a religion. South Korea's population is now about one-fifth Protestant, of whom 69% are members of Presbyterian churches. There are many Presbyterian denominations, varying in size and character. The Presbyterian Church of Korea (PCK, Tonghab) and the General Assembly of the Presbyterian Church in Korea (GAPCK, Habdong) are the largest. The Presbyterian Church of the Republic of Korea (PROK, Gijang) is the most theologically and socio-politically progressive, though numerically a minority.

Based on the pivotal moment of the Great Revival at Pyongyang in 1907, a Pentecostal movement developed. This was shaped during the 1930s by the work of American missionaries who had been influenced by the Azusa Street Revival in Los Angeles. However, it was from the late 1950s that a Korean version of Pentecostalism emerged through the efforts of Choi Jashil and Cho Yonggi with a tent church, now known as the Yoido Full Gospel Church.

South Korea currently contains some of the world's largest Christian congregations, with Yoido Full Gospel Church the outstanding example. There are some mega-churches, but many churches are suffering under stagnation and even face financial debt. Rising standards of living, a growing aversion to institutional religion and greater access to leisure pursuits have resulted in the churches losing members. The reputation of Christianity has also suffered from sex scandals, lack of financial transparency, corruption and association with politicians tainted by questionable ethics.

While domestic numerical growth has slowed, mission activities abroad have increased. Experience of short-term mission awakens spiritual commitment. South Korea has become the second-largest country in terms of overseas Protestant missionaries (after the USA). They are active in many countries worldwide, but focus on areas where Christianity is little represented. The deep rifts within Korea's Protestant Church have been a chronic problem, resulting from the competitive nature of US missionary societies, tension between regions, theological differences and ideological conflict, including an anti-communist stance regarding North Korea.

Main Features of Korean Protestantism

Employing a theological typology, Korean Christians can be considered to fall into three types, in terms of whether they identify primarily with God as Father (as omnipotent heavenly being), Son (as political reformer) or Holy Spirit (as spring of prosperity). The first group, which identifies with God the Father, forms the majority among Protestants and is strongly influenced by the Northeast Asian religious background, which is Confucian and Taoist. It is patriarchal, politically conventional and concentrated in the east coast area. The second group, which identifies with God the Son, tends towards socio-political engagement, as they understand Jesus as a political activist and reformer in the context of Roman imperialism. It is politically progressive, oriented to social salvation and concentrated mostly in the west coast area, which is historically underdeveloped and neglected. The third group, which identifies with God the Holy Spirit as healer and provider of happiness, is focused on the theology of prosperity. It is spread nationwide, is politically conservative and, like the first group, is oriented towards personal salvation.

Another frame of analysis that can be applied to Korean Protestantism is drawn from the classic Christian concepts of kerygma (the message), koinonia (fellowship), martyria (witness) and diakonia (service).

Kerygma

The most popular form of preaching employs a story-telling style of sermon. Instead of following a lectionary, the pastor will choose a Bible text and preach according to the subject rather than using an exegetical method. In terms of the subject and content of the sermon, the first and third groups ('Father' and 'Holy Spirit' Christians) prefer a narrative and emotional approach, while the second group ('Son' Christians) expects to have some political comments regarding burning issues.

Giving a testimony of one's personal experience with God is a favoured contribution to worship services and other meetings. Most church members prefer this kind of personal testimony to a more academic sermon. In accordance with Protestant tradition, Word-centred (or Story-centred) worship services are provided many times during the week, often on a Wednesday or Friday evening. Many worship services are transmitted through Christian television broadcasting.

The Korean Presbyterian standardised form of liturgy with long sermons is rather common, regardless of denominational differences. Conventional worship features more hymns with Western melodies than those with authentically Korean words and melodies. Also popular is contemporary Christian music introduced from the USA. Young people are no longer familiar with traditional hymns. Regardless of denomination, the younger generation are interested in this genre of modern popular music accompanied by electronic instruments. The lyrics tend to be concerned with personal faith rather than any social concerns. Pentecostal worship includes more hymns with body movement.

Koinonia

Korean church life features some important components for building fellowship, such as communal meals, cell groups for Bible study and prayer meetings. The Korean Protestant churches do not have a parochial system. They tend to be pastor-centred. People have freedom to choose their own local church community, even if this involves geographical distance.

Boom towns and satellite cities have been built since the 1980s to accommodate people moving out from the inner cities. This has meant that church members travel long distances to come to church and need to have a communal lunch after the worship service. They have also formed home cell groups and prayer meetings for revival and sharing of faith experience, based on geographical districts. The intimate setting of a home fosters the growth of strong relationships and helps to create organic unity within the church community.

Martyria

The introduction of Christianity to Korea, rather than depending on Western missionaries, was very much driven by indigenous lay people who were active in evangelism. People at the grassroots, women in particular, have continued to be eager to participate in Christian fellowship and to disseminate the gospel.

Regardless of denominational differences, there is a common method of congregation-building: a patriarchal structure, early-morning prayer, common meals, and house visits as well as house groups for prayer meetings and Bible sharing. Mission and evangelism are emphasised, with the aim of increasing numerical growth of the churches. Usually mission is divided into inner/domestic and outer/abroad. Evangelism is understood as spreading the gospel at the local community level. The main denominations place great importance on mission work in other countries. In general, church members prefer to support short-term charity-style initiatives rather than sustainable development with long-term plans. The duration of missionary service is becoming shorter. Short mission trips are very popular. This approach attracts enthusiastic participants but can also have shortcomings, such as lack of gender awareness or lack of understanding of other confessions, such as Orthodox or Catholic, leading to resentment and hostility over apparent proselytisation.

Evangelism is carried out on military bases as well as in hospitals. Evangelisation in the military is important and is carried out on a non-denominational basis. In major Christian hospitals regular worship services are offered, an initiative supported by regional congregations in terms of resources. Religiously neutral hospitals accept Christian activities as well as those of any other religious group. Military service is mandatory and healthy young men spend on average two years in the military. Spiritual care is very important because of the stresses of military service. Besides Christian (Catholic and Protestant) chaplaincy there is a Buddhist chaplaincy system, and the two work hand in hand. Through chaplaincy supported by churches there is active evangelisation, but while many people convert to Christianity during their military service a large proportion do not continue in the faith on their return to civilian life.

In the early period of Korean Christianity, evangelisation by Bible women was an important method of spreading the gospel. They were able to reach other women whose realm was mainly domestic. Door-to-door evangelism or street evangelism still takes place, even when people are reluctant to be disturbed. When South Korea was going through a period of rapid economic growth and industrialisation, progressive churches focused on social outreach programmes like industrial mission and the labour movement. While Evangelical groups were interested in numerical growth through evangelisation, progressive groups were working for structural justice and making political statements.

Diakonia

Korean churches have a major involvement in social welfare. Diaconal work such as medical care, outreach programmes for marginalised people and provision of food for the hungry is undertaken by the churches, with participation by a high proportion of their members. The work ethic associated with Christianity is widely regarded as a driving force of the industrialisation that drove the country's economic growth. This, however, has led to a focus on prosperity as God's blessing rather than considering the structural sin that causes poverty. While progressive churches were addressing structural issues, conservative churches focused on instant social service, which was more attractive to recipients and givers. Increasing interest in public theology and networking of stakeholders assists the development of diakonia.

Christian Influence in Society

Influential theologians and pastors include Han Gyung-Jik (1902–2000) of the Presbyterian Church of Korea (PCK), Kim Jae-June (1901–87) and Kang Won-Yong (1917–2006) of the Presbyterian Church of the Republic of Korea (PROK), Park Hyung-Nong (1897–1978) of the General Assembly of the Presbyterian Church in Korea (GAPCK) and Park Yoon-Sun (1905–88) of the Korean Presbyterian Church (KPC). These all belonged to the Reformed tradition, though their theology and biblical interpretation varied considerably.

All along, women have worked hard to build up the churches at the grassroots level. In the early days of Christianity in Korea, many nameless women served as evangelists and gained access to fellow women who were segregated. Nonetheless, although women played important roles in church and society, they could not occupy a position as minister or presbyter in the decision-making body of the church. The Salvation Army and the Assemblies of God were the first to allow the ordination of women. The Methodist Church started to ordain women in 1931, though with certain conditions. The Presbyterian churches, which form the largest segment of Protestant Christianity, took many years before they began to ordain women as ministers, the PROK in 1977 and the PCK in 1996. Other major Presbyterian churches still reject the ordination of women.

Even today, women form a small minority among theologians holding positions in universities and theological institutions. One influential woman theologian is Park Soon-Kyung, one of the founders of the Korean Association of Women Theologians, who has contributed significantly to the development of a feminist theology for unification in Korea.

The National Council of Churches in Korea (NCCK) is a Christian ecumenical organisation founded in 1924 as the National Christian Council in Korea. It is a member of the World Council of Churches and the Christian Conference of Asia. High on the NCCK's agenda are such social issues as unification, justice, peace and integrity of creation. Its socially oriented approach and ecumenical way of thinking do not sit well with the more conservative churches. The latter have formed their own association, the Christian Council of Korea, founded in 1989 and a member of the World Evangelical Alliance. Its main issues of concern include working together in coalition as Korean churches, evangelism at the national and international levels, preparation for unification and countermeasures against sectarian movements.

Korean churches take a variety of stances in relation to political issues. During the 1970s and 1980s the PROK became known as the most progressive denomination, while the larger churches were generally silent on political matters. Its espousal of Minjung theology is one factor that gave the PROK an international reputation for political engagement. Meanwhile, the vast majority of Korean Christians were not influenced by Minjung theology at all. Most expressed their faith by seeking prosperity rather than pursuing social justice.

Due to the communism and atheism prevailing in North Korea, many Christians fled to the South for the sake of religious freedom. As convinced anti-communists, they looked to the churches to provide ideological support for democracy and capitalism. The question of reunification of the two Koreas has divided opinion. Until recently, anti-communism has been a defining characteristic of Korean Christians regardless of where they stand on the theological spectrum. Those who are influenced by this anti-communist stance tend to be conservative politically.

In the twenty-first century there has been a marked polarisation between the conservative camp and those who espouse a theology of social justice. For instance, during the corruption controversy that led to the impeachment of former president Park Kun-Hye in 2017, there was a clear division between the non-governmental organisations and socially oriented Christians who supported the anti-Park candlelight rallies and the politically and theologically conservative groups who supported the pro-Park Taeggki (Korean flag) rallies.

Minjung theology has been the watchword of those who prize social justice. It arose in the 1970s as an indigenous liberation theology and contributed to the voicing of opposition to social injustice and the dictatorship of President Park Chung-Hee (1961–79). Minjung theology became a trademark of Korean theology and attracted much international interest, though its influence at the level of the local congregation was limited. However, the ideas of Minjung theology influenced such popular social justice movements as the Catholic Farmers Movement and the Protestant Urban Industrial Mission, which fought for better working conditions and just wages. The current generation of Minjung theologians is in dialogue with process theology and is engaged with issues raised by the neo-liberal socio-economic system, such as gentrification, gender injustice and unification.

Inter-faith relations

Inter-faith relations have been harmonious in South Korea, with Buddhism, Christianity and Confucianism all represented at significant public events. Cooperation between different religious communities has been important at some turning points in Korean history, such as the 'March 1' movement against Japanese colonialism in 1919. Inspired by Woodrow Wilson's declaration of the principle of national self-determination and provoked by the mysterious death, apparently by poisoning, of King Gojong, 33 different religious leaders from Christianity, Chondogyo (Donghak) and Buddhism gave their backing to the nationwide movement.

People began to explore the Catholic faith through Western Christian literature. This led to meetings being organised for discussion in the Buddhist Temple of Chonjinam, which became a kind of cradle of the Korean Catholic Church. A combination of academic curiosity and longing for new belief led people to become acquainted with Catholic faith. Due to strict control by the Chosun government, they needed to have a secret place to study Western religious thought. It was the Buddhist monks who provided the required hospitality, a remarkable form of inter-religious cooperation. It proved to be highly costly for the monks, who were accused of being collaborators and were beheaded. In an environment in which the government was anxious to maintain the dynastical order and impose strict classism, one of the points of attraction among those interested in Christian teaching was the equality of people before God.

Inter-religious dialogue is conducted at a high level but has limited influence at the grassroots. For example, there can be religious conflicts within families when members have different faiths. A frequent point of tension is when there is ancestor worship on special occasions. While the Catholic Church provides an alternative integrated form of liturgy, it is only minority churches that have provided a complete replacement for ancestor worship. This reveals a certain lack of indigenisation in Korean Christianity. Funeral practice is rather syncretic, bringing together different religious traditions. Traditional practices of cleansing and clothing are followed, after which funerals take different forms according to religious affiliation.

When Christianity was introduced to Korea it sought to win converts from shamanism and Buddhism. This created inter-religious tension, and conflicts with Confucianism were evident with regard to ancestor worship on major Korean festival and memorial days. To distinguish Christianity from Korean traditional religions and customs, the Christian churches adopted a Western style. In order to avoid suspicion of syncretism with shamanism, Christians wanted to be clearly distinguished. This affected culture, art and music. Western styles of architecture and interior design were adopted. Likewise, people preferred the Western style of hymns to Korean traditional melody for church music. The same preference for Western style is evident in the visual arts, a notable exception being the attempts to depict biblical scenes with Korean costume by Kim Ki-chang and Kim Chang-su. In general, the lack of indigenisation of the faith is evident in art and music, where Western styles continue to prevail.

Current Political Issues

The militaristic tensions between the two Koreas have led to many political incidents and events. In some of these the churches have played an active part. For example, in 2005 in Daechuri, Pyeongtaek, which used to be a small farming village in Gyeonggi Province, some 65 kilometres south of Seoul, people were being forced off their land to allow for the expansion of a US military base. When the villagers resisted the eviction, religious communities like the Catholic Priests Association for Justice (CPAJ), Protestant groups and Buddhists joined the demonstration. In spite of this solidarity of religious groups with the 'Anti-US Military Base in Pyeongtaek' campaign, which organised countless rallies and marches at this rice village area, the Pyeongtaek base has been expanded as US Camp Humphreys. Similarly, when a US naval base was introduced to Gangjeong village on Jeju Island in 2012, religious groups joined together to demonstrate against the construction project. Jeju Island is cherished as the island of peace and ecological diversity. In spite of many demonstrations, construction of the naval base was completed in 2018.

The successive nuclear weapons tests conducted by North Korea and the deployment of the Terminal High Altitude Area Defense (THAAD) weapon system in South Korea led by 2016 to a peak of militaristic and diplomatic tension and conflict in Northeast Asia. The THAAD system is deployed in Sangju, a centre of Won Buddhism. When the Won Buddhists organised protests against the deployment, some socially oriented Christian groups joined them.

Tensions provoked by political uncertainty and militarism are constantly in the minds of Korean people and have a profound effect on them psychologically, culturally and socially. While more conservative Christians focus on upholding opposition to communism in the face of the nuclear threat posed by North Korea, more progressive Christians focus not on military solutions but on the challenge of how to cultivate peace and promote life.

A significant development in November 2018 was the decision of South Korea's Supreme Court to allow conscientious objection to military service. Prior to this, Jehovah's Witnesses and members of the Seventh-day Adventist Church were subject to punishment when they refused to serve in the military on grounds of Christian belief. It is yet to be clarified what form and length of alternative service will be required. Another controversial issue is the introduction of a tax system for Protestant pastors. This might prove to be of assistance to churches in terms of transparency in financial matters.

Contemporary Challenges

Since the Protestant churches do not follow a parochial system, churches are built up around the pastor. Church planting is often an individual matter. Within denominations there are structures that apply, but independent churches can be planted anywhere, regardless of nearby existing churches. The salary paid by congregations to pastors depends on their success in developing the churches. Founder-pastors who are successful and build flourishing churches gain authority and are rewarded financially. Such success, however, carries the risk of the development of a personality cult and authoritarian hierarchical leadership – an issue with which Korean churches are currently grappling, particularly in relation to father–son succession in mega-churches. Tensions and conflicts have often arisen in the latter cases, which often involve political and financial issues and attract considerable public attention. This might be explained by the shamanistic background: as a shaman's followers rely on the mediation of the shaman, so church members depend on their pastors.

Women form a majority in most churches, regardless of denomination and confession. Yet there is still a clear lack of gender justice. Even in denominations where the ordination of women is allowed, women are not guaranteed acceptance as ministers at the local congregational level. Women are in the minority in decision-making bodies and are more often active in diaconal work, particularly food preparation in the kitchen.

By and large, Korean Christians are conservative on matters of sexuality, and there is little tolerance for sexual minorities. The movement to oppose recognition of homosexuality is mostly supported and organised by Christian groups. In some cases this can find expression in open homophobia, supported by a literal interpretation of certain biblical texts. More progressive Christians offer a liberal interpretation of the Bible but are a minority voice in a debate that seems likely to continue.

The prevailing understanding of salvation in Korean Christianity is very much human-centred. Few are alert to the ecological implications of Christian faith and the issue of the salvation of the natural environment. Though there is a Christian environmental movement, it reaches only a small minority and has little impact on the day-to-day life and worship of the Christian churches. So far, little consideration has been given to ways in which churches can demonstrate environmental responsibility in such matters as energy usage. Exceptions include the Hansalim Movement, a federation of Korean organic farmers that has developed since the 1980s as a Catholic movement based on mutual trust between producer and consumer.

The anti-communist sympathies of the pastors and church members who migrated from North to South Korea at the time of the Korean War continue to influence many Christians today. Presbyterians have drawn on Calvinism's doctrine of double predestination to develop a dualistic way of thinking in which North Korea is viewed as evil and categorised as a perpetual enemy. This deep ideological divide is characteristic of the mainline Korean churches, including Korean Pentecostalism. It remains to be seen whether Korean Christians will review such attitudes in light of current hopes for peace and unity on the Korean peninsula.

There is currently a backlash against the confrontational methods employed by more conservative Christians. Repeated attacks on statues in Buddhist temples and Dangun Myth statues have drawn strong criticism. Street missions with loudspeaker slogans such as 'Believe in Jesus, go to heaven. Don't believe, go to hell' are provoking a negative reaction. Corruption scandals involving well known pastors or Christians prominent in public life such as former president Lee Myungbak, who was a Presbyterian elder and found guilty of corruption, have discredited the churches in the eyes of many.

Another controversial issue, particularly since Yemeni refugees arrived on Jeju Island in 2018, has been Christian–Muslim relations. While conservative Christians have viewed Muslims as candidates for conversion or potential criminals, others have argued for a more humanitarian approach.

Conclusion

Pak Nak-Joon, historian and the first president of Yonsei University (1957–60), highlighted issues in Korean Christianity that call for attention: the inherent conservatism of the churches, the lack of social application of Christianity and the low intellectual standard among the Christian community. His comments remain pertinent in the twenty-first century. Although many theologians have trained up to PhD level and there is greater acceptance of a more academic approach to biblical interpretation and hermeneutics, most Christians still prefer a sermon based on appeal to emotion rather than exegesis of the biblical text.

The age profile of Korean church members is rising and the number of young people participating in church life is decreasing. After the spectacular growth of the late twentieth century, there are serious questions today about whether the churches can win a new generation of young people. This is also a challenge for churches in the extensive Korean diaspora. For first-generation Korean migrants, the church was attractive as a cultural centre where they could hear their own mother tongue and experience familiar social customs. The next generation has had an entirely different upbringing and is comfortable in the cultural context of their host country. Often their commitment to their Korean church congregation is much slacker than that of their parents.

Digital technology has made sermons and Christian teaching widely accessible, to the extent that growing numbers choose to satisfy their spiritual needs without becoming part of a local Christian community. Sometimes described as 'paper Christians', they self-identify as Christians but do not participate in communal church life. In order to meet the aspirations of the younger generation, the churches might have to become more hospitable and inclusive, foster a vision of salvation that encompasses the entire creation and not only individual souls, overcome ideological dualism so as to become a force for reconciliation and peace, raise a prophetic voice to transform militaristic politics and militant Protestantism rather than defaming each other among the confessions, and play a dynamic role in the transformation of individuals and society instead of remaining a fortress of outdated convention. The future of Protestantism might depend on how far it can overcome its negative reputation for being in symbiosis with US-oriented capitalism.

Bibliography

Baker, Donald (ed.), *Critical Readings on Christianity in Korea*, 4 vols (Boston, MA: Brill, 2014).

Buswell, Robert E., Jr, and Timothy S. Lee (eds), *Christianity in Korea* (Honolulu, HI: University of Hawaii, 2006).

Min, Kyoung-Bae, *A History of Christian Churches in Korea* (Seoul: Yonsei University Press, 2005).

Oak, Sung-Deuk, *The Making of Korean Christianity: Protestant Encounters with Korean Religions, 1876–1915* (Waco, TX: Baylor University Press, 2013).

Park, Chung-Shin, *Protestantism and Politics in Korea* (Seattle, WA: University of Washington Press, 2003).

Japan

Akemi Kugimiya

A 2015 survey by the Agency for Cultural Affairs on 'the national character of the Japanese' produced a fascinating finding regarding the religious views of the Japanese population. Although 70% of respondents identified as 'non-religious', more than 70% of that group also affirmed that 'the religious mind is important.' Moreover, Japan's 2017 Statistical Survey of Religion includes the strange result that the total number of believers in some kind of religion (182,266,404) is significantly higher than the total population of the country (126,706,000). The breakdown among the different religions is Buddhism 48.1% (87,702,069), Shinto 46.5% (84,739,699), Christianity 1.1% (1,911,196) and other religions 4.3% (7,910,440). Clearly these numbers need to be qualified and many of those identifying with a particular religion would not be recognised by the religion itself as official believers. Nonetheless, it indicates the extent to which the Japanese people are to varying degrees connected to religion in terms of culture, custom and practice, while keeping their distance from formal affiliation or personal commitment. Those who advocate 'non-religion' celebrate Christmas, visit shrines at the beginning of the year and hold funeral ceremonies in the Buddhist style. Such scenes occur quite routinely in Japan.

According to the latest *Japan Christian Yearbook*, which is more reliable regarding Christianity, the total number of Christians in 2018 was 987,070, consisting of 532,183 Protestants, 434,054 Catholics, 10,197 Orthodox Christians and 10,636 clergy and missionaries. This is a mere 0.78% of the total population of Japan. The ratio, which was 0.42% in 1948 (the oldest reliable statistical record), has been consistently within the range of 0.7% to 0.8% since the late 1960s. There are slightly more Protestants than Catholics. The number of clergy and missionaries, which slightly exceeded 20,000 in 1994, has almost halved. On the other hand, Christian universities accounted for 9.5% of all universities in Japan in 2018. Another survey showed that approximately 10% of the total Japanese population are graduates of Christian educational institutions.

Despite Christians being less than 1% of the population in Japan, Christianity has for a long time played important roles and exercised significant influence on society, thought, culture and education. Since the

Meiji period (1868–1912), in particular, Japan has been unable to overlook the Christian faith underlying Western European civilisation, as the modernisation of Japan was promoted by introducing that civilisation. This essay surveys the history of the reception of Christianity in Japan before describing the role of Christianity in modern society.

Beginnings: the Kirishitans

The history of Christianity in Japan begins with the arrival of the Jesuit missionary Francis Xavier on 15 August 1549. During the following 100 years, as many as 300 foreign missionaries came to Japan and lived there according to the Jesuit 'accommodation' policy, based on which they valued the local culture and customs and 'harmonised' with the countries to which they were sent. The missionaries started philanthropic work and introduced Western medicine, culture and objects to Japan. The lords of the warring states benefited from their trade with Spain and Portugal, and in return they gave permission to the missionaries to spread Christianity. As a result, some of the lords were baptised. Amidst the social chaos caused by ongoing war and disaster, the people of Japan sought spiritual redemption. With Buddhism failing to address the crisis, some turned to Christianity. Soon, Christianity gained its highest proportion of adherents in Japanese history. The number of Christians during the 1580s was 350,000, in a total population of 24 million.

However, after unifying the warring states, Hideyoshi Toyotomi (1537–98) announced the *Bateren Tsuiho Rei* (Edict on the Expulsion of Priests) in 1587, and in 1614 the Edo shogunate issued a ban on Christianity. The Japanese feudal thought system was based on the ethics of sovereign–subject/parent–child loyalty, which clashed with Christian teaching about the equality of all before one God. Christianity was considered an obstacle to the unification of Japan to such an extent that one of

Christianity in Japan, 1970 and 2020

Tradition	1970 Population	%	2020 Population	%	Average annual growth rate (%), 1970–2020
Christians	3,100,000	3.0%	2,665,000	2.1%	−0.3%
Anglicans	49,100	0.0%	47,600	0.0%	−0.1%
Independents	617,000	0.6%	1,113,000	0.9%	1.2%
Orthodox	26,500	0.0%	32,000	0.0%	0.4%
Protestants	417,000	0.4%	522,000	0.4%	0.5%
Catholics	361,000	0.3%	535,000	0.4%	0.8%
Evangelicals	258,000	0.2%	310,000	0.2%	0.4%
Pentecostal/Charismatics	349,000	0.3%	430,000	0.3%	0.4%
Total population	**104,926,000**	**100.0%**	**126,496,000**	**100.0%**	**0.4%**

Source: Todd M. Johnson and Gina A. Zurlo (eds), *World Christian Database* (Leiden/Boston: Brill), accessed March 2018.

the Kirishitan lords, Justo Ukon Takayama (1552?–1615), was deported. In 1597, at Nagasaki, a missionary and 26 of his disciples were captured and crucified; these martyrs were canonised in 1861–2 by Pope Pius IX. During this time, the Edo shogunate adopted isolationism, banned Christianity completely within Japan and heavily persecuted Christians. Christianity was seen as an anti-establishment philosophy, and such views formed the foundation of lasting prejudices and the concept of *jashumon* (evil faiths). Christians disguised themselves as Buddhists and secretly continued their Christian faith. They became known as the *kakure Kirishitan* (hidden Kirishitans).

The Modern Missionary Era

At the end of the eighteenth century and the beginning of the nineteenth, Protestant missionaries from Britain and the USA, inspired by the Evangelical movement in the two countries, began to consider Japan. Since they were unable to reach mainland Japan because of the country's isolationist policy, Karl Gützlaff, translator and physician for the East India Company, visited Ryukyu (present-day Okinawa) and distributed Robert Morrison's Chinese translation of the Bible. Another missionary, Bernard Jean Bettelheim, looked after three sailors from the Owari region while in Macau. He learned Japanese from the sailors and after translating the gospel and Epistles of John published them in Singapore in 1837. This became the first Japanese Bible, with God translated as *gokuraku* (heaven or paradise) and *logos* as *kashikoi mono* (the wise being).

In 1858, a Treaty of Amity and Commerce Between the USA and the Empire of Japan was signed, and freedom of faith and worship was permitted in the US living quarters. This enabled the official arrival of foreign missionaries. The first Protestant missionary assigned to Japan, in May 1859, was John Liggins from the Protestant Episcopal Church of America, soon followed by Channing Moore Williams from the same church, James Curtis Hepburn of the Presbyterian Church of America, and S. R. Brown, Duane B. Simmons and Guido H. F. Verbeck from the Reformed Church in America. Based on their experiences of missionary work in China, these men dedicated themselves to missionary work in foreign lands. However, they were not able to overcome their elitist view that they were enlightening an undeveloped country where darkness and unbelief were rampant.

Catholic missionary work was revived through the Société des Missions Étrangères de Paris, under whose auspices Father Théodore-Augustin Forcade landed in Naha, in the Ryukyu kingdom, in 1844. However, he was placed under house arrest because Christianity was banned and he was not able to do any missionary work. In 1846, when Japan was designated a vicariate, Forcade was appointed Vicar Apostolic of Japan, but he soon left for Hong Kong. Among his successors was Father Bernard-Thadée Petitjean, who completed the construction of Oura Cathedral in 1865. On 17 March of that year, Christians in the Urakami region of Nagasaki, who had heard of the cathedral, came to visit. One of the women among the visitors placed one hand on her heart and said to Father Petitjean, 'We here are of the same heart as you. Where is the statue of Santa Maria?' This was a historic event, as Kirishitans in Urakami were discovered 250 years after the ban on Christianity was announced. The hidden Kirishitans of Nagasaki's Sotome, Goto, Amakusa and Hirado regions returned to the church and secretly received instruction from Petitjean. Still today, these areas in Nagasaki are home to many devout Catholics and have produced many priests and nuns.

Despite this turn of events, the Nagasaki Magistrate began to persecute Christians again in 1867. This was the beginning of the so-called Urakami Yoban Kuzure, the large-scale crackdown on the Christians who had remained hidden in Nagasaki's Urakami district. Christians were captured and sent away to places such as Tsuwano, where they underwent severe torture. Following protests from diplomatic representations, the Meiji government finally lifted the ban on Christianity in 1873, and Christianity was tolerated.

From the mid-nineteenth century, British and American Protestant missionaries introduced Western knowledge to Japan by teaching *Eigaku* (provision of English studies as a means to acquire Western knowledge) in private schools, which became the foundation of the 'missionary schools' in Japan. They also emphasised education of girls, to the extent that 60% of the 60 schools that were founded between 1864 and 1889 were girls' schools. The missionaries influenced their students through character-building education based on the gospel, which led some youth to become Christians. Most of the new believers during this time were children of samurai families who had lost out in the Meiji Restoration, and were from feudal domains that supported the Tokugawa shogunate and opposed the new government. Young people who experienced a crisis at this turn of history found a guideline for life and new values in Christianity.

Three groups of worshippers, known as bands, emerged during this period and laid the foundations of Protestantism in Japan. The Yokohama band consisted of worshippers instructed by missionaries such as Hepburn, Brown and James Ballagh. Famous members included Masahisa Uemura (1858–1925), Kajinosuke Ibuka (1854–1940), Masayoshi Oshikawa (1850–1928) and Yōitsu Honda (1848–1912). In 1872, the band founded Nihon Kirisuto Kokai (the Church of Christ in Japan), the largest Protestant denomination in Japan at that time. The Kumamoto band members studied in Kumamoto Yogakko (Kumamoto School of Western Studies) under Leroy Lancing Janes, a former army officer and a devout member of the Congregational Church. With members such as Danjō Ebina (1856–1937), Michitomo Kanamori (1857–1945) and Hiromichi Kozaki (1856–1938), they studied at Doshisha Eigakko (Doshisha School of English Studies) founded by Jō Niijima (1843–90) and laid the foundation of the Nihon Kumiai Kirisuto Kyokai (the Japanese Congregational Church). Members of the Sapporo band, such as Kanzō Uchimura (1861–1930), Inazō Nitobe (1862–1933) and Kingo Miyabe (1860–1951), studied at the Sapporo Agricultural College (the present Hokkaido University Faculty of Agriculture) and were influenced by the character-building education of William Smith Clark. Many of its members played major roles in education, with Uchimura later leaving a significant mark on Japanese Christianity and philosophy from his non-denominational standpoint.

The Protestant missionaries cooperated across denominations and focused their efforts on translating the Bible. A Japanese version of the New Testament was published in 1880, followed by the Old Testament in 1888. Translation of the Bible meant the introduction of new concepts to the Japanese language. Since the times of the Kirishitans, translation of the word 'God' had been an issue for the Japanese because the Shinto concept of 'God' differs from that of Christianity. To avoid misunderstanding, 'God' had previously been translated as *dainichi* (the great sun, or the abbreviated form of the Chinese translation for Mahāvairocana, the supreme deity in esoteric Buddhism), *deusu* (*Deus*, the Latin word for God) or *tenshu* (master of heaven). In the new translation, God was translated with the word *kami* (absolute existence beyond human being), which has been retained until the present.

Another example is the word *ai* (love). Whereas in Buddhism the word had negative connotations such as desire or thirst, in the new translation the word was associated with the Christian concept of neighbourly love or affection. In 1917, the translation was revised and published as the *Bungoyaku seisho* (written Japanese translation of the Bible). This was a phenomenal translation with a refined style of writing and excellent insights that had great influence on Japanese literary works. Many current Japanese idiomatic expressions – such as *semaki mon* (narrow gate), *mayoeru kohitsuji* (lost lamb) and *me kara uroko* (fish scales falling from the eyes) – are taken from the Bible. The translation of hymns also influenced the new style of poetry during the Meiji era, and many songs authorised by the Ministry of Education derive from the hymns.

While the Protestants performed their missionary work through education of the middle and upper classes, the Catholics put more effort into welfare and charity and preached Christianity mainly among the lower class. After becoming bishop, Petitjean invited three organisations from France to come to Japan: les Dames de Saint-Maur (later known as Les Sœurs de l'Enfant-Jésus, the mother organisation of Futaba School) in 1872, la Congrégation des Sœurs de l'Enfant-Jésus de Chauffailles (mother organisation of Osaka Shinai Girl's School) in 1877, and les Sœurs de Saint-Paul de Chartres (mother organisation of Shirayuri University) in 1878. The Catholic sisterhoods played an important role in education and welfare.

The history and the development of the Orthodox Church in Japan owes much to the efforts of the Russian Orthodox missionary Father Nikolai (Ivan Dmitrievich Kasatkin), who arrived in Japan in 1861 as the priest in residence at the Russian consulate in Hakodate. Nikolai learned Japanese and baptised three worshippers, including Takuma Sawabe (1835–1913), in 1868, when Christianity was still banned. In 1871, after baptising 11 more worshippers and spreading the faith in places such as Sendai, Nikolai moved to Tokyo and set up a seminary in Surugadai, making it the base for his missionary work. In 1891, he built the Holy Resurrection Cathedral in Tokyo (known as 'Nikolai do') and engaged energetically in the translation of various prayer books. Although the Orthodox Church had fewer clergy than the Catholic or Protestant denominations, they spread their faith actively among the Japanese under Nikolai's supervision and increased their influence. Among the famous members of the church is the icon artist Rin Yamashita (1857–1939).

Emergence of Nationalism

The Meiji government adopted Westernisation, aiming to modernise Japan. As a result, elites in Japan became interested in Christianity and the number of followers grew exponentially. Christian beliefs, such as freedom, equality and benevolence, also influenced the Freedom and People's Rights Movement in Japan.

After the mid-Meiji period, however, specifically in 1887, Japan adopted 'Rich Country' and 'Strong Army' policies. As nationalism emerged in Japan, Christianity came to be tested. In the constitution of the Empire of Japan, which was declared in 1889, religious freedom was limited to the extent that 'it does not disturb the nation's order and does not go against subjects' responsibilities'. In addition, the Imperial Rescript on Education of 1890 explained the subject's loyalty to the emperor. This rescript became the basis of morality and education in Japan, which were designed to give the emperor and Shrine Shinto a special status in the framework of the nation. This led to the absolutisation/deification of the emperor and state sponsorship of Shintoism. In this climate, Kanzō Uchimura's 'Disrespectful Incident' took place in the first high school in 1891. After he refused to bow deeply enough before the Imperial Rescript on Education during a formal ceremony, Uchimura was accused of profanity. He was driven to resign his post as a teacher. In his 1892 book *Clash Between Education and Religion,* Tetsujirō Inoue (1856–1944), a philosophy professor at Tokyo Imperial University, alleged that Christianity was a crime since it went against the framework of the nation and its education. With attacks from nationalists and the pressure from nationalistic ideas, mission activities stagnated, and many people abandoned Christianity. During the same period, Neo-Orthodoxy based on the 'higher criticism' of the Bible introduced from Germany, brought turmoil and confusion to churches in Japan. Danjō Ebina, who espoused progressive theology, and Uemura Masahisa, who took a hard-line orthodox position, clashed over the question of the deity of Christ.

Christianity in Time of War
As the country moved from the Meiji and Taisho (1912–26) periods to the Showa (1926–89) period, it became more militaristic. With the First Sino-Japanese War (1894) and the Russo-Japanese War (1904) as its triggers, Christianity became incorporated into the framework of the nation and started to take on nationalistic qualities. Many Christians compromised with the government by supporting the wars and cooperating in them. There were only a few pacifists, one of whom was Kanzō Uchimura.

During these transitions, Protestant churches were already promoting indigenisation of Christianity by ending its relationship with foreign religious orders. Based on the resolutions of the 1910 World Missionary Conference, in 1914 they started large-scale cross-denominational missionary activities. With Taisho Democracy, Protestant numbers increased from 79,000 in 1912 to 164,000 in 1917.

The number of Catholics in Japan was 58,800 in 1904 and grew to 67,000 in 1912. By 1891, the four apostolic vicariates had been promoted to become the archdiocese of Tokyo, and the dioceses of Hakodate, Osaka and Nagasaki. Missionary activities, however, stagnated as the Missions Étrangères de Paris lacked personnel and money. The Society of Jesus received a request to establish higher educational institutions in Japan. They despatched missionaries in 1908 and opened Sophia University in 1913.

Sōichi Iwashita (1889–1940) was a famous Catholic priest and theologian who became the leader of modern Catholicism in Japan. Iwashita studied philosophy under Raphael von Koeber at Tokyo Imperial University. After that, while he was studying abroad in Europe at his own expense, he was ordained a priest in 1925 in Italy. He returned to Japan as a missionary. In 1930 he became the head of the Koyama Fukusei Hospital and worked hard for leprosy patients. Simultaneously, in order to gain citizenship,

Catholics in Japan were actively publishing and translating literature on medieval philosophy and Catholic theology. Iwashita also advocated the authority of Catholicism based on the objectivity of the truth it professed.

During the 1930s the Japanese government became militaristic, signalled by the Manchurian Incident of 1931, when Japan took military action against China. Then Japan entered the Second Sino-Japanese War (1937) and the Pacific War (1941). Under an ideology of militarism, freedom of speech and religious freedom were suppressed. There was increased pressure from the military and the public against Christianity as a Western religion, with many incidents of suppression of free speech and repression of religious pacifists. The Religious Association Act of 1940 united 30 Protestant denominations and about 300 congregations to form the United Church of Christ in Japan. Catholic churches became part of the Japan Imperial Public Educational Association. Both were subject to government authority.

Kanzō Uchimura's Non-Church Movement

To provide a full account of Christianity in Japan in the Meiji, Taisho and Showa periods, consideration must be given to the 'Non-Church Movement' (Mukyōkai) of Kanzō Uchimura. Uchimura received a traditional Confucian education before proceeding to Sapporo Agricultural College on government sponsorship. While there, he was influenced by the missionary William Smith Clark and was baptised. As a bureaucrat, he became involved in fishery research. After that, he studied under Julius H. Seelye at Amherst College. This led him to a new understanding of the atonement that resulted from Christ's death on the cross. Uchimura lost his job as a result of the Disrespectful Incident. He moved around and started writing despite being impoverished. He published a number of influential books, including *Representative Men of Japan* (1894) and *How I Became a Christian* (1895). Regarding the Russo-Japanese War, he maintained his pacifist position. In 1900, he created a Christian magazine, *Bible Study* He devoted his life to Bible study and missionary activities, with his weekly Sunday meetings listed in the magazine.

Uchimura advocated the Non-Church Movement, aiming to recover true religious beliefs directly from the Bible. Having neither any official title nor any church association, he presided over Christian gatherings on his own responsibility. The gatherings centred on explanations of biblical teaching instead of official teaching from the clergy. There was no celebration of the sacraments. Uchimura engaged vigorously with the original languages of the Bible. In 1918 these gatherings resulted in a movement focused on Christ's Second Coming. This prophetic belief influenced not only Christians but also Japanese literature and philosophy.

The Non-Church Movement was passed down by Uchimura's pupils, including Toraji Tsukamoto (1885–1973), Takeshi Fujii (1888–1930) and Tadao Yanaihara (1893–1961). Many of these leaders were scholars or teachers. They promoted the study of the Bible in Japan. Today, gatherings associated with the Non-Church Movement are in decline and do not attract the same level of enthusiasm. However, Uchimura's books continue to be widely read.

Social Movements, Welfare, Medical Activity

Christian teachings of God's love and love of neighbour created opportunities to put the faith into practice by serving other people. Christian social movements and social work became significant during the Meiji and Taisho periods. Their work proved to be foundational for medical as well as welfare services in modern Japan. At that time, capitalism grew rapidly and the modern proletarian class emerged. The economic depression caused by the Russo-Japanese War and then the First World War made social and labour issues more visible, for example with the Ashio Copper Mine Poison Incident. In these circumstances many Christians began to express their faith by seeking to solve social problems, rather than just spreading their message only to members of the elite class or to people already attending churches.

Leading proponents of Christian social witness have included: Jūji Ishii (1865–1914), who dedicated himself to the education of orphans and child welfare; Kōsuke Tomeoka (1864–1934), who dedicated himself to educating delinquent youngsters by establishing Home School, a facility supporting children's independence; and Gunpei Yamamuro (1872–1940), who carried out many social welfare business activities, including Christmas kettle (which involved soliciting for donations at the end of the year), the settlement house movement and the Salvation Army campaign for the abolition of licensed prostitution.

The roadside missionary activities of Toyohiko Kagawa (1888–1960) in poor areas by the Kobe Shinkawa became well known around the world. He led a labour union movement and took part in labour disputes with a view to countering poverty. He also developed a farmers' movement and a cooperative movement based on the idea of helping each other out. These activities were based on Christ's 'atonement love' and also the battle to resolve social disintegration and existential crisis, aiming to promote human freedom at an existential level. Kagawa founded the Iesu no Tomo Kai (Friends of Jesus) along with people who were suffering in society. He developed the Million Souls for Christ Movement and the Kingdom of God Movement across the different denominations, the most successful such movements after the Meiji period. However, Kagawa's elite-like thinking and cooperation with the military during the Pacific War have been criticised. His activities have attracted more admiration overseas than they have in Japan.

The Modern Period

On 15 August 1945, through the Potsdam Declaration at the end of the Second World War, Japan accepted defeat. State Shinto was abolished and the Religious Corporation Ordinance replaced the Religious Organisation Law. This enabled each denomination to be reorganised according to its distinctive features, and the Christian community began to recover its vigour.

In 1946, the emperor issued a declaration to make it clear that he was not to be regarded as divine but rather as a human. By article 20 of the 1946 constitution, complete freedom of religion was guaranteed for the first time. The Fundamental Law of Education enacted in 1947 became an indicator of the educational policy of Japan after the war. The commission concerned with its establishment included many who had studied under Kanzō Uchimura and Inazō Nitobe.

As for the shape of Christianity in Japan, Protestant influence was strong before the Second World War, but the activities of Catholic intellectuals were remarkable after the start of the Showa period, especially after the war. The pioneer Sōichi Iwashita, mentioned above, influenced Yoshihiko Yoshimitsu (1904–45), the philosopher and mystic who converted to Catholicism. Another significant figure was Kōtarō Tanaka (1890–1974), a legal philosopher. Meanwhile, the novelist Shūsaku Endō (1923–96) pursued the question of what Christianity means for the Japanese, under Yoshimitsu's tutelage. Likewise, Yōji Inoue (1927–2014), a Catholic priest who worked in the same spirit as Endō, preached the Christian message with sensitivity to Japanese culture and with reference to broad views drawn from Japanese philosophical thought and literature.

On Iwashita's advice, Yoshimitsu studied the philosophy of Augustine and Thomas Aquinas under Jacques Maritain in France and emphasised the universal meaning of the Catholic intellectual history of the Western Middle Ages. Pointing out the misery of the modernistic humans who had lost their faith in God, he criticised the intellectual situation of modern Japan in wartime.

Shūsaku Endō studied under Yoshimitsu and became a novelist on his advice. Endō was baptised at the age of 12 and inherited the Catholic faith from his devout mother. He aimed to 'make it suitable for the body because it is stifling to be put in baggy Western clothing'. In his novel *Silence* (1966), set in the Edo period under the anti-Christian policy, his main character is Father Rodrigo, who was driven to abandon his belief by the persecution and torture of Christians. In the novel, Endō developed the motherhood image of Jesus Christ, who drew close to the suffering and sadness of humans – in other words, God for the weak. This created a sensation. One of the characters in the novel states, 'This country [Japan] is a swamp decaying all the things . . . Christianity won't be rooted in this country', reflecting difficult issues of inculturation. *Silence* was translated into English by a Jesuit, Father William Johnston, and was influential internationally. In 2016 it was made into a film directed by Martin Scorsese. Endō's later work *Deep River* is an ambitious attempt to reconcile Christian monotheism and Japanese pantheism under the image of the flow of the mother Ganges, drawing on John Hick's work on religious pluralism.

Academic research into the philosophy, theology and spirituality of ancient times and medieval times gained momentum after the 1960s and has provided a base for the development of Catholic theology. A steady flow of publications, including some outstanding translations, has stimulated intellectual enquiry and allowed lay believers to deepen their understanding of the faith. The publication of *Corpus fontium mentis medii aevi* (1992–2002), edited by the Sophia University Institute of Medieval Thought under the supervision of Father Klaus Riesenhuber SJ (b. 1938), played an especially significant role. Moreover, through the efforts of Ryosuke Inagaki (b. 1928) and others, the Japanese translation of Thomas Aquinas's *Summa Theologica* was completed in 2012, after 52 years of work.

The spread of Catholicism in Japan owes much to the role and efforts of the missionaries who came to Japan from foreign countries. For example, a member of the Société des Missions Étrangères de Paris, Father Sauveur Antoine Candau (1897–1955), provided insight on post-war Japanese society based on his deep knowledge of the Japanese language and its classical texts. The preaching of German Jesuit missionary Father Hermann Heuvers (1890–1977) touched the hearts of many Japanese people, and Spanish Jesuit Father Mendizabal (1920–2011) devoted himself to his work as a confessor at the St Ignatius Church.

In Protestant theology, Karl Barth's work was received actively and had a significant impact. Japan by this time was also producing its own Christian theologians, with a distinctive contribution to offer. Kazoh Kitamori (1916–98), author of *The Theology of the Pain of God* (1965), regarded salvation by the crucifixion of Christ as the pain of God against the background of Japanese thinking and developed an original dialectical theology. Katsumi Takizawa (1909–84), who developed his 'philosophy of Immanuel' under the influence of Barth and Kitaro Nishida, claimed that all persons belonged to the fact that 'God is with us (Immanuel)'. The presence of God comes first, and a second level of being with God is found when we, as humans, become conscious of that presence. Takizawa explained that the relationship between God and humans was indivisible, unassimilable and irreversible.

In Japan, which has a polytheistic culture, faith in God does not necessarily take a monotheistic form. Therefore, a constant question has been how to explain Christianity to non-believers, and there has been a continuous search for a universal statement that proves convincing. When explaining Japanese spirituality, the philosophy of Kitaro Nishida cannot be disregarded. Nishida explained 'transcendent and immanent, immanent and transcendent God' as the field of 'absolute nothingness', positioned and incarnated as a comprehensive and ontological reality. Although Nishida is not Christian, his viewpoint can open a door to dialogue between Christianity and other religions.

Rapid globalisation of modern society has brought changes to the composition of churches in Japan. Since the 1990s, immigration has greatly increased, and multicultural coexistence with people of different linguistic and cultural backgrounds has become a major issue. Foreigners who came to Japan after 1990 and have settled are called 'newcomers'. Those from such countries as the Philippines, Brazil, Peru and Vietnam are often Catholics. As a result, the Catholic Church has rapidly become multi-ethnic and multilingual. By 2003, the Catholic Commission of Japan for Migrants, Refugees and People on the Move estimated that, in the Catholic Church nationwide, foreign believers totalled 565,712, compared with 449,925 Japanese believers. There are also contrasting demographics, as Japanese believers are older and declining in number, while the 'newcomers' are younger and growing in number. In large churches Mass is celebrated in English, Portuguese, Spanish, Vietnamese, Bahasa and Tagalog as well as Japanese. There can be friction between Catholics from different cultural backgrounds, but they are challenged to find unity in the faith. There are also Evangelical and Pentecostal churches that are made up predominantly of Brazilians and Peruvians.

The essay cannot conclude without some reference to the contribution of women to Christianity in Japan. Mieko Kamiya (1914–79), who was influenced by the Non-Church Movement and by the work of Inazō Nitobe, explored the purpose of suffering in human life in her highly original book *On the Meaning of Life* (1966), based on the experience of psychiatric treatment for sufferers of Hansen's disease. Atsuko Suga (1929–98) was influenced by new Catholic theological thinking in France and Italy, where she studied. Her original essays, literary works and translations, as well as her faithful way of life, have won her an appreciative audience. In addition, Sadako Ogata (b. 1927) and Michiko Inukai (1921–2017), both of whom served as the United Nations High Commissioner for Refugees, contributed significantly to refugee assistance; both are also Catholics.

Advocacy and action on behalf of the socially vulnerable are the most significant role Christianity has played in Japan.

Christianity remains very much a minority faith in the country, yet Japanese Christianity displays both depth and vigour. While the number of baptised Christians remains relatively low, the influence of Christianity on Japanese thought and the role of its educational and social service institutions are not to be underestimated.

Bibliography

Dohi, Akio, *Nihon Purotesutanto Kirisutokyō-shi* [*History of Protestantism in Japan*] (Tokyo: Shinkyō Shuppansha, 1980).

Hanzawa, Takamaro, *Kindai Nihon no Katorishizumu: Shisōshiteki Kōsatsu* [*Catholicism in Modern Japan: Investigation from the History of Thought*] (Tokyo: Misuzu Shobō, 1993).

Kuyama, Yasushi (ed.), *Kindai Nihon to Kirisutokyō* [*Modern Japan and Christianity*], 2 vols (Nishinomiya: Kiriustokyō Gakuto Kyōdaidan, 1956).

Marins, Mark R., *Christianity Made in Japan: A Study of Indigenous Movements* (Honolulu, HI: University of Hawai'i Press: 1988).

Suzuki, Norihisa, *Nihon Kirisutokyō-shi: Nenpyō de Yomu* [*History of Christianity in Japan: Described in Chronological Order*] (Tokyo: Kyobunkan, 2017).

Myanmar

Hrang Hlei

As with many other countries in Asia and Africa, Christianity came to Burma (now Myanmar) on the back of colonialism. It first arrived in southern Burma in the early sixteenth century after Vasco da Gama, a Portuguese who sailed around the Cape of Good Hope, discovered the sea route from Europe to India. Christianity was introduced to Burma by the priests who accompanied the Portuguese merchants and soldiers as chaplains.

Problems ensued when Philip de Brito – a Portuguese captain who was appointed by the king of Portugal to be the governor of Syriam (modern Thanlyin) in 1600 – built a church in Syriam and tried to strengthen his power by pressing the Buddhists to embrace his religion. As a result, the Christian presence in Burma was perceived by the kings and many nationalist Burmans as a threat to their religious and national identity, rather than as a spiritual entity. This became a real challenge when the Protestant missionaries arrived in Burma in the early nineteenth century. Since then, the Christian presence in Myanmar has been a struggle on the one hand and an opportunity to spread the Christian message on the other.

Catholic, Protestant and Pentecostal Missions

The early Christian presence in Burma was brought by the Portuguese, who came seeking opportunities for political expansion and economic development. Catholic missionaries arrived during the rule of the Portuguese and settled in Syriam. They won some converts, including Natshinnaung, a ruler of Taungoo, who was a friend of Philip de Brito. It is reported that de Brito imposed the Catholic faith by destroying Buddhist pagodas, melting gold from the pagodas and turning the monastery bells into guns. This incident, along with other events, provoked the wrath and distrust of the Arakan king, who in 1607 had many Portuguese killed or imprisoned. In short, the early Catholic missionary efforts were rejected by local Buddhists due to fear and distrust of foreigners.

The arrival of Barnabite priests in the eighteenth century brought a more active and sustainable mission to the country. According to the Catholic Bishops' Conference of Myanmar (2017), the Barnabites excelled in their tasks not only as missionaries but also as educators, scientists and scholars. Despite establishing their mission, however, they did not achieve any significant success, as they later faced restriction and even persecution from the Burmese authorities. The arrival of Bishop Paul Bigandet in 1856, after the Second Anglo-Burmese War, and the commitment of succeeding missionaries did, though, help the Catholic mission in Burma to witness remarkable success. This was partly due to a change in their mission approach, as they turned their attention to the ethnic minority groups, especially to the hill tribes, who were culturally more inclined towards Christianity.

The history of Christianity in Burma changed with the arrival of Protestant missionaries in the early nineteenth century. The first Protestant missionaries were Richard Mardon and James Charter, from the Baptist Missionary Society in London, who arrived in 1807. They were later joined by Felix Carey, the son of William Carey, the famous Baptist missionary to India. It was, however, after the arrival of an American Baptist missionary couple, Adoniram and Ann Judson, in 1813 that the Protestant mission was firmly established on the soil of Burma. The Baptists were, much later, followed by other Protestant and Pentecostal missionaries.

The Burmese kings allowed Judson to practise his own religion, but they did not allow the Burmans to be converted to the foreign religion. Consequently, native Burmans were hesitant to embrace the Christian faith, for fear of retaliation and persecution. The Baptists thus switched their attention to minority ethnic groups, expanding their mission work as follows: to the Sgaw Karen in 1828, Pwo Karen in 1836, Karen hill tribes in 1853, Asho Chin in 1856, Shan in 1860, Kachin in 1877 and Chin people in 1899. As a result, Christianity has flourished among the ethnic minority peoples while it has generally not been well received by the Burmans.

The Society for the Propagation of the Gospel (Church of England) started its mission work in Burma in 1854, half a century after its Baptist

Christianity in Myanmar, 1970 and 2020

Tradition	1970 Population	%	2020 Population	%	Average annual growth rate (%), 1970–2020
Christians	1,350,000	5.1%	4,362,000	8.0%	2.4%
Anglicans	27,000	0.1%	72,500	0.1%	2.0%
Independents	84,400	0.3%	680,000	1.2%	4.3%
Orthodox	0	0.0%	0	0.0%	0.0%
Protestants	963,000	3.6%	2,628,000	4.8%	2.0%
Catholics	268,000	1.0%	660,000	1.2%	1.8%
Evangelicals	443,000	1.7%	1,600,000	2.9%	2.6%
Pentecostal/Charismatics	86,900	0.3%	1,160,000	2.1%	5.3%
Total population	**26,381,000**	**100.0%**	**54,808,000**	**100.0%**	**1.5%**

Source: Todd M. Johnson and Gina A. Zurlo (eds), *World Christian Database* (Leiden/Boston: Brill), accessed March 2018.

counterparts. Their initial mission focus was among the English residents in the southern part of Burma. Like the Anglicans, the Methodist mission was started by the British Methodists in 1887 to minister to and educate the Anglo-Burmese and British. Unlike the other Protestant churches, the Presbyterian Church was started in Burma only in the 1950s, by Mizo missionaries in the Kalay and Kabaw valleys in the north-western part of the country. The Pentecostal mission was introduced to Burma in the 1920s by Hector and Sigrid McClean, who worked as missionaries among the Melee people in Upper Burma. The Assemblies of God, established in 1931, is believed to be the largest Pentecostal organisation in Myanmar today. The churches in Myanmar are actively engaged in evangelism and mission, and, amidst their struggles, there has been a steady increase in the Christian population within the country.

Christianity under Successive Military Regimes

The churches in Myanmar have grown under the repressive military regimes that have been in power since the coup of 1962. In 1965 the socialist regime declared the nationalisation of all businesses and schools, including the churches' social institutions and properties. All Western missionaries were ordered to leave the country in 1966, and the local churches had to be on their own, since the country was cut off from the rest of the world. Meanwhile, the churches in the West and the missionaries were understandably concerned for the survival of these churches and feared that their years of mission efforts might have been in vain.

At the same time, the missionaries were hopeful that the indigenous churches would survive and be able to continue to spread the gospel after they had left. In the epilogue of the *Burma Baptist Chronicle* (Rangoon University Press, 1963), the editors – Genevieve and Erville Sowards – stated that God was the one who had helped the Baptists for the past 150 years and that the indigenous leaders could look forward in faith and confidence to the years yet to come and say, 'The future is as bright as the promises of God'. The churches endured enormous pressures from the successive military regimes. Many faithful believers overcame hardship and withstood oppression and persecution, ready to make sacrifices for the sake of their faith. The churches, during the military regimes, had to go through severe difficulties and hardships. But at the same time, they witnessed significant growth.

Christians from minority ethnic groups suffered harassment and discrimination under the repressive military regimes. In many cases, being an ethnic minority Christian was like a crime under the military regime. Numerous villages were destroyed and burned, women were raped and men were forced to go to the front lines of battle as military porters.

Christians were suppressed by the banning of religious activities such as open-air meetings, religious conferences and even worship on Sundays. Ethnic minority Christians also suffered discrimination when they were denied due promotion in various government departments. It has been challenging for Christians, amidst such enormous pressure and so many difficult situations, to remain true to their faith.

However, the post-independence period proved to be a time of church growth under the national leadership as Christians tried to cope with and respond to the political and social changes. Though scattered and deprived of their leaders, Christians continued as much of their work as conditions permitted. The Burmese churches had years of testing and suffered great losses after foreign missionaries left, but they came through with strengthened faith and resolve. They could endure many challenges by adopting the three-self method in their approach to leadership, aiming to be self-supporting, self-propagating and self-governing.

During the post-independence period, indigenous Christian leaders were able to exercise and develop their leadership skills. They proved that they were able to do evangelistic work and lead the church. For example, the Catholic Church, after its missionaries left the country, was able to establish new dioceses; indeed, church membership grew steadily in all dioceses. In the same period, both the Anglican and the Methodist Church were growing and active in evangelism. The Anglican Church was able to establish new dioceses during this period, such as Sittway Diocese in 1984, Toungngu Diocese in 1993 and Myitkyina Diocese also in 1993. The Methodist churches also showed signs of progress during this period. They were able to establish new districts after they became autonomous in 1964.

In the 1970s, the Kachin Baptist Convention launched a historic mission project called the Three Hundred Three Years Mission, which planned to recruit 300 volunteers to serve for three years among the Kachin people. It concluded with great success in 1981. A similar mission project was launched by the Chin Baptist Convention in 1983. The project, called the Chins for Christ in One Century (CCOC), was concluded with great success in 1999 at the centennial celebration of the arrival of Christianity among the Chin people in Hakha. The Karen Baptist Convention also had a two-phase mission project known as the Five Years Mission (1988–92) and AD 2000 Mission (1991–2000). It was concluded in the year 2000 with 5,460 new converts from non-Christian families.

Christian Presence: Challenges and Prospects

The Karen, Kachin, Chin and other churches and organisations, including non-denominational churches, continue to engage in mission projects. For example, the Chin Baptist Convention launched a post-CCOC mission project called Centennial Mission for Christ, running from 1999 until 2013 and focusing on the non-Christian population in various regions in the country. It also continues to engage in a mission project that plans to send 500–1,000 missionaries annually until the year 2028. Similarly, the Karen Baptist Convention and Kachin Baptist Convention have launched mission projects among the Rakhines, Wa, Palaung, Mon, Kayah, Burmans and other groups within the country. The Myanmar diaspora churches also have been actively engaged with similar mission projects in Myanmar and spreading the gospel among the non-Christian population. For example, in 2013 the Chin Baptist Churches, USA, launched an ambitious mission project inside Myanmar called the International Chin Baptist Mission and through the work of those missionaries hundreds of people have become Christians. Similar mission activities have been launched by other churches abroad such as the Karen Baptist Churches, USA; Chin Baptist Association of North America; and Kachin Baptist Churches, USA.

In 2009, Myanmar Missions International, a non-denominational mission organisation, launched a project that aimed to spread the gospel among the 'unreached people who never heard of the gospel in Myanmar'. Significant numbers of new converts have been added to the Christian population through this initiative. Pentecostal churches are also engaged in various mission and evangelism activities, such as open-air revival meetings, crusades and revival conferences. For example, in 2016 the Hebron Brethren Assembly organised the Yangon Love Joy Peace Festival, at which the Reverend Franklin Graham was invited to be the guest preacher. The festival was held for three days at the Myanmar Convention Centre and attracted more than 170,000 people, with more than 7,000 declaring that they accepted Jesus Christ as their saviour during the festival. The Pentecostals in Myanmar have been active in organising similar revival meetings, through which thousands of people have become Christians.

Through the efforts of various denominations and organisations, applying different mission approaches, the Christian population of Myanmar has increased dramatically. The 2014 census showed that the total population had reached 51 million, with Christians accounting for 6.2%. It has been suggested that this is an underestimate. The number of Christians in contested areas such as Kachin and Karen states appears to be under-reported. What is beyond question is that the Christian population in Myanmar has dramatically increased during and after the repressive military regimes. The recent changes in the political landscape in the country have helped to open ways for the Christian churches to freely engage in mission. This has created a situation of opportunity for Christian witness, and it can be expected that the Christian population will continue to increase in number despite ongoing challenges.

As indicated above, the presence of Christianity was perceived by the Burmese kings as a threat to religious and national identity. Buddhist nationalists tend to perpetuate this misperception, which leads them to view Christianity not simply as a spiritual entity but as a Western colonial tool. Hence, ethnic minority Christians are often accused of being unpatriotic and of destroying the values of Buddhist culture. But the 2016 election of Henry Van Thio, a Chin Christian, as second vice president might be an indication that Myanmar has finally overcome this misperception. It appears that since the recent political changes there is a more informed understanding of the Christian faith.

There are, however, still instances of Christians suffering discrimination and subtle repression. For example, a township chief administrator in Chin state was threatened by his superior with removal from office because he was accused of not complying with the mandate to send his subordinates to participate in a Buddhist water festival. The administrator happens to be a Christian, and had the courage to refute the charge against him.

The current constitution, drafted under the strict supervision of the military regime, guarantees 25% of the seats in parliament for the military, which entrenches the military's continuing influence in the new political system. Buddhism is given a special status in the constitution, and it continues to exert its influence not only in politics but also in the public sphere. The Christian presence in such a situation is challenging, and hence the church is confronted with this existential reality. What is important, in this case, is how the church responds to this reality and what role it will play in wider society in such a fast-changing social and political context. Put differently, the question still remains how Christians in Myanmar live out their faith in the public sphere.

Generally, Christians in Myanmar had a very limited role in the public sphere from the 1960s, when General Ne Win took power, until the end of military rule in 2010. During this period, the churches tended to confine their ministry within their own ethnic groups. This was partly due to government restrictions and partly due to the churches' approach to the church–state separation principle. Though the Christian population grew steadily during military rule, the churches' contributions to the social and political spheres were very limited. However, the political landscape in Myanmar has changed significantly since the start of democratic rule in 2011, and doors of opportunity have opened for the churches to freely express their faith in public and to extend their prophetic role by contributing to social transformation in the country.

A significant challenge for the churches in Myanmar today is how they perceive their calling in the current political context and how they view their engagement in wider society. Moreover, as the country is gradually opening to democratic rule, the churches are challenged to be attentive to ways to engage in social and political issues in order to demonstrate that they are not simply the product of Western colonialism. In fact, the churches have the opportunity to be witnesses to God's love by actively engaging in issues that are important for the development of the community as a whole.

As indicated above, Christianity has flourished among the ethnic minority peoples of Myanmar. This is partly because of the strong leadership of early indigenous Christian leaders who were faithful to the gospel that summoned them to live out their faith in difficult situations. It is also partly because the ethnic Christian leaders were well equipped with leadership skills and able to lead their own people when all Western missionaries were forced to leave the country in 1966. Christianity has been the fastest-growing religion in Myanmar since the 1970s, and it is practised today primarily among the ethnic minority peoples, who have effectively applied the soul-winning or church-planting mission approach. As a result, both Protestant and Pentecostal churches in Myanmar have become vibrant missionary-sending organisations, despite economic limitations and geographical isolation.

Myanmar is ringed by the regions where ethnic minorities predominate. The Kachin in the north, the Karen in the south, the Rakhine and Chin in the west and north-west, and the Lahu and Shan in the east surround the centre of the country. The ethnic minority peoples from these regions are socially undeveloped and economically poor. Interestingly, however, the pioneer Christians accepted the gospel when the Burman majority resisted it. They have a sense that they have been chosen by God, like the Israelite people in the Bible, to be a light to the nation. Despite their economic limitations, the ethnic minority churches are active in their mission endeavours, sharing the gospel among the Burman Buddhists. Because of their efforts, a growing number of Buddhists have accepted Christianity as their new religion.

As indicated above, many Western churches were genuinely concerned that the indigenous churches in Myanmar would disappear after the missionaries had left. But because of the faithful commitment and self-determination of the indigenous leaders, the indigenous churches were able to carry on the mission work by themselves. Today, the ethnic minority churches in Myanmar are vibrant in their mission efforts. The Chin, Kachin, Karen and other ethnic churches in Myanmar actively engage in mission among non-Christians, especially in Buddhist-majority areas. People are responding to the gospel on a daily basis and the Christian population has noticeably increased. Significantly, the current government recognises the presence of Christianity in Myanmar. For example, a number of ethnic minority Christian leaders have been invited as special guests at the peace talks between the government and militia groups. Such developments suggest that the Christian presence in Myanmar is being recognised as an accepted element within society.

In fact, the current political system allows Christians to be more proactive in their social and spiritual engagements in society. There seem to be few restrictions on Christians who wish to organise public meetings, open-air preaching and other religious gatherings. They have freedom to engage in God's mission in various respects. Put differently, as the country has embarked on a new democratic era, Christians have opportunities to witness to their faith and to spread the gospel among the people of Myanmar. At the turn of a new democratic era and the opening of the current administration, dozens of mission organisations and missionary training centres have sprouted up throughout the country. As a result, the gospel has reached every part of the country, millions of people have heard about the Bible and Christianity, and thousands have taken the decision to become Christians.

Myanmar has experienced a significant growth of the church during the last decade. Because of the mission efforts of Protestants, Pentecostals, Independent churches and non-denominational mission groups – inside and outside of the country – more and more Burmese people have embraced the Christian faith as their new religion. As a result, thousands have been baptised and added to the Christian population. The Harvard Divinity School's Religious Literacy Project estimates the current Christian population in Myanmar at around 8% of the whole population. If this growth continues at the current rate, the Christian presence in Myanmar is likely to have a significant impact within society at large in the near future.

Hundreds of Christian orphanages have been freely organising and operating in many parts of the country. Some of them are sponsored by churches and Christian organisations from abroad, while others are sponsored by local churches. Many of these orphanages have been accused of being self-serving mission agencies that are looking for financial support from abroad. At the same time, others are genuinely interested in helping the unfortunate by welcoming children and youth, including Buddhists. Their ministry emphasises teaching about the Bible and the Christian message. They offer both Christian education and secular education. The Christian population in the country continues to grow significantly, partly through the commitment of these orphanages and educational institutions.

Many of the mission organisations in Myanmar focus not only on the soul-winning method in their mission efforts. They also recognise the importance of basic education and its impact on the daily life of the people. They strongly believe that education is an essential element for sustaining a community and building the nation. For example, the Chin Baptist Churches, USA, put an emphasis on education in their mission projects by taking the initiative in building boarding schools and sponsoring students from rural areas in the southern Chin state. Other mission organisations have adopted a similar approach and focused on education in their mission endeavours. As the country slowly opens and adopts a more relaxed education system, dozens, perhaps hundreds, of new private schools have appeared. Many of these private schools are run by churches and Christian organisations, which is a sign of progress and promising for the future of the Christian presence in the country.

Conclusion

As indicated in the introduction to this essay, Christianity came to Myanmar on the back of Western colonialism. The early Portuguese Christians appeared to be more interested in economic opportunities and political expansion than engaging in Christian mission in the country. This later resulted in the distrust on the part of the Burmese kings, and since then the Christian presence in Myanmar has been misconceived by nationalist Burmans as a threat to their religious and national identity. Hence, Christians, especially those from ethnic minorities, have been accused of being unpatriotic, their presence in the country regarded as hostile to Burmese culture and religion.

There is no doubt that the presence of the Christian churches in Myanmar has been a struggle both politically and socio-economically. Christians have faced discrimination, oppression and even persecution simply because of their faith. However, with the recent advent of democratic rule, Christianity is no longer perceived as a colonial religion and is gaining respect as a genuine spiritual entity in the country. If the current political situation continues to improve, Christians in Myanmar will have greater opportunities to live out their faith and to share the gospel among their compatriots.

As Myanmar embraces a new political system, the Christian churches are encountering new opportunities to witness to their faith and embody its values in the way they live their lives. This being the case, the Christian presence in Myanmar will likely be defined by how far Christians are missionally informed and socially involved as a force for transformation in the country. There are grounds to expect that the Christian presence in Myanmar in the near future will significantly contribute to the development of the country in many respects.

Bibliography

Augurlion, Saw, *Christian Existence and Issues Related to Nationalism and Religious Identity in Post-Colonial Myanmar* (Yangon: Tin Tin Chit Press, 2017).

Catholic Bishops' Conference of Myanmar, *National Church History of Myanmar* (Yangon: Alpha & Omega Press, 2017).

Ling, Samuel Ngun, *Communicating Christ in Myanmar: Issues, Interactions and Perspectives* (Yangon: ATEM, 2005).

Moffett, Samuel H., *A History of Christianity in Asia, Vol. II: 1500–1900* (Maryknoll, NY: Orbis Books, 2005).

Wa, Maung Shwe, *Burma Baptist Chronicle* (Rangoon: University Press, 1963).

Thailand

Seree Lorgunpai and Sanurak Fongvarin

A distinctive feature of Thailand's history is that it was never colonised by Western countries. Even though neighbouring countries were colonised by France or the UK, Thai people maintained a distinct sense of identity as a traditional society respecting the monarchy. This has helped the country to survive the turbulent politics of modern times. Thai people were united in their respect for King Bhumibol Adulyadej, who died on 13 October 2016. During his long reign he was loved and revered by the people, who mourned his death for an entire year, choosing to dress in black as a mark of respect. He himself was Buddhist but he supported every religion, including Christianity, and every religion conducted ceremonies to mark his passing. The monarchy remains influential in promoting inter-religious harmony.

Freedom from colonial rule allowed Thailand to grow economically, and the national infrastructure has been expanded. In modern times Thailand has become a hub for world travellers. However, even though Thai people have encountered many other cultures, they are able to maintain their own traditions. An important factor in sustaining Thai culture is the Thai language. Almost every person who is Thai by birth is expected to speak Thai. Many tribal people who were born in Thailand are ashamed to speak their own languages in public. They will use Thai even if their Thai is not up to standard. To be a Thai citizen, one has to speak Thai. This mindset discourages people in Thailand from maintaining their tribal languages or learning foreign languages. Even though Thailand is an open country, many citizens cannot communicate in English, and their limited English communication skills affect educational development. For example, most people are unable to access resources on the internet because they cannot read them. Another factor that keeps people in Thailand from developing educational skills is the strength of oral tradition. They prefer to talk rather than to read or write. Government studies conducted to explore Thai citizens' reading behaviour found that when people do read, it is mostly material on social media or email (83.3%), followed by newspapers (68.7%); reading about religion ranked lowest (30.1%). When people were asked why they did not read books, the prevailing answer was that they preferred watching television, while 24.6% said they did not have time.

The impact of internet use on social networking has begun to intensify, creating a new way of life. People tend to avoid personal relationships with family members and focus more on people in online communities. The result is a wider gap between family members. Care and commitment among the family are decreasing. This not only affects relationships but also communication and analytical skills, because those who use social media heavily tend to read casually, without critical thinking, and to forward information without checking the sources to ensure reliability.

Nonetheless, traditional Thai respect for seniors remains highly influential. Thai people tend to trust those whom they regard as having more status. Even if they do not agree, they would not dare to voice a different opinion, because Thai culture honours those who are in a higher position. The Thai term *Kren Jai* indicates the mindset of the people. This term is used in three different ways. It can mean to 'be considerate' when one does not want to disturb another person, even when one needs help. It can mean to 'feel obliged' to do something requested by one's superior, even when one does not wish to do it. It can also mean to 'feel bad' when one does not want to hurt another person. As we shall see, this strong cultural tradition influences the way that people interact at the religious level.

Religion in Thailand

The Thai government under the leadership of Prime Minister Prayut Chan-o-cha on 22 September 2016 issued a protection plan for every religion. In this document are six strategies to protect religions: promoting and supporting education, supporting the correct teaching of each religion, fostering all religions, protecting every religion from harm, creating an opportunity for cooperation among religions, and encouraging communication among religions to understand each other's activities. Even though there is no recognition of Protestantism in the constitution, the Protestant

Christianity in Thailand, 1970 and 2020

Tradition	1970 Population	%	2020 Population	%	Average annual growth rate (%), 1970–2020
Christians	240,000	0.6%	906,000	1.3%	2.7%
Anglicans	700	0.0%	20,000	0.0%	6.9%
Independents	50,600	0.1%	89,300	0.1%	1.1%
Orthodox	0	0.0%	950	0.0%	9.5%
Protestants	34,000	0.1%	449,000	0.6%	5.3%
Catholics	154,000	0.4%	385,000	0.6%	1.9%
Evangelicals	27,000	0.1%	410,000	0.6%	5.6%
Pentecostal/Charismatics	55,000	0.1%	145,000	0.2%	2.0%
Total population	**36,885,000**	**100.0%**	**69,411,000**	**100.0%**	**1.3%**

Source: Todd M. Johnson and Gina A. Zurlo (eds), *World Christian Database* (Leiden/Boston: Brill), accessed March 2018.

churches are recognised by the Thai government. Therefore, the Protestant churches benefit from this protection plan.

Although Buddhism is the major religion in Thailand, people are free to follow other religions. The other major religions in Thailand are Islam, Christianity, Hinduism, Chinese ancestor worship and animism. During important national events, Buddhist monks, Muslim imams, Catholic priests, Protestant ministers and Hindu priests are called to conduct religious ceremonies. In 2004 a tsunami hit the south of Thailand and many lives were lost. Identifying some of the bodies was difficult, so that it was unknown to which religion each victim had belonged. In response, the government called on religious leaders to conduct a multi-faith funeral service. Following an August 2015 bombing incident at Rajaprasong intersection in Bangkok that resulted in many foreigners being killed, the government called on religious leaders to pray for peace in all countries.

In the past, Thai people would do good in order to gain merit according to Buddhist teaching, but modern Thai would use a new term, *Jit-asa*, to indicate volunteering to do good for other people without thinking of gaining merit. This kind of volunteer spirit is a new platform for religious unity. Anyone can join without hesitation or conflict.

The Buddhist worldview and the Christian worldview are, in some respects, opposites. Buddhism teaches that one can gain salvation by one's own effort, whereas Christianity maintains that salvation is the gift of God. Buddhism, however, is not merely a matter of religion but is integral to the culture of the Thai people. Many Thais do not fully understand Buddhism but nonetheless understand themselves to be Buddhists. Although Christians are in a minority, it is possible for them to maintain their faith even in a Buddhist cultural milieu. Many factors, both external and internal, help Christians to remain faithful. One of the most important external factors is that Thailand gives freedom for all people to choose their own religion. Pressures from the communities generally are not life threatening, except from extremist Muslims in the far south. So far as internal factors are concerned, Thais who remain in the Christian faith tend to be those who have had personal spiritual experiences. Some of them opposed Christian teaching for many years but later encountered love among believers. Through listening to sermons, testimonies and sharing, they opened their minds to accept the teaching of the Bible. When they prayed, they often saw unexpected results. Even when they are facing difficulties, they feel a sense of peace through their faith.

Reception of Christianity

The *Kren Jai* factor has been significant when Thai people have encountered Christian missionaries. Their Thai culture inclines them to respond very politely to visiting foreigners, sometimes even to the extent of professing that they accept the message being shared with them. On occasion this has led missionaries to conclude that their Thai hosts have become Christians, when in fact they have not undergone any change of heart and have simply been attempting to put their visitors at ease. There is also a pluralist strain to Thai culture, which fosters the understanding that different faiths may be equally valid. This was evident as early as the Ayutthaya period. When King Narai received visitors from Europe in 1684, he was invited by the representative of France to become a Christian. He politely refused but did not wish to offend the other faith. King Narai said, 'the reason I do not have faith in Christianity may be that God wants each of us to believe in different religions like he has created human beings to be different tribes and races'. Even though he did not convert, he allowed the foreigners to share their faith with Thai people. It is common to hear Thai people saying that every religion teaches human beings to be good. By offering this affirmative assessment of other faiths, Thai people would mean, 'Your religion is good, and my religion is good also; therefore, I do not need to change to believe in your religion.'

Despite the friendly and affirmative response to the Christian message required by *Kren Jai*, Thai people on the whole have considered Christianity to be foreign and not for them. Everything about Christianity marks it as foreign to Thailand. The architecture of its buildings, the structure of its institutions and the nature of its music combine to give Thai people the impression that Christianity is a religion of the Western world. Its emphasis on individual conversion and its drive to separate converts from their original community provide confirmation that it is alien to the Thai way of life. So deeply entrenched is the Thai view of Christianity as a foreign religion that, despite the politeness of their reception, Christian missionaries have consistently met with unyielding resistance to their message.

Nonetheless, since the nineteenth century a small but significant minority of Thai people have chosen to become Christian. American Presbyterian work in Siam (as Thailand was known until 1949) began in 1840. The Presbyterian mission built an extensive network of educational institutions and health-care services as well as churches. Its work continues today as part of the Church of Christ in Thailand. However, the first churches in Thailand were founded not by the Presbyterian mission but by Baptists who started a church among the Chinese in Bangkok. The Chinese church in Thailand began in 1833, when the first three Chinese people professed faith and were baptised. In 1839, the first church building was constructed and two Chinese schools were opened. By 1850 the church had 35 members, and by 1877 six Baptist churches had been established. Based on their location, they adopted the name Wat Koh Church in 1852, the first Protestant church in Thailand and the first Chinese Baptist church in Asia. In 1915, American Presbyterians began to work among the Chaozhou Chinese and the Guangdong Chinese who lived in Thailand. In 1924 the Chinese Church Coordinating Centre was established in Thailand. Through its influence the Maitrichit Baptist Church was built and dedicated on 14 September 1935, after the church moved from Wat Koh to Maitrichit Road. By 1948 its membership had grown to 200. This number has continued to increase and the church has exercised great influence.

Christian Linguistic Diversity and Worship
A feature of Christianity in Thailand is linguistic diversity. Two-thirds (65.4%) of churches worship in Thai, followed by Karen (16.3%), Lahu (5.6%), Akha (4.2%) and Lisu (1.4%). However, these percentages do not necessarily equate to the relative numbers of believers in each group. Since the 1990s, for example, the number of Christians among the Akha people has increased significantly but many of them cannot read Akha, although they have learned to read Thai or Chinese. Some of them migrated from Myanmar and remain unregistered in Thailand. The younger generation of Akha generally speak Thai and English very well, equipping them to go to work overseas.

Churches in Bangkok and other cities have adopted a broadly similar pattern of worship. They begin by singing contemporary Christian songs for half an hour or more, followed by a formal liturgy that uses hymns or devotional songs. In rural areas, many churches do not have musical instruments, so they sing only familiar songs or do not sing at all because they lack musical accompaniment. However, some tribal Christians can sing together in harmony without any instruments. During the early twenty-first century, Christian musicians have joined hands to compose more contemporary worship songs and have encouraged Christians to use these new songs in their worship. For example, a group called W501 promotes their songs through YouTube, social media, CDs and concerts.

Evangelism, Conversion and Church Growth
Both formal and informal evangelism methods are used by individual Christians and churches. When evangelism is formally organised, it is often run by a committee from different churches. The evangelism event normally takes place in a public venue for a few nights, and preachers from outside Thailand are invited. Another formal method is Christian broadcasting on television and the internet. Informal evangelism is normally a matter of sharing the gospel through social media. The most popular

media in Thailand are YouTube, Facebook and Line. (Thai Christians like to share scripture texts with pictures on Facebook and Line.)

A third method of evangelism might be termed indirect evangelism. The Thailand Bible Society has run a Bible competition since 2002. Originally, this project was intended for Christian children from churches or Christian schools. Some Catholic schools have sent non-Christian students to take part as well, however, and many of these students have won prizes. Some of these children have become Christians after reading the Bible.

Several churches have run the Alpha course. This is based on a small group meeting each week in a home, so that people can be relaxed and friendships can be developed while the Christian message is presented in an attractive way. Those attending feel more comfortable than they would at a formal church service. Three organisations focus on school and university ministry: Thai Christian Students Association, Thailand Youth for Christ and Thailand Campus Crusade for Christ. Many churches also work with schools or in universities by planting a church near the campus.

Church planting has recently been emphasised by many churches. Local churches send teams to plant new churches in areas where there is no church. The new church that has been planted becomes a daughter church; it usually uses the same name as the mother church, with the addition of the local place name. The mother church normally sends financial, material, personal and prayer support to the daughter church.

Thai people typically experience conversion to Christianity in one of four ways. The first is through educational activities sponsored by the churches, including opening schools, teaching English and music at church, sports training, vacation Bible studies and Bible day camps. Parents accept these activities because they see the change of behaviour in their children. Most parents are very busy, and they trust the churches to look after their children; in this regard churches are almost like cheap day-care centres. When a church maintains such activities over a long period, it often sees people becoming Christians through these activities.

The second way by which people become Christians is through health care offered at hospitals and clinics. In the past, missionaries started hospitals to help Thai people who were sick and showed them the love of God, giving them the opportunity to share the Christian message. This approach met with considerable success. The sick came to the hospital for healing and received treatment; the hospital and clinics were willing to meet all the cost. Today, however, Christian hospitals have become a source of income for the church rather than a means for evangelism.

Thirdly, social welfare provided through Christian community service centres has been a pathway to conversion for some people. The Baptist mission began its church planting by opening up Christian community service centres and started some worship services on weekdays. When they had enough believers, they worshiped on Sundays and slowly began a new church at the centre. Many Christian organisations promote social welfare. The Compassion ministry gives scholarships to students via local churches. The children who receive the support are required to attend church, and some become Christians. World Vision, a Christian international development organisation, works mostly with local communities and has many development projects. It receives funding from non-Christians and big firms as well as from Christians and is not involved in direct evangelism. Several churches in the north of Thailand established dormitories to host tribal students who come to study in the cities. They have run Bible studies and devotional activities for the students, helping them to grow spiritually.

Fourthly, people have become Christians through direct evangelism, which can involve giving leaflets, approaching people personally, establishing friendly relationships as a means of evangelism, evangelism meetings in local churches, cell-group meetings in educational institutes and large-scale open-air crusades. Relationship evangelism is the most effective method.

Both the Chinese and Thai people who live in Thailand call themselves Buddhist. It is noticeable that Thai citizens who become Christians are more often Chinese or from a Chinese background than ethnically Thai. It seems that the Chinese find it easier than the ethnic Thais to accept the Christian concept of God. This does not mean that ethnic Thais do not believe in divine beings, however. For example, a Thai person who wants to buy a second-hand car will go to a fortune-teller for advice about what to do for good luck and safety while driving the car. The fortune-teller might advise that the colour of the car needs to be changed. However, changing the colour often costs too much, so many second-hand car owners put the colour name on the back of the car instead of repainting the whole car. For example, the owner of a white car will put on a sticker saying 'This car is black'.

Western missionaries have attempted to contextualise the Christian faith as they have sought to increase the number of Christians in Thailand. Catholic churches have been built in the style of Buddhist temples. Instead of using 'Church' in their names, they are called 'Wat', like Buddhist temples. The priests in the Catholic churches are called *Pra*, like Buddhist monks, and Catholic churches use the Buddhist *kathin* ceremony to raise funds for buildings and some big projects. It seems that people are accepting this contextualisation. Contextualisation, however, also involves challenging practices that run counter to the gospel of Christ. For example, in the past, girls were not allowed to study in school, but when the

Protestant missionaries came, girls were given the opportunity to study. At present, more women than men are enrolling in universities. Adoption offers another example. Adoption is not popular in Thailand, as explained by the saying 'Don't eat food that other people have chewed'. Families commonly believe that they should not take children from other parents to raise as their own, because when they grow up, they will not be as grateful for the adoptive parents' love. However, the Bible teaches care for others who are in need. Sadly, many Christians still avoid adoption and keep praying to get their own children. This might be a point at which they need to bring a challenge to the prevailing culture on the basis of their faith.

Christianity in Thailand is now growing at an average rate of 5–6% per year, and one-third of that growth comes from children born into Christian families. Two-thirds of the growth comes from new converts who are baptised into the church. However, the growth rate varies dramatically by region. The most important factor determining how fast a church grows is its age. New churches tend to grow faster than older churches. The new churches tend to be more welcoming to newcomers, who can quickly feel that they are part of the family. By contrast, the older churches, where the congregation has been together for 20 years or more, find it much more difficult to welcome newcomers. There is a sense of excitement among the new members of a new church, and they are very active in sharing their faith. Newcomers get the opportunity to be involved in ministry at an early stage. All these things lead to rapid growth.

The Committee of Protestant Churches in Thailand (CPCT) had set a goal to increase the number of Christians to 1 million by the year 2015, but this was not achieved. However, the Committee has reset the goal, now aiming to have 2 million Christians in Thailand by the year 2020, and by 2030 to have at least some churches in all 80,000 sub-districts in Thailand. In 2017, the population of Thailand was 65,729,098, with 454,127 Protestant Christians worshipping in 5,188 Protestant churches. In 2018, there were 379,975 Catholic Christians worshipping in 517 churches.

When we look at the whole country, we can say that Christian numbers remain relatively small. However, when we look at regional variations, we can see that Christians are concentrated in the north. The biggest Christian population is in Chiang Mai, with 22.73% of Protestants living there. Though Thai people are being influenced by Western culture, most are resistant to the Christian message, which they regard as alien to their culture and their ancestors. The strongest resistance to Christianity derives from family pressure. For example, one high-school boy came to church every Sunday and wanted to become a Christian. He informed his mother of his decision on a Saturday night; upon hearing this, his mother locked him up so that he could not go to church on Sunday.

Organisation and Leadership

Five main Christian organisations are registered with the Thai government. The Seventh-day Adventist Church of Thailand was established in 1919. Their witness has been distinguished by the attention that they pay to questions of health. In particular, they have promoted eating according to biblical teachings. Their teaching on health issues has been well accepted by other Christians.

The Church of Christ in Thailand (CCT), previously named the Church in Siam, was established in 1939. Its administration is organised at three levels: the council of churches, church districts and local churches. An outstanding leader of the CCT is the Reverend Dr Boonratana Boayen, a former general secretary and former moderator of the church. Because he was very popular among church leaders, he was re-elected several times. He is also the first missionary sent by the Thai church to Papua New Guinea.

The Thailand Baptist Convention was established on 24 November 1960. The Reverend Thongchai Pradabchananurat, founder of Nimitmai Christian Church, is the Director of the Baptist Students Centre, Thailand, and president of Thailand Baptist Convention. A former president of the CPCT, he is the pastor of Church of Joy and Church of Love as well as being a writer, broadcaster and president of Alpha Thailand.

The Evangelical Fellowship of Thailand (EFT) was established on 19 June 1969. EFT was started by missionaries who were not affiliated with the CCT. The Reverend Dr Wirachai Kowae has been an outstanding president of the EFT. Founder and senior pastor of the Romyen Church, he is renowned as an evangelist and a church planter. His influence extends far beyond Thailand, as he is planting many Thai churches in other countries.

The Catholic Bishops' Conference of Thailand was established on 9 September 1969. The Roman Catholic Church came to work in Thailand more than 300 years ago. Catholicism in Thailand has been divided for administrative purposes into 10 districts (vicariates). One of its notable leaders was Bishop George Yod Phimphisan (1933–2017), who served as the second bishop of the Diocese of Udon Thani, in the region of Isan, from 1975 to 2009. He was the president of the Bishops' Conference of Thailand for three terms: 1991–4, 1997–2000 and 2006–9. In addition, he played an important role on the board of the Thailand Bible Society.

These five organisations occasionally work together, for example on the board of the Thailand Bible Society. In addition, the CCT, the EFT and the Thailand Baptist Convention formed the Committee of Protestant Churches in Thailand (established on 6 May 1988). The main ministries of these three organisations are evangelism, church planting, building schools, building hospitals and social work.

Major Western denominations, such as Anglicans, Methodists, Lutherans and Pentecostals, belong to the EFT. Besides these denominations, the membership of the EFT had included the Hope of Bangkok Church, founded by local pastor Kriengsak Chareonwongsak on 6 September 1981, but this church had expanded very quickly and created conflict with other churches, which resulted in it losing its membership in 1987. At that point the church became independent and planted many churches in provinces in Thailand. In 2008, the founder decided to become a candidate in the election for governor of Bangkok and used church money to run his campaign. When this was found this out, many members left the church to form new churches under new names. Many joined the EFT and a few of them joined the Thailand Baptist Convention. Some of these new churches expanded very quickly.

Many para-church organisations are registered under the EFT. One of them is Thai Christian Students, established in 1971 and a member of the International Fellowship of Evangelical Students. The students who are involved in the ministry have been trained and become leaders in different churches and Christian organisations. Thailand Campus Crusade for Christ (CCC) is another organisation that is working among students all over Thailand. The former director, the Reverend Yuttasak (Enoch) Sirikul, not only led CCC but also led the Evangelical movement in Thailand. He organised many campaigns to encourage Thai Christians to serve the wider church. Thailand Youth for Christ is another organisation that works among Thai youth and students. It has run Youth Challenge every four or five years, an event that brings together young people from all over Thailand. Each time, at least 1,000 youths participate. Many of them have become leaders, and some of them have gone on to enroll in seminaries.

Since CPCT has set the goal to reach 2,000,000 believers, 10,000 churches and 10,000 Christian leaders by the year 2020, a network of prayer for blessing Thailand has been formed. It has designated 40 days of prayer and fasting every year, and has called on Christians all over Thailand to set the same dates. It has provided a manual with Bible reading and prayer requests each day for Christians to follow. CPCT was formed because of the common interest in evangelism. It has run the Thailand Congress on Evangelism many times. Normally, Christian leaders come for Bible study, workshops, visits to exhibitions of Christian organisations, revival meetings and evangelistic meetings. The number of participants has increased from thousands to tens of thousands.

In recent years, many informal churches, unconnected with the established churches, have been formed, although they have not registered. In these churches, worship and baptisms are usually performed at home. Numbers are difficult to estimate but they are evident on social media.

Even though Thai Christians have a clear and strong vision for evangelism, they are not always successful. Therefore, some Christian leaders have sought a fixed formula for evangelism, and recently a programme called G12 has been used by a number of churches. Though it has attracted large numbers, many churches do not accept this programme, for theological reasons. It is perceived to promote authoritarian church leadership, prosperity theology and the downplaying of biblical authority in favour of spiritual inspiration. The aforementioned Alpha course has gained wider acceptance among the traditional churches.

World Vision is very successful in Thailand. Even Thai Buddhists are willing to donate money to World Vision to support children's projects. In addition, the Thai government has accepted World Vision as a trusted organisation that fights human trafficking. World Vision has worked at the borders and in villages all over Thailand.

Theological training in Thailand is still weak because of limited funds and personnel, and lack of English language skills. Thai Christians do not tend to read theological books, which are often translations of books written in English. Most students who have studied at Bible institutions work in churches. They prefer to be pastors rather than scholars, since pastors enjoy greater respect.

Technology makes the Bible available in many forms, especially in applications promoted by the Thailand Bible Society, such as YouVersion, PocketSword and a programme called 'The Word' that gives Christians more options to read the Bible. However, people still do not read as much as accessibility allows.

Christian books are rarely found in secular bookstores. However, twice a year there are national book fairs in Bangkok. The Thailand Bible Society and other Christian publishers partner to set up a booth called Panyajan to promote Christian literature. These bi-annual occasions help non-Christians to know about Christianity.

Thailand suffers from a lack of Christian scholars. Many seminary graduates do not choose to pursue a formal academic degree but prefer to obtain a doctoral degree without undertaking serious study, simply in order to gain prestige. This trend is harmful to Christian academic institutions. However, there is a positive trend among lay leaders who are willing to spend time studying in seminary part time, while working in their vocation and serving in the church. This trend is more helpful because these people have experience in both worlds.

Conclusion

Christianity in Thailand continues to grow in the midst of diverse cultures. The Thai government is reforming the country in many ways, including support for the activities of all religions. In addition, the religious protection of the government extends to the promotion of inter-religious cooperation for the sake of a harmonious and peaceful society. The effective factors in evangelism in Thai society are strong family nurture and long-term relationships. Thai people often make their decision by following the community in which they live. A significant opportunity for Christian growth lies among Thai people who work overseas. They are often more open to the Christian message than those who remain at home.

Bibliography

Blanford, Carl Edwin, *Chinese Churches in Thailand* (Bangkok: Suriyaban Publishers, 1975).

Martin, Dwight, *Diverse Perspectives on the Protestant Church in Thailand* (Chiang Mai: eStat Foundation, 2016).

McFarland, George Bradley (ed.), *Historical Sketch of Protestant Missions in Siam 1828–1928* (Bangkok: White Lotus Press, 1999).

Poonsakvorasan, A. (ed.), *170 Years of the Maitrichit Chinese Baptist Church* (Bangkok: Maitrichit Chinese Baptist Church, 2017).

Rung, Ruengsan-ajin et al., *The Five Pillars of the Protestant Faith* [in Thai] (Bangkok: Committee of Protestant Churches in Thailand, 2017).

Laos

David Andrianoff

Catholic Christianity

The presence of Christianity in Laos began with the arrival of Roman Catholic missionaries. In 1630 Giovanni Leira, an Italian Jesuit, visited Vientiane, the first person to share the good news of Jesus Christ in Laos. Much later, in 1885, missionaries of the Paris Foreign Mission Society established a church on Ban Dom Don island in the Mekong River – the first church in Laos. Initially, the Roman Catholic work in Laos came under the authority of the church in Siam (as Thailand was then known). In 1899 Pope Leo XIII established the Apostolic Vicariate of Laos, separating the church in Laos from Siam.

The Catholic Church in Laos has four Apostolic Vicariates – Vientiane, Luang Prabang, Savannakhet and Pakse – each with a resident bishop. Because of government regulations, the Luang Prabang bishop lives in Vientiane and periodically visits Luang Prabang. On 21 May 2017, Pope Francis elevated Lao Bishop Louis-Marie Ling Mankhanekhoun, a Khmu, to become a cardinal, the first for Laos.

The approximately 45,000 Catholics in Laos include ethnic Vietnamese in the major urban centres. The church faces a severe shortage of personnel, having only 20 priests for its 218 parishes. Ordination to the priesthood proceeds very slowly. The government does not permit the church to run social institutions, so the approximately 100 sisters work within parishes or in government hospitals and health facilities. The sisters have placed themselves under the authority of the Catholic Church in Thailand.

Beginnings of Protestant Christianity

Throughout its history, the Protestant Church in Laos has expanded at the margins of Lao society. In the late nineteenth century, some Khmu labourers came to faith in Jesus Christ after several visits to Laos by American Presbyterian itinerant missionary Daniel McGilvary, based in Chiang Mai in northern Thailand. The Lao referred to the Khmu as *Kha* (slave). McGilvary planted the first Protestant church in Laos in Vang Mon, a Khmu village, in 1898.

Four years after the planting of the Khmu church in northern Laos, Gabriel Contesse and Maurice Willy, both Brethren missionaries from

Switzerland, moved into southern Laos. They hired Chan Pan, head abbot of the local Buddhist temple, to teach them Lao. He also helped them to translate some of the New Testament gospels from Thai into Lao. As a result, Chan Pan came to faith in Jesus Christ. The first church among the Lao in southern Laos began with an Easter Sunday baptism in 1905.

In 1908, a cholera epidemic took the life of Gabriel Contesse and his wife Marguerite. Their deaths stimulated Fritz Audetat, a close friend of Contesse, to hastily leave Switzerland for Laos. While the sole missionary in Laos for more than three years, Audetat instituted annual Bible conferences for the few believers and established Sunday school programmes for adults as well as children. He translated the Bible into Lao, publishing the Lao New Testament in 1926. He then completed the entire Bible, published in 1932 by the press run by the Christian and Missionary Alliance (C&MA) in Hanoi, Vietnam.

The Swiss missionaries in southern Laos found their strongest response from those Lao accused of spirit possession. The Lao called them *Phii Pop* and evicted them from their villages. The missionaries protected the *Phii Pop*, gave them respect and shared the Christian message with them. The *Phii Pop* responded to this message of Good News. Other Lao people who found themselves ostracised from village society because of their leprosy also responded to the gospel. The villages for people with leprosy more readily received the good news of Jesus's love than the general Lao society.

One young girl, at the very margin of the marginalised people of Laos, illustrated how Christianity can grow from peripheral and unlikely locations. Souphine was born in southern China. When she was five, a travelling merchant purchased Souphine and took her to Savannakhet in southern Laos, to sell cigarettes and sweets. Knowing little Lao, shy Souphine sold very little. She then began to show signs of leprosy. The frustrated merchant thought of leaving her in the forest, but a neighbour suggested offering her to a local Swiss missionary. Eventually Fritz

Christianity in Laos, 1970 and 2020

Tradition	1970 Population	%	2020 Population	%	Average annual growth rate (%), 1970–2020
Christians	62,400	2.3%	199,000	2.8%	2.3%
Anglicans	300	0.0%	200	0.0%	−0.8%
Independents	400	0.0%	1,500	0.0%	2.7%
Protestants	20,200	0.8%	150,000	2.1%	4.1%
Catholics	41,500	1.5%	47,000	0.7%	0.3%
Evangelicals	20,300	0.8%	145,000	2.0%	4.0%
Pentecostal/Charismatics	40	0.0%	18,000	0.3%	13.0%
Total population	**2,688,000**	**100.0%**	**7,165,000**	**100.0%**	**2.0%**

Source: Todd M. Johnson and Gina A. Zurlo (eds), *World Christian Database* (Leiden/Boston: Brill), accessed March 2018.

Audetat and his wife Ida took Souphine in and cared for her. With her leprosy in remission, they sent her to school, where she did very well. When the leprosy returned, Audetat very reluctantly put her in the local leprosy village. In the meantime, Souphine had become a faithful follower of Christ. As a young teenager, Souphine devotedly read her Lao Bible. But her fellow villagers mocked her, even tearing pages out of her Bible. Souphine did not retaliate but instead reacted with quiet love and faithfulness to her Saviour. Attracted by her love and faithfulness, the Lao villagers began to follow Christ themselves, and this was the beginning of a church in the village. It was Souphine, a young girl with leprosy – it is hard to get much lower in Lao society – who planted a church in her village. That church still exists today. Souphine died of complications from her leprosy at the age of 19 but left a legacy that continues to bear fruit today.

At the invitation of the American Presbyterian Mission, which felt it could no longer provide missionaries to oversee its work in northern Laos, and after consultation with the Swiss mission in southern Laos, the C&MA expanded its work from Vietnam into northern Laos. Having completed his French-language studies in Paris, George Edward Roffe arrived in Luang Prabang in 1929 to pioneer the C&MA's work in northern Laos. The Swiss mission sent Saly Kounthapanya to help the C&MA. Saly became the first ordained pastor of the Lao church and the first president of the Lao Evangelical Church (LEC). The Reverend Saly's nephew, Khamphone Kounthapanya, currently serves as the president of the LEC.

The C&MA's greatest impact in Laos came from another marginalised group. In the nineteenth century, in order to escape the increasing incursions by their southern Chinese neighbours, the Hmong ethnic group migrated into Laos and settled on the heights of the mountains, above the reaches of the lowland Lao authorities. Many Hmong lived in Xieng Khouang Province, where Touby Lyfoung, often referred to as the 'king of the Hmong', was appointed deputy governor. In 1949, the C&MA mission sent a young missionary couple, Ted and Ruth Andrianoff (the author's parents), to Xieng Khouang to study the Lao language. The mission then sent Nai Kheng, a Khmu Bible school student, to assist them. Nai Kheng and his wife moved into a cottage belonging to Bua Ya, Touby's personal shaman, which was affordable because it was haunted by evil spirits. After Nai Kheng had successfully lived in Bua Ya's cottage a week, Bua Ya asked Nai Kheng to bring the young missionary to explain this great power over the evil spirits. Andrianoff summarised the teaching of the Bible from creation through the life, death, resurrection and ascension of Jesus. Bua Ya exclaimed, 'I want this power!' He had his spirit paraphernalia destroyed, committing himself and his family to Jesus. Two days later, at the annual mission conference in Vietnam, Ted Andrianoff excitedly informed his colleagues of the first Hmong in Laos to believe. When he returned to Xieng Khouang two months later, Bua Ya and Nai Kheng greeted him with a list of more than 1,000 names – people who had come to faith in Jesus Christ while no foreign missionaries were present. By the time Andrianoff returned to the USA for furlough two years later, a people movement to Jesus Christ had occurred with more than 5,000 – mostly Hmong, but also Khmu – professing faith in Christ in Xieng Khouang Province.

In the late 1960s and early 1970s the Vietnam War spilled into Laos. The US military recruited Hmong to conduct a clandestine sideshow war in Laos. When the communists achieved victory in 1975, virtually all the Hmong who had sided with the USA fled to Thailand. The Thai government quickly set up camps to house the hundreds of thousands of refugees from Laos, Cambodia and Vietnam. Because a sizeable minority of the Hmong were Christians, they erected churches in the camps. Large numbers of Hmong who had lost their sense of identity and found themselves in refugee camps entered these churches. Their trust in Jesus gave them a new identity and a new start in life. Hence a second wave of Hmong entering Christianity occurred, outside Laos.

Gradually, Hmong refugees resettled in the West, particularly the USA. A Hmong church leader in California, Chong Lee, began broadcasting the message of Christianity via shortwave to Southeast Asia. He regularly responded to letters asking questions about the Christian faith. By the mid-1980s, Lee had received many letters from Hmong in northern Vietnam, among whom there were no known Christians. Whole villages came to faith in Christ and asked Lee how to set up churches. By the early 1990s, the approximately 300,000 Hmong Christians in northern Vietnam attracted the attention of and persecution by Vietnamese government authorities.

The Hmong comprise just one of many marginalised ethnic minorities in Laos. These minorities make up more than 50% of the population, and it is they who continue to show the greatest response to the message of Christianity. The ethnic minorities, who are mostly animists, find that faith in Jesus Christ frees them from the constant need to appease the malevolent spirits around them.

Spiritual Practices in the Church

The Lao Evangelical Church (LEC), the umbrella Protestant church in Laos, grew out of the C&MA. While the LEC clearly reflects its C&MA roots, it is distinct from the C&MA denomination. The churches within the LEC have a wide range of practices. The LEC churches in the south, planted by Brethren and Overseas Missionary Fellowship (OMF) missionaries, practise cooperative leadership. The northern churches have a clear hierarchy. The churches in the south mostly serve the Eucharist weekly, while the churches in northern Laos serve it on the first Sunday of the month. Those who have received baptism by immersion, performed by pastors, are entitled to partake of the Eucharist. None of the churches within the LEC currently practise infant baptism. However, the churches do have dedication services for babies, often part of the Sunday morning worship service. Church services include hymns; special music and, occasionally, dances; Bible reading; offering; and a sermon. The sermons often emphasise proper behaviour, which reflects the Lao Buddhist concept of 'if you do good you will receive good', feeding into the rising popularity of prosperity theology.

The LEC encourages Christians to share their faith with friends and neighbours. Church members invite church leaders to their homes and villages to lead special services of thanksgiving for such occasions as weddings, births, healings and harvest. The believers invite their neighbours to these gatherings, which always include the sharing of the Good News of Jesus Christ.

Current Trends in Expanding Christianity
The churches provide training programmes for church leaders, both inside and outside Laos. Pastors from Vientiane (the capital city) and Savannakhet (the largest city in southern Laos) visit more remote provinces and districts to train church leaders. At least once a year, church leaders go to Vientiane to participate in training seminars. Groups of Christians also cross the border into Thailand to receive training in Christian doctrine and in sharing the Good News. Potential church leaders enrol in formal Bible training institutes in Thailand and elsewhere. Meanwhile, in cities and larger villages the churches provide programmes to train disciples and church leaders. The church in Laos continues to grow at a steady rate. Between December 2014 and December 2017 the total number of Protestant Christians increased by 17%.

In addition to attracting people to the Good News of Jesus Christ by their lifestyle, church leaders demonstrate the power of God over the spirit world through healings and deliverances. A historic example illustrates this. One evening in late 1950 in a Hmong village, Ted Andrianoff told the biblical story of Christ. In the midst of his presentation one woman shouted, 'This is it! This is what I told you about two years ago! Listen to him!' The villagers informed Andrianoff that two years previously the village chief had died. As was their custom, this shaman recounted the story of the village chief's ancestors. But she did not stop with his death. She went on to say, 'In two years a white man will come with a special book. He will tell us about a power that is greater than the spirits we fear.' As a result, the entire village came to faith in Jesus Christ.

Not only the animistic tribal people, but also the Buddhist Lao, with an underlying animism, turn to Jesus Christ due to encounters with the spirit world. Miraculous healings attract the attention of fellow villagers. Non-believers have started to call on church leaders to pray for the healing of people with various illnesses. Following a healing, many in their family and village might decide to join the Christian faith.

Gospel radio and recorded Christian programmes in local languages reach people who live in more isolated areas. Recently, many Khmu have come to faith in Jesus Christ as the result of Khmu-language broadcasts. Christian radio broadcasts into Laos in more than half a dozen languages on a weekly basis.

The change in government in Laos in 1975 delayed but did not stop Bible translation projects. The Bible is available in six languages spoken in Laos, and a further six languages have Bible translation projects underway. With an estimated 100 language groups in Laos, not all these languages will ever have the Bible in their language. Representatives from some minority languages receive training in telling stories from the Bible in their own languages. Oral Bible storying is much less time-consuming than translating the Bible into local languages.

Even though ethnic minorities comprise half the population of Laos, lowland Lao provide the basic social and administrative structure for the nation. The Lao consider Buddhism part of their national identity and often view Christianity as counter-cultural. The LEC has taken a strong stance against two Lao practices in particular – drinking of alcohol and participating in the *khwan* rituals. The most commonly practised ritual for Lao people, the *khwan* ritual calls on personal spirits (*khwan*) to increase well-being and re-establish order, thereby strengthening community solidarity. Births, weddings, sicknesses, promotions, visits, moving into a new house and deaths provide occasions for *khwan* rituals. The *khwan* ceremony calls wandering *khwan* back to the individual or community. Strings tied to the wrist symbolise tying the *khwan* to the body. The centrepiece of the ceremony, most often held in homes, is a cone-like structure of banana leaves resembling the Buddhist Mount Meru, with lengths of string attached. Friends and relatives gather around the cone, leaving space on one side for the person(s) honoured and the other side for the master of ceremonies, usually someone of religious significance such as a Brahmin priest or local shaman. The master of ceremonies chants some prayers over the cone and the attendees. People closest to the cone touch it with their right hand; those farther away touch someone touching the cone with their right hand. At the end of a chanted blessing, each person takes strings from the cone and ties them around the wrists of the attendees, saying a blessing for them. By the end, all present have several strings tied around their wrists and feel blessed.

With the *khwan* ritual so integral to Lao society, some churches have started to incorporate *khwan* into the worship service. Instead of a cone they have a basket with lengths of string. The pastor prays a blessing over the strings. Then those gathered take the strings and say a prayer of blessing over each person on whose wrist they tie a string.

Inter-faith Relationships

Laos has two main religions: Buddhism and animism. In general, the lowland Lao consider themselves Buddhist, while most of the ethnic minority peoples are animists. However, the situation is not so clear-cut. The Lao incorporate many animistic beliefs and practices into their Buddhism. For example, virtually all Buddhist temple compounds have a spirit fetish to protect the temple.

Until very recently there has been limited dialogue between Christianity and Buddhism. Generally, Christian leaders have taught that Buddhism opposes Christianity. In practice, Christians more often oppose Buddhism. With recent peace-building workshops, leaders of Christian churches have begun to talk to Buddhist leaders.

Roman Catholics, Protestants (LEC) and Seventh-day Adventists are registered with the government. In addition to Christianity, other registered religions with a following beyond Laos include Islam and Baha'i, but these are smaller minority religions. Occasionally new religions have appeared in Laos. For the most part these have been short-lived and not formally recognised by the government. However, both Lao and ethnic minorities are susceptible to new religious movements.

Conclusion

The government of the Lao People's Democratic Republic proclaims freedom to believe or not believe. Both the Catholic Church and the Protestant churches experience some constraints – from the government, from society and from within and among the church bodies. In the larger urban centres Christian groups experience considerable freedom to practise their faith. More remote areas still report occasional persecution of Christians, including imprisonment, expulsion from villages and forcing individuals to sign documents denying their Christian faith. In spite of delays in the ordination of priests, the elevation of Bishop Louis-Marie Ling Mankhanekhoun to cardinal reflects a vibrant Catholic Church in Laos. Likewise, the pace of growth of the LEC of 17% over three years continues. Overall, Christianity in Laos remains healthy and growing.

Bibliography

Andrianoff, Jean L., *Chosen for a Special Joy: The Story of Ted and Ruth Andrianoff* (Chicago, IL: Wing Spread Publishers, 2012).

Corthay, Charles, *Le Laos: Décourverte d'un champ missionaire* (Yverdon: Henri Cornaz, 1953).

Decorvet, Jeanne and Georges Rochat, *L'Appel du Laos* (Yverdon: Henri Cornaz, 1946).

Dupertuis, Silvain, *The Gospel in the Land of a Million Elephants* (St-Prex: Éditions de Sème, 2013).

McGilvary, Daniel, *A Half Century Among the Siamese and the Lao: An Autobiography* (Bangkok: White Lotus Press, 2002).

Cambodia

Barnabas Mam

Cambodia, formerly the Khmer Empire, is located in the south of the Indochina peninsula. Cambodia is currently the sixty-ninth most populous country in the world, with an estimated 2018 population of 16.25 million. The largest of the ethnic groups in Cambodia are the Khmer, who comprise approximately 90% of the total population. The national language used in Cambodia is Khmer, and the name of Cambodia in Khmer is Kampuchea, which derives from Sanskrit Kambujadeśa (land of Kambuja). During a turbulent 40-year period (1953–93) Cambodia changed its name five times: from Kingdom of Cambodia (1953–70) to Khmer Republic (1970–5), Democratic Kampuchea (1975–9), People's Republic of Kampuchea (1979–89), State of Cambodia (1989–93) and finally Kingdom of Cambodia (1993 to date). It is a predominantly Buddhist country, with Christians forming a small but fast-growing minority.

Christianity Before the Killing Fields

The Roman Catholic Church has the longest history of all the Christian churches in Cambodia. The first known Christian mission in Cambodia was undertaken by Gaspar da Cruz, a Portuguese member of the Dominican Order, in 1555–6. According to his own account, the enterprise was a complete failure; he found the country run by a 'Bramene' king and 'Bramene' officials and discovered that 'the Bramenes are the most difficult people to convert'. He felt that no one would dare to convert without the king's permission and left the country in disappointment, having not 'baptised more than one gentile whom I left in the grave'. But according to Bishop Emile Destombes, Apostolic Vicar of Phnom Penh and president of the Catholic Bishops' Conference of Laos and Cambodia, in his interview with the Vatican news agency Agenzia Fides in 2007, the history of Catholic missions actually began in 1554, with a visit by the Jesuit priest Fernandez Mendez Pinto. The first communities were founded in the seventeenth century by Jesuits, Dominicans and Franciscans. In the mid-1700s, the Catechism was translated into Khmer by priests of the Paris Foreign Missions Society. In 1850 the Apostolic Prefecture of Cambodia was created. The first Cambodian-born priest was ordained in 1957.

In 1972 there were probably about 20,000 Christians in Cambodia, most of whom were Roman Catholics. Before the repatriation of the Vietnamese in 1970 and 1971, possibly as many as 62,000 Christians lived in Cambodia. According to Vatican statistics, in 1953, members of the Roman Catholic Church in Cambodia numbered 120,000, making it, at the time, the second largest religion in the country. In April 1970, just before repatriation, estimates indicate that about 50,000 Catholics were Vietnamese. Many of the Catholics remaining in Cambodia in 1972 were Europeans, chiefly French.

Protestant missions began in 1892 with the Reverend Walter James of the British and Foreign Bible Society, who met Mr Vong, a secretary serving in the royal palace, in Phnom Penh, and had him translate the gospel of Luke from French into Khmer. In January 1923, the Reverend Arthur L. Hammond, with his wife Esther, of the Christian and Missionary Alliance (C&MA), entered Cambodia. He was an American missionary trained at Nyack College who first arrived in Southeast Asia in 1921 and served for two years in Saigon, Vietnam. He began translation of the Bible into Khmer in Battambang in 1925. The New Testament was completed by 1934, but it was not until 1954 that the whole Khmer Bible was finally published.

In March 1923, the Reverend David W. Ellison with his wife Muriel, also of the C&MA, arrived in Cambodia. He also lived and served in Battambang, focusing on evangelism and church planting. In 1932 King Sisowath Monivong imposed an anti-proselytising act upon the church in Cambodia. Ellison hired a small aircraft from Royal Laotian Aviation, filled it with boxes of evangelistic tracts and flew across the sky of Cambodia. He asked the Holy Spirit to bring the tracts to some Khmer people whom God had chosen to follow Jesus and threw the tracts from the aircraft. As a result, five of the people who received the tracts read them, believed in the gospel, made their way to the address printed on the tracts, met the

Christianity in Cambodia, 1970 and 2020

Tradition	1970 Population	%	2020 Population	%	Average annual growth rate (%), 1970–2020
Christians	33,300	0.5%	471,000	2.8%	5.4%
Anglicans	200	0.0%	700	0.0%	2.5%
Independents	2,000	0.0%	180,000	1.1%	9.4%
Protestants	10,600	0.2%	305,000	1.8%	7.0%
Catholics	20,100	0.3%	25,000	0.1%	0.4%
Evangelicals	10,600	0.2%	320,000	1.9%	7.1%
Pentecostal/Charismatics	2,000	0.0%	365,000	2.2%	11.0%
Total population	**6,995,000**	**100.0%**	**16,716,000**	**100.0%**	**1.8%**

Source: Todd M. Johnson and Gina A. Zurlo (eds), *World Christian Database* (Leiden/Boston: Brill), accessed March 2018.

missionary and prayed to accept Jesus as their Saviour. Ellison started a Bible school in Battambang in 1935 with these five students. Four of them – Chao Vouch, Try Hoc, Neak Hom and Sok Chhoum – completed the training course and graduated from the Bible school.

In 1952 the C&MA decided that the national church should take responsibility for supporting its pastors and planned to phase out the missionary subsidy at the rate of one-tenth per year over a decade, beginning in 1952. In May 1955, three years into this scaling-back programme, the subsidy was cut entirely. This took place just after the National Executive Committee met at the National Conference and reassigned many pastors to other congregations. The result was difficult relations between foreign missionaries and Cambodians, as many congregations determined that they could not possibly support a full-time pastor.

During the 1950s, an American Unitarian mission maintained a teacher-training school in Phnom Penh, and Baptist missions functioned in Battambang and Siem Reap provinces. On 1 November 1958 the first Seventh-day Adventist (SDA) church in Cambodia was chartered, with 11 members, who represented many different nationalities. The Cambodian government recognised the SDA mission on 21 August 1959, making possible the construction of a 150-seat church in Phnom Penh, which opened on 3 February 1962. The Jehovah's Witnesses also began their work in Cambodia in 1958. The 1962 census reported 2,000 Protestants in Cambodia.

In 1965, Prince Norodom Sihanouk, head of state of Cambodia, aligned more with China and cut off diplomatic relations with the USA. Most Western missionaries were forced to leave Cambodia by not having their visas renewed. National Evangelical church leaders were jailed on trumped-up charges. The first – Son Sonne, future director of the Bible Society in Cambodia – was arrested while working in a bookshop and held in jail for three months. Three others – San Hay Seng, Yos Aun and Uong Un – followed. Due to financial insufficiency, Westernised expression of worship and weak leadership, the Khmer Evangelical Church remained silent and ineffective for five years without doing any outreach work.

Things changed rapidly after General Lon Nol led a coup d'état to oust Prince Sihanouk from power on 18 March 1970. Many refugees flooded into Phnom Penh and lived there, while others camped outside the city. The US embassy in Phnom Penh was reopened, and foreigners and Western missionaries were warmly welcomed by the new government. Cambodians, especially the youth, were eager to learn English. Large Christian humanitarian organisations such as Catholic Relief Services and World Vision International introduced programmes to demonstrate the love of God to the poor, the needy and the vulnerable. All their leaders, most of their staff officers and many of their staff workers were committed Christians whose quality of life attracted people to Christianity.

Dr Stanley Mooneyham, president of World Vision International, conducted three gospel rallies in Chaktomuk Conference Hall in Phnom Penh, two in 1972 and one in 1973. Each rally was so crowded that Mooneyham had to preach to his audience both outside and inside the hall. In spite of the resentment felt by many Cambodian patriots towards the Roman Catholic Church for giving refuge to the Vietnamese, there was always a good response from the audience when Mooneyham made an altar call. Another influential figure was Edwin Moore, an SDA missionary, who started an English-language school in Phnom Penh that had grown to more than 500 students by 1975.

While the Roman Catholic Church suffered the pain of losing much of its Vietnamese membership through forced repatriation to South Vietnam in 1970 and 1971, by 1975 the Khmer Evangelical Church was experiencing exponential growth, with its membership increasing from around 2,000 to around 10,000. But with the coming to power of the Khmer Rouge, or Red Khmer, all foreign missionaries were expelled again.

Persecution During the Killing Fields

The Khmer Rouge conquered the Khmer Republic on 17 April 1975. They evacuated all the people from the cities to rural areas and banned all banks, shops, restaurants, schools, theatres and religious practices. Cambodia then became an isolated and deprived nation. Pol Pot, prime minister of Democratic Kampuchea, ruled the nation with terror and atrocity. A quarter of the Cambodian population were killed by the Khmer Rouge during the Killing Fields era simply because they were rich, educated, famous or religious; because they had been associated with foreigners or had served any other government; or because they opposed Pol Pot's policy. The Khmer Rouge regarded any religion as opium that weakened the nation. They suspected all Christians of being affiliated with the US Central Intelligence Agency and regarded Catholic priests and Christian ministers as counter-revolutionary people or leeches who sucked the nation's blood.

According to Bishop Emile Destombes, who was quoted by *The Phnom Penh Post* in an article dated 25 March 2005:

> Despite the murder of Cambodian Catholic priests and the expulsion of foreign missionaries, Catholics met to worship in secret during the years of religious repression under Pol Pot. Consecrated Eucharistic bread, which Catholics believe is the body of Christ, was smuggled from Vietnam, often in film canisters, and distributed among the faithful. Catholics would meet in family groups and as a sign of unity with the Church some of them would

kiss a cross that once hung around the neck of Khmer Catholic bishop Joseph Chmar Salas. All Cambodian Catholic priests, including Salas, the first Khmer Catholic bishop, and many members of Catholic religious orders and lay people were killed. Churches were razed and properties seized.

All the members of the National Executive Committee of the Khmer Evangelical Church (KEC) except Pastor Reach Year were killed by the Khmer Rouge, including Chau Uth, Sem Bun, Chhirc Taing, Bible Society director Son Sonne and Minh Thien Voan, president of the Gideons. All SDA Church members perished, except three who left the country just before it fell to the Khmer Rouge.

Christianity Before National Unification
Democratic Kampuchea, or the Killing Fields regime, was terminated by Vietnamese troops and their Cambodian allies on 7 January 1979. The results of a local survey indicated that 1.7 million people lost their lives in the Killing Fields. Only a few hundred Christians survived the genocide. Most of the Christian survivors left the country, but around 200 remained. Pastor Sieng Ang and his wife Bun Sok, Cambodian missionaries who had served the Khmer Krom people in Sóc Trăng (Khleang Province), Vietnam, since 1972, returned to Cambodia to shepherd the church of the survivors that managed to meet secretly on Sundays in three places. Pastor Sieng Ang was arrested in 1984 and was jailed for several months. After his release he continued to strengthen the underground church in Phnom Penh. He planted a church in Prek Talong near Takhmau, about 10 kilometres south of Phnom Penh.

For fear of the new government and communist practice imposed and supported by the Vietnamese, many people fled to Thailand, living in refugee camps for several years before eventually taking asylum in the USA, Canada, Australia, New Zealand and many European countries. In the refugee camps in Thailand, Cambodians were open to the Christian message. Many of them believed in Jesus, were baptised, attended the church and grew in faith. Para-church organisations such as the Catholic Office for Emergency Relief and Refugees, JRS (Jesuit Refugee Service), Don Bosco, Youth With A Mission, COR (Christian Outreach), CAMA Services (Compassion and Mercy Associates), FHI (Food for the Hungry International), OMF (Overseas Missionary Fellowship), Baptist Missions and Campus Crusade for Christ were instrumental in strengthening the faith of the new Christians and training them to build a better future in Cambodia. Together with Sarin Sam, the present author wrote, compiled and edited hundreds of Cambodian indigenous hymns and gospel songs that have been widely used by the Cambodian church worldwide since 1985. Inspired by the Second Lausanne Congress, held in Manila in

1989, Cambodian Evangelical church leaders and Western missionaries connected with the Cambodian churches gathered in Singapore in January 1990 to pray for Cambodia and plan future work.

Christianity After National Unification

The effort for national unification was cemented by the signing of the Paris peace accords by all four Cambodian warring factions on 23 October 1991. After this, Cambodians living overseas, refugees and displaced people were welcomed back to their homeland and were treated equally as citizens of Cambodia. The country was now officially called the Kingdom of Cambodia again. Buddhism was recognised as the state religion, but the constitution provides for freedom of religion, and the government has generally respected this right in practice.

In Asia, the church in Malaysia and the church in Singapore were the first to send missionaries to Cambodia, followed by the churches in South Korea and Thailand. Many individuals, missionaries, mission agencies, denominations and para-church organisations from Asia, the Americas, Europe and Australia came to Cambodia in 1992. Local and international non-governmental organisations offered their programmes to serve Cambodia and its people with child protection, child sponsorship, community development, medical care, health care, caring for people with HIV/AIDS, prison ministry, military ministry, English teaching, vocational training, leadership training and Christian education.

Bishop Emile Destombes told Agenzia Fides in 2007:

> One urgent priority is formation, formation of priests, formation of the community, to help the laity assume greater responsibility. At present we have only 5 Cambodian-born priests, formed after the period of the Red Khmers. We have 96 missionary priests of whom 8 are diocesan and the rest belong to various congregations, and we have 102 women religious. We are forming special Commissions to animate each parish: a Liturgy Commission (to prepare liturgies, hymns etc.); a Catechesis and Education Commission, which is a task not only for priests and religious; a Commission for charity work and social service, to provide assistance for the poor, the abandoned, people with AIDS. We wish every community to have these three commissions.

Around 300 Cambodian pastors and church leaders met together for the first time at the National Church Leaders' Conference in Phnom Penh in April 1994 to promote unity and synergy. On 10 June 1994 around 3,000 Christians joined the Global March for Jesus from Wat Phnom to the Royal Palace in Phnom Penh. Among the Protestants, several church councils were formed. Two of them are inter-denominational with international affiliation: the Evangelical Fellowship of Cambodia (EFC), a member of the World Evangelical Alliance; and the Kampuchea Christian

Council, a member of the World Council of Churches. Three of them are inter-denominational with national affiliation: the Cambodian Christian Evangelical Alliance; National Christian Church Networks Cambodia; and the Cambodian Christian Protestant Community. The rest are mono-denominational church councils, such as the Cambodia Baptist Union, Cambodia Methodist Church and Cambodia Foursquare Church. Of all the church councils, the EFC – which was recognised by the government on 14 January 1996 – is the largest local indigenous umbrella religious organisation, with many denominations, church associations, mission agencies, independent churches and non-governmental organisations joining its membership. The Cambodia government also recognised as church councils the SDA Church, the New Apostolic Church, the Jehovah's Witnesses and the Church of Jesus Christ of Latter-day Saints.

On 12 December 1995, the Bible Society in Cambodia received a permit from the government to operate as a society. The Khmer Standard Version (KHSV), a new translation of the Bible, was completed in April 1997. The dedication of the KHSV Bible was held on 5 June 1998, and the presentation of the KHSV Bible to King Norodom Sihanouk by the board of directors took place a week after the dedication. The board of the Society comprises leaders from the Roman Catholic Church, the SDA Church and most of the main Evangelical denominations.

One hundred and fifty Christian leaders joined the staff of the Far East Broadcasting Corporation (FEBC) on 8 November 2014 to dedicate a new transmitter in the presence of the secretary of the Ministry of Information. Three radio ministries are recognised by the government: Family FM 99.5, Trans World Radio Cambodia and Voice of New Life Radio.

For the first time in the history of the church of Cambodia, on 5 April 2015, the minister of religion attended a joint Easter celebration, in Phnom Penh, in the presence of 3,000 Christians, 150 government officers, 150 Buddhist leaders and 150 Islamic leaders. As Christian ministries concerning child protection are appreciated by the Cambodia government and UNICEF, 1,400 Evangelicals and 600 Catholics were invited to attend the World Day of Prayer and Action for Children on 14 December 2015, together with 1,400 Buddhists and 600 Muslims, in the presence of the prime minister of Cambodia.

On 25 December 2009, after joining a Christmas celebration in Phnom Penh, Mrs Men Sam An, a deputy prime minister of Cambodia, told the minister of religion as they were walking through a row of exhibition booths with two senior Evangelical leaders, 'I just know that Christians in Cambodia have done more good works to rebuild our nation than what was sent to us in their written reports. I am proud to see them wear Khmer costumes and to hear them sing Khmer carols.'

Main Christian Movements

The Khmer Evangelical Church (KEC) of the C&MA is known as the first Protestant church in Cambodia. The KEC is united, well organised, well connected and steadily growing. It is strong in training leaders through Theological Education by Extension and is actively reaching out to tribal people.

The Assemblies of God (AOG) came in with an agreement with the Cambodian government in 1990. The AOG is known for its partnership with primary-school teachers in implementing a full curriculum and teaching biblical values to the students in Takeo Province. AOG Cambodia is also known for the first Christian high school in Phnom Penh. To train Christian workers, AOG Cambodia runs the Cambodia Bible Institute (CBI). All AOG local pastors are CBI graduates.

The New Apostolic Church (NAC) planted more than 200 churches nationwide in the 1990s. Because some of the local leaders left the NAC and joined other Evangelical denominations in the late 1990s, however, membership has decreased, and the NAC is no longer active in church planting.

Southern Baptist missions from the USA also planted more than 200 churches in Cambodia in the 1990s. After some of the first-generation leaders died and others left the movement, the Southern Baptist-affiliated churches in Cambodia decreased in membership and are now less active in church planting. However, other Baptist churches that train and deploy emerging leaders for ministry are growing rapidly.

The Mormons or the Church of Jesus Christ of Latter-day Saints (LDS) began their work in Cambodia in 1994. They are known for their commitment to pay tithes, two-by-two house evangelism, humanitarian projects, nice church buildings and sending students to Brigham Young University in Hawaii. In 2012 the membership of LDS in Cambodia reached more than 14,000, with a steady stream of members recruited to the church each year, according to David Moon, president of the Cambodia mission. In 2009, there were 432 new Mormons in Cambodia, and since then the figure has risen to more than 600 new members per year.

The Methodist missions came to Cambodia from Malaysia, Singapore, Korea, France, Switzerland and the USA in the early 1990s. Multiple Methodist bodies began working together in 2004 to support and plant local churches in Cambodia. In less than a decade, leadership of the Methodist Mission Church has shifted from foreign missionaries to Cambodian Methodists. The local Khmer leadership is strong and local leaders continue to be cultivated. The 154 Methodist faith communities and 140 pastors that make up the Cambodia Mission Initiative are focused on planting new churches and strengthening ministry by women, ministry with street children, Christian education, ministry with youth, economic development and community health.

Various Presbyterian missions from South Korea, Malaysia, Singapore and the USA came to Cambodia in the early 1990s. Korean Presbyterians have planted more churches than the others. Even though they are not yet united as one Presbyterian Church of Cambodia, they have effectively reached out to high-school students and college students. They are known for their Christian university in Kampong Som and their theological seminaries in Phnom Penh.

The Foursquare Church of Cambodia (FCC) claims to be the fastest-growing church in Cambodia. FCC claims to have 5,985 churches and meeting places, and 984,389 members. Many researchers on church growth and church planting in Cambodia find it hard to accept these figures, however. In spite of some tension between missionaries and the local leadership, the FCC is actively planting churches and building orphanage centres all over Cambodia. The FCC is known for love and care for orphans and widows.

New Life Fellowship Phnom Penh was planted by Pastor Eric Dooley, an American missionary, when he came to Phnom Penh in 1993 to do pioneer evangelism. Dooley moved his family to Vietnam in 1997, and leadership passed to Pastor Chuck McCaul. In 1999, New Life Fellowship began planting and resourcing churches throughout Cambodia's remote and rural areas. Pastor Chuck continued to serve as the senior leader in Cambodia until 2004, when he began to transfer the leadership of New Life Fellowship Phnom Penh to his son Jesse and local leaders so he could focus on overseeing rural church plants and development work. More than 60 provincial congregations have been planted. Under the leadership of Jesse McCaul and the local leadership team, New Life Fellowship Phnom Penh has grown to become one of the largest churches in Cambodia.

One of the indigenous church associations that pioneered church planting is Living Hope in Christ Church (LHCC). Paulerk Sar and the present author were called to plant LHCC in Phnom Penh in 1995. During the late 1990s and early 2000s, LHCC grew into an association that today has 132 churches in its membership. The present author established the Institute of Church Planting Cambodia (ICPC) in 1998, training 30 new church planters every year. By 2018, 608 church planters had graduated from ICPC and planted more than 500 churches.

Church Growth in Cambodia Today

'To be Cambodian is to be Buddhist' is a widely quoted saying. The would-be convert's first hurdle to overcome is the feeling that Christianity is in some sense a betrayal of Khmer-ness. The second hurdle is that

Christianity has a reputation for teaching disrespect for parents, although Christians find this difficult to fathom given the biblical injunction to honour one's mother and father. But respect for parents is one of the foundations of Khmer society, and young would-be converts are both surprised and relieved to find that they are not expected to turn their backs on their families. The rapid growth of churches in Cambodia is testimony that these obstacles are increasingly being overcome. A number of factors can be identified to account for this rapid growth.

An analogy used by Cambodian Evangelicals is that their compatriots of Buddhist background see themselves as people drowning in a river but being given a swimming lesson by a good teacher to rescue themselves from the calamity. They have tried their best to follow the teacher's instruction, but they realise that they are too weak to swim. Just as they become desperate, Jesus jumps into the river to rescue them and takes them to safe ground. Then Jesus makes friends with them and gives them useful and practical swimming lessons so that they can enjoy their swims and their travels by boat for the rest of their lives. Their point is that as the drowning need a rescuer rather than a swimming teacher, so Cambodians need a Saviour rather than a religious teacher.

Many Cambodians who never experienced fatherly love or brotherly love, because they grew up in fatherless homes or broken families, through the Christian faith come to feel a strong sense of the fatherly love of God, the brotherly love of Jesus and the love of fellow believers within the church. This offers a strong sense of acceptance, belonging and oneness in God's family (no racial discrimination, no social status discrimination and no gender discrimination). In response to the love of Christ, they worship God's majesty with intimacy. Compelled by this divine love, they pray for one another and passionately proclaim the gospel of Christ to their neighbours. They are set free to forgive the Khmer Rouge who killed their loved ones and even the Vietnamese, whom they once regarded as their bitter enemies.

Cambodian Christians are excited to go to church because they have seen miracles take place in their lives and in those of other believers, including healings, casting out of demons, family reunion, marital restoration, reconciliation, job opportunities, promotions and financial breakthroughs. They believe that they can experience abundant life in Christ through the church.

Students like going to church or a Christian school because of the higher ethical values, the higher training quality, the higher tuition quality, the safer environment and the subsidised school fees or scholarships offered by the churches. Many students from Christian high schools pass the national exam and are accepted for college education every year. Poor students can learn English, music and creative arts or can receive vocational training at church free of charge. Illiterate people in rural areas can learn to read and write Khmer at church. Above all else, emerging leaders are equipped at church and released for ministry at church. They believe that they will have a brighter future in Christ through the church.

Cambodian Christians no longer feel that they lose their national identity. They are proud to wear Cambodian costumes and to integrate indigenous music, hymns, carols, dances and performing arts in their Christian worship. They grow rapidly in number because they have access to contextualised Christian resources in their native language that are easy to read, easy to hear, easy to understand, easy to apply and easy to share with others. They grow in good relationships with their parents by honouring them while they are alive. Cambodian Christians show their love, respect and gratitude to their parents who stay with them by greeting them kneeling on the floor, with closed hands reaching up to the nose and with head bowing down three times. They bring them baskets of fruit, cake, drink and dried food, and give them an envelope with a good amount of money in it on special occasions such as birthdays or anniversaries or on national holidays such as Khmer New Year or Pchum Ben festival. Christians whose parents do not stay with them travel far to visit their parents, greet them with the same level of greeting, bless them with the special gifts and spend a few days with them for family reunion. Christians whose fathers are Buddhist monks go to the Buddhist monasteries, greet them by kneeling on the floor with closed hands reaching up to the forehead and with head bowing down three times, and bless them with special gifts. Cambodian Christians also worship Jesus in a kneeling position, with head up, and with closed hands or open hands above the head.

In the past, the church in Cambodia was known as a community of the foolish, the incompetent and the unemployed, but now the church is known as the community of the wise, the competent and the employed. The church in Cambodia has many contrasts, such as an institutional church versus an organic church, a denominational church versus an indigenous church, an urban church versus a rural church, an 'elephant' church versus a 'rabbit' church, a church that meets in a proper building versus a church that meets at home and a church that meets only on Sunday versus a church that meets every day. Urban churches have five age groups: children, teenagers, young adults, adults and senior people. Rural churches have only three age groups – children, teenagers and senior people – because many young adults go to the city for college education or work and many adults go to the city or overseas for work. Churches vary in size, with the smallest having fewer than 25 members and the largest more than 1,000. Most of the rural churches are house churches or 'rabbit' churches, with fewer than 100 members, mainly peasants, under the leadership of a local pastor and a small team of elders. Most of the urban churches are churches with a proper building and more than 100 members, who may be professionals, business people, students, police officers, military personnel or housewives, under the leadership of a pastoral team and a team of elders. Most rural churches meet for two or three hours on Sunday, use indigenous musical instruments and sing more indigenous hymns and fewer translated hymns and contemporary songs of praise and worship. They pray longer prayers by and for more people, allow two or three testimonies and usually listen to an hour-long sermon on a Bible story that encourages the people's faith and gives direction to their lives. Most urban churches meet for an hour and a half or two hours on Sunday; use both indigenous and modern musical instruments; sing one or two indigenous hymns, one or two translated hymns and several contemporary songs of praise and worship; pray shorter prayers by and for fewer people; allow only one testimony and usually have a 40–60-minute topical sermon that is relevant to the needs of the people.

The recent history of Christianity in Cambodia suggests that missionaries are needed to pioneer the first church plant, to make disciples among the first-generation believers and to produce leaders among them. Missionaries are needed to partner with the local leaders of the first church planted through evangelism, in making disciples among the next generation of believers and in raising leaders among the next generation of Christian disciples. Then the time comes when the church can be left in the hands of local leaders. Tension between influence and resources coming from the mission-sending nations and the development of local leadership arises only when missionaries are not willing to move from the pioneering stage to the parenting stage, then to the training stage and finally to the partnering stage, when appropriate.

Bibliography

Cormack, Don, *Killing Fields Living Fields: Faith in Cambodia* (London: Monarch Books and OMF International, 1997).

Maher, Brian with Uon Seila, *Cry of the Gecko: History of the Christian Mission in Cambodia* (Centralia, WA: Gorham Printing, 2012).

Mam, Barnabas, with Kitti Murray, *Church Behind the Wire: A Story of Faith in the Killing Fields* (Chicago, IL: Moody Publishers, 2012).

Ponchaud, François, Nancy Pignarre, Sharon Wilkinson and Nicole Butcher, *The Cathedral in the Rice Paddy: The 450 Year Long History of the Church in Cambodia* (Phnom Penh: Catholic Catechetical Centre Cambodia, 2012).

Ross, Russell R. (ed.), *Cambodia: A Country Study* (Washington, DC: GPO for the Library of Congress, 1987).

Vietnam

Peter C. Phan

Systematic and organised missions to the Vietnamese people were not undertaken until the arrival of Jesuits in Quang Nam, central Vietnam (then known as Cochinchina), in 1615. From 1615 to 1659, the bulk of missionary work was carried out by the Jesuits, of whom the most celebrated is Alexandre de Rhodes of France (1591–1660). De Rhodes arrived in central Vietnam in December 1624, and after a few months of language study he was sent, together with Pero Marqués, to the north, then known as Tonkin, arriving there on 19 March 1627. De Rhodes was expelled in 1630, went back to Macao, remained there for 10 years, and in 1640 came back to Cochinchina. In 1645, banished from Vietnam for good, he went to Rome to lobby for the establishment of a hierarchy in Vietnam. As a result of tenacious efforts by de Rhodes in the face of fierce opposition by the Portuguese crown, in 1658 Pope Alexander VII appointed François Pallu Apostolic Vicar of Tonkin – bishop under the authority of the Congregation of the Propagation of the Faith (Propaganda Fide) rather than the Portuguese Padroado Real – and Pierre Lambert de la Motte Apostolic Vicar of Cochinchina.

The Church Steeped in Blood

Missionary work in the next two centuries, though highly successful, met with grave difficulties. Some of these stemmed from the political situation of the country at the time. When Christianity first arrived in Vietnam, the reigning dynasty was the Le, which was founded in 1428 and ended in 1788. However, in 1527 power was wrested from it by the Mac dynasty, which ruled the northernmost part of Vietnam until 1592. In 1532, two clans, the Trinh and the Nguyen, defeated the Mac in defence of the Le. Subsequent Le kings were nothing more than puppets, however, and the real power was in the hands of the Trinh and Nguyen clans. Soon rivalries divided the two clans, with the former dominating the north and the latter the south. Military conflicts between the two parts of the country erupted in 1627, the very year de Rhodes went to the north; a total of seven wars lasted off and on for 45 years but failed to produce a victory for either side. The rivalry between the north and the south greatly complicated the work of missionaries as each side, especially the Trinh clan, suspected them of being spies for the other but, when convenient, used them as go-betweens to obtain merchandise and military wares from their Western countrymen, especially the Portuguese.

In addition to external political problems, missions in Vietnam faced two internal church issues. The first was the jurisdictional conflict between missionaries, mostly Spanish and Portuguese Jesuits and Dominicans, operating under the Portuguese *padroado* system and the French ones associated with the Société des Missions Étrangères de Paris (MEP), a missionary society founded by Bishop Pallu, under the supervision of the Propaganda Fide. The second issue was the Chinese Rites Controversy, which was extended to Vietnam, in which Dominicans, Franciscans and MEP missionaries succeeded in having the Jesuits' more liberal attitude towards the practices of offering sacrifices to Confucius and the ancestors condemned as superstitions.

However, the most devastating challenge to the infant church was the numerous persecutions of its members by various Vietnamese rulers. It is estimated that 30,000 Catholics were killed under the rule of the Trinh clan in the north and under the rule of the Nguyen clan and the Tay Son family in the south during the seventeenth and eighteenth centuries. In addition, 40,000 were reportedly killed under the reign of three Nguyen emperors: Minh Mang (1820–40), Thieu Tri (1841–7) and Tu Duc (1848–83). Finally, an estimated 60,000 were killed by the nationalist Van Than (pro-king and anti-French) movement (1864–85). In 1988, Pope John Paul II canonised 117 of these martyrs.

On the Way to Maturity

In spite of these tragedies, the church expanded rapidly. In 1933 the first Vietnamese bishop, Nguyen Ba Tong, was consecrated. In 1934 the first Indochinese council was held in Hanoi, with the participation of 20 bishops, five religious superiors and 21 priests; its policies had extensive

Christianity in Vietnam, 1970 and 2020

Tradition	1970		2020		Average annual growth rate (%), 1970–2020
	Population	%	Population	%	
Christians	3,264,000	7.5%	8,924,000	9.1%	2.0%
Anglicans	2,200	0.0%	200	0.0%	−4.7%
Independents	44,700	0.1%	529,000	0.5%	5.1%
Protestants	159,000	0.4%	1,586,000	1.6%	4.7%
Catholics	2,899,000	6.7%	7,221,000	7.3%	1.8%
Evangelicals	168,000	0.4%	1,650,000	1.7%	4.7%
Pentecostal/Charismatics	32,600	0.1%	800,000	0.8%	6.6%
Total population	**43,407,000**	**100.0%**	**98,360,000**	**100.0%**	**1.6%**

Source: Todd M. Johnson and Gina A. Zurlo (eds), *World Christian Database* (Leiden/Boston: Brill), accessed March 2018.

implications for the life of the church. Unfortunately, no sooner had the church begun its expansion than the country was engulfed in the independence war against colonialist France, and the subsequent Geneva accords (1954) temporarily divided Vietnam into two parts, the north under the communist regime and the south under a democratic and pro-Western government.

As a result of the partition, 860,000 Vietnamese, of whom 650,000 were Catholic, fled the north, thereby decimating the northern church and dramatically swelling the Catholic population of the south. On 8 December 1960 Pope John XXIII established the Vietnamese hierarchy, dividing the church into three ecclesiastical provinces (Hanoi, Hue and Saigon) with 20 ordinaries and no longer merely apostolic vicars. Thus, after 300 years of mission, the Vietnamese Catholic Church became a fully fledged church with its own hierarchy.

North and South: 1954–75
Cut off from the church in the south and the Church of Rome for almost 21 years (1954-75), persecuted by the communist government and devastated by the departure of a large number of clergy and laity in 1954, the church in the north barely survived. With its educational and social institutions confiscated by the government and its clergy practically under house arrest, the church limited its activities to sacramental celebrations and pious devotions. It could not benefit from the great reforms instituted by the Second Vatican Council (1962–5).

Compared with the church in the north, the church in the south was in a far more favourable situation. Not only did it benefit from the massive influx of Catholics in 1954, it also enjoyed 20 years of freedom (1955–75) that fortunately coincided with a period of extensive renewal in the Catholic Church initiated by the Second Vatican Council. It made rapid gains: in 1959 it had 1,226,310 Catholics, 1,342 native priests, 715 brothers and 3,776 sisters. In addition, it exercised extensive influence on society at large through its numerous first-rate educational, health-care and social services.

Religious Freedom: 1975–2015
Like all other religious organisations in South Vietnam, the Catholic Church was caught completely unprepared for the victory of communist North Vietnam on 30 April 1975. Its stance towards communism had been one of rejection and condemnation, consistent with that of the universal church until the end of the Second Vatican Council. The new challenge was how to exist as the church and fulfil its mission under the communist regime.

The most important and widely disseminated document expounding the attitude of the church towards communism and outlining its ministry under the communist regime is no doubt the first pastoral letter of the now-reconstituted Vietnamese Episcopal Conference, composed of 33 bishops from both north and south. It was issued on 5 January 1980 and titled *Living the Gospel in the Midst of the People*. Beginning with an emphatic affirmation that the Church of Jesus Christ must live in the midst of the people, the letter asserts that Vietnam is the place where God calls Vietnamese Catholics to live as children of God and that the Vietnamese people are the community which Catholics must serve as both citizens of the nation and members of the church.

Meanwhile, from 1975 to 1995 the economic condition of Vietnam worsened alarmingly, and the communist government attempted to respond to the economic crisis by adopting the *Doi Moi* (renovation) programme, moving partially from the socialist economy to the market economy. Along with economic innovation, some important changes in the political system were advanced. However, unlike *perestroika* in the Soviet Union, which was officially accompanied by political *glasnost*, *Doi Moi* was not undergirded by a new political ideology of openness. Nevertheless, no doubt it represented the most significant reforms, not only economic but also political, in post-1975 Vietnam.

In spite of all these *Doi Moi* changes towards the free market, the Vietnamese Communist Party (VCP), like the Chinese Communist Party, did everything to retain its status as the only party with power to govern Vietnam. Occasionally, laws and policies were enacted, and ordinances and decrees issued, to protect human rights, including religious freedom, especially if these measures could improve Vietnam's standing in the international community and attract foreign investment. Nothing, however, would be tolerated if it could challenge or jeopardise the party's exclusive grip on power. Nevertheless, it must be acknowledged that in the 1990s there was some relaxation in the government's attitude towards religious freedom and practices in general. New laws and policies on religious matters were issued. With regard to the Catholic Church, diplomatic relations were established between the Vietnamese government and the Vatican.

The 1992 constitution of the Socialist Republic of Vietnam, emended in 2001 and again in 2013, stipulates that:

> citizens have the right to freedom of belief and religion, and may practise or not practise any religion. All religions are equal before the law. Public places of religious worship are also protected by law. No one has the right to infringe on the freedom of belief and freedom of religion or take advantage of the latter to violate state laws and policies. (Article 70; author's translation here and below)

Basic to the VCP's stance on religious freedom is the distinction between religion as faith or belief (*tin nguong*) and religion as religious organisation and activities (*ton giao*). For the former, there is a guarantee of complete freedom of believing and not believing; for the latter, there are restrictions, especially to protect 'national security'. Accordingly, Directive 37-CT/TW of 2 July 1998 of the Central Committee of the VCP requires party committees and administration at all levels 'to encourage religious followers to promote their traditional patriotism, to take an enthusiastic part in the renovation cause, to fulfil religious tasks and citizens' duties, to build and defend the Fatherland, and to continue to implement the policy of the Party and state on religion'.

A detailed and specific list of stipulations regarding what is allowed and what is forbidden was given the following year, in Decree 26/1999/ND-CP of 19 April 1999, especially in articles 6–26. While this Decree marks an advance over the 1998 Directive, inasmuch as it clarifies the kinds of religious activities that can 'cause social disorder and insecurity' and are therefore unlawful, it has been heavily criticised for its attempt to interfere in the normal internal affairs of religions. For example, it requires approval from appropriate government authorities for extraordinary religious activities outside religious buildings (such as procession and pilgrimage), the appointment of religious officials (in particular, bishops and their equivalents), the building of churches, the founding of seminaries and houses of formation, meetings and conferences of religious leaders at the national and local levels, and relations with foreign religious organisations.

On 18 June 2004, the government issued the Ordinance on Belief and Religion, composed of 41 articles. The Ordinance gives precise definitions of terms such as 'belief-related activity', 'belief-related establishment', 'religious organisation', 'grassroots religious organisations', 'religious activity', 'religious association' and 'religious establishment'. A key distinction is again made between 'belief' (for which there is complete freedom, as there is for non-belief) and 'religion' (on which there are restrictions). This Ordinance is a further improvement on the 1998 Directive and the 1999 Decree. Of great interest is article 6, which stipulates that:

> relations between the Socialist Republic of Vietnam and other States and/or international organisations in religion-related matters shall be based on the principle that promotes each other's independence and sovereignty, non-interference in each other's internal affairs, equality, mutual benefit, and in conformity with each other's law and international law and practice.

The Ordinance was shortly followed by the Decree of the Government Guiding the Implementation of the Ordinance on Belief and Religion

(March 2005), which has 38 articles. As implied by its title, this Decree, which is so far the longest and most detailed legal document on religious institutions and practices, sets out procedures for registering 'belief-related festivals' (articles 3–5), 'religious organisations' (articles 6–19) and 'religious activities' (articles 20–35). Again, the overriding concern of the government is control of religions and their activities, particularly by means of 'registration'. Without registration, no religion may legally function. As of 2007, the state, through the Committee for Religious Affairs, officially recognises six religions: Buddhism, Catholicism, Protestantism, Islam, Caodaism and Hoa Hao Buddhism.

Government and the Vatican: 1990–2015
The Vietnamese Catholic Church, differently from other religious organisations, suffered special legal restrictions, especially in the appointment of bishops, because of its institutional connections with what the VCP calls 'foreign elements' – that is, the Vatican State. However, since 1989, after the collapse of the Soviet Union, there has been a remarkable rapprochement between the Vatican and the Vietnamese government.

A turning point in the relationship between Vietnam and the Vatican occurred on 13 January 2011, when Archbishop Leopoldo Girelli was appointed Apostolic Nuncio to Singapore, Apostolic Delegate for Malaysia and for Brunei Darussalam, and non-residential papal representative for Vietnam. He was the first papal representative to be appointed for Vietnam since the expulsion of the resident apostolic delegate in 1975.

Another highly significant event was the government's permission given to the Federation of Asian Bishops' Conferences (FABC) to hold its tenth Plenary Assembly on 10–16 December 2012 in Vietnam, which drew 71 participants hailing from more than 20 Asian countries, Europe, Latin America and Oceania. On 15–20 September 2013, a seven-member delegation from the Vietnam Government Committee for Religious Affairs paid a working visit to the Vatican, during which they met with Pope Francis, to whom they presented a statue of Jesus as a gift. These official events signal a notable improvement in relations between the government of Vietnam on the one hand and the Vatican and the Vietnamese Catholic Church on the other.

Protestant Churches
In most Asian countries, Protestantism (in Vietnamese *Dao Tin Lanh*, 'The Good News Religion') is officially and legally treated as a distinct 'religion' from Catholicism. Introduced into Vietnam in 1911 by Robert A. Jaffray under the aegis of the Christian & Missionary Alliance (C&MA), Protestantism was organised in 1927 into a church known as the

Evangelical Church of Indochina, later changed to the Evangelical Church of Vietnam (ECVN). During the Vietnamese War of Independence (1945–54), the ECVN adopted a policy of neutrality, restricting itself to spiritual activities. After the 1954 Geneva accords, the ECVN was divided into two bodies, ECVN North and ECVN South, and about 1,000 members moved from the north to the south. Soon, and especially during the Vietnam War, other Protestant denominations and groups followed the C&MA, notably the Seventh-day Adventists (1929), the Mennonite Central Committee (1954), the Eastern Mennonite Board of Missions and Charities (1971), the Southern Baptists (1959) and the Assemblies of God (1972).

Despite (or, rather, because of) persecutions by the government, since 1975 the number of Vietnamese Protestants has grown from 160,000 to 1.6 million. The ECVN's missions were highly successful among the ethnic Vietnamese in the south, especially in My Tho and Can Tho, but less so in the north. Later, the church focused its work on the ethnic minorities in the Highland Mountainous Region in the north (notably among the Hmong) and in the Central Highlands in the south (notably among the Koho, Ede, Jarai, Bahnar, Stieng and Mnong). Even though the ethnic minorities make up only 13% of the Vietnamese population, they constitute more than half of Protestants in Vietnam.

A recent phenomenon deserving close attention is the emergence of the house-church movement. In the late 1980s some young ECVN pastors (notably Dinh Thien Tu, Vo Van Lac, Tran Mai and Tran Dinh Ai) were dissatisfied with the accommodating attitude of the church's senior leadership towards the government, and advocated instead for a confrontational approach. In addition, they favoured Pentecostal doctrines of the Holy Spirit and worship style, with emphasis on speaking in tongues and healing. They were subsequently expelled from the ECVN for insubordination. These pastors started the house-church movement, which spread like wildfire. By 2009, an estimated 250,000 Christians in at least 2,500 home-based groups belonged to house-church organisations. These range from single congregations to hundreds of congregations. Some of them have also tried to be connected to international denominations such as Assemblies of God, Nazarenes, Methodists, Mennonites and Presbyterians.

The spread of Protestantism among the tribal people and the rise of the house-church movement present great difficulties for the churches in relation to the government. For example, there was among the Central Highland tribes in the 1960s a liberation movement called FULRO (United Front for the Liberation of Oppressed Races). Most of its members were Protestants who were adamantly opposed to the communists. In 2001 and 2004 there were extensive demonstrations among the Central Highlands tribes against the confiscation of their lands and lack of religious freedom. These protesters, who called themselves 'Dega' (derived from the Ede-language phrase *anak ede gar*, meaning 'children of the mountains'), were accused by the government of working for the USA and were brutally crushed.

Another problem concerns 'registration'. In 2005, as mentioned above, the government issued the Decree of the Government Guiding the Implementation of the Ordinance on Belief and Religion, requiring that religious organisations 'register' for 'recognition' with the government to be allowed to function legally. The following month the prime minister issued Special Directive No. 1 Concerning the Protestant Religion, directing commune- and city-level authorities to expedite the registration of Protestant house churches. Some of these applied for registration and recognition. Two Protestant organisations, the ECVN North and the ECVN South, representing well over half of Vietnam's Protestants, already had full legal recognition, the former since 1950 and the latter since 2001. Only 160 ethnic congregations associated with the ECVN North, out of more than 1,000, received provisional recognition. In 2009, church leaders reported that not more than one-tenth of house churches' applications for recognition had been approved. Other house churches have refused to register, on the ground that such a process allows the government to control their religious activities. Obviously, the combination of the recent mushrooming of Protestant house churches without a central authority and the cumbersome process of registration conspire to make harmonious relations between Vietnamese Protestantism and the Vietnamese government nearly impossible.

Christianity's Contributions to Vietnam

Today, the Vietnamese Catholic Church has 26 dioceses that are grouped in three ecclesiastical provinces: Hanoi, Hue and Ho Chi Minh City (Saigon). Of the current population of nearly 100 million, some 6.8% are Catholics and somewhere between 0.5% and 2% are Protestants; there is one Russian Orthodox parish. Despite its minority status, Christianity has made great and lasting contributions to the country. Until 1975, in addition to several universities, the best high schools were Catholic, the majority of which were run by the Saint Jean-Baptiste de La Salle Brothers of the Christian Schools and were highly esteemed by non-Christians. (In 2016 the communist government permitted the opening of the first Catholic university since 1975.) The church also operated many hospitals, leprosaria and social service centres, especially through the work of religious sisters, notably the indigenous Congregation of the Lovers of the Holy Cross.

One of the most important and lasting cultural contributions made by the Catholic Church is the alphabetisation of the Vietnamese language, which is now the national script (*chu quoc ngu*). This has been accompanied by a large number of works in *chu nom* (southern script), especially by Gerolamo Maiorica, and the composition of dictionaries and grammars, notably those by Alexandre de Rhodes, Pierre Pigneaux de Béhaine and Jean-Louis Taberd. Catholics introduced new forms of literature (especially the poetry of Han Mac Tu), religious art, sacred music and songs, and architecture. Besides the Gothic cathedrals of Hanoi and Saigon, the most famous church is Phát Diệm Cathedral, built in 1892 by the Vietnamese priest Tran Luc (also called Cu Sau or Father Six), which combines Vietnamese traditional pagoda style with Gothic architecture and is described by the novelist Graham Greene as 'more Buddhist than Christian'.

The Catholic Church also played a significant role in politics, producing two presidents (Ngo Dinh Diem and Nguyen Van Thieu) and many political and military leaders. One religious leader deserving special mention is Archbishop Nguyen Van Thuan, who was the nephew of President Diem and was prevented by the communist government from assuming leadership of the Archdiocese of Saigon in 1975. He was put in prison and later under house arrest for more than a decade. Eventually released and exiled abroad, he went to Rome and was made a cardinal and president of the Pontifical Council of Justice and Peace. His case for sainthood has been initiated.

After the fall of South Vietnam, hundreds of thousands of Vietnamese Catholics migrated to the West, especially the USA, Canada and Australia. Currently there are three Vietnamese bishops, one in each of those three countries. The Vietnamese diaspora communities, while lively and influential abroad, with notable achievements in education, science, technology and commerce, continue to maintain close relations with the churches in Vietnam and contribute in many and diverse ways to its well-being and expansion.

As a whole, despite occasional conflicts between the communist government and some Catholic priests (especially in matters regarding the reclamation of church lands and properties) and violations of freedom of speech and religion (which involve not only Catholics and Protestants but also the followers of other religions and which have attracted international attention), it must be acknowledged that the churches, both Catholic and Protestant, do enjoy a measure of freedom of religion as long as they do not engage in public criticism of government policies. The threat to the well-being of Vietnamese Christianity arguably lies less in the restrictions imposed by the communist government than in the corrosion of faith by a new form of economic development fostered by globalisation.

As far as church worship is concerned, Masses are regularly celebrated on weekdays and Sundays and well attended, often with the congregation spilling into the churchyard, especially on Sundays and solemn liturgical feast days. Other sacramental celebrations, such as baptism, confirmation, penance (confession), marriage and ordination, are routinely carried out. Religious education of children is now permitted. Theological education not only of the clergy but also of religious sisters and the laity is also a regular feature. Priests and religious sisters can easily go abroad for higher degrees in all academic disciplines. Bishops can freely travel to Rome on official business with the Vatican. Even large-scale public celebrations, such as religious pilgrimage to the Shrine of Our Lady of Lavang, with hundreds of thousands of participants, are annual events. In sum, despite government restrictions, the Catholic Church in Vietnam is alive and well.

The Future of Vietnamese Christianity

Coexistence between Vietnamese Christianity and the communist regime since 1975 has more than proved that Vietnamese Christian churches have not been a threat to national security as the older political leaders had feared. A generation of new communist leaders have come to realise that the Christian churches have been and certainly can be a powerful and irreplaceable ally in the promotion of economic well-being and social justice for all. It is surprising to read the following statement from the Seventh Plenum of the Ninth Party Central Committee on Religion-Oriented Work (March 2003):

> Beliefs and religions are the spiritual demand of a part of the population, who have been and will be present with the nation in the course of building socialism in our country. Religious believers are a building block of national unity.

It is also encouraging that the same Plenum recognises that religions have a positive role to play in the life of the nation. According to it, one of the tasks of religion-related activities is

> to start a patriotic movement to build a lifestyle of 'good worldly and religious life' among their followers, clergy, and religious practitioners from the grassroots level and to build nationwide solidarity to successfully carry out the cause of renovation, national construction, and defence.

In the meantime, as long as Vietnam maintains a one-party political system, Christianity in Vietnam, both Catholic and Protestant, is challenged to find a peaceful *modus vivendi* with, and to carry out its mission under, a communist-socialist government. The first challenge concerns the relationship between Christianity and the state. Christianity was, and to a certain extent still is, perceived as a Western religion that has colluded with Western colonialism and is associated with foreign powers. The Catholic Church is seen as identical with the Vatican State (whose nature as a sovereign state distinct from the Holy See is recognised under international law), whereas the Protestant churches are perceived as being in collusion with the USA. No doubt the colonialist legacy remains a heavy and scandalous baggage for Vietnamese Christians, which they must honestly acknowledge, even if Christian missions historically have made and continue to make significant contributions to their countries, especially in the fields of education, health care and social welfare.

The second challenge to being Christian under a communist regime concerns religious freedom. Christians around the world continue to press their governments for it, since it is an inalienable human right and not a special favour to be secured through under-the-table deals, or through diplomatic negotiations between their governments and the Holy See in the case of Roman Catholics. Furthermore, this struggle for religious freedom is carried out on behalf of all believers and not just for Christians. It can also be pursued in concert with the followers of other religions, in particular Buddhists, as well as with non-believers, since they too suffer from lack of religious freedom.

The third challenge is internal, albeit originally caused by the communist government's religious policies, and that is the reconciliation of various groups and divisions in the church itself. These may take the form of patriotism – for example, the so-called *quoc doanh* (national enterprise) church – versus allegiance to a foreign power, or competition among different Christian denominations (Catholics versus Protestants), or theological differences (mainline Christianity versus Pentecostals/Charismatics). That these intra-ecclesial disputes have been exploited by various communist governments in their opposition to Christianity is plain and incontrovertible. Fortunately, in recent times, these divisions have been partially bridged through mutual recognition and collaboration, but much work remains to be done. Authentic and full Christian identity depends largely on the success of this ecumenical enterprise.

The fourth issue concerns the role of the Catholic, mainline Protestant and Evangelical/Pentecostal churches of the Vietnamese diaspora, especially in the USA, Canada and Australia. These Vietnamese Christian communities have greater material, academic and personnel resources at their disposal. What is being advocated here is not old-style financial support and control by mission boards (for Protestants) or the Congregation for the Propagation of the Faith, now known as the Congregation for the Evangelisation of Peoples (for Catholics). The Three-Self Movement, whatever the Communist Party's exploitation of it, must remain the norm for Vietnamese Christianity. Rather, what is being suggested is that the Christian churches that enjoy political freedom and economic prosperity have a particular responsibility to and solidarity with their counterparts in Vietnam, especially in matters of human rights.

The fifth challenge is the encounter with other religions. Though there has been a remarkable change in the position of the Roman Catholic Church towards non-Christian religions, at least since the Second Vatican Council, inter-religious dialogue, even among Vietnamese Catholics, is still in its infancy. Moreover, the attitude of Vietnamese Protestants towards other religions remains by and large condemnatory. An adequate theology of religions remains to be developed that acknowledges the positive role of non-Christian religions for the spiritual well-being of their adherents and Christians themselves, beyond the so-called exclusivist, inclusivist and pluralist paradigms made popular in recent decades. In Vietnam, being religious is being inter-religious, and Christian identity cannot be formed apart from a sincere and humble dialogue with the believers of other faiths and from the reality of multiple religious belonging. This dialogue is not only theological but must also involve sharing of life, collaboration for the common good and sharing of religious experiences.

The sixth, and perhaps the hardest, challenge to being Christian in communist countries today, Vietnam included, is, ironically, the rapid encroaching of the market economy and rampant materialism and consumerism, especially among the young. Communism as an ideology, though still spouted and propped up by the Communist Party, is fast becoming an empty shell, and party leaders are quite cognisant of this state of affairs and are busy preserving their interests in an eventual post-socialist state. Today, the greatest threat to Christianity in the Asian socialist countries is not (or no longer) the oppressive religious policies of the Communist Party, or the cultural 'dictatorship of relativism' for that matter. Rather, it is complete indifference to Christianity as well as to any other religious way of life, as the result of a relentless pursuit of wealth and all the pleasures it promises. Religious oppression produces faithful resistance, martyrdom seeds of conversion and relativism at least still takes religion into account by declaring that all religions are equally effective. The threat to Christianity now comes from the newfound faith in the unbounded and unparalleled power of capitalism, whose sole creed is 'greed is good', as the panacea for all ills, the faith that swallows up all other faiths.

Bibliography

Keith, Charles, *Catholic Vietnam: A Church from Empire to Nation* (Berkeley, CA: University of California Press, 2012).

Launay, Marcel, and Gérard Moussay (eds), *Les Missions Étrangères: Trois siècles et demi d'histore et d'aventures en Asie* (Paris: Éditions Perrin, 2008).

Nguyen, Minh Quang, *Religious Issues and Government Policies in Viet Nam* (Hanoi: Gioi Publishers, 2005).

Phan, Peter C., 'Christianity in Vietnam Today (1975–2013): Contemporary Challenges and Opportunities', *International Journal for the Study of the Christian Church,* 14:1 (2014), 3–21.

Taylor, Philip (ed.), *Modernity and Re-enchantment: Religion in Post-revolutionary Vietnam* (Singapore: Institute of Southeast Asian Studies, 2007).

Indonesia

Sulistyowati Irianto

This essay explores the place of Christianity within a Muslim-majority nation that is characterised by vast geographical, cultural and social diversity. The identity of the Christians always has to be considered in relation to multiple identities in terms of race, ethnicity, social class and gender. The Christian community forms a minority within a democratic society, but their presence recognised in the constitution. Yet today freedom of religion is in jeopardy in Indonesia, and at times Christians find themselves being targeted by hostile forces.

The Indonesian archipelago consists of more than 17,000 islands. The largest are Java, Sumatra, Kalimantan, Sulawesi and Papua. The most highly populated island is Java, on which the capital, Jakarta, and many other large cities are located. The country is home to around 272 million people, equivalent to 3.5% of the global population. Indonesia's population is predominantly Muslim, and it has the largest Muslim population in the world. Christianity is Indonesia's second-largest religion. Indonesia also has the second-largest Christian population in Southeast Asia, after the Philippines, as well as the largest Protestant population in the region. Around 33 million Christians live in the country, constituting some 10% of the population: 7% Protestant and 3% Catholic.

The population is characterised by vast diversity in race, ethnicity, religion and social class. Over the course of Indonesian history, racial, ethnic and especially religious conflicts have always had the potential for escalation. However, the state ideology, known as Pancasila, the 1945 constitution, the national motto, 'Bhineka Tunggal Ika' ('Unity in Diversity') and a strong civil society movement have fostered national unity.

Christianity in Indonesia is deeply rooted in history and culture. The faith is perceived and practised mostly in a local way, as the missionaries introduced Christianity through local language and tradition. Christians are found within different ethnic groups in different parts of the archipelago and, for the most part, Christianity has been welcomed in the daily life of the Indonesian people. However, at times Christians have been subject to discrimination, usually because political interests sought to position them as 'other' or 'subaltern' within a predominantly Muslim nation in order to exclude them from power and resources. However, the people who save and protect the Christians are usually their Muslim brothers and sisters.

Christians play an important role in all aspects of national life. They were involved in the fight for Indonesian independence and remain involved in defending the Pancasila philosophy against radicalism and intolerance. Christians are active as professionals in higher education, working as professors, scientists and researchers; as military generals or police officers; as medical doctors and other medical professionals; as entrepreneurs, consultants, accountants and owners of business enterprises; as lawyers and judges; as engineers and technicians; and as government ministers and leaders in the private sector. In short, Christians play important and significant roles in all aspects of Indonesian life.

Unity in Diversity

Indonesia's population consists of more than 300 ethnic and sub-ethnic groups, with 700 to 1,000 languages and dialects. Six religions are officially recognised: Islam, Protestantism, Catholicism, Hinduism, Buddhism and Confucianism. In addition, hundreds of local religious minority groups and beliefs struggle to gain recognition from the state, which they need in order to have access to official registration of births, marriages and property ownership and to be seen as an equal party in a court of law.

Before independence, the *Nusantara* (archipelago) was occupied by the Dutch for around 350 years and was known as the Netherlands East Indies. Christians played a full part in the struggle for independence, notably through the Youth Pledge and Women's Congress, both held in 1928 with the aim of uniting as one nation, one motherland and one language. In 1945 Indonesia was proclaimed a nation by Soekarno and Mohamad Hatta, who became respectively the first president and vice-president of independent Indonesia. Aware of the imperative to unite the

Christianity in Indonesia, 1970 and 2020

Tradition	1970 Population	%	2020 Population	%	Average annual growth rate (%), 1970–2020
Christians	11,233,000	9.8%	33,192,000	12.2%	2.2%
Anglicans	2,000	0.0%	4,200	0.0%	1.5%
Independents	2,192,000	1.9%	6,384,000	2.3%	2.2%
Orthodox	0	0.0%	3,000	0.0%	12.1%
Protestants	6,261,000	5.5%	20,200,000	7.4%	2.4%
Catholics	2,620,000	2.3%	8,100,000	3.0%	2.3%
Evangelicals	1,715,000	1.5%	9,414,000	3.5%	3.5%
Pentecostal/Charismatics	2,179,000	1.9%	11,000,000	4.0%	3.3%
Total population	**114,835,000**	**100.0%**	**272,223,000**	**100.0%**	**1.7%**

Source: Todd M. Johnson and Gina A. Zurlo (eds), *World Christian Database* (Leiden/Boston: Brill), accessed March 2018.

vast and diverse country, Soekarno launched the foundational concept, Pancasila, which was declared as the state ideology. He was inspired by local knowledge and philosophy, which are blended from indigenous Indonesian, Hindu, Western Christian and Islamic traditions. Pancasila consists of five pillars: belief in the one Supreme God, humanity, the unity of Indonesia, democracy and social justice. Pancasila was proclaimed as the highest Indonesian legal principle and the way of life for the Indonesian people.

The 1945 constitution provides for democracy and the rule of law, with freedom for each community to develop its own culture. It also provides that the country's rich natural resources be utilised for the welfare of the people. Concerning religious plurality, article 28 of the constitution grants freedom of religion for all Indonesian citizens. Article 27, very much related to article 28, grants equality before the law for Indonesian people. At independence, the state recognised five religions – Islam, Protestantism, Catholicism, Hinduism and Buddhism. Abdurrahman Wahid added Confucianism as a sixth official religion during his presidency (1999–2001). No formal recognition is given to some 200 local religions or beliefs, nor to the many different streams that are found within Islam and Christianity.

Though the constitution grants freedom of religion, other legal provisions seem to run counter to the constitution. One of these is Blasphemy Law no. 1/1965, article 1 of which prohibits the 'deviant interpretation' of religious teachings. This law is most often used to victimise people from religious minorities, although that was never the intention of its framers. The civil society movement took a case for the judicial review of this law to the Constitutional Court in 2010 and again in 2018 but their cases were rejected on both occasions. Some articles of the Penal Code, inherited from colonial period, also concern blasphemy. Article 156(a) makes it an offence to deliberately, in public, express feelings of hostility, hatred or contempt against religions with the purpose of preventing others from adhering to any religion and targets those who disgrace a religion. The penalty for violating this article is a maximum of five years' imprisonment.

Normatively, Indonesia has a set of legal references, a historical foundation and a national ideology sufficient to recognise and respect diversity and freedom of religion. These ideals and values are reflected in the Pancasila ideology, and further formulated as legal reference in the 1945 constitution. However, legal problems remain, as some legal instruments – ranked lower than the constitution – are not in line with the constitution.

There is always a gap between the normative system and its practices. In this regard, the use of the politics of identity to position Christians as 'other' or 'subaltern', with the aim of excluding them from fair competition and access to power, represents a particular concern. The 2015 presidential election and the Jakarta gubernatorial elections in 2012 and 2017 saw a fragmentation of society as competing political factions resorted to scapegoating tactics in order to gain an advantage.

Protestants

Indonesian Christianity is rooted in the local cultures of many ethnic groups. Because the ethnic groups are diverse, Indonesian Christianity is necessarily diverse. Each church has its own history and local context. Among the most prominent Protestant churches are the Javanese Christian Church, the Sundanese Christian Church, the Batak Christian Church, the Eastern Indonesian Protestant Christian Church and the Western Indonesian Protestant Christian Church – each of the latter three having many branches. Smaller churches also reflect their unique local situations.

To take one example, Protestant Christian churches have been growing rapidly in Batak Land. The Batak are one of the ethnic groups whose identity is closely bound up with Christianity; they include the sub-groups of Toba, Karo, Pakpak, Simalungun, Angkola and Mandailing. Christianity has been planted and has grown among these various groups. Originally from Batak Land, North Sumatra, the Batak have migrated to many regions in Indonesia. Different streams of Protestant Christianity are found in the Batak Land, including some who applied the names of their ethnic sub-groups to their churches (*huria* is the Batak word for church.) The churches that have emerged among the Batak include the Huria Kristen Batak Protestan (HKBP; Batak Protestant Christian Church), Gereja Kristen Protestan Indonesia (Indonesian Protestant Christian), Huria Kristen Indonesia (Indonesian Christian Church), Huria Kristen Indonesia Protestan (Indonesian Protestant Christian Church), Gereja Mission Batak (Mission Batak Church), Gereja Kristen Luther Indonesia (Luther Christian Indonesian Church), Gereja Punguan Kristen Batak (Christian Batak Clan Church), Gereja Protestan Persekutuan Batak Karo (Protestant Batak Karo Brotherhood Church), Gereja Kristen Protestan Simalungun (Protestant Christian Simalungun Church), Gereka Kristen Protestan Angkola (Protestant Christian Angkola) and Gereka Kristen Protestan Pakpak Dairi (Protestant Christian Pakpak Dairi Church).

The largest Protestant church among the Batak is the HKBP. When Batak people settle somewhere, their presence is usually marked by the establishment of an HKBP congregation. Counting the number of Batak people is usually done by tracing the number of HKBP members. The first famous HKBP church, established by migrant Bataks in Jakarta in 1926, is Kernolong Church. At that time, this HKBP congregation, located in Kernolong Street, was the only one in Jakarta. By 1965 the number had increased to 20 and by 1999 to 108.

The first contact of the Toba Batak with the outside world occurred in 1881, with the arrival of the German *Zending*, the Christian Institute of Barmen. Pioneering missionary Ludwig Ingwer Nommensen founded a church in Sait Ni Nuta village in Tarutung District. German missionaries established the first school for local people in a village, and then people from the neighbouring villages also came. A rising awareness among the Batak people that they needed education if they were to participate in the emerging modern economy meant the many schools established by the German *Zending* attracted high enrolments.

Around 1900, the Toba Batak began to migrate extensively to East Simalungun in search of a better life. Later they began to migrate to Medan – today the capital of North Sumatra – and to other regions in Indonesia, including Batavia (now Jakarta). During their migrations, they established many more Batak churches, mainly HKBP. Educated people were urgently needed by the German *Zending* to manage the bureaucracies of the church, as well as by the Dutch administration to function in the offices of the colonial government and of staff companies. In 1926 the *Zending* established Meer Uitgebreid Lager Onderwijs (Junior High School) in the city of Tarutung, North Tapanuli, which has since been known as the student city. Java also developed as a leading educational centre and many able students went to Batavia to continue their education. As a result, the Christian churches in Java grew in strength. The Batak are only one of the ethnic groups in Indonesia to have embraced Christianity and made it integral to their identity. Similar stories could be told of many others.

Catholics

The emergence of Catholicism in Indonesia can be divided into two periods, the Portuguese era and the Netherlands East India period. Catholic missions were embedded within the Portuguese colonisation of Asia. Their first connection was made in the Maluku (or Molucca) Islands, where the Portuguese were searching for herbs and spices. Maluku has been well known for herbs and spices, particularly nutmeg. The Catholic presence began in 1534 when Father Simon Vaz baptised the first convert from among the Moro people, inhabitants of Mamuya village, Halmahera, in Maluku. Other baptisms followed, and soon Halmahera could claim 3,000 baptised Catholics. This early development of the Catholic Church, however, was caught up in a conflict between Muslim forces and the Portuguese; Vaz lost his life and the Christian community was targeted. Eleven years later, the celebrated Jesuit missionary Francis Xavier visited Moro, after his stay in Ambon and Ternate.

In the next century, Portuguese power was weakened as it was replaced by the Dutch, represented by the Verenigde Oostindische Compagnie

(VOC; Association of Trading Companies), established in 1602. During the VOC period (1602–1800) Catholic missions were forbidden. The Catholic villages were destroyed and Catholics were subject to oppression. Only in the eastern part of Nusantara did some Catholic churches survive.

With the bankruptcy and demise of the VOC in 1800, power over the Nusantara archipelago was assumed by the Dutch government, at that time under the influence of France. As a result, Dutch Catholics were allowed to come to Nusantara, particularly to serve Catholics of Dutch and Portuguese descent in Batavia. In 1808 King Louis of Holland appointed Herman Willem Daendels as governor-general of the Dutch East Indies (1808–11) and ordered him to apply freedom of religion to all colonised areas. Thereafter Dutch Catholic missionaries arrived in growing numbers, both to minister to Catholics of European extraction and to bring missions to the indigenous people.

In the twentieth century, the Dutch government introduced a policy called the Politics of Ethics. The aim was to develop the indigenous people. One of its programmes was to relocate people from Java to the outer islands, in order to balance the population density throughout the archipelago. The Catholic Church became a partner of the government in this initiative and was able to greatly extend its missionary outreach throughout the country. This growth in Catholic missions was halted by the Japanese occupation of 1942–5, when many Catholic priests and leaders were arrested and charged with being Dutch spies. It was a difficult period for the Catholic Church, ending only with Indonesian independence in 1945.

Prior to the Second World War, Monsignor Petrus Willekens SJ was appointed Apostolic Vicar of Batavia (now Jakarta), the biggest city on Java. He was concerned about the political situation in Europe and the possibility that the Netherlands could be occupied by the Germans. He therefore took the initiative to separate Central Java, where the Catholics were mostly of an indigenous background, from Batavia, where the Catholics were mostly of European descent. The Catholic Church had been growing in Central Java, with indigenous Catholics starting to outnumber their European co-religionists. It was estimated that of the 60,000 Catholics in the Apostolic Vicariate of Batavia, some 40,000 were in Central Java. Growing Catholic communities could be found in Semarang, Yogyakarta and surrounding districts, some of them served by Javanese priests, products of the recently established seminaries. Willekens made the case for Central Java to become a separate province.

The vitality of Javanese Catholicism was particularly evident at St Yoseph Bintaran Church in Jakarta. The majority of its members were Javanese. Though the language used in the Mass was Latin, the homily was delivered in Javanese. Many spiritual songs, prayers and other texts from the Catholic tradition were translated into Javanese. The parochial leader, Father Albertus Soegijapranata SJ, a Javanese priest, was assisted by a Dutch priest, Father A. de Kuijper. This demonstrated that the church hierarchy was not based on race supremacy. The guiding philosophy was that the indigenous Catholic people would be better led by an indigenous priest, who could better understand the need of the folk. In addition, Soegijapranata was appointed as the chair of the Javanese journal *Swaratama*. Because *Swaratama* was concerned with public matters, Soegijapranata became heavily involved in societal issues. At the same time, he was appointed as supervisor of the Sarekat Jesuits, covering not only Central Java and Batavia but also Flores in East Nusa Tenggara.

On 26 June 1940 the Apostolic Vicariate of Semarang (Central Java) was separated from that of Batavia. Then, on 1 August, the Vatican sent a telegram appointing Soegijapranata Apostolic Vicar. He was consecrated on 6 November, the first indigenous bishop in Java and all of Indonesia.

The development of the Catholic Church in Central Java is well illustrated in the story of Monsignor Soegijapranata. Born into a Muslim family, he asked for baptism at age 13 from a Dutch priest, Father Mertens. The priest told him to get permission from his father first, but Soegijapranata refused, instead convincing the priest that his parents would accept his conversion. His parents' reaction to his baptism surprised him, as they accepted his conversion. So did his sister and brother. Both parents told him that, for a Javanese, all religions are good as long as they are well practised, with the aim of becoming a good person.

Some years later, when he told his parents that he was eager to become a Catholic priest, his mother responded by saying, 'The Javanese knows and is familiar with spiritual exercise. The Javanese is accustomed to be humble in life, practise fasting, control himself, practise meditation to understand himself, and always to be trying to be close to God.' In this respect, Javanese spirituality closely matches Catholic values. During his service to the Catholic people, Monsignor Soegijapranata was well known for his slogan '100% Catholic and 100% Indonesian'. Indonesian Catholics often repeat this slogan today. The Javanese, who form the majority of the Indonesian population, have always been known as a tolerant people. It is common to discover that in a Javanese family the members are affiliated to different religions.

Soegijapranata's ministry owes its origins to the work of Franciscus Georgius Josephus Van Lith (1863–1926), a Jesuit priest from the Netherlands, who paved the way for the emergence of Javanese Catholicism. He baptised the first Javanese Catholic in Sendangsono, Muntilan, Central Java. This place has been memorialised and is today a pilgrimage site for

Indonesian Catholics. Van Lith became well known as a priest with the capacity to harmonise Catholic teachings with Javanese tradition. Catholicism has come to be accepted by Javanese society. On his visit to Indonesia in 1989, Pope John Paul II gave a speech in Yogyakarta in which he said, 'Today, I am in the heart of Java Island to specifically memorise the ones who laid a foundation for Catholic people. Those are Romo (Father) Van Lith sj, and his two students: Monsignor Soegijapranata and I. J. Kasimo.'

Contemporary Pressures

Despite the growth of Indonesian Christianity and the diversity hailed as a social virtue, Christians can be the targets of discrimination and violence. Most often it is political elites who activate religious sentiment as a device to promote their interests. Appealing to religious prejudice is perceived to be the easiest way to win a political contest, rather than promoting concepts and programmes that appeal to voters. Firing up primordial sentiment is preferred to educating people politically, no matter what the risk, including the sacrifice of national cohesion. For the sake of gaining power, political elites are ready to stir up the politics of identity, differentiating between 'us' and 'them' and denying plurality and diversity, thus destroying tolerance, brotherhood and sisterhood within society.

In Indonesian history, those who are constructed as double or triple minorities, such as Christian Chinese women, are invariably the first to be victims of identity politics. Christians, women and people of Chinese ethnicity have been disproportionately represented among the victims whenever large-scale riots have broken out at times of high political tension. Groups perceived to be deviant sects of Islam, such as Ahmadiyya, Shia and Gafatar, and believers in traditional local religions have also been victimised on such occasions. According to a survey by the Wahid Institute in 2015, violations of freedom of religion during the year 2015 reached 190 events, with 249 acts – 20% higher than in 2014. The Institute also found that state actors, particularly from local government, were involved in most of the violations of religious freedom.

The worst human rights violations Christians suffer are the damaging and burning of places of worship/churches, lack of permission to construct church buildings and the forced closure of churches by radical Islamic groups. In the post-Suharto era, more than 1,000 churches have been burned. According to CNN Indonesia, when B. J. Habibie was president of Indonesia (1998–9), the number of cases was 162; under Wahid it was 360; under Megawati it was 160 and under Susilo Bambang Yudoyono it was 500. Churches were burned and destroyed also under Jokowi's administration, with the latest being bomb explosions in three churches in Surabaya, East Java, in 2018.

Another painful situation for Indonesian Christians is when a Christian governor becomes a victim of the Blasphemy Law. An Indonesian court found the Christian governor of the country's capital, Jakarta, guilty of blasphemy against Islam and sentenced him to two years in prison. The case is viewed by many as an unfair trial, as judges were under pressure from a hostile mob. The appeal of this case in the Supreme Court was also rejected by all three judges who handled the case. This case is widely seen as a test of religious tolerance and free speech. The governor, Basuki Tjahaja Purnama (known as Ahok), is not the only victim: there were 88 similar cases, with many other people being victimised in blasphemy cases and sent to jail. Ahok presented a threat to many political elites when he was in power as governor, as he had done much to revitalise Jakarta, mainly by promoting public services, building infrastructure, reforming governance and combating corruption. He lost an election when identity politics was deployed against him. However, he enjoys the support of many moderate Muslims.

An influential factor in Indonesia's chaotic situation is the interpretation of the first principle of Pancasila – *Ketuhanan yang Maha Esa* (belief in one God). This first principle aims to guarantee religious freedom and to accommodate the diverse religious identities of all Indonesians. However, recent interpretation has turned this into a homogeneous doctrine of One God that reflects only a majoritarian (Muslim) perspective. This interpretation is deeply embedded and institutionalised not only among people on the street, but also among government bureaucrats at many levels. Their perception is reflected in their policies and regulations.

Intolerance also affects women, including through the enforcement of regional regulations that place women in the domestic domain. These mainly involve a prohibition against going out at night and an obligation to wear 'proper' dress, which covers women's bodies. Komnas Perempuan in 2016 identified 421 regional regulations throughout the country with discriminatory implications for women. The creep of conservatism into legal institutions and practices could be also identified from some court processes and judicial decisions.

The growth of a culture of hatred and intolerance, loudly provoked by conservative groups in the name of majority religion through their massive activism, is now a well established phenomenon in Indonesia. State officials have played an important role in this, either by omitting to control it or by directly participating as actors in promoting it.

Daily Life of Indonesian Christians

Some observers suggest that a sectarian spirit began to grow in Indonesia during the Suharto era. The Suharto regime maintained its power by a strategy of 'divide and rule' between 'indigenous and non-indigenous' ('non-indigenous' referring primarily to Indonesian Chinese) and 'Muslim and non-Muslim' ('non-Muslim' referring primarily to Christians). This policy continues to have serious consequence for Christians, even though Suharto stepped down in 1998. It has provided a licence for Christians to be targeted, and they have occasionally been the victims of mass riots and bomb explosions, church closures, burning of churches and prohibition against building new churches when they are required to obtain the agreement of village members. They do not enjoy full religious freedom. For example, Christians often have difficulty finding houses to rent in the cities, as owners do not give permission for non-Muslims to stay on their land. Likewise, Christian students often meet with difficulty finding accommodation in a university city like Yogyakarta, simply because of their Christian identity. Christians in government service also suffer discrimination and are often denied promotions on account of their religious identity. It appears that a different standard is applied in their cases, and their performance has to be extraordinary before they can be promoted to a higher rank.

However, Christians remain hopeful that society can come together to build a better future for Indonesia. Christians maintain shared cultural values together with people from other religions, and these give a sense of being fellow members of a family, village and society at large. They look for brotherhood and sisterhood with people from other religions through many common activities. They share a strong sense of coming from the same ancestor, family or neighbourhood. They are united by shared values that teach them to respect one another. When Christians suffer, it is often Muslims who act to protect them and fight on their behalf.

During the twenty-first century, Catholics have developed places of pilgrimage in many locations throughout the country. Sendangsono in Central Java is prominent, but it is not the only one. Usually, such centres are located in remote areas and feature large statues of Jesus or Mother Mary set in beautiful parkland. Such is their popularity that they have a significant beneficial impact on the economy of the surrounding districts as pilgrims require food, souvenirs and other services. Both Catholics and non-Catholics benefit from the economic activity, and relations are harmonious.

The question of the interplay between Christianity and traditional beliefs has been a major point of interest for anthropology postgraduate students at leading universities in Indonesia, such as the University of Indonesia and Gadjah Mada University. Their research has focussed on the ethnic groups in Java and elsewhere in Indonesia who have become Christian but cannot live without their ancestral tradition. Traditional *adat* rituals are observed alongside church ceremonies in marking rites of passage, such as the birth of a child, marriage and funerals, as well as at significant points in the agricultural cycle, such as the planting of rice or the harvest. Christian rituals can be practised in a paddy field, on a beach or in any other public space while, at the same time, celebration of important events in the life cycle can be observed in the church.

Another phenomenon is the practice of syncretism, as seen for example in Kebatinan in Java, rooted in local ancestral religions with their beliefs about the relationship between humans and their God, humanity and nature, and human interrelations. They have adopted principles from the Christian, Muslim and Hindu religions, blending them together in a syncretistic way.

Hope for the Future

The emergence of Christianity in Indonesia cannot be separated from the historical and cultural context of the communities or societies. In contexts like Batak Land in North Sumatra or Central Java, the growth of Christianity is very much integrated with local culture. As a result, Christian faith emerges and grows in a highly diverse society. The principle of unity in diversity remains important to society as a whole, as well as to the government as mandated by the constitution. However, sometimes conflict occurs, usually triggered by the political interest of a certain group. When politicians play the religion card it is often a matter of targeting Christians, as they are perceived to be a minority group.

Though majoritarianism and intolerance are infectious and harmful to democracy and the rule of law, Indonesia has powerful forces to resist such developments and strength to survive them. The civil society movement remains a powerful force. Indonesian nationhood has been supported by powerful social movements, including the feminist movement. These have been evident at every stage of Indonesian history: pre-independence, the Soekarno era, the Suharto era and the recent post-Suharto era. At the beginning of the post-Suharto era, these movements played a significant part in formulating many legal instruments to defend human rights, including freedom of religion. They remain very active in advocacy and launch critiques of the government if there is any policy or action that endangers democracy or violates the rule of law.

Besides, brotherhood and sisterhood are deeply rooted in traditional Indonesian culture. It is common to find that a family or extended family consists of members from different religions. Christians join in the celebration of the Great Ramadan, while Muslims support their family member or neighbour who is celebrating Christmas. In some regions it is common that people work hand in hand to build places of worship, regardless of religion. They also collaborate in maintaining one another's daily livelihoods. In this context, it is not surprising that it is often Muslims, mainly from the moderate Nahdatul Ulama and Muhammadiyah, who guard their Christian neighbours, friends or community from attack by militant groups. Protection of Christianity comes from the Muslim community, within the idea of Unity in Diversity.

Bibliography

Aritonang, Jan Sihar, and Karel Steenbrink, *A History of Christianity in Indonesia* (Leiden: Brill, 2008).

Darmaputra, Eka, *Pergulatan Kehadiran Kristen di Indonesia* [*The Struggle of the Emergence of Christianity in Indonesia*] (Jakarta: BPK Gunung Mulia, 2001).

Farhadian, Charles E., *Christianity, Islam and Nationalism in Indonesia* (Oxford: Routledge, 2005).

Steenbrink, Karel, *Catholics in Independent Indonesia: 1945–2015* (Leiden: Brill, 2015).

van Klinken, Gerry, *Minorities, Modernity and the Emerging Nation: Christians in Indonesia. A Biographical Approach* (Leiden: KITLV Press, 2013).

Malaysia

Hwa Yung

The Malaysian church exists in a nation with a complex mix of ethnicities, languages and religions, and undergoing tremendous socio-political uncertainties today. Malaya, which is now West Malaysia, gained its independence from the British in 1957. Six years later, in 1963, Malaysia came into existence with the incorporation of the two East Malaysian states of Sabah and Sarawak, together with Singapore. However, in 1965 Singapore became a sovereign state of its own.

The population of Malaysia in 2017 was 32 million, broken down into the following ethnic percentages: Bumiputras ('sons of the soil', a term used for Malays and other indigenous peoples) 68.8%, Chinese 23.2%, Indians 7.0% and others 1.0%. Approximately 79% reside in West Malaysia and 21% in Sabah and Sarawak. The last full census, in 2010, recorded the religious breakdown of the country as Islam 61.3%, Buddhism 19.8%, Christianity 9.2%, Hinduism 6.3% and others 3.4%. However, the distribution of Christians is very uneven. In West Malaysia, Christians are a small minority of 3.1%, whereas in Sabah they are a substantial minority of 26.6% and in Sarawak a plurality of 42.6%. Indeed, 72.9% of all Christians are found in East Malaysia, especially among the non-Malay indigenous peoples. These non-Malay Bumiputras constitute a majority of all Christians (59.2%), with Chinese, Indians and others making up only 40.8%. Such a distribution makes for very different religious and social dynamics between East and West Malaysia.

Islam as practised in Malaysia follows the Shafi'i version of Sunni theology and jurisprudence, with all non-Sunni sects like Shiism proscribed. It was accorded a privileged position as the 'religion of the Federation' at the time of independence. Nevertheless, the constitution simultaneously also included clear safeguards for the religious freedom and citizenship rights of all non-Muslims. But, as shall be seen, over 60 years later this delicate balance is now in danger of being destroyed.

The Coming of Christianity

The earliest traces of Christianity in the country date back to the Nestorian presence on the Kedah coast in the seventh century. At the end of the fifteenth century, Christian Armenians were found in Malacca. But it was the Portuguese conquest of Malacca in 1511 that brought Roman Catholicism, and there remains a substantial group of Catholics of mixed Portuguese descent in the country. Protestantism came with the Dutch takeover of Malacca in 1641. The oldest functioning Catholic and Protestant churches in the country are St Peter's Church and Christ Church, built in Malacca in 1710 and 1753, respectively.

The real expansion of the church began only in the late eighteenth century. French Catholic missionaries first came in 1781, to Kedah and Penang. The Anglican presence dates from Francis Light's establishment of Penang as a British colony in 1786, although the first priest arrived only in 1815. Others followed in the nineteenth century in West Malaysia, including the Presbyterians in 1815, Christian Brethren in 1860 and Methodists in 1885. In East Malaysia, James Brooke, a British soldier and adventurer, was made the White Rajah of Sarawak in 1841 and the first Anglican priest arrived in 1848. Catholic missions began when Don Carlos Cuarteron was sent as the Prefect Apostolic to Labuan and Borneo in 1857. But Cuarteron's ministry was less than successful, and a fresh start was made in 1881 through the British Mill Hill Fathers. From the end of the nineteenth century, other missions also began work in the country.

Christianity did not come only through Western missionaries. It also came through migrations of Christians from China and India, many of whom came to meet labour needs in the developing colonies. During the British colonial era, many Tamils from India and Sri Lanka were brought to West Malaysia to work in the plantations, railways and various colonial administrative services. Many of these were Christians. Among Chinese migrants who came in organised groups, the most notable were the Hakkas, who went to Sabah under the Basel Mission beginning in 1882, and the Methodist Foochows, who went to Sarawak in 1900 under the leadership of Wong Nai Siong. Another Methodist Foochow group came

Christianity in Malaysia, 1970 and 2020

Tradition	1970 Population	%	2020 Population	%	Average annual growth rate (%), 1970–2020
Christians	571,000	5.3%	2,991,000	9.1%	3.4%
Anglicans	69,600	0.6%	280,000	0.9%	2.8%
Independents	24,100	0.2%	236,000	0.7%	4.7%
Orthodox	3,700	0.0%	4,500	0.0%	0.4%
Protestants	157,000	1.5%	900,000	2.7%	3.6%
Catholics	301,000	2.8%	1,500,000	4.6%	3.3%
Evangelicals	126,000	1.2%	630,000	1.9%	3.3%
Pentecostal/Charismatics	34,600	0.3%	640,000	1.9%	6.0%
Total population	**10,804,000**	**100.0%**	**32,869,000**	**100.0%**	**2.3%**

Source: Todd M. Johnson and Gina A. Zurlo (eds), *World Christian Database* (Leiden/Boston: Brill), accessed March 2018.

to Sitiawan in 1903. In the past few decades, several million legal and illegal migrants have entered the country to meet the need for workers in plantations, factories, the building industry and the like. These have included many Christians from Indonesia and Myanmar.

Growth since the Second World War

The church grew from 3.0% of the population in 1947 to 9.2% in 2010. The growth was much faster in Sabah and Sarawak than in West Malaysia but has weakened over the last two decades. In West Malaysia, the growth has been steady but slow, increasing from 2.1% of the population in 1947 to 3.1% in 2010. In the 1950s and 1960s, increased Catholic and Protestant missionary efforts in the New Villages and elsewhere, partly through Western missionaries relocated from China after 1949, spurred much growth. Mission schools certainly helped. But in the last few decades the growth has been largely in urban centres, while numbers in small towns and rural areas have stagnated or declined due to urban migration.

From the 1970s onwards, the Charismatic movement has impacted the church significantly. On the Catholic side, it began in 1973 with Sister Cyril, then Principal of Taiping Convent, who experienced 'being filled with the Spirit' while on leave in Ireland. With the bishops' permission, a series of conferences followed that touched many in the church. Though the impact has tapered off somewhat, there remain 11 Catholic Charismatic Covenant Communities throughout the country; the largest, in Kota Kinabalu, has more than 400 members. On the Protestant side, the renewal was driven by visiting speakers, especially from the USA, the UK and India, and through the Full Gospel Business Men's Fellowship. Pentecostal churches, like the Assemblies of God, and independent Charismatic churches, such as the Full Gospel Assembly, grew rapidly until the late 1990s. However, for Protestants the renewal has brought mixed blessings due to the proliferation of prosperity teaching and a lack of accountability in some churches.

Churches in West Malaysia have also made serious attempts to reach the non-Malay indigenous peoples, the Orang Asli, who live mainly in the jungle or on its fringes. Of some 850 villages, more than 250 have been reached. In East Malaysia, the rapid growth of the church was largely the result of mass conversions among the non-Malay indigenous peoples, who were originally ethno-religionists.

In Sabah, Christians were 8.7% of the population in 1951 and continued to grow fairly rapidly in number until the late 1960s. But Mustapha Harun, state chief minister from 1967 to 1975, soon after coming to power initiated an Islamisation policy that put intense pressure on the church. All foreign missionaries were expelled in 1970 or shortly thereafter. The Anglican Church, for example, was left with four clergy for the whole state, an area the size of Scotland. The then Catholic bishop, Peter Chung, although a citizen, was not permitted to reside in Sabah but had to serve his diocese using three-month visitors' passes. Available statistics indicate a slackening in growth in the 1970s, but Christians still reached 27.2% of the population in Sabah in 1980 nonetheless. However, from 1980 onwards growth effectively plateaued, with the proportion of the Sabah population recorded as Christian being 27.8% in 2000 and then declining to 26.6% in 2010. It has been suggested that this dramatic halt to growth was engineered by the government in response to developments in Sabah politics, where a Christian-majority party was in power from 1985 to 1994. Migrations of Muslims from the southern Philippines and Indonesian Borneo were apparently encouraged so as to dilute Christian numbers in the state. Despite all attempts to get to the truth of the matter, no satisfactory answer has ever emerged.

Similarly, in Sarawak all churches grew rapidly after the end of the Second World War. Furthermore, the Charismatic renewal from the 1970s onwards impacted many churches, including the Catholics. This brought a new vibrancy, especially among the indigenous communities. In one Catholic church in Bintulu, for example, from 1992 to 2000 the indigenous Iban congregation grew from 500 worshippers to 4,000 using Iban and another 1,000 using Malay every Sunday. At Christmas, that church's carolling teams visited several thousand homes over two weeks. All that the priest did was to introduce 'Life in the Spirit' seminars, small groups for all members, compulsory catechism classes for adults and children, and family life teachings.

Probably the most exciting story belongs to the Borneo Evangelical Church, or Sidang Injil Borneo (SIB). Australian missionaries of the Borneo Evangelical Mission (BEM) began work in 1928. A breakthrough was soon achieved among the Lun Bawang people, who had been left to die out by the colonial administration because of their social problems. This was followed by a series of revivals in 1952–4, again in 1971–6, and yet again in 1984–5. In every case, the Lun Bawang people were directly involved, although other people groups, like the Kelabits, were also included in some years. Some documented reports from the last two revivals read like the apostolic accounts of signs and wonders in Acts. All these contributed to the rapid and steady expansion of the Sarawak church from 7.9% of the population in 1947 to 42.6% in 2010.

The Churches Today

The Catholic Church in Malaysia is divided into three archdioceses and six dioceses, with one archdiocese and two dioceses in each of West Malaysia, Sabah and Sarawak. About a quarter of the members are in West Malaysia, with the rest distributed over Sabah and Sarawak. The three archbishops and six bishops together constitute the Catholic Bishops' Conference. However, each bishop functions autonomously and is answerable directly to Rome. There are also 30 religious orders serving in the area. In 2013, the Vatican and Malaysia officially agreed to establish diplomatic relations. The Apostolic Nuncio, Archbishop Joseph S. Marino, was officially appointed on 16 January 2013.

In West Malaysia, Catholics used to be primarily Indians, Chinese and Eurasians, but, increasingly, large numbers of Bumiputras from East Malaysia are now included. In Sabah and Sarawak, non-Malay Bumiputras are the majority, followed by the Chinese. The Catholics have two major seminaries. Pride of place must go to College General, which began life in 1665 in Siam (Thailand) but moved several times before settling in Penang in 1809. It was the regional Catholic seminary for Southeast Asia until 1983, but now trains only Malaysians. The other is St Peter's College in Kuching. All ordinands today attend both seminaries consecutively.

After the Catholics, the three largest churches are the Methodist, the Anglican and the BEM/SIB churches. The Methodists are made up of seven conferences: the four in West Malaysia are set up along linguistic lines, Chinese, English, Tamil and Sengoi (Orang Asli); the two in Sarawak are Chinese- and Iban-speaking; and the seventh is in Sabah. Their churches are largely located in the urban areas and small towns, except for the Iban and Sengoi churches, which are predominantly rural.

The Anglicans have three dioceses in West Malaysia, Sabah and Sarawak. Together with Singapore, they form the Province of South East Asia. Numerically, the Anglicans are strongest in Sarawak, followed by Sabah, and are largely rural in both. Generally speaking, Sarawak tends to be more high church, and West Malaysia and Sabah low church.

There are three autonomous BEM/SIB churches that work closely together in Sabah, Sarawak and West Malaysia. Their members are largely indigenous Bumiputras from Sabah and Sarawak, but there is a substantial Chinese presence in the urban centres. They are much stronger in East Malaysia and largely rural, although many of their members are now urbanised. In West Malaysia, they are found mainly in cities where their members have migrated for jobs.

Of the others, the Seventh-day Adventists are found largely in Sabah and Sarawak, while the Basel Christian Church (Lutheran) is primarily in Sabah. The Assemblies of God are much stronger in West Malaysia, where they have some large urban churches, each with several thousand members. Except for the Protestant Church of Sabah (Lutheran), which is rural-based, the rest of the smaller denominations and independent churches are largely urban. The latter include better-known groups such as

Baptists, Presbyterians and Christian Brethren, as well as others of Asian origins, like the historic Syrian Orthodox Church and Mar Thoma Church from India and the True Jesus Church and Assembly Hall Churches (Watchman Nee) from China.

In general, all churches are short of workers. For example, the BEM/SIB in Sarawak has more than 700 churches but little more than 400 pastors. Many local theological schools have been established to meet the training needs of the churches. About 10 of these are accredited to offer up to the master's degree, with three offering doctoral studies and a host of others offering various lower-level programmes. The two oldest seminaries are the Malaysia Baptist Theological Seminary in Penang and the Methodist Theological School in Sibu, both founded in 1954. Other more-established ones include the Bible College of Malaysia in Petaling Jaya, Sabah Theological College in Ranau, Malaysia Evangelical College in both Lawas and Miri, Malaysia Bible Seminary near Rawang, Malaysia Theological Seminary in Seremban and Sabah Theological Seminary in Kota Kinabalu, the last three run ecumenically.

Most churches in the country are linked organisationally. The Catholic Church is overseen by the Catholic Bishops' Conference (CBC). Non-Catholics are affiliated with the Council of Churches of Malaysia (CCM) or the National Evangelical Christian Fellowship (NECF). The older denominations, including Anglicans, Lutherans, Methodists, Presbyterians, the Syrian Orthodox Church, the Mar Thoma Church and the Salvation Army, all come under CCM. The Pentecostal Charismatic and overtly Evangelical groups, including the Assemblies of God and BEM/SIB churches, mostly affiliate with NECF, although some churches are with neither.

Presently, the heads of the CBC, CCM and NECF are respectively the Catholic Archbishop Julian Leow of Kuala Lumpur, the Methodist Bishop Ong Hwai Teik, and independent church pastor the Reverend Eu Hong Seng. In order to relate to the government with a united Christian voice, the Christian Federation of Malaysia (CFM) was formed in 1985, with all three groups as equal partners. The CFM chair is rotated among them and is currently held by Archbishop Julian Leow. The CFM is also a member of the Malaysian Consultative Council on Buddhism, Christianity, Hinduism, Sikhism and Taoism (MCCBCHST), which serves as the public voice of all non-Muslim religious communities in the country.

Given the distinctive needs of East Malaysia, the Sabah Council of Churches (SCC) and the Association of Churches in Sarawak (ACS) were formed to bring together and represent the majority of the churches in the respective states. However, recently the Sarawak Association of Evangelical Churches was formed because many churches in the state, but outside the ACS, felt that their concerns were not represented.

Overall, these structures have worked well to strengthen fraternal relations within and beyond the church. However, at the denominational level, churches tend to run their own programmes separately. Nevertheless, at the ground level there is plenty of grassroots ecumenism at work. Examples of this include inter-denominational student outreaches, joint representation by mission school authorities to the government, Christmas city parades in East Malaysia and inter-denominational prayer networks.

Identity, Theology and Social Engagement

Malaysian Christianity has some distinctive characteristics. The first is its multilingual and multi-ethnic complexities. To begin with, both the Chinese and Indian congregations were originally migrant churches. Sometimes these find their primary Christian identity in race and language, whether Chinese or Tamil, rather than in their denominational distinctions. This is particularly true with Chinese-speaking churches that have strong links with similar churches around the world. On the other hand, many urban churches are English-speaking and rather Western-oriented in ethos and practice. In some of these may be found the latest Western worship fashions and theological trends.

Furthermore, in West Malaysia there are 19 indigenous Orang Asli groups. In East Malaysia there are between 50 and 100 different tribal groups and languages, depending on how these are classified. Many churches among the indigenous peoples use Malay, the national language. But others prefer to worship in their mother tongue, such as the Ibans in Sarawak and the Kadazans and Rungus in Sabah. In urban churches, especially those in West Malaysia, Chinese, English and Tamil are also widely used. Thus, many churches regularly run separate services in two or more languages. All these combine to make the quest for a common Malaysian Christian identity rather elusive.

A second distinction concerns theological orientation. For Catholics, the Second Vatican Council certainly brought fresh challenges, particularly the call for *Aggiornamento* or renewal. In West Malaysia, for example, the whole church experimented with a 'priestless month' in August 1976, with all bishops and priests going on retreat for a whole month. *Aggiornamento* also led to a call for the formation of Christ-centred Basic Ecclesial Communities throughout the church, an increased role for the laity, a greater openness to other Christians and peoples of other faiths, as well as a strong commitment to justice issues, among other things. This also coincided with the coming of the Charismatic renewal in the church, and thus reinforced it. Despite more radical external influences like Latin American liberation theology, the church has remained essentially theologically mainstream.

On the Protestant side, things were less sedate. The years after the Second World War saw the heyday of liberal theology in the West, with all mainline denominations influenced by missionaries of that mindset. On the other hand, there were also Christian leaders, schooled in the earlier fundamentalism, who were both anti-intellectual in temper and discouraging of anything that smacked of the Social Gospel. Yet today, by and large, the leadership in mainline denominations is firmly Evangelical in theology. Similarly, those in the Evangelical and Pentecostal Charismatic churches, with some exceptions, are increasingly open to Christian sociopolitical engagement. Credit for the shift away from the liberal theological influence in the 1950s and 1960s must go to Evangelical mission societies such as OMF International and the Church Missionary Society, as well as to the student movements, including Scripture Union, Campus Crusade and the International Fellowship of Evangelical Students. The Lausanne Movement also helped steer Evangelicals away from their earlier neglect of social engagement. Moreover, over the past few decades, Christians have had to wrestle increasingly with national issues such as poor governance, corruption and restrictions on religious freedom, thus becoming much more socially conscious in the process.

The other major theological issue was the Pentecostal Charismatic renewal. Many in the church had some prior experience with deliverance and healing ministries. But when the renewal first came, in the 1970s, with its overwhelming emphasis on the baptism of the Holy Spirit and tongues, it was met with resistance from large segments of the church. That phase is now largely over. Although there remains a minority holding on to anti-supernatural or cessationist teachings, most churches display varying degrees of openness to the renewing work of the Holy Spirit. Within the Protestant churches, the bigger problem is that many are caught up with the Prosperity Gospel on the one hand and a preoccupation with the miraculous without proper biblical and theological grounding on the other. These, coupled with strong personalities in leadership and weak accountability structures, have spawned multitudes of independent churches around the country. At the same time, few with genuinely powerful gifts of healing, prophecy and godly leadership have emerged.

The third distinctive characteristic of Malaysian Christianity concerns the question of social engagement and nation-building. The churches' record here is rather uneven. In some areas like mission schools, it was brilliant. There are still 448 mission schools in the country. All or most existed at the time of independence, when few good schools were available, with students welcomed irrespective of race or religion. In some of these, very high standards were attained. For example, from the 1950s to the 1970s the four best mission schools in Penang regularly sent students on scholarships to leading US universities like Harvard, Yale, MIT and Wellesley College. But by the late 1960s the schools had been absorbed into the government school system, with churches no longer allowed control. Educational standards have since declined. Recently, the churches have begun asking the government to return some of the schools in order to run them privately.

The churches are also strong on social ministries. Earlier, various mission hospitals and clinics were established, but most of these have been closed with the introduction of a national health service. The few remaining hospitals, including Adventist in Penang and Assunta in Petaling Jaya, are now completely commercialised. Catholics also have various social service ministries under the diocesan human development offices or commissions, Catholic Welfare Services and Society of St Vincent de Paul. They also run senior citizen homes, Montfort training centres for youths, children's hostels and the like. Other denominations also have significant social outreach programmes, such as the St Nicolas Home for the Blind, Salvation Army homes and Malaysian Care. Various churches operate some 40 drug rehabilitation centres, which have high success rates.

The churches' attitude towards social advocacy and political involvement has been rather more ambiguous. There have been and still are both Catholics and Protestants who have risen to high political office. But it is uncertain whether they have been able to bring into their politics a clear Christian social vision. However, there are exceptions. One notable figure was the late Tan Chee Khoon, who was the parliamentary opposition leader from 1964 to 1978 and later was honoured by the government for that role. Moreover, in recent years there have been changes, with many younger Christians with firmer Christian convictions moving into electoral politics. A good example is Baru Bian, a one-time opposition leader in Sarawak but now a minister in the federal cabinet, who has been noted for fighting land rights cases for the rural poor. Christians are also increasingly involved in social advocacy. One outstanding example is the late Irene Fernandez, who founded Tenaganita, an organisation dedicated to helping and 'protecting migrants, refugees, women and children from exploitation, discrimination, slavery and human trafficking'. In 1995, she courageously wrote a piece exposing the mistreatment and abuse of migrants in government detention centres. For that, she was charged by the authorities with spreading false news and shamefully dragged through the courts for 13 years before being finally acquitted.

Living in an Islamic Milieu

The greatest challenge to the Malaysian church today is that of living within a Muslim-majority society. The worldwide resurgence of Islam in the last 50 years has led to an Islamisation agenda that increasingly denies public space and religious freedom to both Muslims and non-Muslims in the country. What happened in Sabah from 1967 to 1975 intensified throughout the nation from the late 1970s. First, it came by way of inconveniences like difficulties in getting land for non-Muslim religious buildings and burial grounds, or visa restrictions on non-Muslim religious workers. But soon more restrictive measures followed that caused non-Muslims to feel increasingly a deep sense of injustice and marginalisation. These feelings were partially expressed in a strong protest note, dated 6 August 2007, sent to the Parliamentary Select Committee on National Unity by the MCCBCHST, representing all non-Muslim communities. It drew attention to

> the personal tragedies of ordinary Malaysians suffering anguish as a result, in one way or another, of the misuse of religion, e.g. persons who are treated as 'Muslims' against their will, some who are being detained for 'rehabilitation' merely because they want the government to recognise their choice of religion and women (and men) who are faced with the loss of their children merely because of the religious conversion by their spouses ... The rule of law appears to be set aside in Malaysia. Our Courts seem powerless to protect non-Muslim rights as we saw in the still unresolved cases of Everest Moorthy, Shamala and now recently Subashini. In Terengganu, the State authorities demolished the Sky Kingdom even though there was a Court order telling them to hold on. Islamic authorities continue to convert non-Muslim students in institutions of higher learning. Prison authorities allow prisoners to be converted to Islam despite prohibitions in the Lock Up Rules against this. Under-aged children still disappear, leaving their parents distraught, only to emerge days after their 18th birthday converted to Islam. Local authorities all over the country continue to act with disregard for the sensitivities of non-Muslims in dealing with their places of worship.

The focus of concern was the increasing marginalisation in the name of Islamisation of the rule of law and constitutional safeguards of citizenship rights.

How did the country get itself into this legal mess? Article 11 of the constitution states that 'Every person has the right to profess and practice his religion'. Further, article 8 affirms the equality of all before the law and prohibits any legal discrimination based on religion, race or descent. These were the constitutional safeguards enshrined at the time of independence from Britain in 1957. Although Islam was given a privileged position as the 'religion of the Federation' (article 4), all the literature of the period clearly affirmed that the state is secular and the constitution supreme. But in 1988 a constitutional amendment of article 121 created a fundamental change by stating that civil courts 'shall have no jurisdiction in respect of any matter within the jurisdiction of the [sharia] courts', without clearly demarcating the boundary between the two. This not only elevated the sharia courts into a parallel system of equal standing with the civil courts but also allows the former to trump the latter by ignoring their rulings whenever conflicting judgements arise. The agenda to subsume civil law under the sharia was slowly but surely being advanced.

On the other hand, the government is worried by another concern, that of Muslims leaving their faith. Despite contrary arguments, most conservative Muslims take the view that there should be no apostasy in Islam. In Malaysia, this was the implicit view taken at the Treaty of Pangkor, signed in 1874 between the Perak Sultan and the British colonial government. It gave the British power to administer the state in all matters except those 'touching Malay Religion and Custom'. This suited the British nicely because they were primarily concerned with their political and economic interests, and not religion. This became the model for all subsequent dealings of the British with other Malay rulers. Consequently, the British discouraged, though they did not forbid, all missionary efforts to the Malays. This also explains why, although the constitution provides for freedom of religion, most states have laws that severely penalise conversion out of Islam and any such efforts directed at Muslims.

In recent years, other restrictions have been directed at the church, in particular through executive fiat. In 1981, the government banned the production and public circulation of the Malay Bible, on the grounds that it is 'prejudicial to the national interest and security', although a year later this was relaxed, with Christians and the church specifically exempted from the ruling. In 1986, Christians were told that they are not permitted to use certain words in the Malay language, to avoid confusing Muslims about their faith. This applies especially to the word 'Allah', which had been used for 'God' in Arabic centuries before the advent of Islam. Notwithstanding that this has become almost a joke among other Muslims worldwide, the government continues to enforce the ban. To outsiders these rulings seem strange and irrational to say the least, especially when the Malay Bible can be downloaded in minutes from the internet nowadays. But underlying these rulings is the great fear that the Malays, who are Muslims by definition in the constitution, will change their religious affiliation and thereby undermine their community's political power in the country.

This is the situation in which the churches find themselves today. How are they to respond? To begin with, Christians are clearly concerned about the restriction of religious freedom for non-Muslims in the country. Historically, every church that has lived under majority Islamic rule has wilted, and many have died – a trend repeated in the fate of many Christian communities throughout the Middle East and North Africa today. The only reversals were those that came through military or colonial interventions, clearly not options for the Malaysian church today. It should be noted that many Muslims in the country are also not happy with the way that Islamisation is moving. They do not subscribe to the ultra-conservative and bureaucratic versions of Islam driving the present agenda. How this will pan out is far from clear.

Secondly, because of the fear of conversion, certain groups have increasingly attacked the church with charges of trying to 'Christianise' the country. Moreover, over the past three decades, the governing coalition, previously in power but now in opposition since the 2018 general election, often played the religious card to garner votes in elections. It is true that some Muslims have attempted to exit Islam for other faiths. But most Christians are not involved in evangelising Muslims, if only because they are intimidated by the law. Yet charges of 'Christianisation' persist, with one state mufti claiming in 2006 that there is a group of 100,000 Muslim converts led by a woman religious teacher, though no evidence was produced. Nevertheless, these two issues have left many Christians rather anxious about their future in Malaysia. One unfortunate consequence is that large numbers of Christians, including many in leadership, have chosen to emigrate.

The Church at a Crossroads

To sum up, the Malaysian church is alive and well, despite being deeply troubled by the challenges it faces. There are many positives. Over the past century, it has come a long way and now even sends 500 or more long-term missionaries abroad. Despite the external pressures, there is much inner vitality and sustained growth. Despite natural fissiparous tendencies within, serious efforts are being made to enhance Christian unity at different levels. Despite the manifest weaknesses of the church, we see new life birthed everywhere through renewed spiritual life and prayer. But doubts persist about its future. Given the continuing pressure of Islamisation, what future does the church have in Malaysia? Will it weaken and die a slow death like many others under Islam in history? Or will it be revitalised and become a powerful source of blessing to the nation and all its peoples?

Bibliography

Chew, Maureen K. C., *The Journey of the Catholic Church in Malaysia, 1511–1996* (Kuala Lumpur: Catholic Research Centre, 2000).
International Panel of Parliamentarians for Freedom of Religion or Belief, 'Country Briefing

on Freedom of Religion or Belief in the Universal Periodic Review Process – Malaysia', 8 October 2017, at <http://ippforb.com/wp-content/uploads/2017/10/FORB-Malaysia.pdf> (accessed 6 December 2017).

Rowan, Peter, *Proclaiming the Peacemaker: The Malaysian Church as an Agent of Reconciliation in a Multicultural Society* (Oxford: Regnum, 2012).

Roxborogh, John, *A History of Christianity in Malaysia* (Singapore: Armour, 2014).

Tan, Jin Huat, *Planting an Indigenous Church: The Case of the Borneo Evangelical Mission* (Oxford: Regnum, 2011).

Singapore

Violet James

Singapore is a small island at the tip of West Malaysia, surrounded by larger islands of Indonesia and the Philippines. It has four main ethnic groups – Chinese, Malay, Indian and 'other' (CMIO); four official languages – Bahasa Melayu (the national language), English (the working language), Chinese and Tamil; and four main religions – Buddhism (and Chinese religions), Islam, Christianity and Hinduism. Chinese comprise 77% of the population, Malays 14%, Indians 7.6% and others 1.4%.

The coming of the Roman Catholic and Protestant missions coincided with the arrival of Sir Stamford Raffles and the beginning of British colonialism. Singapore at the time was only a fishing village with a few hundred indigenous Malay families who exercised loose control over the island. Very soon, Chinese and Indian migrants began to enter the island to find their fortunes and then return to their homelands. Eventually, many remained and became a vital part of the political, economic and social fabric of the community. Today, the Chinese provide the economic backbone of the country.

How did this small, obscure island become a major hub of Christianity? Why was it that the late Billy Graham, who visited Singapore in 1978, referred to its church as the 'Antioch of Asia'? He was comparing Singapore today to the first-century church in Antioch (Acts 11: 19–21). That city was strategically located and was a political and economic hub for Asia. The city and the church were multiracial and multicultural, exercising wide international influence.

It was the foresight of Raffles, who saw Singapore's potential, and the colonisation of the British that transformed the fishing village into a modern city with a free port. Unlike other colonial officials, Raffles allowed missionaries to enter and propagate the Christian faith. His vision was realised when, within two centuries, not only has this island become a thriving cosmopolitan, global city but also Christianity has become the fastest-growing religion.

The early forms of Christianity were transplanted from Britain. Western denominations like the Anglican, Methodist, Brethren and Presbyterian churches came in the nineteenth century. The Baptists, Lutherans, Assemblies of God, Church of Christ, Bible-Presbyterian Church and Salvation

Army entered Singapore in the twentieth century. The traditional churches associated with missionaries have metamorphosed into something quite different in recent decades. While the former denominations are growing, the phenomenal growth in the twenty-first century is seen in the rise of independent mega-churches.

People, Events and Trends

One of the most significant persons involved in shaping Singapore and unifying the indigenous Malay together with the Chinese and Indian migrants was the founding father and first prime minister, Lee Kuan Yew. He was a great visionary and pragmatic leader. With a team of talented leaders, Lee united the three main ethnic groups and laid the foundation for the nation's political and economic infrastructure. Singapore was granted self-governance by the British in 1959 and joined the Federation of Malaysia in 1963. But the many disagreements between Singapore and the federal government, and the fear that the Chinese community might dominate the scene if the merger were continued, led the Malaysian prime minister, Tungku Abdul Rahman, to expel Singapore from the Federation in 1965. Lee was devastated. How could this tiny island survive without any natural resources? However, by 1966 Lee believed Singapore would survive, and he was able to successfully build a nation of diverse cultures, religions and languages. He governed Singapore for more than 30 years. Even at his death in 2015 he continued to unite Singaporeans, as thousands of Chinese, Malay, Indian and other nationalities grieved his loss, out of love and respect for this stalwart 'Father of Singapore'. His son, Lee Hsien Loong, assumed the office of prime minister in 2004, and continues in his father's footsteps by leading with a sense of clarity, mission and purpose.

Christianity in Singapore, 1970 and 2020

Tradition	1970 Population	%	2020 Population	%	Average annual growth rate (%), 1970–2020
Christians	162,000	7.8%	1,205,000	20.3%	4.1%
Anglicans	10,000	0.5%	70,000	1.2%	4.0%
Independents	14,800	0.7%	200,000	3.4%	5.3%
Orthodox	800	0.0%	2,700	0.0%	2.5%
Protestants	35,200	1.7%	180,000	3.0%	3.3%
Catholics	80,000	3.9%	270,000	4.5%	2.5%
Evangelicals	31,100	1.5%	250,000	4.2%	4.3%
Pentecostal/Charismatics	9,900	0.5%	280,000	4.7%	6.9%
Total population	**2,072,000**	**100.0%**	**5,935,000**	**100.0%**	**2.1%**

Source: Todd M. Johnson and Gina A. Zurlo (eds), *World Christian Database* (Leiden/Boston: Brill), accessed March 2018.

Church life in Singapore has also featured outstanding leaders. Some of the most influential leaders today are pastors from the mega-churches, like Joseph Prince of New Creation, Lawrence Khong of Faith Community Baptist Church (FCBC) and Kong Hee of City Harvest. From the traditional denominations Bishop Emeritus Robert Solomon of the Methodist Church and the Reverend Edmund Chan from Covenant Evangelical Free Church (CEFC) are greatly respected.

In 1983 Joseph Prince started New Creation with only a handful of young people. This has grown to over 30,000 and is currently the largest church in Singapore. His famous message on the 'non-judgemental gospel of grace' and on 'God's blessings poured out on all believers' has spread globally, through books and a television programme aired in 150 nations.

Lawrence Khong started FCBC in 1986, as a splinter from Grace Baptist Church. Today this church has around 10,000 members. Khong became the trailblazer as he introduced entertainment into Christian ministry in order to transform communities throughout Asia. He himself is an illusionist. He uses magic, music, drama and dance to share the gospel with non-English-speaking heart-landers, who formerly had rejected Christianity as a Western religion.

In 1989, Kong Hee started City Harvest with 20 young people. By 2007 it numbered 17,000 and it reached 30,000 in 2010. Kong might have learned the secret of church growth from the Reverend Cho Yonggi, the founder of the world's biggest church (in South Korea), as the latter mentored Kong at the start of his pastoral ministry.

Christian leaders attribute the significant growth of these churches to membership transfer from other churches rather than to first-time conversions. However, these charismatic pastors have denied such allegations, affirming that many of the young people who have come to their churches are first-timers who were baptised in their premises.

Mega-churches have several similarities. Their leaders are young, with a charismatic-style of leadership, bold in venturing into initiatives such as the performing arts and entertainment industry. Their members are young, often under 30 years. Many of them are from less privileged, non-English-speaking families who live in public housing managed by the government at reduced cost. This is in marked contrast to members from the Anglican and Methodist churches, who are English-speaking, from the middle and upper classes, and live primarily on landed property or in condominiums. Worship services in the mega-churches are designed like rock concerts, with state-of-the-art acoustics and lighting, attractive back-up singers and skilled musicians, all of which appeal to the younger generation, especially those who are not churched. The theology of these churches seems to orientate towards a 'prosperity' gospel that resonates with the working class and the lower-income groups, many of whom are ambitious to climb the social and economic ladder.

A vital part of their mission is community service. FCBC started Touch Community Service in 1992 and has more than 17 centres that offer a wide spectrum of social services, encompassing children to senior adults. New Creation raised S$2 million to build a kidney dialysis centre to demonstrate God's love to the less fortunate in Singapore. City Harvest distributes S$2 million every year to more than 4,000 needy people through its community services.

As noted above, two other significant voices from the Evangelical denominations are the Edmund Chan and Robert Solomon. The name Edmund Chan is almost synonymous with 'disciple-making churches'. As a pastor of CEFC, Chan has invested his entire life in making CEFC a model for disciple-making and also empowering other churches to do the same. In 2001 he launched the Intentional Disciple-making Church (IDMC) Conference and in 2008 he launched the Global Alliance of Intentional Disciple-making Churches. The former is an annual event at CEFC, and over the years it has drawn thousands of pastors and leaders from hundreds of churches and delegates from more than 20 countries. Chan defines intentional disciple-making as 'the process of bringing people into a right relationship with God and developing them to full maturity in Christ through intentional growth strategies that they might multiply the process in others also'. Solomon was principal of Trinity Theological College, bishop of the Methodist Church for three terms from 2000–12 and president of the National Council of Churches of Singapore. Both these men are popular conference speakers, emphasising the need for discipleship in the marketplace as well as in the church.

LoveSingapore first started as a prayer meeting in 1995, through the initiative of Lawrence Khong of FCBC. The goal was to unite the Protestant churches in order to serve the community and to proclaim the gospel to the unreached. At one such prayer summit, Khong publicly confessed his own sins and sought reconciliation with the pastors who were in attendance. He also desired God's peace and reconciliation for his fellow pastors and church leaders who were present. From 90 leaders in 1996, the numbers grew to almost 700 leaders from more than 100 churches and 37 organisations. In 2015, Singapore celebrated its golden jubilee. Under the leadership of LoveSingapore, a Global Day of Prayer was organised, where 50,000 Christians from various denominations gathered to give thanks to God for Singapore. The guest of honour was the prime minister, Lee Hsien Loong, who thanked the Protestant Church for its contribution to 'nation building' through education and 'building trust and mutual confidence with other religious groups' to establish harmony and mutual respect. The audience sang the Aaronic Blessing (Numbers 6: 22–3), and the prime minister was deeply moved.

During the same period, the Roman Catholic Church, under the leadership of the Archbishop of Singapore, William Goh, together with 10,000 communicants, invited prime minister Lee to attend a thanksgiving Mass as part of the golden jubilee celebration. Lee praised and appreciated the Church for serving society and strengthening racial and religious harmony by 'living your faith through your deeds'.

Christianity, Politics and Religious Harmony
Christianity grew rapidly during the 1980s and 1990s. From 10.1% of the population in 1980 to 12.5% in 1990, the number of Christians increased as a result of intentional and proactive evangelism by the churches. In 2015, as the number of Christians grew to 18.8%, the percentage of Buddhists dropped from 42.5% in 2000 to 31.1% in 2015, and that of Muslims dropped from 14.9% to 14.0% in the same period.

In order to keep the peace among the ethnic and religious groups, the government made it clear that it will take serious measures against any one race that is subversive or intolerant of other religions and races. Evangelism of the unreached has been challenged by laws that have been passed to keep religious harmony among the different ethnic groups. Despite the many challenges, the church has grown significantly over the last 50 years. Besides this aggressive evangelisation in the 1980s, the fear of resentment among other religions and the presence of some social activism forced the government to take stronger measures to prevent possible racial and religious conflicts. In 1987, several leaders, including the then prime minister, Lee Kuan Yew, warned the people not to use their religion as a platform for political gains. Lee 'condemned insensitive evangelisation' as threats to racial harmony and even threatened 'detention without trial for religious extremists'. That same year, Roman Catholic social activists were accused and detained for using the church as a cover for alleged 'Marxist' activities. These fears and concerns resulted in a White Paper on Religious Harmony in 1990, which birthed the Maintenance of Religious Harmony Act (MRHA) in 1992. After 25 years, the government continues to affirm the MRHA as the means of maintaining religious harmony among all the races and religions in order that no one race or religion exploit another. The government intends to use the MRHA to keep in check any apparent subversive tendencies. In 2017, two foreign Christian preachers were banned from entering Singapore because of comments made about other religions that were 'denigrating and inflammatory'. The MRHA aims to keep the state and church separate, based on the assumption that politics and religion do not mix.

Evangelism, Spirituality and Other Faiths

Christianity has flourished in postcolonial Singapore, with conversions primarily among young, affluent and English-educated Singaporean Chinese, as well as a small proportion of Indians. Between 1980 and 2000, the Christian proportion of the population increased by 2.5 percentage points, and in 2010 Christianity became the fastest-growing religion. These conversions were mainly among the affluent, university graduates and professionals. This profile changed with the emergence of the mega-churches, generally attended by younger people from the lower to middle classes, who spoke English and already identified themselves as Christians. Did the 'prosperity' message have anything to do with this increase? One mega-church member teaches that 'the more you give, the more you will get'. Such teaching resonates with the 'millennials' who view investments in the marketplace in the same way as investing in God's kingdom.

Many of the contemporary converts come from Chinese ancestor-worship and animistic backgrounds ('Shenists'). Their understanding of spirituality is often mixed with their former worldviews. The idea of prosperity is evidenced in the Chinese religious worldview, which is 'this-worldly'. Prosperity, longevity and good health are what Chinese religious practitioners embrace. The right kind of food, proper breathing and exercise, the balance of the yin–yang idea, indeed everything in life is somehow linked to the external force. This external force or 'chi' must be harnessed and brought into alignment with one's own chi in order to establish good health, prosperity and harmony. Everything one lives for is found in this life, and one considers the afterlife only when death is imminent. The concept of eternity is alien to their worldview, as what is truly important is the here and now. Physical exercise, diet and whatever prolongs one's life must be embraced. A faith that promotes prosperity, long life, good health, happiness and the absence of suffering is very attractive. As the younger generation find the 'prosperity' gospel appealing, another interesting phenomenon is the conversion of elderly Chinese parents and grandparents of first- or second-generation Christians during times of crisis such as sickness and terminal illness. Such conversions have occurred on their deathbeds because of hope in miracles or greater awareness of their own mortality.

A number of people from Hindu backgrounds have been baptised into the Christian faith. Yet many of these converts merely add Christianity to their inherited Hindu beliefs, resulting in a kind of syncretistic belief and practice. There are many Hindus who in desperation might pray to Jesus because they know that the name of Jesus is powerful. Yet they will remain Hindus because they cannot denounce their deities. The Hindus are tolerant of all religions until they are forced to give exclusive allegiance to Christ. These Hindus, while rejecting the Christian faith, are comfortable in attending Roman Catholic services, where they can retain elements of their Hindu faith and still enjoy the benefits that the church promises to its worshippers. The Church of Saint Alphonsus, better known as Novena Church, attracts Hindus, Buddhists and others.

A more recent phenomenon is the number of people who claim to have no religion and some who profess to be humanists. In the 2010 census, 17% declared that they had no religion. Five years later, that proportion had increased to 18.5%. Sixty-five per cent of those with no religion are aged 15–44, and many of them believe that reason alone is sufficient to determine right from wrong. In July 2011, the local paper, the *Straits Times*, featured an article in which several Singaporeans of various ages shared their humanistic approach to life. In 2008 the Humanist Society was founded with 10 members. By 2010, there were 100 registered members.

The Buddhists, Hindus and Muslims are becoming more intentional in making their faith attractive to young people. The Buddhists have started their own rock band. They also chant Pali scriptures in modern rap style. The Muslims have interactive sessions of Islamic classes in English to boost Quranic literacy skills, build character and foster love for God. The Hindu youth have Saturday workshops and 'Sunday schools' in the temples.

Many Evangelical pastors are equally concerned that despite the growth of the church, many of their members are not rooted in the fundamentals of the Christian faith. These pastors are making genuine efforts to disciple their congregations as they impart biblical theology, teach the cost of discipleship and show them how to live this earthly life with eternal perspectives. Many of these pastors and ministry leaders have attended the IDMC conducted by Edmund Chan and read his books, like *Built to Last* and *Cultivating Your Inner Life,* and also books written by Robert Solomon, such as *Apprenticed to Jesus*. They also seek help from the Singapore Navigators to guide their churches into becoming disciple-making churches. The goal for every believer is to grow in faith and accomplish the Great Commission of Jesus Christ and 'win the world for Christ'.

Contemporary Church Growth

In 2017, of the 5.61 million people in the country, 3.41 million were Singaporeans (this includes permanent residents) and 1.67 million were non-residents. It is estimated that by 2030, Singaporeans will make up 55% of the population, while non-residents will constitute 45%. Many of the migrants are packing the churches today, in both the Roman Catholic and the Protestant denominations. The majority of the Catholics are Chinese and Eurasians, with a minority from Filipino, Indonesian, Indian and European backgrounds. The Archdiocese of Singapore comprises

31 parishes spread throughout the country's five districts, which come directly under the authority of the Roman See. The current Archbishop, Monsignor William Goh, wants the church to be more missionary and evangelistic and to find effective ways to do social mission to help the poor and the marginalised.

But the fastest-growing churches today are those led by charismatic pastors from the independent mega-churches, which entered the scene in the 1980s. Today, they have overtaken the traditional Protestant denominations that were birthed by missionaries in the nineteenth and twentieth centuries. They are called 'mega' because they have more than 2,000 members, their income and staff strength are large, they have multiple programmes, and they and their leaders are known internationally. Currently, there are 19 churches that are considered 'mega'; the top five are New Creation, City Harvest, Lighthouse, Faith Community Baptist and Victory Family Centre. Three other denominational churches – Trinity Christian Centre, St Andrew's Cathedral and Wesley Methodist Church – also have large congregations. St Andrew's Cathedral is the seat of the Anglican Diocese of Singapore, established in 1870, which oversees 27 local parishes and six deaneries: Cambodia, Indonesia, Laos, Nepal, Thailand and South Vietnam. In the 1950s the Singapore Welfare Council was established to provide comprehensive welfare services. It was renamed Singapore Anglican Community Services in 2006 and operates a wide range of centres, from mental health facilities to centres for seniors and families. In 1996 the Diocese of Singapore joined with the Dioceses of West Malaysia, Kuching and Sabah to form the Province of Southeast Asia, a historic moment, when authority was transferred from the Archbishop of Canterbury to the Archbishop of Southeast Asia.

New Creation had more than 30,000 members in 2012. In that year it collected S$75.5 million in tithes alone. In 2010 it raised S$21 million in one day for the purchase of Star Performing Arts Centre. New Creation occupies levels 3–11 of the building and its full cost of $500 million was paid in 2016. It has a 5,000-seat auditorium, which is one of four venues where their services are held.

City Harvest had a membership of 20,000 in 2009. That same year it collected an offering of S$38.6 million. In 2012, it bought a S$97.8 million space at the Suntec City Singapore Exhibition Centre, with a 39.2% stake in that building. Between 2007 and 2010 about S$23 million of church funds was used to finance the singing career of Kong Hee's wife, Yeow Sun. The goal of this Crossover Project was to reach out to Chinese youth in Asia through the use of Mandarin pop music, which was very popular at the time. Eventually this project was aborted as it was not altogether successful. Kong and five other leaders were charged with criminal breach of trust, falsifying accounts for the Crossover Project and using church funds for personal gains. All six of them were given jail sentences. This has indirectly contributed to a decline in City Harvest's membership.

While the mega-churches are growing exponentially, the smaller churches often feel disadvantaged. They meet in rented premises, as they are financially unable to purchase their own buildings. Some of them believe that the only way to grow in number is to mimic the mega-churches, with their external paraphernalia such as state-of-the-art acoustics, singers of the Hillsong kind and stage presence, believing that these contribute to the success and growth of mega-churches. (Hillsong is the largest mega-church in Sydney, Australia. Its music pastors, Geoff Bullock and Darlene Zschech, have written worship songs that have revolutionised their church's music ministry and have also been well received internationally, not least in Singapore.)

In order to fully equip the church through the proper teaching of sound doctrine, two theological seminaries were established to train pastors for the mainline denominations and the Brethren and other inter-denominational and independent churches. Trinity Theological College (TTC) was established in 1948 to serve the traditional historic denominations such as the Anglican, Lutheran, Methodist and Presbyterian churches. The Singapore Bible College (SBC) was established in 1952 to meet the challenges of the Chinese-speaking churches and confront theological liberalism, which was creeping into the churches. Many Chinese churches had a shortage of pastors, as their pastors who had come from China were returning home due to a change of government and the uncertainties that the future held for them. They were looking for Bible-based preachers to equip the congregations but were not comfortable with the graduates from TTC, as some of their foreign lecturers were influenced by liberal theologies and questioned the infallibility of the Bible. It was in this context that SBC was established to meet the urgent needs of the Chinese churches. In October 2018, TTC will celebrate its seventieth anniversary. It has a strong faculty that is Bible-believing and mission-oriented, a far cry from what it was in the formative years. Since 2014, TTC – in partnership with the National Council of Churches and the Bible Society of Singapore – has provided theological education to the laity through the Ethos Institute for Public Christianity, which assists the community to approach societal issues from a theological perspective. In 2017 TTC was invited to teach modules in a local university at the master's level.

SBC celebrated its sixty-fifth anniversary in August 2017 and continues to be church-oriented, Bible-based, mission-minded and context-relevant, integrating theory and practice and theology and spirituality. It is currently considering implementing a 'smarter classroom' in which classes at SBC can have simultaneous teaching connections with alumni and church leaders in other countries in institutions that have similar facilities. This means that on a given day, a professor can be teaching a class at SBC and at the same time be connected with students in another country, have professor–student interactions and also be able to see what is written on white boards on either side of the globe. SBC continues to do theology biblically and contextually to meet the challenges of a new post-millennial generation. These institutions are of strategic importance as they engage with church and society and train both Singaporeans and other Asians in Southeast Asia and beyond.

Denominations such as the Assemblies of God, the Bible Presbyterians, the Baptists and the mega-churches have established their own colleges to train their members for the ministry. Because of the many choices of seminaries today, the number of Singaporean students at TTC and SBC has dropped significantly, and this has warranted administrators to look beyond Singapore to recruit students. Today there are many students from 'Creative Access Nations' (CANs) who are studying in Singapore. The term CANs refers to countries that are 'closed' to any form of evangelism and missionary activities and whose governments do not grant missionary visas of any kind. The majority of these countries are either communist or Islamic. Missionaries have found creative means to enter these countries, through their professional skills. Thus, the term CANs was born. It is from these countries that many students are now coming to Singapore to get an education, in both the secular and the sacred realms. Both TTC and SBC are focusing on master's degree training, while some of the denominational colleges have diploma and bachelor's degree programmes to cater to those without tertiary education. The challenge of the seminaries is to integrate theory and practice, impart a comprehensive understanding of God's truth and be able to engage with a world that is rapidly changing. When they succeed, they enable Christians in the pews to navigate their faith in the marketplace, to be salt and light so that they will be able to fulfil God's mission for the church and the world.

Challenges in Society

There are internal and external challenges that have implications for the state and the church. The arrival of new migrants has brought more diversity into society. Today, there are more than 150 ethnic groups in the country, including professional foreign talent, middle-tiered skilled workers in the service industries and technicians, blue-collar workers at construction sites and domestic helpers. Many of these migrant workers live in communities and ghettos that Singaporeans frown upon and sometimes even consider as threats in their otherwise peaceful environment.

The Malays who are indigenous to the island are somewhat alienated because of their Islamic faith. At times, because of a common faith, they are wrongly associated with the fanatical fringe that has contributed to terrorist activities. The fact that the Islamic State of Iraq and Syria (ISIS) has become a major threat internationally, including to member states of the Association of South-east Asian Nations (ASEAN), and the belief that Malays are automatically Muslims make the latter a potential threat to non-Muslims. In general, the other races and religious groups appear to be paranoid about and suspicious of the Muslims. After the events of 11 September 2001, more attempts have been made at inter-faith dialogues to promote better understanding of and greater appreciation for other faiths, including Islam. The government is more vigilant about terrorism in this region. In 2001, 15 people were arrested, 13 of whom were members of a terrorist group, Jemaa Islamiyah (JI). In the following year, another 21 people were arrested, and 19 were members of JI. Ministers are currently preparing the various religious and public institutions, and the general public, to take necessary steps to protect themselves with the watchword SGSecure. The public is repeatedly warned to be on the alert and be prepared, as these terrorist attacks will certainly happen.

There are also some exclusive identities, such as lesbian, gay, bisexual, transgender (LGBT), that are becoming more pronounced and could cause schism and fragmentation in society. The Pink Dot Movement is a yearly event that attracts tens of thousands and promotes LGBT as an alternative lifestyle with an intention to change the attitude of society and to repeal Penal Code 377A, which forbids same-sex marriage. Lawrence Khong of FCBC speaks against the LGBT agenda, as both spokesman for his own church and also for the church generally in Singapore. Khong believes that the movement has violated God's design for marriage and family and must return to the authority of God's Word and be realigned with God's design.

In 1997, 10 gay Christians met together to pray and study the Bible. Out of this group the Free Community Church (FCC) was born. The FCC welcomes lesbians, gays, bisexuals and others, stressing that the church is both free and inclusive. Their leaders believe that Jesus commanded members of the church to love one another; that everyone, regardless of their orientation, is made in the image of God, and that homophobia is inconsistent with the teachings of the Bible. The late bishop of the Methodist Church, the Reverend Yap Kim Hao, served as advisory pastor of FCC for many years, believing that God had called him to serve the marginalised community.

Although Christianity is growing rapidly, the 2010 census shows that many young people are neither religious nor committed to any religion. Several Evangelical churches are struggling to sustain their youth and young adult ministries because of the many challenges faced by them. Many young Christians are not attending Bible colleges nor are they entering the mission fields. This lack of commitment could be because they are first-generation believers whose parents object to their becoming pastors or missionaries. But not many Christian parents encourage their children to enter full-time ministries, as such ministries are neither lucrative nor something they could boast about to their friends and relatives. In some cases, there seems to be an erroneous belief that people who join Christian ministries have no other option, as they do not have the relevant qualifications to enter the professional sectors.

Prospects

Singapore's demography, identity and landscape have changed over the past 20 years. The four racial groups in Singapore in the past were clearly demarcated as CMIO. With intermarriages between these races and across other nationalities, there are greater varieties and distinctiveness. Singapore has metamorphosed into a new complex mix of numerous national, linguistic, social and religious peoples. As a multicultural, multilingual and multi-religious community, this small nation is surrounded by a crescent of countries that are pursuing an Islamic identity. This location presents both a challenge, with the risk of increasing extremism, and an opportunity, in terms of Christian presence and witness.

Singapore can indeed become an 'Antioch of Asia' because of its multicultural, multiracial character and its strategic positioning in Asia. The church is also becoming more multicultural as migrants enter the country at multiple levels, from the professional white-collar elite to the blue-collar construction workers. Many churches are working among these migrants as they see the mission on their doorstep. Local Christians are taking the lead in pastoral ministries and planting churches and sending missionaries to other parts of Asia and the world. The 'Lion City' has a strategic role to play in Christian mission in Asia and beyond. Its effectiveness in doing so will depend on how far its churches can promote true discipleship among their members, and can become authentic Christian communities where children, youth, young adults and seniors can pursue intimacy with God and reach out to a world that is greatly in need of the churches' reconciling, healing and saving message.

Bibliography

Chong, Terence, and Yew-Foong Hui, *Different Under God: A Survey of Church-Going Protestants in Singapore* (Singapore: Institute of Southeast Asian Studies, 2013).

Lim, Isaac (ed.), *The Christian Church in 21st Century Singapore* (Singapore: National Council of Churches, 2000).

Poon, Michael Nai-Chiu (ed.), *Engaging Society: The Christian in Tomorrow's Singapore* (Singapore: Trinity Theological College, 2013).

Sng, Bobby E. K., *In His Good Time: The Story of the Church in Singapore, 1819–2000* (Singapore: Graduates Christian Fellowship, 2003).

Turnbull, C. M., *A History of Singapore, 1819–1975* (Singapore: Oxford University Press, 1977).

Brunei

Francis D. Alvarez SJ and Kenneth R. Ross

The sultanate of Brunei is located in the north of the island of Borneo and is divided into two separate areas by the Limbang corridor, part of the Malaysian state of Sarawak. Both parts have a coastline on the South China Sea and otherwise are completely surrounded by Sarawak. The unusual geography is explained by history: in earlier centuries the authority of the Sultan of Brunei extended over a much wider area, which shrank to its current proportions during the colonial era, becoming a British protectorate in 1888. When the Federation of Malaysia was formed in 1963, Brunei was the only state that voted to remain under British rule. It was only in 1984 that it became independent from Britain. The same family has been in power for more than six centuries. The current ruler, Hassanal Bolkiah, was crowned sultan in 1968 and became prime minister at the time of independence. He is an absolute monarch and no criticism of the government is permitted. In 1991 he introduced the ideology of Malay Muslim Monarchy, under which the monarch is regarded as defender of the faith. One of the world's wealthiest individuals, he remains the dominant figure in national life.

Brunei continues to have much in common with Malaysia, including the fact that the majority of the population are Malay in ethnicity and Muslim in religion. In terms of both size – 5,765 square kilometres – and population – well under half a million – it is one of the smallest countries in Southeast Asia. However, in terms of per capita income it is among the most prosperous, largely thanks to rapid economic growth during the 1990s and early 2000s as Brunei began to exploit its extensive oil and gas reserves. No personal income tax is levied from its citizens, but it is able to provide a high level of public services, including education and health care that are free at the point of delivery. Its prosperous economy has attracted many migrant workers, who account for most of the Christian presence in this strongly Islamic country.

Sunni Islam has long been the faith of the (predominantly Malay) majority of the population, with significant minorities of (mainly Chinese) Buddhists and Christians from a variety of backgrounds. Although there is freedom of religion to the extent that individuals are free to practise any faith in private, Brunei is officially an Islamic state and Islam shapes its public life. This feature was strengthened in 2014 when Brunei adopted sharia law, despite protests from the international community and human rights organisations. A ban on the public celebration of Christmas was a further indication of the direction being taken.

Even before 2014, Christians were lamenting restrictions imposed on any public display of their faith. Foreigners have been deported for taking part in worship activities in parks and on beaches. Even gatherings and celebrations in private residences, when attended by more than a handful of Christians, have caused problems. A statue of Mary donated in 1999 by the then first lady of the Philippines, Luisa Ejercito-Estrada, and installed in front of the Church of Our Lady of the Assumption, the main church in the capital city Bandar Seri Begawan, had to be re-oriented to face the building, which also serves as the unofficial chancery and cathedral of the Catholics in Brunei. A semi-circular wall also had to be erected to cover the image because the parents of Muslim students attending the church-operated St George's School complained about it.

Anyone converting from Islam to another religion faces severe penalties: the death sentence or a prison term of up to 30 years. Additionally, intense social pressures discourage any Muslim in Brunei from considering a change of religious identity. On the other hand, when people convert to Islam, they are featured on the front pages of the newspapers and are given a cash reward.

The Christian Presence

Christians in Brunei therefore face considerable restrictions. They are forbidden to proselytise or to import Bibles and Christian literature. Churches are required to register with the government. The construction of new church buildings is strictly limited. Marriages between Christians

Christianity in Brunei, 1970 and 2020

Tradition	1970 Population	%	2020 Population	%	Average annual growth rate (%), 1970–2020
Christians	7,300	5.6%	52,000	11.7%	4.0%
Anglicans	4,000	3.1%	3,700	0.8%	−0.2%
Independents	1,900	1.5%	17,500	3.9%	4.5%
Protestants	1,200	0.9%	9,400	2.1%	4.3%
Catholics	100	0.1%	20,000	4.5%	11.2%
Evangelicals	1,900	1.5%	10,200	2.3%	3.4%
Pentecostal/Charismatics	1,000	0.8%	16,000	3.6%	5.7%
Total population	**130,000**	**100.0%**	**445,000**	**100.0%**	**2.5%**

Source: Todd M. Johnson and Gina A. Zurlo (eds), *World Christian Database* (Leiden/Boston: Brill), accessed March 2018.

and Muslims are prohibited. The centrality of Islam to mainstream society means that Christianity remains a marginal presence, despite its significant number of adherents. Christians are found mainly among the Chinese population, the indigenous peoples and the migrant workers.

Most Christians in Brunei belong to the Roman Catholic Church, which has three parishes operating under the Apostolic Vicariate of Brunei Darussalam. Since 2005 Cornelius Sim has been Bishop and Apostolic Vicar of Brunei. The diocese is very small, with just three priests serving under the bishop. The clergy estimate that some 70% of the faithful are Filipino migrant workers, with some 20% coming from other Asian countries such as India, Indonesia and Malaysia, and just 10% being indigenous Bruneians. At the Church of Our Lady of the Assumption, between 5,000 and 6,000 congregants attend Mass each Sunday. Almost every day, prayer groups comprising different ethnicities – Tamils, Malays, Chinese and Filipinos – also meet at the Church of our Lady of the Assumption. A holy hour designated for Eucharistic adoration is also well attended. In 2018 a localisation policy was introduced by the government, leading to fewer work permits for migrant workers and a resultant reduction in the number of participants in church life.

The large Filipino contingent brings vitality and a strong tradition of piety. Though restrained out of regard for the Islamic context, Filipinos are still able to celebrate the *Misa de Gallo*, the traditional nine dawn Masses leading up to Christmas. After these Masses, Filipinos sell traditional Christmas food outside the church. Lately, they have been joined by Malay and Chinese Catholics who bring their own delicacies and make the early-morning gatherings more festive. Processions, of which Filipinos are particularly fond, are also held – but within the church compound and sometimes in the grounds of the nearby St George's School at times when there are no classes. Restrictions imposed on the practice of their faith have made the Catholics more community-oriented. In the Philippines, baptisms are focused on the family, with only close relatives and a few friends invited. In Brunei, they have become occasions for communal thanksgiving and celebration.

The minority Protestant presence includes the Borneo Evangelical Church, the Anglican Church (Diocese of Kuching), the Methodist Church, the Seventh-day Adventist Church and the Korean churches. St Andrew's Anglican Church, centrally located in Bandar Seri Begawan and the only officially registered Protestant church in the country, is a particularly strategic centre of Protestant life and witness. There is also a growing number of Independent churches, often registered as secular organisations and leading a precarious existence, vulnerable to raids from the religious police.

The difficult situation in Brunei has helped bring Christians together. In less challenging contexts, different Christian groups tend to compete with one another. In Brunei, there is more cooperation and collaboration. Other Christians have borrowed and been welcomed into the facilities of the Church of Our Lady of the Assumption. They have even joined some Catholic services during major celebrations. Despite the pressures that result from being a Christian community in an Islamic nation, the churches in Brunei demonstrate much vitality and look to the future with confidence.

Bibliography

De Vienne, Marie-Sybille, *Brunei: From the Age of Commerce to the 21st Century* (Singapore: National University of Singapore Press, 2015).

Rooney, John, *Khabar Gembira: History of the Catholic Church in East Malaysia and Brunei, 1880–1976* (London: Burns and Oates, 1981).

Tan, Jin Huat, *Planting an Indigenous Church: The Case of the Borneo Evangelical Mission* (Oxford: Regnum, 2011).

The Philippines

Jayeel Cornelio

This essay offers new ways of critically assessing the vibrancy of Christianity in the Philippines. The premise is that it is diverse. While it is important to discuss the fortunes of Catholicism, the dominant religion, it is also crucial for new analyses to factor in the emergence of new religious groups. In other words, the analytical way forward is to frame the discussion in terms of Christianities in the Philippines. To spell out their salient attributes is the aim of this essay. In the latter part, consideration will be given to how Roman Catholicism fares in relation to this diversity.

The first point is that Christianity in the Philippines is militant. In the literature, militant Christianity refers to fundamentalism and its triumphalist disposition to different spheres of society. These facets have some local resonances. Although many new groups and denominations have emerged over the years, their general theological character is fundamentalist, which spills over into their political choices. In this sense, the religious economy, while competitive, also has a predictable and dominant trait.

The second characteristic is that it is global. The global expansion of many groups has been made possible by the movement of Filipinos to work around the world. But explaining it only in this manner is no longer adequate. I will argue that the global character of Filipino Christianity is a result too of a postcolonial assertion. Many religious leaders are convinced that Filipinos have a calling to evangelise the world.

Before its concluding section, the essay situates Roman Catholicism in relation to these developments. While other Christian groups are asserting themselves in militant and global ways, there are indications that Roman Catholicism's influence in the public sphere is waning.

Religious Diversity

Roman Catholicism is the religion of the Filipino majority. Recent demographic data from the Philippine Statistics Authority show that Catholics constitute 80% of the population. Only 5% are Muslims, while 10% are Evangelicals and Protestants of different denominations. Iglesia ni Cristo (Church of Christ) and the Philippine Independent Church are indigenous churches that constitute around 2% and 1%, respectively. The rest of the population belong to different religions, including Jehovah's Witnesses,

Latter-day Saints and Buddhism. Different ethnic groups around the country practise indigenous spirituality. In Mindanao (the Southern Philippines), the collective term referring to ethnic groups that did not convert to either Islam or Christianity is *lumad* (native).

In spite of the dominance of Catholicism, other Christian groups are making their presence felt. Religious diversity, after all, is about recognition and visibility. The more competitive a religious environment is, the more assertive the demand for recognition will be. The assertion takes place in different ways. Prominent mega-churches like Victory Christian Fellowship and Christ's Commission Fellowship have the financial resources to build halls to accommodate their members in their thousands. Their financial capacity is not surprising, because their contemporary services attract aspirational students, young professionals and middle-class families. To accommodate attendees in other areas, they even rent cinemas every Sunday to hold worship services. The presence of these mega-churches is a given in urban areas such as Manila, Cebu, Iloilo and Davao.

But Christian diversity is also discernible in rural areas. In every community around the Philippines, it is not uncommon to encounter the neo-Gothic chapels of Iglesia ni Cristo or the worship halls of Jehovah's Witnesses and Latter-day Saints. Rural communities are dotted around, too, with apartments or warehouses renovated for purposes of worship. Many of these communities are independent, calling themselves born-again Christian or non-denominational. Apart from independent Evangelicals, other Protestant denominations, such as Lutherans, Baptists and the Union of the Church of Christ in the Philippines, are very much present in rural areas. Their rural presence has to do with missiological models, which is why in some cases these churches build not just their own halls but also schools. Their religious and educational services directly compete with Catholic parishes and their affiliated parochial schools.

Christianity in the Philippines, 1970 and 2020

Tradition	1970 Population	%	2020 Population	%	Average annual growth rate (%), 1970–2020
Christians	33,607,000	93.9%	99,577,000	90.8%	2.2%
Anglicans	63,300	0.2%	163,000	0.1%	1.9%
Independents	7,142,000	19.9%	19,300,000	17.6%	2.0%
Orthodox	200	0.0%	4,000	0.0%	6.2%
Protestants	1,430,000	4.0%	6,237,000	5.7%	3.0%
Catholics	30,860,000	86.2%	83,000,000	75.7%	2.0%
Evangelicals	692,000	1.9%	3,863,000	3.5%	3.5%
Pentecostal/Charismatics	1,182,000	3.3%	38,000,000	34.6%	7.2%
Total population	**35,805,000**	**100.0%**	**109,703,000**	**100.0%**	**2.3%**

Source: Todd M. Johnson and Gina A. Zurlo (eds), *World Christian Database* (Leiden/Boston: Brill), accessed March 2018.

Furthermore, religious diversity is palpable in politics and the media. Politicians and local celebrities do not shy away from professing their religious affiliations in public to widen their support base. Some celebrities even host local television or radio programmes that are decidedly evangelical. One example is *700 Club Asia*, which is broadcast from Manila. Big religious groups even own their own television stations. Iglesia ni Cristo and Ang Dating Daan (Members Church of God International) are two competing groups that have their respective stations on which they broadcast their religious shows. Their programmes showcase the bitter tension between the two, accusing each other of heresy, for example. The Kingdom of Jesus Christ's Sonshine Media Network International broadcasts from the southern city of Davao. On radio, the Far East Broadcasting Corporation has a long history of doing evangelistic work in the country and in the wider region of Southeast Asia. It is the Evangelical counterpart to DWXI and Radyo Veritas, which are owned respectively by the Catholic Charismatic group El Shaddai and the Archdiocese of Manila.

These are just some illustrations to show that Christian diversity is a social reality in the Philippines. Among observers it is imperative not to dismiss these religious groups as negligible minorities. But there is a caveat. Although other observers might not necessarily neglect these groups, they often categorise them as sects, a term that is loaded with religious and cultural derision. This is the case for many journalistic reports about Iglesia ni Cristo, even though it has become a major religious player around the world. There is also a perception among non-members that many of these churches are not Christian because they do not subscribe to the Trinitarian doctrine found in Roman Catholicism and Protestantism. The bigger issue, then, is not whether diversity is neglected but whether it is approached – wittingly or otherwise – with the biases of dominant Catholic (or Protestant) perspectives. What are the characteristics of this diverse Christianity? There are two that I discuss in the succeeding sections: it is militant, and it is global.

Militant Christianity

Believers who are driven to impose their fundamentalist religious views on society are described in the literature as 'militant' Christians. Although they are not a homogeneous group, there are some shared facets. Many are conservative Evangelicals in the ministry, the media, politics or education. They respond to any ideology that challenges the fundamentalist worldview. In the USA, members of the Christian right have their answers to evolution theory, abortion, same-sex marriage and liberal theology, among other concerns. They also subscribe to dominion theology, which explains their involvement in different sectors of society, including business, legislation and the justice system. Militant Christianity is thus not just intellectual. It also has its own modes of organising. Its militancy has a long anthropological history, which can be traced back to Indo-European warfare.

Some of these attributes resonate with the state of contemporary Christianity in the Philippines. The overarching militant tone has to do with its fundamentalism, which manifests even in its political involvements. I will present my case using a historical perspective. But there is another caveat. It is a mistake to say that Christianity in the Philippines replicates its American counterpart's militancy wholesale. Not all issues are comparable. The American Christian right, for example, has stakes in the supremacy of the USA in global politics. The Philippines, by contrast, plays the role of a small country in international relations. Moreover, fundamentalist Christians in the USA have set up their own colleges and universities in defence of creation science and strict sexual norms. They attract faculty and students who echo these ideas. While there are many Christian tertiary institutions in the Philippines, they are not known for dismissing the theory of evolution or asking students and faculty to sign statements of faith. Finally, militant Christianity is generally associated with conservative Protestantism in the USA. As I have explained above, Christianity is diverse in the Philippines and it is crucial to factor in the theological and political dispositions of groups that are traditionally neither Catholic nor Protestant.

Around the 1980s a fascinating development emerged in the religious history of the Philippines. Various religious groups emerged in this decade, including Evangelical churches, Charismatic fellowships and new religious movements. Some of these churches include Victory Christian Fellowship and Christ's Commission Fellowship. Jesus Is Lord, arguably the biggest Evangelical community in the country, was formed a little earlier (in 1978). Many independent churches that consider themselves born-again were also planted in this decade as the result of the work of foreign missionaries. Catholic Charismatic groups became fashionable too, the most famous of which is Brother Mike Velarde's El Shaddai. One prominent example of the new religious movements is the Kingdom of Jesus Christ, whose leader, Apollo Quiboloy, is believed to be the very embodiment of the Son of God in the present dispensation. It was also in the 1980s that the Iglesia ni Cristo, founded by Felix Manalo in 1914, saw its unprecedented expansion around the country.

What is special about the 1980s? The decade saw the decline of the dictatorship of Ferdinand Marcos, which eventually ended with the People Power Revolution of 1986. During the two-decade presidency of Marcos (1965–86), which was riddled with poverty and human rights violations,

Catholics responded by drawing from liberation theology to organise communities around the country. Jaime Cardinal Sin, then Archbishop of Manila, played a crucial role in galvanising the public against the dictatorship. The Catholic Church's pivotal role in the People Power Revolution would be the high-water mark of its involvement in politics and the national narrative. (In the conclusion I will revisit this moment to reflect on the decline of the Catholic Church's influence in the Philippine public sphere.)

Hence, by the 1980s the time was ripe for a renewal movement to emerge, but one that no longer had the dictatorship as the enemy. The rise of new religious groups coincided with the high hopes about the future of the Philippines and the restoration of its democracy. Interestingly, Iglesia ni Cristo, Ang Dating Daan and the Kingdom of Jesus Christ have all adopted a Restorationist theology, which considers their respective movements as the true and faithful form of Christianity. Salvation is tied to membership. Evangelical churches and Charismatic groups would not state that only their members are saved, but their growth was part of a renewal movement that took place within Catholicism and Protestantism.

Many of these renewal groups looked beyond the country. They also adopted a militant imagery that found its way into spiritual visions. A classic case is Bill Perry's book about the role of the Philippines in the evangelisation of the rest of Asia – *A Prophetic Vision for the Philippines* (1994). This was based on his divine visions as a missionary in the country in the 1980s. In the book, which was widely circulated among Evangelicals, he referred to Asia as a 'war zone' for which Filipino Christians should take up 'swords of the Spirit'. In fact, in one of his visions the shape of the archipelagic Philippines resembled that of a warrior, with the long island of Palawan as the sword. This sword moved and emitted flames towards Southeast Asia, which set the rest of the continent on fire.

Fire was a powerful militant metaphor. No wonder that newly formed religious groups wanted Christians to be 'on fire'. This meant imbibing an unwavering commitment to the faith as a result of either conversion or religious awakening. Thus, the very narrative of their founders was about discovering their religious fervour. In their respective accounts, the Lord delivered Catholic El Shaddai's Brother Mike Velarde from financial ruin and called the Kingdom of Jesus Christ's Apollo Quiboloy to be the 'Appointed Son of God'. When he was still a communist student leader, Brother Eddie Villanueva also had an encounter with God. It inspired him to begin a Bible study group, which eventually became Jesus Is Lord. Interestingly, being on fire manifested too in the drive to proselytise. Among Catholics, Charismatic fellowships were formed around the country. They became a religious ecology in their own right, with their song books, concerts and regular meetings. They arguably arrested the rapid expansion of born-again churches, many of which had the influence of the Charismatic movement. The 1980s, in a nutshell, opened up the competitive environment of Christian diversity that remains to this day.

The Catholic, Protestant and new religious groups mentioned above are just a sample of the many that are now present around the country. While the competition for converts is fierce, the intriguing part is that their theological and moral positions are not necessarily far from each other. They share a literalist view of the Scriptures, which inspires their conservative outlook on divorce, same-sex marriage and abortion. These are just some of the controversies that have generated militant reactions recently. Many of these leaders are also open to the return of the death penalty, a curious position given their hesitation over abortion. Manny Pacquiao, the world-renowned Filipino boxer who is now a senator, believes that reimposing the death penalty is God's will. Being invited to speak to ministers, he is, in a way, the face of fundamentalist Christianity in the country. Even the role of women in religious leadership remains contested for many of these religious groups. So, although they argue with each other about who is genuinely saved, they are in fact on the same side when it comes to a moral crusade. After all, they have a grasp of the sacred calling of the Philippines as a nation whose holiness must be upheld and defended.

It is in the same vein that the political activities of these churches are to be understood. Iglesia ni Cristo is known for voting as a religious bloc according to the endorsements of its leadership. Jesus Is Lord has fielded its own candidates, including no less than Brother Eddie Villanueva himself for the presidency. (His son, Joel Villanueva, is now a senator.) Although many Evangelicals supported him, his base was not big enough for victory. Politicians court the backing of the Kingdom of Jesus Christ during campaigns. One may thus interpret the political activities of these religious groups as a result of their expansion. But that is only one side of the story. That they play a prominent role in local and national politics is also an indication of their conscious militancy. The point is that if the Philippines had a spiritual destiny to fulfil, these groups had to be actively involved in influencing the government so that the country itself could be a 'light to Asia' and the rest of the world. This brings us to the second point.

Global Christianity

Different Filipino religious groups, regardless of tradition or denomination, are very much active around the world. They set up their own congregations, hold massive events and convert other people. In this light, the competition is not confined to local communities in the country. Bringing up this point is crucial because depictions about the move of Christianity to the Global South can be misconstrued as a one-way process. The Philippines has been identified as a centre of Global South Christianity, but that is not to say that it stays there. Migrant workers and missionaries themselves have brought local Christianity outside of the country in different ways. This can be observed historically.

The spread of Christianity among Filipinos outside the Philippines coincided with the government's labour export policy. In the 1970s the country, under President Ferdinand Marcos, began deploying workers when it became clear that the economy could not absorb surplus labour. The government then took advantage of the emerging oil and construction industries in the Middle East to send its mostly male skilled workers. In the succeeding decades the country addressed global demand in the service sector, including domestic work and care-giving. Women generally occupy these jobs. Now Filipinos around the world are in various industries, such as information technology, food and beverages, and seafaring. Since pay is higher, a typical Filipino aspires to work abroad. The education system reinforces this aspiration, which explains the proliferation of training centres and colleges that offer degrees in such fields as engineering, health care and marine transportation. Recent estimates show that more than 10 million Filipinos live overseas, roughly 10% of the Philippine population.

Consequently, they have formed their own Christian communities. Local Catholic parishes in Europe, the USA, Hong Kong and Singapore have Filipino communities that alter the Catholic demographics there. They also bring with them their own practices, such as *Misa de Gallo* during Christmas. In other cases, Filipinos become part of the global outreach of their respective churches. Jesus Is Lord, for example, has grown tremendously among Filipinos in many countries; recent data show that they are present in 60. With more than 2 million members in total, Iglesia ni Cristo is present in at least 100. The same can be said about other indigenous churches, like the Kingdom of Jesus Christ and Ang Dating Daan. Contemporary theological reflections have caught up with this reality by framing the movement of Filipinos as a divine design with missiological implications. At the same time, the global presence of these local groups provides social functions. They offer not just uninterrupted religious socialisation but also support that eases the transition on the part of migrant workers.

However, to continue explaining the expansion of these groups in terms of the global movement of Filipinos is no longer adequate. This is because these churches are also conscious of converting other nationalities. It is a result of a missiological realisation. This idea is quite clear in the experience of Victory Christian Fellowship. It is part of a global movement called Every Nation. Its Philippine unit has taken a large role in evangelising the rest of Asia. In the Philippines alone it has around 80 congregations. Its headquarters, in Bonifacio Global City, is a modern complex that includes a training centre for local and international missionaries, who are expected to plant churches in different places. The church has sent missionaries to such countries as Bangladesh, Cambodia, Vietnam and Afghanistan. The Iglesia ni Cristo is similarly aggressive. Its television programmes are broadcast in different languages, including German, Spanish, Portuguese and French. It has also carried out massive evangelistic events to target locals in such places as South Africa, Thailand and Hong Kong. To meet the needs of their new converts it now buys properties and takes over old worship halls in other countries.

The continuity with religious militancy is evident. In the eyes of these Christians, their global success exemplifies divine calling. But it also has a postcolonial dimension in the twenty-first century: if the Philippines were to be a new centre of world Christianity then it had to be engaged with other cultures. Many of these churches were born in the Philippines, and in a literal sense are now reaching the world. Thus, the postcolonial assertion progresses radically from the older diaspora theology that called for the evangelisation of Filipinos wherever they might be. Instead, Filipinos themselves, formerly colonised and proselytised, are now the bearers of truth for other nations.

In this light, their global outlook is very much tied to the militant character of diverse Christianity in the Philippines. Militant Christianity, it will be recalled, embodies a triumphalist mindset. Whereas this took shape in the form of geopolitical assertiveness on the part of the Christian right in the USA, as far as Filipino Christianity is concerned, it is about massive evangelisation, even among other cultures, by Filipinos themselves. One need only to look at these religious groups' websites, publications and television programmes to see how they celebrate their missiological achievements.

Finally, the global outlook has to do, too, with the growing affluence of these religious groups. A decade ago, El Shaddai opened its International House of Prayer to accommodate attendees in its weekly fellowship. It is touted to be the largest worship hall in Asia. To celebrate its 100th anniversary, Iglesia ni Cristo inaugurated the Philippine Arena, the biggest indoor stadium in the world. The Kingdom of Jesus Christ is now building a bigger one, with a seating capacity of 70,000. The arena is called King Dome. These are just some of the architectural feats of religious groups in the Philippines that showcase their affluence. These are ultimately tied to how they see themselves as key entities in world Christianity. They are architectural achievements at the same time that they are centres for training, missionary work and religious service.

Whither the Catholic Church?

I began this essay by arguing that religious diversity is now a fact of religious life in the Philippines. Christianity has to be discussed in a plural sense because of the assertiveness of religious groups that emerged in the 1980s, many of which are now flourishing. But Catholicism remains the dominant religion. This section of the essay is thus devoted to exploring what has happened to the Catholic Church with respect to these developments. The answer depends on what one looks at.

At the level of the institution, the Catholic Bishops' Conference of the Philippines (CBCP) remains formidable. Although journalistic accounts tend to reduce it to its statements on political issues, CBCP is not only a gathering of bishops who represent the country's more than 80 ecclesiastical territories. The CBCP affects pastoral life through its various commissions in such areas as doctrine, social action and the formation of clergy and lay people. At the level of communities, the Catholic Church has numerous thriving ministries, many of which are led by the laity. Basic Ecclesiastical Communities (BECs), common in rural areas, are an example. Often connected to the local parish, BECs rely on the participation of the laity for evangelisation, liturgy and even social services. Given their limitation in number and resources, parish priests rely on lay Catholics to organise feasts and other religious events, especially in far-flung areas. Furthermore, the most successful BECs have initiated livelihood programmes. They also have organised local people to protest against mining and logging industries that have destroyed the environment. In urban areas, Catholic life is flourishing as well in the form of renewal movements that cater to different demographics. El Shaddai is popular among the urban poor, with an estimated membership of 9 million in the Philippines alone and 2 million more followers among overseas Filipino workers. Its leader, Brother Mike Velarde, is a lay Catholic. By contrast, attracting the aspirational middle class is the Light of Jesus Family, another Catholic Charismatic group known for its weekly gatherings called The Feast. The group claims to have 35,000 members in the Philippines and around the world. It is led by Bo Sanchez, a much sought-after lay preacher who has written books on love, happiness and wealth.

These illustrations are just some of the lay configurations that make Catholicism a vibrant religion for many Filipinos. That they are led by lay people is key to making their activities relevant to particular sectors. These communities and their collective message of hope help their members in navigating the changes that are taking place in Philippine society today. In this sense, these renewal communities add to the already vibrant popular piety that is common among many Filipino Catholics, such as the devotion to the Black Nazarene in Manila, Santo Niño in Cebu and the various icons of the Virgin Mary in different parts of the country. To claim, therefore, that Catholicism is on the decline among Filipinos is a common mistake among observers.

But that is just one side of the story. In relation to the emergence of militant and global Christianity, there are important considerations regarding the Catholic Church's fortunes. One crucial area needs to be unpacked: weekly Mass attendance among Catholic adults has declined significantly, from 64% in 1991 to 40% in 2017, according to a survey by the Social Weather Stations. The figure stands in stark contrast to Iglesia ni Cristo's 58% weekly attendance and other Christians' 67%. But this does not mean that Catholics do not consider their religion important. In fact, 75% of them consider religion 'very important'. Given that the Mass is central for Catholic life, a case may be made that many Catholics have become less institutionally involved over the years.

What could account for this trend? As mentioned above, in 1986 the Catholic Church played an important role in the restoration of democracy in the country. That was its high-water mark in terms of its national and political engagements. That also sealed the church's narrative in the years to come that the Philippines, in spite of its secular constitution, is a Catholic nation that must uphold Catholic virtues. After all, the nation owed much to the Catholic Church. But the public no longer appreciates the church's involvement in politics. In 2008, the International Social Survey Programme revealed that 64% of Filipinos agreed that religious leaders should not influence government. Unsurprisingly, the wider public felt alienated when many Catholic leaders became very vocal in resisting the provision for artificial contraceptives made in the 2012 Reproductive Health Bill. Not only were Sunday homilies devoted to resisting the policy, some parishes even went so far as to dissuade their members from voting for politicians who supported the legislation. This call backfired, with theologians like Father Ramon Echica now admitting that the church has a new social context in which it no longer has a privileged place.

The adjustment has to do not only with the use of public reason in engaging the state and the public. The bigger issue at stake for the Catholic Church is credibility. Over the years, many clergy have been accused of corruption, sexual misconduct and collusion with politicians. Many of these accusations made the headlines, thus affecting the majority population. By contrast, the religious leaders of the other Christian groups I discussed above, even if they are militant in the public sphere, still attract their own loyal converts. One reason is that they are credible as far as their followers are concerned. In other words, it is not only whether religious leaders are morally conservative or whether they use public reason whenever they talk about political matters that counts.

At the same time, Catholics may feel that their leaders are not in touch with realities on the ground, a point repeatedly brought up by Catholic youth. In this light, it is consequential that the greater public no longer associates the Catholic Church with the liberation and social justice that characterised much of its political engagement in the 1970s. Its weak credibility drowns out the many social and community involvements of Catholic groups around the country. This makes it difficult for church leaders to engage the state on various issues of the day, including divorce, human rights and the rise of penal populism.

Conclusion

This essay has been devoted to making sense of the state of Christianity in the Philippines today. The decline of the influence of the Catholic Church in the public sphere has been matched by the rise of militant and global religious groups that continue to attract many converts. From the 1980s onwards, these churches called for new ways of being Christian. Their goal is to be authentic and 'on fire' about the confession and practice of their faith. In some cases their version is Restorationist, seeing themselves as the only church faithful to the principles of the Scriptures. Others have inaugurated the renewal movement, calling for a spiritual awakening that draws from Charismatic gifts or an Evangelical fervour. Regardless of the differences, these movements converge on a fundamentalist view of the Scriptures. To them the Bible is final, authoritative and inerrant. Their fundamentalism thus informs their conservative attitudes towards some of the controversial issues in the country in recent years, such as divorce, same-sex marriage, abortion and even the death penalty. Their militancy has spilled over into their political choices, either by supporting candidates or by fielding their own. It also explains their global outlook, which is why they have taken the competition outside the country to reach Filipinos and even other nationalities.

It is in this manner that they are transforming the Philippines to become a central player in the future of global Christianity, and this is an achievement given that Catholicism remains the dominant religion. This depiction, however, does not mean that all is lost for the Catholic Church. Catholicism remains influential, especially in terms of popular piety. But it has to confront issues with respect to its public engagements and, more importantly, the credibility of the clergy. The reality is that many Catholics are alienated by their own religious institutions. This uneasy situation, coupled with the rise of militant and global Christianity in the country, is what the Catholic Church now faces.

Bibliography

Collantes, Christianne, *Reproductive Dilemmas in Metro Manila: Faith, Intimacies and Globalization* (Singapore: Palgrave Macmillan, 2018).

Cornelio, Jayeel, *Being Catholic in the Contemporary Philippines: Young People Reinterpreting Religion* (London: Routledge, 2016).

Cornelio, Jayeel, 'Popular Religion and the Turn to Everyday Authenticity: Reflections on the Contemporary Study of Philippine Catholicism', *Philippine Studies: Historical and Ethnographic Viewpoints,* 62:3/4 (2014), 471–500.

Echica, Ramon, 'Elements in the Barrel that Produce Rotten Apples', in Stephen Bullivant, Eric Genilo, Danilo Pilario and Agnes Brazal (eds), *Theology and Power: International Perspectives* (New York: Paulist Press, 2016), 137–54.

Francisco, José Mario C., 'People of God, People of the Nation: Official Catholic Discourse on Nation and Nationalism', *Philippine Studies: Historical and Ethnographic Viewpoints,* 62:3/4 (2014), 341–76.

Timor-Leste

Filomeno Jacob SJ

Timor-Leste lies north-west of Australia, at the eastern end of the Indonesian archipelago, and shares a border with West Timor. The country became independent on 20 May 2002, after 24 years of armed resistance against the Indonesian occupation and nearly 500 years of Portuguese colonial rule. According to the 2015 national census, the total population was 1,179,654, with 99.51% identifying themselves as Christian. Of these, 97.57% were Catholics and 1.95% Protestants. The Catholic majority lives side by side with the small Protestant minority and the tiny Muslim community of Arabic descent. At that census, Muslims accounted for 0.23% of the population, Buddhists 0.047% and Hindus 0.023%. Followers of traditional religion accounted for 0.077% and 0.083% of the population was unaffiliated. Nearly 400 years after the baptism of the Queen of Mena (1641), the Timorese state has recognised Christianity as one of the national identity markers of the Timorese.

The nation comprises many ethnolinguistic groups, who speak 11 Austronesian and four non-Austronesian languages. The constitution defines Tetum and Portuguese as official languages, while English and Indonesian are working languages. Mandarin and Hakka are spoken by the small Chinese-Timorese community.

Catholic Missions

The Timorese Catholic Church and the government of Timor-Leste celebrated in 2015 the five hundredth anniversary of the arrival of the first missionaries on the island of Timor, believed to be around 1515. The occasion was marked by the signing of a concordat between the Democratic Republic of Timor-Leste and the Holy See and the unveiling of a monument to the Catholic missionaries in Oe-Cusse.

The first missionaries on the islands of Solor and Timor were Dominican friars who followed Portuguese traders roving the southern seas for sandalwood. Frei Antonio Taveira was among the first Dominican missionaries who crossed the strait from Solor (part of modern Indonesia) to Timor in 1556. On hearing about good news from Timor, the first Bishop of Malacca, Frei Jorge de Santa Luzia, sent more Dominicans to Timor in 1561, under the leadership of Frei António da Cruz. The fall of Malacca in 1640 triggered events on the island in unexpected ways. Muslims took advantage of the circumstances to attack the Christian bases in Larantuka, Solor and Timor. To ensure the safety of Christians in Timor, Frei António de São Jacinto, Frei Crisóstomo de São Tiago and Frei Pedro Manso, together with Captain Francisco Fernandes and 70 soldiers, sailed from Larantuka to the Kingdom of Mena, on Timor, in 1641. The Portuguese expedition of soldiers and missionaries offered protection and earned the trust of the Timorese, resulting in the baptism of the queen, her son and her people on 24 June 1641, the feast day of St John the Baptist. The Christian communities, the Christian way of life and the institutions were cyclically abandoned to their own devices for shorter or longer periods, which did not help the sustained growth of the church. A turning point in the evangelisation of Portuguese Timor occurred more than 200 years later, in 1877, when Father António Joaquim de Medeiros, accompanied by seven missionaries, arrived in the territory. As Superior and Vicar General of the Missions of Timor and later, Bishop of Macau (1884), Father Medeiros was instrumental in establishing Catholic schools and promoting education for women through the work of the Canossian nuns. He passed away on 7 January 1897, at the Central Missions' house at Lahane. His remains are kept in St Anthony's Church at Motael, in Dili.

One of the first decisions of Bishop José Manuel de Carvalho on 15 November 1900 was to create two independent vicariates: the Northern Vicariate covered the missions on the northern coast and the Southern Vicariate those on the southern coast. The latter was entrusted to the Jesuits, while the diocesan clergy retained the responsibility for the Northern Vicariate. Father Sebastião Aparício da Silva and his Jesuit companions arrived in Soibada in 1899 and embarked on a missionary project that combined frequent pastoral visits to the villages and catechesis of children and adults, followed by baptisms and marriages, but, most importantly, formal education. Under Father da Silva's leadership, the Jesuits built the church and a residence and set up two *colégios* in Soibada, one for boys,

Christianity in Timor-Leste, 1970 and 2020

Tradition	1970 Population	%	2020 Population	%	Average annual growth rate (%), 1970–2020
Christians	211,000	34.8%	1,224,000	88.6%	3.6%
Protestants	22,000	3.6%	59,700	4.3%	2.0%
Catholics	207,000	34.2%	1,143,000	82.8%	3.5%
Evangelicals	6,000	1.0%	29,500	2.1%	3.2%
Pentecostal/Charismatics	2,000	0.3%	68,000	4.9%	7.3%
Total population	**605,000**	**100.0%**	**1,381,000**	**100.0%**	**1.7%**

Source: Todd M. Johnson and Gina A. Zurlo (eds), *World Christian Database* (Leiden/Boston: Brill), accessed March 2018.

run by the Jesuits, and another for girls, administered by the Canossian Sisters. Considering the needs of the country, they opened a vocational training school with a carpentry workshop that trained many Timorese at the beginning of the twentieth century. The mission flourished, but events surrounding the Republican Movement in Portugal led to the expulsion of the religious orders and the ensuing contraction of Christianity. The Jesuits and the Canossians left the colony on 23 December 1910, and the diocesan priests took care of the missions. Bishop José da Costa Nunes reorganised the missions in the 1920s; he also founded a teacher-training school for primary-school teachers and catechists. Its graduates were selected to serve in mission centres throughout the country. The Soibada *colégio* became a model replicated in various parts of the country, namely Manatuto, Oe-Cusse, Maliana, Ermera and Ossu. These institutions provided formation and training for the Timorese, many of whom worked in the colonial public administration until 1975.

Father Jaime Garcia Goulart was appointed in 1940 as Vicar General and Superior of the Missions of Timor. One of his main achievements was the establishment of the Minor Seminary of Our Lady of Fatima at Soibada in 1936 to train the native clergy. Four years later, in 1940, the Holy See created the Diocese of Dili and Father Goulart was appointed its apostolic administrator. By then, the Second World War had brought the Japanese and Australian armies to fight the war on Timorese soil. Father Goulart took refuge in Australia and in 1945 was consecrated a bishop in Sydney. There were many Timorese casualties during the war, including four missionaries. Returning from Australia, Bishop Goulart reopened the seminary in 1948, and in 1958 he requested that members of the Jesuit Order came back to Portuguese Timor to take charge of the formation of future priests.

Indonesian Invasion

Indonesia invaded Portuguese Timor on 7 December 1975, one of the most significant and darkest events in Timorese history. The United Nations General Assembly reacted on 23 December 1975 with a resolution calling for the withdrawal of the Indonesian troops and the holding of a genuine referendum on self-determination. Countering the United Nations, the Indonesians carried out a formal annexation of Portuguese Timor on 17 May 1976. The Indonesian occupation was characterised by brutal military oppression, mass internal resettlements, sexual abuse, imprisonment, torture and starvation. Journalist John Pilger wrote:

> In my experience as a reporter, East Timor was the greatest crime of the late 20th century. I had much to do with Cambodia, yet not even Pol Pot put to

death as many people – proportionally – as Suharto killed and starved in East Timor. (<http://johnpilger.com/articles/the-universal-lesson-of-the-courage-of-east-timor>; accessed 8 August 2018)

Throughout this period, the Catholic Church remained a source of strength and hope for the people. The principles behind the church's transformation were outlined in Bishop Ribeiro's 1975 pastoral letter *Perante uma Nova Situação*:

> The position of the Church will be, in any of the options, to accept the situation that the Timorese people choose and to continue its evangelizing mission in the midst of the same people of Timor, no matter what the fate may be.

Bishop Ribeiro was replaced by Monsignor Martinho da Costa Lopes, who firmly believed that the evangelising mission is the theological basis for the church's continued commitment to the people, which includes in all circumstances demanding justice and being at the service of the public good, in respectful cooperation with the legitimately constituted authority.

Protestants

The history of the Protestant denominations in Timor-Leste begins in the late 1950s and is tied to the activities of itinerant pastors. The first prayer meetings took place in private homes, including the family home of the Seabra Gomes family at Balide. Pastor Francisco Coiás helped set up the first prayer meetings at Fatumeta, on the outskirts of Dili, where the first small, thatched-roof provisional chapel was built in August 1968. The most prominent members of this prayer group at Fatumeta included José Gomes and his wife, Maria Gomes, Vicente de Vasconcelos and his wife, Marcelo Cireneu, Alberto Rodrigues, Joaquim Morais, Bernardo Guterres, Florindo Marçal and a few other families, all former Catholics. Soon, as the community grew, a bigger place was required to accommodate them. Despite ongoing characterisations of the Portuguese colonial power as anti-Protestant, the application submitted to the municipal authorities in Dili for land to build a church was granted at Vila Verde in Dili, and construction work started in 1970. The church building was completed and inaugurated in 1971 in the presence of the municipal authorities. It was the first Protestant church building in the country under the Igreja Evangélica Assembleias de Deus (IEAD).

Small communities were by now emerging in Dili, Same, Aileu and Baguia and on the island of Ataúro. After the Indonesian invasion, the Igreja Evangelica Assembleias de Deus changed its designation to the Indonesian-language name, Gereja Sidang Jemaat Allah, and associated with the Indonesian Assemblies of God churches. Around the same period, in 1976, some members of the Fatumeta group, led by Vicente Vasconcelos, set up another denomination with the support of Indonesian Protestants. Initially, they met for prayers at a building in the Mandarin area in Dili. Later they found a permanent location at Vila Verde and built the Hosana church, where Indonesian Protestant pastors, including military chaplains, played essential roles. Thus the Gereja Kristen Timor Timur (Indonesian-language name) was born. Alex Surjadinata, a Protestant pastor based in the USA, stated that one of the negative consequences of the long association with the Indonesian Protestant churches was the perception among Timorese people that the Timorese Protestant churches were 'pro-Indonesian'. The Third General Assembly (2000) adopted the Tetum-language name Igreja Protestante iha Timor Loros'e (IPTL) in a bid to change that perception. Pastors Arlindo Marçal, Francisco de Vasconcelos and Moisés da Silva have been leaders working towards Timorisation and national integration.

Official statistics in 1967 put the overall membership of Protestant churches at 1,471. IPTL membership grew during the Indonesian occupation, to 35,000 in 1996. As Indonesian members left the country after independence, IPTL Timorese membership declined to 17,000; this figure was reduced further due to the emergence of new Christian denominations, drawing from both IPTL's and IEAD's congregations. The Igreja Evangelica Presbyteriana iha Timor-Leste was set up in 2011 by former IPTL members. Many other very small Christian denominations have emerged in the twenty-first century. Most of them came together in 2010 to form the Forum Igreja-Igreja Kristaun Protestante iha Timor-Leste (FIKPTL), as they try hard to develop common organisational and operational values in order to carry out their mission. Significantly, the two largest Protestant churches (IPTL and IEAD) are not active members of the FIKPTL.

Ecumenical relations take time to build and require knowledge and respect to overcome reservations about the political histories and the cultural significance of the churches. Ecumenism requires, moreover, a theological framework that supports religious cooperation at various levels. The Catholic Church and the IPTL, among others, have developed the first steps towards future structures of recognition and possible co-operation. A very strong social platform of recognition shared by leaders and members in both is kinship that binds them in solidarity. However, a future of meaningful formal ecumenical relations might require deeper commitments and focus on religion and society.

Papal Visit and the Santa Cruz Massacre

Pope John Paul II visited Portuguese Timor on 13 October 1989, when it was still under Indonesian occupation. This pastoral visit is significant in the history of Christianity in Timor-Leste for a number of reasons. It was the first time that the leader of the Catholic Church was visiting the small, predominantly Catholic country. For the oppressed and suffering Timorese people, the visit indicated the Pope's solidarity. Before the celebration of the Eucharist, the Pope knelt down and prostrated to kiss the Holy Cross laid on the ground before the altar, blessed the land and paid homage to the many killed in the struggle for freedom and human dignity. For the Timorese Catholic Church and the nationalist resistance, the Pope's actions demonstrated recognition of Timor-Leste as a nation and a people. In his homily, the Pope called on the Timorese to strengthen their unity in faith and reconciliation 'while seeking a just and peaceful solution to current difficulties'.

Two years after the papal visit, on 27 October 1991, Indonesian agents stormed the residential compound of Motael church looking for resistance members suspected of underground activities. A young activist, Sebastião Gomes, was then killed. It was for him that, on 12 November 1991, Father Alberto Ricardo da Silva celebrated a memorial Mass at the Motael church. After Mass, the worshippers joined the procession to the Santa Cruz cemetery, praying and singing nationalist songs, openly defying the Indonesian military. The response of the Indonesian military was not unexpected: they killed at least 271 people within the grounds of the cemetery, and many more disappeared. The facts of the Santa Cruz massacre were caught on camera by Max Stahl for the world to see. Historian Peter Carey summed up the pivotal role of the church in the following statement:

> [I]t is significant that almost all important political manifestations in Timorese territory, especially those organized by resistant students, took place during events related to the Church: for example, the papal mass of 12 October 1989, the celebrations of the 15th anniversary of the diocese of Dili on 4 September 1990, and of course the commemorative service of 12 November 1991 in the cemetery of Santa Cruz. ('Netherlands Indies to Indonesia — From Portuguese Timor to the Republic of East Timor/Timor Loro Sa'e: Two Paths to Nationhood and Independence', *Indonesia and the Malay World*, 25:71 [1997], 15)

Nobel Peace Prize and Independence

Carlos Filipe Ximenes Belo (later Bishop Belo) was appointed Apostolic Administrator in 1983 in very challenging circumstances for the Catholic Church in Timor. Military operations were under way, and many Timorese suffered the direct consequences. While facing intimidation from the Indonesian authorities, Bishop Belo chose to stand up for the people by speaking out on their behalf and offering protection and support to the most vulnerable. He was strengthened in his mission when he was ordained bishop on

19 June 1988. The following year, on 6 February 1989, Bishop Belo wrote a letter to Dr Javier Perez de Cuellar, United Nations secretary-general, calling for a referendum to resolve the Timorese conflict. Moral pressure was applied by the international community when the Nobel committee awarded the 1996 Nobel Peace Prize to Belo and José Ramos-Horta, the two most visible faces and voices of the Timorese plight, and called for a diplomatic solution based on the people's right to self-determination. Finally, Portugal and Indonesia, mediated by the United Nations, signed an agreement on 5 May 1999 by which Indonesia accepted a referendum for self-determination, under the auspices of the United Nations Mission in East Timor. UN secretary-general Kofi Annan announced the results on 4 September 1999. A total of 98.6% of Timorese voted in the 30 August 1999 referendum, and a majority of 78.5% voted for independence. Timor-Leste was, finally, a free nation.

Achieving nationhood meant that the Timorese needed to write their own constitution. In this process, the people of Timor-Leste insisted on recognising the active participation of the Catholic Church in the national resistance when the Constituent Assembly carried out its consultation with communities around the country. In response, the Constituent Assembly included in the preamble of the constitution the following provision: 'In its cultural and humane perspective, the Catholic Church in East Timor has always been able to take on the suffering of all the People with dignity, placing itself on their side in defence of their most fundamental rights'. In section 11, on Valorisation of the Resistance, article 2 states, 'The State acknowledges and values the participation of the Catholic Church in the process of national liberation of East Timor'.

The Holy See continued to follow developments in the country. Cardinal Renato Martino was appointed papal legate to the independence celebrations. He presided at the Eucharistic celebration on Independence Day at Tasi-tolu, the same location where Pope John Paul II had celebrated Mass in October 1989, and blessed the national flag presented by the president elect of the Republic, Xanana Gusmão. The Holy See was present in solidarity with the jubilant people, to continue to offer hope in a better future for all.

The Quality of Catechesis

Membership of the Timorese Catholic Church rose from 31% of the population of 674,550 in December 1973 to 97.57% of 1,179,654 million people in 2015. Numbers are important, but, as noted by many observers, the quality of faith matters, too. During the Portuguese colonial period, catechumens were required, before baptism, to learn by heart the fundamental tenets of the Catholic faith to lead a Christian life. The rituals were learned and understood through participation in community celebrations. Hence, the road to baptism took time, to ensure the structural quality of faith and the fundamental Christian values, to know and to understand what they believed. This traditional approach is in contrast with the phenomenon of mass Christianisation during the Indonesian period, when baptisms took place in record time without proper doctrinal instruction. This course of events caused resistance leader Xanana Gusmão to express concern and to suggest the priority of faith education. In a letter written in 1986 to the Bishop of Dili, he stated, 'We know the difficulties, we know the good intentions and the efforts, but we think that the church must avoid self-satisfaction because the true essence of conversion cannot be relegated to mere statistical data'. The need for continued catechesis was further highlighted when Pope John Paul II reminded Asian bishops that 'if the church in Asia is to fulfil its providential destiny, *evangelisation* as the *joyful, patient and progressive preaching of the saving Death and Resurrection of Jesus Christ* must be your *absolute priority*' (italics mine). A 'patient and progressive preaching' through catechism does not end with the initiation sacrament of baptism, first communion or confirmation; it accompanies people in their journey through life.

How does one reach the most profound spiritual experience of the Timorese? A few steps are required. First, one must walk the long road to the substantive core of systematic evangelisation of the people, as proposed by Pope Paul VI's *Evangelii Nuntiandi* (1975: 18): 'For the church, evangelising means bringing the Good News into all the strata of humanity, and through its influence, transforming humanity from within and making it new'. Secondly, one must aim at interior change as the purpose of evangelisation: the 'Church evangelises when she seeks to convert, *solely through the divine power of the message she proclaims*, both the personal and collective consciences of people, their lives and their context' (italics mine). Thirdly, one must reach out to the spiritual experience accomplished in the liturgy.

Liturgical Developments

For the liturgy to become an act of the people, their language must come to the fore to ensure their full participation and express their deepest feelings, fears, desires and hopes. Most missionaries learned Tetum, the lingua franca of Timor. Jesuit Father Sebastião Aparício da Silva spoke the Soibada Tetum fluently. He wrote the *Catecismo da Doutrina Christã em Tétum* (1885) to help the newly baptised Christians understand the basics tenets of Christianity. He also wrote the *Dicionário Tetum-Portuguez* (1889), which later became the basis to standardise the Tetum language. Father Manuel Fernandes Ferreira SJ wrote the *Catecismo Badac no Oração ba Loron-Loron* (1907) and the *Resumo da Historia Sagrada em Portugues e Tetum para Uso das Crianças de Timor* (1908). Manuel Patrício Mendes and Manuel Mendes Laranjeira published a Tétum–Portuguese dictionary (1935) and a catechism. Finally, in 1980, the Liturgical Commission of the Diocese of Dili, led by Father Alberto Ricardo da Silva, published the official Tetum text of the Ordinary of the Mass and the Liturgical Lectionaries. The adoption of the inculturated liturgy was made possible by the interplay of two factors: the inculturation movement triggered by the Second Vatican Council, including Paul VI's *Evangelii Nuntiandi*, and the political and theological pressure for the Catholic Church to identify with the people during the Indonesian military occupation. The Timorese Christian churches are now in a similar process of inculturation: the IEAD and the IPTL as well the smaller churches have liturgies translated from Indonesian sources into Tetum. However, as stated by Pastor Arlindo Marçal, a former moderator of the IPTL Synod, the translation of texts into Tetum is only the first step. There needs to be a deeper identification of the Christian churches with the local cultures.

Evangelisation and *Lulik*

It is no secret that a sizeable number of Timorese Catholics still follow *lulik* practices alongside their Catholic faith. For some observers, this is a symptom of superficial Catholicism. What is *lulik*? In its most narrow contextual meaning, *lulik* refers to the sacred in the Durkheimian sense. It is the socially constructed system of human relations, including religion as the distinctive space of human practice and belief, which cannot be reduced to any other, although they may overlap or be intertwined. The social, cultural and 'theological' structures of the *lulik* – as indeed in Christianity – are deeply intertwined with the social and cultural systems, such as kinship and alliance structures of wife-givers and wife-takers, without which there is no history and no society. The *lulik* ontology and 'theology' is constructed around the *uma* (house) and the *lia* (word) paradigms. *Uma* (*uma lulik*, sacred house) and *lia* are the root cultural paradigms framing the pervasive and necessary complementary oppositions that are critical for the ritual and political production of history. Life flows in the conjunctural exchanges between the wife-givers and the wife-takers framed by the paradigmatic *uma* and *lia* structures. Wife-givers and wife-takers enact ritual and politics in dyadic, diachronic, fractal and permanent reproductive structures of partnership. *Uma lulik* and *lia* determine, frame and shape the lives of the Timorese and thereby ensure historical continuity, stability and permanency. In other words, the *uma lulik* and the *lia* stand for a historical ideology constructed on the symbiotic platforms of genealogy and religion. The only basis to conceptualise *lulik* as sacred is the *hamulak* (prayer) addressed to the ancestors and the highest *Na'i(n)* (Lord, Owner) of everything, sometimes identified as *Maromak*, an entity similar to the impersonal Unknown God or the *U̲ru-Vatchu* (the sun and the moon) male–female complementary opposition. It is *hamulak* that brings *lulik* closer to the basic sociological meaning of religion, defined as an engineered response to human needs and as the making of humanity.

The controversy with *lulik* came to the fore when the missionary colonial theology labelled Timorese social structures and cultural practices as 'non-Christian'. *Lulik* – an eclectic mix of social practices and religious ideas – came to be seen in opposition to Christianity, which led some Catholic missionaries to actively pursue burning of *lulik* houses and objects, although the Timorese would always rebuild new ones. Even today, some local Protestant churches require their members to turn their back on *lulik* as a logical, Cartesian confirmation of total commitment to Jesus Christ. The burning of *lulik* houses has stopped. Since the 1970s, the Catholic Church has opted for more conciliatory approaches to *lulik*. Based on the Second Vatican Council's overture to cultures, the Catholic Church has pursued inculturated pastoral practices, with a more lenient and gradualist approach to the social and cultural *lulik*, through the appropriation of acceptable traditional Timorese values and symbols and the pastoral care of the *lulik* human and social structures. Becoming and being Christian is a personal choice of total, personal commitment to Christ. It is significant that the late Mau Duan, a ritual leader at the Hohulo-Raimansu *lulik* houses, once stated in symbolic terms that *lulik* is the *(rai) nakukun* (darkness), the past (in the present) and that Christianity is the *(rai) naroman* (dawn), the future (in the present).

Most Timorese are Catholics, and they participate in the Timorese *lisan* (customary social and cultural practices) enacted by the *uma lulik* and *lia* structures and their corollaries. Christianity and *lulik* now live side by side, shaping symbiotic practices and ontologies, without creating any syncretistic third form. Although some political and military movements have made attempts to create such an entity, this proved to be merely an opportunistic and provisional bricolage of symbols and rituals – in other words, a pool of syncretic performances of limited scope. The search for life – which permeates the symbiotic relationship between Catholic and *lulik* ontologies and practices – finds its most striking iconographic display in the *Cruz Jovem* (Youth Cross) event of public veneration of the Holy Cross. Since 1992, the same Holy Cross is carried around the country, attracting large crowds and bringing together people of all ages to pray, sing and dance to celebrate their Catholic faith. *Uma lulik* elders, who might be Catholics as well, participate actively in the celebrations. Individual prayers mix with collective devotions in the context of collective memories.

The Cross has become a powerful ritual attractor, the centre of the crowds' public demonstration of their Christianity, in which the devotion to the Virgin Mary, invoked as *Virgem Peregrina*, has a prominent place. The atmosphere is charged with an emotional and devotional intensity that more often than not leads to profound, personal religious transformations. In the process, the Cross – the Christian icon itself – became *manas* (hot), *lulik* (sacred) in the *lulik* sense: powerful and dangerous.

Participation in social and cultural *lisan* practices does not diminish the Christian faith. There is no reason to think that the Catholic faith of the Timorese is of a lesser quality because they participate in the *lulik* culture. Peter Carey suggested that faith sustained the Timorese in their struggle against the Indonesian military occupation. He wrote:

> At the heart of this struggle has been the East Timorese Catholic Church, a Church which has undergone a remarkable transformation since the mid-1970s from an institution closely linked to the Portuguese colonial order to one which has discovered a new sense of mission as a Church of service, a people's Church able to articulate and defend the interests of the Timorese people. ('The Catholic Church, Religious Revival, and the Nationalist Movement in East Timor, 1975–98', *Indonesia and the Malay World*, 27:78 [1999], 77)

Christianity coexists with *lulik* in the socially constructed ontological, ritual and political frameworks of the complementary opposites that define the metaphysical and cosmological aspects of Timorese social life. The Timorese, as true agents of their culture, have made Christianity an integral part of that culture while keeping the social and cultural structures that make them Timorese.

The Road Ahead

The Catholic Church and all its institutions could do much to shape the cultural and religious experience of the people. It is the deep and personal faith experience of each faithful member of the church that ensures the transformation of the structures of culture into the locus of faith. The church can provide the best of its long tradition of spiritual life through education and formation of the whole person to strengthen the values that underpin the life of the society. If the church is coherent with the values of the gospel it preaches and avoids moral and political corruption, if it keeps its independence and freedom to proclaim justice, the church becomes the critical conscience of the nation. If the church upholds human rights, standing by women, families and the forgotten poor of the rural areas; if it does social solidarity and relies solely on the divine power of the message it proclaims; if the church consistently seeks spiritual depth, it will always have a place in the hearts of the Timorese.

However, if the church allows for mediocrity and runs muddled parish administrations and intolerable low-quality education in its schools; if the church runs reckless and careless pastoral services; if the church's catechesis and moral instructions are superficial; if the church ignores women, families and the poor; if it becomes frivolous and corrupt, and does not discern intelligently to understand the times and the people's plight; if the church seeks its pragmatic interests alone and does not know its place, then the church's human structures will have failed evangelisation and the Christian people. Unless the church finds spiritual depth and moral coherence that come from intellectual wisdom and pastoral humility to touch the deeper layers of the contextual realities of every person and the whole community, the church will morph into irrelevance.

At this juncture, how can the church learn from its history in order to modernise and become a vibrant and relevant institution for the people? The solution lies, first, in the tradition set by Bishop Medeiros and Bishop Goulart to invest in the quality formation of the clergy and the laity and to fully adopt the guiding principles of the Second Vatican Council and subsequent teachings on Christian formation. The strength of the Jesuit and Canossian education in Soibada is a case in point to be revived and amplified to promote faith, education and health of families and communities. Secondly, much will depend on how much the role of lay Catholics is valued and incorporated into the service of the church to promote Christian values in broader society, within the state structures and in everyday life. The clerical temptation to be at the fringes of politics needs to be tempered to ensure the church remains true to its evangelising mission. The issue is leadership. Bill Nicol suggested that dark scenarios in Timorese politics need not happen

> if the right people with the right attitude and the right skills take the political helm. Quality leadership is not just the central *if* for East Timor, it is also *the* key to its future. If capable people with moral integrity and the right leadership qualities assume the reins of power within a constitutional framework that promotes fairness, transparency, accountability, and contestability, the country does have a chance. (*Timor – A Nation Reborn* [Jakarta: Equinox Publishing, 2002], 339)

Mutatis mutandis, that applies to the churches, too.

Bibliography

Durand, Frédéric, *Catholicisme et Protestantisme dans l'Île de Timor: 1556–2003. Construction d'une identité chrétienne et engagement politique contemporain* (Toulouse: Editions Arkuiris, 2004).

Hodge, Joel, *Resisting Violence and Victimisation: Christian Faith and Solidarity in East Timor* (London: Routledge, 2012).

Kohen, Arnold, *From the Place of the Dead: The Epic Struggles of Bishop Belo of East Timor* (New York: St Martin's Press, 1999).

Smythe, Patrick A., *'The Heaviest Blow': The Catholic Church and the East Timor Issue* (Münster: Lit Verlag, 2004).

Traube, Elisabeth G., *Cosmology and Social Life: Ritual Exchange among the Mambai of East Timor* (Chicago, IL: University of Chicago Press, 1986).

Major Christian Traditions

Anglicans

Ken Christoph Miyamoto

Anglicanism is the form of non-Roman Catholic Christianity that emerged from the English Reformation in the sixteenth century. As the result of the movement, the Church of England separated from the Roman Catholic Church and became the established religion of England. In contrast, a non-established form of Anglicanism has its roots in the Scottish Reformation. When Presbyterianism was established in Scotland after the Glorious Revolution, a group of Episcopalians chose to follow their own way and formed the Episcopal Church in Scotland. In the wake of the American War of Independence in the late eighteenth century, Anglicans in the USA organised the Protestant Episcopal Church in the United States of America, independent from the Church of England. Their first bishop was consecrated by the Scottish Episcopalians, thereby inheriting their non-established Anglicanism.

The Anglican tradition is characterised by the biblical faith, liturgical worship based on the Book of Common Prayer and the historic episcopate. Though it originated in the Protestant Reformation, Anglicans consider their church to be continuous with the pre-Reformation Catholic Church and to share many features with Roman Catholicism. They therefore describe it as both Catholic and Reformed. The Archbishop of Canterbury, the leader of the Church of England, is respected also as the spiritual leader of the worldwide Anglican Communion.

Anglicanism has become a significant part of today's Christian presence in East and Southeast Asia. Its expansion to the region took place during the period of British colonialism and American imperialism there, particularly in the nineteenth century. Three major missionary forces contributed to the development: two British societies affiliated with the Church of England and the American Episcopal Church mission. One of the British societies was the Society for the Propagation of the Gospel in Foreign Parts (SPG), incorporated in 1701 and the oldest non-Roman-Catholic overseas missionary organisation. While the SPG was marked by the High Church or Anglo-Catholic tradition, the other, namely the Church Missionary Society (CMS), had the Low Church orientation, because it was founded by a group of Evangelical Anglicans in 1799. As for the American Episcopal Church, it established the Domestic and Foreign

Missionary Society (DFMS) in 1821. However, with the understanding that mission belonged to the entire church, it was legislated in 1835 that every Episcopalian was a member of the DFMS, making the church and the Missionary Society identical.

Introduced by these and other missionary organisations, Anglicanism has taken root in many countries in East and Southeast Asia since the nineteenth century. In this process, it came to take diverse forms, influenced by the way it was brought to a particular country in the region as well as by the way missions interacted with local conditions. Focusing on such a missionary process in various parts of East and Southeast Asia, this essay seeks to understand how Anglicanism arrived in this part of the world and examines how its interactions with local contexts, both historical and social, contributed to the emergence of diversity within Anglicanism in the region.

One note is needed about the name of the American Episcopal Church. While 'The Protestant Episcopal Church in the United States of America' is its original name, the church decided in 1964 to make 'The Episcopal Church' also official. There thus exist two official names of the church. In the rest of the essay, however, it will be referred to with the unofficial yet popular third name, 'The Episcopal Church in the USA' (ECUSA).

Mainland China

No fewer than 12 missionary bodies contributed to the emergence of the Anglican Church in China. The missionary who is considered to be its founder is the American Episcopalian William Jones Boone, who first came to Macau in 1840. After the First Opium War, he moved to Shanghai in 1845, having been consecrated as the first Bishop of China the previous year. He worked there until his death in 1864. In 1844, the South China Mission was established in Shanghai by two English missionaries despatched by the CMS. One of them, George Smith, later became the first Bishop of Victoria (Hong Kong). While the CMS worked mainly in South China, the SPG ministered mainly in the north, namely Beijing and the provinces of Hebei and Shandong. The inter-denominational China Inland Mission founded by Hudson Taylor also sent to China a group of young

Anglicans in East and Southeast Asia, 1970

Region	Total population	Christian population	Anglican population	% of region Anglican	% of Christians Anglican
East Asia	996,425,000	11,456,000	107,000	0.0%	0.9%
Southeast Asia	280,607,000	50,740,000	179,000	0.1%	0.4%
East and Southeast Asia	1,277,032,000	62,196,000	286,000	0.0%	0.5%
Globe	3,700,578,000	1,229,309,000	47,394,000	1.3%	3.9%

Source: Todd M. Johnson and Gina A. Zurlo (eds), *World Christian Database* (Leiden/Boston: Brill), accessed March 2018.

Anglican Evangelicals known as the Cambridge Seven, who landed in Shanghai in 1885 and engaged in various works throughout China. In the early twentieth century, Canadian Anglicans also began their missionary activities in Henan province in central China.

Particularly important among the Anglican missionaries to China was the polyglot Bishop Samuel Schereschewsky of Shanghai, an American Episcopalian born in Russian Lithuania. His major contribution was the translation of the entire Bible into Chinese. Together with Bishop Boone, he founded St John's College in Shanghai. It became a full university in 1905, and many future Chinese leaders, including K. H. Ting, studied there.

In 1912, Anglican missions operating in China merged and formed a single national church called the Chung Hua Sheng Kung Hui (CHSKH) or the Holy Catholic Church in China. A theological seminary was founded in Nanjing, and the first Chinese bishop, Shen Tsai-sen, was elected to be Assistant Bishop of Zhejiang and consecrated in Shanghai in 1918.

After the difficult years of the Sino-Japanese and the civil wars, the Communist Party came to power and established the People's Republic of China in 1949. This development radically changed the situations surrounding Christianity in China. Western missionaries were forced to leave the country. Chinese Anglicans participated in the Three-Self Patriotic Movement (TSPM) under the leadership of Bishop K. H. Ting of Zhejiang. His episcopal consecration in 1955 was one of the last Anglican ones in China, and the CHSKH had ceased all its activities by the end of the 1950s, though it was never formally dissolved. The churches were closed during the Cultural Revolution, but when they resumed worship, all Protestant denominations came together and decided to create the China Christian Council in 1980 as their umbrella organisation, with Bishop Ting as its president. The age of denominationalism thus came to an end in China, and the Anglican Church also ceased to exist as an independent ecclesiastical body.

Hong Kong

As Hong Kong was ceded to the UK under the Treaty of Nanjing in 1842, the Anglican Church there took a distinct course of historical development.

Anglicans in East and Southeast Asia, 2020

Region	Total population	Christian population	Anglican population	% of region Anglican	% of Christians Anglican
East Asia	1,663,619,000	128,787,000	169,000	0.0%	0.1%
Southeast Asia	669,016,000	153,102,000	615,000	0.1%	0.4%
East and Southeast Asia	2,332,635,000	281,889,000	784,000	0.0%	0.3%
Globe	7,795,482,000	2,518,834,000	99,586,000	1.3%	4.0%

Source: Todd M. Johnson and Gina A. Zurlo (eds), *World Christian Database* (Leiden/Boston: Brill), accessed March 2018.

The first missionary to Hong Kong was Vincent John Stanton, who came to the island in 1843 when he was still an undergraduate student. He later became the first colonial chaplain of Hong Kong and founded both St John's Cathedral and St Paul's College. When the Diocese of Victoria was created in 1848, the CMS missionary George Smith was appointed as its first bishop. Initially they ministered to the British communities, but missionary work among the Chinese developed gradually, and the first Chinese church, St Stephen's, was founded in 1865.

In the 1930s, the Sino-Japanese War made the connection between the mainland and Hong Kong, as well as Macau, uncertain. This development led Bishop Ronald Hall to make a memorable but controversial decision: to ordain Florence Li Tim-Oi into the priesthood to work among the refugees who escaped the Japanese occupation of the mainland. Being ordained in 1944, she was the first female priest in the history of the entire Anglican Communion.

As the CHSKH joined the TSPM, Anglicans in Hong Kong and Macau reorganised the Diocese of Victoria. They formed the Diocese of Hong Kong and Macao in 1951, completely separating it from the CHSKH, under the Archbishop of Canterbury. The diocese was abolished in 1998, when the Hong Kong Sheng Kung Hui (the Holy Catholic Church in Hong Kong) was formed as an independent province of the Anglican Communion, with three new dioceses in Hong Kong and a missionary area in Macau. Peter Kwong became the first Archbishop of Hong Kong.

Taiwan

The history of the Anglican Church in Taiwan took yet another course, as Taiwan was under Japanese occupation from 1895 until 1945 as a consequence of the First Sino-Japanese War. It is during this period that Anglicanism reached the island for the first time. The Nippon Sei Ko Kai, or the Anglican-Episcopal Church in Japan, created the Diocese of Taiwan (Taiwan Sei Ko Kai) and engaged in pastoral and missionary work chiefly for the Japanese Anglican communities in Taiwan, establishing churches in Taipei and Tainan. The number of Taiwanese natives who became Anglican was very limited. After the Pacific War ended in 1945, the

Changes in Anglicans in East and Southeast Asia, 1970–2020, growth rate, % per year

Region	Total population	Christian population	Anglican population
East Asia	1.03%	4.96%	0.92%
Southeast Asia	1.75%	2.23%	2.49%
East and Southeast Asia	1.21%	3.07%	2.03%
Globe	1.50%	1.45%	1.50%

Source: Todd M. Johnson and Gina A. Zurlo (eds), *World Christian Database* (Leiden/Boston: Brill), accessed March 2018.

Japanese, including the Anglican clergy and church members, withdrew from Taiwan and the churches in Taipei and Tainan were transferred to the Presbyterian Church.

In 1949, the Republic of China was established in Taiwan by the Kuomintang (KMT), who escaped from the communist takeover of China. Among those who moved to Taiwan with the KMT were a group of Chinese Anglicans, and this group initiated a new Anglican ecclesiastical body in Taiwan. The ECUSA was supportive in this process, and in 1954 it placed Taiwan under the jurisdiction of the Diocese of Hawaii as a missionary diocese. In 1988, John C. T. Chien was consecrated as the first native Bishop of Taiwan, and the missionary diocese was upgraded to full diocesan status. Now the Episcopal Diocese of Taiwan, also called the Taiwan Sheng Kung Hui or Taiwan Episcopal Church, constitutes part of Province 8 of the ECUSA.

Japan

The first Anglican missionary who came to Japan was Bernard Bettelheim, a naturalised British Anglican born in Hungary. Sent by the Loochoo Naval Mission, he arrived at Naha, Okinawa, in 1846 as a medical missionary. Lasting missionary work in Japan, however, began in 1859, when the country's two centuries of national isolation came to an end. As soon as the ports, such as Kanagawa and Nagasaki, opened to foreigners that year, the American Episcopal missionary John Liggins moved from China to Nagasaki as the first non-Catholic missionary to Japan. While he left the land soon because of illness, his seminary classmate Channing Moore Williams, arriving at Nagasaki less than two months later and consecrated as the Bishop of China and Japan in 1866, made a significant contribution to the formation and development of the Anglican Church in Japan. He later moved to Tokyo and founded St Paul's School (today's Rikkyo University) there.

British missionaries also arrived later, sent by both the CMS and the SPG. While the American Episcopal mission worked mainly in Tokyo and Yokohama, as well as Fukuoka in Kyushu, the CMS and the SPG made Osaka and Kobe their bases, respectively. As in Williams's case, they also attached importance to educational mission and founded schools for boys and girls in these cities, some of which later developed into universities and colleges.

The three Anglican missions, one American and two British, cooperated in the translation of the Book of Common Prayer. In 1883, the Japanese Nobori Kanai and Masakazu Tai were ordained by Bishop Williams as the first native deacons. The three missions held the first synod in 1887 under the leadership of Bishop Williams and his British counterpart, Bishop

Edward Bickersteth. At this meeting, it was agreed to form the Anglican-Episcopal Church in Japan, named the Nippon Sei Ko Kai (NSKK) or the Japanese Holy Catholic Church. It was also agreed to drop the 39 Articles and make the Chicago–Lambeth Quadrilateral the confessional basis of the newly formed church. The establishment of the NSKK was a milestone in the history of Anglicanism because it was the first autonomous province of the Anglican Communion outside the lands where British settlers were predominant.

In 1888, the Anglican Church of Canada also entered the missionary work in Japan, with a focus on Nagoya and Central Japan. The first Japanese bishops, John Yasutaro Naide of Osaka and Joseph Sakunoshin Motoda of Tokyo, were consecrated in 1923.

In 1941, Japan's wartime government forced all the existing Protestant denominations in the country, including the NSKK, to merge and form a single religious body in order to make it easy to control them. Thus, the United Church of Christ in Japan, known also as the Kyōdan, was established. However, the Anglican bishops, under the leadership of the Primate Paul Shinji Sasaki, rejected this measure. They chose to dissolve the NSKK rather than join the Kyōdan, despite the persecutions they faced during the war, as the government saw Anglicanism as an enemy religion. After the war, most of those who joined the church union returned to the restored NSKK. Subsequently, its Anglo-Catholic orientation was reinforced because many of those 'lapsed' Anglicans were Evangelicals.

Generally speaking, the present-day NSKK takes liberal stances on the issues surrounding worldwide Anglicanism. However, two dioceses, namely Kobe and Yokohama, maintain more traditional stances. For instance, those two dioceses have not yet recognised women's ordination to the clergy, while the other nine dioceses do.

Korea

The East Asian country where Christianity has taken root most remarkably is Korea. Over 30% of its population are now said to confess the Christian faith. The dominant groups among Korean Christians are Presbyterians and Catholics, whereas Anglicans constitute a minority.

Anglicanism in Korea goes back to Charles Corfe, an Englishman who was a former Royal Naval chaplain and consecrated in 1889 as Missionary Bishop of Korea. He arrived in Korea the following year and established the Church of St Michael and All the Angels in Seoul. He also started hospitals in Seoul and Incheon. Herbert Kelly founded the Korean Missionary Brotherhood in London to train people for missionary work in Korea. This brotherhood, however, soon developed into the Society of the Sacred Mission, an Anglo-Catholic religious order for training clergy for the church in England. A religious order called the Community of St Peter in Kilburn sent its nuns to Korea from 1892 onwards, and made Korea the focus of its mission. In 1925, with the help of Bishop Mark Trollope, it founded the Society of the Holy Cross as a local religious order in Korea. It is thus Anglo-Catholicism that took root there.

The Anglican missionaries in Korea were strongly interested in inculturation. This is shown by the Church of St Peter and St Paul in Ganghwa Island, built under the oversight of Trollope and consecrated by Bishop Corfe in 1900. The church building was a beautiful fruit of an early attempt to harmonise Christianity with Buddhism, Confucianism and Korean religious culture.

Trollope was consecrated as the third Bishop of Korea a year after Japan's colonial rule began in 1910. He had a more cooperative policy on Japan than did the Presbyterians, who strongly identified themselves with the Korean independence movement. As a result, the Anglican mission work had little success during the Japanese period. Nonetheless, even Japanese Anglicans in Korea refused to join the Kyōdan, resisting the forced merger of the churches imposed by the Japanese government.

After liberation from Japan's rule in 1945, the Anglican Church gradually started to grow and expand its work, despite the difficulties caused by the Korean War and the subsequent division of the nation. In 1965, the first native Korean Bishop, Lee Cheon Hwan, was consecrated. In 1992, the Anglican Church in Korea became an autonomous province known as the Tae-Han Song-Kong-hwei (Korean Holy Catholic Church) or the Anglican Church of Korea, with three dioceses, and Simon Songsu Kim became the first Archbishop of Korea the next year.

The Philippines

The Philippines is one of the two Christian nations in East and Southeast Asia, the other being Timor-Leste. According to the 2010 census, more than 80% of its population profess Roman Catholicism and around 11% Protestantism. This is because the islands were ruled by Spain from the sixteenth century to the end of the nineteenth century. Only after the Philippines came under the colonial rule of the USA in 1901 did Protestantism begin to penetrate the islands.

Anglicanism in the Philippines goes back to the first Episcopal worship service held in Manila in 1898 for Americans and other English-speaking residents by Charles Pierce, an Episcopal chaplain of the US Armed Forces that had occupied Manila that year. Later in the same year, the first Episcopal worship was conducted for Filipinos as well.

In 1901, the ECUSA created the Missionary District of the Philippine Islands, and Charles Henry Brent was consecrated as the first bishop of the district. He came to Manila in 1902 with a 'clear-cut missionary policy', although he considered American expatriates and other English-speaking peoples 'as his first responsibility'. Thus, he built a cathedral in downtown Manila (the Cathedral of St Mary and St John), hospitals and schools. Being against proselytising Roman Catholics, he directed his missionary efforts towards the three major non-Christian groups in the Philippines: the Filipino-Chinese in Manila, the Muslims in Mindanao and the Igorot people of north Luzon.

The mission to the Igorot was particularly successful, and they came to constitute 80% of the membership of the Missionary District when it was given the status of diocese and renamed the Philippine Episcopal Church (PEC) by the ECUSA in 1937. Subsequently, the town of Sagada in Mountain Province, the heart of the Igorot mission, has become the only predominantly Anglican town in the Philippines. Ninety-five per cent of the population of Sagada are Episcopalian, with the Episcopal Church of St Mary the Virgin at the centre of town. In 1971, the ECUSA divided the single diocese of the PEC into three, with a Filipino diocesan bishop in each of them, but still kept them under its own jurisdiction. It is only in 1990 that the PEC was officially separated from the ECUSA and became an autonomous province in the Anglican Communion as the Episcopal Church in the Philippines (ECP). The ECP is in full communion with the Philippine Independent Church, which is given the privilege to send delegates to the Council of Churches of East Asia (CCEA).

Southeast Asia

The history of Anglicanism in the rest of Southeast Asia is complicated. The Malay peninsula and the island of Singapore were under British control from the eighteenth century, while Borneo was controlled by the British and the Dutch. The first introduction of Anglicanism into these areas took place at the settlement established by the British East India Company at Penang Island in 1786. The local magistrate, George Caunter, was appointed the lay chaplain there in 1800 under the jurisdiction of the Bishop of Calcutta, and the Church of St George the Martyr in Penang, the oldest Anglican church in Southeast Asia, was consecrated in 1819. In the same year, Singapore was founded as a British colony, and the Anglican Church was established there as well to serve British expatriates.

Anglicans started missionary work in Borneo in 1848, when the SPG responded to the appeal of James Brooke, the Rajah of Sarawak, and sent out Francis Thomas McDougall to Kuching. In 1856, the first Diocese of Labuan was formed, with Singapore as its centre, under the jurisdiction of the Bishopric of Calcutta, and McDougall was consecrated as the first Bishop of Labuan. He was also appointed the bishop for the Diocese of Sarawak created by Brooke. As the British authorities strongly disapproved of evangelism among the Muslim Malays, missionary work was carried out mainly among Chinese and Indian migrants.

In 1867, the Anglican churches in Penang, Malacca and Singapore were organised into the Church in the Straits Settlement, which later was separated from the Bishopric of Calcutta and placed under the care of the Bishop of Labuan as the United Diocese of Singapore, Labuan and Sarawak. In 1909, however, the United Diocese was divided into three dioceses: Singapore, Labuan and Sarawak. During the Second World War, the work of the church fell on the shoulders of local clergy and church workers because the Japanese interned British clergy and missionaries. This development eventually led to the establishment in 1951 of Trinity Theological College in Singapore for training local leaders.

In 1957 Malaya attained independence from British rule. In 1963, it formed the Federation of Malaysia together with North Borneo (Sabah), Sarawak and Singapore, though Singapore was expelled from the Federation in 1965. After several reorganisations of the dioceses, the Anglican churches in these regions eventually became autonomous and formed the Church of the Province of South East Asia in 1996, with four dioceses: Kuching, Sabah, Singapore and West Malaysia. Moses Tay, the Bishop of Singapore, was installed as the first archbishop of the province.

During the late twentieth and early twenty-first centuries, Singapore has been the major centre of growth in Asian Anglicanism. The number of Anglicans there increased fivefold between 1970 and 2010. The Diocese of Singapore has energetically engaged in church planting across Southeast Asia and beyond. Thus, the Province now covers nine countries: Malaysia, Singapore, Brunei, Indonesia, Thailand, Cambodia, Laos, Vietnam and Nepal. Singaporean Anglicanism is conservative Evangelical in theology and Charismatic in spirituality. Archbishop Tay was one of the most outspoken opponents in the Anglican Communion towards the liberalism of the ECUSA. He was involved in founding the Anglican Mission in the Americas in the late 1990s, supporting conservative Anglicans in North America. Together with Bishop Kolini of Rwanda, he consecrated Chuck Murphy and John Rogers as missionary bishops for North America in 2000.

Myanmar

Anglicanism in Myanmar (Burma) goes back to army chaplains who came there with the British army in the early nineteenth century. In 1854, the SPG sent out its first missionary, T. A. Cockey, to begin educational work in Mawlamyine (Moulmein), the centre of British Burma. The SPG then sent A. Shears and J. D. Marks to join him in educational mission, which was later extended to Yangon and Mandalay. The Diocese of Rangoon (now Yangon) was established in 1877.

The nation became independent in 1948, and in the following year Francis Ah Mya and John Aung Hla were consecrated in Calcutta as the first native assistant bishops. In 1962, the military took control of Myanmar through a coup d'etat. In 1966, all foreign missionaries had to depart from the country. Consequently, Francis Ah Mya became the first native Bishop of Rangoon. In 1970, a proposal to form a new Anglican province in Myanmar was approved by the Provincial Council of the Church of India, Pakistan, Burma and Ceylon. Thus, the Church of the Province of Burma (now Myanmar) was created, and the Diocese of Rangoon became one of its dioceses. Francis Ah Mya became the first archbishop of the newly created church.

Conclusion

There are thus in total seven Anglican Churches in today's East and Southeast Asia. Six of them are autonomous: Hong Kong, Japan, Korea, the Philippines, Southeast Asia and Myanmar. The church in Taiwan belongs to Province 8 of the Episcopal Church in the USA. Although Anglicanism was brought to East and Southeast Asia mostly in the nineteenth century, Japan's Nippon Sei Ko Kai alone attained autonomy within the century, whereas the other five became autonomous only in the late twentieth century. The indigenisation of the church leadership also required a considerable period, and it is only in the second half of the twentieth century that most Anglican Churches in the region obtained native bishops.

Depending on by whom and how Anglicanism was transplanted, these churches took different courses of development and, consequently, came to show diverse faces: liberal or conservative, Low Church or High Church, and national or trans-national. For instance, Anglicans in Hong Kong are traditionally liberal, and one of their bishops was the first ordained female priest in the history of Anglicanism, whereas Singaporean Anglicans are quite conservative and have been firmly opposed to the liberalism of American Episcopalians. While Anglicans in Korea cherish the Anglo-Catholic tradition, Japanese Anglicans present a mixture of different tendencies: a few High Church dioceses do not recognise the ordination of women, but others welcome and support them to seek ordination to Holy Orders.

No matter how different they are, however, all these churches share the common tradition that emanates from the English Reformation. For non-Roman-Catholic Christians in the region, the Anglican liturgical tradition based on the Book of Common Prayer offers an important alternative to the less structured Protestant worship normally consisting of scriptural readings, preaching, free prayers and hymn singing. The historical episcopate fundamental to the Anglican tradition also provides a church with a structural stability – the stability displayed remarkably by the experience of the NSKK, which – resisting the pressure of the wartime regime – refused to participate in the merger of the Protestant denominations. The NSKK decided to dissolve itself, but Japanese Anglicans survived the hardship under the leadership of their bishops and successfully restored their ecclesial organisation after the war.

It is not easy to offer a general assessment regarding Anglicanism's impact on society and culture in the region as a whole because of the diversity both of the region and of Anglicanism there. Such an assessment is made even more difficult by the fact that the nations and countries in the region have experienced British and American influence quite differently. For Japan, the Anglican impact was quite positive and productive. Japan now has nine Anglican universities and colleges. Historically, most of them go back to schools originally founded by the Anglican and Episcopal missions to educate boys and girls in the spirit of Christianity. Some missionaries even taught at national universities. Thus, the Anglicans, with their emphasis on education, greatly contributed to the transformation of Japanese society and culture from traditional to modern. Even though the Anglican community in Japan has never been large numerically, one cannot underestimate the role it has played in the modern history of the nation.

As for cooperation among Anglicans in East and Southeast Asia, the seven Anglican Churches form a regional ecclesial council, the Council of Churches of East Asia (CCEA). It was founded in the 1930s and has gained momentum since the 1950s. The Anglican Church of Australia and the Philippine Independent Church also participate in it as associate members. The CCEA holds a full assembly every four years, and the member churches send to it a bishop, clergy, lay and youth representatives from each diocese, while the associates send the same from their province. It is, nonetheless, fair to say that there is little missional cooperation among the churches – perhaps because they had few opportunities to work together in the past, given their separate development. Thus, it remains as their future task to foster closer relations and search for ways to achieve missional cooperation at various levels of church life.

Bibliography

Cox, Jeffrey, *The British Missionary Enterprise since 1700* (New York: Routledge, 2008).
Ion, A. Hamish, *The Cross and the Rising Sun, Vol. 2: The British Protestant Missionary Movement in Japan, Korea, and Taiwan in 1865–1945* (Waterloo, ON: Wilfrid Laurier University Press, 1993).

Jones, Arun W., *Christian Missions in the American Empire: Episcopalians in Northern Luzon, the Philippines, 1902–1946* (New York: Peter Lang, 2003).

Sunquist, Scott W., David Wu Chu Sing and John Chew Hiang Chea (eds), *A Dictionary of Asian Christianity* (Grand Rapids, MI, Wm. B. Eerdmans, 2001).

Ward, Kevin, *A History of Global Anglicanism* (Cambridge: Cambridge University Press, 2006).

Independents

Editorial Note

The Edinburgh Companions to Global Christianity use 'Independents' as an umbrella term to cover those Christians who belong to churches that are not affiliated to the Orthodox, Catholic, Anglican or Protestant streams of Christianity. While some of these are stand-alone local congregations, most belong to organised networks.

This category can be applied to the East and Southeast Asia region but is problematic, since relatively few Christians self-identify as 'Independent'. House churches in China fall within this category and, in this region, constitute by far the largest component within it. Yet Christians who belong to house churches are eager to advance their Protestant credentials, lest they be considered deviant or extreme. Likewise, in much of the rest of the region the minority status of Christianity means that even churches that choose to operate independently of historic denominations are concerned to demonstrate that they belong within the mainstream of the Christian religion.

Hence it is quite unusual for a church to identify as Independent. An exception is found in the Philippines, where the early twentieth century saw churches breaking away from the Roman Catholic Church in order to espouse the cause of independence for their nation. Some of these churches have departed from Christian orthodoxy – for example, on the doctrine of the Trinity or the divinity of Christ – but continue to understand themselves as part of Christianity. In this respect, they are similar to movements or churches like the Jehovah's Witnesses and Latter-day Saints, which have set themselves apart from historic Christian belief.

All of the above forms of Christianity are included when assessing the numbers of Independents in this region. However, out of sensitivity to the particular context of East and Southeast Asia, there is no essay on 'Independents' in this volume. Instead, full consideration is given to the Chinese house churches in the essay 'Mainland China (House Churches)' by David Ro (pp. 63–73). The essays on 'Protestants' by Timothy Lim (pp. 295–309) and 'Evangelicals' by Kang-San Tan (pp. 323–35) sketch characteristics of the Protestants and Evangelicals, and many of these apply equally to Independents, given the concern evident in this region for Independents to align themselves closely with Protestantism. It is hoped that this provides a culturally and contextually appropriate way to present the Independent stream of Christianity in this region.

Independents in East and Southeast Asia, 1970

Region	Total population	Christian population	Independent population	% of region Independent	% of Christians Independent
East Asia	996,425,000	11,456,000	2,793,000	0.3%	24.4%
Southeast Asia	280,607,000	50,740,000	9,557,000	3.4%	18.8%
East and Southeast Asia	1,277,032,000	62,196,000	12,351,000	1.0%	19.9%
Globe	3,700,578,000	1,229,309,000	89,480,000	2.4%	7.3%

Source: Todd M. Johnson and Gina A. Zurlo (eds), *World Christian Database* (Leiden/Boston: Brill), accessed March 2018.

Independents in East and Southeast Asia, 2020

Region	Total population	Christian population	Independent population	% of region Independent	% of Christians Independent
East Asia	1,663,619,000	128,787,000	75,240,000	4.5%	58.4%
Southeast Asia	669,016,000	153,102,000	27,617,000	4.1%	18.0%
East and Southeast Asia	2,332,635,000	281,889,000	102,857,000	4.4%	36.5%
Globe	7,795,482,000	2,518,834,000	391,125,000	5.0%	15.5%

Source: Todd M. Johnson and Gina A. Zurlo (eds), *World Christian Database* (Leiden/Boston: Brill), accessed March 2018.

Changes in Independents in East and Southeast Asia, 1970–2020, growth rate, % per year

Region	Total population	Christian population	Independent population
East Asia	1.03%	4.96%	6.81%
Southeast Asia	1.75%	2.23%	2.14%
East and Southeast Asia	1.21%	3.07%	4.33%
Globe	1.50%	1.45%	2.99%

Source: Todd M. Johnson and Gina A. Zurlo (eds), *World Christian Database* (Leiden/Boston: Brill), accessed March 2018.

Orthodox

Nikolay Samoylov and Ambrose-Aristotle Zographos

This chapter comprises a regional survey by Professor Nikolay Samoylov and a case study of Korea by its serving Metropolitan, His Eminence Ambrose-Aristotle Zographos.

Orthodoxy in East and Southeast Asia: A Regional Survey, by Nikolay Samoylov

The Orthodox presence in East and Southeast Asia is numerically small but has a significant history in China, Japan and Korea as well as interesting recent developments in Southeast Asia. In general, it has depended on the influence of Orthodox countries, particularly Russia, but it is marked today by growing numbers of indigenous people embracing the Orthodox faith. In recent years, Orthodoxy began to spread even in countries where it formerly was practically nonexistent, such as Thailand, Vietnam and Indonesia. This development adds interest to the question of the prospects for Orthodoxy in this part of the world.

China

The Chinese Autonomous Orthodox Church was officially established in 1956, but the history of Orthodox Christianity in China goes back more than three centuries. In 1685, the Orthodox priest Maxim Leontiev came to Beijing with a group of Russians captured from the fort of Albazin by Qing military troops, and as a result the first Orthodox chapel was built in the Qing capital. In 1715–16, the first Russian Ecclesiastical Mission, formed according to Peter the Great's edict, arrived in China, headed by Archimandrite Hilarion (Lezhaisky).

The Mission operated in China for about three centuries. Apart from their religious activities, members of the Mission's staff figured prominently in promoting Sino-Russian cultural exchanges in various fields. It is largely owing to the Ecclesiastical Mission in Beijing that Russian Sinology began to emerge. Russian Orthodox missionaries slowly established a small Orthodox Christian community in Beijing and its suburbs. During the first half of the nineteenth century, some members of the Beijing Ecclesiastical Mission became well known Sinologists and made noticeable contributions to Russian intellectuals' knowledge of Chinese culture, history and language. They acted as interpreters of Chinese culture, and, as its original foreign chroniclers, promoted the Russian formation of what was essentially a new communication mode for sociocultural interaction.

In 1863, Russia separated the Beijing Ecclesiastical Mission from diplomatic activities. In this new situation, the Russian missionaries who served in the Beijing Mission could focus on guardianship and protection of the Albazin Orthodox community and preach Christianity among the Chinese and Manchu. During the Yihetuan (Boxer) Rebellion of 1898–1900, the Mission was destroyed, and more than 200 Chinese Orthodox Christians were killed. In 1902, Archimandrite Innocent (Figurovsky) was consecrated bishop in Russia and returned as the first Orthodox Bishop of China. He spent much effort working to restore Orthodox churches that had been destroyed or burned during the Boxer Rebellion. The number of Chinese priests increased. Bishop Innocent was pessimistic about the possibility of converting people from the educated strata of Chinese society and decided to focus on the common Chinese and the lower strata of society. By 1915 there were 5,587 baptised Orthodox Chinese.

From 1917, the Russian Ecclesiastical Mission in China began to focus on the spiritual care and moral support of a large group of refugees from Soviet Russia. By 1949, parishioners included not only Russians but also approximately 10,000 Chinese converts. The Mission returned to the jurisdiction of the Moscow Patriarchate in 1945. The following year the East Asian Exarchate was formed and included Beijing, Harbin, Shanghai, Tianjin and Xinjiang dioceses. After the Communist Party of China came to power in mainland China in 1949, most of the Russian emigrants left China, and the Moscow Patriarchate headed the creation for the Chinese people of the Chinese Autonomous Orthodox Church, in which most of the bishops were Chinese. By 1951, all the Chinese religious organisations established official 'patriotic unions' that included Chinese believers only, and according to the new law they could not be controlled from abroad. The Holy Synod of the Russian Orthodox Church decided in 1954 to abolish the Russian Ecclesiastical Mission in China and donated

Orthodox in East and Southeast Asia, 1970

Region	Total population	Christian population	Orthodox population	% of region Orthodox	% of Christians Orthodox
East Asia	996,425,000	11,456,000	37,900	0.0%	0.3%
Southeast Asia	280,607,000	50,740,000	4,700	0.0%	0.0%
East and Southeast Asia	1,277,032,000	62,196,000	42,600	0.0%	0.1%
Globe	3,700,578,000	1,229,309,000	141,930,000	3.8%	11.5%

Source: Todd M. Johnson and Gina A. Zurlo (eds), *World Christian Database* (Leiden/Boston: Brill), accessed March 2018.

its territory to the Soviet embassy in Beijing. Chinese authorities agreed to the appointment of the head of the Chinese Orthodox Church, Archimandrite Vasily (Shuang), who was a Chinese citizen. That same year, on 23 November, the Chinese Church received autonomous status from the Moscow Patriarchate. By 1957 more than 100,000 communicants lived in north-eastern China alone, with 200 priests in 60 parishes, several monasteries and a seminary. In other parts of China, there were more than 200,000 Orthodox Christians and 150 parishes.

Unfortunately, many churches were destroyed during the Cultural Revolution – including the famous St Nicholas Orthodox Cathedral in the centre of Harbin – and the number of believers at that time was sharply reduced. In the late 1960s, the Chinese Autonomous Orthodox Church practically ceased to exist, and it has not fully recovered up until now.

After the start of Chinese economic and political reforms following the Cultural Revolution, the official attitude towards religions changed for the better. According to the official sources from the Russian Orthodox Church, about 15,000 Orthodox believers live in China today, and their number is growing, due both to the increasing number of permanent or long-term resident aliens and to growing interest in Orthodoxy among the Chinese. Orthodox believers are concentrated in Heilongjiang Province and in Xinjiang Uyghur and Inner Mongolia Autonomous Regions. Patriarch Kirill, head of the Russian Orthodox Church, paid his first visit to China in 2013 and was well received by Xi Jinping, chairman of the People's Republic of China, as well as by Wang Zuoan, director of the China's State Administration for Religious Affairs. Since then, the activity of the Orthodox Church in China has intensified. In 2016 the Church of the Intercession of the Mother of God in Harbin was reopened, and the Easter service was conducted by the recently ordained Father Alexander Yu Shi, the church's first priest in 15 years.

Japan

The Japanese Orthodox Church is an autonomous church under the omophorion of the Russian Orthodox Church. In 1970 the Russian Orthodox Church granted autonomy to the Japanese church while retaining a

Orthodox in East and Southeast Asia, 2020

Region	Total population	Christian population	Orthodox population	% of region Orthodox	% of Christians Orthodox
East Asia	1,663,619,000	128,787,000	47,000	0.0%	0.0%
Southeast Asia	669,016,000	153,102,000	15,200	0.0%	0.0%
East and Southeast Asia	2,332,635,000	281,889,000	62,200	0.0%	0.0%
Globe	7,795,482,000	2,518,834,000	292,132,000	3.7%	11.6%

Source: Todd M. Johnson and Gina A. Zurlo (eds), *World Christian Database* (Leiden/Boston: Brill), accessed March 2018.

measure of ecclesiastical jurisdiction over it. The election of the head of the Japanese Orthodox Church must be confirmed by the Moscow Patriarchate, but the Japanese Church can elect and ordain its other bishops without such confirmation.

The first Japanese to accept Orthodoxy was Masuda Kosai (Tachibana Kosai), who was baptised in Saint Petersburg in 1858, taking the name of Vladimir and patronymic Iosifovich, after the name of his godfather, Russian diplomat Goshkevich. The Russian Ecclesiastical Mission in Japan was founded by the Russian missionary Archimandrite (later Archbishop) Nicholas (baptised as Ivan Dmitrievich Kasatkin) (1836–1912), who arrived in Japan in 1861. In 1864 Father Nicholas baptised the first three converts in Japan. By 1870, the Orthodox community numbered more than 4,000. The Orthodox Theological Seminary was opened in 1879 in Tokyo in premises adjacent to the cathedral. It remains active today.

By 1880, the Japanese Orthodox Church had 5,377 members, six Japanese priests and 78 Japanese catechists. The most important event in the life of the Japanese Orthodox community was the construction in Tokyo of the Cathedral of the Resurrection of Christ, consecrated on 24 February 1891. This church, erected by St Nicholas of Japan, remains one of the most interesting historical and cultural monuments of the Japanese capital. The Japanese traditionally call it Nikorai-do (Nicholas Temple) in memory of its creator, indicating the popularity of Archbishop Nicholas in Japan. At the time of its completion, it was the tallest building in Tokyo.

After the Russian Revolution of 1917, the Orthodox Church in Japan became virtually self-governing. Japanese parishes, deprived of financial support from Russia, switched to self-financing, which led to a significant curtailment of its missionary and educational work. According to a law passed in Japan in 1939, only those who were born in Japan could lead religious communities. Metropolitan Sergius was forced to retire, transferring the temporary administration of the affairs of the church to the layman Arseniy Iwasawa, who enjoyed the confidence of the Japanese civil and military authorities. Archimandrite Nicholas (Ono) was consecrated as Bishop of Tokyo and Japan on 6 April 1941 by the bishops of the Russian Church Abroad.

Changes in Orthodox in East and Southeast Asia, 1970–2020, growth rate, % per year

Region	Total population	Christian population	Orthodox population
East Asia	1.03%	4.96%	0.43%
Southeast Asia	1.75%	2.23%	2.37%
East and Southeast Asia	1.21%	3.07%	0.76%
Globe	1.50%	1.45%	1.45%

Source: Todd M. Johnson and Gina A. Zurlo (eds), *World Christian Database* (Leiden/Boston: Brill), accessed March 2018.

On 5–6 April 1946, the first post-war Japanese Church Council decided to remove Bishop Nicholas (Ono) from office. In early 1947, Bishop Benjamin (Basalyga) arrived in Japan from the USA. With the support of the civil authorities, he became the head of most of the Japanese Orthodox, as well as of the Korean mission, which in 1955 withdrew from the subordination of the American Metropolia and passed under the omophorion of the Patriarch of Constantinople. A smaller part of the Japanese flock, led by Nicholas (Ono) and Archpriest Anthony Takai, refused to enter American jurisdiction and continued to exist as the Japanese deanery of the Moscow Patriarchate. On 10 December 1967, Hieromonk Nicholas (Sayama) was ordained Bishop of Tokyo and All Japan in Leningrad and declared the head of the Russian Ecclesiastical Mission, continuing the work of Nicholas of Japan and Metropolitan Sergius.

In 1969, complete reconciliation was reached between the American Metropolia and the Russian Orthodox Church, and the decision was taken to establish an autonomous Japanese church within the jurisdiction of the Moscow Patriarchate. In 1970, Archbishop Nicholas, the founder of the Orthodox Church in Japan, was canonised by the Patriarch of Moscow and All Russia and was recognised as St Nicholas, Equal-to-the-Apostles to Japan.

Since 2000, Metropolitan Daniel (Nusiro) has been Archbishop of Tokyo and Metropolitan of All Japan. The residence and cathedral church is the Cathedral of the Resurrection of Christ in Tokyo. Here the church runs the Tokyo Orthodox Seminary and publishes a monthly Japanese-language journal, *Seikyo Jiho*. The Orthodox sisterhood and the society of Orthodox youth are now very active. In 2018, in the town of Ajiro, construction started on the first male monastery in honour of St Nicholas of Japan.

Three dioceses comprise the Japanese Orthodox Church: Tokyo Archdiocese, Eastern Japan Diocese and Western Japan Diocese. It celebrates its liturgy in Japanese though occasionally other languages such as church Slavonic or Greek are used. Many liturgical and biblical texts were first translated into Japanese in the late nineteenth century by Archbishop Nicholas and his Japanese colleague Nakai Tsugumuri. As a result, the language of these texts is heavily influenced by Russian Orthodox usages at that time and sounds archaic today. The Japanese Orthodox Church is active in publishing and its publications include the Japanese Orthodox translation of the New Testament and Psalms as well as liturgical texts.

Southeast Asia: an overview

Today, the number of Orthodox Christians in Southeast Asia is small, the first Orthodox communities having appeared there only in the twentieth century. The Eastern Orthodox Metropolitanate of Hong Kong and

Southeast Asia was set up in November 1996 by the decision of the Holy Great Synod of Constantinople after a visit to Hong Kong by Ecumenical Patriarch Bartholomeos I of Constantinople, the first Patriarch of Constantinople to visit the territory. On 2 December 1996, Archimandrite Nikitas (Loulias) was elected as the first Orthodox Metropolitan of Hong Kong and enthroned the following year, with jurisdiction over Hong Kong, Macau, China, Taiwan, Mongolia, the Philippines, Vietnam, Cambodia, Laos, Thailand, Myanmar, Singapore, Indonesia, Malaysia, Brunei, Timor-Leste, the Maldives, Sri Lanka, Bangladesh, India, Nepal, Pakistan and Afghanistan.

In 2008, the Synod of the Ecumenical Patriarchate took the decision to divide the vast area of the Metropolitanate by creating a new Metropolitanate of Singapore and South Asia, with jurisdiction over Singapore, Indonesia, Malaysia, Brunei, Timor-Leste, the Maldives, Sri Lanka, Bangladesh, India, Nepal, Pakistan and Afghanistan. The remaining territory continued to be under the jurisdiction of the Metropolitanate of Hong Kong. Archimandrite Nectarios (Tsilis) was elected and enthroned as the new Metropolitan of Hong Kong. In 2011 the Holy Synod of the Ecumenical Patriarchate elected Archimandrite Konstantinos (Tsilis) as the first Metropolitan, and he was ordained by Ecumenical Patriarch Bartholomew I of Constantinople. He resides in Singapore, where there is a small Orthodox congregation made up mainly of Greeks, Russians and Ukrainians.

Thailand

The first Thai baptised in the Orthodox faith was Prince Chakrabongse Bhuvanath (Chakkraphong Phuwanat), a son of King Chulalongkorn. He came to Saint Petersburg in 1898 and studied in Russia for about eight years, under the personal patronage of Emperor Nicholas II. Prince Chakkraphong and his associate Nai Phum received higher humanitarian and military education in Saint Petersburg. In 1906, Prince Chakkraphong married Ekaterina Desnitskaya (Catherine Na Phitsanulok), and for this reason he accepted Orthodoxy. Subsequently, Prince Chakkraphong returned to Buddhism, but his associate, Nai Phum, also accepted Orthodoxy, having married a Russian woman, and then rose to the rank of colonel in the Russian army.

Orthodoxy has become widespread in Thailand only since the end of the twentieth century. Beginning in the mid-1990s, a large number of immigrants from the former USSR began coming to Thailand. At that time, not a single Orthodox church was found in the kingdom. Attempts to organise an Orthodox parish in Thailand were made by the Patriarchate of Constantinople. In 1999–2000, with the blessing of Metropolitan Nikita

(Loulias) of Hong Kong and Southeast Asia, a Greek priest was sent to Bangkok. For lack of their own church, services were held in Catholic churches. The congregation of the Patriarchate of Constantinople in Thailand included mainly Greeks, as well as some Romanians.

In response to numerous appeals from Orthodox believers, mainly citizens of the former USSR, the Holy Synod of the Russian Orthodox Church at its meeting on 28 December 1999 decided to open St Nicholas Parish in Bangkok. By the same decision, Hegumen Oleg (Cherepanin) was appointed the first rector of the newly formed parish. Soon after its appearance, the Russian Orthodox community in Bangkok ceased to be mono-ethnic, as Orthodox Romanians joined it. In addition, the conversion of local Thais to Orthodoxy began. The first of these was Danai Bath (who received the baptismal name Daniel), who wished to become an Orthodox priest and was sent to study at Saint Petersburg Theological Seminary.

In 2001, after reviewing the activities of the St Nicholas Parish in Bangkok, the Holy Synod of the Russian Orthodox Church decided to open a Representative Office of the Russian Orthodox Church (Moscow Patriarchate) in the Kingdom of Thailand. Hegemon Oleg (Cherepanin) became the representative of the Russian Orthodox Church in Thailand and also provided spiritual nourishment for Orthodox believers in Cambodia and Laos.

In early 2008, the Thai authorities, having considered the long-term activities of the Orthodox community in Thailand, recognised it as useful, in line with the interests of the Kingdom and strengthening the moral foundations of society. The Orthodox Christian Church in Thailand was officially registered in July 2008. In addition to the main parish of St Nicholas Cathedral in Bangkok, there are Russian Orthodox communities in significant centres throughout the country. Today, around 1,000 people in Thailand are Orthodox Christians (about 0.002% of the population of the country), not counting Orthodox people who come to the country on holiday (about 1 million Russian tourists per year). Thai translations of the Divine Liturgy of St John Chrysostom and the Orthodox Book of Prayer have been completed. At the beginning of 2011, construction of the Assumption Monastery in Ratburi Province was completed. A religious school and an Orthodox cemetery were planned for its territory. Among those who wish to become monks are citizens of Russia, Romania, Thailand and Laos. On 21 March 2012, the first issue of the newspaper *Thailand Orthodox* was published.

Cambodia

An Orthodox church in honour of St George the Great Martyr and under the jurisdiction of the Bulgarian Orthodox Church was built on the territory of the Bulgarian Embassy in Phnom Penh, the capital of Cambodia, in 1993. It was erected in commemoration of Bulgarian peacekeepers who died in Cambodia. However, the Bulgarian Orthodox Church did not send priests for the regular conduct of worship in this church.

In the 2000s, a cleric of the Russian Orthodox Church, Oleg (Cherepanin), with the permission of the hierarchy of the Bulgarian Orthodox Church and the leadership of the Bulgarian diplomatic mission in Phnom Penh, began to hold services in the St George Church during his trips to Cambodia. However, as he noted, 'it is difficult to organise a capable parish at the temple, which is located on the special territory'.

A constituent assembly of Orthodox believers took place in Phnom Penh in 2012 and unanimously decided to establish an Orthodox parish in Phnom Penh in the name of the Holy Great Martyr George the Victorious under the jurisdiction of the Moscow Patriarchate. The same year a constituent assembly of parishioners took place in Sihanoukville. The Orthodox believers in Sihanoukville also decided to establish an Orthodox parish in the name of the Great Martyr and Healer Panteleimon. With the blessing of the head of the Office for Foreign Institutions of the Moscow Patriarchate, Archbishop Mark of Yegoryevsk (Golovkov), and within the framework of the programme for the development of Orthodoxy in Southeast Asia, the website 'Orthodoxy in Cambodia' was launched, to be run by the Representative Office of the Russian Orthodox Church in Thailand. In 2013, the Representation of the Russian Orthodox Church in Thailand, to which Cambodia administratively belongs, received a decree by the minister of cults and religions of Cambodia on the government's favourable decision on state registration as a religious organisation of the Russian Orthodox Church under the name Orthodox Christian Church of Cambodia (Moscow Patriarchate).

At the request of Orthodox believers in Cambodia, in October 2015, the Orthodox Prayer Book was published in the Khmer language. In June 2016, the Liturgy of St John Chrysostom was published in Khmer. In addition to the text of the Liturgy itself, the book also contains prayers for Holy Communion and prayers of thanksgiving after Holy Communion. In addition to the temple in the name of the Great Martyr George the Victorious in Phnom Penh and the temple in the name of the Great Martyr Panteleimon in Sihanoukville, a parish is being developed around the temple of the Kazan Icon of the Mother of God in Siem Reap.

Vietnam

Orthodox Christianity is the smallest Christian community in Vietnam. It is represented by only one parish of the Russian Orthodox Church in the city of Vung Tau, where several hundred Russians are employees of

Vietsovpetro (the joint Russian–Vietnamese enterprise for oil and gas exploration). The parish was opened in 2002 following the visit to Vietnam of the chairman of the Russian Orthodox Church's Department for External Church Relations, Metropolitan Kirill (since 2009 Patriarch of Moscow and All Russia). Metropolitan Kirill was the first Russian Orthodox hierarch to visit the country.

Laos

Orthodoxy is represented in Laos by employees of the Russian embassy and other state and commercial organisations of the Russian Federation. Orthodox citizens of former Soviet republics also reside in Laos. A small number of indigenous Lao people have converted to Orthodoxy. The total number of the Orthodox community is no more than 200. There is no Orthodox church in the country, so they have to meet in temporary accommodation. In 2016, the first Laotian priest, Hieromonk Micah (Phiasayawong), was ordained. In the same year, he translated the textbook *The Law of God* by Serafim Slobodsky into the Laotian language.

Indonesia

Orthodoxy first appeared on the territory of modern Indonesia in the seventh century. The followers of the non-Chalcedonian Christianity of the Syrian-Antiochian tradition appeared in Sumatra in the Majapahit period. Soon, however, the traces of Orthodoxy in Indonesia disappeared. The revival of Eastern Christianity in Indonesia began in the twentieth century. In 1934, in Batavia (Jakarta) on the island of Java, a Russian Orthodox parish was founded, to which priest Vasily Bystrov was appointed. The parish was subordinate to the Harbin Diocese. Upon his arrival in Java, Father Vasily reorganised an Orthodox parish and established a church in Bandung. At the end of the 1940s, the parish in Java became subordinate to Archbishop Tikhon of San Francisco. In May 1950, Father Vasily reported that many Russian parishioners had left Indonesia and, as a result, the parish had ceased to exist. Today, Eastern Orthodoxy in Indonesia is represented by the Indonesian Orthodox Church, headed by Archimandrite Daniel Bambang Dwi Byantoro. It has 2,000 members, who are spread across Java, Bali, Sumatra, Celebes, Timor and Papua.

Conclusion

For the foreseeable future, Central and Eastern Europe will remain the main centre of Orthodox Christianity, with more than three-quarters of the total number of Orthodox believers living in the region. By contrast, the entire Asia-Pacific region is home to a mere 4% of the global Orthodox population. Yet, today, the number of Orthodox Christians is increasing in East and Southeast Asia, mainly due to the migration of people from historically Eastern European Orthodox countries (Russians, Greeks, Romanians, Bulgarians, Ukrainians). In recent years, however, interest in Orthodoxy among the local population has also increased, which creates the potential to increase the number of Orthodox believers in these countries. The example of Japan, where the Orthodox Church over many years has occupied a prominent place among religious denominations, demonstrates what is possible.

Korea: A Case Study in Orthodoxy, by Ambrose-Aristotle Zographos

The Orthodox presence in Korea can be traced back to a decision taken in 1897 by the Holy Synod of the Orthodox Church of Russia to begin a Russian Orthodox mission to 'serve the religious needs of the Orthodox Russians who lived in Korea and the possible spread of the holy Orthodox Faith among the indigenous pagan population'. Two years later, deacon Nicholas Alexeev (1869–1952) arrived in Seoul. On 17 February 1900, at the Russian consulate in Seoul, the first Divine Liturgy was celebrated and a temporary chapel dedicated to St Nicholas was consecrated. In 1911, John Kang-Tak (1877–1939), who had previously served as a teacher at the mission school, was ordained as deacon. He was the first Korean Orthodox member of the clergy and was ordained to the priesthood the following year.

After the Bolshevik Revolution in 1917, the Holy Synod decided to bring the Orthodox mission in Seoul under the jurisdiction of the Russian Archbishop of Tokyo, Sergii Tikhomirov, who was the nearest Orthodox bishop to Korea. In 1932, the Korean cantor Alexis Kim Yi-Han (1895–1950) was ordained as a deacon by Archbishop Sergii and in 1947 he was ordained to the priesthood. On 9 July 1950, after celebrating the Divine Liturgy, Father Alexis was arrested by North Korean soldiers and was never seen again. Shortly before this, Father Polikarp Priimak, who had served as head of the Orthodox mission from 1936 to 1949, had been arrested and expelled from the country. This marked the end of the first period of the Orthodox mission in Korea under the jurisdiction of the Moscow Patriarchate.

During the Korean War (1950–3) Orthodox chaplains to the Greek troops provided pastoral ministry to the scattered community of Orthodox Koreans. The political situation after the war made it no longer possible for the Orthodox Church in Korea to come under the jurisdiction of the Russian Orthodox Church. In 1955 it came under the jurisdiction of the Ecumenical Patriarchate of Constantinople. The Ecumenical Patriarch ensured that pastoral care was provided to the Orthodox Church in Korea through a succession of arrangements until, on 20 April 2004, the Ecumenical Patriarchate established the Holy Metropolis of Korea. Bishop

Soterios of Zela was elected first Metropolitan of Korea, and his enthronement took place on 20 June 2004.

As of 2019, the Holy Korean Orthodox Church has seven parishes in South Korea (in Seoul, Busan, Incheon, Jeonju, Palang-Li, Chuncheon and Ulsan) and one in North Korea (Pyeongyang). In addition there are 13 chapels, a monastery, a publishing house, two bookshops, a kindergarten, a home for the elderly, a cemetery and a training and conference centre. Provision is also made for Orthodox immigrants from Russia and other Slavic lands, with the Divine Liturgy being celebrated in their own languages. The Orthodox Metropolis of Korea, which is under the spiritual authority of the Ecumenical Patriarchate of Constantinople, serves all Orthodox who reside in Korea, without any ethnic, national, linguistic or social discrimination.

Great emphasis is given to the practical application of the gospel in the daily life of the faithful. In other words, the Orthodox Christians of Korea are taught that the Orthodox faith is not a theoretical approach to the doctrinal and moral teaching of the church. On the contrary, they are taught that their Orthodox faith must form and shape their daily actions, so that the Orthodox faith becomes life, not abstract knowledge alone. Catechism lessons for those preparing to join the Orthodox Church stress that the gospel is not a textbook from which one obtains intellectual knowledge but a way of life or mode of being. The Orthodox approach is based on the teaching of the holy fathers of the early church: 'deed is more important than theory' (πράξις θεωρίας επίβασις).

For example, the Orthodox Church's dogma regarding salvation as *theosis* (deification of man), namely that Christ 'became man so that we might be god-like', teaches that Christ is the Saviour of not only the soul but also the body, which has implications for the daily lives of the faithful. Korean Orthodox are taught to respect their own bodies and the bodies of others because Christ deified the human body through his incarnation, and he raised it glorified to the throne of God with his Ascension. One consequence is that the Orthodox faithful object to burning the dead. That is why, in Korea, burial rather than cremation is practised for those who have died. The body of the deceased is delivered to mother earth, looking forward to 'the resurrection of the dead and the life of the world to come'.

Following a catechumen's baptism, great emphasis is placed on participation in the liturgical and sacramental life of the church. The Orthodox Church's rich liturgical prayer and hymnologic tradition is a treasure used in the daily, weekly and annual worship cycles to assist the faithful. However, the liturgical life of the believer is not cut off from everyday practice. After participating in the sacrament of the Eucharist during the Divine Liturgy, which is the centre of the spiritual life of every Orthodox

Christian, the faithful continue to 'live the liturgy' in their everyday lives. The true Light and the Holy Spirit that believers receive by consuming the Body and Blood of Christ – not symbolically but substantially – positively shapes their contact with their fellow human beings. Participating in the liturgy helps Orthodox Christians to see in the face of every other person the image of Christ 'in another other form'; it strengthens them to behave with sacrificial love towards every 'little' brother of Christ, 'for whom Christ died'. Consistent with the example of the God of Love, applied love is the essence of Orthodox Christian life.

Finally, Orthodox Christianity places great emphasis on the ascetic way of life. 'Orthodox spirituality' is by no means words only, but daily struggle – a struggle against fallen human passions and a struggle for the acquisition of the Kingdom, by the grace of God. Fasting, vigilance, philanthropy and other means of spiritual activity contribute to the cultivation of Orthodox spirituality and help the faithful in their effort to become 'partakers of divine nature' (2 Peter 1: 4).

Bibliography

Heliotis, Andreas, Ἡ Ὀρθοδοξία στὴν Κορέα, Συνοπτικὸ χρονικὸ τῆς Ἱεραποστολῆς τῆς Ὀρθοδόξου Ἐκκλησίας στὴν Κορέα [*Orthodoxy in Korea: Concise Chronicle of Orthodox Mission in Korea*] (Athens: Πατριαρχικὸν Ἵδρυμα Ὀρθοδόξου Ἱεραποστολῆς Ἄπω Ἀνατολῆς, 2005).

Huang, Paulos, and Nikolay Samoylov (eds), *International Journal of Sino-Western Studies*, 14 (2018), *Special Issue on Orthodoxy and China*.

Православие на Дальнем Востоке, Выпуски 1–4 [*Orthodoxy in the Far East, Vols 1–4*] (St Petersburg.: СПбГУ, 1991, 1996, 2001, 2004).

Sablina, Eleonora, Саблина Э. Б. 150 лет Православия в Японии. История Японской Православной Церкви и ее основатель Святитель Николай [*150 years of Orthodoxy in Japan. History of the Japanese Orthodox Church and its founder, Saint Nicholas of Japan*] (St Petersburg: Дмитрий Буланин, 2006).

Widmer, Eric, *The Russian Ecclesiastical Mission in Peking during the Eighteenth Century* (Cambridge, MA: Harvard University Press, 1976).

Protestants

Timothy T. N. Lim

During the seventeenth and eighteenth centuries, European Protestants arrived in East and Southeast Asia. Protestant Christianity took root when missionary societies and churches made headway among locals during the nineteenth century. Since the twentieth century, Western-nurtured and indigenous Protestantisms have emerged, developed and matured in various socio-political and postcolonial contexts, decrying oppression, exploitation and unjust treatment of women and the poor. Churches also experimented with educational, entrepreneurial-missional, health-care and social initiatives.

Protestant churches have grown rapidly in China and South Korea. Large and growing churches are also found in Indonesia, Singapore and Taiwan. The late twentieth and early twenty-first centuries have seen the conversion of ethnic groups of Akha, Hmong, Karen and Lahu to Protestantism in Indonesia, Laos, Philippines, Thailand and Vietnam. The Vietnamese governmental Committee for Religious Affairs, for example, reported a sixfold multiplication of Protestants from 1975 to 2013 despite state censuses claiming a declining interest in religious matters between 1999 and 2009. Many smaller-sized Protestant churches also faithfully preach and witness for Christ, theologise and raise disciples in Cambodia, Timor-Leste, Malaysia, Mongolia, Myanmar, Taiwan, Thailand and Vietnam. Protestants in Japan and the Philippines remain few in number. The Christian conversion rate in recent decades has grown more rapidly than the population growth rate in Cambodia, China, Indonesia, North Korea, Laos, Myanmar and Thailand.

Theological Characteristics

During the past 60 years, Asian Protestants have inherited Western Protestant denominational taxonomy and theologies, experimented with indigenisation, faced pushback in contextualisation and experienced theological and ecclesiastical conundrums, such as the conservative–liberal divide among Western Protestants and the reception of Spirit-filled movements. The broad conservative–liberal divide continues sharply today in China, Myanmar, South Korea and Taiwan, while its impact is less intense among churches in Malaysia, Indonesia, Japan, Singapore,

Thailand and Vietnam. Protestants who aligned with the World Council of Churches (WCC) and the Christian Conference of Asia (CCA) were regarded as 'liberals' because of their revisionist reception of Scripture as one among many sources (instead of the only source) for theology. These Protestants also expanded the gospel's salvific witness to include advocacy for the socially, economically and politically oppressed, including women, children and the poor. In the perception of theologically conservative Asian Protestants, the conciliar churches had compromised the faith by embracing theological liberalism, disavowing the authority of Scripture, rejecting Jesus as God's revelation and saviour, accommodating religious pluralism and supplanting the gospel with advocacy in social justice and creation care. The conservative constituency responded by contending for biblical authority. Asian conservative Protestants retrieved local cultures within an *a priori* theological sufficiency of a closed canonical scripture and accepted the agency and finality of Christ to save humanity.

To a great extent, the conservatives have won the debate. Today's mainline Protestants in Asia receive the infallible Bible as normative for belief and conduct, centre their faith in Christ, preach the Evangelical gospel, promote a 'born again' conversion experience and adhere to Evangelical piety and social activism. And although the membership of the Asia Evangelical Alliance registers only national Evangelical associations rather than mainline denominational membership, the national members of the Alliance in Japan, Korea and Singapore include Lutheran, Methodist and Presbyterian denominational membership. Gordon-Conwell Theological Seminary President Scott Sunquist rightly notes the increasingly Evangelical expressions of Asian mainline Protestantism.

Asian Protestants have also been influenced by the Pentecostal/Charismatic movement. While many reacted against non-cessationist theologies between the 1960s and 1990s, mainline denominations today have either accepted sign gifts (and, for some, even the glossolalia) or maintained a revisionist cessationist position (repudiating teaching on tongues but keeping an open mind about God's continuing revelation). Still, the drive of some Korean mega-churches to promulgate an affluent,

Protestants in East and Southeast Asia, 1970

Region	Total population	Christian population	Protestant population	% of region Protestant	% of Christians Protestant
East Asia	996,425,000	11,456,000	3,366,000	0.3%	29.4%
Southeast Asia	280,607,000	50,740,000	9,093,000	3.2%	17.9%
East and Southeast Asia	1,277,032,000	62,196,000	12,459,000	1.0%	20.0%
Globe	3,700,578,000	1,229,309,000	204,506,000	5.5%	16.6%

Source: Todd M. Johnson and Gina A. Zurlo (eds), *World Christian Database* (Leiden/Boston: Brill), accessed March 2018.

consumeristic expression of Christianity has come in for criticism. Nonetheless, the immediate agency of the Holy Spirit has gained ascendancy among the strongly Evangelical mainline and the less expressly Evangelical Protestants.

The Christian Conference of Asia and the Association for Theological Education in South East Asia (ATESEA) have also seen more Evangelically oriented participation by Protestant denominations that previously followed higher critical presuppositions in biblical, theological and missiological scholarship. Particularly, the turnaround at ATESEA is partly attributed to Evangelical faculty joining and leading the Trinity Theological College, Singapore, and its collaborative activity in the region. Though this Evangelical fervour promotes collegiality rather than separatism and seeks wider collaborative witness, a convergence between conciliar traditions and Evangelical Protestant denominations in Asia is not immediately apparent. The staunchly Evangelical Asia Theological Association has leaned towards a Philippine Evangelical contextuality. In recent decades, indigenous theologians and diaspora returnees have engaged theologically with local and inter-religious sources. Sino-Christian and critical cross-religious studies – Christian readings of Asian non-Christian religious canons and traditions as well as using other religious/cultural lenses to read Christian Scripture, traditions and practices – represent innovative Protestant theological engagement. Payap University in Chiang Mai now seeks inter-religious, less exclusive readings in Buddhist Thailand. The development actualises an insight from early-twentieth-century Chinese Christian scholar Ching-yi Cheng: inculturating Christianity might not require that theologians do away with local ideas and cultural customs.

Ecumenism and Ecclesiology

Asian Protestants share a historical-spiritual connection with the European Reformational churches in a threefold theological, liturgical and ecclesiastical separation from Catholicism. They uphold the five '*solas*' of Protestant faith along with a fourfold commitment to world evangelisation, discipleship nurture, transmitting faith and containing/curtailing

Protestants in East and Southeast Asia, 2020

Region	Total population	Christian population	Protestant population	% of region Protestant	% of Christians Protestant
East Asia	1,663,619,000	128,787,000	45,832,000	2.8%	35.6%
Southeast Asia	669,016,000	153,102,000	32,703,000	4.9%	21.4%
East and Southeast Asia	2,332,635,000	281,889,000	78,535,000	3.4%	27.9%
Globe	7,795,482,000	2,518,834,000	486,010,000	6.2%	19.3%

Source: Todd M. Johnson and Gina A. Zurlo (eds), *World Christian Database* (Leiden/Boston: Brill), accessed March 2018.

cultural seduction. However, they share limited historical, ecclesiastical and socio-cultural/political proximity with European Protestantism's ecumenical development, particularly the modern ecumenical movement's attempt to repair the ecclesiological divide.

Thus, at the quincentenary of the Protestant Reformation, apart from a few exceptions – in Japan, Myanmar and Singapore – the Protestant and Catholic Churches in Asia registered their prejudicial, ecclesiological and theological mutual condemnation or indifference, while historic European Christianity ushered in a more conciliatory inter-church era. While the quincentenary was marked in Europe with notes of reconciliation and convergence, it was a very different story in Asia. On 31 October 2017, the learned emeritus Asian Methodist bishop the Reverend Dr Robert Solomon resounded the sixteenth-century Protestant convictions to a multi-congregational Protestant church, Covenant Evangelical Free Church in Singapore, while a well attended Roman Catholic Mass at the Church of Divine Mercy in the same country said nothing about the Reformation. Accordingly, conservative Asian Protestants resist initiatives towards pan-Protestant–Catholic ecclesiality and keep a distance from conciliarism.

Several examples illustrate the spectrum of the Asian Protestant reception of ecumenical efforts. When the WCC held its tenth assembly in Busan, South Korea, in 2013, major South Korean Presbyterian churches protested against what they perceived as the WCC's stances on condoning homosexuality, gravitating towards socialism and denying Jesus as unparalleled mediator of salvation. In contrast, the Hong Kong Christian Council, the Hong Kong Chinese Christian Churches Union and the Vietnamese mainline Protestant churches welcomed the WCC's partnership/connection.

Approaches to Protestant–Catholic relations vary too. In South Korea, *Gidokgyo* (Protestants) do not regard *Chonjugyo* and *Gatolic* (Catholic Christianity) as faith siblings. Cambodian Protestants joined Catholics to translate the Bible into the Khmer language amid their antagonism towards Catholics. On the other hand, the Christian Conference of Asia

Changes in Protestants in East and Southeast Asia, 1970–2020, growth rate, % per year

Region	Total population	Christian population	Protestant population
East Asia	1.03%	4.96%	5.36%
Southeast Asia	1.75%	2.23%	2.59%
East and Southeast Asia	1.21%	3.07%	3.75%
Globe	1.50%	1.45%	1.75%

Source: Todd M. Johnson and Gina A. Zurlo (eds), *World Christian Database* (Leiden/Boston: Brill), accessed March 2018.

and Catholics jointly stood in solidarity for ecumenical formation with regard to social, developmental, gender and political injustices, as well as advocacy to overcome poverty and to respond to HIV/AIDS concerns and other crises and emergencies. At CCA's international consultation for ecumenism in Asia, held in July 2017, the Asia Evangelical Alliance, the Roman Catholic Church's Federation of Asian Bishops' Conferences (FABC) and the CCA agreed to witness a 'more relevant and unique Asian ecclesiology . . . with a vision of seeking to build the Kingdom of God'. The Myanmar Council of Churches and the Catholic Bishops' Conference of Myanmar have started a joint commission, while the Presbyterian Church in Taiwan and the Roman Catholic Church have organised reconciliatory/unity prayers together.

Intra-Protestant fellowship exists for different reasons. In East Asia, the China Christian Council and the union of Three-Self Patriotic Movement (TSPM) Protestant Churches pledge to construct an indigenised Chinese Christian socialism. The National Christian Council of Japan seeks solidarity with the oppressed/discriminated and to promote mutual understanding and peace between people and religions. Meanwhile, the Evangelical Mongolian Church Council, a 2012-established association of Mongolian pastors and elders, collaborates with Intercessory Prayer Network, Word Harvest, Cru, Help International, Youth With A Mission, JCS International, Genesis-AOM and Scripture Union to promote a 24-hour prayer movement. In South Korea, Protestants have been divided between the Korean National Council of Churches (a perceived political and ecumenical-liberal human rights advocacy agency) and an ecumenically conservative Christian Council of Korea (CCK). Recent schisms saw the formation of associations serving the Tonghap, Koryo, Hapdong and Koshin Presbyterian Churches.

In Southeast Asia, the Cambodian Christian Protestant Community seeks to represent 'all denominations and independent churches' to the government of Cambodia. Otherwise, all other national councils represent the churches as needed, serve the cause of intra-Christian unity, bring churches together for common witness and facilitate inter-religious dialogue for peaceful coexistence in their respective socio-political contexts. These councils include: the Communion of Churches in Indonesia (Persekutuan Gereja-gereja di Indonesia); the Council of Churches of Malaysia (Majlis Gereja-Gereja Malaysia), along with the Christian Federation of Malaysia and the National Evangelical Christian Fellowship; the Myanmar Council of Churches; the National Council of Churches in the Philippines (Sangguniang Pambansang Mga Simbahan sa Pilipinas); and the National Council of Churches, Singapore. The Philippines council includes Old Catholic traditions but not Roman Catholics.

Worship and Liturgy

In 1999, a Western liturgical musicologist observed that Asian churches used more Western liturgical resources than local sources. For him, the lack of contextually flavoured worship resources and liturgies did not match an ethno-musicological fact: three of the world's five major musical notation systems originate from Asia (China, India and Indonesia) while the other two originate in the Middle East (Persia) and the West. An appeal by the late Sri Lankan theologian D. T. Niles for more indigenous productions, which began with the *East Asian Christian Council Hymnal* (1963), gave impetus to I-to Loh's pioneering collation of more than 20 Asian hymnals.

Today, indigenous Asian hymnal literature/production is expanding. *Christian Music from Asia for the World* (2014) is revised from *Sound the Bamboo – CCA Hymnal 2000* and selected from hymnals from 20 Asian countries (and in 44 Asian languages) published since *Asian Songs of Worship* (1988). In China, besides *Putian Songzhan*, known largely as *Hymnal of Universal Praise* (Shanghai, 1936), the indigenously composed *Jianan Shige* (*Hymnals/Songs of Canaan*), by Hui-minority born-again composer Lü Xiaomin, has been used throughout Chinese churches. In Taiwan, conservative Lutherans and Presbyterians still rely on the older *Zhangmeizhichuan* (*Stream of Praise*), whereas Hillsong worship songs are sung in newer independent international-styled churches such as Ling Yang Tang (literally translated as Spirit-embracing Temple/Hall). The Evangelical Formosan Church General Assembly (EFCGA) in North America, a Taiwanese-migrant Christian establishment with an indigenous vision, has through its Logos Evangelical Fellowship produced indigenous worship, theological and ministerial literature for use in its 140 congregations in Taiwan, Australia, New Zealand and Asia. The Presbyterian Church of Taiwan produced *Sheng-si* (*Sacred Hymnal*, 2009) after 28 years of editorial collation to provide a wider historical, ecumenical, contextual, multicultural and liturgical representation. *Sheng-si* comprises 50% Western hymns (650 hymns), 25% Taiwanese tribal-language songs and 25% majority-world resources. The production of bilingual English–Korean hymnals also raises issues of contextualising worship.

Observers have regularly noted intense and disciplined pursuit of God and spiritual vibrancy among Asian Protestants, especially those who are subject to religious persecution. Rural churches in China maintain fervent dawn prayers. South Korean Protestants hold ardent daybreak prayers in the mountains. Unlike the Chinese and Korean Protestants who intercede for the world and for national affairs, a recent study of prayers among Protestants in the Philippines reveals that Filipino Protestants see prayer as petition-making or spontaneous appeal to God to improve one's personal conditions; prayer is not conceived as following a formula or reading a (monologue) litany. In Islamic countries, Protestant spirituality is tested as disciples live out their faith. Across these and other churches, spiritual hunger is also evident in believers' active gatherings and participation in Bible-study groups. On creative ministries of worship and service, the Teatro Ekumenikal, a cultural theatre group of the National Council of Churches in the Philippines, expresses worship as doxology through creative arts, using the medium to educate and invite audiences to better understand social justice issues and to provide a wider understanding of prayer, worship and spirituality. Yadong, a Taiwanese Protestant drama group, exercises a similar ministry.

On indigenous worship and liturgy, scenarios vary too. In Vietnam, some Hmong Protestant congregations gather to receive American Hmong Protestant preachers' sermons that are streamed live via Skype. Younger generations in Vietnamese Christian congregations draw readily from Hillsong's YouTube worship resources. Singapore's Chinese-dialect-speaking congregations rely on Mandarin and Chinese-dialect resources from Malaysia, Taiwan and occasionally China. Otherwise, the predominantly English-speaking congregations across various denominations in Singapore use Western hymnals and worship litanies for traditional worship services and contemporary Western worship resources for the contemporary worship services. The pervasiveness of contemporary worship culture presents challenges for nurturing indigenous theologically deep and liturgically rich worship.

Mission and Witness

China, Mongolia and South Korea have all seen exponential Protestant growth as a result of conversion to Christianity. However, the upward growth rates have tapered with secularisation and commercialisation. The conversion growth rate in South Korea has stagnated because of growing distrust and dissatisfaction with aggressive Protestant evangelism and frequent moral/ethical scandals among Protestant ministers.

In Mongolia, criticisms arising from the circulation of suicide notes from Christian youths who wrote 'I gave my life to Jesus' and videos of women in tears praying 'Father, use me' have led social critics to wrongly accuse churches of indoctrinating youths and women to disregard filial piety and familial responsibilities, respectively. Mongolian public misconstrual of Protestantism is also due to a misassociation of Korean-initiated Moonism and Protestantism and a reaction to many disrespectful criticisms of Buddhism by Thomas Terry, owner of Eagle Television, a 24-hour news and overseas Christian broadcasting agency in Mongolia.

Despite these pushbacks on evangelistic fervour, Korean Protestant churches, such as Chunghyeon Church and Gwangrim Methodist Church, have sought a turnaround by planting churches in newer residential complexes, which have generated new conversion growth. Mongolian Protestants have redirected attention to social services. Churches have been learning the correlations between stewardship and witness as they become more discerning in evangelism and in managing public responses to the Christian message. The turnaround will take time.

Asian Protestants continue to be a modernising force for society. In the twentieth century, missionary activities were unwittingly perceived as programmes for Westernising and modernising Asia. This opened doors for Christian outreach (as in Korea) despite concerns about the compatibility of Christian exclusivity with local cultures (for example, in Japan) and misperception of missionary services as tools for Western political agents/spies (as in Vietnam). Nonetheless, Protestant mission was favourably received until there were socio-political outcries for 'de-Westernisation' and 'de-Christianisation'. In Taiwan, Presbyterian outreach to natives (*yuan zuming*) helped indigenous peoples to stay current with the urban populace. Retrospectively, Protestant mission indirectly facilitated a transfer of knowledge and introduced Western models of economic growth, education, health care and modernisation for a developing Asia, which expedited progress (albeit unevenly).

One example of Protestantism's modernising force is the increasing role of women in Christian leadership. Today, women hold leadership roles and ordained ministries in various Protestant denominational churches in Southeast Asia. The Lutheran World Federation reports that 41 of its 54 Asian member churches ordain women in ministry. The World Communion of Reformed Churches' declaration on women in ministry registers that only nine Asian member churches did not ordain women in ministry. Protestant views of gender equality contribute to emancipation of women in paternalistic Asia. In many Chinese house churches and TSPM churches, women hold select leadership roles. Indonesian Protestants – especially in the Gereja Masehi Injili di Timor, the Christian Church of Jawa, the Batak Protestant Christian Church in Sumatra and even the staunchly conservative Christian and Missionary Alliance-founded Gereja Kemah Injil Indonesia – now ordain women ministers. Ordained women ministers serve in congregations of the Methodist Church in Singapore and represent them on international theological commissions. In Taiwan, the Presbyterian and Lutheran churches have women ministers sharing in the pulpit, although theologically trained and gifted women leaders still provide supporting roles to male leaders, unlike their counterparts in Hong Kong. The Church of Christ in Thailand, too, has welcomed gender equality.

Promoting gender-equal leadership will remain challenging. In China, especially in TSPM churches, critical appointments are still held by men.

A recent interpretation of Calvinist theology has swayed Chinese house churches from their long-standing reliance on women pastors and leaders. In Malaysia, Methodist denominational leadership positions are still filled primarily by males. Ironically, in Mongolia, even though women leaders are well received locally, Western missionaries have frowned upon local women in church leadership. In Myanmar, Presbyterian and Baptist women pastors often undertake low-profile services, while Methodist women pastors lead more openly. In South Korea, patriarchal sociality remains the norm despite extensive reporting of ministers abusing and mistreating their wives.

Protestant missions and churches will remain invested in education. Innumerable institutions of higher learning in China, South Korea and Singapore today can trace their origins to the efforts of early missionaries and, later, local Protestants. These Christian schools provide literacy and facilitate upward social mobility for the poor, thereby transforming social, economic and political life for Christians and other residents.

As urbanisation and secularisation take effect across Asia, governments will exercise more leadership in policy-making and providing education. Programmes of modernisation (by-products of historic and ongoing Protestant mission and witness) and educational endeavours started by Protestant missions have, in many cases, come under state jurisdiction or, if they remain as private schools, have lost part or all of their autonomy upon compliance with state policies and the ruling governmental and educational ideologies.

For example, Christian schools in Singapore adhere to the Educational Department's policy and curriculum and are required to employ teachers of other religions. In Malaysia, the 433 Christian mission schools serving 240,000 learners are subjected to restrictions that limit their autonomy. For instance, teachers are hired by the government's educational authorities. In contemporary Myanmar and Vietnam, Christian schools that are independently owned, administered and financed are sought-after educational institutions, although these schools are also subjected to provincial and/or township oversight.

Postcolonial Protestant churches have been facilitating social change. Asian churches that align with the WCC seek to free society and the church from colonial, neo-colonial and Western ideological values and influences. They continue to decry socio-economic exploitation and political oppression as well as the unjust treatment of women, ethnic minorities and the poor. They build upon medical and social missions started by Western missionaries. On the other hand, mainline Evangelical Protestants regularly critique those aligned with the WCC as having supplanted the gospel with advocacy in social justice and creation care.

Despite mutual criticisms of each other's efforts as either too eternally minded or else too justice oriented (to the neglect of offering Christ's eternal salvation), both these streams and many others in between have conscientiously provided social and medical services in an ever-changing, widely diverse and socio-economically unevenly developing Asia. For instance, the Christian Conference of Asia and the Asia Theological Association have been independently supporting programmes to eradicate poverty and prevent economic exploitation. In the last decade, both spectrums have experimented with agricultural–missional–entrepreneurial initiatives known as 'business as mission'.

Fighting poverty and injustice is a response to the region's income gap and problems of urbanisation. Protestantism will perhaps have to rethink its role as an agent of spirituality and societal development, however. In Vietnam, for instance, although Protestantism has reached a sizeable ethnic minority in the lowlands and highlands, the World Bank reports the highest poverty head-counts among ethnic minorities. In Mongolia, Protestants seek social reform to counter vices such as alcoholism, abuse and criminality. Protestants in China will have to come alongside the 30 million rural Chinese in extreme poverty, including Protestants living in rural areas, in their struggle for survival as urbanisation reshapes towns, cities and provinces, and to complement the state's goal to raise the annual income for the poorest by 2020. Protestants will likely expand their education, health-care and social-service provision in Cambodia, Indonesia, Laos, the Philippines, Thailand and Vietnam besides the hundreds of Protestant schools, 40 or more hospitals and many social services in the region.

Opportunities abound for Asian churches to develop and lead boundary-crossing missions as they experience conversion growth, send staggering numbers of missionaries globally (particularly from South Korea), inspire more social entrepreneurs and see indigenous Chinese gospel-heralds bringing the gospel 'back to Jerusalem'. Churches would benefit from studying and implementing trans- and inter-Asian migrations for ministry, such as how Filipinos witness for Christ as migrant workers. Learning from oral traditions will better aid the communication of the gospel to oral cultures and to Asia's increasingly affluent, technologically advanced, secular (or even anti-Christian) society. Asian churches have yet to focus on the emerging areligious, non-religious and 'deconverted' populations. Less denominationally driven 'insider movements' and inter-denominational collaboration will increase. Cross-denominational Protestants will likely receive Pentecostal/Charismatic spirituality as harbingers of evangelism and church growth despite pushback by Evangelicals and mainline Protestants. Perhaps the voluntary ecclesial association of Protestants, as well as the attraction to pragmatism, will lead churches to chart Christianity in the Global South less dogmatically than the theological-ecclesiological structures.

Inter-regional and inter-ethnic opportunities could inspire constructive missions. The need for contextualisation in church life, discipleship and evangelism will remain. For instance, Mongolia might become a base to nurture religious exchange for Northeast Asia, especially North Korea, given its geopolitical and economic goodwill relations with Russia, China and North Korea. Ethnic minority Christians from the Chin, Cachin and Karen people could potentially reach 132 other ethnic minority groups in Myanmar if they could overcome the norm of only evangelising their own ethnic groups and seek social justice for constituencies beyond themselves. In Vietnam, Protestants who have actively won over ethnic groups could broaden their reach by exploring urban ministries and addressing urban poverty to the rising urban middle-class Vietnamese.

Religious Liberty and Inter-religious Relations

Today, humanity does not consistently respect basic human rights regardless of culture, ethnicity, race, religion, language, sexual orientation, social standing and other socio-political identity markers. Protestants continue to experience persecution. As society becomes urbanised and affluent, those 'left behind', including the religious faithful, will face other forms of discrimination. The test of 'lived experience' in discipleship will get tense as the societal cultures of consumerism, selfishness, incivility and godlessness increase.

State policy on religious liberty and inter-religious relations affects religious life in the 17 countries of the region. Christians enjoy relative freedom to practise their religion in Singapore's secular, social-democratic and multi-religious society. Likewise, in predominantly Buddhist-populated Taiwan and Thailand, Christians may practise their faith while respecting Buddhists. In socialist China as well as Confucian-dominated Vietnam, religious groups practise religion with stipulated state sanctions.

However, Christians practise their faith more reservedly in sharia-law Malaysia and Pancasila-Islamic Indonesia, although the constitutions of both countries grant religious adherents freedom to practise their faiths. Violence against Christians occurs frequently. Though some have re-conceptualised cultural civilising (or *adat*) in the aftermath of past conflicts in Sulawesi, south Kalimantan and Ambon, the bombings of churches in Surabaya killed more than 140 in May 2018, testing inter-religious trust. In the Catholic Philippines, religious violence caused by Islamic jihadists is a constant concern of the churches.

In Buddhist-privileged Mongolia, though its constitution permits the practising of select religions, including Christianity, Christians who evangelise actively have unwittingly aggravated Buddhist–Christian tension. Some Buddhist monks criticised Christians for receiving foreign resources and for kowtowing to foreign cultures and religious practices. Christians, on the other hand, attacked the Buddhist religion and the concept of salvation in a karmic worldview. Muslim–Christian relations have been particularly challenging in Bayan-Ulgii, a largely Muslim province in Mongolia. In Theravada-Buddhist Myanmar, roughly 75% of the Burmese are exclusive Buddhists. Some Buddhists regularly antagonise Cachin, Chin and Karen Christians, though in recent decades antagonism has been redirected to the Rohingya Muslims.

In China, the redrawing of state laws on religious practice and monitoring under local township jurisdiction instead of reporting to the religious affairs bureau in February 2018 meant that Chinese Protestants – whether previously TSPM or registered or non-registered house churches – will experience pressures limiting religious practice. The prospect looks bleak for non-registered churches even as TSPM churches in Shanghai, Wenzhou and other towns and provinces have shut down or will have to reformulate orthodoxy for Sinicisation. With regard to North Korea, reports of defectors and foreign workers paint a graphic picture of religious and political restrictions. Whether the North Korean government will enact the constitutional guarantee of genuine freedom of religious practice remains unknown. Mission agencies, however, have reported that death sentences and/or imprisonment are stated penalties for practising Christianity.

Religious persecutions in Cambodia, Myanmar and Vietnam have receded as economic development has helped their governments and people to become better disposed towards Christianity. Formerly, local Christians were regarded as spies for foreign governments. As the Vietnamese government embraces the market economy, its former suspicion has diminished. The recognition of minorities in upcoming years remains uncertain at present, since ethnic minorities continue to experience persecution from dominant groups. In Malaysia and Indonesia, an underlying inter-religious animosity still stirs persecutions and hate crimes against Christians. This was evident in the bombings at Surabaya in Indonesia in May 2018 and the kidnapping of Malaysian Pastor Raymond Koh in February 2017 (he remains missing as of May 2019).

As Asian nations regulate religious practice and inter-religious relations, Protestants will grow in their discipleship and love amid animosity and hatred from the religious other and/or government officials. Responding to threats of religious fundamentalism, Asian Protestants will likely maintain their exclusivistic understanding of faith amid limited collaborations for inter-religious community development. On the opposite end of the spectrum, the Bangkok-based Asian Forum on Cultural Development, which invited Buddhists, Christians and Muslims to serve in community development in several Southeast Asian countries, has blazed an inter-religious trail.

Social and Political Presence

Protestants' socio-political presence contributes a vital moral compass and provides a sanctifying role to society, albeit expressed and felt differently in the region. Having survived the wars, Japanese and Korean Protestants still chart an alternative national consciousness. Protestant churches that received North Korean Christian refugees during the Korean War (1950–3) have grown into mega-churches, such as the Chunghyeon Presbyterian Church, Gwangrim Methodist Church, Somang Church and Youngnak Church. Founding and leading members of these churches have been core members of South Korea's conservative right-wing movement. However, Korean Presbyterians, despite their active nationalistic influence during the Japanese colonial period, have been losing public confidence: many ministers have evaded taxes, been caught in sex scandals and/or embezzled funds and pursued aggressive proselytising policies to finance high-salaried ministers and construct opulent church buildings.

Besides supporting the Mingjing dang (Democratic Progressive Party), Taiwanese Presbyterians' active advocacy for human rights and minority rights, including the rights of indigenous minorities (*yuan zuming*), is widely acknowledged. In recent years, politically inactive Protestants have started to engage public discourse, such as joining the Sunflower Movement to evaluate the legislative procedure in 2014 and contributing to public debate about changing the constitutional definition of the spousal relationship in a civil marriage to possibly accept a 'multi-partner-type familial relationship' (*duoyuan cheng jia*) in 2016.

Asian Protestants continue to offer either active or implicit support to peacekeeping. The National Council of Churches in South Korea, the Korean Christian Federation in North Korea and the World Council of Churches have fervently prayed and sought socio-political reconciliation for the Korean peninsula. At the time of writing, there are hopes that these prayers might by answered by the Panmunjom Declaration of 27 April 2018 in which North and South Korea committed to demilitarise the peninsula and usher in a new period of peaceful and prosperous coexistence.

In many contexts, Protestants struggle to respond effectively to contentious civil-religious issues. Three examples suffice. Chinese Protestants still struggle to accept or repudiate the official position of the China Christian Council and the TSPM churches on Sinicisation (that is, the development of a Chinese Christian socialism/nationalism). In Mongolia, Protestants have refused to join social movements demonstrating against child abuse, opposing corruption, demanding socio-political transparency and expressing concern for ecology. The church has remained silent while witnessing environmental degradation, deforestation and pollution of rivers and lakes caused by urbanisation and irresponsible mining. In Myanmar, ethnic minority Christians from the Chin, Cachin and Karen people still seek social justice only for themselves but not for the 132 other ethnic groups. Such Protestant exclusivity contrasts with Buddhists' active social engagement for the masses.

Protestants can benefit from rethinking their witness, such as how they might contribute to national development amid pressing socio-political concerns and without infringing church–state regulations. Without collective effort, a few Christians elected to public office – in Indonesia, Malaysia, Mongolia, Singapore, South Korea – will produce only sporadic efforts to effect public good. Consider Mongolia again: though the land contains abundant mineral deposits, the mining industry that has been driving economic growth has often done so at the expense of people's livelihoods. Protestants' refusal to seek the nation's development and speak against exploitation leads to a loss of credibility and a missed opportunity to witness to the faith amidst a suffering people.

Conclusion

In Christian witness, postcolonial Protestant emancipatory trajectories will continue to call churches to act on behalf of God and the suffering of marginalised people to restore peace and justice, facilitate reconciliation and care for the voiceless. As the former executive secretary of the Christian Conference of Asia, Hope S. Antone, observes, Christians witness in the midst of massive poverty, powerlessness and pluralism. Hopefully, future Asian Protestant emancipatory programmes, such as Micah Asia, will overcome impasses between the theological/missional shibboleths of the earlier Asian Christian generation, which followed either radical postcolonial, liberational praxis paradigms or the cautious conservative Evangelical aversion to social justice witness. Missional partnership in the future will no longer impose Western ideals or dominate local missions. Observers have also noted a nascent development of philanthropy, a significant rise of ultra-wealthy Asians, as well as a predominant lower-income cluster of churches that contribute in their different ways to social development. If Protestants do not construct a viable Asian Protestant social teaching to inform the churches' social justice service and evangelism, others will soon take the initiative as the rich–poor disparity widens.

Bibliography

Kwan, Simon Shui-Man, *Postcolonial Resistance and Asian Theology* (London: Routledge, 2013).

Ngo, Tam, *The New Way: Protestants and the Hmong in Vietnam* (Washington, DC: University of Washington Press, 2016).

Toh, I-to, *In Search for Asian Sounds and Symbols in Worship*, ed. Michael Poon (Singapore: Trinity Theological College, 2012).

Wilfred, Felix (ed.), *The Oxford Handbook of Christianity in Asia* (Oxford: Oxford University Press, 2014).

Yung, Hwa, 'South-East Asian Protestantism to the Present Day', in Alister E. McGrath and Darren C. Marks (eds), *The Blackwell Companion to Protestantism* (Oxford: Wiley-Blackwell, 2004), 206–9.

Catholics

Daniel Franklin E. Pilario CM

Catholicism is a minority religion in East and Southeast Asia, with the exception of the Philippines and Timor-Leste. In this context, how does the Catholic consciousness coexist with other ancient religions? Let me start with a short narrative. I once taught a theology class for Catholic young people from different countries in Southeast Asia. To start a lesson on the Resurrection, I asked them to identify what 'resurrection' means to them and to give an example. One student from Myanmar volunteered her experience: 'My brother who died years ago was resurrected in my younger brother who was born right after'. Another one from Thailand shared a parallel experience about his cousin who acted, talked and walked like his uncle who had long ago passed away. Their classmates from Laos narrated similar stories. They truly were convinced that their relatives had 'resurrected'. Were these really about resurrection or perhaps reincarnation? Were they examples of incommensurable religious paradigms or syncretic exchange? Did the experiences evince lack of evangelisation or, rather, inculturation? How does the Catholic consciousness endure alongside other ancient religions in this milieu?

Catholic Christianity as Minority Religion

What are the effects of Catholicism's (and Christianity's) minority position? Like all minorities (cultural, political and economic), religious minorities suffer three problems: security, equality and identity.

First, Catholic/Christian minorities experience violence and persecution. Security issues for minorities can be more difficult in authoritarian states, but the everyday lives of religious minorities anywhere can be quite harsh and violent. Take the case of Myanmar. The 2016 *Report of the US Commission on International Religious Freedom* identifies different forms of harassment of Catholic/Christian congregations by the Buddhist military and government: devastation of churches, destruction of cemeteries, land grabbing, arbitrary arrests, forced mass interrogation of believers inside churches, brainwashing and forced conversion, sexual violence in church compounds, forced displacement of villages and torture of church leaders and members. Thus, it is not only the Rohingyas who suffer in present-day

Myanmar as is widely publicised; the Christians too and other cultural minorities suffer with them.

Second, minorities are always in danger of being discriminated against. Opportunities given to the majority are most often not afforded to others. Laws and customs are structured to the advantage of the dominant groups. For instance, government promotion institutionally favours Buddhists in Myanmar. Christians are sanctioned for not supporting Buddhist activities, and Christian employees are forced to work on Sundays without remuneration.

Third, minorities suffer from problems of identity. On the one hand, the minority needs to assert its identity constantly vis-à-vis the hegemonic group. On the other hand, there is also a danger of being co-opted by the majority group and in the process losing one's identity. These directions engender two understandable reactions – aggression and isolationism. Thus, threatened with violence and discrimination, there is a tendency for Christians (including Catholics) to aggressively assert their religious convictions. At the same time, because of fear and anxiety, Catholics might isolate themselves into their own enclaves to protect themselves.

However, in countries such as Indonesia, South Korea, Taiwan, Thailand and Japan, Catholics are also described as a 'creative minority', whose leading institutions are influential in the fields of education, business and social service. It is not all bad news for the Christian minorities.

Catholicism under Communist Regimes

Catholicism in countries under communist rule is numerically insignificant and has not grown substantially in recent decades. For instance, Laos has only 47,000 Catholics, distributed among four apostolic vicariates (small dioceses directly under Vatican supervision) with only three bishops and a few priests in charge. Similarly, Cambodia has only 25,000 members, divided into three apostolic vicariates. Most of these churches are dependent on foreign help, both in theological training and in their human and material resources. Seminary formation is at its barest minimum and local creative theological production is almost nil. These

Catholics in East and Southeast Asia, 1970

Region	Total population	Christian population	Catholic population	% of region Catholic	% of Christians Catholic
East Asia	996,425,000	11,456,000	2,202,000	0.2%	19.2%
Southeast Asia	280,607,000	50,740,000	37,451,000	13.3%	73.8%
East and Southeast Asia	1,277,032,000	62,196,000	39,653,000	3.1%	63.8%
Globe	3,700,578,000	1,229,309,000	658,556,000	17.8%	53.6%

Source: Todd M. Johnson and Gina A. Zurlo (eds), *World Christian Database* (Leiden/Boston: Brill), accessed March 2018.

churches are working closely with NGOs dedicated to empowerment and social transformation. External agents (foreign religious congregations and lay pastoral workers) use NGOs as their entry point into the local life of these churches.

In China and Vietnam, however, official communist atheism holds a dominant position. The relationship between China and the Vatican is well documented. The situation of Vietnam is less publicised. The main issue in both countries is the rejection of external influence in their own religious affairs. The infiltration of 'foreign forces' refers mainly to Vatican incursion and the presence of international missionaries. Religion is tolerated only if it is subservient to the desires of the ruling party. This is enshrined in the countries' constitutions and their laws. In the case of China, two parallel Catholic churches exist – the official Patriotic Church, which is an organ of the Chinese Communist Party, and the so-called 'underground church', which professes its loyalty to the Pope. The animosity and suspicions from both sides are felt in the everyday lives of ordinary Catholic faithful and church leaders on the ground. The underground church blames the Patriotic Church for living a religion of convenience and compromise. Patriotic Church members are convinced that if they want to live their faith in the present context, they need to get out of their isolation and work with the government. The low-grade conflict comes to a head on the issue of the unauthorised ordination of bishops. Some bishops are ordained without Rome's approval and others without the Communist Party's permission. The Vatican, however, has made some diplomatic inroads in recent years. Though still tentative, the Pope signed an agreement with Chinese officials on 22 September 2018 to accept seven bishops whom the Vatican had excommunicated earlier because their nomination was illegal. China for its part is amenable to granting the Vatican more control over underground churches and the appointment of bishops. However, this event also created a stir among underground Catholics, who felt this agreement is a sell-out to the Communist Party.

Though Vietnam has been under communist rule since 1975, Christianity in the country finds itself in a quite different situation. Followers

Catholics in East and Southeast Asia, 2020

Region	Total population	Christian population	Catholic population	% of region Catholic	% of Christians Catholic
East Asia	1,663,619,000	128,787,000	16,901,000	1.0%	13.1%
Southeast Asia	669,016,000	153,102,000	102,371,000	15.3%	66.9%
East and Southeast Asia	2,332,635,000	281,889,000	119,272,000	5.1%	42.3%
Globe	7,795,482,000	2,518,834,000	1,239,909,000	15.9%	49.2%

Source: Todd M. Johnson and Gina A. Zurlo (eds), *World Christian Database* (Leiden/Boston: Brill), accessed March 2018.

of Catholicism, still a minority compared with Buddhists, nonetheless comprise a great number of the Vietnamese population and have shown continuous growth. Unlike China, Vietnam does not have an official church. The Vietnamese Catholic Church keeps a parallel organisational structure with worldwide Catholicism. Dioceses and parishes are quite free to practise their religious and apostolic services. However, religious freedom is understood as freedom within limits imposed by the state. The church is enjoined to ask permission from the government for some crucial activities in exchange for being 'protected'. Not to seek approval first means forfeiture of such protection. As in China, religion is not respected for itself. The state is not convinced that it is intrinsic to social and human existence. Its freedom is tolerated due to the advantages its social services render to the population.

Predominantly Catholic Countries

The relationship between church and state is precarious not only in countries where Catholics are in the minority; the same ambivalence is also present in predominantly Catholic countries. Both the Philippines and Timor-Leste display this ambivalent relationship between religion and the state in different contexts.

After the Indonesian invasion of Timor-Leste in 1975, the Catholic Church – a formidable social force since the Portuguese colonial regime – went on the defensive. It was seen as the main threat to the integration of East Timor into Indonesia. With the Fretilin (Revolutionary Front for an Independent East Timor) driven to the mountains by the invading military, the church almost single-handedly guided the people through the whole occupation (1975–99). The Indonesian government did everything it could to subjugate them. It tried all means at its disposal: co-option (such as bribing teachers to leave Catholic schools and transfer to government schools); discrediting church leaders or fielding Indonesian priests; killing of priests and religious; resettlement and enforced starvation; and sexual victimisation of women. The Indonesian foreign minister at the time, Adam Malik, hinted that around 50,000 or perhaps 80,000 were

Changes in Catholics in East and Southeast Asia, 1970–2020, growth rate, % per year

Region	Total population	Christian population	Catholic population
East Asia	1.03%	4.96%	4.16%
Southeast Asia	1.75%	2.23%	2.03%
East and Southeast Asia	1.21%	3.07%	2.23%
Globe	1.50%	1.45%	1.27%

Source: Todd M. Johnson and Gina A. Zurlo (eds), *World Christian Database* (Leiden/Boston: Brill), accessed March 2018.

killed during the first two years of the occupation, not counting those who disappeared, were tortured or were internally displaced.

But East Timorese Catholics survived and lived what one author calls 'a spirituality of resistance' by taking care of the victims, opening the necessary space for their political ideas, providing development assistance and implementing non-violent protests on the ground. Through the direction and strategic collaboration of their leaders – José Ramos-Horta and Bishop Carlos Filipe Ximenes Belo – they campaigned for international support, leading to the withdrawal of the Indonesian military and the entrance of UN peacekeeping forces. Powerful Christian metaphors served as the resistance's rallying symbols: the suffering God who is vindicated, the glorious death of martyrs and the victory of the cross.

The same role was taken by the Catholic Church during the difficult years of the Marcos dictatorship (1972–86) in the Philippines that led to the famous People Power Revolution. This history has been well documented. At present, the Catholic Church remains the bastion of resistance against the violent regime of Rodrigo Duterte in the Philippines and his 'war on drugs'. Being a threat to political hegemony, the church is easily targeted by any regime's brutal imposition of power. But because of its formidable influence in both people's psyches and everyday practices, it also serves as the centre of resistance against the same regime.

Vatican Directives and Local Churches

At the official level, the Catholic Church follows the Roman structures as stipulated in the Code of Canon Law. Roman Catholics around the world are grouped in geographical units called dioceses. Bigger dioceses are called archdioceses and smaller ones are called prelatures, apostolic vicariates or prefectures. Of the 3,160 dioceses or apostolic jurisdictions worldwide, 357 of them are located in East and Southeast Asia (as of 31 May 2018). Most dioceses in the region are found in China (113), the Philippines (86), Indonesia (39), Vietnam (26) or Korea (21). The lowest numbers are in Laos (4), Cambodia (3) and Singapore and Brunei (a single diocese each). These dioceses are arranged into 11 regional groupings called episcopal conferences, which decide on matters of doctrine, worship and ministry, but always in collaboration with Rome.

A diocesan bishop heads and administers a diocese. 'In the diocese entrusted to his care, the diocesan Bishop has all the ordinary, proper and immediate power required for the exercise of his pastoral office' (Code of Canon Law, 381). Though a diocese and its bishop belong to an episcopal conference, the bishop exercises on his own authority full legislative, executive and judicial power. He shares this power with his episcopal vicars and the presbyterial council. The diocese is composed of several parishes, each administered by a parish priest and his assistants. Manila in the Philippines, one of the oldest and largest archdioceses (1579), is composed of 85 parishes divided into 13 vicariates and 5 districts. On the other hand, the Apostolic Prefecture of Phnom Phen in Cambodia (1850), one of the smallest, has one parish serving only 13,000 Catholics.

At the base of this hierarchical structure in countries where Catholics are dominant, like the Philippines, are small units called the chapels and basic ecclesial communities (BECs). Several BECs comprise a chapel, and several chapels comprise the parish. Depending on his availability, the parish priest visits and celebrates Mass in these chapels once a month or once a year, on the annual fiestas of their patron saints. Volunteer lay liturgical ministers go to far-flung mountain areas that could not be reached by priests. In dioceses where Catholics are a minority, like in Laos and Cambodia, the bishop works directly with the few priests at his disposal to take pastoral care of many isolated parishes in rural areas. Some nuns and religious brothers provide local education through schools they administer; others also help the parish priest in his pastoral duties. Large congregations privately run influential educational institutions where the elite of the country – Christian or not – register to get a 'good Catholic education', while small parochial schools in rural areas catering to the poorer population, especially those who cannot afford to go to the urban centres, struggle to survive.

The parishes normally celebrate sacraments following the Vatican-sanctioned liturgical rituals, but with greater attendance on special occasions like Christmas or Holy Week. The parish priests take concrete directives from their bishops through circulars, which are sometimes read from pulpits. Beyond this, however, the small chapels and basic ecclesial communities are left practically on their own to manage their everyday pastoral and spiritual lives, with little intervention from their pastors. Little formal Catholic formation is given at the base due to the unavailability of priests or pastoral workers. But it is also here that inculturation of the faith (the actual encounter between Catholicism and the local cultures) finds its most flourishing expression. Ecclesiastical structures adopt local forms. Popular religious practices like devotion to Mary and the saints and the celebration of the mysteries of the life of Jesus take on lively colours and intensity, quite opposite to the formal Roman liturgical rites. These community practices, a mixture of Christian teachings and cultural elements, often led by lay people and held in small chapels, individual houses or public places, most often draw more people than the priest-centred official celebrations. Examples of these abound in different places, which raises the following question: Is Catholicism 'foreign', as some have charged, or has it become indigenous and inculturated?

Foreign and Indigenous

Catholicism in East and Southeast Asia is historically linked to the European colonial project. Though China came into contact with Christianity earlier, in the seventh century, the memories of these Christian initiatives were washed away with the changing tides of political history of the region. What persisted were the traces of the Jesuit, Franciscan and Dominican missions during Iberian colonial expansionism, supported as they were by royal patronage (*Padroado*). First came the Portuguese and Spaniards, then the Dutch, French and British at different times from the sixteenth to the nineteenth century. Christianity came to be dubbed a foreign religion, the religion of the colonisers. With its close ties to colonial powers, Catholicism also colluded with them in their pursuit of economic, political and military interests.

El servicio de ambas Majestades (the service of both Majesties) – a phrase present in many official documents – accurately explains the relationship between church and politics during the Spanish colonial regime in the Philippines. The evangelisation project made possible by the *Patronato Real* was both evangelising and civilising. The friar's task was both evangelistic and political. At once, he was the Empire's civil servant and God's missionary. The rule of the friar (frailocracy) dominated the local landscape in the colony. The exaction of tribute, forced labour and military service were direct instruments of exploitation and pacification. Although not directly in charge of the policies' implementation, the friars were closely connected with the system, as they were increasingly entrusted with civil duties – inspector of schools and taxation, of health units and public works, certifier of *cedulas* (a form of identification), and auditing and partitioning of lands, among others. These duties proved to be one source of corruption among the friars. This arrangement transformed the friar missionaries into landowners, who gradually amassed large tracts themselves – some through confiscation of mortgaged lands, others through outright land-grabbing. These properties came to be called 'friar lands' and, together with other friar abuses, fuelled the Filipino revolution against Spain. It was in this context that the Iglesia Filipina Independiente (Aglipayan Church) was born – a local group of patriotic Catholics who rejected its Roman affiliation in favour of the struggle for Philippine independence. Together with their secular revolutionary counterparts, they expelled the Spanish colonisers along with their religion, which was considered 'foreign' and non-Filipino.

The above view is one valid manner in which to read the Catholic historical landscape in the Philippines. But there is another, equally valid view. Though coming from the West, Christianity has become 'indigenous' to the everyday lives of the Filipino Catholics. It has ceased to be 'other' because it has been assimilated and incorporated, adopted and adapted, disrupted and subverted, altered and transformed in order to fit its constantly changing local cultural contexts. Contemporary Catholic events and festivities reveal a skilful combination of Iberian Christianity and indigenous cultures – something beyond the Spanish missionaries' intentions. The formal worship of the Holy Child (*Santo Niño*) in Europe has transformed itself into mardi-gras-like revelry of dancing and feasting in holy abandon, as the faithful utter the deepest prayers of their hearts in the swaying of their hands and hips. The original midnight Mass (*Misa de Gallo*) celebrated on Christmas Eve in Spain has been converted into a series of dawn Masses over the nine consecutive days before Christmas, attended by thousands in joyful anticipation of Jesus's birth. Wherever they are in the world today, Filipinos take these practices as an indigenous expression of their Filipino faith.

Beyond accommodation and adaptation, Filipino Christianity also subverts the original meanings intended by their colonial masters. One example is the recitation of the *Pasyon* or the Passion of Jesus Christ – an extended verse form of the salvation history narrative from Genesis to Revelation. It usually is chanted by people in their homes or in the neighbourhood, a Holy Week tradition practised to this day, especially in rural areas. This religious practice can be viewed as an imposition by the colonisers, to form native minds into submission in the emulation of Jesus's resignation to suffering and death. At the same time, the people's chanting of the *Pasyon* had provided a narrative that served as a rallying symbol for their hopes and aspirations of liberation, a perspective popularised by historian Reynaldo Ileto. Beyond the intentions of the colonisers, the *Pasyon* contains a double truth which, to their surprise, was ingeniously and dexterously utilised by popular leaders to foster solidarity among the oppressed and to promote the revolution. As the unlettered masses dutifully chanted the narrative of the suffering of Jesus during Holy Week, much to the pleasure of the missionaries, these popular revolutionaries were also given the language and vision to articulate their longings for an alternative world far from what the colonisers had ever imagined.

Multiple Religious Belonging

The recent postmodern recognition of multiple voices and perspectives beyond the hegemonic monologue of Western rationality is not at all new to Asian Catholicism. Christianity in Asia has always lived with and negotiated with many religions, cultures and philosophies, not only in the ivory tower of academia but also in the people's everyday lives. The concern for a single unadulterated religious identity is foreign to Asian consciousness. Catholicism in this region, like any other cultural body engaged with its multiple and complex religious-cultural systems, consequently transforms itself in the process.

Three different interpretations from Asian theologians can be summoned to explain this phenomenon. First is Jaime Bulatao's notion of 'split-level Christianity'. Bulatao, a Filipino Jesuit philosopher and psychologist, argued that Filipino Catholicism in general, and the Filipino psyche in particular, display a split-level consciousness. It is described as the coexistence within one person or community of two or more ethical standards, attitudes and worldviews that are inconsistent with one another. For instance, even as a person is baptised Catholic, he or she still believes in spirits present in trees or rivers (*engkanto*), a belief that harks back to the culture's pre-Christian past. In short, that person is not totally converted; he or she suffers from a 'split-level' Christianity. This is also seen in people's inconsistent ethical standards: pious Catholics while in church, but corrupt officials in government; being convinced that bribery is wrong, but quickly paying off a traffic officer if stopped for a violation. Two different theological systems and moral norms exist side by side, receding at some moments but coming back at different times.

Split-level consciousness is an unconscious phenomenon, and is most often taken for granted or is not considered a problem at all. However, this view of Bulatao applied to Catholic Christianity is founded on the belief that a 'pure' religion is possible or that a monolithic worldview exists – a quite abstract and static view of culture that is hardly found in reality. It assumes that if people accept one worldview, they will totally abandon the other. And if they coexist in one community, such an entity is half-bred, a mongrel, deficient as it is not integrated and complete. With psychological categories applied to the theological field, such cultures are also seen as split-level or schizophrenic, socially displaying their bipolar tendencies.

Peter Phan, a Vietnamese theologian working in the USA, thinks otherwise. He argues for a hyphenated Catholic Christianity in East and Southeast Asia – Asian-Christian or Christian-Asian – in which the two poles of the binary equally exert substantive influence. In Phan's reading, the development of Asian-Christian identity has included three phases. The first era was the imposition of Western colonial Christianity on Asian cultures, with the adjective 'Asian' superficially describing 'Christian' identity acting as the main substantive. The second period featured the syncretistic tendencies of Ricci, de Nobili and others who enthroned the Asian cultures as supreme expressions of the Christian faith. The third and final phase is the Christian 'hyphenated' existence, which Phan attributes to the theological developments of the Second Vatican Council. In short, it is not an anomaly for a Catholic to be also Asian and an Asian to be also Catholic if one so desires. The teaching of the Catholic Church opens itself to double belonging. Opposite to Bulatao, Phan argues that 'Christianness' and 'Asianness' can coexist in a culture fully recognising the flourishing of each element both at the level of personal consciousness and in the church community.

Other thinkers, however, argue against Phan's overly conscious and voluntaristic hyphenated Christian. Indonesian thinker Albertus Bagus Laksana prefers the term 'complex religious identity' to 'double belonging' or 'multiple religious belonging'. Hybrid existence is a fact on Asian soil, even beyond the conscious efforts of political or religious leaders 'to form' their people in some exclusive identity. Asian Christians merely live their everyday lives and, in the process, engage in mutual borrowing from the other. Beyond Phan, Laksana thinks that the Asian complex religious identity can be understood as 'what all its members are engaged in the act of living', to borrow a phrase from British neo-Marxist Raymond Williams. Through these complex religious and cultural interactions on the grounds of one's location, a type of hybrid Catholicism is formed. Official theologies exist, but what can be seen with one's eyes is how the people appropriate them in context. Complex religious identities come in many forms: wiping and touching of images; multi-religious shared pilgrimage sites; prayer services from different religious traditions; statues of saints, Vishnu and Buddha side by side on family altars; and offerings of food on the tombs of ancestors on All Souls' Day. Believers do not have qualms of conscience in moving from one religious tradition to another or in belonging to all of them at once. Purists condemn this as syncretism or superstition, but it is all that ordinary people have. Whether in cultural customs, theological reflection or religious practice, it is the grassroots communities – not the cultural virtuosos or religious luminaries – who decide which elements of their everyday religious-cultural encounters shall be assimilated or modified, adopted or subverted, consented to or resisted.

Formal Theologies and Popular Religiosities

Though theological science has always looked up to the West in the field of theological development, significant theological production has been seen in Asia since the Second Vatican Council (1962–5). Important scientific and administrative bodies made the emergence of Asian theologies possible. On the Protestant side, the Association of Theological Schools in South East Asia was established in Singapore in 1957, and the Program for Theology and Cultures in Asia was organised in 1983 in collaboration with the Christian Conference of Asia. Among Catholics, the Federation of Asian Bishops' Conferences (FABC) was set up in the early 1970s as an umbrella organisation of all the episcopal conferences of Asia.

The FABC has exercised great influence on East Asian and Southeast Asian Catholic theology. Since its foundation, the FABC has produced an impressive body of texts from its plenary assemblies and its working commissions – Bishops' Institute on Lay Apostolate (BILA), Inter-religious Affairs on the Theology of Dialogue (BERA), Social Action (BISA), Social Communication (BISCOM), Institute for Theological Animation (BITA) and Office of Theological Concerns (OTC/TAC). Following the commentaries on FABC documents, 10 crucial Asian contributions to theological discourse can be observed.

1. Centrality of dialogue. Already in its first meeting in 1970, the FABC outlined its specific character in the now-famous triple dialogue (dialogue of cultures, dialogue with ancient religions and dialogue with the poor), all relevant dimensions of the Asian context. Dialogue is Asia's manner of proclaiming Jesus Christ and the key interpretive element in the understanding of Asian Catholicism.

2. The local church. Taking its cue from the churches of the New Testament, which are all pluriform and local (the given church in a given place), the FABC considers the local church as the concrete expression of the universal church, not the other way around. 'Each local Church is the Church in its full and integral reality, and the Church universal is a communion of local Churches, a church of churches, a communion of communions' (FABC Papers 60).

3. Harmony. The all-encompassing dimension of harmony, which characterises all ancient Asian religions and cultures, serves as the hallmark of Asian Catholicism. With tensions and conflicts brought about by religious and cultural diversity, all the more is harmony necessary, understood from the perspective of the universe's restoration and recapitulation in Christ.

4. Inculturation. Unless a church is 'incarnate in a people, a church indigenous and inculturated', the people will always consider it an outsider and a foreign religion. This church should be truly Catholic and truly Asian in the way it prays, thinks, lives and communicates Jesus to others.

5. Dialogue with ancient religions. Dialogue finds its deepest dimension in the dialogue with age-old religions deeply rooted in Asia even before the coming of Christianity. It is seen as the distinctly Asian contribution to theological reflection in the whole universal church.

6. Church of the poor. Located on a continent where small pockets of affluence exist side by side with oceans of poverty, the Church in Asia confesses itself to be the Church of the poor, living the evangelical poverty of spirit and professing its option and solidarity with the socially excluded, defending their rights and promoting social justice.

7. Care for the environment. With a sense of harmony and a holistic view of reality as part of the Asian worldview, the FABC sees intimate interdependence between humans and the whole cosmos as the foundation of its spirituality, theology and ecclesial practice.

8. Respect for life. Beyond the Roman Church's discourse of respect for life as centred on abortion and contraception, the FABC talks about the threats to life in all its dimensions as they are experienced in Asia, including patriarchy and gender, genocide and terrorism, the caste system and globalisation. Retrieving the 'image of God' discourse from the Bible, it also takes into account the respect for life in Hinduism, Jainism, Islam, Buddhism and other faiths.

9. Pluralist theological method. Pluralism is not a threat to the church and theology; it is a positive resource. God's creation – humankind, cultures and religions (that is, the whole of reality) – is plural and manifold. So is the history of the church and its theology: not only scholastic and rational but also mystical, apophatic and symbolic; not only within Christianity but also in ancient religions, indigenous peoples and social movements.

10. The Kingdom of God. The central motif of the FABC's theology is not the Christian church but the Kingdom – the 'universal reality, extending far beyond the boundaries of the church'. When people from different faiths search for the transcendent divine mystery and in effect reach out in solidarity with the marginalised, they are not far from God's Kingdom.

Leading Catholic theologians in East and Southeast Asia extensively develop these themes, as is shown in their congresses, conferences and publications, which can now compete with the theological production of other continents. The efforts of Asian theologians can be categorised in the following themes: liberation, inculturation and inter-religious dialogue. But despite this seemingly progressive theological agenda, the situation also appears quite different on the ground. Experience with priestly formation tells us that majority of the seminaries still teach classical Roman theology and philosophy taken from Western sources. Not enough effort has been taken to dialogue seriously with Asian resources. In addition, most of these seminaries do not have enough capable professors and library materials to pursue the Asian theological agenda. It is not true only for countries where Catholics are a very small minority; the same situation prevails in the Philippines and Timor-Leste, where they form a majority. Moreover, many Catholic clergy who presently run the parishes were trained in pre-Second Vatican Council theology and hardly have the time and resources to update themselves. Thus, what is passed on to seminarians and to ordinary faithful in Sunday homilies is most often an echo of their Tridentine manualist deductive theologies still reminiscent of the exclusivist paradigm of the Counter-Reformation.

While Catholic bishops and professional theologians pursue a robust theological agenda for Asia, the lay people are left to their own devices to survive spiritually. Like a parallel theological world with its own coherent system of belief, ritual and ethic, lay people rely on what has been called by manifold and sometimes derogatory names – 'folk religiosity' (as against official Catholicism), 'popular piety' or 'popular devotions' (as against official liturgy). Though tolerated by specialists and the religious elite, most often they are viewed with suspicion and condescension. Magisterial texts exhort that these practices be purified, elevated, renewed and evangelised. These practices often are described as superstitious or syncretistic, bordering on fanaticism and heresy. The officially sanctioned Roman liturgy is still the standard by which all other folk religious practices are to be evaluated. Any deviation would invite some reprimand.

But contemporary thinking brings back the value of popular religiosity as 'theologies of everyday life', 'everyday authenticity', 'theology of the people' and other parallel names. With only 10% of the Catholic population having formal theological training, access to popular religiosity is the only existing theology and spirituality for the non-specialists who comprise the vast majority of the ordinary Catholic faithful. Since they have no access, they also are not heard. But even in the language of classical Catholic theology, these voices from the ground – the *sensus fidelium* – should be listened to, since they are also considered a *locus theologicus*, one of the fundamental sources of the faith.

Back to my first question: How does the Catholic consciousness coexist with its others in the Asian context? This phenomenon can be viewed from many perspectives and the interaction is plural, calling for complex and nuanced answers.

Bibliography

Alberts, Tara, *Conflict and Conversion: Catholicism in Southeast Asia, 1500–1700* (Oxford: Oxford University Press, 2013).

England, John, Jose Kuttianimattathil, John Mansford Prior, Lily Quintos, David Suh Kwang-sun and Janice Wickeri (eds), *Asian Christian Theologies: A Research Guide to Authors, Movements, Sources,* vols 2 and 3 (Delhi: ISPCK, 2004).

Moffett, Samuel, *A History of Christianity in Asia,* vols 1 and 2, (Maryknoll, NY: Orbis Books, 2006).

Phan, Peter, *Asian Christianities: History, Theology, Practice* (Maryknoll, NY: Orbis Books, 2018).

Wilfred, Felix (ed.), *The Oxford Handbook of Christianity in Asia* (Oxford: Oxford University Press, 2014).

Evangelicals

Kang-San Tan

The historian David Bebbington has defined 'Evangelicals' as Christians who share four main qualities: biblicism – a high regard for the Bible; crucicentrism – a focus on Jesus's crucifixion and its saving effects; conversionism – a belief that humans need to be converted; and activism – a belief that faith should influence one's public life. In East and Southeast Asia, the term 'mainline Protestant denominations' is normally used to refer to a stream of churches faithful to Reformation teachings, such as Lutherans, Calvinists or Presbyterians. Methodism and Anglicanism, originating from Britain, are also considered to belong to the mainline denominations associated with the World Council of Churches (WCC). However, in East and Southeast Asia, while many from mainline denominations are associated with the WCC, they are theologically Evangelical in their doctrinal convictions, affirming Bebbington's quadrilateral. Others prefer not to be associated with the WCC and opt instead to identify with the World Evangelical Alliance (WEA). Evangelicalism finds expression in the region through such denominations as Anglicans, Assemblies of God, Baptists, Brethren, Christian and Missionary Alliance, Methodists, Pentecostals and Presbyterians, as well as non-denominational churches.

Evangelical Growth

Though Christians are a small minority in most countries in East and Southeast Asia, there are contexts in which Evangelicals are growing rapidly, such as South Korea, Hong Kong, Singapore, Cambodia, Myanmar and the Philippines. A few examples must suffice to illustrate the kind of growth that has been occurring.

In 1963, the Philippine Federation of Christian Churches was succeeded by the National Council of Churches in the Philippines (NCCP). In 1965, the Philippine Council of Evangelical Churches (PCEC) was established as a group of churches distinct from the NCCP. The PCEC has more than 150 member churches. As of 2011, adherents were estimated to number 11 million. Fifty years after their foundation, the two Councils remain the largest representative groups of mainline and Evangelical Protestants. The NCCP is a member of the WCC, while the PCEC is a member of the

WEA. In 2015, a former national director of the PCEC, Efraim Tendero, was elected secretary general of the WEA.

About 30% of the South Korean population belongs to the Christian faith, with about a quarter of those being Catholic and three-quarters Protestant. Most South Korean Christians identify as Evangelicals, including Pentecostals, Charismatics and those who belong to mainline denominations, such as Presbyterians and Methodists. Christian missionaries to South Korea were mostly Americans, notably Methodists and Presbyterians. Later, small but growing Baptist and independent Evangelical churches were established. After the Second World War, social attitudes of Koreans towards China and Japan became negative due to wartime oppression. Many Korean animists, whose adherence to Buddhism was largely formal, responded positively to the Christian message. From the start, Korean Christians were encouraged to be independent and to serve as evangelists among their own people. Evangelical churches, organised as independent and self-governing, grew rapidly in this enterprising environment.

The growth of the Korean church has also been accompanied by the development of numerous mission agencies and extensive overseas missionary work. In the last decade of the twentieth century, the number of Korean missionaries overseas grew from 1,645 serving in 87 different countries in 1990 to 10,745 serving in some 162 different countries in 2002. By 2018 it was estimated that more than 25,000 Korean missionaries were serving in overseas mission. At the same time, the attitude of the public to Evangelicals has been negatively affected by high-profile scandals, particularly in relation to corruption in financial affairs. For example, one high-profile case concerned David Yonggi Cho, pastor of the Yoido Full Gospel Church in Seoul, reputed to be the largest congregation in the world. In 2014 Cho was convicted of embezzling US$12 million from church funds. He was given a suspended sentence, but his son went to jail. Evangelicals in Korea have faced numerous financial and moral scandals as well as continuing schisms (especially among Presbyterians). In addition, infighting among Evangelicals resulted in the cancellation of a global WEA conference planned for 2014.

Evangelicals in East and Southeast Asia, 1970

Region	Total population	Christian population	Evangelical population	% of region Evangelical	% of Christians Evangelical
East Asia	996,425,000	11,456,000	2,710,000	0.3%	23.7%
Southeast Asia	280,607,000	50,740,000	3,240,000	1.2%	6.4%
East and Southeast Asia	1,277,032,000	62,196,000	5,950,000	0.5%	9.6%
Globe	3,700,578,000	1,229,309,000	111,808,000	3.0%	9.1%

Source: Todd M. Johnson and Gina A. Zurlo (eds), *World Christian Database* (Leiden/Boston: Brill), accessed March 2018.

The Persekutuan Injil Indonesia (Indonesian Evangelical Communion) was formed in 1971, whereas Pentecostal churches in Indonesia are mostly members of the Persekutuan Gereja-gereja Pantekosta di Indonesia (PGPI, or Pentecostal Churches in Indonesia), which was formed in 2001 (formerly Dewan Pentekosta Indonesia, DPI, formed in 1971). Many Reformed churches as well as Charismatic churches in Indonesia are not part of these national Evangelical bodies but participate in international Evangelical movements such as the WEA, the Lausanne Movement and the Asian Evangelical Alliance.

Evangelical Organisations

Founded in 1983, the Asian Evangelical Alliance (AEA) empowers national Evangelical alliances to be agents of transformation in Asia by uniting Evangelical churches for dynamic action in the areas of mission and church planting, theology and church renewal, religious liberty, social concern, women's ministry, youth ministry and leadership development. It was formed as the Evangelical Fellowship of Asia in 1983 and changed its name to Asia Evangelical Alliance in 2009. The AEA exists to promote and nurture networks and collaborations among Evangelicals in Asia for the purpose of strengthening and expanding the Kingdom of God in Asia and beyond. It has held regular consultations and triennial Asia congresses, catering not only for East Asian Evangelicals but also providing cross-regional associations for South Asian Evangelicals. Since 2018, the Reverend Paul Euki, president of the Japan Bible Seminary, has been the chair of the AEA.

In Southeast Asia, members of the Chinese Christian diaspora have played a notable role. With the rise of communism during the 1950s and the subsequent wars and famines, large numbers of Chinese people emigrated to Southeast Asia. In many contexts they have formed the backbone of church life and often have been disposed to adopt Evangelical belief and spirituality.

Since the 1950s, the growth of the Evangelical presence has owed much to the ministries of foreign mission bodies such as the China Inland Mission

Evangelicals in East and Southeast Asia, 2020

Region	Total population	Christian population	Evangelical population	% of region Evangelical	% of Christians Evangelical
East Asia	1,663,619,000	128,787,000	48,675,000	2.9%	37.8%
Southeast Asia	669,016,000	153,102,000	18,322,000	2.7%	12.0%
East and Southeast Asia	2,332,635,000	281,889,000	66,997,000	2.9%	23.8%
Globe	7,795,482,000	2,518,834,000	385,826,000	4.9%	15.3%

Source: Todd M. Johnson and Gina A. Zurlo (eds), *World Christian Database* (Leiden/Boston: Brill), accessed March 2018.

(which later became the Overseas Missionary Fellowship, now OMF International), Worldwide Evangelisation Crusade (now WEC International), Christian Nationals' Evangelism Commission and other international missions. Another group consists of denominational missions such as the Church Mission Society (Anglican) and the Methodist Missionary Society from Britain and the Southern Baptists from North America, which have started local churches. Since the 1950s, the Assemblies of God have played a significant role in the growth of Evangelicalism in Borneo and among the Karen people in Thailand and Myanmar, which has also been strengthened by indigenous revival movements.

Evangelicalism in Asia is primarily a lay mission movement. The Philippine Missionary Fellowship, the Indonesian Missionary Fellowship and the Japanese Overseas Missionary Fellowship have all been marked by lay leadership. In the 1950s several Evangelical ministries were established in Singapore that focused on university students, including the Navigators and Campus Crusade for Christ. In addition, OMF moved its headquarters to Singapore and the World Evangelical Fellowship (now WEA) was based there for many years. All of these bodies have featured lay leadership and have played a significant role in the development of Evangelicalism in East and Southeast Asia.

Among young people, local para-church associations such as the Inter-Varsity Christian Fellowship, Scripture Union and their Inter-School Christian Fellowship, Youth for Christ, Navigator movements and Campus Crusade for Christ (now known as Cru) were influential during the 1970s in producing Evangelical youth leaders. The 1978 Billy Graham Crusade saw the birth of the Evangelical Fellowship of Singapore.

From the 1990s onward, the initiative in national Evangelical leadership steadily moved from national associations to senior pastors of megachurches, such as Lawrence Khong (Faith Community Baptist Church) and Edmund Chan (former senior pastor of the Covenant Evangelical Free Church) in Singapore; Daniel Ho (former senior pastor of the Damansara Utama Methodist Church) in Malaysia; and Pastor Peter Tan-Chi (Christ Commission Fellowship) in the Philippines.

Changes in Evangelicals in East and Southeast Asia, 1970–2020, growth rate, % per year

Region	Total population	Christian population	Evangelical population
East Asia	1.03%	4.96%	5.95%
Southeast Asia	1.75%	2.23%	3.53%
East and Southeast Asia	1.21%	3.07%	4.96%
Globe	1.50%	1.45%	2.51%

Source: Todd M. Johnson and Gina A. Zurlo (eds), *World Christian Database* (Leiden/Boston: Brill), accessed March 2018.

Theological Education

Alongside local churches, the maturing of Asian Evangelicals has also been supported by the formation of theological colleges across Asia. Prominent among them are China Evangelical Seminary in Taiwan, China Graduate School of Theology in Hong Kong, Asian Theological Seminary in the Philippines, Singapore Bible College, Bangkok Bible College, Malaysia Bible Seminary and Malaysia Baptist Theological Seminary. In 1970 these Evangelical seminaries formed the Asian Theological Association (ATA), which has been instrumental in training local pastors and producing younger theologians.

The ATA was established as a direct outcome of the need expressed at several Asia-wide conferences and consultations. It is associated with the International Council for Evangelical Theological Education and plays a significant role in accreditation. Since the 1970s it has grown into a movement committed to serving its members in the development of Evangelical biblical theology by strengthening interaction, enhancing scholarship, promoting academic excellence, fostering spiritual and ministerial formation, and mobilising resources to promote the Christian faith within diverse Asian cultures. ATA seminaries have played a prominent role in nurturing pastors and lay leaders for Evangelical churches. Many of these seminaries welcome students from surrounding Asian countries with limited graduate education and have played a crucial role in supporting and developing Evangelical leaders in Vietnam, Cambodia, China and even parts of South Asia such as Nepal, Bangladesh and India.

The Association for Theological Education in South East Asia (ATESEA), formed in 1957, is another network for seminaries associated with mainline denominations such as Anglicans, Presbyterians, Methodists and Lutherans. Though historically associated with more 'liberal' international partners, the leadership of ATESEA features a significant Evangelical presence and the local congregations of the participating denominations are mostly of Evangelical faith. ATESEA took bold initiatives in contextual education and development of Asian theologies through such prominent theologians as Kosuke Koyama, Emerito Nacpil and Yeow Choo Lak. For example, ATESEA-related seminaries seek to apply the 'Critical Asian Principle' as a framework for theological education, which focuses on identifying what is distinctively Asian and to use such distinctiveness as a critical principle of judgement on matters pertaining to the life and mission of the Christian community, theology and theological education in Asia. As a result, they continue to be at the forefront of the development of indigenous liturgies, engaging with religious fundamentalism in Asia, gender and justice issues, and reclaiming indigenous identity and minority rights in Asia.

The lines between 'liberal' and 'Evangelical' institutions are not as pronounced in Southeast Asia as they are in Northeast Asia or South Asia. For example, Southeast Asian seminaries associated with mainline Protestant denominations, such as Trinity Theological College in Singapore or Malaysia Theological Seminary, are led by strongly Evangelical faculty.

Evangelical Perspectives on Religious Plurality

Asia is undergoing many changes and challenges: the economic and social interdependence that comes with globalisation; a religious resurgence among Hindus, Buddhists and Muslims; and increasing violence between co-religionists in South Thailand and Myanmar (Buddhist and Muslim) and the Philippines (Christian and Muslim).

Asian Christians have lived for centuries with non-Christians. Religious plurality is nothing new. However, what is new is that contemporary society is now more aware of the existence and reality of religious differences as well as the fact of religious plurality. Different religious groupings may either respond by withdrawing into religious separatism and become ghettos or seek to adapt by rethinking their theology, faith and practices in the light of changing contexts. Through globalisation, there are now increasing resources for the church to better understand the nature of being a Christian community in the context of the world religions of Asia.

Hinduism, Buddhism, Taoism and Islam reside within the Asian cultures and psyche, whereas Christianity has struggled, owing to perceptions that it is a Western religion. To become a Christian, one had to leave behind the old religions, and this often included leaving behind being a member of an Asian family, social networks, festivals and cultures. Whenever Christian minorities are unable to integrate into the majority culture, Christianity continues to be treated as a tolerated foreign religion. There are many complex external factors, such as history, politics and social attitudes. There are also internal factors, within Asian Christianity: identifications with Western colonial pasts as well as efforts in evangelism, social engagement and political activism that lack contextual sensitivity. This perceived foreignness of Christianity has contributed to the lack of church growth.

During the Second World War, the Japanese government decided that only three Christian bodies – the Roman Catholics, the Eastern Orthodox and a Protestant amalgam called the United Church of Christ in Japan (Kyōdan) – should be recognised. The majority of Evangelicals and Independent churches refused to join. In addition, some Anglican, Lutheran and Holiness churches refused to join the Kyōdan and lost all legal recognition. After the war, religious freedom was guaranteed in the new constitution of 1947. However, negative social attitudes towards Christians persist and they are often regarded as fundamentalists or religious fanatics. As a result, less than 0.5% of Japanese are Evangelical Christians today.

In societies where national identities are closely tied to specific religions, Evangelical Christianity has found it difficult to attract mass conversions. Whenever Thai or Japanese Christians have converted from Buddhism, or Indonesian or Malay Christians have converted from Islam, Evangelicals tend to demand a radical break from their previous faiths. In these cases, such extractions of individuals from their former communities are seen as crossing not only religious dividing lines but also cultural boundaries. Ethnic and religious identities are closely linked in many Asian societies and conversions to Christianity can pose unique challenges when they are perceived as a betrayal of personal and collective identities.

Evangelicals and the State

Christianity in China comprises three major entities: the Three-Self Patriotic Movement, the Chinese Patriotic Catholic Association and the unregistered house-church movement. Article 36 of the Chinese constitution protects 'freedom of religion', with a restriction that 'no one may use religion to engage in activities that disrupt public order, impair the health of citizens or interfere with the education system of the state'. Underground house churches are those churches that refused to be officially registered with the government. They are spread across both cities and rural areas. Since around 2000, there is a fourth group of Evangelical Christian churches ('Urban Evangelicals'), mostly found in major cities in China, whose leaders were broadly influenced by overseas returnees from the West. From time to time, when Christian communities become too prominent or overtly political, the communist government feels obliged to limit their social influence. For example, hundreds of crosses were removed and church buildings demolished in the city of Wenzhou, in the eastern coastal province of Zhejiang, due to their perceived threat to communist hegemony.

Despite Chinese government restrictions, Christianity has experienced rapid growth. From an estimated 6 million Christians in the early 1980s, Yang Fenggang (2012) suggested that the Christian population in China could have been around 100 million in 2010 and predicted that by 2030 nearly 250 million Christian believers will call China home. Most Christians in China adhere to the Protestant faith, with a third attending officially registered churches. Therefore, the underground house-church movement as well as urban Evangelicals form a formidable group and are influential in terms of rapid growth and future leadership for the churches.

In the post-communist countries of China, Vietnam, Laos and Cambodia, there appears to be a growing spiritual vacuum amidst economic growth and materialism. The sense of Christian fellowship is attractive when compared with the hierarchical structures of other Asian religions and social organisations. With the open doors to trade and foreign relations since the 1980s, younger generations from post-communist nations are attracted to Western cultures, and Christianity is viewed positively as a progressive faith. As communist countries transition into market economies, welcoming foreign traders and social interactions, Christianity has entered into these countries as part of social movements. In the eyes of their governments, Christians can be perceived either as valued partners for national development or hinderances to national unity. They learn to chart a course that allows the former to override the latter.

Since the communist victory in 1975, the Vietnamese government is particularly concerned about evangelism in the highlands. Ethnic minorities are seen as resistant to the state, and unregistered or house churches are regarded as siding with anti-communist sentiment. Likewise, in Laos the communist government is wary of Christianity's association with Hmong hill tribes. In contrast, as Cambodia comes to terms with the tragedy of Khmer Rouge killings, churches there are experiencing rapid growth.

The First World War (1914–18) was a turning point for many Asian Christians, as they witnessed the rise of nationalism and anti-European sentiment and the decline of Western hegemony. A good illustration is the formation of the Hatopen Kristen Batak (HKB, or Batak Christian Association) in Indonesia in 1917, led by Mangihut Hezekiel Mannullang, a student activist who promoted nationalistic sentiment and independence of the church from foreign leadership.

Under the leadership of Jun Vencer, together with Bel Magalit (Asian Theological Seminary) and the Far East Broadcasting Corporation, Evangelicals in the Philippines organised prayer movements and participated in street demonstrations that eventually led to the downfall of the corrupt government of Ferdinand Marcos. At the height of the crisis, the Philippine Council of Evangelical Churches sent out the following statement:

> Our obedience to the State is subordinate . . . to God: . . . where Caesar conflicts with Christ . . . Jesus is Lord. Divine law supersedes human law. Therefore, our obedience is not absolute. Whenever government rules contrary to the will of God, then civil disobedience become a Christian duty.

In Indonesia, Islamic fundamentalism and resentment of aggressive Christian proselytising have led to clashes and physical attacks that have undermined the country's reputation for religious tolerance. Muslim–Christian conflicts in Ambon, bombings in Bali and Jakarta, and the burning of churches in East Java all point to deep-seated suspicions and resentments that can all too easily erupt into violence.

In West Malaysia, Christians come mostly from the migrant populations of Chinese and Indians, while almost 40% of East Malaysians are Christians. Malaysia is a multi-religious society, with the major ethnic groups in 2010 being Malays (60.3% of the population), Chinese (22.9%), Indians (7.1%) and tribal and other races (9.7%). Because religion largely coincides with ethnicity, inter-religious relations are greatly affected by individual racial perceptions of the other ethnic groups. Inter-racial relations become more complicated when they function not only as a sociological category, but also as a tool of the state for resource allocation and political control. In addition, political parties draw their support from ethnic constituencies, making communalism a key political issue since the independence of the country. Though the Chinese and Indians are part of a political alliance in the government, the Malays are in control of the political process. The conjunction of ethnicity and political power (inevitably linked to economic interests) deeply polarised not only the issue of race, but also the religious commitments of the people of Malaysia. Malays who convert to another religion lose not only their ethnic identity but also their social, political and economic privileges. Christians in Malaysia have been facing pressure from Muslims to discontinue the long-standing use of 'Allah' as the term for God in translation of the Scriptures and in hymns. The Malaysian case demonstrates complexities that can be seen in other Asian countries whenever religion is strongly identified with particular ethnic groups.

Indigenous Christian Movements

Significant indigenous Christian movements, carrying the hallmarks of Evangelicalism, have emerged in East and Southeast Asia. Watchman Nee (Ni Tuosheng, 1903–72) founded the Little Flock church in Shanghai. The evangelist John Sung Shang Chieh (1901–44) led campaigns in Southeast Asia that not only converted many overseas Chinese but also ignited a powerful movement of faith that extended across ethnic boundaries. In 1959, the Sidang Injil Borneo (SIB, Borneo Evangelical Assembly) was founded as an inter-tribal conference, and since that time the SIB has established itself as a local-led and indigenous Borneo religion.

Likewise, most Christians in Myanmar and Thailand belong to minority tribes such as the Karen, Chin and Hmong. Christians in Myanmar are estimated to make up around 8.2% of the population: roughly 5.5% Protestant, 1.3% Roman Catholic and the remainder members of Independent churches. About 2.5% of the country's population identify as Evangelicals and 2.1% as Pentecostals. The majority of Bamar people are Buddhists whose cultures and identities are largely unaffected by Christian witness.

From the 1960s onward, Evangelicals in these regions have grown most rapidly among tribal communities in the north-east regions of Thailand, the north-west of Myanmar, Kalimantan in Indonesia, East Malaysia and the northern Philippines, as well as some tribes in the south of the Philippines such as the Manobo tribes. Growth came about primarily through local evangelists who shared about their new-found faith through neighbourhood connections and family ties. In the 1980s, younger people were attracted to Western cultures and ideas as they sought new identities in urban and global contexts. Principally, local church communities are committed to new ethical ideals, challenging traditional structures, and have greater access to education, mission contacts and resources.

During a period when nationalistic ideals hold sway, many foreign mission leaders are not made welcome by Asian governments. Religious visas are no longer renewed, and local churches are forced to develop local leadership, start new training institutions and begin to explore roles for nation-building in the midst of Islam, Buddhism and assertive national identities.

The Future for Evangelical Christianities

Evangelical theology and practice today face significant challenges that will need to be overcome if Evangelical faith is to prove its relevance in these Asian regions. What will be the future shape of Christian mission in these complex regions? Four crucial issues can be identified.

The first is an appropriate contextual theology of mission. There is a growing recognition that, if it is to have credibility, the Christian message must be expressed not only in words but also in deeds. The context calls for a comprehensive mission that includes evangelism, church planting, challenging injustices, caring for creation and showing what it means to be a reconciling community. Given the diversity of the region, there is a need for contextual expression of Christianities in tribal, rural and urban centres.

The second issue is that of a deeper engagement between religions. Generally, few adherents of world religions (Muslims, Hindus, Buddhists and Jews) have turned to Christianity, despite reports of the shift of Christianity toward non-Western peoples. Rapid church growth primarily has been seen either among tribal communities or within secularised urban centres such as Singapore, Seoul and Hong Kong. However, the majority of East and Southeast Asian religious communities remain largely unaffected by Christian witness. Effective outreach calls for new approaches beyond preaching the gospel and planting churches. There is a need for new engagements, such as inter-religious apologetics and living out the faith as a whole-life discipleship that transforms nations. Evangelicals are particularly concerned that many Buddhists or Muslims who might be interested in exploring Christianity have no opportunity to do so because there is no Christian witness within reach.

The third crucial issue to address is the way of the cross and contextualised discipleship. For Christ's followers, the cross indicates that they must be ready for adversity. Evangelicals affirm a cruciform discipleship that enables them to bear faithful witness in the context of persecution and suffering. This commitment can be expected to be highly relevant in East and Southeast Asia in coming years and could yield opportunities for Christian growth in what would otherwise appear to be unpromising or even hostile circumstances.

Finally, Evangelicals need to engage wider society in dialogue. While mainline Christians are more open to engage in inter-religious cooperation, many Asian Evangelicals are still suspicious of closer cooperation with their non-Christian societies, since they fear that this might compromise their Evangelical faith. Our modern world, however, demands deeper engagement with both secular and other religious belief systems. Effective Evangelical witness in the future will depend on deep understanding of the religious belief systems of Buddhism, Hinduism and Islam so as to be able to engage a multicultural setting. In the context of friendships, Evangelicals in these regions could contribute to nation-building and peaceful relationships between communities of different faiths.

Flourishing as a Religious Minority?

The case of Evangelicals in Malaysia can be instructive by way of conclusion. The Malaysian churches encountered a great challenge when the Malaysian government did not renew missionary visas beginning in the early 1980s. As the country went through a process of Islamisation, the young church learned to adapt and had to take over the leadership of local congregations. Foreign mission groups were forced to hand over leadership and had to quickly focus on lay leadership training, on how to preach, lead Bible studies and manage the administration of a fledgling church. Christians in Malaysia had to learn to be sensitive in their witness to their Evangelical faith in the midst of Asian religiosities, especially as regards relating to their Muslim neighbours. Most congregations could not obtain legal permits to build churches and had to meet in commercial buildings, and to move whenever government officials closed these 'illegal buildings'. The church grew in strength through house-church movements, creative use of commercial and warehouse factories and training centres, more imaginative engagements with the poor and the marginalised, and strong discipleship among young people and university students. Groups such as Inter-Varsity Christian Fellowship, the Navigators and church student groups were active in equipping younger leaders for the local churches. Christians were prominent in challenging corruption and unjust government policies as well as being actively involved in social activism, defending the minority rights of indigenous peoples and promoting the use of Bible in Malay languages. Through prayer movements and socio-political activism, a new government that is more sensitive to minority religious rights and racial harmony was elected in 2018.

Both East and Southeast Asia are complex and diverse. Amidst the complexity and diversity, Evangelical Christianity is a growing movement in both regions, seeing steady growth in almost all countries, ranging from mega-churches in cities to house churches among grassroots rural communities. Evangelicals' prospects will likely depend on how far they are able to recover a more holistic understanding of gospel witness, which includes evangelism, social witness and socio-political activism and enables the churches to act as agents of transformation in Asian societies. Key to the future will be the emergence of mature Evangelical leaders who are resilient and able to thrive as they enable local congregations to witness to their faith in plural, multicultural, inter-religious and consumerist Asian societies.

Bibliography

Aritonang, Jan Sihar, and Karel Steenbrink, *A History of Christianity in Indonesia* (Leiden: Brill, 2008).

Kim, Sebastian C. H., and Kirsteen Kim, *A History of Korean Christianity* (Cambridge: Cambridge University Press, 2014).

Laumsdaine, David (ed.), *Evangelical Christianity and Democracy in Asia* (Oxford: Oxford University Press, 2009).

Phan, Peter C. (ed.), *Christianities in Asia* (London: Wiley Blackwell, 2011).

Yang, Fenggang, *Religion in China: Survival and Revival Under Communist Rule* (Oxford: Oxford University Press, 2012).

Pentecostals and Charismatics

Julie Ma

The Pentecostal expression of Christianity has developed in three distinct movements. The first is Classic Pentecostalism, which emerged in the late nineteenth and early twentieth centuries in various parts of the world. In North America it originated within the Holiness Movement, which emphasised fervent revivalism with an eschatological anticipation of the imminent Second Coming of Christ. In 1900, Charles Parham, a Holiness evangelist, began to teach speaking in tongues as the biblical sign of the baptism of the Holy Spirit. The Azusa Street Revival in Los Angeles (1906–9) was led by the African American preacher William Seymour. It played a decisive role in internationalising the movement.

The second movement is the Charismatic renewal, which began in 1960 when members of mainline churches, such as Catholics and Anglicans, experienced the gifts of the Holy Spirit as listed in 1 Corinthians 12: 8–10, including the more spectacular ones. Gradually moving away from the language of the baptism in the Holy Spirit, the Charismatic movement began to emphasise the word of wisdom, word of knowledge, faith, gifts of healing, miraculous powers, prophecy, distinguishing between spirits, speaking in different tongues (languages) and interpretation of tongues.

The third type to emerge in the USA was the 'Third Wave' or the Signs and Wonders Movement. It drew believers from both Charismatic and non-Charismatic churches, particularly from Evangelical groups. The movement emphasised the supernatural power of the Holy Spirit. Its leader was John Wimber, the founder of the Vineyard Church. He later teamed up with Peter Wagner, a church growth specialist of Fuller Seminary, to offer a historic and yet controversial course, 'Signs, Wonders and Church Growth'. However, this 'none of the above' category has expanded in numbers and modalities to include many African Initiated Churches and the majority of Chinese house churches.

Moving our attention to Asia, a century ago the continent struggled because of widespread poverty and substandard health-care and educational facilities as well as the imposition of colonial rule. As the birthplace of all the world's major religions, Asia provided a context in which religions played a crucial role in providing solutions to life's diverse challenges. Notwithstanding the advent of modern education and economic development along with political independence from the middle of the twentieth century, religious faiths, both native and foreign, persist in all the East and Southeast Asian countries.

The Pentecostals' dynamic worship, expectancy of divine intervention, teaching of empowerment by the Spirit and external signs like speaking in tongues and healing have had great appeal. Their unique spirituality has brought the affective dimension of human existence into religious experience. From the outset, Pentecostal and Charismatic beliefs and practices have had a particular appeal to the poor and socially marginalised. The promise of good health and blessing re-established the materiality of Christian salvation to individuals, families and communities. As a result, in many East and Southeast Asian countries upward social mobility has been observed among Pentecostal and Charismatic believers.

Revival Movement

The two major Chinese Pentecostal groups to rise in the 1920s and 1930s were the True Jesus Church and the Jesus Family. Both came into being through the influence of Pentecostal faith. Robust 'nationalist' pressures shaped Chinese churches so that they could stand entirely on their own, without the assistance of Western missionaries. Pentecostalism was no exception. The most extraordinary development was the 1931–2 'Revival' in Shandong peninsula. First of all, the demonstration of the power of the Holy Spirit caused a large revival, through which believers experienced profound empowerment. As a result, they became effective witnesses, bringing a large number of people to faith in Christ. Both the Jesus Family and the True Jesus Church were outcomes of the Shandong Revival. Despite heavy persecution during the communist period, today the True Jesus Church has around 1.5 million affiliates in 60 different countries. The Jesus Family also continues to grow, so that today there are more than 2 million members in Shandong. Its spirituality has drawn heavily from Pentecostalism. The worship of the Jesus Family was distinguished by emphasis on baptism in the Spirit, speaking in tongues, prayer for healing, prophecy and other spiritual gifts. It also included a community pattern

Pentecostals and Charismatics in East and Southeast Asia, 1970

Region	Total population	Christian population	Pentecostal/ Charismatic population	% of region Pentecostal/ Charismatic	% of Christians Pentecostal/ Charismatic
East Asia	996,425,000	11,456,000	1,037,000	0.1%	9.1%
Southeast Asia	280,607,000	50,740,000	3,585,000	1.3%	7.1%
East and Southeast Asia	1,277,032,000	62,196,000	4,622,000	0.4%	7.4%
Globe	3,700,578,000	1,229,309,000	57,637,000	1.6%	4.7%

Source: Todd M. Johnson and Gina A. Zurlo (eds), *World Christian Database* (Leiden/Boston: Brill), accessed March 2018.

of life in which everyone's resources were commonly shared. The Jesus Family was particularly popular in the lowliest strata of Chinese society. As observed by an unnamed present-day believer, the church was a fellowship in love, a gathering avenue for the tired and an area of rest for the despondent – 'no matter where you go, you can find your home'.

In Korea, the prominent 1907 Pyongyang Revival was recognised as the 'Korean Pentecost', and the fire of the Spirit spread all over the country in the following years. The revival was characterised by deep conviction and public repentance of sins, daily dawn prayer meetings, Bible classes, dynamic church worship services, evangelistic meetings, fervent prayer and spiritual renewal. Worship and ministry meetings were accompanied by signs and wonders. Towards the end of the revival, around 1910, many thousands of people reported having gained experience of strong 'religious emotion'. The form of Christianity practised prior to the revival seldom allowed such a display of emotion. Like an unrestrained 'wildfire' the revival expanded and grew in strength until the whole country was affected. One significant outcome was the growth of the church during this time. In 1905 there were 321 churches, 470 evangelists, 9,761 believers and 30,136 catechumens. By 1907 there were: 642 churches, an increase of 100%; 1,045 evangelists, an increase of 122%; 18,964 believers, an increase of 94%; and 99,300 catechumens, an increase of 230%.

As a direct consequence of the 1907 revival, missionaries and nationals of various denominations devised the Million Souls for Christ Movement as a concerted evangelisation programme, with diverse local events connected to all the churches and believers in the given area to reach the community. Theologians of different institutions also focused their efforts to support this nationwide campaign. The net result of this evangelistic programme was the addition of 80,000 members to the Korean churches. Thus, this revival played a significant role in the spread of the gospel and the growth of churches across the country. The revival movement also produced prominent national church leaders such as Sunjoo Kil, Ikdu Kim and Yongdo Lee. All were popular revival preachers, but with varying emphases: Kil on eschatological belief, Kim on supernatural healing and

Pentecostals and Charismatics in East and Southeast Asia, 2020

Region	Total population	Christian population	Pentecostal/ Charismatic population	% of region Pentecostal/ Charismatic	% of Christians Pentecostal/ Charismatic
East Asia	1,663,619,000	128,787,000	38,375,000	2.3%	29.8%
Southeast Asia	669,016,000	153,102,000	52,492,000	7.8%	34.3%
East and Southeast Asia	2,332,635,000	281,889,000	90,867,000	3.9%	32.2%
Globe	7,795,482,000	2,518,834,000	635,260,000	8.1%	25.2%

Source: Todd M. Johnson and Gina A. Zurlo (eds), *World Christian Database* (Leiden/Boston: Brill), accessed March 2018.

Lee on mystical union with Christ. The effect of the revival continued until the 1930s.

Renewal Experiences

In 1973, pastor Hau Lian Kham in Myanmar, along with a tiny group in the Tedim Baptist Church, began praying for renewal. In 1977 Kham became a Pentecostal minister, as his church did not accept the revival that he was initiating, and he is now well acknowledged as the most important figure of the renewal movement among the Chin people. After intensive prayer, he and his group led week-long open-air evangelistic meetings. It was recorded that the move of the Spirit was so strong that numerous non-believers were converted to Christ. The renewal continued over several years and many people were added to the church, while a large number of Chin believers experienced spiritual renewal. The renewal eventually spread through the country. In the revival meetings, many shared their experiences of healing from cancer, skin disease and other sicknesses. Countless miracles were reported to have occurred during and after the evangelistic meetings.

Bethesda Bedok-Tampine Church in Singapore is a good example of the Charismatic renewal. In 1979, as soon as the church was established, it launched various ministries. Through an outreach ministry among young people, the church reached out to its surrounding areas. To reach various language groups, the church has offered a bilingual healing ministry, in both English and Hokkien. It invites non-believing neighbours and loved ones who suffer from illness to experience God's healing touch. The church also provides a counselling ministry with a staff of both pastors and trained lay counsellors. The areas of the counselling ministry range from marital and parenting issues to personal difficulties such as low self-esteem, addiction and anger management. The church mobilises individuals and groups who sense a call to evangelism and are endowed with spiritual gifts. The church also sends out missionaries to Thailand,

Changes in Pentecostal/Charismatics in East and Southeast Asia, 1970–2020, growth rate, % per year

Region	Total population	Christian population	Pentecostal/Charismatic population
East Asia	1.03%	4.96%	7.49%
Southeast Asia	1.75%	2.23%	5.51%
East and Southeast Asia	1.21%	3.07%	6.14%
Globe	1.50%	1.45%	4.92%

Source: Todd M. Johnson and Gina A. Zurlo (eds), *World Christian Database* (Leiden/Boston: Brill), accessed March 2018.

North Sulawesi, the Philippines, Northeast and South India, Mongolia and East Asia.

Catholic Charismatic renewal occurred in Indonesia through those who had encountered similar renewal overseas. Upon their return, they shared their renewal experiences with their fellow Catholics in Indonesia. This initial impetus was strengthened by a renewal seminar for both priests and lay Catholics in 1976. Two speakers were particularly influential: Brandon J. O'Brien sj from Bangkok and Herbert Schneider sj from Manila. They presented on the topic 'New Life in the Spirit'. This occasion served as an introduction and endorsement of the Charismatic renewal within the national Catholic Church. In March 1977, Lambertus Sugiri sj invited some who had completed the seminar run by O'Brien and Schneider to offer a similar seminar on Charismatic renewal to his parish in Mangga Besar Jakarta. Around 300 attended and experienced the baptism of the Holy Spirit in the seminar. Soon the parish experienced renewed spiritual life and the manifestation of spiritual gifts. The move of the Spirit was evident in the lives of the believers. The renewal soon spread to other districts, in both Jakarta and many other parts of Indonesia, and seminars mushroomed. As a result, the Catholic Charismatic Renewal expanded throughout the country.

Although it is difficult to count the number of Charismatic Catholics in the country, they are estimated to reach 1 million believers. As a distinctly lay movement, Catholicism in Indonesia has been revitalised and renewed through the Charismatic movement. The main features of the Catholic Charismatic group's meetings are:

- focusing on Jesus, with the ultimate goal of having a deep, personal relationship with him;
- using a contemporary worship style, which is often found in Pentecostal Charismatic services;
- emphasising Bible study – all members of Catholic Charismatic Renewal groups bring the Bible with them and read and trust it;
- speaking in tongues, with other manifestations of the Spirit also allowed.

Worship

Pentecostal and Charismatic worship is spiritually dynamic. A typical worship service consists of lengthy and lively praise, dynamic preaching, messages of prophecy and in tongues, praying for salvation and healing and the manifestation of various spiritual gifts. The centre of such worship is experiencing God. Accordingly, themes of Pentecostal and Charismatic preaching directly deal with life-connected problems. They range from sickness, poverty and family issues to business matters and relationships. It is important to recall that the majority of Pentecostal Charismatic believers come from the lower strata of a given society. They regularly search for God's direct and immediate help more than their middle-class counterparts would do. Every component of Pentecostal and Charismatic worship is a building block towards the experience with God.

In Pentecostal and Charismatic worship, music plays an important role. Energetic music and passionate singing with various musical instruments draw many young people in particular. With eyes closed during worship and arms frequently raised upward, worshippers are submerged in the presence of God. The dynamic spirituality, immanent expectancy, lively worship, manifestation of the spiritual gifts, prayer with fasting, dawn prayer and all-night prayer meetings all have contributed to its fast growth and spread.

Church Growth and Expansion

The growth and expansion of Pentecostal and Charismatic churches are often attributed to the dynamic spirituality of these churches and their ability to address felt needs of everyday life. However, the mission practice of Pentecostal and Charismatic Christianity, in addition to its focus on evangelism and church planting, is the holistic approach to Christian ministry. The following cases illustrate this.

In 1929, the True Jesus Church, an independent Chinese church characterised by Pentecostal and Charismatic practices, founded congregations in a number of Southeast Asian countries. For instance, in Taiwan the first church was started in March of that year. Within a short period, hundreds of people were baptised. The church grew rapidly, and the membership reached 28,000 in 1968. Charismatic groups such as the True Jesus Church and the Taipei Truth Church from Hong Kong made a significant impact on East and Southeast Asian Christianity, including Pentecostal and Charismatic Christianity.

Yoido Full Gospel Church in Seoul, Korea, is a well known Pentecostal mega-church. It was begun by David Yonggi Cho and Jashil Choi, who later became Cho's mother-in-law, as a tiny tent church with five members in a slum area of Seoul in 1958. Cho was born and raised in a Buddhist home. When he was a teenager, he contracted tuberculosis, which was potentially fatal. At his sickbed, several Christians visited and told him about Jesus. Physically weak, he opened his heart and accepted Christ as his personal Saviour. To his surprise, he experienced God's healing touch. In 1956 he entered Full Gospel Bible College to take theological training. In the winter of 1957, Cho was ill with severe flu. For two weeks Jashil Choi, a former nurse and Cho's classmate, took good care of him in both prayer and medically. Cho recovered completely. By 1962 the tent church had grown to 800 through the message and experience of healing, exorcism and miracles. In 1964, the church moved to Saedamoon and its membership grew to 2,000. The church acquired new land in Yoido in 1969 and completed a 10,000-seat church building in 1973. Today the church has more than 700,000 members.

Cho preaches a positive and uplifting message, presenting Jesus as healer, miracle worker and supplier of all our needs. He offers a 'theology of hope'. Rising from the rubble of the Korean War, the struggling nation desperately needed a message of hope and miracles. It is in this context that Cho's message found a ready reception. The church also emphasises the power of prayer. Taking inspiration from the life of Jesus and the early church, and also from traditional religious practices, the Korean church in general, and Pentecostal and Charismatic churches in particular, have maintained a strong tradition of prayer. Yoido's large 'prayer mountain' has been known for fasting and prayer. There is an expectation of the experience of the Holy Spirit. The church's rapid growth has brought challenges to its organisation and pastoral life, not least the expectation that it will raise a prophetic voice in relation to the life of the nation.

One of the lively and growing Pentecostal Charismatic churches in Indonesia is the Indonesian Bethel Church (Gereja Bethel Indonesia), located in Surabaya. Niko Njotorahardjo has led the church since its founding. In recent decades, the church has been growing exponentially through planting daughter churches in various Javanese cities. Its combined membership reached 100,000 in 1963 and 400,000 by 1968. The current membership is around 12 million. Several unique characteristics of the church are observed. The first is worship, which the church considers to be the foremost part of church life, drawing people to Christ. A modern worship style is used, with outstanding musicians, excellent singers, tambourine dancing groups and flawless sound systems. The second is the pragmatically oriented preaching. Almost all sermons address the immediate concerns of life, to the extent that they are sometimes criticised for being theologically thin. The message is communicated in lively, dynamic and entertaining ways, generously interjected with testimonies, stories and jokes. The third is the focus of church theology on miracles, particularly divine healing. Testimonies of miraculous healing are widely disseminated throughout the church network.

Also in Indonesia, a remarkable revival took place in West Timor in 1964 when several thousand people experienced healing and there was a contest with sorcerers and exorcists. Soon, other revivals followed, for example in Java. Over 2 million Javanese became Christians in 1965–71, with the Pentecostal and Charismatic churches gaining the most members.

In Vietnam, the first Pentecostal church started in Vung Tau in 1972 and grew rapidly to number 10,000 members by 1975. After the North Vietnamese triumph in 1975, churches were suppressed: many were shut down, belongings were removed by the communist government and membership declined rapidly. The impact of the Pentecostal Church was huge during what a historian called the 'Silent Period' (1975–88). For a decade from 1988, still under harsh persecution, Pentecostal churches grew and spread to all parts of the country. An official operating licence was obtained in October 2009, and the church is in the process of receiving official recognition from the Vietnamese government.

Hope Church in Bangkok, Thailand, was started by Kriengsak Charoenwongsak in 1981. In this staunch Buddhist country, the church grew fast and established 430 satellite churches nationwide. Also, this Charismatic church has a plan to plant 120 Hope churches in different parts of the world. The New Creation Church in Singapore began with 25 people in 1984, rising to 150 members in 1990, more than 10,000 in 2004 and 30,000 in 2013.

In September 1980, the Light of Jesus had its initial prayer gathering at a home in Quezon City in the Philippines. In the second prayer gathering of the group, 14-year-old Bo Sanchez preached for the first time. He has not stopped preaching since and has become a crucial figure for the Light of Jesus Family in the Philippines. As a Catholic lay minister, who is biblically oriented and who believes in the work and movement of the Holy Spirit, he has travelled to different parts of the world to preach. Sanchez has been given numerous honours, including being named one of the Ten Outstanding Young Men in the Philippines in 2006 and the Serviam Award, the highest award a lay Catholic can receive in the Catholic Mass Media Awards in 2007. (The Serviam Award is part of the Catholic Mass Media Awards.) In 2016, the community had 35,000 members in the Philippines and different parts of the world. The community organised two large meetings: the annual inspirational convention Kerygma conference and 200 weekly fellowship and worship groups named 'The Feast' in the country and other regions of the world.

Couples for Christ (CFC) was started in 1981 in Manila by the charismatic group Ang Ligaya ng Panginoon (LNP, 'The Joy of the Lord'). The new community invited married couples to private homes for prayer meetings and faith discussions. In 1996, CFC was recognised by the Catholic Bishops' Conference of the Philippines as a national private association of lay faithful, and in 2000 it was acknowledged by the Vatican as a private international association of the lay faithful of *di diritto pontificio*, that is, of pontifical right. CFC has bloomed internationally. It is today present in dioceses across all 82 Philippine provinces as well as in

163 countries. It has become a leading force for energising family life and the church.

In 1999, CFC began the first Gawad Kalinga (GK, 'To Give Care') project, which aimed to provide houses for the poor. During its formal inauguration in 2004, GK777 was unveiled as a campaign to build 700,000 homes in 7,000 communities in 7 years. In 2006, GK set up the Isang Milyong Bayani (GK1MB, 'One Million Heroes'), an international programme of contributing four hours of work per month to support the GK communities. GK1MB volunteers also pledge to come together for a week-long build activity to help poor families construct their own homes. Its 16 area coordination teams are ready to go wherever assistance is most needed. The GK example has also been followed in countries such as Cambodia, Indonesia and Papua New Guinea. It is also at the forefront of peace-building in conflict zones in Mindanao (Southern Philippines) and contributes in post-disaster rehabilitation efforts all over the Philippines. GK began as an outreach of CFC, but disagreements among its leaders resulted in GK becoming a separate group.

Singles for Christ (SFC) is one of several family works of Couples for Christ (CFC). The work began in 1993 to provide support to single men and women (aged 21–40 years), initially in the Visayan Islands of the Philippines. Through three-day workshops, new SFC members are led to experience the empowering presence of the Holy Spirit, helping them hear God's call and commit to the building of a Christ-centred society. SFC spread quickly, and now there are over 65,000 SFC members around the world.

El Shaddai is a large Charismatic Catholic group in the Philippines, led by Mariano 'Brother Mike' Velarde. It claims a membership of some 7–8 million in the country and another 1 million overseas. When he was 37 years of age, Velarde was miraculously healed of heart disease before surgery. In 1982, he received a revelation from God. According to him, God told him, 'Come, and build me a centre'. An estate agent by profession, he initially planned to build an enormous basilica, and he even travelled to Rome to receive a blessing from the Pope. During this period, however, he went through bankruptcy, a family disaster and a crisis at his radio station. Then he came to realise the true meaning of God's call: not building a basilica but establishing a holy temple of people. Soon he used his radio programmes to spread the message of the power of the Spirit to ordinary Catholics. After overcoming financial difficulty in 1988, his work has expanded across the country. Due to the large numbers, Sunday masses are held in large parks and stadiums. International branches were opened in Hong Kong, Canada, the USA, Singapore, the Middle East and Italy, and they continue their national and international expansion.

A commonly asked question is, what is involved in adopting a Pentecostal kind of faith while still remaining a faithful Catholic? A few practical areas of Christian experience have been proposed as a response: healing through the power of God; encounter with God, including receiving direction; and experiencing God's call through the Word or hearing the internal voice of God. One common experience is that God reveals himself to his people, be they Catholics, Pentecostals or Charismatics. Thus, practising this Spirit-initiated faith is a shared experience, whether its proponents remain in their churches, such as Catholics, or become members of Pentecostal churches.

Evangelism

In the 1970s in Malaysia, both the Tabernacle of God and the Latter Rain Church (LRC) actively reached out to young people, particularly in the universities and colleges. As a result, a large number of university students came to faith in Christ in Kuala Lumpur. LRC reached its peak in 1989–91.

Pentecostal and Charismatic emphasis on spiritual practice is ascribed to their unique worldview, close to many Asian animistic counterparts. They assume the dynamic presence and outworking of spiritual beings, both benevolent and malevolent. In such contexts, Pentecostal and Charismatic believers often engage in what is called power encounters, which have served as an effective tool in winning people in East Asia to Christ.

Also, their unique theological identity has shaped Pentecostal and Charismatic believers as zealous, committed and effective missionaries. Their belief in the baptism in the Holy Spirit assumes that every believer is called and empowered to be a witness. The Holy Spirit forms missional people to fulfil God's purpose. As a distinct people of God, they experience a new in-breaking reality through the renewing work of the Holy Spirit. The combination of belief in the gifts of the Holy Spirit and the priesthood of all believers has given birth to this fresh structure of the missionary community. Every believer – including women, the needy, the unschooled, the young and the laity – is called and empowered by the Holy Spirit to serve in leadership positions and to proclaim the gospel. This universal mobilisation with the Spirit's empowerment has resulted in power evangelism, revitalisation and missional community formation.

Mission

Pentecostals and Charismatics have been a missionary movement in both heart and principle. It began with a firm persuasion that the Holy Spirit had endued God's people with signs and wonders to reach the nations with the salvation through Christ before the end of the age. The outburst of the Holy Spirit recorded in Acts has primarily been understood as the Spirit's empowerment for God's mission. The Holy Spirit prepares, according to this belief, men and women for frontline mission even to the uttermost parts of the world. Spirit-endowed missionaries have proclaimed the message of salvation, divine healing, personal holiness and baptism with the Spirit. The early Pentecostals were convinced that the return of Christ was imminent, hence the urgency of the mission.

An exceptional example is that of the missionary work in Japan by Yoido Full Gospel Church. It began with a 40-day evangelistic meeting led by Jashil Choi. The Holy Spirit laid on her heart a burning desire to evangelise Japanese people. The humble initial gathering at a member's home in 1979 soon grew rapidly in number to become Full Gospel Tokyo Church. Then David Yonggi Cho held a two-day crusade at the Nippon Budokan with more than 6,000 people attending the crusade. Today, Full Gospel Tokyo Church has around 1,500 members, leading Cho's ambitious evangelistic campaign 'Salvation for 10 Million Souls' in Japan.

The International Christian Assembly in Hong Kong, under the leadership of Leroy Cloud, undertook highly effective short-term mission work. It played an important role in preparation for the launch of Pentecostal Charismatic churches in Mongolia. In 1993, the church organised a 52-member team comprising gospel singers, musicians and preachers. They held a three-day evangelistic crusade in Mongolia. The response to the very first Christian evangelistic work in Mongolia was beyond anyone's anticipation. Many people came forward to accept Jesus as their personal saviour. Then the team was divided into groups and distributed invitation flyers to the first Sunday worship. Through this effort, the first local church, Hope Church, was born under the leadership of Mike Louton. His teaching was Pentecostal Charismatic, including deliverance, speaking in tongues and healing. The church rapidly grew in number, and its membership reached 1,300 in 1997. The church led the translation project of the Bible into Mongolian. The New Testament was published in 1996, and 10,000 copies were sold within a month. Also, many worship songs were translated into Mongolian, including more than 80 from Hillsong Church in Australia.

Church Planting

Jesus Is Lord Church in the Philippines was planted in 1978 by Eddie Villanueva with a small group of Bible study participants in the Polytechnic University of the Philippines in Manila, where Villanueva, an economics and finance professor, grabbed every opportunity to preach the gospel to his students. A Bible study that began with 15 students grew remarkably every year, and within 10 years the church had 5 million members. It has planted churches all over the Philippines and has turned out to be the largest Charismatic church in the Philippines, with a stress on holistic mission. Soon the church expanded to an international multi-ministry network, establishing churches in various cities around the world. The church maintains 106 Sunday worship sites in Metro Manila, 25 in Bulacan Province and 275 in the rest of the country. Also, there are 72 international sites in 27 countries, totalling 478 worship sites, with 2 million worshippers altogether. The church also runs a television station (ZOE TV-II) that broadcasts church services. At one time, the Jesus Is Lord Church was the only Pentecostal Charismatic group in the nation that operated a school from nursery and kindergarten through primary and high school and to university.

Conclusion

Pentecostals and Charismatics have gained strengths and weaknesses throughout their development. The following are some common criticisms from other Christian groups that they have generally acknowledged and accepted:

- The emphasis on the Spirit-filled, empowered exercise of spiritual gifts in church life can breed spiritual pride over other Christian traditions.
- There has been a tendency to downplay the 'theology of the cross' by focusing on a theology of triumphalism.
- There has been a lack of dialogue with and witness to people of other faiths, who dominate most Asian societies.
- A narrowly focused 'soul-saving' mission practice has neglected the social dimension of Christian mission.

Positively, there is an increasing awareness of the broader work of mission, including church cooperation and unity.

Pentecostals and Charismatics continue to encounter challenges. The emphasis on 'blessings' or 'prosperity' as a theological priority needs to be balanced by bringing out the scriptural teaching of human reality and suffering. They have established hierarchical power centres, which might appeal to many Asian cultures but contradict the 'egalitarian partnership' ethos of Pentecostal Charismatic spirituality. As they experience rapid growth it becomes a challenge to maintain authentic Pentecostal and Charismatic characteristics – theological, spiritual and practical.

Pentecostal and Charismatic Christianity has grown and expanded in the twentieth century and into the current century, and is perhaps the most significant Christian movement in our day. This movement's genius includes its outstanding ability to adjust itself to diverse socio-cultural settings. As a result, it provides realistically contextualised expressions of Christianity in many different situations. This type of faith is intrinsically flexible: the vitality, passion, impulsiveness and spirituality of Pentecostal and Charismatic faith are well known. Also, it is ready to address life's pressing issues, such as illness, scarcity, job loss, loneliness and crisis. With all these combined, its sustained exponential growth is natural.

Pentecostal and Charismatic Christianity in East and Southeast Asia has proclaimed by word and action a practical gospel for daily survival and witnessing. It has addressed straightforward obstacles of life for everyday living, producing the tangible outcome of faith. Pentecostal and Charismatic believers are taught that everyone is called and empowered to proclaim God's good news. Testimonies of healing and supernatural interventions are generously shared with others, and this creates a 'viral' effect in evangelism. With its spirituality of intrinsic flexibility, messages assume a contextual character that allows them to communicate with relevance and effectiveness.

Bibliography

Anderson, Allan, *An Introduction to Pentecostalism* (Cambridge: Cambridge University Press, 2004).

Anderson, Allan, and Edmond Tang (eds), *Asian and Pentecostal: The Charismatic Faces of Christianity in Asia* (Oxford: Regnum Books, 2005).

Ma, Julie C., and Wonsuk Ma, *Mission in the Spirit: Towards a Pentecostal/Charismatic Missiology* (Oxford: Regnum Books, 2010).

Ma, Wonsuk, and Robert Menzies (eds), *Pentecostalism in Context: Essays in Honor of William W. Menzies* (Sheffield: JSOT Press, 1997).

Wilfred, Felix (ed.), *The Oxford Handbook of Christianity in Asia* (Oxford: Oxford University Press, 2014).

Key Themes

Faith and Culture

José Mario C. Francisco SJ

Just as multiple wind and water currents routinely sweep East and Southeast Asia, diverse social forces shape Christianity and the cultures within the region, and thus their interaction. Such forces have emerged, to a great extent, with movements of peoples and their material and cultural baggage within and across the region and have thus generated different modes of interaction throughout history and in today's globalised world.

Both terms of the interaction are themselves complex. Christianity came to this region, as elsewhere, in particular historical incarnations. Early Eastern Christianity influenced by Nestorius (c. 386–450) flourished in ninth-century China, European Catholicism in sixteenth-century colonies and Protestantism in nineteenth-century missions. And despite the endemic attempts to define 'the essence of Christianity', Christianity always exists as lived and living, therefore as subject to these changing currents. Hence the growing preference among contemporary scholars to refer to 'Christianities'.

Furthermore, describing Christianity as religion – that is, as an integrated network of beliefs, moral codes and ritual practices of a clearly delineated community – comes from European historical experience and does not fit Asian faith and wisdom traditions such as Buddhism or Confucianism. With no equivalents for 'religion' in Asian languages, Christianity has been labelled with distorting nomenclature, just as these traditions are not recognised to have the characteristics of religion.

The term 'culture' proves similarly multifaceted. In plural form, it refers to specific ways of life of particular social groups. Given Asia's enormous breadth and extensive history, the number of its diverse interacting cultures is legion. In the singular, 'culture' points to the realm of social life encompassing shared worldviews and ethos, differentiated from politics and economics. This differentiation is based on earlier views of secularisation in European historical experience, where the cultural, political and economic realms constitute 'the secular' in contrast to 'the sacred'.

These views of culture(s) as integrated wholes and as distinct from the political and economic have been questioned on both empirical and theoretical grounds. For instance, cultural, political and economic forces are often interwoven in Asian contexts. Moreover, 'culture' could be ambiguous, as it could take both descriptive and analytical functions. Thus 'culture' is best considered as a heuristic tool for understanding diverse social contexts.

Set within the context of these general considerations, this essay offers a broad overview of the vibrant and multifaceted interaction between Christianity and cultures in East and Southeast Asia. Though the contribution to this interaction of Christian educational institutions is noted, the essay focuses on the platforms of language, social space and mass and digital media, each of which has proved crucial for and representative of the interaction. Sections on each platform describe the modes and outcomes of the interaction between different incarnations of Christianity and local cultures, traditional as well as globalised. The concluding section points to common and emerging currents in the interaction.

Interaction through Language

Interaction between Christianity and culture started with the arrival of Christians in East and Southeast Asia. Whether merchants or missionaries, they brought the Christianity of their places of origin and provided witness in word and deed to the peoples of the diverse contexts they encountered. For this witness to be heard, they had to communicate the gospel through the languages of these contexts in the same manner that earlier Christian expansion first employed Greek and Syriac and then Arabic in West Asia. Thus, language became the first necessary, and arguably most critical, platform in this interaction between Christianity and culture.

This interaction through language, which occurred during successive waves of Christian mission, required the appropriate linguistic infrastructure involving the region's multiple languages. In a little-known instance during the seventh-century T'ang dynasty in China, churches of the East, commonly named Nestorian by the Western churches, embraced the highly developed Chinese script and language in preaching the gospel.

However, during the sixteenth-century missionary movement accompanying European colonisation, regional languages had to be transformed to facilitate their use by missionaries. Thus, the construction of a linguistic platform became a deliberate, systematic and widespread strategy. For example, the very first Synod of Manila (1582–6) voted to evangelise using native languages rather than Spanish. This strategy in the Philippines, as elsewhere, often required that grammars and vocabularies of these languages be codified after European models and non-Roman scripts like the Philippine syllabic *baybayin* or the Vietnamese *chu nom* be alphabetised.

With the linguistic platform established, interaction between Christianity and the region's diverse cultures ensued, particularly through the mode of translating Christian discourse. Needed devotional texts like prayers and instructional materials like catechisms were first translated from European texts and later written by missionaries and Christianised natives.

Multiple factors shaped the creation of native Christian discourse, such as the fear of making Christianity appear equivalent to 'false' or 'inferior' local traditions or the concern about whether a translation was intended for the 'literati' or 'folk' among the natives. Some nomenclature was directly transliterated from European languages; an example is the word *grasya*, from the Spanish *gracia*, referring to God's grace, in many Philippine languages. Others were approximations from local usage, as in the unusual use of *binyag*, originally referring to Muslim purification before prayers, instead of the Spanish *bautismo* for the sacrament of baptism in the Philippine Tagalog vernacular.

The dynamic of this interaction between Christianity and the region's cultures through the platform of language is most profoundly illustrated in the local renditions of the Christian term 'God'. Subject to not only linguistic but also theological concerns, the challenge of translating God's name is indicative of the complex interaction between Christianity and local cultures. Extant texts and relics from the brief tenure of Nestorian Christianity, like the famous bronze Nestorian Inscription, attest to their efforts at translating 'God' into Chinese and their consideration of existing vocabulary derived from Taoist, Buddhist and other traditions; even 'Buddha' was initially appropriated for God's name. This search for the equivalent translation became more pronounced with the sixteenth-century wave of Christian mission. Jesuit Francis Xavier (1506–52), the 'Apostle of Asia', settled for the Japanese rendition of the Latin *Deus* instead of his native informant's *Dainichi*, a Buddhist deity's name. Another prominent Jesuit, Matteo Ricci (1552–1610), appropriated *Shangti* ('Lord on High') in consideration of his Chinese Confucian audience.

Translating the divine name clearly points to what is at stake in the interaction between Christianity and native cultures through language. Translation is not just the product of matching words with pre-existing realities or of finding equivalences, literal or functional, between different languages. Contrary to earlier philosophies of language and translation, it is more commonly described today as the mediation between social worlds involving texts, semiotic systems and other elements. Thus, translating both God's name in particular and Christianity in general into these local languages proves to be a multidirectional process.

Christian texts in these languages integrate not only native vocabulary but also local views and ethos in communicating the gospel. Some well known examples are *Doctrina Christiana* (1582–91?) by Franciscan Juan de Oliver (?–1599) for lay Tagalogs and the Vietnamese–Latin *Catechismus*

(1651) of Jesuit Alexandre de Rhodes (1593–1660). This Vietnamese catechism, influenced by Ricci's approach, shows keen awareness of Vietnamese religious thought and employs vernacular proverbs and sayings to explain Christian doctrine.

Other native Christian texts like novenas chronicle lives of exemplary Christians and use local rhetorical forms for prayer. In the enduring Philippine tradition of chanting the epic of Christ's life, available in all major languages, biblical characters come to life as natives in thought, feeling and behaviour and thus serve as native Christian models. For instance, ordinary natives during the 1896 Philippine Revolution perceived their struggle as participation in Christ's Passion.

Thus, the interaction between Christianity and local cultures through the mode of translation truly becomes a two-way rather than a unilaterally controlled process that integrates the preaching and the reception of the gospel. Inasmuch as language is the primary carrier of culture, the interaction translates what is brought by foreign missionaries and gives birth to Christianity in East and Southeast Asian cultures – a Christianity through which their people could witness to their own Christian faith.

Moreover, as cultures change through time, this process of translating Christianity becomes constitutive and ongoing. Thus, the work of translation has continued beyond earlier missionary movements. From the late nineteenth century, efforts of newly arrived Protestant groups to translate the Bible into Chinese had to overcome factors such as the variety of levels and dialects as well as denominational and theological differences. They succeeded in producing a common translation only in 1919.

Then, with the development of modern social science in the latter half of the twentieth century, Christian churches became more aware of and knowledgeable about the nature and dynamics of cultures. The World Council of Churches began to employ anthropological concepts like 'indigenisation' or 'acculturation' in its theological and pastoral reflections. The Catholic Church's Second Vatican Council allowed the general use of vernaculars in church liturgies and applied a social science view of culture in analysing the contemporary situation in its major document *Gaudium et spes* (1965).

Given these recent developments, efforts at deepening the interaction with cultures within the region became deliberate and extensive. Pioneer scholars from the region begin to publish theological works in their native languages; for example, Korean theologians used the concept of *han* (woundedness, suffering) for the liberation of the *Minjung* (poor, oppressed). Others integrated native cultural ethos in their theologising; C. S. Song incorporates Chinese folk tales, and Filipino José de Mesa the Tagalog understanding of *loob* (interiority).

At present, this interaction through the platform of language remains dynamic within the region and sets various strategies for and outcomes in translation. Some differences in translation have been accepted as a sign of diversity, but others have led to conflict. For instance, the prayer 'Our Father' has two versions in Korean, corresponding to differences between the Protestant and Catholic traditions. It has had many different Javanese translations throughout the twentieth century because of differing theological views.

The Christian use of 'Allah' has recently proved contentious in Malaysia. It has historical roots in the first Christian communities in West Asia and is currently accepted in Indonesia and Malaysian Sarawak. But because the political status of Islam in peninsular Malaysia has had a different historical configuration, Christians have been ordered by federal courts not to use 'Allah' in their publications.

Apart from the many forces at play in specific cases, these current differences in translations simply indicate the central importance of language as platform and translation as mode of interaction. They illustrate the continuing growth of Christianity as constituted in and through the cultures of the region.

Interaction in Social Space

Social space, both geographical and cultural, is another important platform where Christianity and East and Southeast Asian cultures interact. In certain parts of the region, this space has been severely limited by different forms of dominant political power. Such power from traditional leaders, nationalist and communist regimes or strong ethnic or religious majorities have restricted, if not prohibited, Christian interaction with local communities. During certain periods in their past and even in the present, such has been the case in Laos, Cambodia and even Myanmar. Thus, Christian missions have often concentrated on marginal groups, such as ethnic minorities, or oppressed sectors.

But in more open social spaces, Christianity has been able to interact with culture and to show its public face through communal practices and in material artefacts. This interaction occurs in three modes: when Christianity encounters deeply embedded cultural practices and artefacts, when local cultures shape Christian practices and artefacts, and when Christian practices and artefacts move into new contexts. These modes of interaction illustrate how the constitutive strands of these cultures – ethnicity, class, or other religious and wisdom traditions, among others – come into play.

The first mode of interaction consists in Christianity's encounter with existing social contexts. Upon its relatively recent arrival, it encountered a rich repertoire of cultural practices, like common rituals and symbolic objects, all of which had evolved in the enduring traditions of diverse local communities. Christianity, though identifying itself as 'true religion', was not reticent in appropriating whatever was helpful for evangelisation. In the colonial Philippines, for instance, Spanish missionaries taught catechism through local musical idioms. In Java, Catholics consider their pilgrimages to major Marian shrines as part of the long-standing local *ziārah* pilgrimage tradition, in the same spirit that Muslims visit tombs of prominent Islamic missionaries. Given this inclusive tradition, Catholics and Muslims visit each other's shrines without compromising their own religious identities.

This first mode of interaction is best illustrated by the Christian encounter with the traditional ethos of filial piety and its ritual expressions, beginning with Ricci's China mission and enduring in parts of the region with Chinese and/or Confucian influences.

Contemporary studies still discuss this complex encounter, memorialised in the so-called Chinese Rites Controversy and concerned with their compatibility with Christian faith. Given Ricci's Renaissance humanist background and serious study of Chinese thought, he viewed them as cultural and ethical practices, not religious, and thus compatible with Christianity. However, following their 1635 arrival in Fuan, Dominicans and Franciscans, who preached to Christian converts rather than Confucian scholars, opposed Ricci's position and sent an indictment to church authorities in the Philippines and Rome.

What was initially a theological dispute proved to be a conjuncture of various forces within the Catholic Church and Chinese society. Ancestral rites were intertwined with power relations between lineages and thus implicated in political hierarchy and social harmony. Subsequently, even the Kangxi emperor and his courtiers became concerned about this conflict. Within the church, the continuing dispute involved various power centres in Asia and Europe, among them religious congregations and orders, theological commissions, papal legates and even several popes. In 1704, Pope Clement IX issued a ban on the rites, which Pope Benedict XIV reaffirmed in 1742. However, in 1939 Pope Pius XII reversed the ban. At present, these rites have been accepted and even integrated into liturgies among some Catholic communities across the region, but not among the more reticent Protestant groups.

Though commentators see this controversy as 'a missed opportunity' for Christianity in Asia and beyond, the more fundamental issue in this interaction is Christianity's presence in the social space of native communities. More than just an issue of ritual practice and its theological status, this tradition is deeply woven into the social fabric of many East and Southeast Asian societies, and therefore Christianity's response delineates its public place vis-á-vis local cultures.

The second mode of interaction through social space consists in how native cultures adapt and appropriate Christian forms and artefacts as their own. In line with Christianity's traditional view of mission as transplanting the church, foreign missionaries and native clergy brought church practices familiar to them or from their places of origin. Church architecture and art provide the most obvious examples. Malaysia's St George's Church, the earliest Anglican Church in Southeast Asia, completed in 1818 by the East India Company, is modelled after its namesake in Chennai along the Georgian Palladian style common then.

Despite this importation of foreign styles in constructing sacred spaces, the native, unlike passive platforms, asserted its materiality and character in different, even subtle, ways. First, materials for these churches came from local resources. In the colonial Philippines, missionaries built European-style churches in cities and towns with improvised local materials like red clay, volcanic tuff (*adobe*) and dressed coral stone (*tabliya*). Moreover, other factors, such as local topography and climate, forced European church designs to be modified; because of the recurrent earthquakes, colonial churches could not be as high as their European models, hence their being termed 'earthquake' or 'squat' baroque.

Native forms and motifs appear in churches throughout the region. For instance, though Singapore's Catholic Church of Saints Peter and Paul was built in colonial neo-Gothic style, its exterior neo-Gothic columns feature lotus details. Vietnam's Phát Diệm Cathedral, designed by local priest Tran Luc and built in 1892, is a stone cathedral with traditional Vietnamese roofs. Though these design details might appear simply ornamental and therefore superficial, they show the intrusion of native cultural ethos and suggest a subtle subversion of colonial Christian design. In many Philippine colonial churches, botanical motifs like familiar banana and papaya fruits abound, hinting at a lush tropical environment.

This mode of interaction is most evident in the depiction of Christian images in painting, relief and statuary. Although these images, like church architecture, borrowed European representations, native artists crafted them using traditional expertise and styles. Facial features, especially the eyes, bear resemblances to those of the natives, thus projecting them as their own. In the *retablo* (altarpiece) of the Jesuit church in Silang, the Archangel Gabriel's Annunciation to Mary takes place in a room complete with what appears to be the mosquito net ubiquitous in ordinary Filipino houses.

This localisation of Christianity becomes more widespread and deliberate in the second half of the twentieth century, with greater Christian openness to local cultures. Jesus and the saints are represented in native dress and within local settings. But even with such openness, Christianity's interaction with local cultures has not been free of tension and conflict, because other forces also shape these cultures. Korean Christians have disagreed about whether the Holy Family should be represented in elaborate royal robes or in ordinary peasant attire. More striking is the Redemptorist Church building in Pattaya, Thailand, completely rendered in the Buddhist tradition. Not only does the church itself look like a temple, but Christ is also portrayed through Buddhist iconography. Some Thai Catholics feel completely at home in it, while others cannot pray in what they see as a Buddhist temple.

The third mode of interaction in social space began with recent widespread, sustained and systematic movements of peoples who bring their Christian practices and artefacts into new contexts. Its most documented instance relates to the migration of Catholic Filipino workers within the region and beyond, which affects the dynamic between Christianity and culture in their places of destination.

While local churches in Korea and Taiwan, for example, have shown concern for Catholic migrants, differences between the migrants' ethos and practice, rooted in Filipino Christianity, and those of local Christian communities have made negotiations necessary and challenging. Filipino traditions like patronal feasts and Christmas novena Masses are given religious space at local parishes, as in the Kuala Lumpur Cathedral, but these traditions do not become part of the local community. In other instances, migrants are integrated into parish life, singing at regular Sunday Masses and welcoming other parish members to typically Filipino religious celebrations.

This mode of interaction involving Christian practices and artefacts from different local contexts raises an important issue regarding the public place of different Christian forms within a particular church and society. In Japan, for instance, migrant Catholics from the Philippines and Latin America exceed native Catholics in number, thus making Japanese Catholics a minority in society and also in the Catholic Church itself. At the same time, the presence of Filipino Catholic women as wives or nannies sometimes leads to baptism, first of the children and subsequently of other family members. These situations pose practical challenges to the catholicity of Christianity.

Beneath these modes of interaction on the platform of social space lies the dynamic between Christianity's appropriation of local cultures and its concern over the integrity of its tradition. How this dynamic is negotiated in each case – for example ancestor veneration, Buddhist representations of Christ and differing forms of Christian practice – shapes Christianity's public presence in local societies. These negotiations, however, also take place through and within Christian educational institutions in many rural and urban areas across the region. Envisioned as a strategic base for reaching the large Asian youth population, these schools and universities not only facilitate interaction between the Christian minority and those from other religious, ethnic or economic backgrounds but also provide formal education to sectors without traditional access, such as women and the poor.

Interaction through Media

With advances in transport and communications technologies in the second half of the twentieth century, movements of peoples within and beyond borders and the consequent increase in the number and density of urban centres brought profound changes within a Christianity confronted by modernity and in East and Southeast Asian cultures no longer represented by traditional rural communities. Thus, their interaction has taken new modes through the equally new platforms of mass and digital media.

The first mode of interaction emerged with radio and television, early forms of mass media that provided means for evangelising those beyond geographical reach, either because of their remote locations or due to political restrictions. Initially cautious, but also conscious of mass media's potential, Christian churches and groups established international and local radio stations. Among the most prominent internationally were the Catholic Vatican Radio in 1931 and Radio Veritas Asia in 1969, as well as the Protestant Evangelical Far East Broadcasting Corporation (FEBC) in 1945, all of which later expanded coverage by broadcasting in various languages. Though initially focused on religious themes, they have also responded to critical historical circumstances and provided news information independent of government control. For instance, Radio Veritas supported the 1986 People Power Revolution against the Marcos dictatorship in the Philippines.

But the greater impact of Christianity's interaction with cultures through the mass media platform has been in the transformation of Christian presence and of the social fabric of local communities themselves. Through mass media, Christianity and local cultures interact in new ways. The voice of Christianity is no longer just that of the resident foreign missionary or native pastor; those from across local and national borders are now heard. Through radio and television, Christianity speaks in multiple voices heard by local communities, bringing about what has been called the 'de-territorialisation' of Christianity. Transformation also occurs within local communities, once isolated villages but now connected to and in conversation with others, both Christian and non-Christian.

For instance, the spread of Evangelical Protestantism among indigenous Hmong communities in Vietnam and other parts of Southeast

Asia began in the 1980s through FEBC radio programmes in Hmong. Mountain villages heard through transistor radios Hmong preachers using traditional folk tales to explain Christian faith, so much so that they accepted Christianity as their new tradition. In response, listeners sent cassette tapes to FEBC radio stations to ask questions express and their concerns. This interaction has fostered Christian community and a sense of religious identity transcending geographical boundaries.

This mode of interaction has also been present among Charismatic or Evangelical groups in urban centres like Seoul, Taipei and Manila. Groups such as the Korean Yoido Full Gospel Church and the Filipino El Shaddai use mass media to enhance interaction between Christianity and rapidly developing cultures. Their religious ethos is often a mixture of imported and traditional sources, bringing about either modification or reinforcement of traditional values. On the one hand, such groups preach an American-style 'prosperity gospel' to local city-dwellers influenced by Confucian tradition and now searching for better opportunities and build community fellowship with loud electronic music, television videos and new gestures and body movements. On the other, the common prominence of male Charismatic leaders within them reinforces traditional patriarchy in many Asian cultures. These illustrate how Christianity and cultures interact in the region's urban centres through the platform of mass media.

The second mode of interaction between Christianity and culture operates on the platform of digital space. Given the movements of peoples in our globalised world, connectivity through digital space has become a valued and central platform for all areas of contemporary life, including the interaction between Christianity and culture. Following the birth of the World Wide Web, Christian churches and groups initially employed its countless applications as a more far-reaching means of preaching the gospel, just as they did through radio and television. They put up websites to provide basic information about Christianity and to share religious reflections on Christian themes.

But as websites have become interactive and social media increasingly popular (especially among the young, urban-based and technologically fluent), interaction between Christians has taken new forms on the digital landscape. Religious practices like spiritual accompaniment, recollections and even the Filipino Holy Thursday tradition of visiting seven churches are offered interactively on the Web. The blogsite DiscipleSFX, created and curated by Malaysian Catholics, provides a forum for exchange open not only to Christians but also to those with other or no religious affiliation. Its recent discussion of the 'Allah' controversy illustrates its cogency and role in Christianity's interaction with contemporary culture.

A similar example from the Philippines shows the importance and impact of social media. Since the 1970s, efforts to pass reproductive health legislation have failed because of official Catholic opposition, expressed in numerous pastoral letters from the Catholic Bishops' Conference of the Philippines read during Sunday services. However, from 2010 onwards, Catholic groups and individuals argued in favour of the current legislative proposal through social media. This platform provided an alternative voice and created a Catholic constituency for the legislation. Thus, the proposal was subsequently passed by Congress and signed into law by President Benigno Aquino III.

Though these interactions on the platform of mass and digital media are not hermetically sealed from traditional face-to-face situations and often have links to Christian institutions, they alter the dynamics of Christian connectivity and identity. No longer is community solely structured along geographical proximity, or the public voice of Christianity limited to its official leaders.

Common and Emerging Currents

This essay on 'Faith and Culture' has discussed the interaction of Christianity in its various historical incarnations with diverse traditional and contemporary cultures in East and Southeast Asia along the platforms of language, social space, and mass and digital media. Though these platforms give rise to different modes of interaction, one finds certain common and emerging currents related to the dynamic and outcome of this interaction.

First, the interaction between Christianity and local cultures of the region involves all aspects of individual and social existence. Inasmuch as these cultures are practically inseparable from the economic, political and religious forces in each local context, their interactions with Christianity are often subject to these same forces. Christianity's relations with historical colonial and commercial interests or with modern nationalist and modernising sentiments influence its encounter with local communities and determine its appropriation or rejection. All these forces are at play, for example, in Christianity's complex interaction with contemporary China, with its traditional heritage, tumultuous encounters with Western and other Asian nations in both past and present, ever-changing relations with the Catholic Church and rapid modernisation under communist leadership. Moreover, the dominant status of other religious and wisdom traditions in parts of the region and Christianity's regard of them affect the dynamic and outcome of this interaction. As a result, this interaction has been subject to social forces based on nation, ethnicity, class and other factors. This too is evident through Christianity's public presence in the region's social space through ritual, art and architecture and in mass and digital media, where its encounters with traditional practices and urbanised cultures are played out. What all these indicate is Christianity's significant place within the region despite its minority in number.

Second, this manifold interaction is multidirectional and thus transformative of both Christianity and local cultures. Whether this interaction is spontaneous, as shown in the use of native materials, expertise and motifs in Christian architecture and art, or is deliberate, like the translation of Christian nomenclature and belief into native languages, Christianity and local cultures encounter each other in all their concreteness and materiality and together give birth to the incarnation of Christianity in each local culture. This dynamic and outcome belie earlier views of inculturation or contextuality that ignore this constitutive mutuality. Thus, despite Christianity's initial entry through 'outsiders', its stature within the region cannot be reduced to that of colonial imposition. Throughout history and at present, the witness of Christian churches and individuals, as well as their native voices in prayer and reflection, call into question the popular view that Christianity, despite its birth in West Asia, is foreign to Asia. At Mass in some Malaysian Catholic parishes, one hears Bible readings and liturgical songs in Malay, Tamil, Mandarin and English.

Third, the interaction on the different platforms is nevertheless characterised by a dynamic tension between the centripetal pull towards localisation and the centrifugal push towards de-territorialisation of both Christianity and local cultures. On the one hand, Christianity is subject to the compelling force of local cultures; its vocabulary, rituals and other forms of practice are pulled to take native incarnations. On the other, local cultures and Christianity itself are linked to others beyond geographical boundaries. Even before communications technologies, local churches, no matter how isolated, became part of the wider Christian network, and communities are subject to entities and influences in society at large. The interplay between these centripetal and centrifugal forces could be illustrated in the interaction with what is commonly seen as Asian traditions of authoritarianism and patriarchy. Clericalism of traditional Christianity has reinforced this in many instances in local churches. But in recent decades, Asian Christian women have articulated Christian discourse that interrogates these traditions in Christianity and local contexts and, at the same time, respects the integrity of Christianity and their own cultures.

Fourth, this tensive interaction not only transforms Christianity and local cultures but also renews incarnations of Christianity in the diverse spaces of the region. Asian Christian representations of Jesus as guru, the traditional master, or as 'the enlightened' open different avenues towards a richer understanding of who Jesus is.

Furthermore, greater and faster mobility across geographical and digital spaces provides more far-reaching means of preaching the gospel as well as different structures for communication and of community. Christianity's interaction on these constantly developing platforms challenges its reliance on geographical proximity and traditional structures for governance and belonging. All these diverse instances of interaction between Christianity and local cultures attest to Christianity's vibrant presence and promising future in East and Southeast Asia.

Bibliography

Evers, Georg, *The Churches in Asia* (Delhi: ISPCK, 2005).

Federation of Asian Bishops' Conferences, *For All the Peoples of Asia*, 3 vols (Quezon City: Claretian Publications, 1992, 1997, 2002).

Phan, Peter C. (ed.), *Christianities in Asia* (Oxford: Wiley-Blackwell, 2011).

Tirimanna, Vimal (ed.), *Harvesting from the Asian Soil: Toward an Asian Theology* (Bangalore: Asian Trading Corporation, 2011).

Wilfred, Felix (ed.), *The Oxford Handbook of Christianity in Asia* (Oxford: Oxford University Press, 2014).

Worship and Spirituality

Wonsuk Ma

Spirituality is bi-dimensional. It has an inner dimension consisting of personal beliefs (based on the Scriptures and traditions) forming values and attitudes, and an outer dimension, which is the expression of these in one's life, in community worship and mission to the world. At least two elements play an important role in the formation of individual and communal spirituality: the role of the social, cultural and religious context, and the transcendent realm that Christians understand in terms of the work of the Holy Spirit.

In East and Southeast Asia, Christianity has, in general, a shorter history than other religions. In this religiously rich region, many still view Christianity as a Western religion, despite its Asian origin. The process through which Christianity was introduced to different parts of the region is varied and often entangled with tumultuous socio-political events. The shaping of Christianity, therefore, is deeply rooted in its engagement with long-standing and still prevailing religious traditions and practices. Christianity's exclusivistic claim to be the only true religion often meets with reaction, rather than interaction, on the part of other religions.

The spread of Christianity in the region is extremely uneven. With two exceptions (Timor-Leste, with around 89% of its 1.3 million population identified as Christians, and the Philippines, with 93% of its over 100 million population claiming to be Christian), most Christians live as religious minorities in countries where other religions are dominant. In the three Islamic states in the region – Brunei, Indonesia and Malaysia – freedom of religion is constitutionally recognised. However, various social and political measures are in place to limit Christians' social, political and religious engagement. Treatment of Christians in Buddhist-dominated nations varies. Christians in Cambodia, Mongolia and Thailand are repressed less than those in Laos, Myanmar and Vietnam. Equally prominent in the region are several political systems that are inclement or hostile towards Christians. In addition to legal restrictions, in some areas the frequency of mob attacks, church burnings and terrorist attacks is on the rise. For example, Christian presence is almost nonexistent in North Korea due to that country's socialist system, which completely denies freedom of religion except for a few 'showcases'. The unregistered churches in China practise their faith and mission 'underground'. In parts of the region, however, the struggling state of Christianity cannot be explained by such hostility alone. In completely free environments, such as Japan and Thailand, Christianity is still trying to establish itself even after many centuries of mission.

Despite the challenging circumstances of the region, Christians and churches have developed a vibrant spirituality, worshipping lifestyle and missionary engagement. In many countries in the region, Christianity historically has brought much-needed social change. Challenging long-standing social traditions and customs – such as taking concubines, the use of narcotics like opium and unjust social-class systems – has led many to see modernity as naturally concomitant with Christianity. Still, in other countries, Christianity is often perceived as the religion of the Western imperial powers. Christian self-identity in each context is, therefore, the result of an active process wherein Christian belief, missionary tradition, socio-cultural context and local religious beliefs interact with and against each other.

Worship: Centre of Christian Spirituality

Worship expresses the spirituality of believing individuals and communities. Consider a lively worship scene where local and global influence comes together. The All Gospel Church in San Fernando, the Philippines, gathers between 120 and 150 members for Sunday morning worship. They range from fish vendors to a city clerk, from students to the elderly. After a short prayer, a group of young musicians and singers leads the congregation in worship. There are no hymn books, and the songs are highly 'contemporary' (such as the music originating from Hillsong in Australia). The atmosphere is lively and the music loud. Several young girls dance with cymbals in their hands, and the congregation moves along clapping and raising their hands. The music slows down, and the pastor extends a warm welcome, shares announcements and gives updates on recent missionary trips. Being Pentecost Sunday, the message traces the appearance of God through 'fire', especially the appearance of 'tongues of fire' on the day of Pentecost. The congregation continually responds with various expressions of agreement. The sermon concludes with a prayer for baptism in the Holy Spirit, which eventually turns into a communal prayer as the audience divides into groups of three and four to pray for one another. The congregation then spends some time in *koinonia* (fellowship), as the pastor acknowledges and prays over birthday celebrants. After the collection of tithes and offerings, the pastor pronounces a benediction, and the worship service ends with a burst of applause and another period of joyous singing.

This is just one example of the many types of worship practised in the region. It is important to recognise the powerful influence of globalisation on the formation of spirituality and the practice of worship. Contemporary worship music, often from Pentecostal and Charismatic communities, has spread across geographical and ecclesial boundaries.

Central to this widespread culture of worship is simple and yet contemporary worship music, such as that produced by Hillsong or Bethel Music. This modern Christian culture is closely related to the spread and popularisation of Charismatic spiritual experiences, forms of spirituality and worship. Extremely modern in their look, sound and environment, many church gatherings resemble rock concerts. Such worship gatherings naturally attract the younger generation, which otherwise would have been left out by traditional worship. A guitar, instead of a pipe organ, creates a worship atmosphere, promoting a casual, friendly and mobile environment for the Christian community. This supra-denominational culture has also presented a context in which fellowship across denominational lines takes place by sharing common worship songs and prayers. In the coming years, therefore, Christian spirituality will draw from both local and global experiences.

Spirituality Shaped by Christian Status

With large numbers of Asians having not yet heard the Christian message, there is no other continent in the world for which the call for mission is more pronounced. The meagre footprint of Christianity has sharpened the church's sense of mission. Individual Christians might exercise their faith away from their families, who might not support their new-found faith. Frequent accounts of persecution are part of the East and Southeast Asian Christian experience. Such circumstances encourage Christians and churches to set evangelism as their mission priority. While people of dominant religions might not feel a need for conversion, ethnically or socially marginalised groups tend to be more open to the Christian message. For example, in the Buddhist nation of Myanmar, the Chin tribe in the north are predominantly Christian, and the majority of Malaysian Christians are either Chinese, indigenous or Indian. These groups also develop a stronger sense of missionary call to reach out to the rest of the nation for Christ. Fervent prayer and commitment for mission often spark a series of revivals, which frequently result in large evangelistic programmes. For example, the 1907 Pyongyang Revival gave birth to the Million Souls for Christ Movement in Korea during the harsh colonial era. When Korea was divided after independence (1945), Christian refugees from the communist North formed congregations in Seoul, praying and preparing for the restoration of churches in North Korea. The majority of

Korean Christians have remained politically conservative and missionally committed due to this historical experience.

The Bario Revival in the Island of Borneo in Malaysia is another case. Begun among students in 1973, the revival resulted in a missionary fervour, and many evangelistic teams were formed to reach out to nearby communities. The revival eventually gave birth to the largest Protestant denomination in Malaysia, Sidang Injil Borneo. The church today maintains its missionary commitment, sending out missionaries to many parts of the world. Perhaps the most enduring case of Christian spirituality shaped by a sense of mission is post-Cultural Revolution Christianity in China. Through the harsh socio-political turmoil, people were more open to the message of an alternative community with a new identity, and so both registered and unregistered churches mushroomed. The unregistered churches soon became a missionary force, mobilising young believers to form missionary teams to spend months doing evangelism. The outcome was a rapid spread of the Christian faith. Many mission movements in China today, including the well known Back to Jerusalem Movement, are a natural outgrowth of spirituality shaped by the struggling status of Christianity there and the self-awareness created by the missionary mandate to bring the good news of Christianity to their communities.

Mission, Church, Spirituality: New Understandings

The traditional concept of Christian mission was introduced and exemplified by Western missionaries. As a result, Christian mission came to be understood as a programme only rich (Western) Christian countries could undertake. This historically shaped mission understanding and practice, however, have recently been challenged by a rediscovery of the biblical teaching that every believer (and therefore church) is sent to the world and called to witness, both locally and beyond. The inherited unhealthy notion of mission has slowly been challenged and broken among East and Southeast Asian churches. Several important factors have caused this change. The first is increasing awareness of the church's missionary call. This awareness is linked to the increasing study of the Bible. For example, Gipung Lee – one of the seven members of the first graduating class of the Chosun Presbyterian Theological Seminary of Pyongyang in 1907 – initiated a missionary tradition that continued for many years, going to Jeju Island as the first ever Korean missionary. The theological consciousness of mission (by every believer) best explains this missionary awareness in the very early years of Christian presence in Korea. The Back to Jerusalem missionary movement is another example of indigenous mission impetus.

The second factor is contextual. East and Southeast Asia, as the home of many religions, finds the church in a setting ripe for mission. Living with other religions, adversity and marginalisation help the church to sharpen its missionary mandate.

The third factor is the (possible) influence of missionaries. Through the intentional work of missionaries (including non-Westerners), national missionary movements have spread. It is not clear how much influence Western missionaries exerted on the early years of Korean Christianity, for example. However, it is clear that the new mission movement in Nagaland, India, was fostered by national church leaders, assisted by Korean missionaries.

Finally, the fourth factor is the drastic increase in mobility. Christian mission has been positively affected by globalisation. In so-called 'creative access' regions, professional Christians best serve as mission actors. Hundreds of thousands of Christian immigrant workers from the Philippines, for example, have been effective gospel bearers in homes, factories and hospitals. In large cities such as Hong Kong, these – sometimes very large – gatherings are a conspicuous demonstration of Christian faith in social settings where it is restricted. The net result is a serious revision of the traditional understanding and practice of mission, allowing the church in East and Southeast Asia to emerge as a committed mission actor in global Christianity.

Engagement with Culture

The relationship between Christianity and other religions has been complex. The 'foreign' nature of Christianity and its exclusive claim for truth have placed the church on a collision course with other religions. Conservative Christians simply condemn other religions and their related cultural practices as 'pagan', while more progressive Christians detect 'pre-evangelism' elements in a given culture. In East Asia, where Confucian influence has loomed large, how Christians deal with the traditional ancestor veneration has served almost as a litmus test to gauge the 'purity' of their Christian faith. Many early believers were ostracised, persecuted or disowned by their families for refusing to participate in the family rite of offering a table to the spirits of deceased ancestors. At some point, state-sanctioned persecutions were carried out to reinforce the Confucian practice, and thousands of Christians lost their lives. In their minds, if any spirits are present around the table, they are evil spirits. The whole practice of ancestor veneration was considered to be a violation of the first commandment given through Moses. This attitude of complete separation has established Christianity as a radical 'other' faith against all the traditional beliefs and increased the distance between Christianity and Asian religions, perpetuating the perception of it being a Western religion. On the other hand, some East Asian churches, such as the Anglican Church, tend to lean towards formal (or High Church) worship, connecting with Confucian and Taoist traditions that regard formality and propriety as the foremost elements in their civic and religious rites.

More progressive Christians view some elements of culture and religions as the manifestation of the presence and work of the Holy Spirit. One well publicised example is the Spirit/spirit(s)-invoking dance performed by a Korean woman theologian at the General Assembly of the World Council of Churches in Canberra, Australia, in 1991. In this provocative performance, she called the spirits of those killed by oppression and of the earth and rainforests. After calling 'the spirit of the Liberator, Jesus Christ', she claimed that through these spirits we could experience the Holy Spirit. Although this might be considered an extreme case, it symbolised a quest to present the Christian message through the existing religious symbols and categories. Indeed, openness to regional cultures and religious ideas has been surprisingly common throughout the history of Christianity. For example, in almost all Bible translations, the traditional name of the supreme deity in the given context has been adopted for 'God'. Even in the controversial issue of ancestor veneration, churches in various socio-cultural contexts have developed Christian responses to social needs. For example, at an early stage of the Protestant mission in Korea, the Methodist Church modified the traditional ancestor rite into a Christian family memorial. The Korean Catholic Church issued a formal statement admitting its teachings 'misled' early believers to refuse the ancestor rites. Generally, there is a growing awareness of God's ongoing presence and work in creation, including culture.

Prayer and Worship: Contextually Informed

The intensity of spirituality is a major characteristic of East and Southeast Asian Christianity, and this is particularly visible in worship, prayer life and mission commitment. The generally conservative attitude also reflects the spiritual commitment. Many denominations whose Western counterparts are theologically and behaviourally liberal remain rather conservative in Asia. Several factors contribute to this. The first is the minority social status of Christianity. In many settings where Christians are numerically a minority, or socially or legally marginalised, local churches are the focal points of spiritual life. In addition to many weekend and weekday meetings for worship and prayer, various informal gatherings – including the famous early-morning prayers – take place. Homes, however, are not conducive to such spiritual practices. Marginalisation and persecution bring division to some families. It is the Christian community that supports and strengthens the faith. Naturally, their prayer and worship are intense and their commitment to mission strong.

The second is the deeply rooted religiosity of East and Southeast Asians. All the region's religions – including Buddhism, Hinduism, Islam, Taoism and animism – feature deep devotion and dedicated prayer as part of their spiritual values. The region is dotted with mosques, temples, shrines and prayer huts, in both the mountains and urban centres. In Japan, Shinto shrines are found in every community. Worship days and festivals are immediately noticeable as the whole community changes in attire, decoration and activities. However, religious activities are not limited to formal locations. The Chinese offer food at their family shrines, while many taxis in the Philippines carry statuettes of Mary. Shamanistic Korean families maintain a corner in their homes to offer clean water and food to the spirits. Considering that first-generation Christians have made a change in their religious affiliation, it is natural for them to bring their existing religious orientations to Christianity. Therefore, the influence of other religions is greater than the average Christian wishes to admit.

The pervasive influence of regional realities impacts the forms of worship, especially the music. During the Pre-Assembly Event of the Commission on World Mission and Evangelism of the World Council of Churches held in Manila in 2012, participants were introduced to Christian music drawn from indigenous resources. The prolific introduction of Chinese Christian music among unregistered churches is often in stark contrast to the registered churches, whose worship is still dominated by old Western hymns. It was said that the early-morning prayer initiated in the Korean Pyongyang Revival was inspired by the Buddhist practice of early-morning prayer. More convincing, however, is the suggestion that the Buddhist practice of prayer motivated the prayer mountain movement in Korean Christianity. In parts of Indonesia the main Sunday worship service is held early in the morning, in part accommodating the agricultural cycle but also following the practice of Islam.

The third factor is the influence of missionaries. In settings where Christianity was part of the colonial experience, dominant churches such as the Spanish Catholics in the Philippines, French Catholics in Indochina and Anglicans in Malaysia tended to preserve the spiritual tradition and worship forms of the 'mother churches'. However, in settings where missionaries were not associated with the ruling power, as in Korea and China, many early missionaries tended to be pietistic in spirituality. Their unrelenting commitment to Christian faith and an altruistic lifestyle resulted in the intensity of Christian worship, prayer and mission.

Openness to the Spirit/Spirit(s)

Related to the general religious fervour among Christians in East and Southeast Asia is their openness to the work of the Holy Spirit. Because they are keenly aware of the spiritual world and its impact on daily life, the person and work of the Holy Spirit have found an open reception. This consciousness stands in contrast to the general tendency to downplay pneumatology in the West. The biggest contribution to this strong pneumatological consciousness has to do with general religious expectations. Although major Asian religions might not contain a strong belief in healing and miracles, animism – which undergirds practically all religious beliefs – has shaped a powerful understanding that the spiritual world is the main cause of all human experiences. Consequently, to correct any ills in life, one needs to investigate the spiritual world, identify any spirits that are responsible for misfortune, and appease them with an appropriate ritual or offering. By similar logic, in any aspiration in life – such as success in business, a good marriage, or childbearing – spirits (often benevolent) are called to act on behalf of the worshipper.

In each context, the number of spirits called ranges from hundreds to millions, and this widespread and persistent belief system has permeated almost every religion in East and Southeast Asia. For example, many Buddhist temples include statues of major spirits and gods of the local folk beliefs. Fortune-tellers and shamans often claim that the source of their supernatural ability comes from major religious figures, such as the Buddha. Faith healers in the northern Philippines attribute their supernatural ability for claimed healing incidents to Jesus, Mary and José Rizal, the Filipino national hero of the independence movement. Similarly, around large Catholic churches in the Philippines, local vendors sell plants, dried seeds, snake spines and small bottles of unknown liquids along with holy water for the purposes of healing, pregnancy and warding off evil spirits. Examples abound, and they all point to the pervasive influence of the religious orientation and expectations in East and Southeast Asia, often regardless of formal faith affiliations.

The Holy Spirit, as the Spirit of God and Christ, therefore occupies a special place in East and Southeast Asia's religious psyche. It was the national Christians who explored the dynamic work of the Holy Spirit, which frequently was curtailed by the traditional downplaying of pneumatology among missionary churches. Considering that religious expectations among East and Southeast Asians include supernatural encounters like healing, Christians, regardless of denomination, anticipate similar experiences, especially from the God who claims to be supreme above all other gods and spirits. The Holy Spirit has naturally been viewed as the primary agent of such religious experiences, and healing movements began to appear even among churches that evade the topic of the Holy Spirit.

During the early twentieth century, John Sung spread revival in China and Southeast Asia, and his meetings frequently were accompanied by testimonies of supernatural healing and miracles. After the Cultural Revolution in China, around half of Christians among unregistered church networks attributed their (or a known) experience of healing as the primary motivation for conversion. In the 1950s, Ig-du Kim, a Presbyterian minister in Korea, led a large-scale healing movement, gaining the attention of a national newspaper. 'Prayer mountains' in Korea, regardless of denominational links, have promoted encounters with the Holy Spirit through healing and miracles. The higher proportion of Pentecostal and Charismatic Christians in Asia than in the rest of the world also points to this openness to the Spirit.

Church and Society

The age-old but famous 'Critical Asian Principle' takes the colonial experience as a critical principle in the process of theologising in Asia. Most states in East and Southeast Asia were under colonial rule, generally by Western powers, though also by an Asian power, Japan. In the independence process, perceptions of the church were rather ambivalent in nations where the dominant church was part of the colonial experience. On the other hand, churches in contexts where Christianity was not part of the colonial package but where Christians shared the colonial suffering with their fellow nationals played a different role in the nation-building process.

In Korea, Christians, including Western missionaries, were political targets of the Japanese colonial power. During the democratisation process, the Catholic cathedral in downtown Seoul served as the haven for the movement. Generally, Christianity has opposed communist ideology in support of democracy. In places where an authoritarian or socialist system dominated, the church led a resistance movement. The Catholic Church in the Philippines raised a prophetic voice during the Marcos dictatorship, and some clergy joined the New People's Army, the armed resistance movement of the Philippine Communist Party. In Myanmar, Christians led the Karen resistance in the struggle for independence. Christian influence and leadership were so strong in the Karen National Liberation Army that Buddhist members decided to form a separate armed movement in 1994.

Excelling in education, moral discipline, medical service and volunteerism, church and missionary communities have worked with the state during social transition and nation-building periods, as was the case in Cambodia after the fall of Pol Pot and in post-socialist Mongolia in the 1990s. However, the church still struggles to negotiate its relationship with the state in some nations of East and Southeast Asia. South Korea witnessed the growth of Christianity, but the North practically eliminated the Christian presence there. During Mao's revolution in China, the

Christian Nationalists retreated to Taiwan. In East Malaysia (traditionally Christian), aggressive Islamisation has been sanctioned or supported by the state.

Missionaries in East and Southeast Asia traditionally have paid much attention to education. They invented writing systems and translated the Bible into vernacular languages. In Korea, the Bible was translated into Korean, the language that common people, including women, used in reading and writing. In China, due to the social system, most children of urban immigrant families do not have access to public education, as residency is not easily and legally transferred to urban addresses. It is Christians, often from unregistered churches, who open (often unregistered) schools to provide education to such children. In the Philippines, it was local church-operated Catholic schools that formed the backbone of the national educational system until public education was introduced. Even today, an increasing number of Protestant churches open and operate Christian schools.

Christianity has also excelled in demonstrating the value of life. Its messages and actions of love are widely perceived to carry high moral value compared with animistic religion or the traditional teachings of Asian religions. The introduction of modern medicine and hospitals is part of the Western missionary movement. More than life-saving new knowledge, it is the sacrificial care for a 'stranger' that has most impressed East and Southeast Asians. When a powerful earthquake shattered the Sichuan Province of China in May 2008, house churches promptly organised, supplied and deployed a large contingent of relief volunteers and medical professionals. These large teams of volunteers made a powerful impact not only on the victims but also on the governmental authorities. Not only were they unregistered (and thus illegal) entities, but they challenged the national law that does not grant the right of association.

Christian spirituality and its expression in worship constantly evolve in interaction with contextual forces. The onslaught of materialism and secularism poses a formidable challenge to the church. For this reason, Christian spirituality is closely linked to the church's mission. And this keeps Christianity a dynamic living faith in a region crowded with traditional religions.

Bibliography

Anderson, Allan, and Edmond Tang (eds), *Asian and Pentecostal: The Charismatic Face of Christianity in Asia*, 2nd edn (Oxford: Regnum Books, 2011).

Chan, Simon, *Spiritual Theology: A Systematic Study of the Christian Life* (Downers Grove, IL: InterVarsity Press, 1998).

Ma, Julie C., and Wonsuk Ma, *Mission in the Spirit: Towards a Pentecostal/Charismatic Missiology* (Oxford: Regnum Books, 2010).

Phan, Peter C., *In Our Own Tongues: Perspectives from Asia on Mission and Inculturation* (Maryknoll, NY: Orbis Books, 2003).
Ringma, Charles R., and Karen Hollenbeck-Wuest (eds), *Walking with God: Christian Spirituality in the Asian Context* (Manila: OMF International, 2014).

Theology

Alexander Chow

Theology is often understood in terms of the systematising of Christian thought in the ivory tower: an academic enterprise, with little value for the real world. We think of figures like Karl Barth, with his unfinished 14-volume *Church Dogmatics*, or Thomas Aquinas's *Summa Theologiae*, which uses Aristotelian philosophy to speak about God as 'unmoved mover' and 'first cause'. When we consider theology in East and Southeast Asia – as well as in other regions – we see that theology is conveyed in different ways and is based on different kinds of resources. The genre of a *summa* – that is, a text that tries to coherently summarise the doctrines of the Christian faith – has rarely been attempted by Asian Christians. Moreover, instead of invoking Platonic, Aristotelian or Kantian terms and philosophy, some have turned to Confucian, Buddhist or Marxist expressions and reasoning. Other Asian Christians have drawn from more 'popular' modes of theologising, such as stories, songs and drama.

While it is impossible to cover every development in East and Southeast Asian theology in the space allowed, this essay will begin with a discussion of the resources used to articulate theology in this region, before giving a brief overview of the two theological themes of Christology and ecclesiology.

Theological Resources

The history of Christianity in Asia has been instrumental in promoting the idea that theology should be shaped by one's context. Two of the most important academic terms associated with this idea – 'inculturation' and 'contextual theology' – were articulated with Asia in mind.

The theological understanding of inculturation was introduced into Catholic circles in the 1960s and 1970s, mindful of pioneer Jesuit missionaries such as Francis Xavier in Japan, Matteo Ricci in China, Alexander de Rhodes in Vietnam and Robert de Nobili in India. The Society of Jesus later codified the term in Decree 4 of the Society's General Congregation 32, held in 1974–5. It was also key in the formation of the Federation of Asian Bishops' Conference (FABC) in its first assembly, in Taipei in 1974, which described the local church as 'a church indigenous and inculturated' that is in dialogue with Asia's living traditions.

The latter notion of contextual theology was propagated by Shoki Coe (1914–88) through the World Council of Churches (WCC) in the 1970s. Taking the 'divine contextualisation' of the incarnation as his basis, Coe described contextuality and contextualisation as a necessary part of theology and theological education. In contrast with inculturation's engagement with 'living traditions', his focus was largely on the historical moment of a particular context. However, the idea was clearly informed by the life experiences of Coe, also known in Taiwanese as C. H. Hwang – born in a Taiwan under Japanese imperial rule (1895–1945), which would soon be followed by 'White Terror' under Nationalist rule (1949–87).

Despite the recent coinage of the terms inculturation and contextual theology, these ideas were produced through the yearnings of generations of Asian Christians. Historically, they have tended to be embraced by more progressive Roman Catholics and Protestants, respectively. In recent years, they have often been used interchangeably and have been appropriated by others, including Orthodox Christians and Evangelical Protestants, although with somewhat different meanings. The terms have also tended to emphasise two foci of theology in Asia: on the one hand, Asia's cultures and religions, and on the other hand, Asia's socio-political and economic crises. The East and Southeast Asian contexts have been moulded by the religious and political pressures of various civilisations – not only from Europe with Western Christianity, but also from China with Confucian and Taoist traditions and from India with Hindu and Buddhist traditions. We should also not forget the role of the Persian and Russian Empires in introducing Eastern Christianity to these regions, as well as the traders and mariners from Arabia, Persia, India and western China, who brought with their spices the religion of Islam. These movements of peoples and ideas, along with the more recent concerns of nation-building and the momentum gained by communism and capitalism, have offered important theological resources for Asian Christianity.

Much of Asian Christianity is shaped by a very long tradition of written languages and written scriptures. Christian missionaries have needed to contend with these multiple scriptural traditions, especially Protestants, with their deep convictions of *sola scriptura*. Mahayana Buddhism, found predominantly in East Asia, has a relatively open canon, which has resulted in new texts such as the *Lotus Sutra* or the *Heart Sutra*. Contrastingly, the relatively closed nature of the Qur'an, the Theravada Buddhist *Tipiṭaka* and the Confucian *Four Books and Five Classics* (*Sishu Wujing*) have resulted in the flourishing of important commentary traditions. These Asian scriptures have never existed in isolation but have required dialogue and debate and the creation of different hermeneutical approaches that shape engagement with the more recent introduction of the Christian Bible. Archie C.

C. Lee (b. 1950), K. K. Yeo (b. 1960) and others have therefore argued that Asian Christians cannot read the Christian Bible alone but need to read it alongside the multiple scriptures of Asia, advocating for what has been termed cross-textual or cross-cultural hermeneutics.

Asian textual traditions, however, tend to be associated with 'high culture' as opposed to 'popular culture'. Many groups within East and Southeast Asia do not have as strong a written culture. Mindful of aboriginal Christians in Taiwan, C. S. Song (b. 1929) has argued that Asian Christians should develop a 'story theology' based on indigenous stories. Kwok Pui-lan (b. 1952) has likewise spoken about how Asian Christian women often use poems, songs, dances and rituals to convey theological ideas. Theology is sung by the Chin in Myanmar and the Lisu in southwest China, as studies by Denise Ross and Aminta Arrington have shown. Theology is preached by revivalists such as Kil Son-ju (or Gil Seon-ju; 1869–1935), considered by some to be the father of Korean Protestantism, and John Song (or Song Shangjie; 1901–44), who conducted evangelistic tours throughout China and Southeast Asia. We must also consider the material culture found in folk Catholicism, such as rites associated with self-flagellation in the Philippines or Marian devotion associated with the Virgin's apparition in La Vang (Vietnam) or Sheshan (China). Oral and material cultures have also been connected to the rapid rise of Christian forms often described as 'Pentecostal' or 'Charismatic', which emphasise prophecy, healing and talismanic uses of the Bible or the cross.

The task for the rest of this essay is to explore two classic theological loci, Christology and ecclesiology, from the vantage point of East and Southeast Asia. Mindful of what we have just discussed, this is not an easy task. Along with basing this on more 'theological' writings, these overviews will also attempt to provide theological reflections on historical and social scientific studies on these expressions of the Christian faith.

Asian Faces of Christ

'Who do you say I am?' Responding to Jesus from a first-century Jewish perspective, Peter immediately responds with the answer, 'You are the Messiah' (Matthew 16: 15–16). Jesus asks this question not only of Peter, but of countless Christians who have walked the earth over the last two millennia. Christology is perhaps the theological subject that has produced the most copious amounts of theological writings in Asia, as well as in other parts of the globe. This is not surprising, given that Christ, who reveals God through the Incarnation, is the central figure of the Christian religion. The New Testament itself includes four portrayals of Christ. We can also consider the approaches of various theologians, such as Eusebius and John Calvin, who spoke of the threefold offices of Christ (prophet, priest and king) or the Pentecostal fourfold or fivefold gospel (saviour, [sanctifier,] baptiser, healer and coming king). However, when we turn to more recent Christologies around the globe, the answer is often shaped by the ways in which Christ is first encountered. Is he a coloniser, a rich and powerful white man, or only concerned with my well-being beyond death? But the answer is also guided by one's experiences and existential concerns. Is Christ a sage, a neighbour or a fellow sufferer?

One Christology which has been the focus of many studies is that of the eminent Chinese theologian T. C. Chao (or Zhao Zichen; 1888–1979). The *Life of Jesus* (*Yesu zhuan*, 1935), his most famous work on this subject, is described by Chloë F. Starr as 'imaginative nonfiction' in the Chinese genre of *zhuan* – a biography that focuses on a figure's outward achievements, serving commemorative and didactic functions. Chao's *Life of Jesus* paints a portrait of Jesus as a great Confucian sage (*junzi*), an exemplar of moral perfection. Though this would change in Chao's later thinking, this text breaks with the Chalcedonian formulation, tending to underscore only the human nature of Christ. Jesus is not a political figure looking to restore the nation of Israel through social and economic revolution; neither is he an apocalyptic prophet who preaches an imminent doom followed by a new Heaven and a new Earth. Instead, Jesus came to establish the Kingdom of God, a spiritual kingdom built in the here and now by lives changed by and embodying the love of God.

The *Life of Jesus* offers us a snapshot into Chao's Christology, written in the 1930s when Chinese society was rethinking the foundations of its civilisation and antagonistic towards the foreignness of Christianity. Understood more broadly, Chao held to a universality of Christianity through the cosmic dimension of God. This pre-dated many of the debates about the 'cosmic Christ' in the 1960s and 1970s through the WCC and through South Asian ecumenical debates. In the 1980s and 1990s, the cosmic Christ became a dominant expression among Christian leaders of the state-sanctioned Three-Self Patriotic Movement (TSPM) such as K. H. Ting (or Ding Guangxun; 1915–2012) and Wang Weifan (1927–2015). For Ting, it is the theological basis for Chinese Christians to work together with non-Christians (especially communists) in Christ's work; for Wang, it offers a mediating position for Chinese Evangelicals to uphold the priority of Christ's salvific work on the cross and to be involved in the socio-political and spiritual crises of present-day China. Among various Chinese Christians in the twentieth century, a cosmic Christology has underscored the universal extent of Christ's domain and concern and the great love of God as expressed through the life of Jesus and his followers.

Another important East Asian example can be found in South Korean Minjung theology, originally developed in the 1970s and 1980s in response to Park Chung-hee's military regime. Minjung theologians were socially concerned Christians: professors and writers who positioned themselves in solidarity with social activists in support of justice and human rights. Ahn Byung-mu (1922–96), a New Testament professor at Hanshin University, articulated his understanding of Christ in the gospel of Mark as being on the side of those described in Greek as the *ochlos* (the crowd made up of the tax collectors and the sinners marginalised in society). For Ahn, the term 'sinner' is ideological language used by the rich and powerful ruling class to rob and to oppress and can never properly be applied to the poor or the weak. The equivalent to the Markan *ochlos* in the South Korean context were the *Minjung* – the 'masses', who were oppressed by the dictatorial government and dismissed by conservative South Korean churches. Ahn, along with another Minjung theologian, David Kwang-sun Suh (b. 1931), has noted the particular plight by women. Not only do they face oppression from the state and from religious structures; women also face patriarchal oppression in society and in the homes of South Korea. They are the '*Minjung* of *Minjung*'.

These examples from China and South Korea help us to see a theme that arises throughout much of Asia – the need to coexist and to be in solidarity with those who do not self-identify as Christians. Often this coexistence focuses on Christ as an exemplar of one who suffered on the cross and one who continues to suffer alongside those who suffer today. Other examples of this include Kazoh Kitamori's (1916–98) *Theology of the Pain of God* (1946) and C. S. Song's *Jesus, the Crucified People* (1990).

Another major way of understanding this coexistence is in terms of loving one's non-Christian neighbour – what Kosuke Koyama (1929–2009) describes as 'neighbourology'. Arising from his work as a Japanese missionary in Thailand, Koyama explains in *Water Buffalo Theology* (1974) that neighbourology is an incarnational principle of communication. As minorities in Asia, Christians need to step back from the use of theologically dense Christological language and step first into the lives and experiences of their Asian neighbours. Koyama's idea was further developed in the Malaysian context by Sadayandy Batumalai's (b. 1946) *A Prophetic Christology for Neighbourology* (1986) and *A Malaysian Theology of Muhibbah* (1990), the latter appropriating an Arabic idea meaning 'goodwill'. Even more so than in Thailand, Batumalai argues that the sharpness of Christian–Muslim relations in Malaysia requires a Christology of neighbourology in which Christians offer both a prophetic voice and an experience of neighbourly hospitality with their Muslim neighbours. Like the Chinese and South Korean Christians mentioned above who provide a theological rationale for working in solidarity with non-Christians for societal change, Batumalai sees these Christological understandings as offering Christians tools for working alongside Muslims in pursuit of the common good and the transformation of Malaysian society.

In contrast with these more 'elite' Christologies, a very different understanding can be found within popular Catholic spirituality in the Philippines. We can consider the important Santo Niño (the Holy Child), an icon said to have been given by Ferdinand Magellan to Queen Juana of Cebu at her baptism in 1521. In Cebu City, the Santo Niño is venerated in a festival every January as crowds gather at the Basilica Minore del Santo Niño to celebrate in ritual dance known as *Sinulog*, Visayan for 'moving like a current'. Such celebrations are practised elsewhere throughout the Philippines. Moreover, replicas of the Santo Niño can be found in Catholic homes and businesses and are thought to bring blessings to devotees. On the other end of Christ's earthly ministry, another popular image is the suffering Christ. Spanish colonisers used religious imagery such as the *Pasyon*, Tagalog for Christ's Passion, to control the colonised by inculcating loyalty to Spain and to the church and by instilling a preoccupation with morality and the afterlife, as opposed to the concerns of the day. According to Reynaldo Clemeña Ileto's *Pasyon and Revolution* (1979), this also unexpectedly offered Filipinos an epic story – one that replaced the indigenous epic stories destroyed by the same Spanish colonisers. Filipino folk songs, poems and plays have therefore invoked this Christological imagery to critique the colonial situation and to call for change and revolution.

A number of Filipino women theologians have offered new engagements with these popular Christological expressions. Muriel Orevillo-Montenegro (b. 1954) raises questions about how the images of Christ in the Santo Niño and the *Pasyon* connect with the daily lives of devotees. She sees these images as problematic and believes the doctrine of the incarnation needs to be revisited for its moral and religious power, especially for Asian women. Likewise, Virginia Fabella has critiqued the *Pasyon* as a 'dead-end theology' in which there is suffering but no resurrection or liberation in sight. According to Fabella, Asian women need to recognise their status of gendered oppression as contrary to the will of a just and loving God and the need to reclaim the image of Christ as a saviour and a liberator. Lydia Lascano has helpfully distinguished between Christ's 'passive' and 'active' suffering. His passive suffering is reflected in women's experiences of colonialism, militarism and patriarchy; but Christ also experienced active suffering, which mirrors Filipino women's struggle for justice and freedom.

These Christological examples highlight some of the themes arising in East and Southeast Asia when faced with Jesus's question, 'Who do you say I am?' It is instrumental that one of the major Chinese renderings of 'contextual theology' is *chujing shenxue* (theology of plight). Christ is met when Christ meets one's greatest needs. Yet if one were to describe this Christ, the truest descriptions use the language of one's heart, often a deeply spiritual language. For others, Christ is described through the acts of exemplars in our midst. In the next section, we shift from the central figure of Christianity to the people who represent this central figure on earth for others to encounter – that is, the church.

An Asian and Autonomous Church

Very little has been written on ecclesiology in East and Southeast Asia when compared with the vast amount written on Christology. Many of the theological questions around the nature and expression of the church have arisen due to the keen awareness of East and Southeast Asian Christians that, with the exception of the Philippines and Timor-Leste, the vast majority of peoples of the region do not consider themselves Christians. The body of believers would therefore need to articulate their dual loyalties to Asia (independent of Western imperialism) and to Christ (as the central figure of a minority faith). Moreover, disproportionate to their numbers, Christians would also need to offer a particularly strong public voice to engage the socio-political matters of the day. Hence, ecclesiological ruminations of the past couple of centuries offer us an important vantage point for understanding what it means to gather and to identify as Christians and to be the church in East and Southeast Asia.

Perhaps the most pressing critique of Christianity that has been experienced by East and Southeast Asian Christians is related to its foreignness – a 'foreign' religion, supposedly different from those 'indigenous' religions of Buddhism, Islam or even communism. For many parts of Asia, this was due to the complex relationships between missionaries and foreign governments. In the Dutch East Indies, for instance, Dutch colonial policy focused on converting Catholics to Protestantism and chose to not engage regions with a Muslim majority. In China and Japan, Christian missionaries were allowed entry in the nineteenth century only after unequal treaties were forced upon them by Western military might. Moreover, denominational and theological differences between missionaries presented a divided Christian message. Should one follow the 'Romish' Catholics, who worship Mary and the Pope, or the 'deceitful' Protestants, who simply toss Bibles from their boats? How should one render 'God' into a local language? What was the appropriate mode of baptism? Are we to hold to the true fundamentals of the faith or embrace the social gospel in lieu of the 'true' gospel? Despite mission policies that encouraged the establishment of indigenous churches and the raising up of indigenous leadership based on the three-self principle of self-government, self-support and self-propagation, in most East and Southeast Asian countries local Christians were often subordinated to the paternalism of foreign denominations and mission agencies.

In the Philippines, one of the few Asian countries with a Christian majority, the church is often found at the crossroads of Christianity's relationship with nationalism. When we consider the period of the Philippine Revolution (1896–8), we see how divisions formed along partisan lines, with Spanish friars tending to side with Spanish colonial powers and Filipino clergy tending to support nationalist and revolutionary forces. These lines were more blurred when considering lay Catholics, many of whom participated in the Revolution but also protected Spanish friars. Later, under American sovereignty, the struggle for equal rights for local clergy led to the establishment of the Philippine Independent Church (Iglesia Filipina Independiente), a schism from the Roman Catholic Church in 1902 led by the nationalist Isabelo de los Reyes (1864–1938), who named Gregorio Aglipay (1860–1940) its Supreme Bishop (*Obispo Maximo*). However, Aglipay was initially quite reluctant to split the church, and the Philippine Independent Church has struggled to maintain a strong following. Part of this was undoubtedly due to the Roman Catholic Church's recognition of these conflicts in the Philippines, resulting in a restructuring of church leadership through the 1902 papal constitution *Quae Mari Sinico* and, eventually, consecration of its first Filipino bishops, beginning with Jorge Barlin in 1906.

A different example can be seen with the growing spirit of Protestant ecumenism in China, where there was a shift of power from foreign to local ecclesial bodies. When the 1910 World Missionary Conference met in Edinburgh, the Chinese pastor Cheng Jingyi (1881–1939) declared that Chinese Protestants wanted to see 'a united Christian Church without any denominational distinctions' and that denominationalism 'never interested the Chinese mind'. Cheng would return to China and lead a movement alongside foreign missionaries and other Chinese Protestants to establish a national Chinese church, which was formed in 1927 as the Church of Christ in China (Zhonghua Jidu Jiaohui). Cheng was elected the first moderator of this national union of more than 15 church bodies, including Presbyterian, Reformed, Baptist, Congregational, Methodist and Independent churches. However, while it produced the largest Protestant denomination during this time, in its cooperative ventures the new church chose to set aside doctrinal differences; institutional unity was sought, not theological uniformity. Conservatives who saw this as a liberal development built their own Chinese-run denominations or denomination-like networks, such as Yu Guozhen's (1852–1932) China Christian Independent Church (Zhongguo Yesujiao Zhilihui), Watchman Nee's (or Ni

Tuosheng; 1903–72) 'Little Flock' (Xiao Qun) and Wei Enbo's (1877–1919) True Jesus Church (Zhen Yesu Jiaohui). Others chose a different route to independence, by establishing their own indigenous churches or evangelistic ministries, such as Wang Mingdao's (1900–91) Christian Tabernacle (Jidutu Huitang) and Andrew Gih (or Ji Zhiwen; 1901–85) and John Song's Bethel Worldwide Evangelistic Band (Boteli Huanqiu Budao Tuan). While the Church of Christ in China aspired to establish a national church that had a strong relationship with foreign Christians, these other developments underscored the need to be fully independent of foreign control.

In other examples, the questions of independence from foreign powers were imposed from above. This was clearly the case of the Japanese Empire from the Meiji Restoration period (1868–1912) until the end of the Second World War in 1945. Various policies were employed to control the development of Christianity in its colonies. For instance, Japanese authorities saw Presbyterians in Taiwan as encouraging education and literacy on the island and introducing advances in Western medicine, but the colonial government was also concerned with the problems that might arise with the multiplicity of denominations. Hence, Japanese authorities gave Presbyterianism a monopoly in Taiwan from 1895 to 1925 and, by 1920, there was a fully independent and Taiwanese-run Presbyterian church.

In the Japanese state itself, authorities wanted to sever Japanese Christianity from foreign ties and, in 1941, pushed for the union of more than 30 Protestant denominations to form the United Church of Christ in Japan (Nihon Kirisuto Kyōdan). This pattern was also pursued after the Japanese occupation of the Dutch Indies in 1942. The few local evangelists in Protestant regions were hurriedly ordained on the eve of the Japanese takeover and were given charge of mission funds. Furthermore, the colonial power imposed ecumenical organisations, requiring all Protestant churches to join regional councils of churches. After the war, these councils collapsed, but the foundations had been laid for indigenous leadership and the eventual development of Indonesian ecumenism.

A similar practice of regional councils of churches was brought by Japanese authorities to the Chinese mainland. While the developments of the Church of Christ in China in the 1920s and 1930s made great strides towards a national church, it still had a long way to go. Timothy Brook has argued that the developments in Japanese-occupied China brought an independent national church closer to reality, resulting ultimately, under the People's Republic of China, in the TSPM in 1954 and the Catholic Patriotic Association (CPA) in 1957.

In an ironic turn of events, Japan, an Asian colonial power that did not have a vested interest in Christianity, accelerated the process of ecumenism and ecclesial independence in all these regions.

It is worth clarifying that these ecclesiological shifts were not only imposed from above but also arose from Christians fighting for national independence. There is the case of contributions made by Korean Protestants in the 'March 1' movement of 1919, who made up 16 of the 33 signatories of the Declaration of Independence and, overall, had nearly as many clergy involved as Cheondogyoist and Buddhist clergy combined. During Indonesia's struggle for independence from Japanese and Dutch power, Christians died alongside Muslims in the fight. This collaboration between Christians and Muslims continued under the Sukarno administration, which resulted in the five principles of the Pancasila as the basis of a state that would be both secular and theistic. In both these efforts, they proved that they were not only Christians, but that the church can and should work alongside of those who are not Christians, for the common good. In other contexts after the Second World War, a number of military regimes rose to power from within, often aspiring to achieve political stability and economic growth. In Taiwan, South Korea and the Philippines, this came at the cost of many social ills against the lower strata of society. In the face of these injustices, the church became one of the main voices to speak out against these authoritarian regimes.

However, these examples of Christian participation in the fight for independence or social justice have tended to offer less theologically formulated views on public engagement. In other examples, Christians draw from the social or public theology of their denominational backgrounds. We can see this in the place of Anglican or Catholic social teaching in Singapore and Hong Kong, which has empowered the church to contribute to civil society through the provision of educational and medical infrastructure. Yet at times this has resulted in ambiguous understandings of the relationship between church and state. In the Chinese mainland, Anglican social teachings (combined with ecumenical backgrounds) have informed individuals such as T. C. Chao and K. H. Ting in their support of the TSPM. Contrastingly, a growing number of urban Chinese churches in the twenty-first century have turned towards Dutch neo-Calvinist public theology, arguing that the church needs to have a public presence as a 'city on a hill' and be involved in God's cultural mandate through Chinese civil society. A number of these churches see themselves as being a 'third church' – a new ecclesiology that transcends the historical impasse between a clandestine and illegal existence as 'house churches' and an open position through the 'adulterous' TSPM. Hence, while K. H. Ting has applauded Chinese Christianity's developments in a 'post-denominational era', a number of 'house church' Christians have been establishing Presbyterian and Congregationalist denominations to network with one another in their engagement with China's broader civil society.

As stated at the outset of this section, writings on ecclesiology are far fewer than those on Christology. However, as we have seen, this in no way suggests that considerations of the nature and expression of the church have been absent from the minds of East and Southeast Asian Christians. One major theme that we have seen is the desire to underscore an Asian and autonomous church. At times this has also produced forms of ecclesiology that are seemingly idiosyncratic to Asian religiosity, such as the more discursive expressions like the Non-Church (*Mukyōkai*) in Japan, Korea and Taiwan and the 'cultural Christians' (*wenhua jidutu*) of mainland China, as well as grassroots movements of house churches and basic ecclesial communities. A second theme that has been underscored is to be God's people, gathered together and existing in a dominantly non-Christian Asia. In many Western contexts, church institutionalism is seen as a problematic relic of the past. In many of the examples discussed here, however, the institution of the church has enabled Christians to work together, offering a collective voice in solidarity together against both outside imperial pressures and inside authoritarian regimes. Along with the rise of national churches, we must not forget the growth of various pan-Asian organisations such as the FABC and the Christian Conference of Asia. The final theme we have seen in the discussion above is that the church exists as a public body. At times this is expressed through the church's attempt to be a people set apart to reveal God's goodness in this world; at other times, the church must work with those outside the church for the greater common good of these Asian societies.

Conclusion

At the outset of the twenty-first century, the future holds many unknowns in the development of theology in East and Southeast Asia. New questions may be raised, but, more often than not, old questions will be repeated in one form or another. We may consider, for instance, the two foci of theology: Asia's cultures and religions and Asia's socio-political and economic crises. Firstly, cultures and religions are not static but change and develop over time. While many forms of 'traditional' culture and religion are waning due to the course of industrialisation and modernisation, there are also reverse responses, through revivals and renaissances in Confucianism, Hinduism and Islam. Not only does this raise questions around inter-religious engagement, but it also suggests that Christians more often than not must seek critical intra-religious engagement – the interplay, conscious or not, of multiple religious imaginations in a given Christian individual or Christian community. Secondly, it is nearly impossible for Asian Christians to ignore the ills experienced in their local societies. This will undoubtedly also include theological engagements with the broader cosmos, sometimes drawing from non-Christian sources to enrich theological understandings. As has been witnessed in regions such as Latin America and sub-Saharan Africa, Christians of all theological traditions need to address this-worldly questions alongside other-worldly aspirations.

Additionally, migration is an age-old matter that will increasingly be important for Asian Christians. We may consider the long history of ethnic Chinese migrating to Southeast Asia, the Asian diaspora in Western and African countries, the influx of Westerners or Africans to various parts of Asia or even the movement of peoples from rural to urban centres and vice versa. We may also consider the development of trans-regional and trans-national networks and relations. Furthermore, the creation of nation states in this region has severely simplified many matters, whether we speak about the Korean peninsula – where many South Korean Christians can trace their lineage to the North – or about China, Burma, Indonesia and the Philippines – all empires in their own right, with a multiplicity of peoples within each of their borders.

Theology (or theologies) in East and Southeast Asia reflects the complexities and diversities of this vast region. This has highlighted the importance of contextuality in theological enquiry. Yet it cannot be forgotten that the Asian church is part of a larger community with a need – dare I say, a mission to – engage and be engaged by the Church Universal. What draws East and Southeast Asian Christianity together is more than geography; it is the common worship of one God, as revealed through the person of Christ and through the people gathered under his name.

Bibliography

Batumalai, Sadayandy, *A Prophetic Christology of Neighbourology: A Theology for a Prophetic Living* (Kuala Lumpur: Seminari Theoloji Malaysia, 1986).

Chow, Alexander, *Chinese Public Theology: Generational Shifts and Confucian Imagination in Chinese Christianity* (Oxford: Oxford University Press, 2018).

CTC–CCA (ed.), *Minjung Theology: People as the Subjects of History* (Maryknoll, NY: Orbis Books, 1983).

Schumacher, John N., *Revolutionary Clergy: The Filipino Clergy and the Nationalist Movement, 1850–1903* (Quezon City: Ateneo de Manila University Press, 1981).

Starr, Chloë F., *Chinese Theology: Text and Context* (New Haven, CT: Yale University Press, 2016).

Social and Political Context

Sebastian C. H. Kim

In the 1980s, when Third World theologians were inspired to express their theology locally, Asian theologians characterised their context as featuring religions and poverty. Today, following the end of the ideological conflict of the Cold War, religions have been strengthened across Asia, and they have increasingly filled the ideological gap left in the political sphere. Furthermore, following processes of democratisation, civil society has grown, and faith-based organisations are active in the space created between the state and people. Poverty persists for the masses of citizens of Asia. Today, however, great wealth, the pursuit of prosperity and associated inequalities are also part of Asian experience. In this essay, we will treat all four dimensions that shape the context of Christian witness in East and Southeast Asia: religion and politics; the emergence of civil society; poverty and marginalisation; and prosperity and economic growth.

East and Southeast Asia is a densely populated region, home to more than 30% of the world's people. From a study-of-religions perspective, Eastern Asia, as defined by the United Nations, roughly corresponds to the historic sphere of influence of China and to the traditions of Confucianism, Mahayana Buddhism and Taoism; that is, the modern nations of China (including Tibet), Mongolia, Korea (North and South) and Japan. The countries of the United Nations' South-Eastern Asia region were, on the whole, more influenced by India, and consequently by Hinduism and Theravada Buddhism. These include Cambodia, Laos, Myanmar (Burma), Thailand, Malaysia, Singapore, Brunei, Indonesia and Timor-Leste. In contrast, although Vietnam is part of South-Eastern Asia, it inherited a strong Confucian tradition. Japan, Taiwan (both Eastern Asia) and the Philippines (South-Eastern Asia) were at the extremity of these religious movements and retain stronger indigenous traditions. From the sixteenth century, the Philippines, whose people were not yet incorporated into a 'world religion', was evangelised by Spanish priests from Latin America and became Asia's first Catholic nation. It and most other Southeast Asian nations were more affected by the spread of Islam along eastern trade routes than were their neighbours to the north.

Religion and Politics

In East Asia, the pattern for the relationship of religions with the state was drawn from neo-Confucianism: for the sake of societal harmony, there is a strong centralised state, and religions are expected to be subservient to it. Religious belief and practice are subject to the favour of the rulers and are closely regulated. In the twentieth century, both China under communism and Japan under fascism insisted on conformity to state rituals, sometimes to an extreme extent. During the Cultural Revolution in China (1966–76), Maoism was a substitute for religion, and the performance of Shinto rituals was enforced throughout the Japanese Empire, which at its peak in 1942 included Korea, large parts of China, the whole of Southeast Asia, and most Pacific islands. Today, China, Japan and other nations in the region exhibit a variety of models for the relationship between religion and politics.

In China, religious faith is officially incompatible with membership of the Chinese Communist Party and, therefore, with social advancement. Nevertheless, Christian belief and practice have become widespread in China, and some party members are willing to declare themselves Christian. Since the 'Christian fever' of the 1980s, when thousands of churches (re)opened among the Han Chinese, the faith has become especially strong in urban areas and among the middle class, although figures for the number of Christians vary widely. Government statistics include only those registered with the two national bodies – about 2% of the population. Other recent surveys give figures two or three times that number. Christianity has also taken a cultural form disconnected from the churches. Centres for the study of Christianity in university departments of religion have stimulated the emergence of an intellectual Christianity with a distinctive theology of modernisation.

Since the communist revolution, the Chinese state's approach to religions has gone through several stages. Initially (1949–57) it attempted to co-opt religion to support the revolution. For Christians this was through the formation of national bodies separated from Western churches: the (Protestant) Three-Self Patriotic Movement (TSPM) and the Catholic Patriotic Association (CPA). From 1958, the state attempted to suppress religion and – from 1966, under the Cultural Revolution – even eradicate it. However, many Christians had refused to join the official bodies. When religious practice was once again permitted from 1979 in the context of the economic liberalisation, it was clear that Christianity had spread as an underground movement. Protestantism had even grown in a de-institutionalised and de-clericalised form in the prison camps and in underground or 'house' churches in rural areas and had overtaken Catholic numbers. In global terms, the underground churches were mostly Evangelical free church or Pentecostal in form. In the new climate, many churches were reopened or founded, and Christianity grew faster during what was referred to as 'Christian fever'. Since then, the policy has been to recognise Christianity but to attempt to weaken it by criticism and the promotion of ancient Chinese religions, or merely to contain it by regulation.

The distinction between official and underground or unregistered Protestant churches has largely broken down at the local level. There is overlap in membership between them. Moreover, many of the unregistered churches have their own buildings, thanks to wide variations in planning permission across regions. However, nationally there is continuing tension and mutual suspicion between unofficial forms of Christianity and the two official bodies. The TSPM-controlled China Christian Council, which describes itself as 'post-denominational', is well recognised internationally. The Holy See is treading a delicate path between the CPA – which rejected the authority of the Vatican and appointed leaders outside the apostolic succession, but which was never declared heretical – and the underground Catholic Church, whose leaders asserted their loyalty to Rome.

Christians in China are afforded religious freedom, provided they do not interfere with government policies, proselytise, baptise or teach religion to children, or contact foreign organisations without permission. Churches that contravene these rules, or do not register, risk censure by the authorities and are at the mercy of local officials. For example, the mid- to late 2010s have seen high-profile local cases in which crosses have been removed from the roofs of churches and whole church buildings have been demolished. In Hong Kong, which was returned to China by Britain in 1997, there is continued religious freedom, despite fears to the contrary. Christians played an active role in negotiations for the return of the territory to China, although their attempts to ensure greater democracy are suppressed.

In Taiwan in the 1970s, leaders of the Presbyterian Church, which drew its main support from among the majority population who lived in Taiwan before 1949, campaigned vigorously – and at the cost of imprisonment – for the rights of the Taiwanese against the Nationalist Chinese government of the Mainlanders, who ruled Taiwan as a one-party state from 1949 to 2000. The historic churches continue to be active politically.

Vietnam was strictly controlled in the socialist republic, but since 1988 religions have enjoyed more freedoms, although religion remains highly controlled. Today, Vietnamese Christianity, mainly Catholic, is a minority of about 8% of the population but is growing significantly.

Religious freedom is enshrined in Japan's post-war constitution, but religious diversity is low. Shintoism continues to play a political role, especially through the remembrance at the Yasukuni Shrine of those who died in battle, but Buddhism has by far the largest number of adherents. Protestant Christianity in Japan has not shed its image as a foreign religion, despite a history of reaction against Western denominational divisions, institutionalism and exclusivism. The strong sense of national identity continues to make conversion to Christianity appear un-Japanese, and social pressures cause high defection rates from churches. At the same time, one can find prominent Christians with a long Christian heritage, going back in some cases to the Catholic martyrs of the seventeenth and eighteenth centuries. Although Japanese Christians are a small minority, they have contributed disproportionately to education and social welfare. Moreover, Christians actively campaign for the rights of other minorities, such as the indigenous Ainu people in Hokkaido.

The peninsula of Korea is divided into two nations in which the political conditions for Christians are at opposite ends of the spectrum. The communist regime in North Korea accommodated religion for only a few years after the partition in 1945 by the USSR and Allied forces, before suppressing it almost entirely, consigning religious people to the lowest social strata and holding many in labour camps. Official Christianity re-appeared in North Korea in the 1970s, and some churches were built from the late 1980s. The opening of the North since the natural disasters and famine of the 1990s has led to increased contact of foreign Christians with North Koreans. Christian missions and faith-based organisations have been doing humanitarian work in the North or helping people escaping the regime. South Korean Christians have also been involved in longer-term industrial and educational initiatives. However, the extent and state of underground Christianity in the North are difficult to determine. Under the leadership of Kim Jong-un, grandson of the founder of the nation, there are no signs of religious freedom, but the economic liberalisation he is pursuing might make controlling religions more difficult for him.

South Korea, by contrast, was founded as part of the US policy to contain communism, and the promise of religious freedom was a major reason why Christian leaders – many of whom were exiles from the communist North – eventually supported the division of the peninsula in 1948. Church leaders committed themselves to evangelistic work and supported the undemocratic and military-backed governments of the 1950s, 1960s and 1970s for the sake of national security. In South Korea, as in Singapore and among the Chinese diaspora across Southeast Asia, Evangelicalism and Roman Catholicism were strengthened by their anti-communist stance. Christianity grew rapidly until in the twenty-first century around 30% of Koreans declared themselves Christians, eclipsing the other main organised religion, Buddhism. Such Christian growth is unparalleled anywhere else in Asia. It must be understood in light of the resistance to communism but also of the vision for a nation founded on Christian values that was articulated by the political leaders, many of whom were Christians, which encouraged evangelism and Christian service to society.

One reason for the lack of such growth elsewhere in Asia might be that, historically, Christian mass movements have occurred only in societies without allegiance to one of the other 'world religions'. Mass movements to Christianity have generally arisen in contexts where the main form of religion is a local or indigenous one, and these have continued into recent times among isolated peoples. Another reason might be that in few other Asian countries has Christianity been associated with nationalism as it was in South Korea. The fact that, in most cases, Christianity was contemporaneous with Western colonialism, and even implicated in it, undermines its credibility in the eyes of many.

In the two nations in East and Southeast Asia with the most Christians – South Korea and the Philippines – churches played an important role in democratisation movements that eventually overthrew military-backed governments. From the 1970s, other radical Korean Christians, influenced by Minjung theology towards humanisation and liberation, challenged authoritarianism on the grounds of human and civil rights. They soon discovered that religious freedom did not extend to challenging the government. Nevertheless, Christian theologians and clergy – Protestant and Catholic – were prominent in the labour and democratisation movements that brought down the military-backed regimes. In the Philippines, Catholic priests and other Christians were influential in the People Power Movement that in 1986 overthrew the military dictator, Ferdinand Marcos, and his wife, Imelda, and also in a second movement in 2001 that toppled President Joseph Estrada. In the late 2010s, churches are again working together in the context of the strongman rule of President Rodrigo Duterte.

In Malaysia and Indonesia, political life is significantly influenced by forms of Islam that claim a political role and social dominance. A gradual process of Islamisation in Malaysia has been aided by the fact that in 1957 the constitution of independent Malaysia was set up to favour the majority Malay community, who are identified by it as Muslim. Many denominations cooperate in the Christian Federation for political purposes, especially to oppose the more radical Islamic reforms and to promote communal peace by working together for the common good and engaging with Islamic thought. Singapore, which separated from the rest of the Malay peninsula in 1965, is dominated by the Chinese community. The government of Singapore has been strongly anti-communist and also very conservative, in a Confucian way. As in South Korea, this strengthened conservative forms of Christianity, and more than 16% of Singaporeans are Christians (including some from the Tamil and other communities). However, radical and progressive Christianity was suppressed.

Indonesia is the fourth most populous country in the world and is overwhelmingly Muslim. Nevertheless, it resisted Islamisation when it gained independence. The constitution is based on five principles (Pancasila) that begin with belief in one God but guarantees equal rights, regardless of faith. In the mid-1960s, the government counteracted the threat of atheistic communism by requiring everyone to belong to one of five different religions – Islam, Protestantism, Catholicism, Hinduism or Buddhism. Partly as a reaction against Islamisation, tribal peoples, nominal Hindus and Muslims – among them communist sympathisers – and also members of the economically powerful Chinese minority flocked to join the churches in some parts of the country. According to census data, Christians form nearly 10% of the population. A legacy of colonialism is that Protestant Christians still exert influence in the economy and the military.

In most countries in Asia, the number of Christians is a politically sensitive issue. Religions, including Christianity, create communities, but powerful interests can easily play them off against one another. Christians might be associated with particular subgroups, such as Chinese and certain indigenous peoples in Indonesia. Unless, as in Malaysia, Asian Christians emphasise their unity across ethnic and denominational divides and work together, their political and social influence is limited.

Christianity, Democracy and Public Life

The liberalisation of communist economic systems and the democratisation of many East and Southeast Asian systems of government have opened up a public sphere and allowed for the development of civil society in many countries that had previously been strongly centrally controlled. Often, this has provided opportunities for Christians to play a role in public life, from which they formerly were excluded.

The most striking example of this is China. The Three Self Patriotic Movement and China Christian Council have created space for Christianity in the public sphere by emphasising social service and social care. Moreover, the intellectual form of Christianity in China is particularly interested in the moral and ethical contributions to society that Christianity can bring. At first, local churches and informal groups simply served the needs of those around them, but wider networks subsequently developed. Since 2011, non-governmental organisations have been encouraged to register with the government as long as they are social, not political, in orientation, and many Christian-inspired groups have been among them. In

Hong Kong, Protestant denominations play an active role in society. This includes running educational institutions, including three universities and seven hospitals dating from the colonial period.

Peace and reconciliation is another area of public life in which Christians have a significant impact in East Asia. The historic Japanese churches have been active in peace-building since the end of the Second World War. From the 1960s they admitted wartime collaboration, although the nation has a whole has yet to deal with the militarist past to the satisfaction of neighbouring countries. In Hong Kong, church leaders feel a responsibility to work for reconciliation between Hong Kong and the rest of China. This means overcoming the suspicion that exists between the Hong Kong Chinese brought up in the Western system and the Chinese Communist Party (CCP). Whether this can be achieved depends on whether Christians perceive the CCP as having the interests of the people at heart. In the current situation of strongman leadership and allegations of corruption, this looks increasingly difficult. Some parts of Indonesia have since the 1990s seen outbreaks of Muslim–Christian violence. A group of women – Protestant, Catholic and Muslim – played a significant role in bringing about reconciliation in Ambon after the worst episode, in 1999. In the Philippines, the Ecumenical Peace Platform, which brings Protestants, Catholics and other Christians together, encourages greater democracy and reconciliation. For example, it supports peace negotiations with the Moro Islamic Liberation Front in Mindanao. It also challenges hard-line policies that would suppress or exclude groups from participation in the public sphere.

Conflict between China, Japan and Korea threatens the peace of the region, and the recent militarisation of these nations is a matter of increasing concern, especially in the South China Sea, where many of the national interests collide. The nuclearisation of North Korea has raised the possibility of even wider conflict. The instability of the Korean peninsula is at the heart of security issues in East Asia. South Korean Christians are sharply divided over how to address the issue of unification. Nevertheless, they are at the forefront of efforts at reconciliation. Different churches have responded in different ways. Evangelicals have seen prayer, underground evangelism, relief and development as the chief means to achieve this. They were the first to send aid to the North in the late 1980s. Ecumenicals made links with the Chosun Christian Federation, which was re-established by the North Korean regime in the 1970s. The first North-South meeting of any non-governmental agency took place in 1986 when Christians from both nations celebrated Communion together in Geneva under the auspices of the World Council of Churches. Catholic social teaching motivated South Korean President Kim Dae-jung to initiate the 'sunshine policy' that first brought about a meeting of the leaders of the two nations in 2000, and two further summits in 2007 and 2018 were influenced by it.

The emergence of the public sphere since 1989 in South Korea has affected Christians in rather the opposite way to those in China. Whereas Chinese Christians are participating in civil society for the first time since the communist revolution, Korean Christians are finding that their voice is diminished. Christians were leaders in politics and in the democratisation movement in South Korea. However, since democracy has been achieved and a vibrant civil society has developed, Christians find that their voice is only one among many interest groups. Moreover, the internet and social media have helped expose corruption by powerful Protestant pastors and challenged aggressive forms of evangelism. As a result, Protestants can no longer expect a hearing. In contrast, the Catholic Church has largely avoided scandal. Another reason for its high credibility rating is its prominence in the overthrow of military regimes. A further explanation is that it has shown commitment to social service. As well as its own initiatives, it delivers a large proportion of government-funded services.

Poverty, Marginalisation and Persecution

As well as the plural religious context, most of the Christian communities of East and Southeast Asia suffer from poverty and marginalisation. In most cases it was among the poor and outsiders that Christianity first found a foothold, and although some Christians are now very wealthy, in most nations they have a minority status. In countries that have been destabilised or occupied in recent centuries, and where religious identities are resurgent, Christians are often seen as an ideological and security threat, and persecution is a feature of life for them.

Most Chinese Christians come from the majority Han community. In the nineteenth century, Catholic missions and the Evangelical China Inland Mission drew some of the largest responses from their work in rural areas. Converts lived in isolated Christian villages. During the violence of the twentieth century, these villages not only survived but even flourished and developed indigenous expressions of the faith. However, both church and government authorities are uneasy with the way many have syncretised Christianity with folk religion. The future of these rural communities is threatened by the rapid urbanisation of China, which has rendered them increasingly elderly as well as poor.

From about 1900, resistance to Western imperialism stimulated the formation of Chinese-founded churches through local fellowships on a house-church pattern. Since these were active in evangelism, networks of independent churches soon emerged that are still influential today. These included: the Little Flock led by Watchman Nee (Ni Tuosheng), who emphasised spiritual life as the key to bodily holiness in what he saw as the end times; the Jesus Family of Jing Dianying, who, with his wife, set up a cooperative or commune, which was then replicated across northern and north-western China; the True Jesus Church, a Pentecostal group; and the Christian Church in Christ of Wang Ming-Dao, who exercised a strictly moral and prophetic ministry that had no time for the social gospel or enthusiasm for indigenisation of missionary Christianity. Most of these congregations, suspicious of the China Christian Council as a government organisation, have chosen to remain 'unregistered'. The religious enthusiasm has generated even more new groups, some of which are radically sectarian. Many of the indigenous Chinese churches migrated to Taiwan with the Nationalist Chinese after the communist victory on the Chinese mainland. Recently they have been growing fast and are re-evangelising China from a Taiwanese base. Chinese migrants in diaspora have spread Chinese churches throughout the region, including to Malaysia.

Christianity has sometimes helped minority populations to forge an identity in the modern world by preserving their language through Bible translation and by encouraging them to think of themselves as a people, like the Israelites. Once Christianity was permitted again in China, some minority groups, such as the Lisu in Yunnan Province, who had been evangelised by China Inland Mission before 1949, even claimed Christianity as a mark of their ethnic identity.

The Lisu people are split by current borders between China and Myanmar, where they are also recognised as a minority. Here and in several other countries of Southeast Asia – Cambodia, Laos and Thailand – Christians mainly belong to minority ethnic groups among majority Theravada Buddhist societies. The majority Burmese population of Myanmar have been resistant to centuries of Catholic and Protestant attempts at evangelisation. Nevertheless, Christians might make up 8% of the Myanmar population due to the conversion of several tribal groups, chiefly to a Baptist expression of the faith. The main groups are the Karen, Kachin and Chin. However, the assertion of a distinctive Christian identity by these minority groups was seen as a threat by the Burmese, who used Buddhism to create a national identity. Despite international protests, the Burmese authorities have oppressed other religions, including these Christians, by policies of disinformation, discrimination and violent persecution.

The situation is similar in Thailand, which has the distinction of being the only nation in Southeast Asia that has never submitted to colonial rule and where Thai ethnicity is synonymous with being Buddhist. Most of the Christians (who form less than 2% of the population) are not of

Thai descent. Some are from tribal minorities and others are Chinese or Vietnamese.

In Malaysia, the majority Malay population is defined as Muslim and their conversion is forbidden; nor are Christians allowed to evangelise them. Christians, who form about 9% of the total population, are from the other major communities: Chinese, Indians, Eurasians and indigenous peoples whose presence predates Malay migration. The indigenous are a tiny minority in peninsular (West) Malaysia but form a two-thirds majority in East Malaysia – a separate territory on the island of Borneo. Churches tend to be organised along ethnic and language lines. The indigenous people, who make up two-thirds of Malaysia's Christians, are marginalised in the churches as well and are hardly represented in denominational leadership. Malaysian Christians face a particular challenge in transcending ethnic differences and expressing their common faith in the Malay language: the laws that protect Malays from proselytisation forbid, for example, a Malay translation of the Bible and Christian use of the word 'Allah' for 'God'.

Indonesia is the most ethnically diverse nation in the region. Catholic theologians particularly have sought to recognise and celebrate the diverse cultures of Indonesia in the church, and Protestants have emphasised human equity regardless of religious or racial background. As elsewhere in Southeast Asia, those who converted to Christianity were mainly from groups not incorporated into the major religious systems. In states of largely tribal population, there are large numbers of Christians. For example, the state of Papua, which shares an island with Papua New Guinea, is more than 60% Christian.

When Timor-Leste, which lies close to Australia, was annexed by Indonesia in 1975, 90% of the indigenous people to whom it belonged declared themselves Catholic. Their resistance against Indonesia not only increased their poverty but led to widespread suffering and violence at the hands of the Indonesian military. Various agencies of the Catholic Church supported the Timorese – first by humanitarian aid and eventually by advocacy of the people's rights. When it was recognised as an independent state in 2002, it became the second predominantly Catholic nation in the region. In the other mostly Catholic nation, the Philippines, most of the population, of over 100 million, continue to live in poverty. The story of Jesus's passion is popularly retold in verse form. His suffering and death at the hands of the powerful inspires ongoing struggle and resistance.

Suffering and persecution are not just recent developments in the history of Christianity in East and Southeast Asia. The first Catholic Christians in the region, from the sixteenth century, encountered repeated and widespread persecution in most countries. Cults of the martyrs developed, and these play a prominent role in the Catholicism of the region. Some of the martyrs – local Christians and some foreign priests – have been beatified and canonised. Pope Pius IX canonised 26 Japanese martyrs as far back as 1862, but Pope John Paul II especially encouraged this form of popular religiosity. For example, he canonised 16 more martyrs in Japan in 1987, 120 martyrs in Korea in 1984, 117 in Vietnam in 1988, and 120 in China in 2000. Protestants also commemorate their martyrs, many of them killed by communists, but in a less systematic way.

Christians, Prosperity and Economic Development

East and Southeast Asia is home to many economic success stories: Japan, Hong Kong, Singapore, South Korea, Taiwan, Brunei and now China. Although many Christians in East and Southeast Asia remain poor, in some places Christians have been active in the region's economic development. The post-war growth of US missions in the region has included Evangelical missions that are adapted to capitalism. Furthermore, in the era of neo-liberal economics, new Christian movements have emerged that are oriented to help members achieve success, and some church leaders have developed types of prosperity theology that legitimise the accumulation of wealth. For example, the Chinese in Hong Kong and Taiwan, and in diaspora in many parts of Southeast Asia, were mostly anti-communist, and many have been extremely successful in capitalist systems. Singapore, for instance, boasts many large Chinese churches that use English and have global outreach programmes. Singaporean culture and politics discourage Christian involvement in wider society, except in the form of service, while Evangelical and Pentecostal worship and evangelism flourish.

South Korean Christians were similarly motivated towards capitalism because of their fear of communism, but also because of their vision for the kingdom of God, which they understood in terms of modernisation for the national good. That the growth of Protestantism was closely linked to modernisation is shown by the way post-war Korean churches were built in modern styles and made use of the latest technology to convey a future-oriented message of good news. Most Korean Christians regard both the growth of the church and the economic miracle of twentieth-century Korea as blessings from God and see a close connection between the two. Christians who fled communism before and during the Korean War had economic skills, an acquaintance with Western culture and an admiration for US society that enabled them to take a leading role in reconstruction in the South, together with others who returned from exile. The mega-churches that arose in the context of mass evangelism, urbanisation and religious market competition encouraged participation in nation-building, disseminated education and facilitated business networking. The

Charismatic and Pentecostal churches – most famously Yoido Full Gospel Church – developed techniques of prayer and evangelism to guarantee health, well-being and prosperity. Such large churches now run extensive social and educational programmes to support development. As in the case of Singapore, these business-oriented churches support and encourage the extensive overseas missionary movement from South Korea, which ranks among the largest in the world.

It cannot be argued that Christians in other parts of the region have made such a direct contribution to economic development as in South Korea, but the Pentecostal and Charismatic churches that thrive in late modernity have been growing throughout the region. Some are linked to Northern American, Australian or other Western missions and some to Korean and Chinese movements; others are indigenous responses to these. Although many Pentecostals are from tribal groups, such churches are also well adapted to the urbanisation of the region. They are growing not only in liberalised communist countries such as China, Vietnam, Cambodia and Laos but even in resistant communities such as among the Thai. Many such churches do empower their congregations by building community and providing educational and leadership opportunities that enable upward social mobility. However, the fear is that many are so compromised with capitalism and the spirit of the age that they become vehicles of prosperity for the few at the expense of the many.

Many Filipinos were attracted to US-style Evangelicalism, and the growth of these churches contributed to the reduction of the Catholic population to just over 80% of the total population. Pentecostal Charismatic Christianity has reached perhaps more than 40% of the population but has provoked a backlash that stigmatises it as the refuge of the gullible and insecure. Because of the openness in the Catholic Church to Charismatic renewal, the rise of Pentecostalism has blurred denominational boundaries rather than resulting in a separate movement of independent Pentecostal churches. But whereas Pentecostalism has had something of a unifying effect in the Philippines, in a situation of religious tension such as Indonesia, observers fear that initiatives led by outsiders and local Christian enthusiasm could endanger existing balances between communities.

Christians in East and Southeast Asia continue to form a small minority of the region's vast population. Moreover, in most cases Christians are economically poor and politically marginalised. Nevertheless, Christianity is flourishing in many parts. It is missionally engaged in the region and beyond it, and increasingly East and Southeast Asian leaders are rising to prominence in global Christian organisations. The churches of the region negotiate especially challenging social and political contexts in which some are oppressed by governments or by social pressure, and even persecuted. However, while the region as a whole is increasingly economically successful, perhaps the greatest challenge to the church in East and Southeast Asia today is not repressive systems but indifference to religion due to pursuit of wealth.

Bibliography

Bays, Daniel H., *A New History of Christianity in China* (Chichester: Wiley-Blackwell, 2012).

Kim, Sebastian C. H., *Christian Theology in Asia* (Cambridge: Cambridge University Press, 2008).

Moffett, Samuel H., *A History of Christianity in Asia*, vols I and II (Maryknoll, NY: Orbis Books, 1998, 2005).

Phan, Peter C. (ed.), *Christianities in Asia* (Chichester: Wiley-Blackwell, 2011).

Yong, Amos, and Vinson Synan (eds), *Global Renewal Christianity: Asia and Oceania* (Lake Mary, FL: Charisma House, 2016).

Mission and Evangelism

Septemmy E. Lakawa

The ever-changing realities of East and Southeast Asia shape the increasingly complex picture of mission and evangelism there today. This essay accentuates the complexity of mission and evangelism through contemporary Asian Christian narratives that are multidimensional and multidirectional. The following five themes – the ecumenicity of mission and evangelism; violence, inter-faith dialogue and hospitality; Pentecostalism, Roman Catholicism and everyday Christianity; empire, resistance and discipleship; and terrorism, spirituality and public theology – reflect the interconnected features of mission and evangelism as they find various expressions in the countries of contemporary East and Southeast Asia.

Ecumenicity of Mission and Evangelism
Mission and ecumenism have discovered refreshing interconnections in the ways in which churches use ecumenical platforms in their missional response to the Asian realities of poverty, ecological crisis, economic injustice, violation of human rights and the war on terrorism. The Asia Mission Conference, with the theme of 'Journeying Together: Prophetic Witness to the Truth and Light in Asia', was held under the auspices of the Christian Conference of Asia in October 2017 in Yangon, Myanmar. This conference urged both the churches and the mission bodies in Asia, as well as Christian communities outside Asia, to respond through an ecumenical framework to the emerging questions and challenges to mission arising in Asia. The call to be in mission is defined as the call to churches to journey together in witnessing to God's truth and light in the living realities of Asia today.

The site of the conference, Yangon, symbolised in a unique way the new challenges facing mission and evangelism in Asia. Myanmar, like many other countries in East and Southeast Asia, has a long and complex history of the intertwining of religion, ethnicity, violence and politics. Two of the four subthemes of the conference, 'Mission as Prophetic Accompaniment' and 'Mission as Embodying the Spirituality of the Cross', clearly speak to the situation at the time of the conference, when the story of the Rohingya people complexified the narrative of figures such as Aung San

Suu Kyi. Being church in mission in places such as Myanmar, Indonesia and Malaysia requires a process of discerning how a prophetic mission might place minority religious communities in risky and even dangerous situations.

The cross has been a central symbol of mission for East and Southeast Asian churches – as in the theology of the pain of God of Kasoh Kitamori and the water buffalo theology of Kosuke Koyama, both of Japan, and the compassionate God theology of Choan Seng Song of Taiwan – and it continues to be relevant today. It has also become an ecumenical symbol that connects different mission theologies and practices across churches and mission bodies.

Christianity in South Korea provides an example of the distinction between mission and evangelism. The rapidly growing church, which reveals the role of Korean churches in shaping the economic growth of modern Korea, has been criticised for an overemphasis on individual salvation that disconnects the church from the reality of unjust systems and from its own historical roots as a forerunner in social transformation. Korean churches' long tradition of taking social responsibility as their missional task is embedded, for many, in the Korean concept of Minjung (the oppressed, the poor, the sick and the marginalised). Minjung theology as a theology of resistance, especially in its formation and development in the 1970s and 1980s, looks at Minjung as subjects of social transformation and provides a theological basis for the church to influence the people's movement to shape a democratic South Korea.

The ecumenicity of mission and evangelism in East and Southeast Asia is also shown in the Korean churches' response to the quest for peace and reconciliation between South Korea and North Korea. The use of ecumenical platforms – the World Council of Churches, Christian Conference of Asia, Korean National Council of Churches and other similar approaches – has become a model for the effectiveness of mission as a prophetic accompaniment that overcomes divisions while respecting differences in the churches' responses to one of the most complex historical, socio-cultural, military and political problems that have affected and will affect not only the future of Asia but also that of the world, including the future of Christianity in the region. The ecumenical platform provides a way for churches in South Korea to overcome the dualistic aspects of being church in mission by reclaiming their missional role in shaping a just peace process for the future of the country and the peninsula.

Violence, Inter-faith Dialogue and Hospitality

A history of violence has significantly influenced the changing contours of the East and Southeast Asian religious landscape in the twenty-first century. The impact of violence on harmonious inter-faith living, which for centuries had characterised the Asian religious landscape, is made more complex by the current phenomena of religious radicalism and violations of human rights.

Between 1995 and 2005, Indonesia – the country with the world's largest Muslim population and also a country known for its claim to be an example of a harmonious pluralistic society – suffered from massive communal violence in many areas. Other Southeast Asian countries, such as Singapore, Malaysia and Thailand, survived the Asian economic crisis at the turn of the century, but Indonesia faced a slow road to economic recovery in the face of riots, pogroms and violence in the context of a national political crisis. Stories of communal violence that involved religious communities were highlighted in many media outlets, including social media. Many did not realise that this long history of violence would affect the shape of inter-faith relationships, particularly the discourse on mission and inter-religious dialogue, in the coming years.

The story of Indonesia is not isolated. The changing global economic and political landscape, which often goes hand in hand with regional political upheaval, affects inter-religious relationships in various ways at the grassroots level. In countries where the presence of one of the world's religions not only is predominant but also shapes the contour of the public space – such as Malaysia with Islam as the state religion, Myanmar with Buddhism and the Philippines with Roman Catholicism – communal violence, human rights violations, and impunity are often associated with religious motives or agendas. Moreover, religious violence or communal conflicts that are shaped by religious claims, symbols and narratives contradict claims of religious harmony and peace and, as a result, put into question the ability of people of different religions to live together harmoniously.

Narratives of local religious communities in the aftermath of violence not only detail the horrors of violence and point to the unspeakability of trauma but frequently also tell of the hospitality that a community either received or offered to religious 'others' who once were their enemies. The history of violence has challenged religious communities and religious leaders, including Christian theologians and mission practitioners, to rethink the relevance of mission and evangelism in the context of religious violence.

Peter C. Phan's concept of 'being religious inter-religiously' or 'being Christian inter-religiously' challenges the binaries of evangelism and social transformation and of conversion and religious pluralism by promoting a new way of looking at the complexity of mission from within the reality of East and Southeast Asian multicultural and multi-religious society. Furthermore, Phan's inter-cultural perspective on mission, which is built on the Vietnamese Catholic Church's experience, provides a unique understanding of the role of culture in shaping and accommodating the process of crossing borders, of being the church in mission in Asian ways.

Border crossing is a model of mission that is predominant in Asian mission discourse, and it becomes more relevant in the context of the history of violence and its long-term impact on inter-religious relationships. The local practice of hospitality in post-conflict situations, in particular, illustrates the riskiness of mission as a border-crossing practice. As an example, the stories of Muslim and Christian women who survived the politically and economically based religious violence in Poso and Ambon, two of the areas that suffered religious violence in Indonesia, reveal the interlacing of bravery, caring for 'others' and fears for their own safety as they offered and received hospitality from one another.

During the period of violent conflict, a Christian family in Poso who protected a Muslim neighbour, or a Christian family who hid their Muslim relatives in their house while feeding them out of their own limited resources, risked being accused of being traitors and even being harmed by their own Christian community. Gerakan Ibu Peduli (the Movement of the Caring Mothers) was initiated by Muslim and Christian women in the early phase of the Ambon conflict. The women reconnected their communities despite knowing the dangers they brought to their lives and communities by visiting other women in the 'enemy territories' – in the marketplace, segregated neighbourhoods and so forth. The stories of these women testify to the dimensions of vulnerability and resilience that are embedded in the practice of hospitality as an inter-religious practice. Hospitality as a practice of embracing others requires the ability to acknowledge the risk of putting oneself in a vulnerable situation when the religious other is one's enemy. This embracing is also an act of resilience, as the women from both religious communities persist in crossing the borders of fear, suspicion, hatred and violence in order to meet each other and, as a result, have inspired their communities, including youths, to be persistent in finding ways to be hospitable to each other even in the midst of violent conflict and its aftermath.

The aftermath of communal violence has challenged not only the understanding of mission and its relationship to inter-religious dialogue but also, essentially, the discourse and practice of inter-religious dialogue. New models have arisen alongside acknowledgement of inter-religious dialogue as a women's practice, including local communities' initiatives of healing and social transformation. Lian Gogali, a young female theologian and an activist for peace from Poso, exemplified these dimensions when she launched the first initiative of a women's school called the Mosintuwu

Institute. She gathered Muslim and Christian women survivors of the Poso conflict and provided them a safe space for facing their own fears, misconceptions of each other and trauma caused by the conflict. This school provides a model of inter-religious hospitality and of inter-religious education where local women's voices and leadership are recognised as the foundation of the transformation of communities wounded by years of communal violence. The women of the Mosintuwu Institute witness to each other's trauma and healing as they continue to sustain one another and testify to the possibility of healing and transformation in the aftermath of one of the most violent communal conflicts that Indonesia has ever witnessed. Furthermore, the narratives of these local women provide a contextual model of mission in the aftermath of religious communal violence as a practice of inter-religious hospitality.

Pentecostalism, Catholicism and Everyday Christianity

The growth of Pentecostal and Charismatic movements has changed the landscape of Catholic and Protestant churches in East and Southeast Asia. Pentecostal movements in South Korea have played a significant role in making Protestantism the second-largest religious group in the country after Buddhism, followed by Catholicism. Yonggi Cho's Yoido Full Gospel Church is an example of the magnitude of the growth of Pentecostals in East and Southeast Asia and their role in shaping social movements. Indonesia witnessed an increase in Pentecostals at the turn of the twenty-first century, when they represented approximately 3% of the total population of the Muslim-majority country. The Philippines, the only Catholic-majority country in Asia, experienced a significant shift in its Christian landscape as the proportion of Catholics declined due to the influence of Pentecostalism.

In addition to South Korea, Indonesia and the Philippines, China has witnessed a phenomenal expansion of Pentecostalism. J. M. Prior's study 'The Challenge of the Pentecostals in Asia' (in *Exchange*, 36 [2007]) predicts that in the twenty-first century, China might become the Asian country with the largest number of Christians as well as the country with the largest number of Pentecostals, Charismatics and neo-Pentecostals. Today, more than 40% of Asian Christians are Pentecostal or Charismatic.

Allan H. Anderson argues that Asia has more Evangelicals than the entire Western world. He describes Pentecostalism in China through house-church movements that reflect the process of the indigenisation of Christianity in China, which is characterised by its informality, spontaneity, flexibility and evangelistic outreach ('Pentecostalism in East Asia: Indigenous Oriental Christianity?', *PNEUMA: The Journal of the Society for Pentecostal Studies*, 22:1 [2000], 116).

The house-church movements also epitomise Pentecostalism as a religious and social phenomenon, which positions China as key to understanding the Asian face of Pentecostalism.

The importance of Pentecostal movements in the context of church unity has become a primary concern for the Roman Catholic Church and for ecumenical bodies such as the World Council of Churches. Prior's study reveals the complex relationship between Pentecostals and the Catholic Church, one that not only shapes the contours of Asian Christianity but also determines the direction of mission and ecumenism in East and Southeast Asia today.

Prior's identification of the stark differences between the Pentecostal and Charismatic theological and cultural undertaking – which is oral, inclusive and narrative – and conventional Christianity – which is literary, exclusive and conceptual – provides both challenges and opportunities for dialogue. Furthermore, the demographic shift of Christianity that is predominantly shaped by Pentecostal movements and the Catholic Church implies the urgency of dialogue between Roman Catholics and Pentecostals, including dialogue on the understanding and practice of mission and evangelism. The Philippines has witnessed the challenges that Pentecostal movements have brought to the Catholic Church by reshaping the Christian demographics and the grassroots movements in the country. The country has also witnessed growth in the number of Charismatic Catholics, which renders the everyday practice of Catholic teachings more complex.

Many have argued that the rapid growth of Pentecostalism in Asia is due to its Spirit-oriented practices that are attuned to Asian religiosities. East and Southeast Asian Pentecostal movements reveal the unique dimensions of Christianity in the region as, to use Nancy T. Ammerman's term, an 'everyday religion'. In each of the four countries – South Korea, Indonesia, the Philippines and China – where Pentecostal movements have growth rapidly, many similar dimensions of Pentecostalism are exhibited: it is a grassroots, indigenous and Spirit-oriented phenomenon; the Bible is used as a source of everyday hope for healing and justice; and Pentecostalism emphasises the independence and autonomy of local congregations, the importance of the personal experience of salvation and the roles of women and lay people. These characteristics are addressed in a recent study on mission and migration. Maraike Bangun, in her master-of-theology thesis 'From Soul Evangelism to Compassionate Presence: Migration, Missional Presence, and the Migrant Church in Malaysia' (Jakarta Theological Seminary, 2015), identifies the ordinariness of Christianity as a characteristic of the religion of migrants. She highlights the roles of Indonesian and Filipino women migrants in Sabah, Malaysia, in shifting their local Charismatic church's understanding from evangelism as a soul-saving practice to evangelism as Christian presence. Her study showcases the fluidity of Pentecostal and Charismatic movements in their theology and mission practices, highlighting the openness of Pentecostals and Charismatics to dialogue with other branches of Christianity in the contexts of mission and ecumenism in East and Southeast Asia today. As dialogue has become one of the major tenets of Asian religious practices, the coming together of churches in the region through dialogue is a significant feature of contemporary East and Southeast Asian Christianity as an everyday religion.

The encounters of Pentecostals and Charismatics with other churches in the region have also shown the importance of arts and Asian cultural practices. In various Christian communities, it has become a common practice to sing Pentecostal or Charismatic songs. Dialogue through the arts is increasing. In ecumenical seminaries, various Christian traditions are being studied, and Pentecostal and Charismatic spiritual practices are being introduced in the context of student formation for church ministry.

Empire, Resistance and Discipleship

Mission in the context of empire is one of the central features of the global conversation on mission. Joerg Rieger's characterisation of empire as massive concentrations of power, uncontrollable and affecting all parts of life, reveals the multifaceted nature of empire, which can take form in nations, corporations, the military, the economy, culture and politics. Today, empire has taken on multiple shapes, both in East and Southeast Asia and globally.

Although the discourse on empire is not foreign to the study of Christianity, exposing the massive concentrations of economic, political and military powers that affect all life globally has made it obvious that any conversation on mission has to take into consideration this reality. The Asian mission discourse has always been embedded in the three interconnected features of Asian society – widespread and extreme poverty, cultural diversity and religious plurality. The contemporary conversation on mission in the context of empire has disclosed the delicate thread of concentrated power that permeates these three intertwined layers. Therefore, analyses of widespread poverty, for example, cannot overlook the economic imperialism that has maintained the unjust structure of the economy that degrades the humanity of the poor and the oppressed.

Stories of congregations reverberate with the complex dynamics of empire and its repercussions on the church's understanding and practice of mission. The three interconnected layers of power – state, corporation and religion – in the above stories of migration manifest the grip of empire on the lives of ordinary people. They also display the multiple roles of the church in providing a safe space for migrants. However, the church often plays a role in maintaining a form of religious imperialism by not protesting, for example, about the domestication of women.

Resistance is one of the central themes in the discourse of mission in the context of empire. Forms of resistance to widespread religious, economic and political imperialism are witnessed in the daily lives of religious communities, including churches and civil society. In the church and civil society in South Korea, the Philippines and Taiwan, movements for resistance against political, economic and religious imperialism have shaped mission discourse and practice.

In the 1980s and 1990s, the Mission and Evangelism Desk, and the Education Desk of the Christian Conference of Asia had a joint programme called 'Reading the Bible with New Eyes'. The premise was that reinterpreting the Bible from the perspectives of the poor, the marginalised, the feminist and the religious other would provide a contextual biblical basis for creating inclusive communities that would resist every form of violence. In one of the workshops in 1997 in Pattaya, Thailand, a Dalit participant reinterpreted the story of Jesus healing an ill man at the pool of Bethesda, in John 5: 1–18, from a Dalit perspective. He read the gospel story of healing as a story of empowerment, of the power to speak to the powers that be by redefining discipleship as a resistance against the religious imperialism that denies the humanity of Dalits. The healing of the Dalit man at Bethesda became a symbol of resistance to the power of religious, cultural, political and economic dominance.

Resistance as a form of discipleship is a pivotal theme in the development of mission theology and evangelism in the context of empire. In the case of China, the issue of empire takes another route. Rapid social change has opened up China to the world but also has changed the future of religion in the country and, by implication, the nature of mission. Ambivalence towards the effects of the revolution – the restriction of religious activities and their presence in the public sphere, on the one hand, and the overthrowing of the unjust class structure, on the other hand – raises the existential question of discipleship as a form of mission. Richard P. Marsden responds to this dilemma by placing the theme of discipleship in parallel with the unlikely theme of domination. The question, therefore, is whether discipleship as mission – understood both as Christian proselytism and as social transformation – can become a way of life without falling into the practice of domination.

Mission has always been a practice of power – power to change, power to influence and so forth. Resistance to the powers that be, which has been demonstrated throughout the history of mission and in contemporary mission practice in East and Southeast Asia, needs to be critically examined in conjunction with the vision of Christianising the world as a fundamental aspect of discipleship. Evangelism as conversion, which adheres to a sense of religious domination, juxtaposes the idea of evangelism as a form of social transformation, which adheres to a practice of resistance to the powers that be. Both dimensions are paradoxically present throughout the mission history of East and Southeast Asia.

China is now one of the world's largest economic powers. When speaking about mission and evangelism in China today, one cannot disregard the nation's global, imperial, economic and political power. The missional presence of the church in China is more crucial than ever before, as China will also determine the future of world peace. Being in mission in China requires the practice of a discipleship that resists every form of domination.

Churches and Christian and inter-religious communities have had ambivalent responses to the modern South Korean missionary venture. The economic boom of South Korea has positioned it as one of Asia's leading economic powers, which has affected the development of the missionary movement of Korean churches throughout Asia. This missionary enterprise, which is widely depicted as a movement of evangelising Asia and the world for Christ, undeniably carries with it an image of South Korea as an economic giant. Economic dominance becomes one of the lenses through which the missionary enterprise is perceived. Economic imperialism goes hand in hand with religious imperialism, which positions mission as a risky undertaking.

The presence of South Korean churches and missionaries in many Asian cities, small towns, and even remote and dangerous areas, which is embedded in the missionaries' strong commitment to sharing the Christian message with the world, has raised questions. It is undeniable that their presence continues to bring insights for the betterment of communities. Their presence and ministry, however, have raised suspicion among religious communities and even resistance by local churches. The Korean missionary enterprise, with its theological emphasis on evangelisation, has opened up educational access for many local communities, partnership with local churches regarding women's right issues, and so forth. The evangelism paradox of conversion and social change is present in this movement. The long-lasting prejudice against and stereotype of the missionary movement as a colonial and Western enterprise might overshadow this modern form of missionary movement. It might also jeopardise long-term efforts to build and maintain harmonious inter-religious relationships. In this context, discipleship as a form of mission remains an ambivalent concept.

Terrorism, Spirituality and Public Theology

The year 2001 marked the beginning of the global war on terrorism. The global landscape of the human network has been changed radically because of the misuse of power and religion in an ideology called terrorism. The Philippines, Indonesia and Malaysia are considered safe harbours for terrorist cells. The recent war on terrorism on the island of Mindanao, in the Philippines, has demonstrated the dangerous and catastrophic nature of the ideology of terrorism. The 2018 suicide bombings of three churches and several other places in the city of Surabaya, Indonesia, stunned society because the perpetrators were women and children as well as men; this is an unfamiliar aspect of terrorism.

The war on terrorism has placed Islam in a very difficult position, both globally and locally. The spread of radical Islam at various levels of society and the use of social media for religious campaigns are considered conducive to the spread of terrorist ideology. Blaming Christian evangelisation for the rise of Muslim fundamentalism, the spread of hate speech, attacks at minority worship spaces and public facilities that have caused widespread trauma and wounded the long tradition of inter-religious relationship – all of these have shaped the contours of the East and Southeast Asian religious landscape in recent years.

The 2017 Asia Mission Conference stated that mission is an embodiment of the spirituality of the cross. Using the cross as a symbol of Christian spirituality in the context of daily terror, religious enmity and suspicion, however, faces complex challenges. The current theological discourse on mission spirituality has brought Christology into conversation with pneumatology. Pentecostalism is playing an important role in reintroducing and reclaiming the role of the Holy Spirit in mission spirituality. The conversation allows for the emergence of new perspectives on the role of the Spirit in the midst of violence and terror and their aftermath. The discourse and practice of healing as a form of mission spirituality are not seen as merely a domestic affair that takes place in the internal circle of Christian communities. Healing becomes a public affair. Mission spirituality becomes a search for God that cuts through the binaries of private and public.

The old metaphor of carrying the cross is being extended to include the biblical metaphors of breathing, dancing and embracing the Spirit (Septemmy Lakawa, 'Risky Hospitality: Mission in the Aftermath of Religious Communal Violence in Indonesia', ThD Dissertation, Boston University, 2011). Cultural stories, symbols and metaphors are being reclaimed. The world that is imbued with fear of difference is faced with a spirituality of resilience that welcomes and respects differences. In 2017, the Council for World Mission held a series of seminars with the theme

'De-centring Perspectives on Evangelism'. A seminar was held in Jakarta, with participants representing various dimensions of difference – countries, religions, denominations, ethnicities, genders and socio-economic backgrounds. The seminar provided a unique platform where evangelism was discussed across differences that in many cases have caused pain and trauma. A Muslim transgender participant expressed her gratitude for having experienced such a welcoming space where her voice was heard. A Christian participant's perspective on Islam was changed as she listened to the stories of a Muslim activist sharing his experience of building a grassroots youth movement for inter-religious dialogue as a platform for facing the challenges of religious radicalism. In this space, evangelism is extended and the mission spirituality of welcoming difference and being resilient in the midst of hatred and violence is embodied.

The public space has become a contested site in many East and Southeast Asian countries. Several years ago, the government of Malaysia officially prohibited non-Muslim Malays from using the word 'Allah' ('God'); it defined Allah as an exclusively Muslim word, since it is in Arabic. In countries such as Malaysia and Indonesia, which use the word 'Allah', Arabic is considered an Islamic language. In contrast to the situation in Malaysia, however, in Indonesia the issue remained insignificant in circles of conversation. The Malaysian case is one of many examples of the ways the religion of the majority plays a central role in shaping the character of the public space. In the past several years in many cities in Indonesia, banners that declare the refusal to accept those who are different are being displayed along public roads, in residential neighbourhoods, in front of worship spaces and at other public sites.

In Malaysia, non-Muslim communities fought for their right to use the word 'Allah', with which they were familiar and which they had used for centuries. The Catholic Church in Malaysia, which owned the newspaper *The Herald*, appealed to the Malaysian High Court for the right to use the word 'Allah' in the newspaper. After five years, it lost its case, marking the end of this long struggle for the rights of non-Muslim citizens. The response of Christians along with other non-Muslim communities in Malaysia models a spirituality of resilience.

The story of the congregations of Gereja Kristen Indonesia (GKI) Yasmin, and of Huria Kristen Batak Protestan (HKBP) Bekasi, of Indonesia, reflect the public face of mission spirituality. They have been holding their Sunday worship together every other week since 2012 in front of the presidential palace in Jakarta as a sign of protest for the lack of action by the government to afford them the right, which has been guaranteed by the Indonesian High Court, to worship in their own buildings. A few years previously, their Muslim neighbours had prohibited them from worshipping in their church buildings. One of the reasons was that the neighbourhood was majority Muslim. Many similar stories of contested public space could be told.

The role of religion in the public space, which indicates that mission is public discourse, raises the question of the compatibility of religion and democracy in East and Southeast Asia. Robert W. Hefner, a leading scholar on Islam in Asia, has claimed that Islam is compatible with democracy. In a similar tone, churches in East and Southeast Asia have constructed their missional responses by looking at the compatibility of Christianity and democracy. Churches in this region have struggled to shape the public space as a just space through which a model of mission as public theology has been lived out. One of the profound challenges for churches and Christian communities in East and Southeast Asia today is to continue to be in mission by shaping the public space of their nations and by shaping a just and peaceful future for Asia.

Conclusion

This essay has identified five interconnected themes of mission and evangelism in East and Southeast Asia today – the ecumenicity of mission and evangelism; violence, inter-religious dialogue and hospitality; Pentecostalism, Roman Catholicism and everyday Christianity; empire, resistance and discipleship; and terrorism, spirituality and public theology. The essay has also sketched the multiple angles – theological, political, economic, cultural and artistic – from which mission and evangelism can be envisioned, discussed and lived out contextually. These themes emphasise the multidimensionality and multidirectionality of mission and evangelism in East and Southeast Asia today. They mirror the changing contour of mission and evangelism in the region that is playing a significant role in shaping the landscape of Asian Christianity in the twenty-first century. Questions of mission and evangelism in the context of Asian religiosities and the socio-economic and political landscapes are responded to by highlighting the similar as well as the unique approaches that each East and Southeast Asian country brings to shape the face of mission and evangelism today.

Bibliography

Freston, Paul, *Evangelicals and Politics in Asia, Africa and Latin America* (Cambridge: Cambridge University Press, 2001).
Hefner, Robert W. (ed.), *Global Pentecostalism in the 21st Century* (Bloomington, IN: Indiana University Press, 2013).
Phan, Peter C., *Being Religious Inter-religiously: Asian Perspectives on Interfaith Dialogue* (Maryknoll, NY: Orbis Books, 2008).
Phan, Peter C., *In Our Own Tongues: Perspectives from Asia on Mission and Inculturation* (Maryknoll, NY: Orbis Books, 2003).

Prior, John Mansford SVD, 'The Challenge of the Pentecostals in Asia Part One: Pentecostal Movements in Asia' and 'The Challenge of the Pentecostals in Asia Part Two: The Responses of the Roman Catholic Church', *Exchange,* 36 (2007), 6–40; 115–43.

Gender

Sharon A. Bong

The intersection of gender and Christianity finds myriad expressions across East and Southeast Asia, where Christians are a minority (with the exceptions of the Philippines and Timor-Leste in Southeast Asia). An analytical review of this important intersection draws from the rich literature of Asian feminist theologies and, to a lesser extent, queer theologies, whereas most historical documentation on Christianity in this region (such as mission studies and early church history), including contemporary trends such as mega-churches (in Singapore, Indonesia, the Philippines, South Korea), are often gender blind (without a gendered or feminist perspective).

This review tangentially considers the corpus of gender and sexuality studies in Islam and in Confucianism, Buddhism and Chinese folk religions, as Muslims are the demographic majority in Indonesia (which hosts the most populous *ummah* or Muslim community in the world), Malaysia and Brunei in Southeast Asia (where both Brunei and Aceh, Northern Indonesia, are Islamic states), while a syncretic mix of Confucianism, Buddhism and Chinese folk religions are still influential in Thailand, Vietnam, Laos, Cambodia, Myanmar and Singapore in Southeast Asia and in China, Taiwan, Hong Kong, Macau and South Korea in East Asia.

Politically, this intersection is negotiated within communist frameworks (Vietnam and Laos in Southeast Asia, China and North Korea in East Asia) as well as current and past military dictatorships or incursions (Myanmar, the Philippines, Indonesia and Timor-Leste in Southeast Asia, and China, Japan, and North and South Korea in East Asia). This intersection is also embedded in narratives of colonisation, beginning with the introduction of Christianity in this region through colonisation (Catholicism via the Portuguese, French and Spanish; Protestantism via the British and Dutch) and neo-colonisation (such as Korean Protestantism founded on American far-right conservatism and Protestantism).

A consideration of the intersection of gender and Christianity in this region is made more complex by the broader intersectional frameworks and ideologies as outlined above. In navigating these private–public, individual–institutional and local–global matrices, this essay is divided into three sections: conformity, challenge and controversy. The section on conformity shows how the basic tenets of Christianity complement, even augment, gender ideologies in this region. The second section, on challenge, foregrounds the under-quoted scholarship of Asian feminist theologians who call into question many of these gender ideologies as they negotiate the tension between being dutiful daughters and becoming defiant daughters in the home, church and nation. The final section, on controversy, builds on the transgression of gender ideologies for LGBTQ (lesbian, gay, bisexual, transgender and queer) communities in Asia.

Conformity

The category of 'gender' is largely differentiated from 'sex', as the latter is deemed to be biologically determined (one is born male or female) while the former is socially constructed (one becomes masculine or feminine). A cisgender person refers to one whose 'sex' is aligned with his or her 'gender' identity and expression. A person born male thus becomes masculinised and one born female becomes feminised. These are also generally accepted to be mutually exclusive categories, as a person is either male or female, masculine or feminine, not both–and. Gender binaries or dualisms as such are denoted as male/female and masculine/feminine. Across time and space, these have given rise to other dualisms that have come to be aligned with male and masculinity – such as the mind, rationality, muscularity, hairiness, aggression, agency, good – while the body, emotion, slenderness, hairlessness, docility, passivity and evil have come to be aligned with female and femininity. The first terms of each of these dualisms—mind/body, rationality/emotion, muscularity/slenderness, hairiness/hairlessness, aggression/docility, agency/passivity and good/evil—are dominant categories (because they are aligned with the male and masculinity) and the second terms, secondary and subordinate ones (because they are aligned with the female and femininity).

Gender binaries as a construct play up differences between the sexes that are ontological (for example, one is logical and the other is given to excesses of emotion), physical (one is muscular; the other, slender – hence the beauty myths that more women than men historically have been subjected to), and behavioural (one is aggressive; the other, docile – which problematically feeds into rape cultures). Gender binaries as a construct are premised on oppositional differences (being female is not being male, and vice versa) and this leads to gender statuses under which men are generally perceived and treated as superior to women, who are, consequently, inferiorised and even infantalised. The gender work involved in sustaining the purposeful and systemic marginalisation of not only women (and girls) but also qualities or attributes associated with femininity, principally the body and emotions, takes the form of patriarchy.

Gender binaries that are the foundational bases of gender ideologies are thus premised on differences and mutual exclusivity (oppositional differences) that cement the superiority of most men over most women, most of the time and in most spaces.

These spaces are largely constructed as heteronormative spaces that enforce the naturalness and rightness of heterosexuality or opposite-sex attraction. If one is born male, one ought to become masculinised, and, conversely, if one is born female, one ought to become feminised – and for both opposite-sex attraction is prescribed, with same-sex attraction proscribed. This gives rise to a corresponding gender (and sexuality) dualism, heterosexuality/homosexuality or heteronormative/non-heteronormative, with legitimacy accorded to the first terms and the second terms constructed as unnatural, deviant, even sinful. Bodies and sexualities are disciplined and heterosexuality made compulsory, especially for LGBTQ persons, by both secular and religious laws with (worldly and other-worldly) rewards for conformity and sanctions for non-conformity. Gender as a category thus becomes intimately intertwined with sexuality.

In the context of East and Southeast Asia, Confucianism, past and present, ascribes to the girl-child and woman 'Three Obediences and Four Virtues'. Where obedience is concerned, a woman is required to obey her father as a daughter, her husband as a wife and her son in widowhood. The feminine virtues comprise wifely virtue, wifely speech, wifely manner or appearance and wifely work. What are apparent are not only the presumed heterosexuality of women in general (as the roles of wife and mother are naturalised) but also the gender ideologies at work. Obedience as a feminine virtue is accorded inter-generational legitimacy, which, in turn, sustains gender dualisms of a man's lifelong dominance over a woman's lifelong subservience.

To many, these obediences and virtues might seem archaic, but to scholars who work on trafficking in human persons, such expressions of feminine gender identity, compounded by another key Confucian trait, filial piety, exacerbate the vulnerability of the girl-child and woman whose virginities and bodies are knowingly sold into prostitution by their families. These willing daughters manifest ambivalent positions: shame at their defilement, pride as providers to their poverty-stricken families and hurt by familial rejection upon returning. In addition, Vietnamese folklore romanticises women's unconditional devotion and loyalty to their families and in doing so institutes an inter-generational inferiority of women in relation to men, which some impute as a perversion of family and Asian values.

The unquestioning daughter's filial piety, with its Confucian basis, finds a haunting parallelism, in discourses on prostitution, with the feminised martyr complex in the Philippines, which is overwhelmingly Catholic. The cultural-religious construction of the 'Filipino woman' as a dutiful wife, mother and daughter, not unlike the three obediences of Confucianism, finds its highest expression in ideal victimhood, in imitation of Jesus as the archetypal sacrificial lamb. A machismo culture aggrandising gender inequality and gender inequity between men and women, and a Christianised machismo culture as a Spanish legacy of Catholicism in the Philippines, aggravate the plight of the 'Filipino woman' destined to a life of suffering and silent acquiescence, with her gaze directed at other-worldly redemption. The Filipino woman is further oppressed by two inaccessible Christian female role models: the thoroughly chastened ideal of a virgin-mother in the form of Mary and the thoroughly castigated nemesis, the evil seductress that Mary Magdalene is often portrayed to be.

Feminist theologians like Mary John Mananzan OSB courageously speak out against Christianity as the root of women's oppression in the Philippines. Feminist theologians, including the contingent of the 1994 Ecumenical Association of Third World Theologians, denounce the masculinised image of God as a tyrannical father that could be interpreted as legitimising domestic abuse (as the sacrifice of a son is entailed) and fostering a victim attitude among women. The practice of such endemic gender ideologies in the home is further fuelled by Christian ideology that, in turn, reinforces the distortion of family values that are lopsidedly borne by the dutiful daughter in selling her body to feed her family. Against the cultural-religious signification of ideal femininity as the embodiment of passive victimhood, the Filipino women's movement GABRIELA, had to deploy a victimhood narrative to better relate to girls and women as prostitutes before deploying an agentive narrative intended to re-socialise prostitutes in empowering them to gradually transition from victims to agents who are imbued with self-determination.

The global movement of consecrated women against trafficking in human persons (TIPs), Talitha Kum (meaning 'little girl, arise'), deploys another tenet of Christianity, the fundamental dignity of the human person as created in the image of God (*imago dei*). This is a core goal of Talitha Kum Asia, which articulates *imago dei* from a gendered lens: 'To renew the values of the church to respect and uphold the dignity of women and men created in the image and likeness of God'. Talitha Kum Asia's vision (formed by chapters in Timor-Leste, Indonesia, Malaysia and Thailand in Southeast Asia and Japan, Korea and Taiwan in East Asia) lies in its commitment to eradicate 'human trafficking, modern-day slavery, forced labour and debt bondage, especially among children and women, in the Southeast/East Asia region'. A Christian framework in this regard affords Talitha Kum Asia not only a faith-based but also a rights-based framework within which to operate. Whereas a faith-based framework is premised on the (biblical and doctrinal) dignity of the human person, a rights-based framework is premised on human rights of the individual as universal (applicable to all persons, at all times, at all places), indivisible (economic, social and cultural rights are inseparable from civil and political liberties) and inalienable (integral to being human).

However, the challenge of bridging the chasm between an ideological understanding and praxis of human dignity and the everyday trampling of human dignity – especially the human dignity of women, who suffer TIPs differently and disproportionately – persists. In addition to gender ideologies at work, this is a challenge that involves other binaries, which include, but are not limited to, Western ideology (Christianity) versus Asian values (unconditional filial piety more onerously borne by the girl-child and woman) and atomistic individualism (individual rights) versus communitarian spirit (personal sacrifice for familial or common good, again more onerously borne by the girl-child and woman). As the bases of both human rights and human dignity have historically and theologically been gender biased (androcentric), as argued by feminist theologians and women's human rights activists, the composite challenge is a postcolonial and feminist one.

Challenge

The prior and more fundamental challenge is a feminist one as gender ideologies in Christianity find expression not only in sexism (such as Augustinian positioning of women as the devil's gateway) but also the (deceptively egalitarian notion of) gender complementarity of the sexes embedded in the concept of 'feminine genius'.

The term 'feminine genius' gained visibility in Pope John Paul II's 1995 'Letter to Women' in conjunction with the fourth (and last) UN World Conference on Women, held in Beijing in that year. A fuller sense of the 'feminine' is an intrinsic feature of his 1988 Apostolic Letter *Mulieris Dignitatem*, on the dignity and vocation of women in the Marian year. The term is back in circulation as used by Pope Francis to facilitate women's greater leadership role in the church. Although women continue to be excluded from priestly ordination, the Vatican had initiated a commission to study the historical precedence of female deacons in the Catholic Church, with a view to the potential resuscitation of this practice in this millennium. The 'feminine genius' of women encapsulates three inter-related effects: it is complementary, essentialising and regulatory.

First, in 'Letter to Women', Pope John Paul II notes that: 'Womanhood expresses the "human" as much as manhood does, but in a "different and complementary way"'. The complementarity of womanhood and manhood are not only physical and psychological but also ontological: 'It is only through the duality of the "masculine" and the "feminine" that the "human" finds full realization'. The 'gender complementarity' that is also the bedrock of the church's theology of the body makes sacred gender and sexual differences – from the very beginning 'male and female' were created (Genesis 1: 27) – thereby justifying gender dualisms: the 'unity of the two'. In doing so, it effectively brackets off gender and sexual divergences, dissonances and diversities. There are only two ways of being in the world: the human is created male or female and gendered masculine or feminine.

Secondly, from this foundational principle of the gender complementarity of womanhood and, by extension, 'feminine genius', Pope John Paul II contextualises the 'genius of women' as 'a specific part of God's plan' where the 'creation of woman is thus marked from the outset by *the principle of help*: a help which is not one-sided but *mutual*'. In other words, the essence of womanhood is that of a 'helper fit for [man]' (Genesis 2: 18), to assist him in reproductive ways (propagating the species) and productive ways (exercising dominion over the earth and all living creatures). The concomitant qualities that have become essentialised (naturalised and fixed) as feminine are nurturing, life-giving and subsidiary; that is, woman assists rather than initiates. One may argue that the gender dualism inherent in a feminised 'principle of help' is 'one-sided [rather than] mutual'. Mutuality in this context does not mean reciprocity, as the Pope adds that 'Their most natural relationship, which corresponds to the plan of God, is the "unity of the two", a relational "uni-duality"'. Woman is man's helpmate. In contrast, man does not, cannot and therefore should not serve in this capacity. This is woman's singularity, her 'genius', her 'feminine genius'.

Thirdly, the 'feminine genius' puts 'every woman' in her place. The cautionary note glimpsed in John Paul II's 'Letter to Women' finds clearer expression in *Mulieris Dignitatem* in relation to the quest and 'question of women's rights':

> Consequently, even the rightful opposition of women to what is expressed in the biblical words 'He shall rule over you' (Genesis 3: 16) must not under any condition lead to the 'masculinization' of women. In the name of liberation from male 'domination', women must not appropriate to themselves male characteristics contrary to their own feminine 'originality'. There is a well-founded fear that if they take this path, women will not 'reach fulfilment', but instead will *deform and lose what constitutes their essential richness*.

The 'feminine genius' is femininity made proper. It is to exercise her 'originality', which is her essential acting and being in the world as a 'helper fit for [man]'. It is to stay in place within the dualisms of man/woman, masculine/feminine, Christ/church, bridegroom/bride and ministerial/common priesthood. It is to emulate the impossible ideal of virgin-mother (as Mary, Mother of God, embodies the 'highest expression of the "feminine genius"'), beginning with the feminised quality of obedience to man and God. The 'question of women's rights' risks women overreaching their place, of overstepping the boundaries of male/female and active/passive. To do so, in misappropriating 'male characteristics', is a transgression of the boundaries set up within the economy of gender dualisms and risks the '"masculinization" of women'. What is revelatory is that 'male "domination"' is masked as 'mutuality'. The full import of John Paul II's 'Letter to Women' is now made clear. While all believers share in the 'common priesthood', only the elect male may rise to 'ministerial priesthood' — in fidelity to the complementarity of these principles, 'entrusted only to men the task of being an "icon" of his countenance as "shepherd" and "bridegroom" of the Church'.

The genius, feminine or otherwise, of feminists theologising from the bowels of Asia has been precisely and necessarily to 'overreach' their place in challenging untenable gender ideologies that form the bedrock of how Christianity has come to be interpreted and practised. As Christianity in Asia is understood and experienced as the religion of the colonisers, feminists theologising in Asia are triply marginalised: on accounts of their sex, faith and ideological persuasion. Where the overriding rhetoric of many postcolonial states positions Christianity as not only foreign but Western, and hence potentially polluting Asian values and morality, feminist theologians risk being triply branded: as unfilial daughters (and sons, for men who identify as feminist), unpatriotic citizens and masculine women. They embody the socially marginal (insider–outsider) and socially marginalised identities of belonging but not quite within the home, church and nation. To find her place – after all, women hold up half the sky (as the Chinese proverb goes) – women paradoxically need to lose their place, to cross over and inevitably transgress boundaries, especially those steeped in gender binaries. In this way, the related and no less fundamental challenge for feminists theologising in Asia becomes a feminist postcolonial one, as they reflexively seek ways to reconcile the conflicting ideologies and ontologies of being feminist, being Christian and being Asian.

For a feminist, finding her place entails, firstly, a coming into her own. On the one hand, there is humble recognition of those who had paved the way, given that Asian feminist theologies are a successor epistemology or later body of knowledge inherited from – or at least richly informed by – Western feminist theologians such as Elisabeth Schüssler

Fiorenza, Rosemary Radford Ruether, Mary Daly, Carter Heyward, Sallie McFague and many others. Asian feminist theologies are also successor epistemologies to Asian postcolonial theologies featuring Burakumin, Dalit and Minjung theologies (such as those of C. S. Song from China, David Kwang-Sun Suh from Korea, Kuribayashi Teruo from Japan, R. S. Sugirtharajah and Aloysius Pieris from Sri Lanka, and Arvind P. Nirmal from India) and liberation theologies (from Latin America and Africa).

On the other hand, there is a critical distancing from white feminists' colonising representation of the 'Asian woman', often as poor, multiply oppressed and in need of being rescued. Such skewed representation is ominously reminiscent of civilising missions that exaggerate the differences between Christian missionaries and godless natives with the intent to inferiorise and the concomitant justification to conquer the latter. To illustrate, Asian feminist theologians such as Angela Wong Wai Ching from Hong Kong critique the Western missionaries' intention to save Chinese heathens, especially women, by depicting the latter as hapless victims of arranged marriages, polygamy, concubinage, slavery and foot binding and by emphasising the complicity of Chinese religions, which include Confucianism, Taoism and Buddhism, in affording gender ideologies cultural and traditional legitimacy. The inverse strategy of othering (Chinese women as culturally oppressed and Chinese traditions as debased) lies in romanticising Asian religious traditions as extensions of exoticising their foreignness. The hardening of West/East, centre/margin and Christian/heathen binaries, infers the eminent Kwok Pui-Lan in *Postcolonial Imagination and Feminist Theology*, inadvertently obscures the suffering of Asian women, as these representations are not grounded in the lived realities of Asian women, who are, to begin with, not a monolithic group (not all Asian women are poor or oppressed, or poor and oppressed, in the same way).

There is also internal critique from Asian feminist theologians that is consonant with the internal dissent constituting the various waves of feminist thought that is an integral component of what sustains rather than fragments a women's movement. Where the quest to come into one's own necessitates finding both one's voice and a collective voice that seeks uniqueness of the 'Asian' in Asian feminist theologising, others have noted the limits of such identity politics – it is at once empowering but also reductionist and potentially exclusive. For example, Namsoon Kang, from the first wave of Korean feminist theologians (1980s to 1990s), cautions feminists on the pitfalls of essentialising the Asian subject and subjectivity, which inadvertently reifies a binary of us (Asian) versus them (West). In doing so, one risks Orientalising oneself – not unlike the colonising strategy of constructing the 'Oriental' (East) – to borrow from the postcolonial theorist Edward Said – as other, different and oppositional from the 'Occident' (West) – which narrows the complexities of what it means to be Asian. Instead, Kang's theologising moves beyond identity politics or group-based affinities and differences such as nationality, ethnicity, religion, gender and sexuality. This inclusive vision is prophetic, given the acceleration of trans-nationalisation today that compresses time-space for all, bringing the point home of how we are all intimately connected.

In going beyond the binaries of West/Asia, given the myopia of not doing so, finding one's place entails, secondly, having a place to call one's own (to paraphrase Virginia Woolf). This is the quest to eke out a sense of belonging within the home, the church and nation by negotiating the tension between being a dutiful daughter and becoming a defiant daughter. Aye Nwe, for instance, notes the parallelism with the deeply gender hierarchised society and church in Myanmar that are premised on the belief that men embody *phon* (male power, glory or holiness). This cultural construct of *phon* drives a divisive wedge in the differentiated treatment, position and status of men and women, sons and daughters, in the home and church, which are manifest not only in gender-based discrimination (such as denial of women's ordination in most churches) and gender-based violence (rape used as a weapon of war, particularly to subdue ethnic minorities such as the Karen, Kachin and Chin) but also in misogyny. Yet women remain as the bedrock upon which the home, church and nation are built, amid Myanmar's political turmoil (its military dictatorship and turbulent transitioning to democracy) and economic insecurity. Nwe affirms Wa women (one of the 135 minority groups in Myanmar, found also in China, Laos and Thailand) as agents of transformation, in the spirit of the Syro-Phoenician woman (Matthew 15: 21–8, Mark 7: 24–30) who persists in imploring Jesus to heal her spirit-ridden daughter (and would not take 'no' for an answer).

Christian feminist conscientisation extends a place to call one's own to the streets or the grassroots and trans-nationally, as embodied by the evolution and revolution of Filipino feminist nuns (Virginia Fabella, Maryknoll, Mary John Mananzan OSB and Amelia Vasquez RSCJ, among others). They traverse the interstices of local–global in having the privilege of a theological education abroad, deploying this education by facilitating gender-sensitising workshops among the grassroots in the post-Marcos era reminiscent of the mobile consciousness-raising classrooms during the martial law of the Marcos dictatorship regime (1970s to 1980s) and living among the churches of the poor following the Second Vatican Council (1962–5). The nun's habit becomes a signifier not only of religious piety – where individual identities were obliterated to foreground collective identities – but also the symbolic capital of religious integrity alongside street demonstrators against draconian laws and tyrannical state leaders. As both dutiful and defiant daughters to the home, church and nation, these feminist trans-national nuns stand in solidarity with other dutiful and defiant daughters, such as Filipino comfort women or former military sex slaves of the Japanese occupation of the Philippines and domestic workers, including *Japayuki* (overseas contract entertainers in Japan), resulting from the feminisation of poverty and labour.

Beyond the spatiality of having a local–global place of one's own, Asian Christian feminists transcend the temporal by bequeathing a legacy in the form of a body of theology based on the bodies and sexualities of women especially, who suffer, resist and heal. Their 'genius' is embedded in the setting up of theological bodies where inter-generational voices can be heard, documented and circulated. Noteworthy are the Korean Association of Feminist Theologians (1985) and Korean Association of Christian Women for Women Minjung (1986), which were established during the period that witnessed the rise of Korean feminist theology and the movement towards democracy and an end to authoritarian rule; and the Asian Women's Resource Centre for Culture and Theology (1988), which is committed to promoting Asian women's theology chiefly through its feminist theological journal, *In God's Image*, in realising the vision of Sun Ai Lee Park. There is also the Centre for Feminist Theology and Ministry in Japan, which was jointly established by Satoko Yamaguchi and Hisako Kinukawa as second-generation Japanese feminist theologians, to reclaim and restore into the home, church and nation the memories of women leaders in the Bible (such as Deborah) in sync with Korean women of the past, present and future and to do theology as Jesus did by affirming women whom he had encountered.

Finding her place entails, finally, transgressing her allocated space in expanding the 'feminine genius' and unsettling the gender complementarity of the sexes. The Ecclesia of Women in Asia (EWA), conceived in 2001, are Catholic feminists, both religious and lay women, theologising in Asia. EWA embodies an Asian women's ecclesiology, reimagines the *ekklesia* as it affords a dialogical space (through its biennial conferences and seven edited volumes) that critically interrogates what it means to be a woman-church in Asia. EWA's theology draws from and is sustained by the lived realities of women, men and LGBTQ communities in negotiating their identities in conversations with diverse ethnicities, cultures and religions in political economies that range from communism to neo-liberalism impacted by fundamentalisms, both political and religious, ecological sustainability and the bioethical limits of trans-humanism and post-humanism accelerated by technological advances.

Controversy

The ethos of transgression among Asian feminist theologians is made more visible through the ethos of inclusivity of some that runs counter to heteronormative ideologies within the feminist movement itself. This is because the Asian Christian feminist movement is predominantly a movement of, for and by (presumed) heterosexual women with a dedicated focus on dismantling the male/female and masculine/feminine gender binaries. A feminist movement, as such, is necessarily gender biased in leaning towards women, given the disproportionate and different ways that women and girls live out poverty, gender-based discrimination and violence compared with men and boys. While the Christian feminist movement is neither necessarily nor wholly heterosexist, there has been unwitting erasure of internal differences, especially gender and sexual diversities, from among Asian Christian feminists themselves.

Where dutiful and defiant daughters perform their genders and sexualities that intersect with their faith, the home, church and state become the loci of not only sexism, as consequences of the zeal to empower women and girls, but also homophobia and transphobia. Pope Francis, for instance, denounces 'gender ideologies' as 'terrible', as 'God created man and woman... and we are doing the exact opposite', thereby putting down the valuable work of feminist-queer theorists and theologians in deconstructing sex/gender/sexuality as fixed and unchanging categories. As a counter-discourse to the Pope's denouncement of 'gender ideologies', the theologising of Yuri Horie, an ordained lesbian minister of the United Church in Christ of Japan, is instructive here. She advocates for a 'lesbian continuum' (to borrow from Adrienne Rich) within the Asian feminist movement that recognises the diversity of heteronormative and non-heteronormative women who form the Christian feminist movement. She does so as she is cognisant of the parallelism between sexism and homophobia within the feminist movement. The sexist element reinforces the boundary between male/female and elides differences among women (where not all women are oppressed in the same way or to the same degree). The homophobic element reinforces the binary of heteronormative/non-heteronormative, resulting in LGBTQ persons from within and without the women's movement being stigmatised.

Horie's 'lesbian continuum', which imbibes an ethos of inclusivity that serves as a counter-narrative to feminist-based sexism and homophobia, however unintended, finds expression in the queer-feminist theologising of an 'epistemology of the sacred body' of LGBTQ persons in Malaysia that is predominantly Muslim. With (British) colonial legacies not only of Christianity but also sodomy laws (such as section 377 of the Penal Code of Malaysia), LGBTQ persons are not accorded full citizenship rights, bereft as they are of a spectrum of sexuality rights enshrined in the Yogyakarta Principles (the right to found a family; the right to freedom from criminalisation and sanction on the basis of sexual orientation, gender identity, gender expression [SOGIEs] and sex characteristics). The marginalisation of LGBTQ persons in modern Asia, which includes Malaysia, following the conquest of the region not only by Christianity but also by Islam, is a marked departure from the legitimacy accorded to those with diverse SOGIEs that was affirmed in pre-modern Asia.

A recuperation of such affirmation is articulated in an 'epistemology of the sacred body', which is premised on the lived experiences of LGBTQ persons of various religious persuasions and ethnicities, given the heterogeneity of Malaysians (Muslim gay-identifying man, Christian lesbian, Tibetan Buddhist bisexual mother, New Age Spiritualist female-to-male transsexual or transman and Hindu intersex mystic). Epistemic privilege is accorded to these who inhabit the margins as they negotiate, as an everyday reality, what it means to be not only spiritually queer but also queerly spiritual. The use of queer is to make strange the familiar and make sacred the profane. A queer-feminist theologising of their bodies that suffer, resist and heal renders them as the embodiment of the sacred, *imago dei*.

The way forward in solidarity with the LGBTQ community for Asian Christian feminists would be to rethink the category of 'woman', which, as Horie posits – based on Judith Butler's (a feminist post-modernist theorist) contention that not only is 'gender' a construct (therefore unstable) but also, and quite problematically, 'sex' is as well – is a contested and sometimes divisive one.

Bibliography

Brazal, Agnes M., and Andrea Lizares Si (eds), *Body and Sexuality: Theological-Pastoral Perspectives of Women in Asia* (Quezon City: Ateneo de Manila University Press, 2007).

Chan, Lúcás Yiu Sing, James F. Keenan and Shaji Geoge Kochuthara (eds), *Doing Asian Theological Ethics in a Cross-cultural and an Inter-religious Context* (Bengaluru: Dharmaram Publications, 2016).

Chung, Hyun Kyung, *Struggle to Be the Sun Again: Introducing Asian Women's Theology* (Maryknoll, NY: Orbis Books, 1990).

Gallares, Judette A., and Astrid Lobo-Gajiwala (eds), *Practicing Peace: Feminist Theology of Liberation Asian Perspectives* (Quezon City: Claretian Publications, 2011).

Kwok, Pui-Lan, *Postcolonial Imagination and Feminist Theology* (Louisville, KY: Westminster John Knox Press, 2005).

Religious Freedom

Paul Marshall

East and Southeast Asian countries vary tremendously. What they have in common is that they share an area of the globe containing almost one-third of the world's population and are tied together by trade and diplomacy. China has the world's largest population, while Brunei has among the smallest. The area has major maritime and continental states and some of the world's leading democratic states, as well as some of its most authoritarian.

The same diversity marks the religious freedom situation. North Korea is arguably the most repressive country for Christians, while Japan and Mongolia are largely religiously free. Each country has, of course, its own idiosyncrasies and regional variations, but, for the purposes of comparison, they can be divided broadly into four groups:

- the remaining communist, or self-described communist, states – China, Laos, North Korea and Vietnam;
- other authoritarian states – Cambodia and Myanmar;
- Muslim-majority countries – Brunei, Indonesia and Malaysia;
- largely religiously free countries – Japan, Mongolia, the Philippines, Singapore, South Korea, Thailand and Timor-Leste.

Each will be considered in terms of their compliance with, or violation of, international standards with regard to observance of religious freedom.

Self-professed Communist Countries

The remaining communist countries in the area are China, Laos, North Korea and Vietnam. Their economies vary, but they still profess anti-religious ideologies that foster state repression of religion. In recent decades, with the exception of North Korea, their ideological rigidity has been tempered, but they remain highly repressive. Governments still control all political and most civic activity, including religion, but now the aim is not to eradicate Christianity but to register, regulate and restrict it. North Korea has made no substantial reforms regarding religious freedom since its founding.

China remains officially atheist and under the presidency (now for life) of Xi Jinping, control of religion has become a greater priority. President

Xi stresses making religion more Chinese in orientation and, consequently, the regime has begun favouring Buddhism, Taoism and folk religions and is reviving Confucianism, in part to counter Christianity's rapid growth. Meanwhile, Christianity is routinely criticised in official media as a foreign and potentially subversive religion.

The major agencies controlling religion have been the Communist Party's United Front Work Department and the Religious Affairs Bureaus (RAB). These have exercised control through what are called patriotic religious associations, including the Catholic Patriotic Association and, for Protestants, the Three-Self Patriotic Movement. These associations are not truly independent organisations and, while their personnel may be committed Christians, they have functioned as extensions of the RAB. However, in March 2018 the Party disbanded the RAB in order to bring religion directly under the Party's Central Committee, one sign of the regime's increased attention to religion. The Ministry of State Security also monitors religious groups, particularly those thought to be cults, and Christian sects or Christianity-inspired cultic groups have been banned.

Seminary students may be examined on political conformity as well as theological knowledge. Religious literature is regulated, while religious schools for children are banned. Meetings with foreign co-religionists require state authorisation. Even the selection of church leaders must meet government approval. There has also been a tightening of restrictions on student and youth work, with children being banned from attending Christian camps and, in some cases, children and their teachers barred from attending church. Meanwhile, unofficial Catholic and Protestant churches, comprising most of China's Christians, remain illegal. Since churches are forbidden to be under the authority of an overseas body, Roman Catholicism is outlawed because it is in communion with Rome. Those who follow the church magisterium and papal authority might pay a steep price.

While Taiwan, Hong Kong and Macau remain religiously free, China now persecutes Christians at the highest rate since the Cultural Revolution, with continuing arrests, disappearances and imprisonment. The US Congressional Executive Committee on China reported that, 'In 2011, at least 40 Roman Catholic bishops remain imprisoned, detained, or disappeared'. Many had not been seen or heard from since their arrests, and some have spent decades in prison camps. As of the end of May 2018, almost 100 house churches had been shut down in Henan province alone. In 2018, more than 100 ethnic Uyghur Christians who had converted from a Muslim background were sent to 're-education' camps in Xinjiang, where they are pressured to follow communist ideology. Comparing 2016 to 2015, China Aid found that cases of persecution rose 20.2%, numbers detained rose 147.6%, numbers arrested rose 11%, numbers of people sentenced rose 30%, numbers of abuse cases rose 42.6% and the number of people abused rose 69.5%.

Even government-approved Three-Self churches have been attacked, with some forcibly demolished. Between 2013 and 2015 more than 1,200 crosses were pulled down from official churches in Zhejiang, where there is a strong Christian presence. Zhang Shaojie, a prominent pastor of the state-sanctioned Nanle County Church in Henan, was jailed for 12 years in 2014 for 'gathering crowds to disturb public order'. He has been tortured, and his daughter reports that in 2018 he was 'barely alive'.

Vietnam's constitution guarantees freedom of religion; however, laws allow the government to restrict religion to protect 'national security' and 'social unity'. There is a tendency to identify Catholics with French colonialism and Evangelicals with the USA, a former enemy. The government also tends to see religion, especially Christianity, as a threat, and so there is continuing state discrimination against Christians.

The government manages Christians through the Committee on Religious Affairs within the Ministry of the Interior, which issues regulations even on theological orthodoxy. There are also specific religion-focused units within the security forces and in the Communist Party. Special police units monitor groups the state considers extremist, including unregistered Protestants, especially among ethnic minorities, some Mennonite church leaders, and some Catholic priests and orders, particularly the indigenous Redemptorists.

A 2018 law on religion might streamline church registration and allow Christians more easily to establish medical and educational institutions and to work with foreigners. Private schools are required to follow a government-approved curriculum, which does not allow for religious instruction. Unlike China, Vietnam does not have state-controlled 'patriotic churches', but it vets Catholic bishops and monitors priests and seminaries. It has now accepted a papal nuncio, although he resides outside the country.

Few of the dozens of house-church organisations started in recent decades have received legal recognition. The government had said that its 2013 Religion Decree would speed up registration, but half of Protestant groups remain unregistered. Registration applications for about half of the 950 Hmong congregations affiliated with the government-recognised Evangelical Church of Vietnam have been denied or ignored for decades. The government is afraid that widespread conversions among the Hmong might trigger an independence movement. Given these problems, many house churches do not bother seeking legal recognition.

Evangelical leaders have occasionally been imprisoned for 'disturbing public order' or 'harming national unity'. Christian human rights defenders, including priests and pastors, are imprisoned and often serve long sentences. In 2017, nearly 100 suspected plain-clothes police in Thua Thien-Hue Province broke into the Catholic Thien An Monastery, pulled down a cross and smashed its figure of Christ in order to pressure the monastery into surrendering its land for a tourism project.

Problems are greater in rural areas, especially among communities that are not ethnically Vietnamese. Catholics and Evangelicals can suffer persecution if they evangelise or start churches in areas where Christians had been absent. There is harassment of Catholics by local authorities in the north central area, especially Nghe An and Ha Tinh provinces, and police have beaten priests. Converts to Christianity might be pressured to recant and denied government benefits if they refuse, and often they cannot register their new religion on their ID cards. Some have been severely beaten by police and had their belongings taken and homes destroyed. Among ethnic minorities, converts might suffer persecution from fellow ethnic animists, and security officials do not protect them and sometimes even support the attacks.

In Laos, evangelising and distributing religious literature is allowed legally, but in practice many restrictions remain. Some officials in the ruling Pathet Lao Movement see Christianity as a Western, particularly American, imperialist religion since the USA had supported the previous government against the communists. An additional reason for hostility is a cultural ideal of social cohesion, seen as threatened by the presence of disparate beliefs. Furthermore, while the country is nominally Marxist-Leninist, the majority of the population, including government officials, is Theravada Buddhist, which is seen as the unifying religion. Buddhism is increasingly common in official ceremonies, and the government sometimes encourages people to convert from animism to Buddhism. Christian converts from Buddhism or animism are often deemed to bring shame to their community. Government permission is required for all conversions, evangelism and church activities.

In recent years, many previously closed churches have reopened; there are reduced arrests of Christians and a public condemnation of forced renunciations of Christianity. However, forced renunciations still occur, including arrests and forced evictions from villages. In 2017, six church leaders were arrested for showing a film about Jesus as part of a Christmas programme. They were part of the registered Lao Evangelical Church (LEC), but when they failed to show village officers that they had LEC permission for the event, they were arrested (they were released in early 2018).

North Korea is an extreme communist state with a ruler who is held to be divine. Under constitutional changes in 1998, the position of president was abolished, and Kim Il-sung, the founder and first president, who had died in 1994, was named 'Eternal President'. A 2013 decree stated that the party and revolution must be carried 'eternally' by the '*Baekdu* bloodline' – that is, the Kim dynasty. The state energetically promotes this personality cult, along with lessons denigrating religion, in weekly indoctrinations at state study halls, replete with photographs of the Kims and shrines. People caught worshipping another god, or carrying a Bible, can be sent to a prison camp (along with their entire families).

The government has formed and controls the Korea Christian Federation and the Korean Roman Catholic Association. No Catholic priests live in the country, so the sacraments can be administered only by a visiting foreign priest, which now occasionally occurs. There are no ties to the Vatican and no following of the church magisterium.

Tens of thousands of Christians are incarcerated in labour camps. Thousands more keep their faith a secret, even from their families. Defectors report that Christian prisoners are given the heaviest work, the least food and the worst conditions. Those caught praying in prison are beaten and tortured. Singing a hymn can be punished by death. Those who have foreign contacts are singled out for especially harsh persecution.

In 2018, Hea Woo, a Christian escapee from the camps, described them as a 'living hell'. When people died, often their bodies were piled up outside a crematorium too small to dispose of them, so she and other prisoners would have to chop them into smaller pieces. In one prison, she lived with 50 other inmates in a cell that had 'only a hole in the floor' as a toilet. Her husband died in prison, having reportedly been arrested for being a Christian. She said she was once tortured for three days in a row, just for speaking about her faith.

Other Authoritarian States

Myanmar (Burma) and Cambodia can be as repressive as nominally communist states, but their repression is driven less by ideology than by a desire to maintain power and privilege. They have been heavily militarised states with rulers determined to stamp out any opposition. As in the nominally communist states, the state is the prime persecutor.

Cambodia has an authoritarian government with widespread human rights violations but with few specific restrictions on religion, including on the small Christian community, many of whom are ethnic Vietnamese, unless it is believed to be politically active. Buddhism is the state religion and the state supports Buddhist education and other activities, benefits denied to other religions. The constitution guarantees freedom of religion, provided it does not interfere with other religions or violate public order, and forbids discrimination based on religion. The law forbids religious groups to openly criticise other groups and bans non-Buddhists from door-to-door evangelism; non-Buddhist literature may be distributed only inside religious institutions. The law also prohibits offers of money or materials to induce people to convert.

All religious groups, including religious schools, must register with the Ministry of Cults and Religions and provide information on leaders and funding. The registration process can be laborious. There is no explicit punishment for not registering, but unregistered groups cannot claim tax exemption. New places of worship must be at least two kilometres from existing ones, although this does not apply to smaller 'offices of prayer'.

Myanmar moves between religious nationalism and general authoritarianism, now perhaps tempered by an elected government. The military regime repressed Buddhists, especially those who opposed it, but also used a policy of *Amyo, Batha, Thatana* (One Race, One Language, One Religion) to privilege Buddhism. The 2008 constitution guarantees 'freedom of conscience and the right to freely profess and practice religion' but also enshrines 'the special position of Buddhism'.

After decades of military rule, in 2015 democratic elections were held, and the opposition National League for Democracy (NLD) won an overwhelming majority. However, NLD leader Aung San Suu Kyi was barred from the presidency, though she continued to hold very significant power in the party. The constitution gives the military 25% of parliamentary seats and control over the key ministries of Home Affairs, Border Affairs and Defence.

Legal restrictions have included bans on house churches, evangelisation, and imported literature, while domestically produced literature is subject to censorship. Churches and Christian schools are allowed but face tight government surveillance and restrictions. The regime sometimes uses fines, denials of foreign aid and imprisonment to oppress Christians. Religion is also intertwined with ethnicity. The majority is ethnic Burman, and Burmans tend to be regarded as necessarily Buddhists. In contrast, while there are Burman Christians, the Christian population is largely from the Kachin, Chin, Karenni, Karen and other ethnic minorities, which have often fought for autonomy. Consequently, Christians in these areas have suffered harassment, violence and forced labour for overlapping religious, ethnic and political reasons.

Until recently, religious intolerance came from the military. Since 2012, however, there has also been intolerance from society at large, much driven by militant Buddhists. Their attacks have focused largely on Rohingya Muslims, but some Buddhist monks have called Christianity a 'guest religion' and Christians have found it harder to build churches. In July 2017, about 150 Buddhists attacked newly converted Christians in Sagaing

Province, destroying their homes and injuring seven people. In Chin and Kachin states the army had a policy of forcing Christians to replace crosses with Buddhist pagodas. In April 2018, it bombed predominantly Christian, ethnic Kachin civilians, sending 2,000 fleeing from their homes, and then restricted aid to them.

Muslim-majority Countries

The Muslim-majority countries in East and Southeast Asia include one of the world's smallest, Brunei, and the largest, Indonesia. Brunei is repressive, while Indonesia is comparatively free, though suffering from increasing radicalism. Malaysia has become more repressive. A common thread is increased radicalisation, taking different forms in each country.

Sultan Hassanal Bolkiah of oil-rich Brunei is an absolute monarch and also head of religion. He has adopted the platform of *Melayu Islam Berja* (MIB), which claims that Brunei is Malay in culture, Islamic in religion and a monarchy. All schools must propagate MIB. Non-Muslims may not use the term 'Allah', and Christian symbols, even in Christian schools, have been denounced as offensive to Muslims. The first stage of the Sultan's introduction of Islamic law began in 2014 and requires all purported Muslims, including converts to Christianity, to attend Muslim worship. The authorities restrict churches, including registered ones, and an official *fatwa* bans construction or renovation of churches. Christian evangelism and importing Bibles are prohibited, as is celebrating Christmas. The state plans to introduce capital punishment for conversion from Islam.

Malaysia has prided itself on developing a forward-looking 'civilisational Islam' (*Islam Hadhar'i*) but has become increasingly repressive toward non-Muslims. The constitution gives the right to profess, practise and propagate religion but makes Islam 'the religion of the Federation' while 'other religions may be practised in peace and harmony'. The constitution provides that nobody can be taxed to support another's religion but also that individual states may 'assist in establishing or maintaining Islamic institutions' and 'providing instruction' in Islam.

Ethnic Malays are given special economic preferences: property developers must allocate at least 30% of new housing units to them, and at a 10% discount. There is similar discrimination in education and business. Since ethnic Malays are defined as Muslim, the result is pervasive discrimination in favour of Muslims. State governments often use their authority over construction of non-Muslim places of worship and cemeteries to impede Christian activity. Federal and state governments can restrict the propagation of any religious belief among Muslims.

The large 'Jerusalem Jubilee' prayer gathering was banned in 2017 by the home minister, who argued it would hurt Muslims' feelings. Shortly afterward, the chief executive officer of the Centre for Human Rights Research and Advocacy argued that Evangelicalism should be banned since it 'threatens religious harmony'. Christians are banned from using the word 'Allah' on the grounds that this might confuse Muslims. The government and Christian leaders reached a compromise on this in 2011, but in 2014 Selangor State religious authorities raided the Bible Society of Malaysia and confiscated Malay-language Bibles.

Conversion from Islam is a major problem. Malaysia's sharia courts have exclusive jurisdiction over such conversions, and they refuse to recognise them. Those who attempt to convert can be detained for more than three months in 'Faith Purification Centres'. Dispute remains over whether children converted to Islam by their parents but who never practised it can leave the faith.

There is ongoing state-backed proselytisation of indigenous Christians in the East Malaysian states of Sabah and Sarawak. Teachers in state schools, and even kindergartens, have pressured Christian children to convert. Since the 1980s, Muslim refugees and illegal immigrants from the Philippines and Indonesia have altered Sabah's religious composition so that the large Christian minority has been reduced to political irrelevance.

Restrictions on religious freedom in Malaysia have usually been legal rather than violent, but that might be changing. In 2016 and 2017, three Christian workers disappeared. CCTV footage shows that one, Pastor Koh, was abducted in a very professional operation. The disappearances appear to be faith-related; Pastor Koh had been suspected of evangelising Muslims, and the two others were converts. The professional abduction and the casual approach taken by the police prompt fears that the state was involved.

Since the fall of the dictator Suharto in 1998, Indonesia has been on a broadly upward path politically and economically. However, the trajectory of religious freedom has been more varied. In the period 2004–14, during the presidency of Susilo Bambang Yudhoyono (SBY), the situation deteriorated. The national government consistently refused to intervene when local governments restricted religious freedom, and SBY also boosted the authority of the semi-official Indonesian Ulama Council (MUI). In 2005, he spoke at the MUI's national congress and promised to increase its authority to define proper Islam. Shortly afterwards, the MUI issued *fatwas* prohibiting inter-faith prayer, mixed marriages, inter-faith inheritance and religious pluralism. Since 2014, under President Joko Widodo, there have been positive changes in religious freedom, but, because of growing radical movements, the situation on the ground has worsened.

The 1945 constitution outlines the broad state ideology of Pancasila, whose first article is belief in one God, and combines this commitment to monotheism with religious freedom. Religious organisations are required to uphold the national ideology and are prohibited from criticising it or committing blasphemous acts against or spreading hatred of other religions. According to a 1979 decree from the Ministries of Religion and of Home Affairs, evangelism is illegal, but conversions are legal and accepted. Catholicism and Protestantism are among the six recognised religions and their adherents have the right to establish churches, obtain identity cards naming their religion and register marriages and births.

A 2006 Joint Ministerial Decree stipulates that building churches requires local community agreement, but can be in areas where another religion is the majority. Permission to build a church requires production of a list of 90 members of the congregation, signatures from 60 local households of a different faith and positive recommendations from the local religious affairs office. These conditions have empowered Islamist vigilante groups, who block construction or close churches in the name of the local community. In 2016, Muslim hardliners closed the Santa Clara Catholic Church in Bekasi only weeks after it had opened. In October 2015, a mob destroyed 11 Christian churches in the province of Aceh, and thousands of Christians fled temporarily into the neighbouring province of North Sumatra.

ISIS-inspired attacks on Christians are increasing. In November 2016, a bomb at the Oikumene Church in Samarinda killed a two-year-old girl and injured three other children. In August 2016, a man attempted but failed to detonate a bomb at a Catholic church in Medan. In May 2018, three churches were bombed in Surabaya, Indonesia's second-largest city, by ISIS-linked terrorists. There were failed attempts on two other churches.

Another major concern is Indonesia's blasphemy law. Article 156(a) of the criminal code provides for a sentence of up to five years for those 'who purposely express their views or commit an act that principally disseminates hatred, misuses or defames a religion recognised in Indonesia . . . '. This can be applied to any religion, but the most high-profile case was an accusation against Ahok, the Christian governor of the capital, Jakarta. After massive politically charged demonstrations during an election, he was sentenced to two years in prison. In May 2018, Abraham Ben Moses was sentenced to four years in prison for religious defamation for quoting a Quranic verse about marriage and for trying to convert a taxi driver to Christianity.

There are particular problems in Papua, which has a large Christian population and is the least developed part of the country. Many Papuans are worried that they are being swamped by Muslim immigrants from other parts of Indonesia, who are getting the best jobs and giving Islam increasing influence.

Largely Religiously Free Countries

Almost half of the countries in East and Southeast Asia are comparatively religiously free. These include the two Christian-majority countries in the region, Timor-Leste and the Philippines, and also include countries largely shaped by Buddhist and other Eastern religions – Japan, Mongolia, Singapore, South Korea and Thailand. Their governments do not exert much control on Christians or others, although there are problems with terrorist attacks in the Philippines.

Timor-Leste has a large Christian (overwhelmingly Catholic) majority. While it has no official state religion, the constitution commends the Catholic Church for its role in the country's liberation, and a concordat with the Holy See provides tax benefits and safeguards the church's cultural heritage. Non-Catholics, who are usually Protestant, have sometimes objected to the state's support for Catholicism, though they may apply for government funds designated for civil society organisations. There are also ad hoc incidents of individual public servants refusing Protestants service, and the civil code regulates the legal procedure only for Catholic marriages. Some government officials have refused to accept the validity of Protestant marriage and birth certificates for registering for schools and other services. The government has said that it will address these issues.

The constitution of the Philippines provides for religious freedom and prohibits the establishment of a state religion. The law requires religious groups to register if they wish to receive tax-exempt status. The Catholic Church has criticised the large number of extrajudicial killings associated with President Duterte's war on drugs. In turn, the president has labelled some church leaders 'corrupt' and 'womanisers' and warned against the influence of religion.

The principal problem facing Christians comes not from the government but from extremist Muslim terrorists operating in the south. In 2017, the Maute Group and related factions seized the southern city of Marawi. These ISIS affiliates bombed hospitals and schools. The groups went house to house searching for Christians and killing them and also burned churches and took hostages, including a priest and staff members of a Catholic church. Militants killed nine Christians at a checkpoint and killed at least one Christian man when he failed to recite the Shahada, a Muslim proclamation of faith. They also targeted Christians who refused to convert to Islam. The specific targeting of priests led some priests to arm themselves, something that Catholic church leaders have rejected.

In Japan, the USA-imposed 1946 constitution vested legislative authority in parliament, ended the emperor's divine status and brought religious freedom. Religious bodies do not have to be licensed, although doing so can bring tax benefits. Christians and others have freedom to worship and propagate their faith and freedom to train and appoint clergy. They also have rights of self-government, of religious education, to carry out charitable activities, to own and acquire property and to maintain social institutions. They can produce, import and distribute literature, receive donations and have contact with co-religionists overseas. Individuals can adopt and change religion freely.

The Mongolian constitution provides for 'freedom of conscience and religion' and prohibits religion-based discrimination, although it gives Buddhism a privileged position. Religious institutions must register with the authorities, and there are low-level restrictions on religious freedom, although these appear to be bureaucratic holdovers from the communist years rather than deliberate policy. Some Christian groups have not tried to register because they cannot meet the legal requirements, due to insufficient size or lack of dedicated worship sites. The government requires different congregations of the same church to have separate registrations, which creates problems for churches with centralised administration. Unregistered religious groups can often still function, though government officials press them to register. Evangelism is allowed unless it involves pressure, deception or spreading 'cruel' religious ideology. The government can restrict unaccompanied minors from participating in religious services, sometime requiring their parents' written permission. Obtaining visas for foreign religious workers can be difficult, and there is sometimes negative coverage of Christians in the media.

Singapore's constitution and laws provide for religious freedom, subject to restrictions relating to public order, health and morality, and also prohibit religious discrimination by the government. Religious instruction is allowed in the country's government-subsidised religiously affiliated schools if it does not include evangelism. The government stresses the need for 'religious harmony' and the Ministry of Home Affairs restrains any religious action that it believes might disturb that harmony. It is illegal to wound 'the religious or racial feelings of any person' or knowingly promote 'disharmony or feelings of enmity, hatred, or ill will between different religious or racial groups'. In 2017, the government refused entry to two foreign Christian preachers whom it said had previously made 'denigrating and inflammatory comments' about Muslims and Buddhists. The National Council of Churches advised its churches to exercise 'careful discernment' before inviting preachers, in order to preserve the 'harmonious religious environment' that currently exists. There is no legal provision for conscientious objection to military service, which creates problems for Christians committed to non-violence.

South Korea's constitution guarantees freedom of religion and forbids religion-based discrimination. The Religious Affairs Bureau of the Ministry of Culture, Sports and Tourism manages relations with the larger religious groups and seeks to promote religious freedom and mutual understanding. Religious groups do not have to register, but there are tax benefits if they do. As of 2018, a revision to the Income Tax Act discontinued some benefits for Christian clergy and other religious workers. The country does not allow for conscientious objection to military service, which creates problems for Christians committed to non-violence, although the burden has fallen almost exclusively on Jehovah's Witnesses.

Thailand's 2017 constitution provides for religious freedom and forbids religious discrimination. However, it also requires that the monarch be a Buddhist and that the government 'patronise and protect Buddhism and other religions', and it prevents 'the desecration of Buddhism in any form'. Christianity is one of five legally recognised religions and so may register to receive state benefits regarding taxes, visas or subsidies. Registration is not mandatory and non-registered groups operate freely. The government sets a limit on the number of foreign missionaries. In 2017, this was 1,357 Christian, six Muslim, 20 Hindu and 41 Sikh. However, many unregistered missionaries work freely. In an unusual quirk, Christian clergy are prohibited from voting if they are wearing religious dress.

The Future

While it is always difficult to give intelligent predictions concerning religious freedom, in a region this diverse it is doubly so. China is likely to become more repressive in coming years, while Laos and Vietnam show some signs of opening up. The North Korean government has talked of emphasising the economy rather than security, and this might presage some relaxation of control. The political coalition that had governed Malaysia since independence lost a national election in 2018 to a broadly based opposition, and this might halt its increased control of Christians. In Indonesia much depends on whether its moderate forces can resist radicalisation, and the 2019 presidential election will be a bellwether for this. Brunei is likely to stay repressive as long as the sultan, currently in his seventies, lives. There are no clear trends in Cambodia and Myanmar, and the currently largely religiously free countries are likely to stay that way in the near future. Despite high levels of repression in several countries, Christians have shown great resilience and the church is growing. This is also likely to continue in the future.

Bibliography

Fattore, Elisa, *Alleged Violations of the Human Right to Religious Freedom in Vietnam: A Case Study on the Montagnards' Minority Group* (Saarbrücken: Editions Accademiche Italiane, 2017).

Johnson, Ian, *The Souls of China: The Return of Religion After Mao* (New York: Pantheon, 2017).
Marshall, Paul (ed.), *Religious Freedom in the World* (Lanham, MD: Rowman and Littlefield, 2008).
Marshall, Paul, Nina Shea and Lela Gilbert, *Persecuted: The Global Assault on Christians* (Nashville, TN: Thomas Nelson, 2013).
Shah, Dian A. H., *Constitutions, Religion and Politics in Asia: Indonesia, Malaysia and Sri Lanka* (New York: Cambridge University Press, 2017).

Inter-religious Relations

Sivin Kit

Southeast Asia, with 11 countries stretching from the Indochina mainland to the Malay Archipelago, is located at the crossroads of Indian and Chinese civilisations, where Hinduism, Buddhism, Confucianism and Taoism have long histories. The later growth of Islam in the twelfth century and the intensified presence of Christianity with the missionary movement and foreign colonial powers in the 1500s further complicate how these religious communities historically interacted with each other and the local indigenous population. Some might describe inter-religious relations in this context as a melting pot of conflicting and complementing beliefs, values and practices; however, the reality might be closer to a mosaic of religions in constant contestation and adaptation to not only local cultures but also the impact of modernity. The influence of migration, trade and the flow of ideas cannot be underestimated, even without attributing too much to political and colonial factors. In the twenty-first century, while inter-religious relations in Southeast Asia continue to be affected by the legacy of historic cultural conditions and the impact of colonialism in the past, forces of globalisation and ongoing local internal dynamics both constrain and contribute to harmonious inter-religious relations in the respective countries.

The East Asian countries include the historically influential China and South Korea, of rising prominence and where much attention has been on the growth of Christianity. In Taiwan it appears that the development of contemporary forms of Buddhism is increasingly influential. Japan remains unique, with its fusion of developments since the Second World War and traditional Shintoism. Hong Kong offers another exceptional case of the impact of colonialism and trade on religious developments. In North Korea and Mongolia interaction with outsiders is more restricted, and thus information much more limited.

Any comprehensive account of inter-religious relations must include consideration of cultural coexistence, social cohesion, inter-faith dialogue, religious belonging, inter-religious engagement, mission and evangelism, and the role of religion in society. This essay will first offer an overview of the religious landscape, framed mainly by majority–minority dynamics. Secondly, it will present a range of key concerns that condition and to some extent constrain inter-religious relations at all levels, both structurally and culturally. Thirdly, it will highlight contributions that have sought to address these concerns. Finally, it will offer some closing reflections and remarks.

Overview of the Religious Landscape

With the exception of Singapore, which has more equal representation of different religions, the countries in Southeast Asia have a significant Buddhist, Christian or Muslim majority. In these contexts, it is often the religious minorities who articulate challenges that hinder inter-religious relations among the citizenry. However, it is also important to note that religious identities are closely associated with ethnicity. Therefore, media reports of events as inter-religious conflicts often mask underlying ethnic tensions.

The Buddhist-majority countries of mainland Southeast Asia show the dominant influence of Theravada Buddhism over religious minorities, who are mostly Christians or Muslims. Religious and ethnic identities are frequently closely intertwined. Indonesia is the largest Muslim-majority country in the world but allows relative freedom to the Christian minority. The great majority of Muslims are Sunni, with Shia and Ahmadi minorities. Often, intra-religious relations are brought to the surface when the plight of these non-Sunni Muslim minorities is highlighted. Therefore, besides the ethnic–religious combination and the legal and cultural dimensions, internal dynamics within the majority religious communities also affect inter-religious relations. In particular, the Shia and Ahmadi minorities might face more social hostility and government restrictions than the Christian minorities.

Both Brunei and Malaysia have an added legal and cultural dimension to the ethno-religious identity of Muslims. An important feature of Malaysian Islam is that ethnic Malays are Muslims by birth, which is the only ethno-religious identity stated in the Malaysian federal constitution; non-Muslim minorities do not have an ethno-religious identification in the constitution, even though the majority of Buddhists are ethnically Chinese and Hindus are majority Indian. Christians comprise a mixture of all the ethnic groups, particularly in Sabah and Sarawak, where most Christians are from the indigenous tribal communities, which also have a special position in socio-economic affirmative action policies in the nation. In Brunei, a small nation with a total population of 445,000, Malay Bruneians are presumed to be Muslims, while the Chinese populations include both Buddhists and Christians. The indigenous tribes of the Dusun, Bisaya and Murut consist of a mixture of mostly Muslims, with the rest Christians and other religious groups. Additionally, Brunei expounds an official national philosophy described as *Melayu Islam Beraja* (Malay Islamic Monarchy). Brunei is self-defined with strong Malay cultural and Islamic religious influences that are the overarching norm for not only law but also policies and regular social relations.

The only two Christian-majority countries, the Philippines and Timor-Leste, are predominantly Roman Catholic. In both cases, the non-Catholic religious minorities are smaller in percentage terms than their Christian counterparts in Buddhist- and Muslim-majority countries. The Philippines is the larger Christian-majority country in Southeast Asia. There is a significant minority of Muslims – who are mainly from various minority ethnic groups – residing mostly in the southern islands, particularly in Mindanao. The main issue of conflict for the Philippines has been the government's attempt to address the grievances and aspirations of these Muslims in Mindanao, especially in negotiations with groups such as the Moro Islamic Liberation Front. Timor-Leste has the lowest religious diversity in the region, with an overwhelming majority of the population Roman Catholic.

In contrast to all the above, Singapore can be considered the most religiously diverse country in the world. Even in a small country like Singapore, however, the religious and ethnic combination is evident. Singapore appears to be the model of inter-religious harmony compared with the rest of Southeast Asia, but this picture of peaceful coexistence of religious communities may mask latent frustrations of religious minorities.

For East Asian countries, any assessment of religious membership is fraught with difficulties. In Japan, the reported membership of religious groups is larger than the total population, suggesting that respondents self-identify with multiple religions, such as being both Buddhists and participants in religious practices of Shintoism. In China and North Korea, it is notoriously difficult to estimate the numbers adhering to different religions accurately. However, the majority–minority dynamic is evident in East Asia also, with South Korea offering an exceptional case of a balance between Buddhists, Christians and non-religious.

In sum, while the majority–minority dynamics might be a starting point for understanding inter-religious relations, one cannot neglect the cultural and ethnic roots of each religious community, especially in cases of social conflict. This is evident explicitly in countries with clear religious majorities but is present even in religiously diverse contexts such as Singapore. Attention to what is often labelled 'religious conflict' does not necessarily bring the ethnic dimension explicitly to the surface, yet, as this brief overview has shown, the religious identities of religious majorities and minorities are fundamental conditions that cannot be ignored. For instance, it is evident that while China, Japan, North and South Korea,

Hong Kong and Taiwan have deep Confucian, Taoist and Buddhist roots, the dynamics that have arisen from religious diversity, multiple belonging and non-religion feature prominently as well. Therefore, any understanding of inter-religious relations in each country and in both regions more broadly resists simplistic generalisations.

Challenges and Constraints

Since 2000, hostile relations between religious communities have not been widespread, at least not compared with the situation in parts of the Middle East, Africa and South Asia. However, neither have tensions and conflicts been totally absent from Southeast Asia and, to some extent, East Asia, particularly China. Arguably, deeper latent legal, political and socio-cultural conditions shape – and are shaped by – the majority–minority ethno-religious dynamics. Furthermore, how religious communities respond to the influence of modernisation in East Asian countries needs to be considered. Historic and modern conditions that are structural and institutional often intersect with cultural symbolic aspects of religion. The following four themes are especially important in the discussion of inter-religious relations.

First, most of the Southeast Asian countries have heightened governmental restrictions on religious communities. In some cases, these tightened regulations not only affect individual religious freedom but also discourage the cultivation of hospitable organic inter-religious encounters. Despite constitutional differences between highly restrictive countries such as Malaysia and Myanmar and relatively free countries such as the Philippines and Singapore, religious minorities generally have some space to profess and practise their religions. Many restrictions are related to concerns about religious conversions and to security issues involving public order, safety and morality.

Although Malaysia has relative freedom of religion – which means that while Islam is named as the 'religion of the federation', other religions may be practised 'in peace and harmony' – government restrictions continue to constrain the religious practices of non-Muslim minorities. Besides the power 'to control and restrict the propagation of any religious doctrine or belief among persons professing the religion of Islam', federal and state laws have provisions that tightly regulate Islamic religious affairs even for the Muslim majority. Muslims who seek to convert to another religion must first apply to a sharia court for approval to declare themselves 'apostates'. In some states, enforced 'rehabilitation' and penalties are imposed on apostates; in other states, conversion out of Islam is a criminal offence for which apostates may face a fine or even a jail term. Therefore, while inter-religious dialogue in the public sphere often addresses questions of coexistence and the common good of fellow citizens in Malaysia, conversion is a lingering theme that affects inter-religious relations, especially when questions of mission and evangelism are raised. This has been a thorny issue for Christian–Muslim relations in recent years because of allegations by Muslim groups about unethical proselytisation by Christians; Christian groups have also raised concerns over unethical missionising among indigenous tribes who were originally Christians.

In East Asia, China is well known for the severity of its restrictions and regulations on religious communities, by both the central government and local governments, compared with the rest of the region (with the exception of North Korea). Admittedly, religious freedom has not been totally absent in China, but religious revivalism – especially Christian groups who spread messages with a strong apocalyptic tone – can be deemed 'sensitive', and public proselytising is forbidden. Keeping one's religious beliefs private is the preferred option advocated by the state, for national and local 'stability'. There continue to be reports of state authorities asserting more control in confrontation with not only segments of the Christian minorities but also new religious movements such as Falun Gong, as well as restrictive policies for the religious practices of Uyghur Muslims and the religious expressions of Tibetan Buddhists. Thus, any optimism for greater religious freedom is tempered by more reports of harassments, detentions and other violations of human rights.

Second, religious nationalism in various degrees of intensity has become a growing concern. For example, Indonesia is often showcased as a model of unity in diversity among religious communities in a Muslim-majority context. Six religions have an official status in the country: Islam, Catholicism, Protestantism, Buddhism, Hinduism and Confucianism. Its national philosophy, Pancasila, which is required to be upheld, encompasses belief in one God, justice, unity, democracy and social justice. However, the inclusive nature of Indonesia is nonetheless struggling to balance contradictory tendencies. For example, Bali island is often highlighted as a historic site where Hindu influences remain strong culturally; but at the same time, Aceh is an example of increased implementation of sharia regulations. These two cases within a country show how inter-religious relations are further complicated by provincial developments in which historic and demographic factors impact the conditions affecting mutual interaction among people of different faiths. In the case of Aceh, unlike Bali, the direction of policy decisions has been unfavourable towards non-Muslim minorities. Even in the cosmopolitan capital, Jakarta, the high-profile case of Governor Basuki 'Ahok' Tjahaja Purnama's political defeat in 2017 under tremendous pressure from Muslim groups has raised concern over the mobilisation of conservative Muslim groups as well as the role of the media in generating what some have termed 'hate spin'. In the midst of changing political dynamics, there is an ongoing tension between a national philosophy that promotes tolerance and local practices that hinder hospitable relations.

In Japan, neither freedom of religion nor the secular constitution is in question. Yet in practice, perhaps to the surprise of outside observers, government leaders appear to succumb to pressure to participate in prayer for the spirits of the war dead and other related religious rituals at Shinto shrines. While Japanese citizens might identify with other religions, such as Buddhism, Shintoism is deeply rooted in Japanese culture, and its public visibility in the political sphere has caused concern for religious minorities. In China, recent studies have suggested that in contrast to its hostile response to Falun Gong, the Communist Party has favoured the development of Buddhism through institutions such as the Buddhist Association of China. In particular, both political and religious actors converge in their shared interest, on the one hand, to implement government policies, and, on the other, to define the contours of Buddhist beliefs, practices and organisation. Neither of these East Asian neighbours displays a full-blown religious nationalism, but religious favouritism, especially by state actors, hinders the cultivation of healthier inter-religious relations. Taiwan seems able to resist this trend with a version of 'twin toleration', in which the state refrains from interfering with religious affairs and vice versa. While the Taiwanese experience is not without its own controversies due to the fraudulent activity and political involvement of some religious leaders, the contribution of religious institutions to a vibrant civil society has been largely positive.

Third, the role of religion in the public sphere sheds light on the significant place of religion in the socio-cultural imagination of the majority of Southeast Asian countries. Religion continues to be a deeply rooted force, both explicitly in public discourse and implicitly in daily life. In Thailand, explicit political support for the majority religion is visible when the government is mandated to promote Theravada Buddhism through education, propagate its principles in the public sphere, and establish structural measures and mechanisms 'to prevent the desecration of Buddhism in any form'. Although there is no official state religion, there is a requirement for the king to be a Buddhist, who nonetheless also serves as the 'upholder of religions' – which includes five officially recognised religious communities: Buddhists, Muslims, Brahmin Hindus, Sikhs and Christians. All students at both the primary and the secondary level are required by law to undergo religious education that includes information about the five recognised religious groups in Thailand. Both the Christian and the Muslim communities have advised on the development of the national curriculum. The Christian community also offers private educational options up to the university level.

In contrast, Singapore appears to minimise the place of religion in the public sphere, or at least seeks to limit its influence to the socio-cultural arena. Interestingly, in 1991 the notion of 'Singapore's Shared Values' reframed social cohesion under the notion of a primary loyalty to the nation over religious identity. Religious communities are free to express themselves within this national framework, but when religious beliefs challenge Singaporean norms, offenders face severe consequences. For example, both the Jehovah's Witnesses and the Unification Church are banned by the government. The Jehovah's Witnesses object to the mandatory national service in Singapore and refuse to recite the national pledge and to sing the national anthem. The Unification Church was banned because it was considered a 'cult'. In both Thailand and Singapore, the shaping of socio-cultural imagination with more or less emphasis on religion is a top-down, government-dominated initiative.

At the grassroots level, the scenes arising from the Umbrella Movement in Hong Kong during 2014 suggest the emergence of a liberating imagination for religious participation in the public sphere – one of resistance rather than subservience. Protesters drew on religious sources and symbolism from both Christianity and Chinese religions as points of reference in their public demonstration of civil disobedience against the mainland Chinese government's antidemocratic decisions. In a rare moment of inter-religious solidarity, an image of Jesus and an open Bible were exhibited close enough to a bamboo and metal barricade shrine dedicated to the ancient Chinese general Guan Gong to signify how religious inspiration converged with the democratic aspirations of the protestors. Dialogues and debates around the role of religion in this significant citizens' movement, and the government's reaction to it, will continue to shape the future of inter-religious engagement and cooperation.

Fourth, the celebration of religious diversity and acknowledgement of religious vitality are complemented by growing concern about religious fundamentalism. In some cases, violent extremism has reached an alarming level. This concern has gained more public attention in Southeast Asia than in East Asia. In Indonesia, the religious tensions in Maluku between Christians and Muslims have received international attention both for the violence reported and for the significant peace-building initiatives. The rise of religious extremism in a Buddhist-majority context in Myanmar has surprised those who do not normally associate intolerance, even violence, with Buddhism. Debates around the 'propagation of conflict' by the Buddhist Committee for Protection of Race and Religion, a group denounced by the government, shed light on the struggle towards more peaceful approaches to inter-religious relations. Additionally, the use of anti-Muslim campaign slogans marred the 2015 elections in this emerging democratic country.

Since 2004, there has been violence between Buddhists and Malay Muslims in the deep south of Thailand. There have also been reports of authorities detaining asylum seekers and undocumented workers, mostly Pakistani Christian refugees overstaying their visas. A serious issue in the Philippines is the government's attempt to address the grievances and aspirations of Muslims in Mindanao. Inter-religious harmony is often hindered in a climate of conflict generated by violent extremism and then counter-terrorist operations where the dividing line between ethnicity and religious identity is blurred. Nonetheless, important inter-religious initiatives such as the Philippines Council of Evangelical Churches in dialogue with the leaders of the Moro Islamic Liberation Front complement official initiatives, such as the Presidential Task Force on Inter-religious and Inter-cultural Concerns.

The cases of Indonesia, Myanmar, South Thailand and the Philippines have brought to the surface complex ways in which normative religion is in tension or contradiction with lived religion on the ground – especially when socio-political and economic factors are taken into account, such as in the Rohingya crisis in Myanmar and the long-extended conflict in the far south of Thailand with the Malay Muslims. The militancy of either a majority or a minority community generates a hostile environment, making healthy inter-faith relations virtually impossible. Yet even in the midst of seeming impasse, there appears to be some progress. Minority Christian groups such as the Philippines Council of Evangelical Churches are reaping some preliminary positive results. The experience of Maluku, Indonesia, also offers lessons in peace-building and reconciliation among Christians and Muslims.

Significant Contributions and Responses

The assemblage of structural and cultural aspects of religious communities at times suggests a pessimistic outlook for inter-religious relations, particularly for religious minorities in Southeast Asia. However, contributions that restrain inter-religious conflicts from escalating into violent extremism or, more positively, efforts to re-imagine inter-religious solidarity, are important interventions for both the short-term and the longer-term well-being of religious communities. Although concerns similar to those in Southeast Asia also exist in East Asia, there are also distinctive features, due to cultural and linguistic homogeneity combined with historical trajectories entangled with the reality of the impact of modernity, that resist any reductionist understanding. A number of noteworthy areas that are significant for inter-religious relations in both regions can be identified.

First, religious leaders have initiated or participated in various institutional bodies in order to engage governing authorities. For instance, the Myanmar Inter-religious Council has risen in prominence as the nation struggles in its democratic maturity and governance. In the wake of tensions from the Rohingya crisis, there have been important initiatives to monitor and counter hate speech. One representative from the Inter-faith Dialogue Group, Catholic Cardinal Charles Maung Bo, raised awareness within the Burmese press and the international community of the need to address actions that incite hatred and hostility towards religious minorities, as well as the importance of celebrating religious diversity. In Malaysia, Christians organise themselves around the Christian Federation of Malaysia, the Association of Churches in Sarawak and the Sabah Christian Council, from which they speak on issues related to Christian interests and religious freedom. Christian leaders also played a key role in the founding and ongoing work of the Malaysian Consultative Council of Buddhism, Christianity, Hinduism, Sikhism and Taoism. All these religious bodies and leaders have voiced increasing concern over matters of religious practice, freedom, coexistence and conversion. Interestingly, these initiatives often have been led by representatives of religious minorities.

In Taiwan, the Taiwan Inter-faith Foundation, created by Buddhist, Taoist and Yiguandao associations, works in parallel with the Association for Inter-Faith Dialogue, which also includes Christian churches and other new religious communities. The two have worked together with government authorities to address matters of law on religion. In South Korea, the Korean Council of Religions of Peace has worked with Buddhist groups and the Catholic Church not only in inter-faith dialogue programmes but also in issue-centred campaigns.

In cases of controversy and conflict, religious leaders are often the first to advocate calm and peaceful responses. In some cases, however, these religious leaders have also chastised the ruling powers for politicising religion through public statements. Thus, religious institutions and religious leaders, especially for minorities, have to navigate through difficult terrain, depending on the particular context. Some who prefer religion to be private have also criticised religious leaders from both religious-majority and religious-minority communities for getting involved in politics. In times of peace and calm, religious leaders strengthen social cohesion through bridge-building initiatives for mutual understanding. Although one might argue that the role of religious leaders within these bodies is necessarily elitist and focused on religious leadership and government authorities, nonetheless their public voice provides unifying material for collective action from religious communities and civil society actors.

Second, Christian theologians in Southeast Asia and East Asia have pioneered significant theological resources – frameworks, approaches and contextual theologies – that address issues and concerns relevant to inter-religious relations. In the practice of inter-faith dialogue, practitioners from the Protestant traditions and religious traditions from other faiths drew inspiration from the comprehensive approach proposed by the Federation of Asian Bishops: dialogue of life, dialogue of action, dialogue with the poor and marginalised, dialogue of religious experience and dialogue of theological exchange. These basic distinctions allow for participation at all levels, from the leadership to the congregation. The Association of Theological Education of Southeast Asia has championed the transformation of the Critical Asian Principle into Guidelines for Doing Theology in Asia. This continues to be important in the development of contextual theologies that are relevant to the social, economic, political and religious realities of Christians in the region. The Centre for the Study of Asian Christianity at Trinity Theological College in Singapore has drawn attention to the value of the popular religiosity of Southeast Asian Christianity for theological reflection and historical work. However, these important contributions have not necessarily trickled down to the weekly sermons in the pulpit. There remains a gap between the rigorous and often constructive theological production and day-to-day Christian experience at the grassroots level.

Nonetheless, contextual theologians have consistently given attention to dialogical approaches to contextual theologising. For example, the early works of Asian theologians such as Kosuke Koyama advocated for – and modelled – doing theology with an inter-religious sensibility, inspired by his missionary experience in Thailand and his work in Japan. The contributions of C. S. Song encouraged theological reconstruction informed by Asian cultures and socio-political realities, particularly in Taiwan. Subsequent Southeast Asian theologians have followed up with the notion of 'neighbourology'. This seeks to move beyond Christian–Buddhist relations in Thailand to encompass Christian–Muslim relations, as in the work of Albert Walters in Malaysia. Recent work by Joas Adiprasetya is informed by Trinitarian theology, aiming to relate the notion of mutuality and perichoresis to questions of religious belonging and identity in the context of the multi-religious lived experience in Indonesia.

The works of Catholic Filipino Daniel Pilario push Christian thought towards more a more grounded approach to contextual theologising and inter-faith dialogue. Similarly, Pentecostal Simon Chan, speaking from a Singaporean context, proposes a grassroots theology that interacts with Confucianist concepts and values, such as the family and other social relations. Malaysians such as Methodist Hwa Yung have raised concerns over the lack of attention to power encounters and the spiritual dimension, which are relevant not only to Charismatics and Pentecostals in Asia but also to their neighbours from other faiths (especially in the context of folk religious practices). While more work remains to be done to sustain inter-religious and inter-cultural openness, Christian theologians across a variety of confessions have advocated or produced contextual theological contributions shaped by inter-religious concerns. As emerging contextual theologies mature, they will continue to wrestle with the challenge of forging a confident Christian identity that will engage the religious other, whether Christians are in the majority or the minority.

Third, the participation of religious people through educational initiatives suggests more inclusive interactions for emerging leaders and at the grassroots level of religious communities. This is particularly true for youth and university students. For example, since 2000, mutual exchange programmes at the undergraduate and graduate levels have been intensified and more intentional. The National University of Singapore has brought students to the region for inter-faith exposure programmes, thus grounding the reflection of inter-religious round-table dialogues in lived realities. The University of Malaya and the Malaysia Theological Seminary have had mutual visits for students from the Islamic department and the theological departments, in which religious leaders and religious officers in training exchange ideas, values and personal narratives. The Inter-religious Studies Programme of the Consortium of Inter-religious Studies based in Indonesia is a formalised academic programme with inter-religious relations at the centre of its research and academic production. The Kyoto Graduate Union of Religious Studies, founded in 2005 by one Christian university and six Buddhist universities in Japan, offers opportunities for academic exchange between students as well as scholars from different strands of Buddhism and other religions. While academic freedom varies from country to country, these programmes and events suggest that educational institutions are intentionally and strategically incorporating an inter-religious dimension into their educational efforts.

Besides these local, national and regional collaborations, complementary training programmes such as the World Council of Churches' Youth in Asia Training for Religious Amity support local initiatives to develop leadership in the area of religious peace-building. The Tao Fong Shan Centre in Hong Kong is renowned for its early work in Buddhist–Christian dialogue, inculturation in Chinese culture and Christian spirituality. The Centre continues to be an important collaborator regionally and internationally through conferences, workshops and relevant capacity-building programmes. Additionally, with the support of the Lutheran World Federation, efforts are being made in Indonesia to empower youth through social media, thereby bringing inter-religious concerns to the emerging digital culture. These and other innovative approaches offer more promising ways to invite the participation of the younger generation of Christians as well as other like-minded youth who are keenly aware of the threat posed by inter-religious hostility.

Inter-religious cooperation via educational institutions and the training arms of religious bodies provides an important opportunity for dialogue, understanding and learning without the legal and political pressure that often plagues controversial engagements. This is an important safe space in which students and faculty have relative freedom to experiment with new approaches in a friendlier environment. However, it must be noted that there have been occasions when programmes that were perceived to be apologetic in nature or, worse, polemical against other religions (usually minority groups) have been condemned in the public sphere.

Crossroads for Religious Communities

The narrative of inter-religious relations in Southeast Asia and East Asia is characterised not only by diversity but also by complexity, and includes ambiguity, fluidity, tension and even, at times, inter-religious hostility. Religious communities are confronted with the reality that they will be coexisting with each other, at times with harmonious friendly neighbourliness and, yet, at other times with controversies and conflicts. In the light of both discouraging and encouraging developments around inter-religious relations, religious communities might find themselves at a crossroads where they must decide how they will respond to the various conditions and constraints in a given context.

The tendency for religious minorities is to seclude themselves in a ghetto-like mode of existence or to descend into a disempowered victim mentality. Where there is limited religious freedom – at least to profess and practise (if not propagate) their faith – Christians are challenged to find ways to re-imagine fresh expressions of faith that are nonetheless still faithful to their core Christian identity. This challenge to reflect on one's religious identity and practice is also experienced by Muslim, Buddhist and Hindu minorities and, even more so, by those with no religious affiliation or practitioners of indigenous religions. However, when both majority and minority religious communities, from the grassroots to the leadership, are able to move beyond an inward self-preservation and defensive mode and intentionally draw on the best of their religious resources, collaborating with people of other faiths or life stances for inter-religious (and inter-cultural) solidarity and engagement, then we might envision a brighter future for all the people of Asia.

Bibliography

Anderson, Emily (ed.), *Belief and Practice in Imperial Japan and Colonial Korea* (Singapore: Springer, 2016).

Bouma, Gary, Rodney Ling and Douglas Pratt (eds), *Religious Diversity in Southeast Asia and the Pacific: National Case Studies* (London: Springer, 2009).

Clart, Philip, and Charles B. Jones (eds), *Religion in Modern Taiwan: Tradition and Innovation in a Changing Society* (Hawai'i: University of Hawai'i Press, 2003).

Liow, Joseph Chinyong, *Religion and Nationalism in Southeast Asia* (Cambridge: Cambridge University Press, 2016).

Welter, Albert, and Jeffrey Newmark (eds), *Religion, Culture, and the Public Sphere in China and Japan* (Singapore: Springer, 2017).

Migration

Maruja M. B. Asis

After more than four decades, international migration has become an enduring feature of the social landscape in East and Southeast Asia. Migrants move for work, marriage or study. The region also has its share of migrants who have been forcibly displaced due to war, conflict or environmental change. Because it involves the largest numbers and raises many policy challenges, the temporary labour migration of workers in less-skilled occupations has dominated discussion of international migration in Asia.

Asia is home to 79.6 million international migrants, or about 30% of the total international migrant population of 257 million. Most international migration in Asia takes place within the vast continent. The Gulf Cooperation Council countries and other countries in Western Asia together are the destination of more than half (54%) of the international migrants in Asia, while East and Southeast Asia combined host one-fifth (22.2%). East and Southeast Asia have a diverse migration profile. East Asia consists primarily of destination countries and areas that are among the more attractive labour market destinations in the region: South Korea, Japan, Taiwan and Hong Kong. Of the four, Japan has remained wedded to its policy of not admitting foreign workers in less-skilled occupations. Nonetheless, less-skilled migrant workers have been present in Japan, but they enter the country as trainees or technical interns or as descendants of former Japanese emigrants, the *Nikkeijin*. After decades of guardedness, Japan's lawmakers passed a bill on 8 December 2018 to admit foreign workers in sectors facing severe labour shortages such as construction, nursing, farming, transport and tourism. Japan may have stalled bringing in foreign workers who perform less skilled work, but, like other developed economies, it did not escape the need to turn to labour migration.

China is an origin country – largely of students, the highly skilled and investors – but in recent years it has been attracting international migrants, who are drawn to the opportunities offered by China's vibrant economy. It is also attracting return migrants, who are pulled by the country's impressive growth while simultaneously contributing to China's development.

Southeast Asia, on the other hand, is a patchwork of origin countries (the Philippines, Indonesia, Vietnam, Cambodia, Myanmar and, to some extent, Laos), destination countries (Singapore and Brunei) and countries that are both origin and destination (Malaysia and Thailand). Destination countries in the region are also receiving migrants from other regions in Asia and beyond, while significant labour migration from Southeast Asia has been directed towards the oil-rich Gulf countries since the 1970s.

Compared with Europe and, to some extent, the USA, the migration–religion nexus has not been a focus of attention in terms of policy and research interest in East and Southeast Asia. This might be due to migration not generating tensions or debates in Asia in the way that religion has ignited deep cleavages, mostly driven by unease over Muslim immigrants, in Europe. The temporary labour migration regime in Asia is perhaps a key factor in minimising concerns over the influx of the foreign population in the region: migrants are allowed to work and stay only for the duration of their employment contracts; they are not supposed to settle; and they generally bear the onus of adjusting to the lifeways of their intended destination country. In relation to the last factor, in origin countries in the region many migrants undergo pre-deployment orientation seminars to prepare themselves for the working and living conditions that they will likely encounter overseas. In some origin countries – such as the Philippines, Vietnam and Cambodia – similar preparations for marriage migrants going to South Korea (overwhelmingly women) are offered as well.

By comparison, employers or families of marriage migrants in the destination countries do not have to know about the culture of the migrant workers or foreign spouses. A few examples of initiatives introduced in destination countries are worth noting. In Singapore, the government requires first-time employers of foreign domestic workers, as well as employers who change foreign domestic workers frequently, to complete the online Employers Orientation Programme to provide them with basic information for hiring and dealing with foreign domestic workers in their employ. In Hong Kong, the Mission for Migrant Workers introduced the Happy Homes Programme to disseminate positive experiences of employers and foreign domestic workers; to produce information materials on Christian values of love, care and fellowship among churchgoers; and to raise employer awareness. South Korea has established multicultural centres to ease the adjustment of foreign spouses to Korean society. Despite their name, however, the programmes and supports offered by these centres are aimed at training foreign spouses on how to be Korean, and no mention is made of orienting Korean families to the cultural background of their new members.

Migration in the region involves the movement of people from and to societies of diverse religious traditions. The primary country of origin, the

Philippines, is distinctly Christian (largely Roman Catholic). Indonesia is Muslim. Vietnam is officially an atheist state, although it has adherents of Buddhism, Confucianism and Taoism. Myanmar, Cambodia and Laos are mainly Buddhist. On the destination side, Malaysia and Brunei are predominantly Muslim. Singapore's Chinese, Malay and Indian composition results in a mosaic of faith traditions with a layer of secularism. Thailand is Buddhist. Japan, South Korea, Hong Kong and Taiwan are secular.

The results of three surveys conducted by WIN/Gallup between 2008 and 2018 reveal varying degrees of religiosity among countries in the region. In general, between 82% and 97% of respondents in the origin countries considered themselves religious; Vietnam is the exception, ranking among the 20 least religious countries in the world, with only about a third describing themselves as religious. Religiosity in destination countries diverges between the highly religious (Thailand and Malaysia) and the less religious (ranging from 13% in Japan to 45% in Taiwan). Only 7% considered themselves religious in China, the lowest globally, although, given China's huge population (1.4 billion), 7% translates into some 98 million people in absolute figures. Despite its official stance as an atheist state, since the reforms instituted by Deng Xiaoping in the early 1980s, the number of Christian adherents has grown. In the early 1980s, an estimated 6 million Christians lived in China. Current estimates vary, but they all point to a surge. In 2010, the Pew Research Center estimated 67 million Christians; others suggest between 100 and 130 million. The renewed interest in religion has been attributed to the rise of the modern, wealthier China and a people in search of meaning in their lives.

This essay explores the interface between migration and religion in East and Southeast Asia, focusing specifically on encounters between migration and Christianity. Although a minority religion in the region, Christianity has inspired highly visible initiatives in the promotion of the dignity of migrants. The resulting discourse and actions contribute to the predominantly market-driven view of migration and migrants. This essay examines the migration–Christianity nexus by discussing how migration bears on Christian churches' practices in response to the phenomenon of migration and by exploring how Christianity affects the religious practices and faith life of migrants. Due to data gaps and limitations, the essay cannot provide a comprehensive overview of how this nexus operates in the different origin and destination countries, migrant groups and Christian theologies and churches. That some sites, migrants and churches are discussed more than others is more a reflection of extant literature than an indication of differential importance. As an exploratory piece, the essay aims to generate more critical conversations and further research on migration and Christianity in this highly mobile region.

International migration presents challenges and opportunities to the witness of Christian churches and communities in East and Southeast Asia. From a pastoral point of view, the weakening or erosion of the faith of Christian migrants who find themselves in a non-Christian and/or secular milieu is a concern. On the other hand, migrants also possess an evangelising or theologising potential: by their faithful witness, they can be bearers of the Good News to all peoples. As the succeeding discussions suggest, Christian institutions at home and overseas are rising to address both the alienating and the evangelising potentials of migration.

A Ministry of Accompaniment

As mentioned above, Christian migrants in the region are largely from the Philippines, which is one of two countries in Asia as a whole (the other is Timor-Leste) where Christians, mostly Roman Catholics, comprise the majority of the population. At one level, the unabated migration of Filipinos since the 1970s reflects the continuing search for better opportunities in the global labour market. Seen through the lens of religion, Filipino migration is also the movement of Christians from the Philippines to the rest of the region and beyond. This large-scale and sustained migration has alerted Christian churches in the Philippines that their flocks are no longer contained within the Philippines.

In light of this, Christian churches in the Philippines have taken a trans-national turn in tending to their flocks, which entails accompanying Filipinos in their diasporic journeys while also looking after the families left behind in the Philippines. The policy of strictly temporary labour migration of destination countries in the region has kept migrant workers and their families apart. To ensure that temporary labour migration will not develop into permanent settlement, family reunification is not allowed for migrant workers in less-skilled occupations (who account for the majority of migrant workers in the region). In the Philippines and other origin countries, the migrant ministry includes programmes supporting the families left behind, such as psychosocial support for children, or parenting classes for fathers, mothers or grandparents who have assumed care-giving responsibilities. In the early years of the Philippines' labour migration experience, Christian churches and related organisations were among the pioneering providers of services addressing the myriad concerns of overseas Filipino workers and their families. One example is the information and education programme to prepare migrants for their departure; this was later adopted by the government and was made mandatory for departing migrant workers. In addition, Christian churches and organisations also number among the persistent voices promoting the protection of migrants.

In the Philippines, the response of the Catholic Church in shepherding its flock has been shaped by the realities of Filipino migration and the response of the Universal Church to the global phenomenon of migration. The social teaching of the Catholic Church on migration and the structures that link the Universal Church and local churches provide the 'software' and the 'hardware', respectively, for collective reflections and actions. At the institutional level, church engagement with Filipino migration is manifested in the work of the Episcopal Commission for Migrants and Itinerants of the Catholic Bishops' Conference of the Philippines, religious congregations and their counterparts overseas, and a host of Catholic-inspired organisations as they engage with relevant stakeholders. The global distribution of Filipinos prompted the Catholic Church in the Philippines to send priests, religious and pastoral workers to bring the church to those migrants. Another approach is to coordinate with its counterparts in destination countries. The church also makes use of technology to enable Filipinos abroad to participate in key religious activities in the Philippines, such as the online *Visita Iglesia*, the practice of visiting seven churches following the Mass on Holy Thursday, which is made available during the Lenten season.

Philippine-based Protestant and other Christian churches have been equally attentive to the needs of overseas Filipinos, by coordinating with affiliated churches, by developing a specific ministry for this particular population, or by establishing a church overseas. The last has nourished the expansion of two homegrown churches. The Iglesia ni Cristo (INC; Church of Christ), registered in 1914, was local until 1968, when it established its first overseas congregation in Hawaii. With the migration of Filipinos to other countries, the INC followed its flock and now counts 6,000 local congregations and missions in 142 countries and territories around the world. Similarly, sociologist Jayeel Cornelio attributes the expansion of the Jesus Is Lord Church Worldwide outside the Philippines to the migration of Filipinos. Founded by Brother Eddie Villanueva in 1978, the church has grown to an estimated membership of 5 million and has established some 60 churches overseas. In establishing a presence overseas, these homegrown churches also aim to evangelise and convert non-Filipinos as well as Filipino migrants of other faith traditions.

A Ministry of Welcome

In the highly industrialised societies of Japan, South Korea, Hong Kong, Taiwan and Singapore, the biblical teaching of hospitality and welcome to the foreigner goes against state policies hinged on border control and a welcome mat that extends only to foreigners with skills and capital while imposing a conditional welcome to less-skilled migrant workers. The call for Christian churches to welcome foreigners is the call to be a missionary church to peoples who are at their very doorstep.

For Catholic migrants, the widespread presence of the church presents access to a familiar institution in a strange or even hostile environment. Migrants gravitate to the church not only for spiritual reasons but also to meet co-ethnic believers and to avail themselves of support. One reason why Filipino migrant workers are better protected than other Asian migrant workers is the former's tendency to seek out the church wherever they are. Initially, Filipinos attend the 'international' Sunday Mass (usually the English mass for foreigners). At some point, they will request a Tagalog mass. Then they will organise choirs and prayer groups and introduce religious traditions from the Philippines (such as the nine-day Christmas Masses, the devotion to the Holy Child and the block rosary). In addition to religious activities, the local church and the Filipino community develop programmes and services to help migrants encountering problems in destination countries. Usually, these programmes provide legal assistance, psychosocial support, shelter, skills training programmes and social activities, such as sports-fests and cultural events. Specific Masses and ministries involving other groups, such as Indonesians and Vietnamese, follow similar phases of development. The Catholic Church in Korea has introduced a continuing training programme called Exodus for those involved in the pastoral care of migrants to develop skills, to have a forum for exchange and to enhance coordination.

Coordination between origin and destination churches has forged trans-national cooperation. One recent example is the agreement between the Catholic Church in Vietnam and that in Japan to work together to provide pastoral care to migrant workers and diaspora populations in both countries. Although the two have small populations of Catholics, the church saw the need to establish pastoral programmes to serve the needs of 200,000 Vietnamese workers in Japan and 100,000 Japanese in Vietnam.

The service-delivery aspect of Christian churches and organisations is well established across the region. To reach non-Christian migrants, some organisations establish centres outside the church premises and recruit laypersons so as not to prevent non-Christians from accessing needed services. In destination countries, Christian churches and organisations also actively participate in the advocacy and promotion of the protection of migrants' rights. In Korea, many Christian NGOs played a leading role in the reform of migration policies, and eventually the Korean government established a formal system for bringing in and protecting foreign workers. The advocacy role of faith-based organisations is tempered by the political climate in destination countries. In places like Hong Kong, Japan, Taiwan and South Korea, civil society organisations in general and faith-based organisations in particular have more freedom to push for the promotion of migrants' rights. Where this is not possible, faith-based organisations concentrate on less political activities, such as counselling and skills formation.

Gifts Migrants Bear

Migrants are not just the recipients of what the church can offer. They also contribute to the local church in various ways. Given the generally small and ageing population of Christians in these countries, the arrival of Christian migrants boosts the membership and brings new life to the congregations. Japan is a case in point: Catholic migrants from the Philippines and Vietnam have been described by foreign missionaries as a 'breath of fresh air'. Migrants not only increase membership but also add their youth to the profile of believers.

Managing cultural diversity in the church, however, is a more difficult ground to tread. With the arrival of migrants, the usual ways of doing things are unsettled, and migrants also have to adapt to different practices and traditions. The building of a multicultural church thus calls for dialogue and inter-cultural mediators to bridge migrant members and local members. In recent fieldwork in Kaohsiung, Taiwan, the author witnessed a multicultural Mass conducted in both Chinese (for the local parishioners) and English (for the migrant parishioners) and songs in Chinese, English and Tagalog. To facilitate understanding, when the priest used Chinese for some parts of the Mass, the English translation was projected, and vice versa.

Welcoming migrants who come bearing religious traditions from their home countries makes visible the diversity of religious expressions in the receiving churches. Under conditions of dialogue and understanding, the different religious expressions of the same faith can be enriching, attesting to the reality of the proclamation of God's kingdom to all. Alternatively, the differences can result in 'othering' and even contentions about 'proper' practices and 'true' faith among the community of believers.

Migrants as Faith Bearers

Migrants embark on their journeys in the hope of achieving transformation – in most cases, a better life for themselves and their families. For this reason, migration has been described as a kind of secular pilgrimage. The road to the hoped-for better life is fraught with many challenges. In the context of labour migration in Asia, the odds are stacked against migrant workers in less-skilled occupations, as documented by the many violations of migrant workers throughout the migration process. The vulnerabilities of migrants increase when they migrate outside of the legal channels or, worse, when they fall victim to traffickers. Marriage migrants, particularly those arranged by commercial marriage brokers, also face risks and vulnerabilities. Abuse, exploitation, prejudice and discrimination can sorely test the faith of migrants, as does exposure to different value systems in non-Christian or culturally diverse environments.

In the region, the impact of migration on the faith, religiosity or spirituality of Filipino migrants has received research attention, much of which focuses on the faith life of migrants in the destination countries. Actually, faith surfaces in different phases of migration. Before leaving, praying for safety during overseas employment is part of the preparation of overseas Filipino workers. Novenas or prayers to the Mother of Perpetual Help Shrine, the Black Nazarene and the *Santo Niño* (Holy Child Jesus) are among the devotions that are popular with Filipino migrants, who invoke their help and guidance before they leave. While they are overseas, as mentioned above, Filipinos seek out churches. They are visible in churches in destination countries not just as Mass-goers but also in church-related organisations, including those that provide support for fellow migrants. Filipino migrants often cite faith in God as helping them cope with the challenges of working overseas, separated from their families.

Anthropologist Nicole Constable observed that migration can have both an alienating and a theologising impact on migrants confronted with multiple challenges of working and living in a foreign environment: some opt to join religious groups that remind them of religious practices from their home country, some join a new group, and some ignore religion or shut it out of their lives. Based on their study of Filipino migrants in Hong Kong, Jonas Nakonz and Angela Wai Yan Shik suggested that migration challenges can incline migrants towards more Charismatic religious groups, which they might find more attuned to helping them cope with their conditions. The families left behind in the Philippines similarly cite faith in God as the main factor that keeps their families intact despite the distance. Faith thus can be empowering for migrants, as it gives them courage, provides them with a moral compass and buoys their hopes.

A study of Filipino domestic workers underscored spirituality as an important personal resource in dealing with various stresses. Praying and reading the Bible were among the coping strategies to which migrants resorted. Through these means, God is not distant but is rather part of the migrants' 'network' who provides an anchor and a refuge from their isolation and difficult circumstances in a foreign land.

The discourse and the literature on migrant empowerment, however, tend to focus solely on the political aspects of empowerment and view faith or anything related to spirituality as disempowering because it does not lead to changes in the structural conditions of migrants.

While some migrants turn to God to face their challenges, others can find their faith life diminished by the demands or requirements of their occupation and by encounters with different value systems in foreign lands. Christian migrants in destination countries that are predominantly Muslim might not have easy access to Christian churches. Catholic migrants might be prevented from attending Mass on Sundays if they are not given a day off. Female Christians who work in the entertainment sector might find their faith compromised by having to entertain male clients. The religious practices of those who work in private homes can be subject to the surveillance of their employers.

In Hong Kong, for example, an Indonesian migrant worker could not practise praying five times during the day, as is the custom in Islam, and was chastised by her employer, who told her that she came to Hong Kong to work, not to pray. Some scholars propose that, although marginalised in Hong Kong society, Indonesian migrants have made Islam visible in the city through their expressions of Islamic piety through prayer, the use of the veil and adherence to a halal diet. The same argument can be advanced about Filipino workers, whose faith expressions make visible the Christian or Catholic faith in the destination countries, also conveying that Filipino migrants are not just workers. Religious celebrations in public spaces allow migrants to visibly assert their space, albeit temporarily, in the destination. In Taipei, St Christopher's Parish introduced *Santacruzan*, a religious procession held during the month of May to commemorate the finding of the Holy Cross by Empress Helena, the mother of Emperor Constantine. The annual procession has become part of the May events in Taipei and has received support from the City of Taipei in its programmes to support the cultural activities of various migrant groups. Previously, *Santacruzan* was a Filipino event, but in more recent editions, Vietnamese migrants also had representatives who served as *sagalas* (women who portray historical or biblical characters) and consorts. In the last *Santacruzan* organised by Our Lady of the Miraculous Medal Church in Kaohsiung, several Buddhist monks walked with parishioners during the procession. According to the priest who invited them, the monks readily accepted the invitation because they believe that 'while we differ in how we worship, there is only one God in heaven'.

In foreign lands, migrants are freed from the norms and mores of their home countries, which can lead to practices and behaviours that are subject to social control at home. Overseas, migrants meet other migrants, which can lead to friendships or romantic relationships with people of other faiths or no faith. In Hong Kong, conversion to Islam has been observed among Filipino women migrants due to their romantic relationships or inter-marriage with Pakistani men. Pastoral workers in Korea and Taiwan have shared concerns about extramarital affairs, children born out of these relationships, and incidences of abortion and same-sex relationships.

Chinese Migration

The link between migration and Christianity is also contributing to the rise of Christian believers in China observed since the 1980s. This trend is a reversal of the narrative of religious persecution in China, which led to different waves of emigration of Christians, particularly after China embraced communism in 1949. Although China became an atheist state, Christianity was not completely stamped out, as 'underground' churches kept the faith and state-sanctioned or registered churches were allowed to operate. The opening of China to the world since the 1980s has been accompanied by increasing international migration. Initially, those who emigrated were government-supported officials or scholars, but as China's economy improved, more Chinese started to migrate independently. China is the number-one source country of international students, and like the trend observed for Korea, well-off families are starting to send their children for international education even at the pre-university level. The migration of students, the highly skilled and investors is a departure from the unauthorised migration of Chinese to Europe and the Americas in the 1990s.

Several scholars have commented that international migration leads Chinese migrants to encounter religion and exposes them to religious freedom. The migration experience can also engender questions about identity and the search for meaning in a new environment that could provide openings for exploring religion. It is important to point out that the receptivity of destination countries plays a significant role in the conversion of Chinese migrants to Christianity. In the USA, for example, the welcome, assistance and fellowship provided by campus ministry programmes have paved the way for Chinese migrants to encounter and embrace Christianity. Some campus ministries and churches in the USA are reported to have a specific focus on Chinese migrants. A study by the Singapore Management University examines how Chinese Christian converts in Singapore reconcile being Chinese and being Christian and how their conversion affects their relationships with other Chinese migrants, Singaporeans, family and friends. According to the study, many Christian groups in Singapore focus their evangelisation efforts on Chinese migrants. The implications of conversion on Chinese migrants' social relationships and their integration in Singaporean society suggest multifaceted outcomes. Some converts had less interaction with non-Christian Chinese migrants; others felt a sense of in-betweenness upon their return to China.

The role of religion, particularly Christianity, in integration is an interesting question to pursue further in the Asian context. In Australia, where an increase in Christian affiliation among the Chinese had been noted previously, the 2016 census revealed that the decline in Christian affiliation seen in the general Australian population was also observed among the Chinese population. One of the reasons could be that conversion to Christianity and church affiliation, which traditionally played a part in the acculturation of first-generation immigrants, might not be as important a source of support for the younger generation. Another reason could be that the churches are not responding to the concerns and interests of their young members. Other issues to explore are the return of converts to China and their experiences, and the trans-national links between Chinese Christians overseas and Christianity in the homeland.

The social and political landscape in China cannot be ignored. Although some doors had been opened, recent reports indicate renewed persecution of Christians and other religious adherents in China. It is for this reason that some observers consider China to be a 'religious wild card'. The notion that the future of Christianity is moving away from the West and shifting to Asia means that, politics aside, imagining the future will inevitably have to include the migration of people as well as the migration of faith.

Conclusion

This essay has outlined the ways in which migration and Christianity impact on each other by considering the responses of Christian churches and organisations to the phenomenon of migration and how the migration experience affects the faith life and practices of migrants. Although Christianity is a minor religion in East and Southeast Asia, the migration of Christian migrants, mostly from the Philippines, has allowed Christianity to be spread to some extent in non-Christian destination countries in the region. Given the temporary labour migration regime in the region, only migrant workers move: they leave their families behind, and migrants are not expected to settle and to integrate in destination countries. Thus, unlike permanent migrants who become residents and/or nationals of destination countries, temporary labour migrants are trans-national subjects who are not full members of either origin or destination countries. Under this migration regime, institutions in origin countries, including Christian bodies, are drawn into accompanying migrants and the families they leave behind through the different phases: preparing migrants before they leave, supporting migrants and their families at home while the former are overseas, and supporting the reintegration of returning migrants. Christian churches and organisations have become trans-national in tending to their flocks, and in the process some homegrown Christian churches have expanded to other countries. At the destination side, Christian institutions are called to welcome migrants, a commandment with biblical foundation addressed to all Christians. Christian churches and organisations are one of the spaces of welcome for migrants in destination countries. This is significant not least for the growing number of migrants from China. In their welcoming, Christians have the opportunity to share the Good News with migrants and to show that a more compassionate society can be possible.

Bibliography

Asia Pacific Mission for Migrants (APMM), *Faith in Action: Faith-Based Programs and Institutions for Migrants in Asia Pacific and the Middle East* (Hong Kong: APMM, 2014).

Asis, Maruja, *Advocacy and Networking on Migrants' Issues* (Quezon City: Scalabrini Migration Center, 2010).

Baggio, Fabio, and Maurizio Pettena (eds), *Caring for Migrants: A Collection of Church Documents on the Pastoral Care of Migrants* (Strathfield: St Paul's Publications, 2009).

Ho, Wai-Hip, 'The Emerging Visibility of Islam Through the Powerless: Indonesian Muslim Domestic Helpers in Hong Kong', *Journal of Asian Anthropology*, 14:1 (2015), 79–90.

Scalabrini Migration Center, *Directory of NGOs for Migrants in Asia* (Quezon City: Scalabrini Migration Center, 1997).

Colonial and Postcolonial Context

Wai Ching Angela Wong

Historians have agreed that Christianity reached the Ganges in the first century and crossed the Gobi Desert to China in the fifth century. Unfortunately, Christianity's major expansion in modern times in what we call Asia today has been tainted by colonialism. While Western companies and their traders enjoyed privileges of sovereignty in lands they occupied, the missionaries they brought also enjoyed extraterritorial protection in cities and ports opened to evangelistic activity by force. Conflicts between these missionaries and local residents eventually turned into military attacks and resulted in wars and unequal treaties for the occupied territories. In short, with almost every territorial annexation of the Western powers in Asia, Christianity arrived in the company of artillery and gunboats. In the perception of many Asians, therefore, missionaries went hand in hand with the deployment of troops and administrators of the colonial powers, and the gospel was an instrument of Western imperialism. Whereas the military made territorial and material advances in the occupied territories, missionaries championed the superiority of Western cultures and values and undermined indigenous religions and cultures. Beginning in the 1950s, however, critiques of a Christianity tinged with imperialism and racism gave rise to a post-war movement for Asian Christianity.

Paradoxically, it is the very history of colonialism that gave birth to the notion of 'Asia as one'. An Asian-American historian, Joseph Kitagawa, has pointed out that 'Asia' was unknown until the latter half of the twentieth century. K. M. Panikkar, an Indian theologian, also argues that the emergence of an Asian identity did not result from any international agreements but rather a collective process of nationalistic resistance by the colonised peoples against Western colonial aggression. In contrast to the European process of formation of nation states, the rise of nationalism in Asia is better understood as a form of struggle against colonial exploitation, with the aim of replacing the structure of colonial power with a new order, namely, that of national power. While national independence movements dominated the Asian political scene of the 1950s and extended to the 1970s, they varied from one another regarding historical processes, ideological references and resultant political structures. Despite their common goal of decolonisation, Asian nations were founded on very diverse – and sometimes divisive – grounds, with borders arbitrarily imposed by colonial powers without reference to, or even the knowledge of, their inhabitants. Many of these artificial borderlines were drawn across tribal neighbourhoods, dividing families and communities and forcing them into becoming 'national' enemies. In order to inculcate loyalty to the young nation and to legitimise its authority and power, the state made considerable effort to bind people of entirely different languages, customs and religions into the so-called one nation. Inevitably, this arbitrary process of Asian nation-building planted seeds of deep suspicion and hostility among peoples of different origins, which grew into never-ceasing ethnic rivalries, with a dominant group trying mercilessly to suppress or even wipe out the languages, religions and cultures of the others.

What Postcolonial Context?

'Postcolonial' has been used popularly as a self-designated position for the formerly colonised peoples in Africa, Latin America and Asia. In current circulation it carries at least three meanings. First, it is used as a historical indicator referring to the period that followed American and European colonisation and began with the independence of the respective nations, largely by the middle of the twentieth century. When this meaning is adopted, historical attention is given to the establishment of national governments, constitutions, militaries and all other structures for social and cultural functions. The key to these new establishments is the transference of the ruling power from the former colonisers to the local peoples – primarily the elites who were trained and brought into leadership positions by their colonisers.

Second, and the most popular use of the term, is its political deployment. It is not only about the end of colonisation but also about the process of resistance to the legacy of colonialism, well beyond the historical period. Elleke Boehmer tries to distinguish these first and second meanings by designating a hyphenated 'post-colonial' for periodical reference and a non-hyphenated 'postcolonial' for the dynamic textual and political practices that critically scrutinise colonial relationships. The latter is aimed to destabilise the structures of imperialism by re-examination, writing back and deconstructing the very basis of colonial knowledge to re-establish the colonised peoples as historical subjects. Destabilising Western colonial knowledge is the meaning that has been widely adopted by 'Third World' theologians.

There is yet a third and more ambivalent meaning of 'postcolonial' that has been largely under-utilised but which would have implications for historical studies of Christianity in Asia. Building on the key literary and cultural critiques of theorists such as Edward Said, Homi Bhabha and

Gayatri Chakravorty Spivak, the postcolonial context meant much more than a ground for the champion of an anti-colonial battle against the West. It is also a continuing battle internal to the formerly colonised peoples and within the mind of each who lives and grows up in the formerly colonised world. In other words, colonisation is about not only foreign domination of territories or political dependency of national governments, but also the internalised values and thought structures within and among the newly independent national subjects. When Bhabha underscores the colonial production of hybridity in the colonised world, none can take it lightly as something that could be easily purged or dismissed upon national independence. Instead, it is something that has infiltrated not only local political and socio-economic structures but also art, culture and philosophical minds. It impacts on people's everyday lives regarding architectural designs, urban and social organisations, and perception and reception of religious and cultural values. In other words, there cannot be a clear line of demarcation between what is colonial – something to be resisted or fought against – and what is 'purely' indigenous – something to preserve and lift for local identification in the postcolonial world. Hybridity, once produced, is there to stay and even proliferate.

Christian Missions to Asia
East Asia is diverse in terms of languages, cultures and religions; yet it also sees some major common influences from Confucianism, Taoism and Buddhism, with Confucianism providing the basis of much of the social organisation of the various countries and areas, including China, Hong Kong, Taiwan, Japan and Korea. As mentioned above, the first record of Christianity in East Asia is the arrival of Nestorian monks in 635. They set up the first monasteries and churches in Xian, then the capital of the Tang dynasty. The next introduction of Christianity to China was led by Franciscan missionaries in 1294, followed by the arrival of the Jesuits and the Dominicans until the peak of the Rites Controversy in 1744, which resulted in the Vatican's prohibition of Christian mission in China. When full-scale missionary activities were launched with the backing of colonial governments in the nineteenth century, not only China but also other countries in East Asia were confronted with an imperialistic Christianity that left many countries and peoples deeply affected.

While Christianity was accused of complicity with Western colonialism, its early missionaries had made significant sacrifices. Portuguese forces arrived in Japan in 1542, bringing with them gunpowder and Jesuit missionaries. These missionaries were initially welcomed and successfully converted some members of the ruling class. However, a period of persecution of the missionaries followed from the sixteenth to the eighteenth century, first for fear of their political influence and later for their competition with Shintoism and Buddhism for believers. When Japan was forced open by the Americans in the nineteenth century, Japanese Christians were criticised by Shinto nationalists as betrayers of their own country and culture.

Christianity first reached the Korean peninsula through returned Korean captives during the Japanese invasion of 1592–7. Several systematic persecutions of Christians took place before 1900, when Korea was forced open. At their peak, Presbyterian and Methodist missionaries took charge of nearly 80% of the Korean population and more than 70% of all land. Because of their broad influence, the Korean churches led the independence movement against Japanese occupation in 1919 and later the opposition to Russian communist encroachment in northern Korea in 1945. In each case, Christians suffered severe loss and persecution. The history of Korean Christianity is intriguing, as Christians' holding onto their American missionary faith had been, ironically, a means of exercising national resistance.

In Taiwan (Formosa), the Dutch implanted Christianity in 1624 through the Dutch Reformed Church, which took over Keelung and Tamsui from Spanish Catholic missionaries. After a period of prohibition during the rule of Cheng Cheng-Kung, a general from the mainland, the English Presbyterian mission arrived in 1860 and founded medical services and provided education for tribal women. Similar to the case of Korea, the Japanese severely persecuted Christians and left a deep imprint on Taiwan's language and culture.

The cases of Macau and Hong Kong have been entirely different. Missionaries first arrived in the former in 1557 and the latter in 1841. Both cities were initially taken not as destinations in their own right but as stepping stones for missionary work in China. Unexpectedly, the Portuguese and British respectively ended up with 99-year leases on the two cities, allowing special privileges to the Catholic Church in Macau and the Anglican and other missionary churches in Hong Kong. The impact of Christianity in these two cases has been outstanding, not only in the religious but also in the political landscapes, especially before their respective handovers to China at the end of the twentieth century.

Southeast Asia lies in a strategic region between the Indian continent and South China and has been deeply influenced by the convergence and interaction of several major cultures: Hinduism, Buddhism and Islam from the Indian subcontinent and Confucianism and Taoism from China. The early presence of Nestorian Christians as traders and travellers to the Malay peninsula, Java and South Sumatra is also generally assumed. Countries in this region include Vietnam, Laos, Cambodia,

Myanmar (Burma), Malaysia, Singapore, Brunei, Indonesia, Timor-Leste and the Philippines. As with East Asia, Christian missionaries came to Southeast Asia in the company of European traders and soldiers in the sixteenth century. The first Christian missionaries arrived in Malacca in 1511 with the Portuguese. The Spanish took over the Philippines in 1565. The missionaries were mainly from the Franciscan, Dominican and Jesuit orders. As Protestant missions joined the scene in the seventeenth and eighteenth centuries, the political rivalry between the Catholic countries of Spain and Portugal and the Protestant countries of England and Holland was aggravated by confessional diversity. While the Dutch colonial officers supported Christian missionaries only when they aligned with their political intentions, the British in Burma and Malaysia played down Christianity in order to stay at peace with traders who belonged to other religions. In the Philippines, Catholics advanced their mission exclusively under Spanish rule, with Protestant missions pre-eminent under the Americans after the USA defeated Spain in 1898.

Yet even if missionaries made significant sacrifices concerning physical deterioration and material deprivation in their evangelistic missions to bring medical service and education to the remote areas, they were generally seen as collaborators with the colonial masters, enjoying military protection against the power of local authorities. Furthermore, missionary policy varied from country to country in Southeast Asia. French missionaries in Indochina enjoyed exclusive protection from their colonial officers, while the Dutch administration in Indonesia was more careful about not offending the Muslims, and so allowed Catholics and Protestants to evangelise only in specific districts. In Singapore, Malakka and Penang, where the British took control, Christian missionary activities were generally most free.

Similar to the experience in East Asia, Christians faced difficulties during the Japanese occupation from 1941 to 1945. Except for missionaries from Germany and Italy, which were allies of Japan in the Second World War, all foreign missionaries were interned. Unexpectedly, it proved to be a time when the leadership of some young churches was transferred to local Christians.

After the war, independence movements were successful in Indonesia in 1945; Burma in 1948; Vietnam, Laos and Cambodia in 1954; and Malaysia in 1957. Each of the independence battles was fought differently. Some ended up with communist insurgencies, as was the case in Vietnam, while others, like that in Burma, turned into bitter ethnic rivalries. Christians in Southeast Asian countries took part in the movements for nation-building in their respective countries, but their efforts were not always welcomed or later appreciated.

Christianity: Anti-colonial Force and More

Apparently, nationalism did not sit squarely with Christianity given the latter's alleged foreign origin and association with Western imperialism. However, the tide of independence movements and, with it, the rise of nationalism spread widely and affected a significant group of Christian intellectuals and church leaders in Asia. At the Edinburgh 1910 missionary conference, Asian representatives, though few in number, resolutely made their voices heard. They sharply questioned the dominance of the Western missions over the young churches in Asia and the divisions that Western denominationalism inflicted on the young nations. Back home, many local Christian leaders began to denounce the missionary churches as Western imports and strove to establish autonomous local churches, rejecting denominationalism and rigid theological systems. With the success of the movements of national independence in Asia after the Second World War, a movement of indigenisation for churches and theology gained prominence.

As stated above, because of the non-unifying understanding of the 'nation' in Asia, resistance to imperialism played a defining role in the forming of 'national' identities in Asian countries in the twentieth century. In other words, anti-colonialism constituted the ground of 'nationalism' in the newly independent countries in Asia. In East Asia, the postcolonial milieu of Christianity in the second sense of the term – resistance to colonialism – started from the early twentieth century, and indigenous churches sprouted with innovative structures and organisation for self-reliance, self-governance and self-propagation. And yet, as we shall see, Christianity moving along with the nation against colonial dominance has not always meant independence of church governance in East Asia.

In the face of the encroachment of the West, East Asian countries responded with very different strategies, including the comprehensive reform of the Meiji modernisation of Japan and the scientific and military modernisation of China. The most drastic and lasting changes in the region, led by the Soviets, were two communist revolutions leading to regime change in China and the partition of North and South Korea. With the Cultural Revolution set forth by Mao Zedong from 1966 until 1976, the landscape of Christianity in East Asia completely changed.

In China, Christian intellectuals were conscious of the ambiguity of their dual loyalty to Christianity and the Chinese nation, and started early on with an indigenous 'three-self' movement in the 1920s, the idea of which was taken up and developed into the Three-Self Patriotic Movement in 1954, a unifying organisational framework for all churches under Chinese communist rule. In Japan, besides the coming together of 32 churches to become the United Church of Christ during the First World

War, the Non-Church Movement (*Mukyokai*), founded in 1910, adopted an anti-colonialist agenda and rejected denominationalism, doctrines, ordination or sacraments of the Western churches. For the Korean churches, two significant phases of anti-colonial struggles took place, against Japan and the Americans, successively. After leading the national movement against Japanese control, Korea was thrown immediately into the Cold War and became the battleground between the Americans and the communists. From the 1960s to the 1970s, when American-backed military regimes ruled South Korea, the churches were once again at the forefront of the struggle against dictatorship and championed human rights and the welfare of the workers. In short, the anti-colonial war for Korea in the twentieth century had multiple fronts: Japanese occupation, communist encroachment from the Soviets and China, and American-backed military government. The result was an imposed division between the north and south of the country that has lasted until today.

After Japan's defeat in the Second World War, Taiwan was taken over by the Kuomingtang when the Chinese Republicans retreated from Nanjing to Taipei in 1949 and has remained separated from China. As with the general population in Taiwan, Christians, many of whom came from the mainland, were divided into pro-reunification and pro-Taiwan camps. An outstanding representative of the latter was the Presbyterian Church of Taiwan, whose leaders also led the Taiwan indigenous movement for self-determination. Many of its churches adopted the Taiwanese language in their services and considered ministries to the aborigines as one of their critical missions. For the churches that claim to have rooted themselves in Taiwan, nationalism has been immensely problematic. China is politically and ideologically too remote to be identified as the 'nation', and an independent Taiwan is not be possible due to obstruction from China. In this sense, more than Japan, China has been identified as the target for Taiwan's 'anti-colonial' struggle in recent decades.

The rising consciousness of Asian Christians of the colonial complicity of Christianity has generated an indigenous movement in the churches of East Asia. From the 1920s on, extensive efforts were made to integrate local architecture styles, cultural symbols and music into church buildings, decoration of altars and hymns for worship in China and Korea. However, these were soon found insufficient, and contextual theology arose and took the lead. Minjung (literally the mass of the people) theology was a contextual theology that took up the issues of a post-war Korea. It scrutinised problems such as militarisation and dictatorship, economic and labour exploitation; it underscored the abuse of human rights and foregrounded people's social biography of suffering at the centre of theologising work. At about the same time, another contextual theology, this one led by theologians of the Presbyterian seminaries of Taiwan, was undertaken under the name of 'Homeland' theology. It called for people's renewed sense of belonging to the land, whose ownership the Taiwanese have long been denied.

The Catholics, who arrived much earlier, had a more difficult time in China as the country was taken over by the communists. Priests and believers who would not submit to the Chinese Patriotic Catholic Association in place of the Vatican suffered and went underground as house churches. There were no official consecrated priests and bishops until 2018, when the Vatican reached a ground-breaking agreement with the Chinese government. Except for similar difficulties in North Korea, Catholics in other East Asian countries have fared well. In Japan, Catholics tried to integrate Zen Buddhist practices into Christian spirituality, and Jesuit missionaries learned to become Zen masters.

Incongruously, colonialism in East Asia was not only exercised by Dutch, British, Soviet and other European powers in parts of China, but it was also, for a significant period, applied by Japan, a coloniser within the same region. The battle of anti-colonialism was therefore filled with contradictions when the missionary churches became the base for Korean Christians to fight against Japanese colonialism and the Soviet communist aggression from the north. Moreover, in the cases of Japan and Taiwan, neither nationalism nor anti-colonialism could be taken straightforwardly. Rather than a tool against colonialism, Japanese nationalism, with its militarism, had been the major obstacle to the formation of an independent indigenous church locally. As for Taiwan, it was, in fact, the successive colonisation by the Dutch and Japan that made possible the growth of a local church determined to ground itself firmly with the people against further outside intrusion.

In Southeast Asia, the process of nation-building differs from country to country. The shape and composition of the population in countries of the region today are primarily a result of European colonial rule. Even after national independence, the area remained the playground of the ideological battles of the Cold War. The USSR, China, France and the USA all played a part. Vietnam was divided and Cambodia suffered most extensively with the Pol Pot regime from 1975 to 1979. Malaysia and Indonesia both felt the pressure from communist insurgency and brutally suppressed members of their communist parties. Since independence in 1948, the ethnic minorities in Burma have never been free from conflict. A central state of national unity in Myanmar, as with other Southeast Asian countries, has been a site of struggle for the government as well as the people.

The role of Christianity in fighting colonialism was further complicated by the 'migrant' status of Christians. In countries such as Malaysia and

Indonesia where Islam has been dominant and in several countries where Buddhism prevails, Christianity has mostly thrived as a community of immigrants. In Malaysia, Christians are usually of Chinese or Indian descent; in Cambodia, they are mainly Vietnamese; and in Thailand, indigenous Thai are expected to be Buddhist. Nevertheless, Christians made a significant contribution to the anti-colonial war against the Dutch in Indonesia and against the Spaniards in the Philippines. The Asian Christian movement led by ecumenical bodies such as the Christian Conference of Asia, established in the 1950s, has continued to champion contextualisation of the churches and theology, so that new generations of Christians might shed the image of being a transplant of Western churches and ground themselves in the soil of Asia.

Nevertheless, contextualisation of Christian churches and theology has been easier said than done. Independence from missions and colonial associations can still leave the question of dual or even triple identities unresolved. Much more complex than in East Asia, in the context of Southeast Asia Christians are often viewed as representing a particular national or ethnic identity. Even if Christians would like to identify with the nation and adopt the national language, in countries such as Malaysia where Islam is the dominant religion, the government would be suspicious of the Christians' motives. The Malaysian government would prefer to isolate Christians from national life and culture and to protect Malays from their influence. Some Thai, Filipino and Indonesian churches feel comfortable using local or regional art to express their faith, but peoples of the dominant faiths might resent their 'syncretic' practices and prefer the lines of demarcation to be clearly drawn. As such, the presence of Christianity in multi-religious and multi-racial countries does not necessarily lead to theologising about the issues involved when different religions align with ethnic groups and complicate the situation. Christians are afraid of losing freedom and rights, and Muslims or Buddhists are afraid of losing ground. For those who speak the language of an original migrant community, ethnic identity and geographical origins remain more important than crossing boundaries. In a context where Christian identity, national identity and ethnic identity can easily come into conflict, efforts at contextualisation have touched only the surface.

One of the main questions for Christianity in Southeast Asia has been its role in the process of modernisation and hence its influence in the inter-cultural formation of the region. Georg Evers argues that missionaries, often bringing with them technology, medicine, education and social service to the mission fields, have served as agents of modernisation. Moreover, with the colonial introduction of a different economy and ways of living in the Southeast Asian countries, they were also agents of change to people's traditional norms and values, causing disruption to the original patterns of behaviour and living in society. The activities of the Christian missionaries and churches have not only brought relief to many poor and marginalised communities but also opened up education for girls and women, giving them the possibility to rise above the confines of domesticity. Most controversially, however, Christian education brought to the region the strong influence of Western ideas, which often radically undermined traditional religions and cultures.

The Deeper Postcolonial Question

With an examination of the dilemma between nationalism and colonialism in both East and Southeast Asia, the equivalence of a postcolonial position to anti-colonialism is insufficient. In other words, the postcolonial milieu is not complete without a deeper reflection on the evolution of Christianity in the two regions with regard to the third meaning of the term, as it relates to hybridity. Threads of Christianity have been so entangled with a series of variegated political, social, economic and cultural specificities that as many internal as external questions remain to be answered. For example, it is undeniable that more than a few indigenous churches have been established in various countries/areas in the region, but to what extent has Christianity been rooted in local cultures and society? In what ways are indigenous churches resistant to the influence of Western churches? Colonial rule ended for most Asian countries at least three decades ago. What does it mean to identify the Asian context as postcolonial?

When R. S. Sugirtharajah first adopted the postcolonial framework to position Asian Christianity, he aimed to bring about an ideological tool to debunk Eurocentrism, colonialism and imperialism in the doing of theology and biblical interpretation by Asians. In his later work, nonetheless, he wrote about the history of Christianity in India and explained the negotiations between Christianity and nationalism and the rich cultural encounters between missionaries and Indian converts under the British Empire. Rather than a binary approach of blaming the colonialists for their oppression of the colonised peoples, his postcolonial intervention has complicated the understanding of the missionary history from both the side of the colonisers and that of the Indian natives. Although his main concern was to expose the privileged position that missionaries often occupied in the history of Asian Christianity and to recover the voices of the Indians, what he did has generated postcolonial historical writing that is more complex. It has not only troubled one's knowledge of Christianity and imperialism but it has also highlighted the complicity of local Christians, drawing attention to not only the missionaries' destruction of local religions and cultures but also the double-edged nature of their contribution to the community. There are many more contradictions and and much more inconsistency than a strict postcolonial (meaning anti-colonial) agenda would assume.

Despite the successive declarations of independence in many Asian countries, there is no doubt that the dominance of politics and the economy by the First World over the Third World remains. Many national economies in Asia today are open to the control of trans-national companies not only from the West but also from Japan, Korea, Taiwan and China. Today, expansion of the global economy is coupled with the expansion of many Asian churches praying for national wealth and personal prosperity. Some Protestant churches in Korea took over the model of the American mega-church and built up their multi-billion-dollar enterprises. Before the latest round of persecution of churches in Zhejiang, Hunan and Hubei, churches in the eastern coastal cities of mainland China celebrated their tremendous success with the burgeoning business class. Today, some of the largest mega-churches are found in Korea, India, Indonesia, Singapore and the Philippines, with Korean churches sending large numbers of missionaries out to the world. These churches are arguably both copies and hybrids of Christian expansion in the east.

Politically, the newly independent nations are embroiled in the mess left by their colonial rulers, with unbalanced development between the urban centres and the rural villages and economic and social disparities between different ethnic and linguistic groups. Deep corruption in local and national governments perpetuates the problems. Because of the prevalence of communal conflicts, ethnic rivalries and religious disputes, independence wars against foreign aggressors have been turned into internal battles aimed at suppressing minorities. Political oppression, social devastation and sometimes genocide occur in countries across both regions, not necessarily instigated by external factors. In the name of national security, stringent control has been exercised over minority Christian communities such as those in Indonesia, Myanmar and Malaysia. In socialist countries such as China and Vietnam, Christianity is subjected to scrutiny for foreign infiltration and churches are kept under tight surveillance. For them, rather than cutting off entirely from the support of international churches, 'foreign associations' have been essential for the struggle and survival of local congregations in cases of human rights violations and suppression of religious freedom. Struggling with basic survival, these Asian churches choose to adopt a disengaged spiritual approach to living the faith, with less concern about contextualising the gospel with social involvement. The bloom of Pentecostalism in these countries can be understood in this light. Ironically, indigenisation of Christianity (or 'Sinicisation' in the case of China) in these countries has been a state agenda rather than the churches' independent exercise of postcolonial resistance to Western imperialism.

Furthermore, increasing globalisation of national economies has continued to force people to migrate from the rural villages to the urban slums and from less affluent Asian countries to more affluent ones, such as Hong Kong, Taiwan, Korea, Singapore, Malaysia and Japan. In the latter case, this has resulted in a late insurgency of migrant churches or congregations. In many cases, these represent an effort of the local churches to reach out to the migrant population, such as offering special Filipino church services to domestic helpers in Hong Kong or the organisation of Bahasa ministry for Indonesians in Singapore. In light of the increasing diversity of Christian communities because of the growth of migrant populations, adding to the existing tension and conflict between Islamic revivalism and Christian fundamentalism in some countries, the enhancement of the Christian capacity to cohabit well with peoples of other faiths becomes a matter of urgent concern. Ecumenical platforms for multi-faith ministry and inter-religious dialogue have been created over recent decades for education as well as experimental communal worship. Moreover, following the principle of inclusiveness, churches for sexual minorities have also recently been formed in contexts such as Hong Kong, Taiwan and Malaysia.

The postcolonial context of Christianity is a complex one and should not be reduced to the battle to dismantle Western colonialism. It is vital for Christianity in Asia to reposition itself on the Asian plane rather than always looking to the West as its referent. The fact that Japan was a coloniser of many of its East Asian and Southeast Asian neighbours has ironically complicated the critique of colonialism by refuting the formulaic accusation of the West as colonisers and Asia as colonised. The imperialism narrative has been further complicated by the rise of China, as its political and economic power has begun to weigh heavily on the diplomatic and trade relations of its Asian neighbours. The Belt and Road Initiative for which China invested heavily in West Asia and some maritime countries has been an emerging target of criticism. It is therefore timely to review what is meant by the postcolonial context of East Asia today. Unless the politics between the East and the West can be placed alongside other emerging issues in Asia, East and Southeast Asian Christianity will risk remaining the 'other' of the West and be seen only through the colonial (albeit with the prefix 'post') lens.

Bibliography

Evers, Georg, *The Churches in Asia* (Delhi: ISPCK, 2005).
Goh, Robbie B. H., *Christianity in Southeast Asia*, Southeast Asia Background Series, no. 7 (Singapore: ISEAS, 2005).

Jongeneel, J. A. B. (ed.), *Christian Presence and Progress in North-East Asia: Historical and Comparative Studies* (Frankfurt: Peter Lang Gmbh, Internationaler Verlag Der W, 2011).

Moffett, Samuel H., *A History of Christianity in Asia, Vol. II: 1500–1900,* American Society of Missiology Series no. 36 (Maryknoll, NY: Orbis Books, 2006).

Wilfred, Felix (ed.), *The Oxford Handbook of Christianity in Asia* (Oxford: Oxford University Press, 2014).

Conclusion

The Future of Christianity in East and Southeast Asia

Mary Ho

To gauge the future trajectory of Christianity in East and Southeast Asia, we must first grasp how historically textured and pluralistic this mosaic region is. East Asia is more homogeneous, defined by Confucianism, folk religion, Mahayana Buddhism and Taoism. Confucianism emphasises social harmony under a strong central state in which religion is subservient to the ruler. This state-control dynamic continues to suppress Christianity in many Asian countries today. Nevertheless, since Protestantism arrived in the nineteenth century, Christianity has grown in every East Asian country.

The Southeast Asian countries are more varied and complex, influenced by Hinduism and Theravada Buddhism and by China and India. Beginning in the thirteenth century, Islam also came through the eastern trade routes and has especially shaped Indonesia, Malaysia and the Philippines. Southeast Asia has since been heavily influenced by various Western colonial powers, which brought Christianity, including the Dutch Protestants who colonised Indonesia; the Spanish in the Philippines; the French in Indochina; and the British in Singapore, Malaysia and Myanmar. Today, Christianity continues to be viewed as foreign and Western in these countries (with the exception of the Philippines). The only country in Southeast Asia that has never succumbed to a colonial power is Thailand.

During the Second World War, Japan dominated Asia. After the war, Southeast Asian countries, one by one, gained independence. Several countries, including Vietnam, Laos and Cambodia, became communist. Currently, every country in Southeast Asia has a dominant religion, except Singapore, which has maintained a balance of religions. However, irrespective of the predominant religion and governmental structure, Christianity is growing throughout East and Southeast Asia. The countries can be roughly divided into four categories: (1) communist states – North Korea, China, Vietnam and Laos; (2) authoritarian states – Cambodia and Myanmar; (3) predominantly Muslim countries – Indonesia, Malaysia and Brunei; and (4) religiously free countries – Taiwan, Japan, South Korea, Mongolia, the Philippines, Timor-Leste, Singapore and Thailand.

Today, Asia is defined by ethnic and religious pluralism. The population is rapidly increasing and is gravitating towards the urban centres. Additionally, the digital age of the internet, social media, travel and trade partnerships have brought the countries and cultures closer than ever before, intensifying cross-pollination but also inducing conflict between ethnic and religious groups. As we survey this complex region through both a historical lens and its current trajectory, there are 12 prevailing trends that can be expected to shape the future of Christianity in East and Southeast Asia.

(1) Christianity will likely grow in every country and become one of the two largest religions, along with Islam

Christianity is rapidly expanding in every country in East and Southeast Asia, growing two to four times faster than the population. It is currently the third-largest religion in Southeast Asia and the fourth in East Asia. Even in Japan, where Christianity has not taken root in society as a whole, partly as a result of inward migration the percentage of Christians has doubled in the past century. In Mongolia, where there were only a handful of Christians in 1990, the Christian faith has grown rapidly.

During the past century, Christianity and Islam have been the two fastest-growing religions both globally and in Asia. Even in the predominantly Muslim country of Indonesia, Christianity has grown to be the second-largest religion, representing around 10% of the population. Christianity can be expected to continue to grow in every predominantly Muslim country. It is also likely that Christianity will grow in the predominantly Buddhist countries of Mongolia, Laos, Myanmar, Thailand and Vietnam, while Buddhism and folk religion can be expected to continue to decline.

The likely challenge for Christians is that while population growth will lead to an increase in their numbers, younger generations will not necessarily hold on to their faith in the same way that their forebears did. Millennials and members of Generation Z appear more fluid in their commitments than older generations. What will this mean for the future of Christianity?

Due to the rise of communist governments, there has been an increase in atheism and agnosticism over the past few decades. However, as some of these countries open up economically, there will be a decline in agnosticism and atheism. It appears that Christianity fills a spiritual void left by atheism and provides answers to the meaning of life. Agnosticism and atheism will continue to be present mostly because of an increase in secularism, economic growth and attendant materialism. Christianity will almost certainly expand in every communist country except North Korea, where it is hard to gauge. Nevertheless, recent summit dialogues with South Korea might open this reclusive country to new opportunities.

(2) Christianity will grow significantly through the Pentecostal and Charismatic movements

In East and Southeast Asia, the Pentecostal and Charismatic movements are the fastest-growing branches of Christianity, catalysing exponential church growth, conversions and vibrant faith across denominations. The Charismatic and Pentecostal movements emphasise the personal empowerment of the Holy Spirit, a living relationship with Jesus and the appropriation of the Word of God, thereby solidifying the priesthood of all believers even among the impoverished. In Asia, which remains one of the neediest and least-evangelised regions of the world, the emphasis on supernatural healing, miracles, deliverance and the promise of divine assistance have strong appeal among the poor and socially marginalised. Consequently, in the past few decades, mass renewal movements have swept through Asian countries, including Indonesia, Vietnam, Thailand, Myanmar, Borneo (Malaysia), China, South Korea and Cambodia.

Asia is the birthplace to many of the world's major religions and countless folk religions. Therefore, Asia has a deep-seated worldview fraught with good and bad spirits that orchestrate all human events. In the Asian psyche, religion is the solution to life's ills through prayer and offerings to spiritual beings. Charismatic beliefs – centred on the Holy Spirit, who aids, enlightens and performs miracles – tap into the Asian worldview. For example, Christianity grew among the Hmong and Khmu peoples in Laos through power evangelism, deliverance from evil spirits and miracles. In Asia, Christianity will continue to abound through the Charismatic and Pentecostal movements across denominations. The Catholic Charismatic renewal can also be expected to grow, especially in the Philippines and Indonesia.

Christianity will also grow among the youth through the Charismatic and Pentecostal movements. Among the mega-churches in the cities, the lively worship, dynamic messages, testimonies and authentic experience have proved attractive to young people. In the future, the Charismatic experience will attract the youth, along with cause-driven activism, fervent 24/7 prayer rooms and authentic community.

(3) Christianity will continue to grow through indigenous house-church movements

The fastest Christian growth will probably be through the multiplication of house-church movements and informal church networks. In Asia, the Christian faith often began among ethnic minorities or marginalised populations who were persecuted, creating a fertile ground in which house-church movements could emerge. For example, in Vietnam, thousands of house churches spread among the persecuted Hmong minority. In China, there are now conservatively more than 100 million Christians, predominantly part of the house-church networks. In North Korea, unofficial house-church networks might comprise between 100,000 and 300,000 believers. Accompanying this growth will be a rise in persecution and radicalism (see Trend 7, below), which will spur the spread of Christianity through church-planting movements.

There will also be a growth of disciple-making movements among the young generation, who, as products of the Uber culture, do not want to fight traffic to attend a large church with prescribed programmes. As materialism unravels family values and increases the divorce rate, young people yearn for personal, authentic communities that social media cannot provide. In the digital age, young people want to belong to authentic communities, know their purpose in life and change the world by giving back through social causes. Consequently, there will be a rise of small youth communities in cities and universities. These might have names other than 'church' but they will be essentially the same.

(4) Christianity will be reinterpreted through indigenised worship, theology, stories and social codes of honour

Christianity will continue to spread mainly through indigenised forms. Although all the major religions are imported, only Christianity is seen as Western, while the others are seen as 'Asian', except in the predominantly Catholic countries of Timor-Leste and the Philippines. In the past, Christianity had the advantage of superior educational standards, but in the future, there will be a resurgence of Islamic and Buddhist intellectuals articulating their cultural classical roots. Therefore, Christian theology will need to increasingly incorporate Asian culture, oral traditions, and Confucian and Buddhist philosophy. Christianity also needs to be socially relevant and address issues specific to Asia. For example, South Korean theology has already incorporated the concept of Minjung (the suffering masses) to portray Jesus championing the oppressed, and Asian theology has adopted the Confucian concept of *junzi* (the gentleman-scholar) to portray an 'Asian' Christ. Asian theology will increasingly employ indigenous concepts, oral traditions and inter-religious traditions.

The indigenisation of Christianity is also seen in music, art and rituals. In the Chinese underground church movement, indigenous worship songs have proliferated. In Cambodia, Christians worship Jesus in the traditional kneeling position, with hands above their heads. In Myanmar, a church-planting movement was ignited using the Burmese-style illustration of

Bible stories. In the Himalayan Tibetan region, workers have produced a set of 63 'biblical' *thankas* (a Tibetan Buddhist art) to chronicle Genesis to Revelation. Consequently, many Tibetan Buddhist monks, nuns and ethnic minorities have embraced the Christian faith. Throughout Asia, Christianity has empowered minority populations and preserved their culture through oral recordings, Bible translations, and redeeming cultural traditions, fables and symbolism.

Most Asian cultures feature deep religious symbolism, practices and celebrations. Instead of condemning local practices, Christianity will grow by finding culturally acceptable alternatives to pagan rituals, such as honouring ancestors. The Cambodian churches have found redemptive expressions of honouring parents by greeting them with bowing and kneeling and bringing food and money for special occasions. Korean churches have transformed the Buddhist early-morning prayer into dawn church prayers. In Laos, some churches now incorporate the animistic *khwan* rituals by the pastor blessing a basket of strings. In Timor-Leste, Christianity now coexists with the traditional *lulik* (holy) practices. In Mongolia, the fastest Christian growth started as national leaders began to replace missionaries and they aim to disciple 10% of Mongolia's population by 2020. Churches are now writing indigenous worship songs to replace Western and Korean music in order to reach herders in remote regions. Christianity will continue to grow through indigenous networks using indigenous practices.

(5) Christianity will grow through the migration of displaced peoples, labour migration and reverse migration

There are more migrants today than ever before, numbering around 250 million people globally, of whom about a third are in Asia. Migration has been the norm in Asia, as the Chinese have long migrated to other Asian countries and as the various ethnicities spill over borders. Today, there is also migration from the rural to the urban areas and by refugees displaced by conflict to other countries. Currently in Asia, the most serious refugee crisis stems from the displacement of the Rohingya in Myanmar. Labour migration and reverse migration are also key contemporary trends. There are other sources of migration as well. For example, both China and Taiwan have offset the gender ratio imbalance by importing 'brides' from countries like Vietnam. Because Asian countries are closely clustered together, there will be an increase in migration, triggering demographic changes and tension in a complex region.

Labour migration is significant in Asia. Taiwan is currently experiencing a drainage of professionals, business people and academicians to China. Since the 1970s, the Philippines has sent some 10 million labour migrants to other countries, fuelling both the national economy and a global missions movement. For example, about 70% of Christians in Brunei are migrant workers from the Philippines and other Asian countries.

The effects of migration are complex. While migration due to labour has brought Christianity to many places in Asia, the feminisation of migration also means that more mothers are separated from their families, possibly affecting the handing on of the faith in the migrants' home countries. Another factor is that Islam is also systematically spreading through labour migration. In Malaysia, the Christian growth in Sabah and Sarawak has plunged since 2000 due to Muslims migrating from the Philippines and Indonesia. Similarly, Muslim migrants are flooding into predominantly Christian Papua in Indonesia and are awarded the best jobs.

Christian influence will spread through reverse migration, especially Chinese professionals and scholars drawn by career opportunities in China. China is the world's largest source of international students. Many of them embrace the Christian faith overseas and return to China for long-term employment. Additionally, a large contingent of overseas Chinese Christians is making regular trips back for business and short-term mission assignments.

(6) Christianity will grow through socio-economic initiatives and political advocacy in a cause-driven younger generation

Poverty remains a significant challenge in many contexts within this region. Therefore, the social role of Christianity will continue to play a pivotal role. Historically, Christianity has entered Asian countries through socio-economic initiatives, including education, literacy, medicine and advocacy. For example, the first Protestant missionary to Taiwan, Dr George Mackay, established the first hospital and school, as well as planting the first church in the country. Similar patterns opened up much of Asia. In the future, both evangelism and social transformation will continue to spearhead the spread of Christian faith. However, social missions are unlikely to operate on a Western model of aid. As Asian churches develop sustainable local ways of addressing social issues, Christianity will continue to be a major driver of modernisation through socio-economic initiatives.

In Asia, Protestant and Catholic churches unite around social initiatives. In Japan, Christians advocated for the rights of the Ainu minority in Hokkaido. Currently, in the Philippines, where the sex industry is the fourth-largest source of income, Christian organisations are banding together to eliminate the trafficking of up to 100,000 children and 400,000 women. Today, churches and denominations across Taiwan have united to counter the legalisation of gay marriage through nationwide petitions, prayer vigils and rallies. Such socio-political advocacy will continue to define the future of Asia.

Christians can be expected to play a key role in political advocacy. In the Philippines, the Catholic Church was instrumental in bringing down Ferdinand Marcos in 1986 and Joseph Estrada in 2001. However, the controversial anti-contraceptive campaign in 2012 created a backlash that has diminished the church's role in addressing socio-political issues, such as the penal system. Despite some highly publicised scandals in South Korea, churches will continue to exert an influential conservative platform in national politics. Christian leaders will play a key role in future unification dialogues, as the National Council of Churches continues to advocate for reconciliation between South and North Korea and the demilitarisation of the peninsula.

Education will continue to reach the marginalised populations in Asia. In China, Christian-backed colleges draw ethnic minorities from rural areas restricted to foreigners. As Burmese policies become more relaxed, churches and Christian organisations are offering basic education and starting private schools. In Cambodia, many from impoverished rural areas have opportunities to learn through Christian schools and churches.

Social initiatives are increasingly focused on sustainability, including agricultural projects and business-as-mission initiatives to close the economic gap. A key Chinese church-movement leader predicts that whereas Christianity has traditionally grown through evangelism, future growth will be predominantly through business and social initiatives that serve society.

(7) There will likely be an increase in persecution and martyrdom, along with a surge in radicalism, terrorism and violence

There will be an increase in persecution, radicalism and violence in Asia. In some countries, the political system is hostile to Christians through the government's enforcement of 'stability', forbidding the public sharing of faith. In other countries, religious radicals target Christians through terrorism and violence. Nevertheless, indications are that Christianity will continue to grow and thrive in these persecuted contexts.

Persecution is tied to the political system. Most Asian countries have emphasised economic growth without a parallel political development, thereby restricting Christian activities. China has been posting breathtaking economic growth while strengthening the authority of the Communist Party and tightening control of religions. Political development in the Philippines, Brunei, Cambodia and Laos also lags behind economic development. However, economic development has helped Vietnam, Myanmar and Cambodia become more open to Christianity and the level of persecution can be expected to decrease in these countries. Thailand is posting strong GDP growth but has been under military rule since the 2014 coup. The Muslim countries of the region – Brunei, Indonesia and Malaysia – will continue to limit Christian public activities. Similarly, Christian evangelistic activities are prohibited in Myanmar, Vietnam, Laos and Cambodia. In Asia, political and religious freedom is most advanced in Taiwan, Japan, Singapore and South Korea.

In pluralistic Southeast Asia, religious radicalism and violence will rise as various ethnicities subscribe to different religions. Given the majority–minority dynamic, ethnic minorities will continue to experience repression, hate crimes and persecution from the majority ethnic and religious groups. For example, the predominantly Catholic nation of the Philippines continues to clash with Islamic Jihadists in the southern islands, especially Mindanao, with an increase in kidnappings, killings and bombings. Currently, every country in Southeast Asia has a dominant religion – whether Buddhism, Christianity or Islam – except Singapore, which has a peaceable representation of multiple religions. The following are some of the countries that give cause for concern.

In North Korea, tens of thousands of Christians are detained in labour camps. Since 1994, anyone caught worshipping other gods besides North Korea's 'divine' ruler is imprisoned, beaten or killed. However, the natural disasters and the famine in the 1990s and the government's recent focus on economic advancement have slightly cracked open the country. Furthermore, summit talks between North and South Korea and between North Korea and China might create new opportunities in North Korea.

China is officially atheist and will become increasingly repressive. In March 2018, the government eliminated the Religious Affairs Bureau and put religion directly under the Communist Party's Central Committee. The Chinese government is especially targeting Christianity. While Communist Party membership is around 90 million, the Christian population conservatively exceeds 100 million, representing about 7% of the total population. The government has shut down many house churches and even the state-sanctioned Three-Self churches, especially in Henan province, where the house-church movement was birthed. Crosses have been forcibly removed. Arrests, imprisonments and disappearances of both Protestants and Catholics have increased. Since September 2018, the government has passed rules further regulating religious texts, images and videos through mobile apps and websites. Another key government strategy is to 'Sinicise' religion to be 'Chinese in orientation' by fostering folk religion, Confucianism, Buddhism and Taoism. Christianity, including Catholicism, is seen as subversive and foreign. In past decades, the Chinese government allowed only state-sanctioned Catholic churches and bishops, while Vatican-appointed clergy operated underground. In September 2018, the Vatican and the Chinese government signed a landmark accord permitting the Pope to appoint bishops in return for the recognition of seven state-appointed bishops. However, many Catholic communities representing the 10–12 million Catholics in China believe that this 'sellout' gives the government control of Catholic churches.

In Vietnam, there is still persecution of Christian ethnic minorities, who constitute more than half of the Christian population, including beatings, confiscations and destruction of homes. Registration applications for more than 1,000 Hmong churches remain unprocessed by the government for fear of a possible independence movement.

Myanmar is controlled by a military government that strongly favours Buddhism and restricts Christian evangelism, house churches and foreign literature. In 2018, government forces bombed the Christian Kachin areas. Ethnic minorities, which make up most of the Christian population, continue to suffer violent attacks, fines and imprisonment, especially the Chin, Kachin, Karenni and Karen peoples. Currently, the most widespread persecution is among the Muslim Rohingya refugees, who have been subjected to systematic ethnic cleansing since 1972.

Radicalism is on the rise in Indonesia, the country with the largest Muslim population in the world. It is also home to more than half of the world's Christians who live in Muslim-majority countries. It boasts one of the world's top economies, but the economy is dominated by the Chinese, a situation which has created racial tension and violence. The constitution guarantees freedom of religion and resists Islamisation, but the Blasphemy Law and the Penal Code undermine this constitutional provision and penalise those who are perceived to be speaking against Islam. In a highly publicised case in 2017, Basuki Tjahaja Purnama (popularly known as Ahok), the Chinese Christian governor of Jakarta, was controversially indicted and imprisoned for insulting Islam. Radicalism, terrorism and violence, including riots, killings and car bombings, have increased in regions dominated by Islamic fundamentalists. Religious atrocities committed in Maluku between Christians and Muslims have drawn international attention. Non-Muslim minorities in states like Banda Aceh are subjected to sharia law and churches have been destroyed. In May 2018, three churches were bombed in Surabaya, the country's second-largest city. Increasingly, violence and bombings will change how Christians gather for worship, because 'mall churches' and large buildings will continue to be targeted.

Radical messages are grabbing hearts worldwide, especially among the youth. Social media has been a conduit to tap into economic discontent and spread radicalism, terrorist ideology and hate campaigns. A recent survey shows that 38% of college students in Indonesia have been exposed to radical groups. There is a network of mosques, schools and imams significantly funded to promote an extremist interpretation of Islam. Despite that, a positive outcome from Ahok's imprisonment has been that the public has awakened to the destructive effect of radicalism and is stepping up security and preventive measures. The future of Christianity in Indonesia will be shaped by the growth of Muslim extremists and the outcome of the presidential election in 2019.

In Malaysia, Islam is the official religion and Muslims are given educational and economic preference. Although the constitution guarantees freedom of religion, the civil law is subjugated by sharia law. Conversion from Islam to Christianity is severely penalised. More than 100 radical groups continue to demand a stricter interpretation of Islam. Christians are banned from using 'Allah' to describe God. Evangelism is illegal in most states and public circulation of the Malay Bible is forbidden. Since 2016, violence has increased, including the abduction of Christian pastors and converts from Islam. However, a more tolerant opposition defeated the incumbent party in the 2018 elections, which might relax the legal impositions on Christians and create new opportunities.

Brunei is officially a Muslim country, with the sultan as the head of religion. Under sharia law, non-Muslims are not allowed to use 'Allah'. Christmas celebrations in public places, evangelism, importing Bibles and building new churches are banned. Conversion from Islam is punishable by death. This country will be repressive towards Christians as long as the sultan continues to reign.

(8) Increasing urbanisation will exacerbate socio-economic issues, while smart cities with digital technologies and disruptive innovations will widen the socio-economic gap

Many of the countries in East and Southeast Asia will be among the world's most populous states, including China, Indonesia, Japan, Vietnam, the Philippines and Thailand. Much of the population growth will be in urban areas. Therefore, there will be a significant rise in the urban poor, slum dwellers and women and children at risk. Since 2000, the globalisation of markets and technological development have been widening the income disparity. Asian policy-makers must focus on inclusive growth to stimulate equality of opportunity.

As urbanisation continues, Asian cities are leading digital initiatives and disruptive innovations, including biomedical breakthroughs, artificial intelligence, quantum computing and unmanned land and aerial vehicles. China, through its sheer volume of start-ups, will lead in processing big data. Hong Kong, Singapore and Tokyo will become smart cities that build digital technology into their infrastructure. However, this explosion in technology will widen the skills and income gaps in both rural and urban areas.

A positive development is that digital technology and social media enable information to reach rural areas and allow multiple voices to be heard. In Asia, there are 1 billion active users of social media, and mobile-phone usage has penetrated remote regions. Therefore, Christian discipleship will no longer be defined by geographical proximity. In the past, radio and television broadcasts disseminated the Christian message to remote areas, for example among the Khmu people of northern Laos. While these methods will continue, digital media will increase exponentially. Many churches in Asia now conduct discipleship through interactive websites, blog sites, online forums and social media. Digital technology can also hurdle governmental barriers. For example, the 1,300 congregants of a church in Beijing recently shut down by the government now download the sermons on their cellphones.

(9) Inter-religious dialogue will play a key role for peace and prosperity in this ethnically pluralistic region

Christians will play a key role in reconciliation in this region fraught with ethnic conflict and religious nationalism. In times of conflict, religious leaders are often the first to dialogue through inter-religious forums and Christians are often the first to initiate reconciliation. For example, a Christian church-planting network in Indonesia has conducted 'peace camps' between Christians and Muslims throughout Southeast Asia to build common ground. Similarly, church leaders have facilitated summits between North and South Korea, and between Christians and Muslims after the violence in Ambon, Indonesia, in 1999. In Cambodia and Laos, there are inter-religious talks between Christian and Buddhist leaders. In Myanmar, since democratic rule started in 2011, ethnic minorities are included in peace talks between the government and armed ethnic groups. In Singapore, inter-faith dialogues have built bridges among the 150 ethnic groups in the country. Inter-faith dialogues can be expected to contribute to the weaving of a tapestry of peace and understanding in this mosaic region.

(10) The main threat to Christianity is the rise of secularism, materialism and the pursuit of wealth

As Asian countries grow economically, the main threat to Christianity is not persecution: it is secularisation and commercialisation. While persecution fuels spiritual fervour, materialism breeds a new faith that wealth can solve all problems. In the context of Asia's economic growth, prosperity theology, which claims to guarantee divine provision, health and well-being, has gained popularity, validating the accumulation of wealth in capitalist economies. In many cities, wealthy churches encourage Christian business networking. Nevertheless, the focus on wealth breeds secularism. In Hong Kong, there has been negative Christian growth, especially among the younger generation of churchgoers, since the 1970s. In Singapore, there is a growing number of atheists and agnostics, who now represent 18.5% of the population. Churches are losing their youth and young adults.

However, it is not just the wealthy cities and countries that are struggling. Even in communist states such as Vietnam, commercialism and materialism pose a greater threat to Christianity among young people than government restrictions. In Laos, prosperity theology is gaining popularity. Even among other religions, secularism is on the rise. As young people pursue wealth and are turned off by radicalism, there is a rise in 'Muslim atheists' in Indonesia and Malaysia. Faith in wealth negates all other religious beliefs. As Asian economies become more bullish, this pressure will be brought to bear on Christianity in the region.

(11) Indigenous mission movements will increase in Asia

In Asia, the gospel began mainly among marginal groups, but these marginal groups will be the future impetus of indigenous mission movements. In many Asian countries, oppressive governments and majority religions have suppressed the gospel among the mainstream population. Consequently, mission efforts have focused on marginal groups, including the Chin people in Myanmar; the lepers and the Hmong and Khmu peoples in Laos; the Chinese, Indians and Eurasians in Malaysia; and ethnic minorities in Vietnam. However, these same groups will be the catalyst for indigenous missions in Asia. For example, in Malaysia, Christianity came through Christian migrants from India and China. Now, Malaysia is sending out about 500 missionaries. In Myanmar, Chin churches are sending up to 1,000 missionaries annually, mostly to other ethnic groups and the Buddhist Burmans. Karen and Kachin missionaries are also working among the Rakhine, Wa, Plaung, Mon, Kaya and Burmans. Similarly, Chinese Christians are engaging in missions under the 'Back to Jerusalem' banner and might be further catalysed by the government's One Belt, One Road policy. In Thailand, Christians from the Akha people are sharing with other minorities, such as the Akeu people. Taiwanese aborigines are working in China to reach ethnic minorities who have been oppressed by the dominant Han Chinese for centuries. Unlike the Han Chinese, the Taiwanese aborigines are free of historical baggage, are closer in culture and face similar socio-economic issues, including discrimination, poverty and animistic oppression. Now many of these ethnic minorities reached by Taiwanese aborigines are reaching neighbouring ethnic minorities.

Mission in Asia is often cross-cultural within national boundaries. Although both India and China have produced large-scale missionary movements, these missionaries mainly stay within the national borders or focus on diaspora populations. There could be a trend in the future towards wider global outreach. Currently, South Korea leads the region in sending missionaries to foreign countries. The Philippines is Asia's second-largest sender of workers to other countries through its formidable force of mission-minded migrant workers. Both Protestants and Catholics have established their own Filipino churches and evangelism programmes throughout the world. Given their unique sense of identity as the centre of Christianity in Asia, churches in the Philippines will almost certainly continue to send many missionaries to other countries.

(12) Christian professionals will be the main impetus of missionary outreach, using business platforms, career opportunities and trade routes to open doors of opportunity

As 27 of the 30 countries with the fewest Christians are Muslim and three are Buddhist, the future of missionary outreach will be dominated by businesspeople and professional 'tent-makers' gaining creative access to mild- to high-persecution countries. A growing number of Asian missionaries from Singapore, the Philippines, Indonesia and Malaysia are already going as teachers, engineers, medical professionals and businesspeople. South Korean missionary initiative has also grown in tandem with its economic growth, because, historically, countries with strong economies have a higher sending capacity. This continues the trend of missionaries following trade routes, which has been evident since the colonial period. This will continue to be the case as China launches its ambitious One Belt, One Road initiative, linking the ancient Silk Road route by land (belt) and sea (road) with Central Asia, the Middle East, Russia and Europe. So far, 68 countries have joined. This creates an ideal platform for Christian professionals to exercise missionary influence in regions that have long been resistant to the Christian message.

Conclusion

Asia is a region of clashing extremes, where polar forces hang in fragile tension. It houses some of the fastest-growing economies but is home to two-thirds of the world's poor. It hosts the world's most populous atheistic state but also vast numbers of Buddhists, Muslims and Christians. Asia leads the world in digital technology, big data and disruptive innovation and yet swarms with a large unskilled population. It has the world's most ambitious economic expansion plan (One Belt, One Road) and yet has the most protectionist country, North Korea. Culturally, the region ranges from the formalised Japanese norms to those of the effusive, vibrant Filipinos. The region is dominated by all the major religions of the world and yet teems with a cornucopia of animistic religions. East Asia includes the world's second-largest sender of missionaries to foreign lands in South Korea yet is also a hotbed for Islamic radicalism and terrorism. With North Korea's quest to develop intercontinental ballistic missiles, the region is tottering on the brink of nuclear conflict. China is also destabilising the region by establishing bases in the South China Sea to which neighbouring countries also have rights. Asia is a region where polar forces pivot in precarious balance. It could become the world's most explosive region. Or it could take the global lead economically, technologically and spiritually as the most advanced region in the world. For Christians, the stakes are high as they navigate pressure points and exploit new opportunities to share their vision of the reign of God.

Bibliography

Economy, Elizabeth, *The Third Revolution: Xi Jinping and the New Chinese State* (New York: Oxford University Press, 2018).

Granberg-Michaelson, Wesley, *Future Faith: Ten Challenges Reshaping Christianity in the 21st Century* (Philadelphia, PA: Fortress Press, 2018).

Hayes, Peter, and Chung-In Moon (eds), *The Future of East Asia* (London: Palgrave Macmillan, 2017).

Khanna, Parag, *The Future Is Asian: Commerce, Conflict and Culture in the 21st Century* (New York: Simon and Schuster, 2019).

Phan, Peter, *Asian Christianities: History, Theology and Practice* (Maryknoll, NY: Orbis Books, 2018).

Appendices

Christianity by Country

The table that begins overleaf provides a quick-reference, country-by-country listing for Christianity and its major traditions for all the countries that appear in this volume. These statistics are found in the *World Christian Database* (see Methodology and Sources) and all figures relate to 1970 and 2020. Small numbers are left unrounded to distinguish known small populations from zero but do not represent precise estimates.

The columns are as follows:

- Country (name of country in English)
- Region in which country is located
- Total population of country (United Nations estimate, 1970, 2020) and total numbers and percentage of population in each tradition
- Percentage mean annual growth rate, 1970–2020.

The last page of the table presents regional totals.

Country	Region	Tradition	1970 Population	%	2020 Population	%	Growth rate (%), 1970–2020
Brunei	Southeast Asia	Total population	130,000	100.0%	445,000	100.0%	2.5%
		Christians	7,300	5.6%	52,000	11.7%	4.0%
		Anglicans	4,000	3.1%	3,700	0.8%	−0.2%
		Independents	1,900	1.5%	17,500	3.9%	4.5%
		Protestants	1,200	0.9%	9,400	2.1%	4.3%
		Catholics	100	0.1%	20,000	4.5%	11.2%
		Evangelicals	1,900	1.5%	10,200	2.3%	3.4%
		Pentecostal/Charismatics	1,000	0.8%	16,000	3.6%	5.7%
Cambodia	Southeast Asia	Total population	6,995,000	100.0%	16,716,000	100.0%	1.8%
		Christians	33,300	0.5%	471,000	2.8%	5.4%
		Anglicans	200	0.0%	700	0.0%	2.5%
		Independents	2,000	0.0%	180,000	1.1%	9.4%
		Protestants	10,600	0.2%	305,000	1.8%	7.0%
		Catholics	20,100	0.3%	25,000	0.1%	0.4%
		Evangelicals	10,600	0.2%	320,000	1.9%	7.1%
		Pentecostal/Charismatics	2,000	0.0%	365,000	2.2%	11.0%
China	East Asia	Total population	824,788,000	100.0%	1,424,548,000	100.0%	1.1%
		Christians	876,000	0.1%	106,030,000	7.4%	10.1%
		Anglicans	100	0.0%	950	0.0%	4.6%
		Independents	183,000	0.0%	62,000,000	4.4%	12.4%
		Orthodox	5,000	0.0%	10,000	0.0%	1.4%
		Protestants	254,000	0.0%	33,999,000	2.4%	10.3%
		Catholics	400,000	0.0%	10,000,000	0.7%	6.6%
		Evangelicals	59,300	0.0%	35,000,000	2.5%	13.6%
		Pentecostal/Charismatics	93,400	0.0%	28,000,000	2.0%	12.1%
Hong Kong	East Asia	Total population	3,873,000	100.0%	7,548,000	100.0%	1.3%
		Christians	623,000	16.1%	1,146,000	15.2%	1.2%
		Anglicans	23,200	0.6%	29,200	0.4%	0.5%
		Independents	57,200	1.5%	170,000	2.3%	2.2%
		Orthodox	50	0.0%	100	0.0%	1.4%
		Protestants	193,000	5.0%	411,000	5.4%	1.5%
		Catholics	256,000	6.6%	590,000	7.8%	1.7%
		Evangelicals	122,000	3.1%	259,000	3.4%	1.5%
		Pentecostal/Charismatics	82,300	2.1%	320,000	4.2%	2.8%
Indonesia	Southeast Asia	Total population	114,835,000	100.0%	272,223,000	100.0%	1.7%
		Christians	11,233,000	9.8%	33,192,000	12.2%	2.2%
		Anglicans	2,000	0.0%	4,200	0.0%	1.5%
		Independents	2,192,000	1.9%	6,384,000	2.3%	2.2%
		Orthodox	0	0.0%	3,000	0.0%	12.1%
		Protestants	6,261,000	5.5%	20,200,000	7.4%	2.4%
		Catholics	2,620,000	2.3%	8,100,000	3.0%	2.3%
		Evangelicals	1,715,000	1.5%	9,414,000	3.5%	3.5%
		Pentecostal/Charismatics	2,179,000	1.9%	11,000,000	4.0%	3.3%

Christianity by Country

Country	Region	Tradition	1970 Population	%	2020 Population	%	Growth rate (%), 1970–2020
Japan	East Asia	Total population	104,926,000	100.0%	126,496,000	100.0%	0.4%
		Christians	3,100,000	3.0%	2,665,000	2.1%	−0.3%
		Anglicans	49,100	0.0%	47,600	0.0%	−0.1%
		Independents	617,000	0.6%	1,113,000	0.9%	1.2%
		Orthodox	26,500	0.0%	32,000	0.0%	0.4%
		Protestants	417,000	0.4%	522,000	0.4%	0.5%
		Catholics	361,000	0.3%	535,000	0.4%	0.8%
		Evangelicals	258,000	0.2%	310,000	0.2%	0.4%
		Pentecostal/Charismatics	349,000	0.3%	430,000	0.3%	0.4%
Laos	Southeast Asia	Total population	2,688,000	100.0%	7,165,000	100.0%	2.0%
		Christians	62,400	2.3%	199,000	2.8%	2.3%
		Anglicans	300	0.0%	200	0.0%	−0.8%
		Independents	400	0.0%	1,500	0.0%	2.7%
		Protestants	20,200	0.8%	150,000	2.1%	4.1%
		Catholics	41,500	1.5%	47,000	0.7%	0.3%
		Evangelicals	20,300	0.8%	145,000	2.0%	4.0%
		Pentecostal/Charismatics	40	0.0%	18,000	0.3%	13.0%
Macao	East Asia	Total population	246,000	100.0%	652,000	100.0%	2.0%
		Christians	32,600	13.2%	44,600	6.8%	0.6%
		Anglicans	200	0.1%	150	0.0%	−0.6%
		Independents	50	0.0%	2,800	0.4%	8.4%
		Protestants	5,400	2.2%	10,200	1.6%	1.3%
		Catholics	27,000	11.0%	31,200	4.8%	0.3%
		Evangelicals	3,100	1.2%	6,800	1.0%	1.6%
		Pentecostal/Charismatics	1,800	0.7%	2,800	0.4%	0.9%
Malaysia	Southeast Asia	Total population	10,804,000	100.0%	32,869,000	100.0%	2.3%
		Christians	571,000	5.3%	2,991,000	9.1%	3.4%
		Anglicans	69,600	0.6%	280,000	0.9%	2.8%
		Independents	24,100	0.2%	236,000	0.7%	4.7%
		Orthodox	3,700	0.0%	4,500	0.0%	0.4%
		Protestants	157,000	1.5%	900,000	2.7%	3.6%
		Catholics	301,000	2.8%	1,500,000	4.6%	3.3%
		Evangelicals	126,000	1.2%	630,000	1.9%	3.3%
		Pentecostal/Charismatics	34,600	0.3%	640,000	1.9%	6.0%
Mongolia	East Asia	Total population	1,279,000	100.0%	3,209,000	100.0%	1.9%
		Christians	3,500	0.3%	62,400	1.9%	5.9%
		Independents	100	0.0%	24,000	0.7%	11.6%
		Orthodox	3,400	0.3%	2,600	0.1%	−0.5%
		Protestants	0	0.0%	34,000	1.1%	17.7%
		Catholics	50	0.0%	1,300	0.0%	6.7%
		Evangelicals	10	0.0%	9,000	0.3%	14.6%
		Pentecostal/Charismatics	100	0.0%	17,000	0.5%	10.8%

Country	Region	Tradition	1970 Population	%	2020 Population	%	Growth rate (%), 1970–2020
Myanmar	Southeast Asia	Total population	26,381,000	100.0%	54,808,000	100.0%	1.5%
		Christians	1,350,000	5.1%	4,362,000	8.0%	2.4%
		Anglicans	27,000	0.1%	72,500	0.1%	2.0%
		Independents	84,400	0.3%	680,000	1.2%	4.3%
		Orthodox	0	0.0%	0	0.0%	0.0%
		Protestants	963,000	3.6%	2,628,000	4.8%	2.0%
		Catholics	268,000	1.0%	660,000	1.2%	1.8%
		Evangelicals	443,000	1.7%	1,600,000	2.9%	2.6%
		Pentecostal/Charismatics	86,900	0.3%	1,160,000	2.1%	5.3%
North Korea	East Asia	Total population	14,410,000	100.0%	25,841,000	100.0%	1.2%
		Christians	142,000	1.0%	99,000	0.4%	−0.7%
		Independents	8,000	0.1%	90,000	0.3%	5.0%
		Protestants	119,000	0.8%	6,000	0.0%	−5.8%
		Catholics	15,000	0.1%	3,000	0.0%	−3.2%
		Evangelicals	8,800	0.1%	10,000	0.0%	0.3%
		Pentecostal/Charismatics	8,600	0.1%	90,000	0.3%	4.8%
Philippines	Southeast Asia	Total population	35,805,000	100.0%	109,703,000	100.0%	2.3%
		Christians	33,607,000	93.9%	99,577,000	90.8%	2.2%
		Anglicans	63,300	0.2%	163,000	0.1%	1.9%
		Independents	7,142,000	19.9%	19,300,000	17.6%	2.0%
		Orthodox	200	0.0%	4,000	0.0%	6.2%
		Protestants	1,430,000	4.0%	6,237,000	5.7%	3.0%
		Catholics	30,860,000	86.2%	83,000,000	75.7%	2.0%
		Evangelicals	692,000	1.9%	3,863,000	3.5%	3.5%
		Pentecostal/Charismatics	1,182,000	3.3%	38,000,000	34.6%	7.2%
Singapore	Southeast Asia	Total population	2,072,000	100.0%	5,935,000	100.0%	2.1%
		Christians	162,000	7.8%	1,205,000	20.3%	4.1%
		Anglicans	10,000	0.5%	70,000	1.2%	4.0%
		Independents	14,800	0.7%	200,000	3.4%	5.3%
		Orthodox	800	0.0%	2,700	0.0%	2.5%
		Protestants	35,200	1.7%	180,000	3.0%	3.3%
		Catholics	80,000	3.9%	270,000	4.5%	2.5%
		Evangelicals	31,100	1.5%	250,000	4.2%	4.3%
		Pentecostal/Charismatics	9,900	0.5%	280,000	4.7%	6.9%
South Korea	East Asia	Total population	32,209,000	100.0%	51,507,000	100.0%	0.9%
		Christians	5,747,000	17.8%	17,277,000	33.5%	2.2%
		Anglicans	32,400	0.1%	90,000	0.2%	2.1%
		Independents	1,718,000	5.3%	11,330,000	22.0%	3.8%
		Orthodox	3,000	0.0%	2,300	0.0%	−0.5%
		Protestants	2,117,000	6.6%	10,400,000	20.2%	3.2%
		Catholics	838,000	2.6%	5,500,000	10.7%	3.8%
		Evangelicals	2,132,000	6.6%	12,855,000	25.0%	3.7%
		Pentecostal/Charismatics	324,000	1.0%	9,150,000	17.8%	6.9%

Country	Region	Tradition	1970 Population	%	2020 Population	%	Growth rate (%), 1970–2020
Taiwan	East Asia	Total population	14,693,000	100.0%	23,818,000	100.0%	1.0%
		Christians	933,000	6.3%	1,463,000	6.1%	0.9%
		Anglicans	2,100	0.0%	1,100	0.0%	−1.2%
		Independents	210,000	1.4%	510,000	2.1%	1.8%
		Protestants	261,000	1.8%	450,000	1.9%	1.1%
		Catholics	305,000	2.1%	240,000	1.0%	−0.5%
		Evangelicals	127,000	0.9%	225,000	0.9%	1.1%
		Pentecostal/Charismatics	178,000	1.2%	365,000	1.5%	1.4%
Thailand	Southeast Asia	Total population	36,885,000	100.0%	69,411,000	100.0%	1.3%
		Christians	240,000	0.6%	906,000	1.3%	2.7%
		Anglicans	700	0.0%	20,000	0.0%	6.9%
		Independents	50,600	0.1%	89,300	0.1%	1.1%
		Orthodox	0	0.0%	950	0.0%	9.5%
		Protestants	34,000	0.1%	449,000	0.6%	5.3%
		Catholics	154,000	0.4%	385,000	0.6%	1.9%
		Evangelicals	27,000	0.1%	410,000	0.6%	5.6%
		Pentecostal/Charismatics	55,000	0.1%	145,000	0.2%	2.0%
Timor-Leste	Southeast Asia	Total population	605,000	100.0%	1,381,000	100.0%	1.7%
		Christians	211,000	34.8%	1,224,000	88.6%	3.6%
		Protestants	22,000	3.6%	59,700	4.3%	2.0%
		Catholics	207,000	34.2%	1,143,000	82.8%	3.5%
		Evangelicals	6,000	1.0%	29,500	2.1%	3.2%
		Pentecostal/Charismatics	2,000	0.3%	68,000	4.9%	7.3%
Vietnam	Southeast Asia	Total population	43,407,000	100.0%	98,360,000	100.0%	1.6%
		Christians	3,264,000	7.5%	8,924,000	9.1%	2.0%
		Anglicans	2,200	0.0%	200	0.0%	−4.7%
		Independents	44,700	0.1%	529,000	0.5%	5.1%
		Protestants	159,000	0.4%	1,586,000	1.6%	4.7%
		Catholics	2,899,000	6.7%	7,221,000	7.3%	1.8%
		Evangelicals	168,000	0.4%	1,650,000	1.7%	4.7%
		Pentecostal/Charismatics	32,600	0.1%	800,000	0.8%	6.6%

Region	Tradition	1970 Population	%	2015 Population	%	Growth rate (%), 1970–2015
East Asia	Total population	996,425,000	100.0%	1,663,619,000	100.0%	1.0%
	Christians	11,456,000	1.1%	128,787,000	7.7%	5.0%
	Anglicans	107,000	0.0%	169,000	0.0%	0.9%
	Independents	2,793,000	0.3%	75,240,000	4.5%	6.8%
	Orthodox	37,900	0.0%	47,000	0.0%	0.4%
	Protestants	3,366,000	0.3%	45,832,000	2.8%	5.4%
	Catholics	2,202,000	0.2%	16,901,000	1.0%	4.2%
	Evangelicals	2,710,000	0.3%	48,675,000	2.9%	5.9%
	Pentecostal/Charismatics	1,037,000	0.1%	38,375,000	2.3%	7.5%
Southeast Asia	Total population	280,607,000	100.0%	669,016,000	100.0%	1.8%
	Christians	50,740,000	18.1%	153,102,000	22.9%	2.2%
	Anglicans	179,000	0.1%	615,000	0.1%	2.5%
	Independents	9,557,000	3.4%	27,617,000	4.1%	2.1%
	Orthodox	4,700	0.0%	15,200	0.0%	2.4%
	Protestants	9,093,000	3.2%	32,703,000	4.9%	2.6%
	Catholics	37,451,000	13.3%	102,371,000	15.3%	2.0%
	Evangelicals	3,240,000	1.2%	18,322,000	2.7%	3.5%
	Pentecostal/Charismatics	3,585,000	1.3%	52,492,000	7.8%	5.5%
East and Southeast Asia	Total population	1,277,032,000	100.0%	2,332,635,000	100.0%	1.2%
	Christians	62,196,000	4.9%	281,889,000	12.1%	3.1%
	Anglicans	286,000	0.0%	784,000	0.0%	2.0%
	Independents	12,351,000	1.0%	102,857,000	4.4%	4.3%
	Orthodox	42,600	0.0%	62,200	0.0%	0.8%
	Protestants	12,459,000	1.0%	78,535,000	3.4%	3.8%
	Catholics	39,653,000	3.1%	119,272,000	5.1%	2.2%
	Evangelicals	5,950,000	0.5%	66,997,000	2.9%	5.0%
	Pentecostal/Charismatics	4,622,000	0.4%	90,867,000	3.9%	6.1%

Methodology and Sources of Christian and Religious Affiliation

Todd M. Johnson and Gina A. Zurlo

Unless otherwise designated, the demographic figures in this book, both in the full-colour section and in the tables throughout, are from the *World Christian Database* (Boston, MA: Brill). This essay offers a concise explanation of methods and sources related to the database. It is adapted from longer treatments in Todd M. Johnson and Brian J. Grim, *The World's Religions in Figures: An Introduction to International Religious Demography* (Oxford: Wiley-Blackwell, 2013) and David B. Barrett and Todd M. Johnson, *World Christian Trends* (Pasadena, CA: William Carey Library, 2001). The *World Christian Database* (*WCD*) includes detailed information on 45,000 Christian denominations and on religions in every country of the world. Extensive data are available on 234 countries and 13,000 ethno-linguistic peoples, as well as on 5,000 cities and 3,000 provinces. Information is readily available on religious activities, growth rates, religious literature, worker activity and demographics. Sources are evaluated and reviewed on a weekly basis by a professional staff dedicated to expanding and updating the *WCD*, and the database is updated quarterly.

The Right to Profess One's Choice

The starting point of this methodology is the United Nations 1948 Universal Declaration of Human Rights, article 18:

> Everyone has the right to freedom of thought, conscience and religion; this right includes freedom to change his religion or belief, and freedom, either alone or in community with others and in public or private, to manifest his religion or belief in teaching, practice, worship and observance.

Since its promulgation, this group of phrases has been incorporated into the state constitutions of a large number of countries across the world. This fundamental right also includes the right to claim the religion of one's choice, and the right to be called a follower of that religion and to be enumerated as such. The section on religious freedom in the constitutions of very many nations uses the exact words of the Universal Declaration, and many countries instruct their census personnel to observe this principle. Public declaration must therefore be taken seriously when endeavouring to survey the extent of religious and non-religious affiliation around the world.

Religious Demography

The origins of the field of religious demography lie in the church censuses conducted in most European societies. For many years and in many countries, churches produced the most complete censuses of the population. They achieved this largely by recording baptisms and funerals. These data, however, were seen not as referring to specific religious communities, but rather to the larger homogeneous societies. With the decline of national churches in Europe beginning in the nineteenth and continuing into the twentieth century, governments began tracking births and deaths, eventually replacing churches as the main bodies collecting detailed information on human populations. Although thousands of sources for international religious demography are available, ranging from censuses and demographic surveys to statistics collected and reported by religious groups themselves, little has been done by scholars in religion, sociology, or other disciplines to collect, collate and analyse these data.

Sources

Data for religious demography fall broadly under five major headings:

1. Censuses in which a religious question is asked

In the twentieth century, approximately half the world's countries asked a question related to religion in their official national population censuses. Since 1990, however, this number has been declining as developing countries have dropped the question, deeming it too expensive (in many countries each question in a census costs well over US$1 million), uninteresting or controversial. As a result, some countries that historically included a religion question have not done so in their censuses since 1990. National censuses are the best starting point for the identification of religious adherents, because they generally cover the entire population.

2. Censuses in which an ethnicity or language question is asked

In the absence of a question on religion, another helpful piece of information from a census is ethnicity or language. This is especially true when a particular ethnic group can be equated with a particular religion. For example, over 99% of Somalis are Muslim, so the number of Somalis in, say, Sweden is an indication of a part of the Muslim community there. Similarly, a question that asks for country of birth can be useful. If the answer is 'Nepal' there is a significant chance that the individual or community is Hindu. In each of these cases the assumption is made (if there is no further information) that the religion of the transplanted ethnic or linguistic community is the same as that in the home country.

3. Surveys and polls

In the absence of census data on religion, large-scale demographic surveys such as MEASURE (Monitoring and Evaluation to Assess and Use Results) and Demographic and Health Surveys (DHS) often include a question about the respondent's religious affiliation. In some instances, demographic surveys by groups such as UNICEF (the United Nations Children's Fund) include a religious affiliation question. Demographic surveys, although less comprehensive than a national census, have several advantages over other types of general population surveys and polls. Demographic and Health Surveys (DHS) are highly regarded by demographers and social scientists, and provide valuable nationally representative data on religion. Surveys can also be commissioned in light of a dearth of data on a particular subject and results can be used to search for correlations between different variables.

4. Scholarly monographs

Every year, scholars publish hundreds of monographs on particular religions or religions in particular countries or regions. Such monographs differ from other sources in that they attempt to provide an overall profile of religion in an area or country, bringing to light local sources of quantitative data as well as qualitative information that provides layers of context and background.

5. Religion statistics in yearbooks and handbooks

Religious communities keep track of their members, using everything from simple lists to elaborate membership reports. The most detailed data collection and analysis is undertaken each year by some 45,000 Christian denominations and their 4.7 million constituent churches and congregations of believers. The latter invest over US$1.1 billion annually for a massive, decentralised and largely uncoordinated global census of Christians. In sum, they send out around 10 million printed questionnaires in 3,000 different languages, covering 180 major religious subjects reporting on 2,000 socioreligious variables. This collection of data provides a year-by-year snapshot of the progress or decline of Christianity's diverse movements, offering an enormous body of data from which researchers can track trends and make projections. Statistics collected by religious communities often enable researchers to distinguish between two categories of religionists – practising and non-practising – based on whether or not they take part in the ongoing organised life of the religion.

In addition to the above categories, there are governmental statistical reports, questionnaires and reports from collaborators, field surveys and interviews, correspondence with national informants, unpublished documentation, encyclopaedias, dictionaries and directories of religions, print and web-based contemporary descriptions of religions, and dissertations and theses on religion. The best practices in determining the religious affiliation of any population utilise as many sources as possible.

Affiliation

There are at least two different perspectives on what it means to be a Christian: professing Christians and affiliated Christians. Utilising the United Nations Universal Declaration of Human Rights as a foundation, 'professing Christians' means all those who profess to be Christians in government censuses or public-opinion polls, that is, who declare or identify themselves as Christians, who say 'I am a Christian' or 'We are Christians' when asked the question 'What is your religion?'

However, not all those who profess to be Christians are affiliated to organised churches and denominations. Therefore, 'affiliated Christians' are those known to the churches or known to the clergy (usually by names and addresses) and claimed in their statistics, that is, those enrolled on the churches' books or records, with totals that can be substantiated. This usually means all known baptised Christians and their children, and other adherents; it is sometimes termed the 'total Christian community' (because affiliated Christians are those who are not primarily individual Christians but who primarily belong to the corporate community of Christ), or 'inclusive membership' (because affiliated Christians are church members). This definition of 'Christians' is what the churches usually mean by the term (and thus the *WCD*), and statistics on such affiliated Christians are what the churches themselves collect and publish. In all countries, it may be assumed with confidence that the churches know better than the state how many Christians are affiliated to them. This therefore indicates a second measure of the total Christians that is quite independent of the first (government census figures of professing Christians).

Children

The family is by far the most important instrumentality through which individuals acquire personal, cultural and social self-identification. In consequence, children of church members are more likely to remain members than those whose parents are not church members. Children of ardent and practising Christians usually are, to the extent that their years permit, ardent and practising Christians. However, many churches do not enumerate children under 15 years. One reason is that it has been widely noted that most conversion crises occur in the 13–20-year age group in Christian families or in majority Christian contexts. On this view, therefore, children who have not yet reached 15 cannot reasonably be expected to be practising and believing Christians. The *WCD* takes the opposite view: children and infants also can properly be called Christians, and can actively and regularly (to the extent of their ability) practise the Christian faith. Consequently, where Christian denominations do not count children in their membership rolls, their membership is reported in our adult category. A total community figure is calculated (in the absence of any additional information from the denomination) by adding in the average number of children reported in United Nations statistics for the given country. Thus, the total community figures are comparable from one denomination to the next whether or not they count children in their membership.

Choice of Best Data Available

Religious demography must attempt to be comprehensive. In certain countries where no hard statistical data or reliable surveys are available, researchers have to rely on the informed estimates of experts in the area and subject. Researchers make no detailed attempt at a critique of each nation's censuses and polls or each church's statistical operations. After examining what is available, researchers then select the best data available until such time as better data come into existence. In addition, there are a number of areas of religious life where it is impossible to obtain accurate statistics, usually because of state opposition to particular tradition(s). Thus it will probably never be possible to get exact numbers of, for example, atheists in Indonesia or Baha'i in Iran. Where such information is necessary, reasonable and somewhat conservative estimates are made.

Reconciling Discrepancies in Survey Data

There are post-survey strategies that help general population surveys better reflect the actual composition of a particular country. For instance, if in a survey of 1,000 people, 60% were women and 40% were men, but we know that women and men are each 50% of the country's total population based on a recent census, then each woman's response on the general population survey would be weighted down by a factor of 500/600 and each man's response would be weighted up by a factor of 500/400. Such adjustments are called weighting.

Other adjustments made to general population surveys may require taking into account that they are meant to be representative of only adult populations. Therefore their results require adjustments, particularly if some religious groups have more children than others in the same country. This requires either a complete roster of members of each household or some other way to estimate of the number of children living in the household with the adults. When a complete roster is unavailable, most estimates of religious affiliation of children assume that they have the same religion as their one of their parents (usually assumed by demographers to be the religion of the mother). Differences in fertility rates between religious groups are particularly useful in estimating religious differentials among children. This is because demographic projections carry forward children born to women. It may introduce some bias to the degree that the father's religion is more likely to be the religion of the children than the mother.

Example: Coptic Church in Egypt

At times, the results from government censuses and information from religious communities can be strikingly different. For example, in Egypt, where the vast majority of the population is Muslim, government censuses taken every 10 years have shown consistently for the past 100 years that a declining share of the population declare themselves as or profess to be Christians. In the most recent census, some 5% identified as Christian. However, church estimates point to a percentage figure three times larger (15%). This discrepancy may be due to overestimates by the churches or attributed, at least in part, to social pressure on some Christians to record themselves as Muslims. Further, according to news reports, some Egyptian Christians have complained that they are listed on official identity cards as Muslims. It also might be that church reports include Egyptian Christians working as expatriates outside Egypt, while the census does not, or that the churches simply overestimate their numbers.

Such a lack of clarity is compounded by media reports and even Egyptian government announcements repeatedly claiming that Christians make up 10% or more of the country's approximately 80 million people, despite the fact that the census repeatedly reports only 5%. The highest share of Christians found in an Egyptian census was in 1927 (8.3%). Figures for Egyptian Christians declined in each subsequent census, with Christians seemingly making up 5.7% of the Egyptian population in 1996. The report from the most recent census, conducted in 2006, does not, however, provide data on religious affiliation, but a sample of the 2006 census data is available through the Integrated Public Use Microdata Series, International (IPUMS). They sample the same Christian share (about 5%) as the latest Egyptian Demographic and Health Survey, with a sample size of 16,527 women aged 15–49 years.

According to the Pew Forum's analysis of Global Restrictions on Religion (see www.pewforum.org), Egypt has very high scores for government restrictions on religion as well as high scores for social hostilities involving religion. These factors might lead some Christians to be cautious about revealing their identity. Regardless of the actual number, it is very likely that Christians are declining as a proportion of Egypt's population, even if their absolute numbers are not falling. On the one hand, Christian fertility in Egypt has been lower than Muslim fertility. On the other, is possible that large numbers of Christians have left the country, although a 2012 study by the Pew Forum on the religious affiliation of migrants around the world has not found evidence of an especially large Egyptian Christian diaspora.

Dates of Statistics

It is important, in changing situations, to know the exact date (year, perhaps also month and sometimes even day) to which particular statistics apply. This methodology compares government statistics of religion with statistics from religious communities themselves; but in doing so, it must be remembered that a government census (or a public-opinion poll) is almost always taken on a single, known day; whereas, by contrast, religious statistics are compiled over a lengthy period – perhaps three, four or even five years from the local grassroots counting of heads to final compilation of totals by a large denomination or church. Denominational totals published in 2020 therefore probably refer to the situation in 2017, 2016 or even 2015.

Counting Pentecostals

Three types of Pentecostals

For the purpose of understanding the diverse global phenomenon of Pentecostalism, it is useful to divide the movement into three kinds, or types. First are denominational Pentecostals, organised into denominations in the early part of the twentieth century. Second are Charismatics, individuals in the mainline denominations (primarily after the mid-twentieth century). Third are Independent Charismatics, those who broke free of denominational Pentecostalism or mainline denominations to form their own networks.

Pentecostals (Type 1)

Pentecostals are defined as Christians who are members of the explicitly Pentecostal denominations whose major characteristic is a new experience of the energising ministry of the Holy Spirit that most other Christians have considered to be highly unusual. This is interpreted as a rediscovery of the spiritual gifts of New Testament times and their restoration to ordinary Christian life and ministry. Classical Pentecostalism usually is held to have begun in the United States in 1901, although most scholars have moved to a 'multiple origins' theory of the birth of modern Pentecostalism, emphasising early activity outside of the Western World. For a brief period, Pentecostalism expected to remain an interdenominational movement within the existing churches, but from 1909 onwards its members increasingly were ejected from mainline bodies and so forced to begin new organised denominations.

Pentecostal denominations hold the distinctive teachings that all Christians should seek a post-conversion religious experience called baptism in the Holy Spirit and that a Spirit-baptised believer may receive one or more of the supernatural gifts known in the early church: the ability to prophesy; to practise divine healing through prayer; to speak (glossolalia), interpret or sing in tongues; to sing in the Spirit, dance in the Spirit, pray with upraised hands; to receive dreams, visions, words of wisdom, words of knowledge; to discern spirits; and to perform miracles, power encounters, exorcisms (casting out demons), resuscitations, deliverances, or other signs and wonders.

From 1906 onwards, the hallmark of explicitly Pentecostal denominations, by comparison with Holiness/Perfectionist denominations, has been the single addition of speaking in other tongues as the 'initial evidence' of one's having received the baptism of the Holy Spirit, whether or not one subsequently experiences regularly the gift of tongues. Most Pentecostal denominations teach that tongues-speaking is mandatory for all members, but in reality today not all members have practised this gift, either initially or as an ongoing experience. Pentecostals are defined here as all associated with explicitly Pentecostal denominations that identify themselves in explicitly Pentecostal terms, or with other denominations that as a whole are phenomenologically Pentecostal in teaching and practice.

Among Protestants (coded as 'P-') are Pentecostal denominations such as the Assemblies of God. Sub-categories of Oneness, Baptistic, Holiness, Perfectionist and Apostolic were retained from earlier research. Each minor tradition within Pentecostalism is considered to be 100% Pentecostal (all members of Pentecostal denominations are counted as Pentecostals).

Charismatics (Type 2)

Charismatics are defined as Christians affiliated to non-Pentecostal denominations (Anglican, Protestant, Catholic, Orthodox) who receive the experiences above in what has been termed the Charismatic movement. The Charismatic movement's roots go back to early Pentecostalism, but its rapid expansion has been mainly since 1960 (later called the Charismatic renewal). Charismatics usually describe themselves as having been 'renewed in the Spirit' and as experiencing the Spirit's supernatural and miraculous and energising power. They remain within, and form organised renewal groups within, their older mainline non-Pentecostal denominations (instead of leaving to join Pentecostal denominations). They demonstrate any or all of the *charismata pneumatika* (gifts of the Spirit), including signs and wonders (but with glossolalia regarded as optional).

Type 2 recognises the existence of Pentecostal individuals within the Anglican, Roman Catholic, Orthodox and Protestant traditions. These are designated 'Charismatic' and evaluated by country as Catholic Charismatics, Anglican Charismatics and so on, designating renewal within an existing tradition. For example, the beginning of the Charismatic movement in Anglican churches is described by Episcopal priest Dennis Bennett in *Nine O'Clock in the Morning* (Alachua, FL: Bridge-Logos, 1970). Traditions are assessed to determine what percentage of adherents identify themselves as Charismatics, ranging from 0% to 100%. Self-identification percentages for Charismatics were calculated by contacting renewal agencies working within denominations.

Independent Charismatics (Type 3)

While the classification and chronology of the first two types is straightforward, there are thousands of churches and movements that 'resemble' the first two types but do not fit their definitions. These constitute a third type and often pre-date the first two types. For lack of a better term, these are called 'Independent Charismatics'. Part of the rationale for this term is the fact that they are largely found in the Independent category of the overall taxonomy of Christians. Thus, Type 3 includes Pentecostal or semi-Pentecostal members of the 250-year-old Independent movement of Christians, primarily in the Global South, of churches begun without reference to Western Christianity. These indigenous movements, although not all explicitly Pentecostal, nevertheless have the main features of Pentecostalism. In addition, since Azusa Street, thousands of schismatic or other Independent Charismatic churches have come out of Type 1 Pentecostals and Type 2 Charismatic movements. They consist of Christians who, unrelated to or no longer related to the Pentecostal or Charismatic denominations, have become filled with the Spirit, or empowered by the Spirit and have experienced the Spirit's ministry (although usually without recognising a baptism in the Spirit separate from conversion), who exercise gifts of the Spirit (with much less emphasis on tongues, as optional or even absent or unnecessary) and emphasise signs and wonders, supernatural miracles and power encounters; but also do not identify themselves as either Pentecostals (Type 1) or Charismatics (Type 2). In a number of countries they exhibit Pentecostal and Charismatic phenomena but combine this with rejection of Pentecostal terminology. These believers frequently are identified by their leadership as Independent, Postdenominationalist, Restorationist, Radical, Neo-Apostolic or 'Third Wave.'

Thus, the third type is Independent Charismatics (also known in the literature as neo-Charismatics or neo-Pentecostals) who are not in Protestant Pentecostal denominations (Type 1) nor are they individual Charismatics in the traditional churches (Type 2). Type 3 is the most diverse of the three types and ranges from house churches in China to African Initiated Churches to white-led Charismatic networks in the Western world. It includes Pentecostals who had split off from established Protestant denominations (Type 1) and who were then labelled as Independent. Independent churches formed by Charismatic leaders (Type 2) who founded new congregations and networks are also included. Some Independent Charismatics speak in tongues, but healing and power evangelism are more prominent in this type than in the other two.

Three types together
One difficulty that has plagued all researchers and historians of Pentecostalism is what to call the overarching movement. Some have used 'Pentecostalism' or 'Global Pentecostalism', while others have used 'Charismatic'. Still others have used 'Pentecostal and Charismatic'. David Barrett originally used the lengthy phrase 'the Pentecostal and Charismatic Renewal of the Holy Spirit', which he later shortened to 'Renewal'. He then coined the term 'Renewalist' to refer to all three waves or types. For the purposes of this series, we use the term 'Pentecostals/Charismatics' to refer to all three types.

A demographic overview of Pentecostals/Charismatics (all types) illustrates the complexities of both the spread of the movement across the countries of the world and the striking diversity of the churches themselves. While current ways of understanding Pentecostals, Charismatics and Independent Charismatics reveal a global movement of immense proportions, perspectives on classification, counting and assessment of the movement are likely to continue to evolve. In the meantime, hundreds of millions of Christians across all traditions will continue to participate in the movement – bringing vitality in some denominations and schism in others. They will also promote social transformation in some communities and show little participation in others. What is certain is that, for the foreseeable future, Christianity as a whole will continue to experience the growth pains of this global phenomenon.

Counting Evangelicals

Any effective and comprehensive method for counting Evangelicals must take into consideration denominational affiliation, self-identification and theology. The results of counting Evangelicals are directly related to denominational membership figures. Strictly speaking, denominational affiliation means official membership on a church roll.

Method 1: Individuals in denominations that are 100% Evangelical

The first category of Evangelicals includes individuals who are found in denominations that are coded 100% Evangelical. That is, membership of an Evangelical council (national, regional or global) is assessed for every denomination and those denominations that have Evangelical affiliations are classed as 100% Evangelical. Consequently, 100% of the members of these denominations are considered Evangelical. Using this method alone, the *WCD* estimates there are 150 million Evangelicals in the world. As of 2010, the nine largest 100% Evangelical denominations in the world were all Protestant, and the five largest 100% Evangelical denominations were found in Brazil, Ethiopia, Nigeria and Indonesia, reflecting the global scope of the movement.

Method 2: Individuals who self-identify as Evangelical in non-100% Evangelical denominations

For those denominations not identified as 100% Evangelical, an estimate is made of the percentage (0–99%) of members who self-identify as Evangelical. Self-identification percentages for Evangelicals in non-100% Evangelical denominations are verified by contacting key figures within each denomination, and each estimate is sourced in documentation housed at the Center for the Study of Global Christianity. Adding together figures from both 100% and partially Evangelical denominations gives a total of 285 million Evangelicals worldwide. Looking at both 100% and non-100% Evangelical denominations reveals that the movement has a significant presence beyond Western Protestantism. Some of the denominations with the most Evangelicals are within Anglicanism in the Global South, such as the Anglican Church of Nigeria and the Church of Uganda. Chinese house churches (classified as Independents) taken together constitute the denomination with the third most Evangelicals globally. The United Kingdom (the Church of England) and the United States (the Southern Baptist Convention), however, are still important locations of the movement.

Method 3: Evangelicals not affiliated with any denomination (Unaffiliated Evangelicals)

To date, no studies have addressed directly how many Evangelicals are denominationally unaffiliated. However, two well known realities (in Western Christianity, in particular) appear to provide indirect evidence for this undocumented trend. The first is reflected in recent research indicating the unaffiliated are not uniformly non-religious. The Pew Research Center reported that 68% of America's unaffiliated believe in God. It is reasonable to assume that a notable proportion of Christians is among the ranks of the unaffiliated by virtue of Christianity being the largest religion in many of the countries studied. The second reality is the acknowledged fact that unaffiliated Christians often attend and are active in churches, including Evangelical churches, without becoming official members. These unaffiliated Christians profess allegiance and commitment to Christ but do not maintain church affiliation.

Dynamics of Change in Religious Populations

The question of how and why the number of religious adherents changes over time is critical to the study of international religious demography. It is more complex than simply 'counting heads' via births and deaths – a well established area in quantitative sociological studies – but in addition involves the multifaceted areas of religious conversion and migration. The migration of religious people has only in the past few years become a more researched area of demographic study, and issues surrounding religious conversion continue to be under-represented in the field. Data on religion from a wide range of sources – including from the religious communities themselves, as well as governments and scholars – must be employed to understand the total scope of religious affiliation. Given data on a particular religion from two separate points in time, the question can be raised, 'What are the dynamics by which the number of adherents changes over time?' The dynamics of change in religious affiliation can be reduced to three sets of empirical population data that together enable enumeration of the increase or decrease in adherents over time. To measure overall change, these three sets can be defined as follows: (1) births minus deaths; (2) converts to minus converts from; and (3) immigrants minus emigrants. The first variable in each of these three sets (births, converts to, immigrants) measures increase, whereas the second (deaths, converts from, emigrants) measures decrease. All future (and current) projections of religious affiliation, within any subset of the global population (normally a country or region), will account for these dynamics, and the changes themselves are dependent on these dynamics.

Births

The primary mechanism of global religious demographic change is (live) births. Children are almost always counted as having the religion of their parents (as is the law in Norway, for example). In simple terms, if populations that are predominantly Muslim, for example, have more children on average than those that are predominantly Christian or Hindu, then over time (all other things being equal) Muslims will become an increasingly larger percentage of that population. This means that the relative size of a religious population has a close statistical relationship to birthrates.

Deaths

Even as births increase their memberships, religious communities experience constant loss through the deaths of members. Although this often includes tragic, unanticipated deaths of younger members, it most frequently affects the elderly members. Thus, changes in health care and technology can positively impact religious communities if members live longer.

Births minus deaths/total fertility rate

The change over time in any given population is most simply expressed as the number of births into the community minus the number of deaths out of it. Many religious communities around the world experience little else in the dynamics of their growth or decline. Detailed projections rely on a number of estimated measures, including life expectancy, population age structures and the total fertility rate. This means that any attempt to understand the dynamics of religious affiliation must be based firmly on demographic projections of births and deaths.

Converts to

It is a common observation that individuals (or even whole villages or communities) change allegiance from one religion to another (or to no religion at all). Unfortunately, one of the problems in studying conversion is the paucity of information on it. Reliable data on conversions are hard to obtain, for a number of reasons. Although some national censuses ask people about their religion, they do not directly ask whether people have converted to their present faith. A few cross-national surveys do contain questions about religious switching, but even in those surveys it is difficult to assess whether more people leave a religion than enter it. In some countries, legal and social consequences make conversion difficult, and survey respondents might be reluctant to speak honestly about the topic. In particular, Hinduism is for many Hindus (as is Islam for many Muslims) not just a religion but also an ethnic or cultural identity that does not depend on whether a person actively practises the faith. Thus even non-practising or secular Hindus may still consider themselves, and be viewed by their neighbours, as Hindus.

Converts from

Conversion to a new religion, as mentioned above, also involves conversion from a previous one. Thus, a convert to Islam is, at the same time, a convert from another religion. In the twentieth and twenty-first centuries, the most converts from Christianity were and continue to be found largely among those in the Western world who have decided to be agnostics or atheists.

Converts to minus converts from

The net conversion rate in a population is calculated by subtracting the number of 'converts from' from the number of 'converts to'. Conversion to and conversion from will likely continue to play a role in changing religious demographics in the future.

Immigrants

Equally important at the international level is how the movement of people across national borders impacts religious affiliation. Once religious communities are established through immigration they often grow vigorously (for a time) via high birth rates.

Emigrants

In a reversal of nineteenth-century European colonisation of Africa, Asia and parts of the Americas, the late twentieth century witnessed waves of emigration of people from these regions to the Western world. The impact on religious affiliation is significant.

Immigrants minus emigrants

In the twenty-first century, international migration continues to have a significant impact on the religious composition of individual countries. One can try to anticipate the way in which expected immigration and emigration trends will affect a country's population over time. One profound change to be expected is the increase of religious pluralism in almost every country of the world. Increasing religious pluralism is not always welcomed and can be seen as a political, cultural, national or religious threat.

The six dynamics discussed above determine changes in religious demographics. Gains are the result of three positive dynamics: births, conversions to, and immigration. Losses are the result of three negative dynamics: deaths, conversions from, and emigration. The net change in religious demographics is the result of gains minus losses. The balance of dynamics can be reflected in any proportions (for example, mainly births for gains, mainly conversions from for losses) but can also be represented by pairing the gains and losses by type: births versus deaths, converts to versus converts from, and immigrants versus emigrants. In each case, the net change (either positive or negative) will be the difference between the two. This means that any attempt to understand religious affiliation in the past, present or future must be firmly based on demographic dynamics. A proper awareness of these dynamics as well as their significance is thus vital both for undertaking and for interpreting studies of the future of religion.

Measuring Growth Rates

The rates of growth, increase, decrease or decline of membership in many congregations can readily be measured from their annually reported statistics. This has been done by obtaining the statistics for two different years, where possible five years apart (to minimise the effects of roll-cleaning and other annual irregularities), usually 2000–5 and 2005–10, and working out the average annual growth rate as a percentage. Great care must be taken in such computations to ensure that the statistics used are measuring exactly the same entity (especially geographically) for each of the two years concerned. Growth, as a percentage increase or decrease per year, must be measured by dividing any annual increase by the identical category of total. Thus a church, for example, in a particular country with 500,000 total adherents (including children) in 2005 which grows to 600,000 total adherents (including children) in 2010 shows an increase of 600,000 minus 500,000 = 100,000, which divided by 5 = 20,000 a year, which divided by the mean membership of 550,000 gives an increase rate of 3.64% per year. In practice, the methodology follows a more accurate method by using the 1970 to 2020 figures for each denomination to arrive at average annual growth rates.

There are different ways of measuring the growth of a religious body. First, one can measure either adults only, or total community including children. Secondly, the growth rate of a church or religious grouping can be measured over a single day, or a month, a year, a decade, or 50 years – and all will yield differing results. This survey is concerned primarily to measure long-term rates. A growth rate measured for a specific religious body over a two- or three-year period may not be sustained over a decade.

Projecting Religious Populations

The starting point of future studies is natural growth of the total population of the country or region of interest, using demographic projections as a baseline. Three major areas beyond natural growth are utilised to improve the projections. First, birth and death rates vary among religious communities within a particular country. Secondly, increasing numbers of people are likely to change their religious affiliations in the future. Thirdly, immigration and emigration trends will impact a country's population over time. The highest-quality projections for religious communities are built on cohort-component projections – ones that use differential rates for each religion: age-specific fertility rates by religion, age structure in five-year age-and-sex cohorts by religion, migration rates by religion, and mortality by religion.

Unfortunately, this kind of detail is not yet available for many countries (half of censuses do not ask a question about religion). Fortunately, the process of filling in missing data using demographic and smaller-scale general population surveys is underway, and as these data become available through the Pew–Templeton Global Religious Futures Project, researchers will have access to these data through the *World Religion Database*, where they will be archived in full, with summary results available at the Pew Forum's website. In the meantime, projections cannot solely rely on the cohort-component method. Instead, they use a hybrid projection method. First, the 2020 religious composition of each country is established as the baseline. Then, utilising the United Nations medium variant cohort-component projections of populations for five-year periods up to 2050, future religious shares are modestly adjusted from the 2020 baseline. Adjustments are based on analysis of past differential growth rates of religious groups, factoring in historical patterns of religious switching and possible future attenuation of past trends. Finally, these projections take into account how immigrants might alter the future religious composition of country populations.

Ethno-linguistic People Groups

A problem for social science research is the lack of available survey and polling data in non-Western countries. While the United States and many European countries have a long history of engaging in this kind of research, many – often more underdeveloped – countries can be difficult to access and/or speak languages difficult for Western researchers. The *WCD*'s method directly addresses this methodological challenge through its additional taxonomy of the world's ethnic groups, which are paired with religious statistics.

A 'peoples' taxonomy must take into account both ethnicity and language. The approach taken in 'Ethnosphere' in Part 8 of the *World Christian Encyclopedia* was to match ethnic codes with language codes, which produced over 13,700 distinct ethno-linguistic peoples. Not all combinations of ethnicity and language are possible, but nevertheless every person in the world can be categorised as belonging to an ethno-linguistic people (mutually exclusive). For example, there are ethnic Kazaks who speak Kazak as their mother tongue and ethnic Kazaks who speak Russian as their mother tongue. These, then, are two separate ethno-linguistic peoples.

The work of determining the religious breakdown of ethno-linguistic peoples was begun in the 1970s in Africa, where many Christian churches reported the ethnic breakdown of their congregations. Utilising data gathered by religious bodies and in government censuses, estimates of religious affiliation for all peoples was completed in the mid-1990s and published in the second edition of the *World Christian Encyclopedia*. These data continue to be updated and published in the *World Christian Database* and *World Religion Database*.

Each distinct ethno-linguistic group in a country is assigned varying shares of the 18 categories of religion. For example, the Japanese in Japan are reported as 56% Mahayana Buddhist, 23% various New religionist, 10% agnostic, 3% atheist, 2% Shinto and 1% Christian. Each group is traced throughout the world with the assumption that whatever their religious breakdown is in their home country will be the same abroad. This allows researchers to locate Christian people in predominantly non-Christian countries. For example, the *WCD* reports that Pakistan – a majority-Muslim country – is also home to over 3.9 million Christians. While Christians are found among Muslim-majority people groups (for example, Punjabi at 4% Christian), they are also present in the country as ex-pats, such as French (65% Christian) and British (70% Christian).

Conclusion

There are a variety of issues related to finding and choosing the best data sources of religious affiliation. Censuses are generally accepted as the most reliable, but there are times when they fail to present the full picture, for example because they omit certain regions of a country or because they do not ask clear or detailed questions about religion. General population surveys can often fill the gap, but, depending on their quality, they may also have some bias. At times, religious groups may have very different estimates of their sizes than are found by censuses and surveys, but for some types of data, such as denominations of Protestantism, estimates by the groups may be the best information available. Finally, for religions such as Islam, Hinduism, Buddhism and Judaism, subgroup information is routinely missing from censuses and surveys. Estimates for the subgroups of these religions often rely on indirect measures, such as ethnic groups likely to adhere to a particular subgroup or expert analysis of multiple ethnological and anthropological sources. Thus, it is important to take into consideration many different kinds of data in order to arrive at the best estimate of a particular religious population in a country.

Index

Aaronic Blessing, 229
aborigine(s), 99–100, 104, 109, 469, 490–1
abortion, 244, 247, 252, 321, 460
abuse, 52, 220, 256, 304, 308, 316, 416, 427, 458, 469
acculturation, 354, 461
Aceh, Indonesia, 413, 433, 442, 487
activists, 229, 379, 417
Adam (biblical), 44
Addai (Thaddeus), 31, 244–6, 249–50, 343, 360
Adiprasetya, Joas, 447
adoption, 80, 162, 262
Adoration of the Magi, 35
adult(s), 93–4, 168, 185, 215, 228, 236, 251, 255, 317, 384, 490, 505–6, 515
Adventist(s), 76, 104, 129, 163, 173, 177, 193, 216, 220, 240
affiliation(s), 64, 95, 127, 132, 180–1, 222, 244, 360, 370–1, 461, 502, 504, 506, 510, 512, 514, 516
Afghanistan, 249, 288
Africa(ns), 31, 72, 145, 223, 249, 335, 386, 420, 441, 464, 510, 514, 516
African Americans, 335
African Initiated Churches (AICs), 335, 510
Agenzia Fides, 175, 180
Aggiornamento, 218
Aglipay, Gregorio, 316, 382
Aglipayan Church, 316
agnostic(s), 480, 490, 513, 517
agriculture, 28, 94, 136
Ahmadiyya, 207, 439
Ahok (Basuki Tjahaja Purnama), 208, 433, 442, 487–8
Ai, Tran Dinh, 193
AIDS, 180, 299, 481
Aileu, Timor-Leste, 257
Ainu, 390, 484
Ajiro, Japan, 287
Akeu, 490
Akha, 159, 295, 490
Albazin Orthodox, 283–4
alcohol(ism), 28, 62, 84, 93–4, 107, 120, 131, 172, 202, 304, 308, 381, 407, 411, 413, 465, 472
Alexei, Father, 292

All Gospel Church, 365
All Souls' Day, 319
Allah, 222, 257, 331, 355, 360, 396, 410, 431–2, 488
Allen, Horace Newton, 120
Alliance Church, 104
Alopen, 17, 21
Alpha course, 160, 163, 165
altar (s), 25, 178, 259, 319, 357, 469
Amakusa, Japan, 135
Ambon, Indonesia, 204, 305, 330, 393, 403, 489
America(ns), 18–19, 47, 76–7, 93, 101, 103–4, 107–8, 120–1, 134–5, 146, 149, 158–9, 167, 169, 176–7, 180, 183, 192, 218, 245, 269–71, 273, 275–9, 287, 300–1, 324, 326, 335, 358, 360, 382, 386–7, 398, 413, 420, 428, 460, 463–4, 466–7, 469, 473, 511, 514
American Baptist Mission, 76, 146
American Episcopal Church, 269–71, 273, 278
American Metropolia, 287
American Presbyterian(s), 158–9, 167, 169
American War of Independence, 269
Amherst College, 139
Ami (tribe), 108
Amity Press, 66
Ammerman, Nancy T., 405
Amoy, Philippines, 100
An, Chang-ho, 121
An, Men Sam, 181
An, Nghe, 428
ancestor(s), 26, 51, 90, 92, 105, 127, 157, 162, 171, 188, 209, 230, 262, 319, 358, 368–9, 483
Anderson, H., 404
Andrianoff, Ruth, 169
Andrianoff, Ted, 170–1
Ang Dating Daan, 244, 246, 248
Ang Ligaya ng Panginoon, 342
angels, 274
Angkola, 203
Anglican(s), 33, 75–6, 84–5, 89, 104–5, 147–8, 164, 213–14, 216–17, 225, 227, 232–3, 240, 270, 272, 274, 276, 278, 281, 323, 326–8, 335, 357, 368, 370, 384, 466, 508–9, 511
Anglican Communion, 89, 269, 274, 276–7
Anglican Diocese of Singapore, 232
Anglican Mission, 271, 273, 275, 277

Anglo-Burmese War, 146
Anglo-Catholic (s), 269, 274–5, 278
Anglo-Chinese College, 79
Anglo-Chinese War, 74
Anhui, China, 63, 67–9
animists, 157, 170, 172–3, 324, 370–1, 428
Annan, Kofi, 260
Antakya, Turkey, 16
Anthony, Saint, 26
anthropology, 209
Anti-imperialist Patriotic Movement, 75
Anti-Mui Tsai, 79
Antioch, 16
Antioch of Asia, 225, 236
Antone, Hope S., 308
Antonio, Dom, 254
António, Frei, 254–5
Aparício, Sebastião, 255
apologetics, 332
apostasy, 222
Apostle of Asia, 353
apostolate, 320
Apostolic Administrator, 256, 259
Apostolic Delegate, 192
Apostolic Nuncio, 192, 216
Apostolic Prefecture of Cambodia, 175
Apostolic Prefecture of Phnom Penh, 315
Apostolic Vicar of Phnom Penh, 175
Apostolic Vicariate of Batavia, 205
Apostolic Vicariate of Brunei Darussalam, 240
Apostolic Vicariate of Laos, 167
Apostolic Vicariate of Semarang, 206
Appenzeller, Henry Gerhard, 120
Aquinas, Thomas, 141–2, 375
Aquino III, President Benigno, 361
Arabia, 376
Arabic, 222, 254, 352, 379, 410
Arakan, 145
Arawa, Bougainville, 212–18, 220, 238, 276–7, 355, 432, 439, 446, 484
Archbishop of Canterbury, 49, 269
Archbishop of Manila, 246
Archbishop of Singapore, 229
Archbishop of Southeast Asia, 232
Archbishop of Tokyo, 287
Archdiocese of Guangzhou, 75
Archdiocese of Manila, 244
Archdiocese of Saigon, 195
archdiocese(s), 75, 119, 138, 195, 215, 231, 244, 314–15
Archimandrite Innocent (Figurovsky), 284
Arianism, 77, 210, 362, 391, 430
Armenia, 212
army(ies), 74, 80, 125, 136–7, 140, 217, 220, 226, 277, 288, 372, 431
Arrington, Aminta, 377
arts, 27, 28, 30, 35, 46, 49, 94, 97, 106, 128, 185, 195, 227, 232, 233, 301, 357, 362, 406, 465, 471, 482–3

Ashio Copper Mine, 140
Asho Chin, 146
Asia Church Leaders' Forum, 71
Asia Evangelical Alliance, 296, 299, 325
Asia Mission Conference, 400, 409
Asia Theological Association, 97, 297, 304, 327
Asian Theological Seminary, 327, 330
Asian Women's Resource Centre, 422
Assemblies of God, 76, 97, 125, 147, 182, 193, 214, 216–17, 234, 257, 323, 326, 508
Assembly Hall (little flock), 104, 217, 331, 383, 395
Association for Theological Education in South East Asia (ATESEA), 47, 297, 327
Association of Churches in Sarawak (ACS), 217, 446
Association of Southeast Asian Nations (ASEAN), 29, 31, 235
Association of Theological Schools, 319
Association of Trading Companies, 205
Assumption Monastery, 289
Assunta, Malaysia, 220
Assyrian Apostolic Church of the East, 17, 20, 92
asylum seekers, 445
Ataúro, Timor-Leste, 257
atheist(s), 64–6, 89, 92, 126, 312, 392, 425, 453, 460, 480, 486, 490–1, 505, 513, 517
Athens, Greece, 420
ATLAS, 47
attendance, 69, 78, 102, 112, 251, 315
Audetat, Fritz, 168–9
Augustine, 141
Aun, Yos, 177
Aung San Suu Kyi, 29, 430
Australia, 18, 47, 77, 179–80, 195, 197, 215, 233, 254, 256, 279, 300, 345, 365, 369, 396, 398, 461
Ayutthaya, Thailand, 158
Azusa Street, 121, 335, 509

Back to Jerusalem (B2J), 51, 55, 66, 72, 85, 124, 177, 260, 298, 304, 314, 332, 367, 378, 390, 417, 436, 490, 502
Badma, 96
Baekdu, 429
Baghdad, Iraq, 92
Baguia, Timor-Leste, 257
Baha'i(s), 173, 505
Bahasa Melayu, 225
Bahnar, 193
Balcombe, Dennis, 68
Bali, 31, 105, 107, 143, 195, 257, 291, 321, 328, 330, 351–2, 360, 366, 368, 438, 442, 474, 488
Balide, Timor-Leste, 257
Ballagh, James, 135
Bamar, 331
Ban Dom Don, Laos, 167
Banda Aceh, Indonesia, 442, 487

Bandar Seri Begawan, Brunei, 239–40
Bandung, Indonesia, 291
Bangkok Bible College, 327
Bangkok, Thailand, 157–9, 164–5, 289, 307, 327, 339, 342
Bangladesh, 249, 288, 327
Bangtan Sonyeondan (BTS), 19
Bangun, Maraike, 405
baptism(s), 16, 42, 60, 68, 164, 168, 171, 196, 204, 206, 219, 240, 254–5, 260–1, 289, 293, 335–6, 339, 344–5, 353, 358, 365, 380–1, 502, 508–9
Baptist(s), 27, 49, 60, 69, 76, 89, 95, 104, 108, 146–9, 153, 158–60, 163–4, 177, 179, 181–2, 193–4, 217, 225, 227, 232, 234, 243, 255, 303, 323–4, 326–7, 338, 382, 395, 508, 511
Baptist Missionary Society (BMS), 146
Baptist Union (Britain), 181
Baptist World Alliance (BWA), 49
Bario Revival, 367
Barlin, Jorge, 382
Barmen (Rhenish) Mission, 76, 204
Barnabites, 145
Barrett, David B., 501, 510
Barth, Karl, 103, 142, 375
Bartholomew, Patriarch, 288
Baru Bian, 220
Basalyga, Bishop Benjamin, 287
Basel Christian Church, 216
Basel Mission, 76, 213
Basic Law of Macau, 90
Basilan, Philippines, 29
Basilica Minore del Santo Niño, 380
Basuki, Tjahaja Purnama, 208, 442, 487
Batak Christian Church, 203
Batak Protestant Christian Church, 203, 302
Batak(s), 203–4, 210, 330, 410
Batavia, 99, 204–6, 291
Bateren Tsuiho Rei, 133
Bath, Danai, 289
Batha, 430
Battambang, Cambodia, 176–7
Batumalai, Sadayandy, 379
Bayan-Ulgii, Mongolia, 306
Bebbington, David, 323
Beifang Jinde Social Service Centre, 60
Beijing Ecclesiastical Mission, 283–4
Beijing Shouwang Church, 65
Beijing Zion Church, 73
Beijing, China, 60–1, 64–6, 70–3, 85, 90, 96, 110, 119, 270, 283–5, 417, 489
Bel Magalit, 330
Belgium, 61
bells, 145
Belo, Carlos Filipe Ximenes, 259–60, 314
belonging, 24–5, 40, 59–60, 64, 83, 104, 169, 184, 198, 319, 342, 363, 419, 421, 428, 438, 441, 447, 470, 516
Ben Moses, Abraham, 433
Benedict XV, pope, 57
Benedictines, 61, 84
Bennett, Dennis, 509
Bethel Music, 366
Bethesda Bedok-Tampine Church, 338
Bhabha, Homi, 464–5
Bhineka Tunggal Ika, 200
Bible(s), 16, 24, 29–30, 41–4, 46–9, 54, 63–4, 66–7, 70, 81–2, 88, 94, 97–8, 100, 119–20, 122–4, 129, 134, 136, 139–40, 151–2, 157, 160–5, 168–9, 171–2, 176–7, 179, 181–2, 186, 217, 222, 225, 233–6, 239, 246, 252, 271, 296, 298, 301, 321, 323, 325, 327, 333–4, 337, 339–40, 345, 354, 362, 367, 369, 373, 376–7, 381, 395–6, 405, 407, 422, 429, 431–2, 444, 458, 483, 488
Bible College of Malaysia, 217
Bible Presbyterians, 225, 234
Bible schools, 29, 46–8, 94, 9, 169, 177
Bible societies, 94, 96, 160, 163, 165, 176–7, 179, 181, 233, 432
Bible Society of Malaysia, 432
Bible Society of Singapore, 233
Bible study, 42, 66–7, 94, 123, 139, 164, 246, 345
Bible Theological College, 97
Bible translation, 98, 172, 369, 395, 483
Bickersteth, Edward, 274
Bigandet, Bishop Paul, 146
Bintulu, Malaysia, 215
birth(s), 15, 32, 64, 88, 113, 155, 171–2, 185, 201, 210, 223, 229, 232, 317, 326, 335, 344, 354, 360, 362, 365–7, 433–4, 439, 463, 481, 486, 502, 507, 512–15
Bisaya, 439
bishop(s), 21, 23, 31, 44–5, 49, 51, 53, 55–9, 74–6, 85, 87–8, 90, 92, 103, 105, 137, 145–6, 163, 167, 173, 175, 178, 180, 187–8, 190–2, 195–6, 206, 214–18, 227–9, 232, 235, 240, 246, 250, 254–7, 259–61, 265, 269–79, 284, 286–7, 290–2, 298–9, 311–12, 314–15, 319–21, 342, 361, 375, 382, 426–7, 447, 455, 470, 487
Bishop of Calcutta, 276
Bishop of China, 270, 273
Bishop of Dili, 261
Bishop of Korea, 274–5
Bishop of Labuan, 276–7
Bishop of Macau, 87–8, 255
Bishop of Malacca, 254
Bishop of Rangoon, 278
Bishop of Shenyang, 58
Bishop of Singapore, 229, 277
Bishop of Taiwan, 273
Bishop of Tokyo, 286–7, 292
Bishop of Victoria, 270
Bishopric of Calcutta, 276
Bishops' Conference of Thailand, 163
Bishops' Institute on Lay Apostolate (BILA), 320

Black Nazarene, 24, 32, 250, 458
blasphemy, 202, 208, 433, 487
blind, 80, 220, 413
blood, 15, 24, 80, 178, 294, 429
Blood of Christ, 294
Bo, Cardinal Charles Maung, 446
Boayen, Boonratana, 163
Boehmer, Elleke, 464
Bolkiah, Hassanal, 238, 431
Bolshevik Revolution, 292
bombing(s), 157, 305–6, 330, 409, 486–7
Bongsu Church, 113–14
Bonifacio Global City, 249
Book of Acts, 63
Book of Common Prayer, 269, 273, 278
Boone, Bishop William Jones, 270–1
Borneo, 213, 215, 238, 240, 276–7, 326, 331, 367, 396, 481
Borneo Evangelical Assembly, 331
Borneo Evangelical Church, 215
Borneo Evangelical Mission (BEM), 215–17
Boteli Huanqiu Budao Tuan, 383
boundaries, 22, 25, 28–9, 33, 59, 321, 329, 331, 360, 362, 366, 398, 419, 491
Boxer rebellion, 19, 52, 247, 284
boys, 120, 255, 273, 279, 423
Brahmin(s), 172, 443
Braille, 42
brainwashing, 310
Brazil, 23, 143, 511
Bread of Life Christian Church, 104, 108
Brent, Charles Henry, 275
brethren, 67, 77, 149, 167, 170, 213, 217, 225, 233, 323
Brethren Movement, 67
bribe, 318
Brigham Young University, 182
British, 33, 74, 76–7, 83–5, 96, 102, 120, 135, 147, 176, 212–13, 222, 225–6, 238, 269, 272–4, 276–7, 279, 316, 319, 413, 423, 466–7, 470, 472, 479, 517
British and Foreign Bible Society (BFBS), 176
British East India Company, 276
British empire, 74, 472
British Mill Hill Fathers, 213
Brook, Timothy, 383
Brooke, James, 213, 276
brotherhood(s), 203, 207, 209–10, 274
Brown, S.R., 134–5
Brunei, 29, 34, 192, 240, 277, 288, 314, 364, 387, 397, 413, 425, 431, 436, 439–40, 452–3, 467, 479, 484–6, 488
Bua Ya, 169–70
Buddhist(s), 16–17, 20, 25, 29–30, 48, 69, 84, 115, 124, 127–8, 130, 132, 134, 145, 150–2, 155, 157, 161, 165, 168, 171–3, 175, 181, 183–5, 195, 197, 229, 231, 238, 254, 297, 305–8, 310–11, 313, 328, 331–2, 340, 342, 353, 358, 364, 366, 370–2, 375–6, 384, 395, 424, 428–31, 434–6, 439–49, 453, 459, 470–1, 480, 482–3, 489–91, 517
Buddhist Association of China, 443
Buddhist Mount Meru, 172
Buddhist School, 115
Buddhist Temple of Chonjinam, 127
Bulacan Province, Philippines, 346
Bulatao, Jaime, 318–19
Bulgan, Mongolia, 92
Bulgarian Orthodox Church, 289–90
Bullock, Geoff, 233
Bumiputras, 212, 216
Bun Sok, 179
Bungoyaku seisho, 136
Bunun, 108
Burakumin, 420
Burkhan, 96
Burma, 145–7, 149, 151, 153, 277–8, 386–7, 429–30, 467, 470, 490
Burma Baptist Chronicle, 147
Buryatia, 96
Busan, South Korea, 293, 298
Bush, George W., 100
business, 24, 28, 63, 69, 71, 94, 117, 140, 147, 186, 196, 201, 214, 245, 304, 311, 340, 371, 380, 397–8, 431, 473, 483–5, 490
Bystrov, Vasily, 291
Byung-mu, Ahn, 379

Cachin, India, 305–6, 308
Calcutta, India, 276–8
Calvinist(s), 69, 99, 130, 303, 323, 384
CAMA Services, 179
Cambodia, 17, 19–20, 23, 27, 30, 34, 170, 176, 178, 180, 182, 184, 186, 232, 249, 277, 288–90, 295, 298–9, 304, 306, 314–15, 323, 327, 330, 343, 355, 364, 372, 387, 395, 398, 413, 425, 429, 436, 451–3, 466–7, 470–1, 479, 481–3, 485–6, 489
Cambodia Baptist Union, 181
Cambodia Bible Institute (CBI), 182
Cambodia Foursquare Church, 181
Cambodia Methodist Church, 181
Cambodian Christian Evangelical Alliance, 181
Cambridge Seven, 271
Campus Crusade for Christ, 160, 164, 179, 326
Can Tho, Vietnam, 193
Canada, 77, 179, 195, 197, 274, 343
Canberra, Australia, 369
Candau, Father Sauveur Antoine, 142
candles, 24
Canon Law, 55–6, 61, 314
Canossian Sisters, 77, 79–80, 255–6, 265
Canton, 74, 83–4, 88
Cantonese, 83–4, 88
Cape of Good Hope, 145
Cape Town, South Africa, 70–1
capitalism, 126, 131, 140, 198, 376, 397–8

captives, 466
Carey, Felix, 146, 259, 264, 501
Carey, William, 146, 501
Caritas, 80–1
caste, 163, 321
Castilians, 25
catechism, 99, 175, 215, 261–2, 293, 353–4, 356
cathedral(s), 17, 29, 58, 67, 95, 113, 135, 137, 195, 232, 239, 272, 276, 286–7, 289, 357–8, 372
Cathedral of St Mary, 276
Cathedral of the Resurrection of Christ, 286–7
Catholic(s), 16–19, 21–3, 26–8, 30–3, 35, 42, 48, 52, 54, 56, 58, 60, 62, 69, 74–6, 78–85, 87–90, 92–3, 95, 99–100, 103, 105, 112–13, 115, 119, 124, 126–8, 130, 132, 134–9, 141–3, 146, 148, 157, 160–3, 173, 175–8, 181, 188–90, 192, 194–8, 200–2, 205–7, 209, 213–18, 220, 225, 229, 231, 239–48, 251–2, 254–5, 257–60, 262–5, 269, 271–6, 278, 281, 289, 297–9, 305, 312, 314, 316, 318, 320, 322, 324, 328–9, 331, 335, 339, 342–4, 351, 354–62, 369–73, 375–7, 380–4, 387–8, 400, 402–3, 405, 410–11, 416–17, 422, 426–9, 433–4, 440, 442, 446–7, 453–5, 457, 459, 466–7, 470, 481–2, 484–7, 491, 508–9
Catholic Bishops' Conference, 145, 163, 175, 216–17, 250, 299, 342, 361, 455
Catholic Bishops' Conference of Laos, 175
Catholic Bishops' Conference of Myanmar, 145, 299
Catholic Bishops' Conference of Thailand, 163
Catholic Bishops' Conference of the Philippines, 250, 342, 361, 455
Catholic Charismatics, 31, 214, 244, 250, 339, 481
Catholic Commission of Japan, 143
Catholic Farmers Movement, 126
Catholic Patriotic Association, 53, 75, 383, 388, 426
Catholic Priests Association, 128
Catholic Relief Services, 80, 177
Catholic Welfare Services, 220
Catholicos of the Church of the East, 92
Caucasians, 16
Caunter, George, 276
Cebu (Philippines), 243, 250, 380
celebrations, 189, 196, 239, 241, 260, 263, 315, 358, 380, 459, 483, 488
cemeteries, 310, 431
censorship, 430
census(es), 76, 78, 149, 177, 212, 231, 235, 254, 275, 295, 392, 461, 501–7, 513, 515–17
Central Asia, 491
Central Committee of the KCF, 115
Central Committee of the VCP, 191
Central Java, 205–6, 209–10
ceremonies, 102, 105, 132, 155, 157, 172, 210, 428

Ceylon, 278
Chaktomuk Conference Hall, 178
Chalcedon, 291, 378
Chan, Edmund, 227–8, 231, 326
Chan Pan, 168
Chang, Aloysius B., 105
Changchun, China, 113
chants, 145, 172, 352
Chao, Jonathan, 68
Chao, T. C. (Zhao Zichen), 378, 384
Chao, Vouch, 177
Chaozhou Chinese, 159
chapel(s), 243, 257, 283, 292–3, 315
chaplain(s), 24, 124, 145, 258, 272, 274–7, 292
Charismatic(s), 29, 31, 33, 49, 66–8, 73, 77, 95, 105, 108, 197, 214–15, 217–19, 227, 232, 244–7, 250, 252, 277, 296, 304, 324–5, 336, 338, 340, 342, 344, 346, 360, 366, 372, 377, 398, 404–6, 448, 458, 507, 509–10
charity, 48, 77, 124, 136
Charter, James, 146
Chau, Uth, 179
Chen, Nan-Jou, 106
Cheng, Cheng-Kung, 466
Cheng, Jingyi, 382
Chengdu, China, 69
Chennai (madras), India, 357
Cheondogyoists, 384
Cherepanin (Hegumen Oleg), 289
Chhirc, Taing, 179
Chhoum, Sok, 177
Chi Tao Church, 89
Chiang Kai-shek, 103
Chiang Mai, Thailand, 71, 162, 167, 297
Chiang, Generalissimo, 106
Chien-Jen, Dr Chen, 21, 105
Chien, John C. T., 273
children, 28, 54–5, 69, 81, 93–4, 101, 113, 135, 140, 152, 160–2, 165, 168, 181, 183, 185, 190, 194, 196, 215, 220, 228, 236, 255, 296, 358, 373, 389, 409, 416, 426, 432–3, 454, 460, 484, 488, 503–6, 512, 515
Chilgol Church, 114–15
Chin Baptist Association of North America, 149
Chin Baptist Churches, 149, 153
Chin, 21, 100, 146, 148–51, 153, 305–6, 308, 331, 338, 366, 377, 395, 421, 430–1, 487, 490
China, 17–20, 23, 25, 27–8, 30–4, 40, 42, 44, 46, 48, 50, 52, 54, 56, 58, 60, 62, 64, 66, 68, 70, 72, 74–9, 83–4, 87–90, 92–4, 99–107, 110, 116–19, 134, 139, 168, 175, 177, 187, 193, 213–14, 217, 233, 238, 271, 273, 281, 283–5, 288, 295, 299–304, 306–7, 312–14, 316, 324–5, 327, 329, 351–2, 356, 361, 365, 367, 370–3, 375–9, 381–9, 393–5, 397–8, 404–5, 407–8, 413, 420–1, 425–7, 436, 438, 440–3, 451, 453, 460–3, 465–70, 473–4, 479, 481–8, 490–2, 510

China Aid, 426
China Christian Church, 76–7
China Christian Council (CCC), 41–2, 45–9, 110, 164, 271, 299, 307, 389, 395
China Evangelical Seminary, 327
China Gospel Fellowship, 68
China Graduate School of Theology, 327
China Inland Mission (CIM), 67, 270, 325, 394–5
China Peniel Missionary Society, 83
Chinese Autonomous Orthodox Church, 283, 285
Chinese Catholic Patriotic Association (CCPA), 53, 55–60, 329
Chinese Catholic(s), 51–3, 57–8, 60, 240
Chinese Church Coordinating Centre, 159
Chinese Church of Christ, 76
Chinese Communist Party, 22, 57, 75, 190, 312, 388, 393
Chinese Overseas Christian Mission, 77
Chinese Regional Bishops' Conference, 103
Chinese religion, 84, 90, 225, 389, 420, 444
Chinese Rites Controversy, 188, 356
Ching, Angela Wong Wai, 420
Ching Empire of China, 100
Chins for Christ in One Century (CCOC), 148
Chiuchow, 83
Cho, David Yonggi, 108, 227, 324, 340, 345, 404
Choi, Jashil, 121, 340, 345
choirs, 456
cholera, 168
Chonjugyo, 28
Chosen Christian College, 120
Chosun Christian Federation, 393
Chosun Presbyterian Theological Seminary of Pyongyang, 367
Christ's Commission Fellowship, 243, 245
Christian and Missionary Alliance (C&MA), 168, 176–7, 182, 302, 323
Christian Batak Clan Church, 203
Christian Brethren, 213, 217
Christian Church of Jawa, 302
Christian Conference of Asia (CCA), 49, 125, 296–8, 299–300, 304, 308, 319, 385, 400, 407, 471
Christian Council of Asia, 106
Christian Council of Korea (CCK), 126, 299
Christian education, 132, 152, 180, 183, 352, 472
Christian Federation of Malaysia (CFM), 217, 299
Christian Fellowship Church (CFC), 342–3
Christian Institute of Barmen, 204
Christian Nationals' Evangelism Commission (CNEC), 326
Christian Outreach, 179, 302
Christian Shuen Tao Church of Macau, 89
Christian Study Center, 84
Christian Tabernacle, 383

Christian television, 123
Christmas, 29, 42, 132, 140, 181, 210, 215, 218, 239–40, 248, 315, 317, 358, 428, 431, 456, 488
Christmas Masses, 456
Christology, 30, 375, 377–9, 381, 385, 409
Chrysostom, John, 289–90
Chuang Tzu, 15, 19, 27, 30, 34–5
Chuncheon, Korea, 293
Chundokyo, North Korea, 115
Chung, Peter, 215
Chung Hua Sheng Kung Hui, CHSKH, 271–2
Chunghyeon Presbyterian Church, 307
Chungjin, 116
church architecture, 18, 357
Church Dogmatics, 375
Church Doubling Movement, 103
Church Missionary Society (CMS), 76, 219, 269, 272–3
Church of Christ in Thailand (CCT), 163
Church of Christ of Congo (ECC), 107
Church of Christ, 76, 89, 102, 104, 135, 139, 158, 163, 225, 242–3, 274, 302, 328, 382–3, 455, 468
Church of Divine Mercy, 298
Church of England, 146, 269, 511
Church of God, 244
Church of Jesus Christ of Latter-day Saints (LDS), 182
Church of Joy, 163
Church of Love, 163
Church of Our Lady of the Assumption, 239–41
Church of Saint Alphonsus, 231
Church of Saints Peter, 17, 357
Church of St George the Martyr, 276
Church of St George, Limassol, 276
Church of St Michael and All the Angels, 274
Church of St Peter, 275
Church of the East, 17, 20, 92
Church of the Province of Burma, 278
Church of the Province of South East Asia, 277
Church regulations, 50
Church Union, 274
Church Universal, 320, 386
Church World Services, 80
Cireneu, Marcelo, 257
citizen(s), 47, 54, 57, 64, 69, 102, 138, 155, 161, 180, 190–1, 202, 212, 215, 220–1, 238, 285, 289, 291, 329, 387, 410, 419, 423, 439, 442–4
citizenship, 138, 212, 221, 423
City Harvest, 227–8, 232–3
civil war(s), 271
civilisation, 79, 133, 376, 378, 438
clan(s), 187–8, 203
Clark, William Smith, 136, 139
cleansing, 127, 487
Clement, 356, 364

clergy, 45, 49, 51, 53–4, 59–60, 76–7, 85, 132, 137, 139, 189, 196, 214, 240, 250–2, 255–6, 265, 273–4, 277, 279, 292, 321, 357, 372, 382, 384, 391, 435–6, 487, 504
clinics, 81, 160, 220
clothes, 33, 428
Club Asia, 244
clubs, 81
CNN Indonesia, 207
Cochinchina, 187
Cockey, T. A., 277
Code of Canon Law, 314
Coe, Shoki, 106, 376
cohorts, 515
Coiás, Francisco, 257
Cold War, 105, 121, 387, 469–70
colleges, 102, 234, 236, 245, 248, 273, 279, 327, 344, 485
Colloquium of the Six Religious Leaders of Hong Kong, 84
colonialism, 21, 54, 109, 127, 145, 151, 153, 197, 225, 269, 380, 391–2, 427, 438, 463–4, 468, 470, 472, 474
combat, 208
commerce, 134, 195
Communalism, 331
Communion of Churches, 299
communion, 30, 42, 49, 51, 53, 56, 89, 261, 269, 272, 274, 276–7, 290, 299, 302, 320, 325, 393, 426
communism, 126, 128, 189–90, 198, 325, 376, 381, 388, 390–2, 397, 422, 460
Communist Party, 20, 22, 41, 57, 64–6, 69, 75, 190, 197–8, 271, 284, 312, 372, 388, 393, 426–7, 443, 485–6
Communist Party's United Front Work Department, 426
Communist(s), 20, 22–3, 28, 32, 34, 41, 52–4, 57, 64–6, 68–9, 75, 85, 92, 94, 96, 99, 103, 105–6, 112, 122, 126, 130, 170, 179, 189–90, 193–8, 234, 246, 271, 273, 284, 312, 329–30, 336, 342, 355, 361, 366, 372, 378, 388, 390–5, 397–8, 413, 425–9, 435, 443, 466–70, 479–80, 485–6, 490
Community of St Peter, 275
compassion, 28, 66, 105, 161, 179, 401, 405, 462
Compassionate Presence, 405
competition, 22, 29, 160, 197, 202, 247, 252, 397
Cone, James, 172–3
confession, 107, 124, 129, 131, 196, 252, 274, 448, 467
conflict(s), 20–1, 51, 58, 79, 83, 90, 107–8, 122, 127–9, 157, 164, 187–8, 195, 200, 204, 210, 222, 229, 260, 305, 312, 320, 343, 355–6, 358, 382, 387, 393, 402–4, 419, 438–41, 444–6, 449, 451, 463, 470–1, 473–4, 480, 483, 489, 492
Confucian Four Books, 376

Confucian(ism), 20, 84, 90, 119, 122, 127, 139, 201–2, 275, 305, 351, 353, 356, 360, 368–9, 375–6, 378, 385, 387–8, 392, 413, 415, 420, 426, 438, 441–2, 447, 453, 465–6, 479, 482, 486
congregation(s), 40, 42–3, 49, 55–6, 60, 67, 77–8, 81, 89, 104, 113, 115–16, 124, 126, 129, 131, 136, 139, 162, 177, 183, 193–4, 196–7, 203, 215, 218, 231–3, 247, 249, 258, 281, 288–9, 298, 300–2, 310, 312, 315, 324, 327, 333–4, 340, 356, 365–6, 375, 382, 384, 395, 398, 406, 410, 427, 433, 435, 447, 455, 473, 503, 515–16
Congregation for the Evangelisation of Peoples, 197
Congregational Church, 136
conservative(s), 33, 64, 66, 89, 105, 111, 122, 125–6, 128–30, 208, 222–3, 244–5, 247, 251–2, 277–8, 295–6, 298–300, 302, 307–8, 367–9, 379, 382, 392, 442, 482, 485–6, 505
Constable, Nicole, 458
Constantine, 459
Constantinople, 287–9, 292–3
Constituent Assembly, 260, 290
Constitution(s), 22, 41, 82, 137, 141, 150, 156, 180, 190, 200, 202, 210, 212, 221–2, 251, 254, 260, 305–7, 312, 328, 364, 382, 389, 391–2, 427–32, 434–6, 439, 441, 443, 464, 487–8, 501
Constitutional Court, 202
Contesse, Gabriel, 167–8
Contesse, Marguerite, 168
contextualisation, 45, 50, 105, 161, 295, 305, 376, 471
Converse, Charles Crozat, 16
conversion(s), 21, 25, 31, 43, 63–4, 82, 100, 130, 158, 160, 198, 206, 214, 223, 230, 246, 261, 289, 295–6, 301–2, 304, 310, 329, 366, 372, 390, 395–6, 402, 408, 427, 431–3, 441, 446, 459–60, 481, 488, 505, 508–9, 512–14
Cooke, Eliza C., 101
Corfe, Bishop, 275
Corinthians, 16, 335
Cornelio, Jayeel, 455
Cornelius Sim, 240
Cornelius, Justice Alvin Robert, 240
Cosmic Christ, 44–5, 378
Costa Nunes, 256
cotton, 18
Council of Churches of East Asia (CCEA), 276, 279
Council of Churches of Malaysia (CCM), 217, 299
councils, 41, 180–1, 299, 323, 383
counselling, 61, 338, 457
Counter-Reformation, 321
Couples for Christ (CFC), 342–3
couples, 16, 18, 342–3
Covenant Evangelical Free Church (CEFC), 227–8, 298, 326

creation, 101, 125, 131, 169, 227–8, 232, 245, 284, 296, 303, 321, 332, 342, 353, 369, 376, 386, 418
Crete, 83, 315, 320, 362
crime, 138, 147, 306, 486
Crisóstomo, Frei, 255
Critical Asian Principle, 327, 372, 447
cross, 22, 29, 32, 66–8, 70, 73, 77, 110, 138–9, 171, 194, 259, 263–4, 275, 297, 304, 314, 325, 333, 346, 377–9, 400–1, 409, 419, 428, 459, 480, 491, 513
Crossover Project, 232
Crossroads, 83, 382, 438
Cross-Strait Service Trade Agreement, 110
Cross-Straits Christian Forum, 110
Crown Colony, 74
Cru, 299, 326
crucifixion, 142, 323
crusades, 149, 160–1, 164, 179, 219, 247, 326, 345
Cruz Jovem, 263
Cu Sau, 195
Cuarteron, Carlos, 213
Cuellar, 260
cults, 18, 60, 290, 396, 426, 430
Cultural Affairs, 132
Cultural Organization (UNESCO), 87
cultural revolution, 53, 55, 59, 61, 64, 69, 73, 75, 87, 271, 285, 367, 372, 388, 468
curriculum, 46–7, 50, 182, 303, 427, 444
customs, 79, 83, 119, 127, 131, 133, 297, 311, 319, 365, 464
Cyrillic, 92, 96

Daechuri, South Korea, 128
Daendels, Herman Willem, 205
dainichi, 136, 353
Dalit(s), 335, 407, 420
Daly, Mary, 420
Daman, India, 193, 326
Damien, David, 68
dance, 42, 47, 69, 78, 82, 94, 97, 102, 112, 114, 123, 171, 185, 227–8, 251, 263, 315, 365, 369, 377, 380, 458, 508
Dangun Myth, 130
Davao, Philippines, 243–4
Day of Pentecost, 365
De Béhaine, Pierre Pigneaux, 195
De Brito, Philip, 145
De Carvalho, Bishop José Manuel, 255
De Cruz, Gaspar, 175
De La Salle Brothers, 27, 194
de Nobili, Roberto, 318, 375
De Rhodes, Alexandre, 187, 195, 354, 375
deacons, 114–15, 273, 417
deaf, 46
death, 26, 51, 127, 139, 155, 168–9, 171–2, 223, 226, 230, 239, 247, 252, 261, 270, 306, 314, 317, 378, 396, 429, 488, 502, 512, 514–15

debate(s), 15, 45, 83, 85, 96, 107, 129, 296, 307, 376, 378, 444, 452
Deborah, 422
debt, 122, 416
declaration of human rights, 106, 501, 504
Declaration of Independence, 384
decolonisation, 463
Deep River, 142
Dega, 194
deity, 96, 119, 136, 138, 353, 369
deliverance, 171, 219, 345, 481, 508
democracy, 45, 79, 85, 93, 106, 110, 126, 138, 210, 246, 251, 372, 389, 393–4, 411, 421–2, 430, 442
Democratic Kampuchea, 178–9
Democratic Progressive Party, 105, 107, 307
demographics, 236, 248, 250, 405, 501, 503, 505, 506, 512, 514
demons, 24, 43, 45, 61, 94, 106, 108, 114, 128, 130, 171, 177, 184, 193, 206, 228, 241, 259, 264, 281, 292, 308, 330–1, 368, 373, 407, 409, 422, 433, 444, 508
Deng Xiaoping, 57, 453
denominations, 39–40, 63–4, 68–9, 75–7, 89, 99, 103, 121, 124, 129, 136–7, 139–40, 149, 164, 180–2, 193, 197, 216, 219–20, 225–8, 233–4, 242–3, 257–8, 271, 274, 279, 281, 292, 296–7, 299, 301, 323–4, 327–8, 337, 369, 382–4, 392, 410, 481, 484, 501, 504–5, 507–10, 517
depression, 84, 140
Desnitskaya, Ekaterina, 288
Destombes, Bishop Emile, 175, 178, 180
Deus, 136, 257, 353
Devi, Renuka, 54, 202, 207, 255, 281, 321–2, 337, 415, 417
devil, 54, 417
devotees, 24, 32, 380
Dewan Pentekosta Indonesia, DPI, 325
diakonia, 122, 125
dialects, 83–4, 92, 201, 354
dialogue, 30–1, 48–9, 54, 57–8, 61, 84, 110, 113, 117–18, 126–7, 143, 173, 198, 235, 299, 320–1, 333, 346, 375–6, 400, 402–3, 405–6, 410–11, 438, 441, 444–9, 457, 474, 481, 485
Diana, Lady, 16
Dias, Cardinal Ivan, 77–8, 94, 98, 131, 149, 195, 197, 249, 297, 325, 386, 390, 395, 397, 454, 456, 491, 504, 507
Dias, Priya, 77–8, 94, 98, 131, 149, 195, 197, 249, 297, 325, 386, 390, 395, 397, 454, 456, 491, 504, 507
diaspora, 94, 98, 131, 149, 195, 197, 249, 297, 325, 386, 390, 395, 397, 456, 491, 507
dictators, 21, 198, 246, 314, 372, 413, 421, 469
Diem, Ngo Dinh, 195
Dili, Timor-Leste, 255–8, 261–2
Ding Guangxun, 378
Dinh Thien Tu, 193

diocese(s), 58–61, 74–8, 81–3, 85, 87, 89–90, 119, 138, 148, 163, 194–5, 215–16, 231–2, 240, 244, 256, 262, 272–9, 284, 287, 291, 313–15, 342
Diocese of Dili, 256, 262
Diocese of Hawaii, 273
Diocese of Kuching, 240
Diocese of Labuan, 276
Diocese of Rangoon, 278
Diocese of Singapore, 231–2, 277
Diocese of Taiwan, 272–3
Diocese of Udon Thani, 163
Diocese of Victoria, 89, 272
disasters, 39, 390, 486
disciples, 68, 92, 95, 97, 134, 171, 186, 231, 236, 295, 298, 301, 305–6, 332–3, 360, 400, 407–8, 411, 489
Discipling a Whole Nation (DAWN), 240, 263, 300, 317, 337, 340, 483
discrimination, 55, 113, 148, 153, 184, 200, 207, 220–1, 293, 305, 311, 395, 421, 423, 427, 429, 431, 435–6, 458, 491
disease, 143, 338, 343
dissidents, 109
diversity, 42, 77–8, 128, 200, 202, 207, 210–11, 234, 242–4, 247, 250, 270, 279, 320, 332, 334, 355, 389, 406, 423, 425, 440–2, 444, 446, 449, 457, 467, 474, 510
divinity, 152, 281
divorce, 247, 252, 482
Doctor of Ministry, 47
Doctor of Theology, 47
doctors, 24, 201
Doctrina Christiana, 353
doctrine(s), 20, 45, 60–1, 64, 68, 119, 130, 171, 193, 208, 233, 244, 250, 281, 314, 354, 375, 380, 441, 469
dogma, 25, 111, 293, 305, 375
Doi Moi, 190
Dominican(s), 77, 99–100, 103, 175, 188, 254, 316, 465, 467
Dong, Bishop, 59
Donghak, 127
Dooley, Pastor Eric, 183
Doshisha Eigakko, 136
dreams, 508
drugs, 314, 434
drums, 97, 295
Dusun, 439
Dutch, 21, 33, 99–100, 201, 204–6, 213, 276, 316, 381, 383–4, 413, 466–7, 470–1, 479
Dutch East Indian Company, 99
Dutch Reformed Church, 99, 466
Duterte, Rodrigo, 314, 391, 434
Dwi Byantoro, Archimandrite Daniel Bambang, 291

Eagle Television, 301
Early Rain Covenant Church, 69
earthquake(s), 17, 357, 373
East Asian Christian Council Hymnal, 300
East Asian Exarchate, 284
East Malaysia, 212–14, 216–18, 331, 373, 396, 432
East Nusa Tenggara, 206
East Simalungun, 204
East Timor, 260, 313–14
Easter, 17, 19–20, 31, 42, 54, 57, 83, 102, 114, 168, 181, 193, 203, 205, 254, 285, 287, 291–2, 328–9, 351, 376, 387, 434, 473, 479
Eastern Europe, 54, 57, 291–2
Eastern Indonesian Protestant Christian Church, 203
Eastern Japan Diocese, 287
Eastern Mennonite Board of Missions, 193
Eastern Orthodox, 19, 287, 291, 328
Eastern Orthodox Metropolitanate of Hong Kong, 287
Ebenezer Home, 80
Ecclesia of Women, 422
ecclesiology, 50, 67, 107, 299, 375, 377, 381, 384–5, 422
Echica, Father Ramon, 251
ecology, 246, 308
Ecumenical Consultative Committee, 107
Ecumenical Patriarchate, 288, 292–3
Ecumenical Peace Platform, 393
ecumenism, 42, 44, 75, 77, 81–2, 84, 104, 106–7, 110, 126, 197, 217, 258, 288, 292–3, 298–300, 378, 383–4, 393, 400–1, 405–6, 416, 471, 474
Edinburgh, Scotland, 281, 382, 468
education, 21, 28–30, 39, 45, 47–50, 52, 55, 60, 63, 68, 72, 78–81, 85, 89–90, 93–4, 97–8, 100–2, 113, 115, 120, 132, 135–41, 144, 152–3, 155–6, 160–1, 180, 182–5, 189, 195–7, 201, 204, 220, 228, 233–4, 238, 243–4, 248, 255, 261, 264–5, 273, 277, 279, 286, 288, 295, 297, 302–4, 311, 315, 329, 332, 335, 352, 358–9, 372–3, 376, 383–4, 390, 393, 397–8, 404, 407–8, 421, 426–7, 429, 431, 435, 443, 447–9, 454, 460, 466–7, 471–2, 474, 482, 484–5
Egypt, 68, 507
Eigaku, 135
Ejercito-Estrada, Luisa, 239
El Shaddai, 31, 244–6, 249–50, 343, 360
elderly, 48, 78, 81, 230, 293, 365, 394, 513
elders, 32, 42–3, 49, 65, 70, 97–8, 112, 114–15, 186, 263, 299
elections, 203, 223, 430, 445, 488
elites, 79, 101, 111, 137, 207–8, 395, 464
Ellison, David W., 176
empire, 74, 92, 96, 100, 134, 137, 175, 316, 376, 383, 386, 388, 400, 407, 411, 472
employment, 34, 55, 452, 458, 484
empowerment, 41, 312, 336, 344–5, 407, 458, 481
Enbo, Wei, 383

England, 146, 269, 275, 467, 511
English-educated Singaporean Chinese, 230
English language, 16, 19–20, 31, 79, 83, 88, 93, 97, 100–2, 135–6, 142–3, 147, 155, 159–60, 165, 177–8, 180, 185, 216, 218, 225, 227, 230–1, 254, 269–70, 274–6, 278, 300–1, 338, 362, 397, 456–7, 466, 495
English Presbyterian Mission, 100, 102, 466
English Reformation, 269, 278
Enlightenment, 25, 101
Enoch, 164
entrepreneurs, 47, 63, 304
environment, 24, 41, 55, 70, 72, 84–5, 127, 129–30, 184, 234, 243, 247, 250, 308, 320, 324, 357, 365–6, 435, 445, 449, 456, 458, 460
Episcopal Church, 134, 269–70, 272–4, 276, 278
episcopate, 269
epistemology, 423
Epistles of John, 134
equality, 31, 45, 119, 127, 133, 137, 202, 221, 302, 310, 416, 488
Ermera, Timor-Leste, 256
eschatology, 30
Esther, 176
Estrada, Joseph, 391, 485
ethics, 25, 32, 61, 94, 122, 133, 205
Ethiopia, 511
ethnicity, 23, 27, 200, 207, 238, 305, 331, 355, 361, 395, 400, 421, 430, 439, 445, 516
Ethos Institute, 233
Eucharist, 60, 171, 240, 259–60, 293
Euki, Paul, 325
Eurasians, 216, 231, 396, 490
Eurocentrism, 472
Europe, 25, 27, 47, 54, 57, 94, 99, 101, 133, 138, 145, 158, 176, 179–80, 192, 205, 231, 245, 248, 291–2, 295, 297–8, 316–17, 330, 351–3, 356–7, 376, 452, 460, 463–4, 467, 470, 491, 502, 514, 516
Eusebius, 377
Evangelical(s), 25–6, 49, 64–5, 76, 81–2, 89, 95, 97, 101, 108, 124, 126, 143, 163–4, 169–70, 177–82, 184, 193, 197, 215, 217, 219, 227–8, 231, 235, 242–7, 252, 269, 271, 274, 277, 281, 296–300, 303–4, 308, 320, 324, 326, 328, 330, 334–5, 359–60, 376, 378, 389–90, 393–4, 397–8, 404, 427–8, 432, 445, 512
Evangelical Church of Vietnam, 193, 427
Evangelical Covenant Church, 108
Evangelical Fellowship of Asia, 325
Evangelical Fellowship of Singapore, 326
Evangelical Fellowship of Thailand, 163
Evangelical Formosan Church General Assembly, 300
Evangelical Mongolian Church Council, 299
evangelisation, 51, 58, 60, 70, 82–3, 89, 124, 197, 229, 246, 249–50, 255, 261, 265, 297, 310, 316, 326, 337, 356, 395, 460
Evangelisation of Peoples, 55–6, 197

evangelism, 39, 41, 43, 52, 67, 70, 79, 100, 123–4, 126, 147–9, 160–1, 163–6, 176, 182–3, 186, 229, 234, 277, 301–2, 304–5, 326, 328, 330, 332, 334, 338, 340, 347, 366–8, 370, 391, 393–4, 397–8, 402, 406, 408, 410, 428, 430–1, 433, 435, 438, 442, 481, 484–5, 487–8, 491, 510
Evangelize China Fellowship, 104
evil, 24, 130, 134, 169, 368, 371, 414, 416, 481
evolution, 53, 55, 59, 61, 64, 69, 73, 75, 79, 87, 113, 178, 233, 244–6, 269, 271, 285–6, 292, 313–14, 316–17, 354, 359, 367, 372, 378, 380, 382, 388, 394, 407, 421, 429, 468, 472
Ewha Hakdang, 120
exegesis, 130
exile, 113, 195, 390, 397
exodus, 88, 100, 456
exorcism(s), 341, 508
extremism, 236, 444–5

Fabella, Virginia, 380, 421
Facebook, 160
Faith Community Baptist, 227, 232, 326
Faith Purification Centres, 432
Falun Gong, 442–3
families, 23, 31, 81, 94–5, 97, 101–2, 112–17, 127, 135, 148, 162, 184, 225, 227, 232, 243, 257, 264–5, 336, 343, 366, 368–70, 373, 415, 429, 452, 454, 457–8, 460–1, 464, 484, 505
Family Guardian Coalition, 111
famine, 116, 325, 390, 486
Fang, Mark, 105
Far East Broadcasting Corporation, 244, 330, 359
farmers, 126, 130, 140
fascism, 388
fasting, 164, 206, 294, 340–1
Fatima, Portugal, 256
Fatumeta, 257–8
fatwas, 432
feasts, 94, 250, 358
Far East Broadcasting Corporation (FEBC), 181, 360
Federation of Asian Bishops Conference (FABC), 31, 192, 299, 319, 375, 385, 447
female(s), 120–1, 263, 272, 278, 403, 414–19, 423–4, 459
feminist theology, 125, 420, 422
Fernandes, Captain Francisco, 255
Fernandez, Hilary, 175, 220
Fernandez, Irene, 220
fertility, 506–7, 515
festivals, 192, 328, 370
Filipino(s), 16–17, 19, 23, 27, 83, 88, 105, 231, 240, 242, 246–52, 275–6, 300, 304, 316–18, 354, 357–8, 360, 371, 380, 382, 398, 405, 416, 421–2, 447, 454–6, 458–9, 471, 474, 491–2
finance, 21, 39, 42, 53, 75, 232, 303, 307, 345
fire, 17, 87, 246, 252, 337, 365

First Opium War, 74, 270
First Sino-Japanese War, 272
First World War, 140, 330
fishing, 83, 225
Five Classics, 376
Five Years Mission, 148
Five-Year Outline Plan, 45
Five-Year Plan, 66
Flores, 206
food, 40, 125, 129, 162, 179, 185, 209, 230, 240, 248, 319, 370, 429, 483
Food for the Hungry, 125, 179
Forcade, Father Theodore-Augustin, 134–5
Foreign Bible Society, 176
Foreign Institutions of the Moscow Patriarchate, 290
foreigners, 26, 87, 102, 145, 157–8, 177–8, 239, 273, 427, 455–6, 485
forests, 369
Formosa, 99, 111, 300, 466
forts, 22, 39, 44, 83, 94, 96, 100, 105, 111, 120–1, 136–7, 142, 145, 147, 149, 151–2, 187, 214, 222–3, 231, 261, 276, 298, 303–4, 308, 319, 321, 328, 337, 343, 353–4, 361, 384, 393, 408, 445, 448–9, 460, 467, 469, 471, 490
Forum Igreja-Igreja Kristaun Protestante, 258
Four Virtues, 415
Foursquare Church, 181, 183
fragmentation, 203, 235
France, 77, 137, 141, 143, 155, 158, 182, 187, 189, 205, 470
Francis, Pope, 51, 58, 167, 192, 417, 423
Franciscan(s), 61, 96, 175, 188, 316, 353, 356, 465, 467
Francisco, José Mario C., 20
Free China, 106
Free Community Church, 235
Free Methodists, 104
freedom, 22, 34, 40–1, 45, 48, 63, 65, 70, 84–5, 90, 102, 114, 123, 126, 134, 137, 139–41, 152, 155, 157, 173, 180, 189–91, 194–5, 197–8, 200, 202, 205, 207–10, 212, 219, 221–2, 238, 259, 264, 305–6, 310, 313, 328–9, 364, 380, 389–91, 424, 430, 432, 434, 436, 439, 441–3, 446, 448–9, 457, 460, 471, 473, 486–8
freedom of religion, 102, 141, 180, 195, 200, 202, 205, 207, 210, 222, 238, 329, 364, 427, 429, 435, 441, 443, 487–8
French, 33, 119, 169, 176, 188, 213, 249, 316, 370, 413, 427, 467, 479, 517
Fretilin, 313
Friends of Jesus, 140
friends, 32, 44–5, 48, 59, 93, 140, 160, 171–2, 184, 211, 236, 240, 333, 459–60
Fuan, 356
Fujian, 64
Fujii, Takeshi, 140
Fukuoka, 273
Full Gospel Assembly, 214

Full Gospel Bible College, 340
Full Gospel Church, 121, 324, 340, 345, 360, 398, 404
Full Gospel Tokyo Church, 345
Fuller Theological Seminary, 335
Fundamental Law of Education, 141
fundamentalism, 28, 33, 36, 62, 68, 219, 242, 245, 252, 306, 327, 330, 409, 422, 444, 474
funding, 161, 430
funerals, 127, 210, 502
Futaba School, 137
future, 27, 50–1, 57, 65, 70, 85, 90, 106, 131, 147, 152–3, 177, 179–80, 185, 209, 223, 233, 241, 246, 252, 256, 258, 260, 263, 271, 279, 291, 308, 329, 333–4, 363, 385, 394, 397, 401, 407–8, 411, 422, 444, 449, 461, 480, 482, 484, 488, 490, 510, 512, 514–16
Fuzhou, China, 83

G12 strategy, 165
Gabriel (angel), 357
GABRIELA, 416
Gadjah Mada University, 209
Gafatar, 207
Gallo, 240, 248, 317
Gallup, 453
Gama, Vasco da, 145
gambling, 90
Ganges River, 142, 463
Ganghwa Island, 275
Gangjeong, 128
Gatolic, 28, 298
Gaudium et spes, 354
Gawad Kalinga, 343
gender equality, 302
gender-based violence (GBV), 421
gender, 15, 97, 106, 110, 124, 127, 129, 184, 200, 235, 299, 302, 311, 321, 327, 380, 410, 414, 416, 418, 420, 422, 424, 460, 483
genealogy, 262
Generation Z, 480
Genesis, 36, 299, 317, 483
Geneva, Switzerland, 189, 193, 393
genocide, 179, 321, 473
geography, 238, 386
Georgian Palladian, 357
Gereja Bethel Indonesia, 341
Gereja Kemah Injil Indonesia, 302
Gereja Kristen Indonesia, 410
Gereja Kristen Luther Indonesia, 203
Gereja Kristen Protestan Indonesia, 203
Gereja Kristen Protestan Simalungun, 203
Gereja Kristen Timor Timur, 258
Gereja Masehi Injili, 302
Gereja Mission Batak, 203
Gereja Protestan Persekutuan Batak Karo, 203
Gereja Punguan Kristen Batak, 203
Gereja Sidang Jemaat Allah, 257
Gereka Kristen Protestan Angkola, 203

Gereka Kristen Protestan Pakpak Dairi, 203
German(s), 104, 119, 142, 204, 249
Germany, 57, 467
Germany, East, 57
ghettos, 234, 328
Gibbens, John, 96
Gideons, 179
Gidokgyo, 28
Gih, Andrew, 383
Gijang, 121
Gilmour, James, 93
Giovanni of Montecorvino, 96
Girelli, Archbishop Leopoldo, 192
Global Day of Prayer, 228
globalisation, 31, 105, 107, 143, 195, 321, 328, 366, 368, 438, 474
Glorious Revolution, 269
glossolalia, 296, 508
gnosticism, 480
Gobi Desert, 463
Goddess of Macau, 90
Goh, William, 229, 232
gold, 27, 145
Gomes, Anima Mukti, 257, 259
Gomes, José, 257
Gomes, Major General John, 257, 259
Gomes, Maria, 257
Gomes, Seabra, 257
Gomes, Subrata Augustine, 257, 259
gong, 442–4
Good Friday, 24
Goshkevich, 286
gospel, 19, 21, 32, 39, 44, 63, 68–70, 72–3, 81–2, 93–4, 101, 108, 111, 121, 123–4, 134–5, 146–7, 149, 151–3, 159, 161, 168, 172, 176, 178–9, 184, 190, 214, 219, 227–8, 230, 264, 269, 293, 296, 303–4, 324, 332, 334, 337, 340, 344–5, 347, 352–4, 360, 363, 365, 368, 378–9, 381, 395, 398, 404, 407, 463, 473, 490
Gothic, 17, 195, 243, 357
Goto, 135
Goulart, Jaime Garcia, 256, 265
Grace Baptist Church, 227
grace, 44, 55, 64, 68, 73, 202, 227, 294, 353
Graham, Angus Charles, 15
Graham, Billy, 15, 82, 149, 195, 225, 326
Graham, Franklin, 149
grassroots, 58, 64, 109, 123, 125, 127, 191, 218, 319, 334, 385, 402, 405, 410, 421, 444, 447–9, 507
Great Commission, 82, 231
Great Harmony, 42
Great Martyr, 289–90
Great Missionary Movement, 99–100
Greek(s), 287–9, 292, 352, 379
Greene, Graham, 195
Gresnigt, Dom Adelbert, 84
gross domestic product (GDP), 34, 40, 486
Guan Gong, 444

Guangdong, 69, 74, 159
Guangqi Press, 61
Guangzhou, China, 64, 74–5
Guinea, 163, 343, 396
Guiyang, China, 69
Guizhou, 69
Gulf Cooperation Council, 451
guru(s), 362
Gusmão, Xanana, 260
Guterres, Bernardo, 257
Gutheinz, Luis, 105
Gützlaff, Karl, 134
Gwangrim Methodist Church, 301, 307
Gyeonggi Province, 128

Habibie, B. J., 207
Hainan, 83
Hakdang, 120
Hakha, 148
Hakka, 83, 213, 254
Hakodate, 137–8
Hall, Bishop Ronald, 272
Halmahera, 204
Hammond, Arthur L., 176
Han Chinese, 388, 490
Hangul, 119–20
Hanoi, Viet Nam, 168, 188–9, 194–5
Hansalim Movement, 130
Hansen's disease, 143
Hao, Yap Kim, 235
Happy Homes Programme, 452
Happy Valley Racecourse, 83
harassment, 147, 310, 428, 430, 442
Harbin, China, 284–5, 291, 304
Harun, Mustapha, 214
Hatopen Kristen Batak, 330
Hatta, Mohamad, 201
Hau Lian Kham, 338
Hawaii, USA, 182, 273, 455
He Qi, 35, 74, 87, 283
Hea Woo, 429
Healer Panteleimon, 290
healing, 32, 51, 54, 63, 108–9, 160, 171–2, 184, 193, 219, 236, 335–6, 338–41, 344–5, 347, 371–2, 377, 403–5, 407, 409, 481, 508, 510
health, 28–9, 35, 45, 48, 52, 88, 94–5, 120, 124, 158, 160, 163, 167, 173, 180, 183, 189, 197, 220, 230, 232, 238, 248, 251, 265, 295, 302, 304, 316, 329, 335–6, 361, 367, 398, 435, 443, 445, 490, 503, 506, 513
Heart Sutra, 376
heaven, 44, 119, 122, 130, 134, 136, 378, 459
Hebei, 56, 69, 270
Hebron Brethren Assembly, 149
Hede, Bishop Liu, 59
Hee, Kong, 227, 232
Hefner, W., 411
hegemony, 314, 329–30
Heilongjiang Province, 285

Helena, 459
hell, 130, 429
Help International, 299
Henan, China, 63, 67–8, 70, 271, 426–7, 486
Hepburn, James Curtis, 134–5
herbs, 204
heresy, 244, 322
hermeneutics, 35, 43, 130, 377
heroes, 343
heterogeneity, 424
Heuvers, Father Hermann, 142
Heyward, Carter, 420
Hi-Eng, Gou, 102
Hick, John, 142
High Church, 216, 269, 278, 369
Hilarion, Archimandrite, 283
Hillsong, Australia, 18, 233, 300–1, 345, 365–6
Himalayan Tibetan, 483
Hindu(s), 157, 202, 210, 230–1, 376, 424, 436, 442, 449, 503, 512
Hinduism, 157, 201–2, 212, 217, 225, 321, 328, 333, 370, 385, 387, 392, 438, 442, 446, 466, 479, 513, 517
Hirado, Japan, 135
HIV/AIDS, 180, 299
Hla, John Aung, 278
Hmong, 21, 169–71, 193, 295, 301, 330–1, 359–60, 427, 481–2, 487, 490
Ho Chi Minh City, Vietnam, 194
Hoeryong, North Korea, 116
Hohulo-Raimansu, 263
Hokkaido, Japan, 136, 390, 484
Hokkien, 83, 338
Holiness Church, 76, 83, 101, 103–4, 328
Hollywood, 34
Holy Great Synod of Constantinople, 288
Holy Korean Orthodox Church, 293
Holy Metropolis of Korea, 292
Holy Orders, 278
Holy Resurrection Cathedral, 137
Holy See, 51, 53, 55, 57, 87, 105, 197, 254, 256, 260, 389, 434
Holy Synod of the Ecumenical Patriarchate, 288
Holy Synod of the Russian Orthodox Church, 284, 289, 292
Holy Thursday, 360, 455
Holy Trinity Church, 84
Holy Week, 315, 317
Hom, Neak, 177
Home Affairs, 430, 433, 435
Homeland Theology, 106
homeless, 82
homosexuality, 129, 298, 415
Hong Kong, China, 27, 31, 47, 49, 51, 60, 68, 71, 76, 78, 80, 82, 84, 86, 88–90, 96, 135, 248–9, 272, 278, 287–9, 298, 302, 323, 327, 332, 340, 343, 345, 368, 384, 389, 392–3, 397, 413, 420, 426, 438, 441, 444, 448, 451–3, 455–6, 459, 465–6, 474, 488, 490

Hong Kong Catholic Social Welfare Conference, 80
Hong Kong Chinese Christian Churches Union, 77, 298
Hong Kong Christian Council, 77, 298
Hong Kong Christian Industrial Committee, 79
Hong Kong Christian Services, 80
Hong Kong Christian Welfare, 80
Hong Kong Church Census, 76
Hong Kong Council of Social Services, 80
Hong Kong Harbor Mission Church, 83
Hong Kong Mutual Christian Improvement Society, 79
Hong Kong Sheng Kung Hui, 89, 272
Hope African University (HAU), 338
Hope Church, 342, 345
Hope of Bangkok Church, 164
Horie, Yuri, 423
hospice, 94
hospitality, 16, 94, 127, 379, 400, 402–4, 409, 411, 455
hospitals, 27, 81, 85, 102, 105, 124, 160, 163, 167, 194, 220, 274, 276, 304, 368, 373, 393, 434
hostel, 81, 220
house church(es), 19, 22, 32, 43, 64, 66, 70, 72, 115, 185, 194, 281, 302–3, 306, 329–30, 334–5, 373, 384–5, 426–7, 430, 470, 482, 486–7, 510–11
Hsu, Francis, 76
Huang, Po-Ho, 106
Hubei, 473
Hue, 189, 194, 428
Hui, 89, 271–3, 300
Huiyang, 74
human rights, 106, 110, 190, 207, 210, 239, 245, 252, 264, 299, 305, 307, 379, 400, 402, 417, 427, 429, 432, 442, 469, 473, 501, 504
Human Rights Research, 432
humanism, 31, 62, 422
Humanist Society, 231
humanists, 231
Hunan, 69, 473
Hungary, 273
hunger, 301
Hungry Ghost Month, 24
Hungry International, 179
Huria Kristen Batak Protestan, 203, 410
Huria Kristen Indonesia Protestan, 203
Huria Kristen Indonesia, 203
Hwang, C. H., 376
Hyesan, 116
Hymnal of Universal Praise, 300
hymns, 18, 123, 128, 136, 159, 171, 179, 185–6, 300, 331, 370, 469

iban, 215–16, 218
Iberia, 316–17

icons, 250
identity, 21, 60–2, 83, 85, 105–7, 110, 145, 150, 153, 155, 170, 172, 185, 197–8, 200, 202–4, 207–9, 236, 239, 254, 305, 310–11, 317–19, 327, 331, 344, 360–1, 365, 367, 390, 395, 414–15, 420–1, 424, 433, 439, 444–5, 447–9, 460, 463, 471, 491, 506–7, 513
ideology, 81, 105–6, 121, 139, 190, 198, 200, 202, 238, 244, 262, 372, 409, 416–17, 426, 429, 432–3, 435, 487
idioms, 356
Iesu, 140
Ig-du Kim, 372
Iglesia Filipina Independiente, 316, 382
Igorot, 276
Igreja Evangélica Assembleias, 257
Ileto, Reynaldo, 317
illness, 172, 230, 273, 338, 347
Iloilo, Philippines, 243
imagery, 246, 380
imagination, 385, 420, 443–4
imams, 157, 488
immigrant(s), 23, 83, 88–9, 293, 368, 373, 432–3, 452, 461, 512, 516
immigration, 143, 514–15
Imperial Rescript, 137
imperialism, 39, 75, 122, 269, 381, 394, 406–8, 463–4, 468, 472, 474
imprisonment, 173, 202, 256, 306, 389, 426, 430, 486–8
Inagaki, Ryosuke, 142
incarnation, 293, 310, 351–2, 361–2, 376–7, 379–80
Incheon, South Korea, 274, 293
inclusivity, 423
income, 40, 160, 228, 232, 238, 304, 308, 436, 484, 488–9
Income Tax Act, 436
inculturation, 19, 34, 51–2, 57, 62, 142, 262, 315, 320–1, 375–6, 448
Independent Churches, 104, 106, 181, 216, 233, 240, 245, 299, 331, 382, 510
Independent(s), 29, 33, 39, 42–3, 54, 57, 63, 75–6, 89, 95, 104, 106, 108, 110, 117, 164, 181, 201, 214, 216–17, 226, 232–3, 238, 240, 242–3, 245, 254–5, 269, 271–2, 276, 278–9, 299–300, 303–4, 313, 324, 331, 340, 359, 381–3, 391, 394, 398, 426, 460, 465, 468–9, 473–4, 504, 507, 510–11
India, 23, 51, 77, 99, 134, 145–6, 204, 212–14, 216–18, 225–6, 230–1, 240, 276–8, 288, 300, 327, 331, 339, 357, 366, 368, 375–6, 387, 396, 420, 438–9, 453, 463, 466, 471–3, 479, 490–1
Indians, 212, 216, 225, 230, 331, 396, 472, 490
indigenisation, 84, 105, 110, 127–8, 138, 278, 295, 395, 404, 468, 473, 482
individualism, 32, 417
Indochina, 87, 175, 193, 370, 438, 467, 479

Indonesia, 19–22, 28–9, 31, 33–4, 109, 202, 204, 206, 208, 210, 214–15, 225, 231–2, 240, 254, 257–62, 264, 277, 283, 288, 295, 299–300, 302, 304–6, 308, 311, 313–14, 319, 325–6, 329–30, 332, 339, 341, 343, 355, 364, 370, 383–4, 386–7, 391–3, 396, 398, 401–5, 409–10, 413, 416, 425, 431–3, 436, 439, 442, 444–5, 447–9, 451, 453, 456, 459, 467, 470–1, 473–4, 479–81, 484, 486–91, 505, 511
Indonesian Assemblies of God, 257
Indonesian Bethel Church, 341
Indonesian Christian Church, 203
Indonesian Evangelical Communion, 325
Indonesian High Court, 410
Indonesian Missionary Fellowship, 326
Indonesian Orthodox Church, 291
Indonesian Protestant Christian Church, 203
Indonesian Ulama Council, 432
Industrial Relations Institute, 79
Industrial Training Center, 95
industrialisation, 104, 124, 385
inequality, 31, 416
infant(s), 35, 171, 188, 414, 505
infrastructure, 57, 60, 155, 208, 226, 384, 489
Ing-wen, Dr Tsai, 110
Injil, 215, 302, 325, 331, 367
injustice, 54, 69, 109, 126–7, 221, 299, 304, 332, 384, 400
Inner Mongolia, 92–3, 285
Innocent, Archimandrite, 284
instability, 393
Institute for Theological Animation (BITA), 320
Institute of Church Planting Cambodia, 183
Institutio Generalis Missalis Romani, 105
intellectuals, 28, 52, 63–4, 68, 73, 79, 141, 284, 468
Inter-Faith Dialogue, 49, 235, 400, 438, 446–7, 489
Inter-religious Affairs on the Theology of Dialogue (BERA), 320
Inter-Varsity Christian Fellowship, 326, 333
intermarriage, 236
International Christian Assembly, 345
International Council of Christian Churches, 105
International Social Survey Programme, 251
Internet, 155–6, 159, 222, 394, 480
interventions, 223, 347, 445
intolerance, 201, 208, 210, 430
Iran, 505
Iraq, 235
Ireland, 77, 214
isan, 163
Isang Milyong Bayani, 343
Islam, 25, 30, 48, 84, 92–3, 157, 173, 181, 192, 201–2, 207–8, 212, 214, 221–3, 225, 231, 234–6, 238–41, 243, 301, 305, 321, 328–30, 332–3, 355–6, 364, 370, 373, 376, 381, 385,

387, 391–3, 402, 409–11, 413, 424, 431–4, 438–42, 445, 448, 459, 466, 471, 474, 479, 482, 484, 486–8, 492, 513, 517
Islamic law, 431
Islamic State, IS, ISIS, 19, 72, 235, 364, 413, 433–4
Island of Borneo, 238, 367, 396
Israel, 151, 378, 395
Italian, language, 16, 59, 167
Italy, 77, 138, 143, 343, 467
Itinerants of the Catholic Bishops' Conference of the Philippines, 455
Iwasawa, Arseniy, 286
Iwashita, 138–9, 141

Jainism, 321
Jakarta, Indonesia, 99, 200, 203–5, 208, 291, 330, 339, 405, 410, 433, 442, 487
Jakarta Theological Seminary, 405
James, Walter, 176
Janes, Leroy Lancing, 136
Japan, 16, 18–21, 23–5, 27, 30–4, 39, 76, 78, 83–4, 87, 89, 99–104, 111–12, 120–1, 127, 134, 136, 140, 142, 144, 205, 256, 271–5, 277–9, 283, 286–7, 292, 295–6, 298–9, 302, 307, 311, 324–6, 328–9, 345, 353, 358, 365, 370, 372, 375–6, 379, 381, 383–5, 387–90, 393, 397, 401, 413, 416, 420, 422–3, 425, 434, 438, 440, 443, 447–8, 451, 453, 455–7, 465–70, 473–4, 479–80, 484, 486, 488, 492, 517
Japan Bible Seminary, 325
Japan Christian Yearbook, 132
Japan Imperial Public Educational Association, 139
Japan's Nippon Sei Ko Kai, 278
Japanese, 16, 18–20, 23, 25, 27, 30, 76, 78, 83–4, 89, 100–4, 111–12, 120–1, 127, 132–4, 136–44, 205, 256, 271–5, 277–9, 285–7, 307, 326, 328–9, 345, 353, 358, 372, 376, 379, 383–4, 388, 390, 393, 397, 422, 443, 451, 456, 466–7, 469–70, 492, 517
Japanese Congregational Church, 136
Japanese Holy Catholic Church, 274
Japanese Nobori Kanai, 273
Japanese Orthodox Church, 285–7
Japayuki, 422
Jarai, 193
Java (Indonesia), 200, 204–7, 209–10, 291, 330, 341, 356, 466
Jehovah's Witnesses, 129, 177, 181, 243, 281, 436, 444
Jeju Island, 98, 128, 130, 367
Jemaa Islamiyah, 235
Jeonju, 293
Jerusalem, 20, 66, 72, 121, 304, 367, 431, 490
Jesuit(s), 18, 51–2, 77–8, 87, 133, 142, 167, 175, 179, 187–8, 204, 206, 255–6, 265, 316, 318, 353–4, 357, 375, 465, 467, 470

Jesus Family, 67, 250, 336–7, 342, 395
Jesus film, 93
Jesus Is Lord Church, 25, 345–6, 455
Jews, 332
Jianan Shige, 300
Jiangsu, 69
jihad, 305, 486
Jin, Bishop, 58
Jin, Tianming, 71
Jinping, Xi, 62, 69–70, 72, 285, 425–6
Jit-asa, 157
Joaquim, Father António, 255
jobs, 216, 248, 433, 484
John Paul II, Pope, 56–7, 188, 207, 258, 260–1, 397, 417–19
John the Baptist, 255
John XXIII, Pope, 189
Johnston, William, 142
Jorge, Frei, 254
jubilee, 228–9, 431
Judaism, 517
judgement(s), 108, 222, 227, 327
Judson, Adoniram & Ann, 146
Justice and Peace Commission, 82
justice, 45, 54, 59, 69, 82, 105–6, 109–10, 124–9, 195–6, 218, 221, 245, 252, 257, 264, 296, 299, 301, 303–5, 308, 320, 327, 332, 379–80, 384, 400, 405, 442

Kabaw, 147
Kachin Baptist Churches, 149
Kachin(s), 146, 148–9, 151, 395, 421, 430–1, 487, 490
Kadazans, 218
Kagawa, Toyohiko, 140
Kajinosuke Ibuka, 135
Kalay, 147
Kalgan, 93
Kalimantan, 200, 305, 332
Kalmucks, 96
Kambuja, 175
kami, 136
Kamiya, 143
Kampong Som, 183
Kampuchea, 175, 178–80
Kanagawa, 273
Kanamori, Michitomo, 136
Kang-Tak, John, 292
Kang, Namsoon, 420
Kang, Won-Yong, 125
Kao, C. M., 106
Kaohsiung, 457, 459
Karen (Kayin), 146, 148–9, 151, 159, 295, 305–6, 308, 326, 331, 372, 395, 421, 430, 487, 490
Karen Baptist Convention, 148–9
Karen National Liberation Army, 372
Karenni, 430, 487
Karo, 203
Kasatkin, Ivan Dmitrievich, 137, 286

Kaya, 490
Kayah, 149
Kazakh(s), 92, 516
Kazan, Russia, 290
Kebatinan, 210
Kedah, 212–13
Keelung, 466
Kelabits, 215
Kernolong Church, 203
Kerygma, 122, 342
Ketuhanan, 208
Khalkh Mongolian, 92
Kham, 338
Kheng, 169–70
Khleang Province, 179
Khmer, 175–8, 181–5, 290, 298, 330
Khmer Evangelical Church, 177–9, 182
Khmer New Year, 185
Khmer Rouge, 178–9, 184, 330
Khmu Bible, 169
Khmu, 167, 169–70, 172, 481, 489–90
Khong, Lawrence, 227–8, 235, 326
kidnappings, 486
Kil, Son-ju, 337–8, 377
killing(s), 179, 313, 330, 434, 486–7
Killing Fields, 179
Kim, Chang-su, 128
Kim, Ikdu, 337
Kim, Jae-June, 125
Kim, Kyu-sik, 121
Kim, Maria, 121
Kim Il-sung, 113, 429
Kim Jong-un, 390
kindergartens, 81, 432
King Bhumibol Adulyadej, 155
King Dome, 249
King Gojong, 127
King Louis of Holland, 205
King Narai, 158
King Norodom Sihanouk, 181
King of Portugal, 87, 145
King Sisowath Monivong, 176
kingdom, 17, 134, 140, 175, 180, 230, 244–9, 255, 288–9, 294, 299, 321, 325, 378, 397, 457, 511
Kingdom of Cambodia, 175, 180
Kingdom of God, 140, 299, 321, 325, 378, 397
Kingdom of Mena, 255
kings, 24, 145–6, 150, 153, 187
Kinmen, Taiwan, 68
kinship, 258, 262
Kinukawa, Hisako, 422
Kiribati Protestant Church (KPC), 125
Kirill, Patriarch, 285, 291
Kirishitans, 134–6
Kitamori, Kazoh, 142, 379
Kobe, Japan, 140, 273–4
Koh, Pastor, 432
Koho, 193

Kolkata (Calcutta), India, 276–8
Korea, North, 34, 114, 116, 118–20, 122, 126, 128, 130, 292–3, 295, 305–7, 364, 366, 390, 393, 401, 413, 425, 428, 436, 438, 440, 442, 470, 479–80, 482, 485–6, 492
Korea, South, 27–8, 31–2, 34, 70–1, 94–5, 98, 103, 114–15, 117–18, 122, 124, 128, 130, 180, 183, 293, 295, 298–301, 303–4, 307–8, 311, 323–4, 372, 378–9, 384, 386, 390–4, 397–8, 401, 404–5, 407–8, 413, 425, 434–5, 438, 440, 446, 451–3, 455–6, 468–9, 479, 481–2, 485–6, 489, 491–2
Korean Association of Christian Women, 422
Korean Association of Women Theologians, 125
Korean Buddhist Federation, 115
Korean Catholic Association, 115
Korean Chondoist Association, 115
Korean Council of Religions of Peace, 446
Korean Missionary Brotherhood, 274
Korean National Council of Churches, 299, 401
Korean Orthodox Church, 115, 293
Korean Presbyterian Church, 125, 298
Korean Religionists Council, 115
Korean War, 103, 112, 121, 130, 275, 292, 307, 341, 397
Koreans, 18–19, 33, 67, 116, 119–20, 292, 324, 390
Koryo, 299
Kosai, Masuda, 286
Kosai, Tachibana, 286
Koshin Presbyterian Churches, 299
Kota Kinabalu, 214, 217
Kounthapanya, Khamphone, 169
Kounthapanya, Saly, 169
Kowae, Wirachai, 163
Kowloon, 74
Koya, 30, 138, 327, 379, 401, 447
Koyama Fukusei Hospital, 138
Koyama, Kosuke, 30, 327, 379, 447
Kozaki, Hiromichi, 136
Kren Jai, 156–8
Kriengsak Chareonwongsak, 164, 342
Kuala Lumpur, Malaysia, 217, 344, 358
Kuching, 216, 232, 240, 276–7
Kumamoto School of Western Studies, 136
Kumamoto Yogakko, 136
Kuomintang, 105, 273, 469
Kuribayashi Teruo, 420
Kuzure, Urakami Yoban, 135
Kwok, Pui-Lan, 377, 420
Kwong, Peter, 75, 272
Kyoto Graduate Union of Religious Studies, 448
Kyushu, 273

La Salle Brothers, 27, 194
La Vang, 377

labour, 15, 33, 41, 79, 82, 105, 124, 140, 167, 213, 248, 316, 390–1, 416, 422, 429–30, 451–2, 454, 457, 461, 469, 484, 486
Labuan, 213, 276–7
Lady of the Assumption, 239–1
Lahane, 255
Lahu, 151, 159, 295
Lai, Bishop José, 88
laity, 51, 67, 189, 196, 218, 233, 250, 265, 344
Lak, Yeow Choo, 327
Lakawa, Septemmy, 409
Laksana, Albertus Bagus, 319
Lam, Domingos, 88
Lam, Chung-kong, 89
Lam, Yam-man, 89
Lamb, Samuel, 64
land, 23, 83, 92, 99, 107, 128, 175, 203, 209–10, 220–1, 257, 259, 273, 308, 310, 316, 341, 428, 458, 466, 470, 488, 491
Langham, 97
language(s), 18, 25, 33, 42, 60, 72, 88, 92, 96, 119–20, 136, 139, 142, 155, 165, 169, 172, 175, 178, 185, 187, 194–5, 200–1, 205, 212, 218, 222, 225–6, 249, 254, 257–8, 284, 287, 290–1, 293, 298, 300, 305, 317, 322, 334–5, 338, 351–5, 359, 361–2, 373, 376, 379, 381, 395–6, 410, 430, 432, 464–6, 469, 471, 503, 516
Lanzhou, 69
Lao Evangelical Church, 169–70, 428
Laos, 20, 24, 31, 34, 168, 170, 172, 175, 232, 277, 288–9, 295, 304, 310, 314–15, 329–30, 355, 364, 387, 395, 398, 413, 421, 425, 428, 436, 452–3, 466–7, 479–81, 483, 485–6, 489–90
Laranjeira, Manuel Mendes, 262
Larantuka, 255
Lascano, 380
Latin America, 192, 218, 358, 386–7, 420, 464
Latter Rain Church, 344
Latter-day Saints, Mormons, 181–2, 243, 281
Lausanne Congress, Third, 70
Lausanne Movement, 70, 219, 325
Lausanne World Congress, 71
law(s), 43, 45, 55–6, 61, 65, 76, 85, 90, 104, 107, 109–10, 116, 141, 197, 201–2, 208, 210, 222–3, 239, 284, 286, 291, 305, 314, 340, 361, 373, 421, 427, 429–31, 433–4, 440, 443, 446, 487–8, 512
Lawas, 217
lawyers, 201
Lay Apostolate, 320
leadership, 25, 33, 39, 41–3, 54, 56, 61, 89, 93–6, 108, 112, 129, 148, 151, 156, 165, 171, 177, 180–3, 186, 193, 195, 213, 219, 223, 227–8, 247, 254–5, 265, 271, 273–4, 278–9, 290, 302–3, 325–7, 329–30, 332–3, 344–5, 361, 372, 381–3, 390, 393, 396, 398, 404, 417, 447–8, 467, 509
lectionaries, 262

Lee, Stephen, 88
Lee, Cheon Hwan, 275
Lee, Chong, 170
Lee, Gipung, 367
Lee, Kuan Yew, 226, 229
Lee, Myungbak, 130
Lee, Yongdo, 337
Leira, Giovanni, 167
Lenin, Vladimir, 287, 428
Leningrad, 287
Lenten, 455
Leo XIII, Pope, 167
Leontiev, Maxim, 283
Leow, Archbishop Julian, 217
leprosy, 15, 138, 168–9
Les Sœurs, 137
Leuven, Belgium, 61
LGBTQ, 414–15, 422–4
Li Tianen, 64
Li Xinheng, 19, 72
Liaoning, 69
liberalisation, 388, 390, 392
liberation, 24, 39, 107, 112, 126, 193, 218, 246, 252, 260, 275, 308, 317, 321, 354, 372, 380, 391, 393, 420, 434, 440, 445
liberation theology, 126, 218, 246
liberty, 325
Life Fellowship Phnom Penh, 183
Liggins, John, 134, 273
Light of Jesus Family, 250, 342
Lim, Timothy, 281
Limbang, Malaysia, 238
Ling Liang World-Wide Evangelistic Mission Association, 104
Lisi, Meng, 19, 72
Lisu, 159, 377, 395
literacy, 152, 231, 303, 383, 484
literature, 41, 78, 127, 139, 141, 165, 195, 221, 239, 242, 244, 300, 426, 428, 430, 435, 453, 458, 487, 501, 509
Lith, Van, 206–7
Lithuania, 271
Little Flock, 331, 383, 395
Little Sisters of the Poor, 78, 80
Liturgical Commission of the Diocese of Dili, 262
Liturgical lectionaries, 262
liturgy, 43, 60, 84, 123, 127, 159, 250, 261–2, 287, 289–90, 292–4, 301, 322
Liturgy of St John Chrysostom, 289–90
Living Hope in Christ Church, 183
Lock Tao Christian Association, 77
Logos Evangelical Fellowship, 300
London Missionary Society, 76, 88–9
London, UK, 76, 88–9, 146, 274
loneliness, 347
Loochoo Naval Mission, 273
Los Angeles, California, 121, 335
Lotus Sutra, 376

Louton, Mike, 345
Love Singapore, 228
Luang Prabang, 167, 169
Luc, Tran, 17, 195, 357
Luke, 176
Lun Bawang, 215
Luther Christian Indonesian Church, 203
Lutheran(s), 49, 80, 95, 103, 105, 108, 164, 216–17, 225, 233, 243, 296, 300, 302, 323, 327–8, 449
Lutheran World Federation, 49
Lutheran World Services, 80
Luzon, Philippines, 99, 276
Lyfoung, Touby, 169

Macanese, 88, 90
Macau, 32, 49, 88, 90, 134, 255, 270, 272, 288, 413, 426, 466
Macau Anglican Church, 89
Macau Baptist Church, 89
Mackay, Australia, 101, 484
Mackay, George, 484
Madame Song, 103, 106
Madras (Chennai), India, 357
Magellan, Ferdinand, 380
magic, 24, 227
Maha Esa, 208
Mahayana Buddhism, 84, 376, 387, 479, 517
Mai, Tran, 193
Maiorica, Gerolamo, 195
Maitrichit Baptist Church, 159
Majapahit, 291
Majestades, 316
Majlis Gereja-Gereja Malaysia, 299
Malacca, Malaysia, 87, 212–13, 254, 277, 467
Malay Archipelago, 438
Malay Bumiputras, 212
Malay Islamic Monarchy, 440
Malay-language Bibles, 432
Malay Muslim Monarchy, 238
malaya, 212, 277, 448, 483
Malaysia, 16, 19–20, 23, 31, 33–4, 180, 182–3, 192, 214, 216, 218, 220, 222, 225–6, 232, 238, 240, 277, 288, 295, 299, 301, 303, 305–6, 308, 326–8, 331–3, 344, 355, 357, 360, 362, 364, 366–7, 370, 373, 379–80, 387, 391–2, 395–6, 401–2, 405, 409–10, 413, 416, 423–5, 431–3, 436, 439, 441–2, 446–8, 452–3, 467, 470–1, 473–4, 479, 481, 484, 486, 488, 490–1
Malaysia Baptist Theological Seminary, 217, 327
Malaysia Bible Seminary, 217, 327
Malaysia Evangelical College, 217
Malaysia Theological Seminary, 217, 328, 448
Malaysian Consultative Council of Buddhism, 446
Maldives, 288
Maliana, 256

Malik, Adam, 313
Maluku, 204, 444–5, 487
Mamdu, Dom Joseph, 84, 167
Mamuya, 204
Manalo, Felix, 245
Mananzan, Mary John, 421
Manas, 264
Manatuto, 256
Manchuria, 119, 139
Mandailing, 203
Mandalay, 278
Mandarin, 36, 42, 83, 104, 232, 254, 258, 301, 362
Mangga Besar Jakarta, 339
Mangihut Hezekiel Mannullang, 330
Manichaeism, 20
Manila, Philippines, 24, 56–7, 100, 179, 243–4, 246, 250, 275–6, 315, 339, 342, 345–6, 352, 360, 370
Mankhanekhoun, Bishop Louis-Marie Ling, 167, 173
Mankin, Pramod, 321
Manobo, 332
Manso, Frei Pedro, 255
Manuel, Bishop José, 255
Mao Zedong, 468
Maoism, 388
Mar Thoma Church, 217
Marawi, 434
Marçal, Arlindo, 258, 262
Marçal, Florindo, 257
Marcos, Ferdinand, 245, 248, 330, 391, 485
Mardon, Richard, 146
marginalised, 31, 79, 82, 103, 105, 108–9, 121, 124, 168–70, 232, 235, 321, 333, 336, 366, 369, 379, 396, 398, 401, 419, 447, 459, 472, 481, 485
Marian devotion, 377
Mariano, 343
Marino, Archbishop Joseph S., 216
Maritain, Jacques, 141
Mark of Yegoryevsk, Archbishop, 290
markets, 488
Maromak, 263
marriage, 24, 94, 110–11, 196, 201, 210, 235–6, 239, 244, 247, 252, 255, 307, 371, 420, 432–4, 451–2, 458–9, 484
Marsden, P., 407
Martino, Cardinal Renato, 260
martyr(s), 19, 22, 65, 70, 72–3, 112, 119, 122, 134, 188, 198, 276, 289–90, 314, 390, 396–7, 416
martyrdom, 65, 72, 198
Marxist(s), 62, 229, 319, 375, 428
Mary Magdalene, 416
Maryknoll, 77, 80, 421
Maryknoll Sisters Catholic Welfare Centre, 80
masculinity, 414

mass, 18, 28, 32, 54, 58, 60, 83, 88, 100, 112, 143, 205, 209, 214, 229, 240, 251, 256, 259–62, 298, 310, 315, 317, 329, 342, 352, 359–62, 391, 397, 455–9, 469, 481
materialism, 198, 330, 373, 480, 482, 490
Matthew, Apostle, 377, 421
Mau Duan, 263
Maute Group, 434
Mawlamyine, 277
May Fourth Movement, 52
Mbour, Senegal, 341
McCaul, Jesse, 183
McCaul, Chuck, 183
McClean, Hector, 147
McClean, Sigrid, 147
McDougall, Francis Thomas, 276
McFague, Sallie, 420
McGilvary, Daniel, 167
McIntire, Carl, 105
Medan, Indonesia, 204, 433
Medeiros, Father, 255, 265
media, 28, 49, 56, 69, 79, 83, 104, 129, 155–6, 159–60, 164, 244, 260, 297–8, 314, 340–2, 352–3, 360–2, 370, 377–8, 394, 402, 409, 426, 435, 439, 443, 449, 457, 469, 480, 482, 487, 489, 506
medicine, 39, 101, 133, 373, 383, 471, 484
meditation, 206
Meer Uitgebreid Lager Onderwijs, 204
mega-church, 18, 31, 108, 122, 129, 226–7, 230, 232–4, 243, 296, 307, 334, 340, 413, 473, 481
Megawati, 207
Meiji empire, 133, 135–40, 383, 468
Mekong River, 167
Melayu Islam Beraja, 431, 440
Melee, 147
Mendes, Bonnie, 262
Meng Lisi, 72
Mennonite (s), 104, 193, 427
merchants, 145, 352
Mercy Associates, 179
Mertens, Father, 206
Merton, Thomas, 15, 19
Meru, 172
Mesa the Tagalog, 354
Methodist(s), 76–7, 95, 97, 103–5, 112, 120, 125, 147–8, 164, 181–2, 193, 213, 216–17, 225, 227–8, 232–3, 235, 240, 296, 298, 301–3, 307, 323–4, 326–7, 369, 382, 448, 466
Methodist Missionary Society, 326
Methodist Theological School, 217
methods, 95, 97, 130, 159, 489, 501
Metropolitan Archdiocese of Seoul, 119
Metropolitan Daniel, 287
Metropolitan Kirill, 291
Metropolitan of All Japan, 287
Metropolitan of Hong Kong, 288
Metropolitan of Korea, 293
Metropolitan Sergius, 286–7
Metropolitanate of Hong Kong, 287–8
Mexico, 77
Micah Asia, 308
Micah, Hieromonk, 291
Michelangelo's *Pietà*, 35
Middle East and North Africa (MENA), 27, 31, 72, 92–3, 223, 248, 300, 343, 441, 491
migrant(s), 23, 27, 49, 80, 83, 88–9, 94, 131, 143, 203, 213–14, 218, 220, 225–6, 231, 234, 236, 238, 240, 248, 277, 284, 288, 293, 300, 304, 331, 358, 368, 373, 395, 405, 407, 432–3, 451–62, 470–1, 474, 483–4, 490–1, 507, 512, 516
Migrant Church, 218, 405, 474
migration(s), 32, 64, 143, 204, 213–15, 292, 304, 358, 386, 396, 405–6, 438, 452, 454, 456, 458, 480, 484, 512, 514–15
militants, 434
military, 99, 102–3, 110, 119, 124, 128–9, 139, 141, 149–50, 170, 180, 186–8, 195, 201, 223, 256, 258–9, 262–4, 278, 283, 286, 288, 310, 313–14, 316, 379, 381, 384, 390–2, 394, 396, 401, 406, 413, 421–2, 430, 435–6, 463, 467–9, 486–7
Military Ordinariate, Australia, 119
Military Ordinariate of South Korea, 119
Million Souls, 140, 337, 345, 366
Mindanao, Philippines, 243, 276, 343, 393, 409, 440, 445, 486
Ming-cheung, Bishop Michael Yang, 51
Mingjing, 307
Minh Mang, 188
Minh Thien Voan, 179
Ministry of Cults, 430
Ministry of Education, 47, 136
Ministry of Home Affairs, 435
Ministry of Information, 181
Ministry of the Interior, 427
Minjung theology, 19, 126, 378, 391, 401
Minor Seminary of Our Lady of Fatima, 256
minorities, 24, 129, 151, 153, 170, 172–3, 193, 202, 207, 238, 244, 303–4, 306–7, 310–11, 328, 330, 355, 364, 379, 390, 396, 421, 427–8, 430, 439–42, 445–6, 449, 470, 473–4, 481, 483, 485–7, 489–1
miracle(s), 33, 64, 104, 184, 230, 338, 341, 371–2, 397, 481, 508–9
Miri, 217
Misa, 240, 248, 317
missiles, 492
Mission Batak Church, 203
Mission China, 66, 69, 71–2
missionaries, 19, 21, 26–7, 39, 44, 51, 66–7, 69, 71–4, 76–7, 79, 82–3, 87, 92–7, 99–103, 105–6, 119–23, 132–6, 138, 142, 145–9, 151, 157–8, 160–3, 167–71, 177–80, 182–3, 186–8, 200, 204–5, 213–15, 219, 223, 225–6, 232, 234, 236, 245, 249, 254–6, 263, 270–1, 273, 275, 277–9, 283–4, 303–4, 312, 316–17, 324,

336–8, 345, 352–4, 356–7, 367–8, 370, 372–3, 376, 381–2, 408, 420, 436, 457, 463, 465–7, 470, 472–3, 483, 490–2
Missionary Alliance, 168, 302, 323
Missouri, 18
Miyabe, Kingo, 136
mizo, 147
Mnong, 193
mobility, 303, 336, 363, 368, 398
models, 82, 243, 302, 352, 354, 357, 388, 403, 410, 416
modernisation, 21, 28, 31, 55, 79, 133, 302–3, 361, 388, 397, 441, 468, 471, 484
Moi, Daniel Arap, 190
Moisés, 258
Molucca, 204
Mon, 94, 136, 149, 167, 490
Mon, Vang, 167
monarchy, 79, 87, 155, 238, 431, 440
monasteries, 20, 90, 185, 285, 465
money, 138, 164–5, 185, 430, 483
Mongol Empire, 92, 96
Mongol(s), 18, 28, 34, 87, 94, 96, 98, 285, 288, 295, 299, 301–6, 308, 339, 345, 364, 372, 387, 425, 434–5, 438, 479–80, 483
Mongolia, 18, 28, 34, 87, 94, 96, 98, 285, 288, 295, 299, 301–6, 308, 339, 345, 364, 372, 387, 425, 434–5, 438, 479–80, 483
Mongolian Bible Translation Committee, 96
Mongolian Evangelical Alliance, 97
Mongolian Research Institute, 98
Mongolian Standard Version, 96
Mongolian Union Bible Society, 96
monks, 16, 115, 127, 157, 161, 185, 289, 306, 430, 459, 465, 483
monotheism, 142, 433
Montfort, 220
Moody, Dwight Lyman, 111
Moody, N., 111
Moon, David, 182
Mooneyham, Stanley, 178
Moore, Edwin, 178
Morais, Joaquim, 257
morality, 51, 94, 137, 380, 419, 435, 441
Moravia, Czech Republic, 96
Moravian(s), 96
Moro Islamic Liberation Front, 393, 440, 445
Morrison, Robert, 74, 134
mortality, 230, 515
Moscow, Russia, 284–7, 289–92
Moscow Patriarchate, 284, 287, 289–90, 292
Mosintuwu Institute, 404
mosques, 370, 488
Motael, 255, 259
Mother of Perpetual Help Shrine, 458
mothers, 97, 403, 454, 484
Motoda, Joseph Sakunoshin, 274
Moulmein, 277
Movement of the Caring Mothers, 403
movements, 29, 40, 52, 94, 103, 105–6, 108–9, 121, 126, 173, 210, 219, 245–6, 250, 252, 263, 281, 295, 304, 308, 321, 325–6, 330, 333–5, 351, 354, 358–60, 367–8, 371, 376, 385, 387, 391, 397–8, 404–7, 432, 442, 463, 467–8, 482, 491, 503, 509
Muhammad (prophet), 25, 29, 211
Muhammadiyah, 29, 211
Muhibbah, 379
Mukyokai (non-church movement), 469
multidimensionality, 411
Muntilan, 206
Murut, 439
Musan, 116
music, 18–19, 29, 46–7, 49, 84, 97, 123, 128, 158–60, 171, 185–6, 195, 227, 232–3, 300, 340–1, 345, 356, 360, 365–6, 370, 469, 482–3
Muslim(s), 21, 25, 28–30, 34, 48, 69, 130, 157, 181, 200–1, 204, 206, 208–12, 215, 217, 220–3, 229, 231, 235, 238–40, 242, 254–5, 276–7, 306–7, 328, 330–3, 353, 356, 379–81, 384, 391–3, 396, 402–4, 409–11, 413, 423–6, 430, 432–6, 439–45, 447, 449, 452–3, 459, 467, 471, 479–80, 484, 486–91, 502, 506–7, 512–13, 517
My Tho, 20, 193
Mya, Francis Ah, 278
Myanmar, 16, 20–1, 27, 29, 31, 34, 150, 152, 159, 214, 278, 288, 295, 298–9, 303, 305–6, 308, 310–11, 323, 326, 328, 331–2, 338, 355, 364, 366, 372, 377, 387, 395, 400–2, 413, 421, 425, 429–30, 436, 441, 444–6, 451, 453, 467, 470, 473, 479–83, 485–7, 489–90
Myanmar Council of Churches, 299
Myanmar Missions International, 149
Myitkyina Diocese, 148
myths, 414

Na'i, 262
Nacpil, Emerito, 327
Nagaland, India, 368
Nagas, 134–5, 138, 273
Nagasaki, 134–5, 138, 273
Nagasaki Magistrate, 135
Nagasaki's Urakami, 135
Nagoya, 274
Naha, 134, 273
Nahda, 211
Nahdatul Ulama, 29, 211
Nai Kheng, 169–70
Nai Phum, 288
Naide, John Yasutaro, 274
Nak-Joon, 130
Nakai Tsugumuri, 287
Nakonz, Jonas, 458
nande, 175, 220, 255
Nanjing Union Theological Seminary, 46
Nanjing, China, 46, 74, 271, 469
Nanle County Church, 427

Narai, 158
Nasarah (Nazarenes), 193
nation-building, 219, 332–3, 372, 376, 397, 464, 467, 470
National Chinese Christian Conference, 45
National Christian Church Networks Cambodia, 181
National Christian Council (China), 125
National Christian Council of Japan, 299
National Council of Churches of Singapore, 228
National Council of the Mongolian Church, 95
nationalism, 121, 271, 308, 330, 382, 391, 430, 442–3, 463, 468–70, 472, 489
Natshinnaung, 145
nature, 17, 44, 51, 106, 122, 158, 197, 210, 294, 328, 354, 368, 376, 378, 381, 385, 406–7, 409, 433, 442, 449, 473
Navigators, 326, 333
Nazarene(s), 24, 32, 193, 250, 458
Ndoni, Nigeria, 298
Nectarios, 288
Nee, Watchman, 67, 104, 217, 331, 395
neighbourology, 29–30, 379, 447
neighbours, 29–30, 33, 169, 171, 184, 211, 333, 338, 379, 387, 410, 443, 448, 474, 513
neo-Confucianism, 388
Nepal, 232, 277, 288, 327, 502
Nestorian(s), 17, 20, 212, 352–3, 465–6
Nestorius, 351
Netherlands, 201, 204–5
New Age Spiritualists, 424
New Apostolic Church, 181–2
New Century Mission Movement, 103
New Creation Church, 342
New Life Fellowship (NLF), 183
New People's Army, 372
New Religious Movements (NRMs), 173, 245, 442, 517
New Testament, 96, 136, 168, 176, 287, 320, 345, 377, 379, 507
New Zealand, 179, 300
newspapers, 155, 239
Nguyen, Ba Tong, 188
Nguyen, Van Thieu, 195
Nicholas, Archbishop of Japan, 286–7
Nicholas, Hieromonk, 287
Nicholas Alexeev, 292
Nicholas II, 288
Niger, 511
Nigeria, 511
Nihon Kirisuto Kokai, 135
Nihon Kumiai Kirisuto Kyokai, 136
Nihongo, 16
Nikitas, Archimandrite, 288
Nikkeijin, 451
Nikorai-do (Nicholas Temple), 286
Niles, D. T., 300

Nimitmai Christian Church, 163
Nippon Budokan, 345
Nippon Sei Ko Kai, 272, 274, 278
Nirmal, Arvind P., 420
Nishida, Kitaro, 142–3
Njotorahardjo, Niko, 341
Nobel Peace Prize, 260
Nobili, Roberto de, 318, 375
Nol, General Lon, 177
Nommensen, Ludwig Ingwer, 204
non-church movement, 140, 143, 469
non-governmental organisation(s) (NGOs), 27, 88, 93, 312, 456
North Africa, 31, 223
North America, 47, 101, 107, 149, 277, 300, 326, 335
North Borneo, 277
North Tapanuli, 204
North Vietnam, 189, 342
Norway, 512
Norwegians, 84
Novena Church, 231
nun(s), 53, 135, 255, 275, 315, 421–2, 483
nurses, 24
Nusantara, 201, 205
Nusiro, 287
Nwe, 421
Nyack College, 176

O'Brien, Brandon J., 339
Obispo Maximo, 382
Occupied Territories, 463
Oceania, 192
Oe-Cusse, 254, 256
Office of Theological Concerns, 320
Ogata, Sadako, 143
Oikumene Church, 433
oil, 238, 248, 291, 431, 452
Okinawa, Japan, 134, 273
Okryu, 115
Old Catholic(s), 251, 299
Old Testament, 96, 136
Oleg, Hegumen, 289–90
One Belt, One Road (OBOR), 72, 474, 490–2
One Million Heroes, 343
Ono, 286–7
Open Doors, 330
oppression, 20–1, 113, 120, 147, 153, 198, 205, 295, 303, 324, 369, 379–80, 416, 472–3, 491
orality, 51, 94, 137, 380, 419, 435, 441
Orang Asli, 214, 216, 218
Order of Friars Minor, 77
Order of Preachers, 77
Ordinary of the Mass, 262
ordination, 23, 42, 56, 59, 67, 76, 90, 125, 129, 167, 173, 193, 196, 274, 278, 287, 312, 343, 417, 421, 456
Orevillo-Montenegro, 380
orphanages, 94, 152

orphans, 140, 183
Orthodox, 19, 33, 49, 95, 115, 119, 124, 132, 137, 194, 217, 281, 284, 286, 288, 290, 292, 294, 306, 328, 376, 427, 508–9
Orthodox Book of Prayer, 289
Orthodox Metropolis of Korea, 293
Orthodox Prayer Book, 290
Orthodox Theological Seminary, 286
Orthodoxy, 119, 281, 285–6, 288–92, 306, 427
Osaka Shinai Girl's School, 137
Osaka, Japan, 137–8, 273–4
Oshikawa, Masayoshi, 135
Ossu, 256
Our Lady of Mount Carmel Cathedral, 29
Our Lady of the Miraculous Medal Church, 459
Oura Cathedral, 135
outreach, 28, 71, 93–4, 124, 177, 179, 205, 218, 220, 248, 302, 332, 338, 343, 397, 404, 491
Overseas Missionary Fellowship (OMF), 170, 179, 219, 326
Owari, 134

Pacific Ring of Fire, 17
Pacific War, 102, 139, 141
Pacquiao, Manny, 247
Padroado Real, 187
Padroado, 187–8, 316
Paiwan, 108
Pakistan, 19, 72–3, 278, 288, 445, 459, 517
Pakpak, 203
Pakse, 167
Palang-Li, 293
Palaung, 149
Palawan, 246
Palestine, 16
Pali, 231
Pallu, Bishop, 188
Palmerston, Lord, 74
Pamba, India, 299
Pancasila (five principles), 21, 200–2, 208, 305, 384, 392, 432, 442
Panginoon, 342
Panikkar, K. M., 463
Panyajan, 165
Papua New Guinea, 343, 396
para-church organisations, 63, 93–4, 164, 179–80
paradigms, 30, 198, 262, 308, 310
Parham, Charles, 335
Paris Foreign Missions Society, 167, 175
parishes, 81, 88, 95, 167, 231–2, 240, 243, 248, 251, 285–6, 293, 313–15, 321, 358, 362
Park Chung-hee, 126, 379
Park Hyung-Nong, 125
Park Kun-Hye, 126
Park Soon-Kyung, 125
Park, Sun Ai Lee, 422
Park Yoon-Sun, 125

parliament(s), 92, 150, 220–1, 430, 434
Parliamentary Select Committee, 221
Parolin, Cardinal Pietro, 58
partnership(s), 182, 233, 262, 298, 308, 346, 408, 480
pastors, 22, 24, 26, 42–3, 59, 63–5, 67–72, 97–8, 103, 110, 112, 125, 129–30, 165, 171, 177, 180, 182, 193, 217, 227–8, 231–3, 236, 257–8, 299, 303, 315, 326–7, 338, 394, 428, 488
Pasyon, 317, 380
Pathet Lao Movement, 428
Patriarch of Moscow, 287, 291
Patriarchate of Constantinople, 287, 288–9, 292–3
patriotism, 40, 45, 102, 191, 197
Patronato Real, 316
Pattaya, Thailand, 358, 407
Paul VI, Pope, 83, 261–2
Pchum Ben, 185
peace, 36, 69, 82–3, 109, 125, 128, 130–1, 149, 152, 157, 166, 173, 180, 195–6, 228–9, 234, 259–60, 290, 299, 307–8, 314, 333, 343, 391, 393, 401–3, 408, 411, 431, 440–1, 444–6, 448, 467, 486
Peduli, Ibu, 403
Peixian, Jin, 58
Penang, Malaysia, 213, 216–17, 219–20, 276–7, 467
Pentecostal(s), 23–4, 29–30, 33, 62, 66–8, 76, 83, 95, 108, 121, 123, 130, 143, 146–7, 149, 151–2, 164, 193, 197, 214, 217, 219, 296, 304, 323, 325, 331, 336, 338, 340, 342, 344, 346, 366, 372, 377–8, 389, 395, 397–8, 400, 405–6, 409, 411, 447–8, 473, 508–10
Pentecostal Holiness Church, 76, 83
People Power Movement, 391
People Power Revolution, 245–6, 314, 359
People's Rights Movement, 137
Perak Sultan, 222
percussion, 17, 34, 110, 406
Perempuan, 208
Perestroika, 190
Pero Marqués, 187
Perry, Bill, 246
persecution, 20, 23, 30, 36, 53, 64–8, 70, 72, 100, 103, 119, 142, 146–7, 153, 170, 173, 188, 193, 274, 300, 305–6, 333, 336, 342, 366, 368, 395–6, 426, 428–9, 460, 466, 473, 486–7, 489, 491
Persekutuan Gereja-gereja, 299, 325
Persekutuan Injil Indonesia, 325
Persia, 300, 376
Peru, 143
Petaling Jaya, Malaysia, 217, 220
Peter the Great, 283
Peters, Andrej, 286, 288–9
Petitjean, Father Bernard-Thadée, 135
Pew Research Center, 453, 506–7, 511, 516
Phan, Peter, 318–19, 402–3

Phiasayawong, 291
Phii Pop, 168
Philippine Communist Party, 372
Philippine Council of Evangelical Churches, 323, 445
Philippine Episcopal Church, 276
Philippine Federation of Christian Churches, 323
Philippine Independent Church, 242, 276, 279, 382
Philippine Missionary Fellowship, 326
Philippine Statistics Authority, 242
Philippines, 17, 21, 23–5, 29, 31, 33–4, 77, 99, 143, 200, 215, 225, 239, 244, 246, 248, 250, 252, 276, 278, 281, 288, 295, 299–301, 304–5, 310, 313–16, 321, 323, 326–8, 330, 332, 339, 342–3, 345–6, 352, 356–9, 361, 364–5, 370–2, 377, 380–2, 386–7, 391, 393, 396, 398, 402, 404–5, 407, 409, 413, 416, 422, 425, 432, 434, 440–1, 445, 451–8, 461, 467, 471, 473, 479, 481–6, 488, 491
philosophy, 21, 101, 119, 134, 136, 138–9, 141–3, 201–2, 321, 375, 440, 442–3, 482
Phimphisan, Bishop George Yod, 163
Phitsanulok, Catherine Na, 288
Phnom Penh, Cambodia, 175–83, 290
Phoenicia, 421
Phuwanat, Chakkraphong, 288
Pierce, Charles, 275
Pieris, Aloysius, 420
pietism, 33, 67
Pigneaux, Pierre, 195
Pilario, Daniel, 447
pilgrimage, 191, 196, 206, 209, 319, 356, 457
Pink Dot Movement, 235
Pinto, Fernandez Mendez, 175
Pius IX, Pope, 134
plantations, 213–14
Plaung, 490
Plenum, 196
pluralism, 142, 296, 308, 321, 402, 432, 480, 514
PocketSword, 165
poetry, 97, 136, 195
pogroms, 402
Pol Pot, 178, 372, 470
Poland, 54, 57
police, 116, 186, 201, 240, 427–8, 432
politics, 25, 27–8, 32, 54, 65, 109, 131, 150, 155, 195, 202, 205, 207–8, 215, 220, 244–7, 251, 262, 265, 316, 328, 351, 387, 394, 397, 400, 406, 420–1, 446, 461, 473–4, 485
Politics of Ethics, 205
polls, 504–5
polygamy, 420
Polytechnic University of the Philippines, 345
Pontifical Commission, 82
Pontifical Council of Justice, 195
poor, 28, 31, 61, 78, 80, 82, 93, 95, 140, 151, 177, 184, 219–20, 232, 250, 264–5, 295–6, 303, 308, 320, 333, 336, 343, 354, 359, 379, 394, 397–8, 401, 406–7, 420–1, 447, 472, 481, 488, 491
Pope Alexander VI, 187
Pope Benedict XIV, 356
Pope Clement IX, 356
Pope Francis, 51, 58, 167, 192, 417, 423
Pope John Paul II, 56–7, 188, 207, 258, 260–1, 397, 417
Pope John XXIII, 189
Pope Leo XIII, 167
Pope Paul VI's Evangelii Nuntiandi, 261
Pope Pius IX, 134, 397
Pope Pius XII, 356
Portugal, 87, 133, 145, 256, 260, 467
Portuguese, 16, 87–8, 90, 143, 145, 153, 175, 187–8, 204–5, 213, 249, 254–8, 260, 262, 313, 316, 413, 465, 467
Portuguese Bishops' Conference, 90
Poso, 403–4
Potsdam Declaration, 141
poverty, 34, 40, 48, 82, 125, 140, 245, 299, 304–5, 308, 320, 335, 340, 387, 396, 400, 406, 415, 422–3, 484, 491
Pradabchananurat, Thongchai, 163
prayer, 24, 32, 42, 54, 66–7, 97, 107–8, 115, 123–4, 137, 160, 164, 172–3, 181, 186, 206, 218, 223, 228, 240, 249, 257–8, 262–3, 269, 273, 278–9, 289–90, 293, 299–301, 307, 317, 319, 330, 334, 336–8, 340–2, 353–5, 362, 365–6, 370, 372, 393, 398, 430–2, 443, 456, 458–9, 481, 483, 485, 508
Prayer Mountain, 108, 370, 372
preaching, 42, 67, 81, 97, 99, 108, 122, 142, 152, 261, 279, 332, 339, 341–2, 352, 354, 360, 363
Prefect Apostolic, 213
pregnancy, 371
Prek Talong, 179
Presbyterian(s), 69, 95, 97, 100–4, 108, 112, 120–1, 123, 125, 130, 134, 147, 158–9, 167, 169, 183, 193, 213, 217, 225, 233–4, 258, 269, 273–5, 296, 298–300, 302–3, 307, 323–4, 327, 367, 382–3, 389, 466, 469–70
priest(s), 24, 31, 53–61, 65, 79, 87, 89, 93, 95, 100, 119, 128, 133, 135, 137–8, 141, 145, 157, 161, 167, 172–3, 175, 178, 188–9, 195–6, 205–7, 213, 215, 218, 240, 250, 256, 272, 278, 283–7, 289–92, 311, 313, 315, 321, 339, 344, 357, 378, 387, 391, 397, 417, 419, 427–9, 434, 455, 457, 459, 470, 481, 509
Priimak, Father Polikarp, 292
Prince, Joseph, 227
Prince Chakkraphong, 288
Prince Chakrabongse Bhuvanath, 288
Prince Charles, 16
Prince Norodom Sihanouk, 177
printing, 66

prison, 28, 51, 53, 56, 63–5, 72, 82, 94, 106, 112, 173, 180, 195, 202, 208, 239, 256, 306, 388–9, 426–30, 433, 486–8
privacy, 113
Propaganda Fide, 187–8
properties, 87, 147, 195, 249, 316
prophecy (gift), 219, 335–6, 339, 377
proselytising, 176, 276, 307, 330, 442
prosperity, 31, 45, 49, 108, 122, 125–6, 165, 171, 198, 214, 219, 227, 230, 346, 360, 387, 398, 473, 490
prostitution, 140, 415
Protestant(s), 16–18, 21, 28, 30, 33, 40, 42, 48, 50, 52–3, 59–60, 64, 69–70, 74–5, 78–85, 87–90, 93, 95–6, 108, 112–17, 119–26, 128–9, 131–2, 134–9, 141–2, 145–7, 151–2, 156–7, 159, 162–3, 170, 173, 176–7, 180–2, 192–8, 200–2, 213–14, 216, 219–20, 225, 228, 231–2, 240, 242–7, 254, 258, 263, 269–71, 274–5, 278–9, 281–2, 296, 298, 300, 302, 304, 306, 308, 319, 323–4, 328–9, 351, 354–6, 359, 367, 369, 373, 376–7, 381–3, 388, 390, 392–7, 404, 413, 426–7, 433–4, 442, 447, 455, 467, 473, 479, 484, 486, 491, 508–11, 517
Protestant Batak Karo Brotherhood Church, 203
Protestant Christian Simalungun Church, 203
Protestant Church of Sabah, 216
Protestant Episcopal Church of America, 134
Protestant Reformation, 269, 298
Protestant Urban Industrial Mission, 126
protests, 128, 135, 239, 314, 395
proverbs, 354
Provincial Council of the Church of India, 278
psalms, 96, 287
Public Christianity, 233
Public Welfare Charitable Activities, 48
publishing, 61, 139, 168, 287, 293
pulpits, 315
Punjab, India, 517
purification, 353, 432
Putian Songzhan, 300
Putonghua, 88
Pwo Karen, 146
Pyeongtaek, 128
Pyongyang, North Korea, 114–16, 120–1, 337, 366–7, 370
Pyongyang Revival, 337, 366, 370
Pyongyang Theological Seminary, 115

Qing dynasty, 20, 52, 74, 79
Quae Mari Sinico, 382
Quakers, 104
Quang Nam, Vietnam, 187
queen(s), 254–5, 380
Queen Juana of Cebu, 380
questionnaire(s), 503–4
Quezon City, Philippines, 342
Quiboloy, Apollo, 245–6

Quito, Ecuador, 357
Qur'an, 231, 376, 433

race, 23, 200, 206, 218–19, 221, 229, 305, 331, 430, 444
radicalism, 201, 402, 410, 431, 482, 486–8, 490, 492
radio, 56, 94, 172, 181, 244, 343, 359–60, 489
Radio Veritas Asia, 359
Raffles, Sir Stamford, 225
Rahman, Tungku Abdul, 202, 226
Rai, D. R., 263
raids, 240
railway, 213
rain, 69, 344
Rajah of Sarawak, 213, 276
Rajaprasong, 157
Rakhine, 149, 151, 490
Ramadan, 29, 210
Ramos-Horta, José, 314
Ranau, 217
Ranchi, India, 60
rape, 414, 421
Raphael, 138
Ratburi Province, 289
Rawang, 217
Ray of Hope, 32
reconciliation, 58–9, 61, 131, 184, 228, 259, 287, 307–8, 393, 401, 445, 485, 489
reconstruction, 41, 44–5, 50, 397, 447
Red Hero, 92
Redemptorists, 427
Reformation, 269, 278, 297–8, 321, 323
Reformed Baptists, 69
Reformed Churches, 49, 69, 73, 106, 302, 325
refugee(s), 77–8, 80–2, 88, 103–4, 113, 116–17, 130, 143, 170, 177, 179–80, 220, 272, 284, 307, 366, 432, 445, 483, 487
Regional Bishops' Conference, 103, 105
Regulating Religious Circles' Participation, 48
regulations, 23, 50, 69, 102, 167, 208, 308, 427, 441–2
rehabilitation, 81, 220, 343, 441
Reichelt, Karl L., 84
relief, 48, 61, 78, 80, 177, 179, 357, 373, 393, 472
Religion Decree, 427
religiosity, 32, 35, 322, 370, 385, 397, 447, 453, 458
Religious Affairs Bureau, 306, 426, 435
religious affiliation, 127, 222, 244, 360, 370, 502, 504, 506, 512, 514, 516
Religious Charity Week, 48
Religious Corporation Ordinance, 141
religious diversity, 243–4, 250, 389, 441, 444, 446
religious freedom, 34, 48, 84–5, 90, 114, 126, 137, 139, 190–1, 194, 197, 207–9, 212, 219, 221–2, 310, 313, 328, 389–91, 432, 434, 436, 441–2, 446, 449, 460, 473, 486, 501

Religious Organisation Law, 141
renaissance, 356, 385
renewal, 63, 84, 105, 109, 189, 214–15, 218–19, 246, 250, 252, 325, 335, 337, 339, 398, 481, 508–10
research, 98, 112, 139, 142, 183, 201, 209, 432, 448, 452–3, 458, 503, 505, 508, 510–12, 516–17
respondent(s), 24, 132, 440, 453, 503, 513
restoration, 48, 100, 135, 184, 246, 251–2, 320, 366, 383, 507, 509
resurrection, 137, 169, 261, 286–7, 293, 310
returnees, 297, 329
revival(s), 43, 67, 72, 81, 101, 108, 115, 120–1, 123, 149, 164, 215, 291, 326, 335, 337–8, 341, 366–7, 370–1, 377, 385, 442, 474
revolution, 53, 55, 59, 61, 64, 69, 73, 75, 79, 87, 113, 178, 233, 245–6, 269, 271, 285–6, 292, 313–14, 316–17, 354, 359, 367, 372, 378, 380, 382, 388, 394, 407, 421, 429, 468
Reyes, Isabelo de los, 382
Rhenish (Barmen) Mission, 76, 204
rhetoric, 354, 419
Rhodes, Alexandre de, 187, 195, 354, 375
Ricardo, Father Alberto, 259, 262
Ricci, Matteo, 53, 318, 353–4, 356, 375
Rich, Adrienne, 423
Rieger, Joerg, 406
Riesenhuber, Father Klaus, 142
Ritchie, Hugh, 101
Rites Controversy, 25, 51, 87, 105, 188, 356, 465
rites, 16, 18–19, 25, 51, 87, 105, 188, 210, 315, 356, 369, 377, 465
ritual(s), 32–3, 41, 43, 45, 49, 60–4, 67, 73, 78, 81, 94, 98, 102, 105, 108–9, 111, 122, 124, 131, 133, 142–3, 145, 150, 152–3, 157, 161, 165, 172–3, 193, 198, 206, 210, 223, 233, 243, 246–7, 252, 260–5, 269, 277, 284, 289, 293–4, 297, 300–1, 304, 314–15, 321–2, 325, 327, 329, 336–40, 344, 346–7, 351, 355–6, 360, 362, 366, 370, 377–8, 380–1, 388, 395, 400, 406, 410–11, 424, 443, 448, 456, 458, 470, 473, 480–3, 489, 492, 507
rivers, 308, 318
Rizal, José, 371
Rodrigo, Michael, 141, 314, 391
Rodrigues, Alberto, 257
Roffe, George Edward, 169
Rohingya, 29, 306, 310, 400, 430, 445–6, 483, 487
Roman Catholic(s), 74–5, 81, 163, 167, 173, 175–6, 178, 181, 197–8, 213, 225, 229, 231, 240, 242, 244, 269, 275–6, 281, 299, 314, 328, 331, 376, 382, 390, 400, 402, 405, 411, 426, 429, 440, 453, 509
Romania, 57, 289, 292
Rome, 51, 53, 55–60, 96, 187, 189, 195–6, 216, 312, 314, 343, 356, 389, 426

Romyen Church, 163
rosary, 456
Ross, Denise, 377
Ross, John, 119
Royal Citizen Movement, 102
Royal Laotian Aviation, 176
Royal Letters Patent, 89
Rubinstein, Murray, 108
Ruether, Rosemary Radford, 420
Rungus, 218
Runi, 92
Russia, 49, 92, 94–5, 119, 137, 194, 271, 283–93, 376, 466, 491, 516
Russian Ecclesiastical Mission, 283–4, 286–7
Russian Orthodox Church, 49, 95, 284–5, 287, 289–92
Russians, 283–4, 288, 290, 292
Russo-Japanese War, 138–40
Rwanda, 277
Ryukyu, 134

Sabah, Malaysia, 212–18, 221, 232, 277, 405, 432, 439, 446, 484
Sabah Council of Churches, 217
Sabah Theological Seminary, 217
sacraments, 30, 42–3, 54–6, 58, 139, 315, 429, 469
sacrifice, 19, 67, 72, 96, 147, 188, 207, 416–17, 465, 467
Saedamoon, 341
Sagada, 276
Said, Edward, 421, 464
Saigon, Vietnam, 176, 189, 194–5
St Andrew's Anglican Church, 240
St Andrew's Cathedral, 232
St Anthony's Church, 255
St Christopher's Parish, 459
St Francis' Canossian College, 79
St George Church, 290
St George's Church, 357
St George's School, 239–40
St Ignatius Church, 142
Saint Jean-Baptiste, 27, 194
St John the Baptist, 255
St John's Cathedral, 272
St John's College, 271
St Joseph's College, 79
St Louis Jesuits, 18
St Mary's Church, 84
Saint-Maur, 137
St Nicholas Cathedral, 289
St Nicholas Orthodox, 285
St Nicholas Parish, 289
St Paul's College, 79, 87, 272
St Paul's School, 273
Saint Petersburg, Russia, 286, 288–9
Saint Petersburg Theological Seminary, 289
St Peter's Church, 213
St Peter's College, 216

St Savior's College, 79
St Stephen, 272
St Vincent, 80, 220
St Yoseph Bintaran Church, 205
saints, 17, 19, 22, 30, 35, 70, 111, 181–2, 243, 281, 315, 319, 357
Saipan Island, 109
Sait Ni Nuta, 204
Salesians, 77
salvation, 44, 80–1, 122, 125, 129, 131, 140, 142, 157, 217, 220, 225, 246, 293, 298, 304, 306, 317, 336, 339, 344–5, 401, 405
Salvation Army, 80, 125, 140, 217, 220
Saly, Reverend, 169
Samarinda, 433
Sanchez, Bo, 250, 342
sanctification, 45
sanctions, 305, 415
sanctuary, 70
Sangju, 128
Sanjiang Church, 23
Sanskrit, 175
Santa Cruz massacre, 259
Santa Isabel Cathedral, 29
Santa Luzia, 254
Santacruzan, 459
Santo Niño, 250, 380, 458
São Jacinto, 255
São Tiago, 255
Sarawak, Malaysia, 212–18, 220, 238, 276–7, 355, 432, 439, 446, 484
Sarekat Jesuits, 206
Sarin Sam, 179
Sasaki, Paul Shinji, 274
Savannakhet, 167–8
Sawabe, Takuma, 137
Sayama, 287
Scandinavia, 93
Schereschewsky of Shanghai, Bishop Samuel, 271
schism(s), 53, 56–7, 109, 235, 299, 324, 382, 509–10
Schmidt, I. J., 96
Schneider, F. E., 339
Schneider, Herbert, 339
schools, 27–9, 42, 46–8, 79–81, 85, 88–90, 94, 97, 101–2, 105, 112, 135, 147, 153, 158, 160, 163, 178, 184, 194, 204, 214, 217, 219–20, 231, 243, 255, 265, 273, 276, 279, 303–4, 313, 315–16, 319, 359, 373, 426–7, 430–2, 434–5, 485, 488
science, 64, 101, 103, 119, 195, 245, 261, 264, 319, 354, 430, 435, 516
scientists, 145, 201, 503
Scorsese, Martin, 142
Scotland, 215, 269
Scottish Enlightenment, 101
scripture(s), 96, 160, 219, 231, 247, 252, 296–7, 299, 326, 331, 364, 376–7

Scripture Union, 219, 299, 326
Scriven, Joseph, 16
Second Vatican Council, 18, 53, 60–1, 76, 82, 84, 105, 189, 198, 218, 262–3, 265, 318–19, 321, 354, 421
Second World War, 101, 104, 108, 141, 205, 215, 219, 256, 277, 324, 328, 383–4, 393, 438, 467–9, 479
sect(s), 207, 212, 244, 426
sectarianism, 77
secularism, 373, 453, 480, 490
seekers, 445
Seelye, Julius H., 139
Seikyo Jiho, 287
Selangor State, 432
Sem Bun, 179
Semarang, 205–6
seminaries, 29, 46–9, 54–5, 61, 63, 69, 78, 85, 103, 164, 191, 205, 216–17, 233–4, 321, 327–8, 406, 470
Sendai, 137
Sendangsono, 206, 209
Seng, Eu Hong, 217
Seng, San Hay, 177
Sengoi, 216
Seo Sang-ryun, 119
Seon-ju, Gil, 377
Seoul, South Korea, 71, 119, 128, 274, 292–3, 324, 332, 340, 360, 366, 372
Seremban, 217
Sergii, Archbishop, 292
sermons, 45, 60, 123, 131, 157, 171, 301, 341, 447, 489
Serviam, 342
settlement(s), 83, 94, 140, 256, 276–7, 313, 454
Seung-hun, 119
Seventh-day Adventist(s), SDA, 76, 104, 163, 177, 193, 216, 240
Seymour, William, 335
Sgaw Karen, 146
Shafi'i, 212
Shahada, 434
shamanism, 18, 92, 95, 119, 127–8
Shan, Tao Fong, 84, 448
Shandong, 64, 270
Shanghai, China, 61, 64, 71–2, 83, 270–1, 284, 300, 306, 331
Shangti, 353
Shaojie, 427
sharia, 222, 239, 305, 432, 441–2, 487–8
Shears, A. 277
Shen Tsai-sen, 271
Sheng-si, 300
Shenists, 230
Shenyang, China, 58, 69
Sheshan, 377
Shia, 207, 439
Shijiazhuang, 60
Shik, Angela Wai Yan, 458

Shinto, 16, 18, 25, 102, 132, 136–7, 141, 370, 388–9, 438, 440, 443, 466, 517
ships, 21, 32, 42, 47–8, 75, 94, 123, 147, 156, 160–1, 166, 184–5, 220, 245–6, 333, 340, 381, 394, 402–3, 408, 413, 459–60, 464, 480, 513
Shirayuri University, 137
Showa, 138–9, 141
Shrine of Our Lady of Lavang, 196
Shrine Shinto, 137
shrines, 102, 132, 356, 370, 429–30, 443
Shuang, 285
Siam, 158, 163, 167, 216
Sibu, 217
Sichuan, China, 69, 373
sickness, 172, 230, 338, 340
Sidang Injil Borneo, 215, 331, 367
Siem Reap, 177, 290
Sieng Ang, 179
Sihanoukville, 290
Sikhs, 217, 436, 443, 446
Silang, 357
Silk road, 491
Silva, 255, 258–9, 262
Simalungun, 203–4
Simmons, Duane B., 134
sin, 36, 44, 55–6, 111, 125, 246
Sin, Cardinal, 246
Singapore, 17, 19, 23, 31, 34, 71, 107–8, 134, 180, 182–3, 192, 212, 216, 226, 228, 230, 232, 234, 236, 248, 276–7, 288, 295–9, 301–3, 305, 308, 314, 319, 323, 326–8, 332, 338, 342–3, 357, 384, 387, 390–1, 397–8, 402, 413, 425, 434–5, 439–41, 444, 447–8, 452–3, 455, 460, 467, 473–4, 479, 486, 488–91
Singapore Bible College, 233, 327
Singapore Management University, 460
singing, 97, 159, 232, 259, 279, 340, 358, 365, 429
Sinicisation, 62, 66, 73, 306–7, 474
Sino-American Mutual Defense Treaty, 103
Sino-British Joint Declaration, 76
Sino-Japanese War, 76, 78, 139, 272
Sinuiju, 116
Sinulog, 380
Siong, Wong Nai, 213
Siraya, 99
Sirikul, 164
Sister Cyril, 214
Sisters of St Paul, 77
Sisters of the Precious Blood, 80
Sitiawan, 214
Sixth Party Congress, 113
Skype, 301
slavery, 220, 416, 420
slums, 474
Smith, George, 270, 272
social action, 33, 250, 320
Social Service Department, 48

Social Weather Stations, 251
socialism, 45, 298–9, 308
Society for the Propagation of the Gospel (SPG), 146, 269–70, 273, 276–7
Society of Jesus, 138, 375
Society of St Vincent, 80, 220
Society of the Holy Cross, 275
Society of the Sacred Mission, 274
sociology, 502
Soegijapranata, Archbishop Albertus, 21, 206–7
Soekarno, 201–2, 210
Sœurs, 137
Soibada, 255–6, 265
soldiers, 145, 255, 292, 467
Solnae, 119
Solomon, Robert, 227–8, 231, 298
Solor, 254–5
Somalis, 502
Somang Church, 307
Son, Tay, 188
Song, Choan Seng, 106, 354, 377, 379, 401, 420, 447
Song (Sung), John, 67, 331, 371, 377, 383
Song Shangjie, 377
Songbun, 112
Songs of Canaan, 300
Sonne, Son, 177, 179
Sophia University, 138, 142
Souphine, 168–9
South Africa, 249
South Asia, 288, 325, 327–8, 378, 441
South China Boat Mission, 83
South China Mission, 270
South China Sea, 238, 393, 492
South Sudan, 119, 377
South Sumatra, 466
South Vietnam, 178, 189, 195, 232
Southern Baptist Convention, 511
Soviet Union, 190, 192, 468–9
Sowards, Erville, 147
Sowards, Genevieve, 147
Spain, 33, 77, 87, 133, 275, 316–17, 380, 467
Spanish, language, 99–100, 142–3, 188, 249, 316–17, 352–3, 356, 370, 380, 382, 387, 413, 416, 466–7, 479
spirituality, 43, 60–2, 64, 67, 142–3, 206, 233, 243, 277, 294, 301, 304, 314, 321–2, 325, 336, 340, 346–7, 366, 370, 380, 400, 410–11, 448, 458, 470
Spivak, Gayatri Chakravorty, 465
Sri Lanka, 213, 288, 300, 420
Stahl, Max, 259
Stallybrass, Edward, 96
Stanton, Vincent John, 272
Starr, Chloë F., 378
statistics, 78, 82–3, 121, 176, 215, 242, 258, 388, 495, 502, 504–5, 515–16
stewardship, 302

Stieng, 193
stigma, 20, 22, 61, 398, 423
students, 46–7, 49, 71, 85, 95, 110, 135, 153, 160–1, 163–5, 177–8, 182–6, 204, 207, 209, 219, 234, 239, 243, 245, 326–7, 333, 344–5, 365, 367, 426, 443, 448–9, 451, 460, 484, 488
sub-Saharan Africa, 386
suffering, 30, 32, 57–8, 63–5, 67–8, 73, 103, 107, 111, 122, 140, 142–3, 150, 230, 259–60, 308, 314, 317, 333, 346, 354, 372, 380, 396, 416, 420, 431, 469, 482
Suga, 143
Sugiri, Lambertus, 339
Sugirtharajah, R. S., 420, 472
Suharto, 207–10, 432
suicide, 301, 409
suicide bombing, 409
Sukarno, 384
Sulawesi, 200, 305, 339
Sultan of Brunei, 238
Sulu, 29
Sumatra, 200, 203–4, 210, 291, 433, 466
Sun, Yeow, 232
Sundanese, 203
Sunday Mass, 343, 358, 456
Sunday school, 168, 231
Sunflower Movement, 307
Sunni(s), 212, 238, 439
Sunquist, Scott, 296
superstition, 188, 319
Supreme Bishop, 382
Supreme Court, 128, 208
Surabaya, Indonesia, 207, 305–6, 341, 409, 433, 487
Surjadinata, 258
Surugadai, 137
surveillance, 70, 112, 430, 473
survey(s), 43, 97, 111–12, 132–3, 179, 207, 251, 283, 388, 453, 480, 488, 502, 504–6, 513, 515–17
survival, 39, 72, 147, 304, 347, 473
Susilo Bambang Yudhoyono, 207, 432
sustainability, 422, 485
Swaratama, 206
Sweden, 502
switching (religious), 513, 516
Switzerland, 168, 182
swords, 246
Sydney, Australia, 233, 256
symbols, 263, 314, 369, 402, 409, 431, 469
syncretism, 24, 49, 128, 210, 319
Synod of Manila, 352
Synod of the Ecumenical Patriarchate, 288
synods, 102, 104
Syria, 17, 92, 145, 217, 235, 291, 352
Syriac, 17, 92, 352
Syriam, 145
Syrian Orthodox Church, 217
Syro-Phoenician, 421

T'ang dynasty, 352
Taberd, Jean-Louis, 195
Tabernacle of God, 344
Tagalog, 25, 143, 353–4, 380, 456–7
Tai, Masakazu, 273
Tai, Northern, 99
tai, Southern, 99–100
Tainan, 272–3
Taipei, Taiwan, 272–3, 340, 360, 375, 459, 469
Taipei Truth Church, 340
Taisho Democracy, 138
Taiwan, 19, 21, 25, 27, 31–2, 47, 49, 60, 68, 87–8, 102, 104, 106, 108, 110, 273, 278, 288, 295, 299–302, 305, 307, 311, 327, 340, 358, 373, 376–7, 383–5, 387, 389, 395, 397, 401, 407, 413, 416, 426, 438, 441, 443, 446–7, 451, 453, 455–7, 459, 465–6, 469–70, 473–4, 479, 483–4, 486, 490–1
Taiwan Inter-faith Foundation, 446
Taizhou, 69
Takai, Archpriest Anthony, 287
Takeo Province, 182
Takhmau, 179
Takizawa, 142
Talitha Kum, 416
Tamil(s), 213, 216, 218, 225, 240, 362, 392
Tamsui, 466
Tan, Chee Khoon, 220
Tan, Kang-San, 281
Taoism, 15, 20, 26, 48, 84, 90, 217, 328, 370, 387, 420, 426, 438, 446, 453, 465–6, 479, 486
Tarutung District, 204
Tasi-tolu, 260
Tau, Vung, 290, 342
Taungoo, 145
Taveira, Fr. Antonio, 254
Tayal, 108
Taylor, Charles, 24
Taylor, Hudson, 67, 270
teachers, 92, 98, 140, 182, 256, 303, 313, 426, 432, 491
Teatro Ekumenikal, 301
technology, 79, 131, 165, 195, 248, 397, 455, 471, 489, 491, 513
Tedim Baptist Church, 338
television, 29, 94, 123, 155, 159, 227, 244, 249, 301, 346, 359–60, 489
Temple, Nicholas, 286
temples, 17, 20, 115, 130, 161, 231, 370–1
Tenaganita, 220
Tendero, Efraim, 324
Tenth National Christian Conference, 50
Terminal High Altitude Area Defense, 128
Ternate, 204
Territorial Abbey of Tokwon, 119
terrorism, 235, 321, 400, 411, 487, 492
Terry, Thomas, 301
testimonies, 63, 157, 186, 341, 347, 372, 481
Tetum, 254, 258, 262

Thai, 17, 19, 25, 155–66, 168, 170, 288–9, 329, 358, 395–6, 398, 471
Thai Christian Students Association, 160
Thailand, 17, 25, 30–1, 33–4, 71–2, 109, 158, 160, 162, 164, 167, 170–1, 179–80, 216, 232, 249, 277, 283, 288–90, 295–7, 302, 304–5, 310–11, 326, 328, 331, 338, 342, 358, 364–5, 379, 387, 395, 402, 407, 413, 416, 421, 425, 434, 436, 443–5, 447, 452–3, 471, 479–81, 486, 488, 490
Thailand Baptist Convention, 163–4
Thailand Bible Society, 160, 163, 165
Than, Van, 188
Thanlyin, 145
Thapa, Agatha, 169
Thatana, 430
theologians, 19, 120, 125–6, 130, 142, 251, 297, 318, 321, 327, 337, 354, 377, 379–80, 387, 391, 396, 402, 414, 416–17, 419–20, 422–3, 447–8, 464, 470
theological education, 45, 47, 49, 78, 97–8, 101, 182, 196, 233, 297, 376, 421
theology, 19, 30–1, 44–7, 49–51, 53, 61, 64–5, 67–9, 89, 101, 103, 105–6, 108, 122, 125–6, 138–9, 142, 165, 171, 198, 212, 219, 227, 231, 233–4, 244, 246, 249, 262–3, 277, 296, 303, 310, 319–22, 325, 327–8, 332, 341, 346, 376, 378, 380, 384, 386–8, 391, 397, 400–1, 405–7, 411, 418, 420, 422, 447, 468–72, 490, 510
theory, 28, 99, 233–4, 244–5, 293, 507
Theravada Buddhism, 387, 443, 479
Thien An Monastery, 428
Thieu Tri, 188
Thomas, Apostle, 15, 19, 141–2, 276, 301, 375
Three-Self Patriotic Movement (TSPM), 22, 39, 64, 75, 271, 299, 329, 378, 388, 426, 468
Thua Thien-Hue Province, 428
Tian Feng, 47
Tiananmen Square, 63, 69
Tianjin, China, 284
Tibet, 30, 69, 387, 424, 442, 483
Tibetan Buddhist(s), 30, 69, 424, 442, 483
Tikhomirov, Sergii, 292
Tikhon of San Francisco, Archbishop, 291
Tim-Oi, Florence Li, 89, 272
Timor-Leste, 22, 26, 34–5, 88, 256, 258, 260, 262, 275, 288, 291, 295, 302, 310, 313, 321, 341, 364, 381, 387, 396, 413, 416, 425, 434, 440, 454, 467, 479, 482–3
Ting, Bishop K. H., 44, 271, 378, 384
Tinh, Ha, 428
Toba Batak, 204
Tokugawa, 135
Tokyo Imperial University, 138
Tokyo Orthodox Seminary, 287
Tokyo, Japan, 137–8, 273–4, 286–7, 292, 345, 488
tolerance, 40, 129, 201, 207–8, 210, 330, 430, 443

tombs, 319, 356
Tong, Stephen, 68
tongues, 30, 193, 219, 296, 335–6, 339, 345, 365, 508–10
Tonkin, 187
torture, 57, 135, 142, 256, 310, 314, 427, 429
Touch Community Service, 228
Toungngu Diocese, 148
tourism, 428, 436, 451
Toyotomi, Hideyoshi, 133
trade, 74, 87, 92, 99, 110, 126, 133, 254, 330, 376, 387, 425, 438, 463, 466–7, 474, 479–80
tradition(s), 16, 18, 27–9, 32, 42, 61, 63–4, 66–9, 72–3, 76, 81–4, 88, 95–6, 107, 114, 119–20, 123, 125, 127–8, 155–6, 165, 191, 195, 200, 202, 206–7, 209–10, 226, 232–3, 240, 245, 247, 254, 261, 263–5, 269, 274, 278–9, 286, 291, 293, 297, 299, 301, 304, 317, 319, 332, 341, 346, 351–71, 373, 375–7, 385–7, 401, 406, 409, 420, 438, 447, 452–3, 455–7, 461, 472, 482–3, 485, 495, 505, 508–10
trafficking, 165, 220, 415–16, 484
training, 42, 45, 48–50, 54, 57, 59, 61, 93, 95, 97–8, 101, 115, 152, 160, 165, 171–2, 177, 179–80, 182–6, 217, 220, 234, 248–9, 256, 274, 277, 293, 311, 322, 327, 332–3, 340, 448–9, 452, 456
trances, 108
Trans World Radio, 181
Transitional Justice Commission, 109
trauma, 402, 404, 409–10
treaties, 381, 463
Treaty of Amity, 134
Treaty of Nanjing, 74, 271
tribal(s), 155, 159, 161, 172, 182, 193, 218, 300, 331–2, 392, 395–6, 398, 439, 464, 466
Trinh, 187–8
Trinity Christian Centre, 232
Trinity Theological College, 228, 233, 277, 297, 328
Trollope, Bishop Mark, 275
True Jesus Church, 76, 101, 103–4, 108, 217, 336, 340, 383, 395
Truku, 104
Truth Lutheran Church, 108
Try Hoc, 177
Tsilis, 288
Tsukamoto, Toraji, 140
Tsuwano, 135
Tu, Han Mac, 195
Tu Duc, 188
Tulu, India, 215
Tunis, Tunisia, 263
Turkey, 16
Tuva, 92

Uber, 482
Uchimura, Kanzo, 20, 136–8, 140–1
Uemura, Masahisa, 135

Uganda, 511
Ukrainians, 288, 292
Ulaanbaatar, Mongolia, 92
Ulsan, South Korea, 293
Umbrella Movement, 444
ummah, 413
Un, Uong, 177
underground church, 32, 53–4, 56–9, 71, 76, 113, 117, 179, 312, 388, 482
Underwood, Horace Grant, 120
unemployment, 34
UNESCO World Heritage Site, 87
Unification Church, 444
Union of Soviet Socialist Republics (USSR), 288–9, 390, 470
Union Theological Seminary, 46
Unitarian(s), 177, 417
United Bible Societies, 96
United Church of Christ, 102, 139, 274, 328, 468
United Nations Children's Fund (UNICEF), 181, 503
United Nations General Assembly, 256
United Nations High Commissioner for Refugees (UNHCR), 143
United Nations, 32, 106, 143, 256, 260, 387, 495, 501, 503–5, 516
United States (USA), 18, 21, 27, 31, 33, 77, 94, 118, 120, 122–3, 134, 149, 153, 170, 177, 179, 182–3, 194–5, 197, 214, 244–5, 248–9, 258, 269–70, 275, 278, 287, 318, 335, 343, 427–8, 434, 452, 460, 467, 470
unity, 32, 42, 44–5, 50, 57–8, 61–2, 77, 98, 123, 130, 143, 157, 180, 200, 202, 210–11, 221, 223, 259, 299, 330, 346, 382, 392, 405, 418, 427, 442, 470
Universal Declaration of Human Rights (UDHR), 501, 504
University of Indonesia, 209
University of Leuven, 61
University of Malaya, 448
unregistered church, 367, 370, 372–3, 389
Upper Burma, 147
urbanisation, 43, 49, 63, 104, 303–4, 308, 394, 397–8
Uyghur, 285, 426, 442

validity, 27, 56, 434
values, 45, 62, 79, 90, 107, 121, 135, 150, 153, 182, 184, 202, 206, 209, 258, 260–1, 263–5, 303, 360, 364, 370, 391, 415–17, 419, 438, 444, 447–8, 452, 463, 465, 472, 482
Van Lith, Franciscus Georgius Josephus, 206
Van Thio, Henry, 21, 150
Van Thuan, Archbishop Nguyen, 195
Vancouver, Canada, 68
variable(s), 503, 512
Vasconcelos, Vincente, 257–8
Vasily, Father, 285, 291

Vasquez, Amelia, 421
Vatican, 18, 21–2, 51–8, 60–1, 65, 76, 82, 84, 105, 175–6, 189–90, 196–8, 206, 216, 218, 262–3, 265, 312, 315, 318–19, 321, 342, 354, 359, 389, 417, 421, 429, 465, 470, 487
Vatican Radio, 359
Vaz, Father Simon, 204
Velarde, Brother Mike, 31, 245–6, 250, 343
Vencer, Jun, 330
veneration, 263, 358, 368–9
Verbeck, Guido H. F., 134
Veritas, 56, 244, 359
vernacular(s), 18, 60, 353–4, 373
vestments, 230
Vicar Apostolic of Japan, 135
vicariates, 138, 163, 167, 255, 311, 314–15
victims, 69, 207, 209, 314, 373, 416, 420
Victory Christian Fellowship, 243, 245, 248
Victory Family Centre, 232
video, 301, 360, 486
Vientiane, Laos, 167, 171
Vietnam, 16–17, 20–1, 23, 27–8, 31, 34, 88, 143, 167–70, 178–9, 183–4, 188, 190, 192, 194, 196, 198, 232, 249, 277, 283, 288, 291, 295–6, 301–6, 312–14, 318, 327, 329–30, 342, 352–4, 357, 359, 364, 375, 377, 387, 389, 396–8, 403, 413, 415, 425, 427–9, 436, 451–3, 456–7, 459, 466–7, 470–1, 473, 479–83, 485–8, 490
Vietnam War, 170, 193
Vietnamese Episcopal Conference, 190
Vietnamese War of Independence, 193
vigils, 485
Vila Verde, 257–8
Villanueva, Eddie, 246–7, 345, 455
Villanueva, Joel, 247
Vineyard Church, 335
violence, 35–6, 207, 305, 310–11, 328, 330, 393–4, 396, 400, 402–4, 407, 409–11, 421, 423, 430, 435–6, 444–5, 486–9
Virgem Peregrina, 264
Virgin Mary, 35, 251, 264
virtue, 207, 251, 415, 512
Visayan, 343, 380
vishnu, 319
Vladimir, Archbishop, 286
Vo Van Lac, 193
vocations, 54, 59
Voice of New Life Radio, 181
Volga, Russia, 96
volunteers, 148, 343, 373
Vong, 176

Wagner, Peter, 335
Wahid Institute, 202, 207
Walters, Albert, 447
Wang, Hsien-Chih, 106
Wang, Mingdao, 64–5, 67, 383
Wang, Weifan, 378
Wang, Yi, 69

Wang, Zuoan, 285
war, 39, 74, 76–8, 80, 101–2, 104–5, 108, 112, 121, 130, 133, 139–42, 146, 170, 189, 193, 205, 215, 219, 246, 256, 269–70, 272, 274–5, 277, 279, 287, 292, 307, 314, 324, 328, 330, 341, 383–4, 387, 389, 393, 397, 400, 409, 421, 434, 438, 443, 451, 463, 467–71, 479
Warri, Nigeria, 133, 180, 246
Wat Koh Church, 159
Wat Phnom, 180
Water Buffalo Theology, 379, 401
water, 21, 24, 30, 36, 116, 150, 246, 251, 351, 370–1, 379, 401
Wati, Imachaba Bendang, 207
Watson, Burton, 15
Way of the Cross, 67, 70, 73, 333
wealth, 31–2, 90, 198, 238, 250, 308, 387, 394, 397, 399, 453, 473, 490
WEC International, 326
weddings, 16, 18–19, 171–2
Wednesday, 123
Wellesley College, 220
Wenzhou, China, 20, 23, 63–4, 66–7, 69–70, 306, 329
Wesley Methodist Church, 232
Wesleyan Methodist Mission, 76
Western Europe, 133
Westernisation, 137, 302
White Rajah of Sarawak, 213
White Terror, 109, 376
Widodo, President Joko, 432
widows, 183
Willekens, Monsignor Petrus, 205
Williams, Channing Moore, 134, 273
Wilson, Daniel, 127
Wilson, Woodrow, 127
Wimber, John, 335
Win, General Ne, 150
wisdom, 30, 72, 265, 335, 351, 355, 361, 508
witnessing, 19, 308, 347, 400
women, 16, 21, 33, 43, 79, 97, 101, 108, 110, 114, 120–1, 123–5, 129, 135, 143, 147, 162, 182, 201, 207–8, 220, 247–8, 255, 264–5, 274, 278, 295–6, 301–3, 313, 325, 343–5, 358–9, 362, 373, 377, 379–80, 393, 403–5, 407–9, 414–23, 452, 459, 466, 472, 484, 488, 505–6
Won Buddhism, 128
Woolf, Virginia, 421
Word Harvest, 299
World Alliance of Reformed Churches (WARC), 106
World Bank, 31, 304
World Christian Database (WCD), 495, 501
World Christian Encyclopedia (WCE), 516
World Communion of Reformed Churches (WCRC), 49, 302
World Council of Churches (WCC), 49, 64, 104–5, 125, 181, 296, 307, 323, 354, 369–70, 376, 393, 401, 405, 448

World Day of Prayer, 181
World Evangelical Alliance (WEA), 49, 126, 180, 323, 326
World Human Rights Day, 106
World Missionary Conference (Edinburgh 1910), 138, 382
World Presbyterian Alliance, 104
World Vision International, 161, 165, 177
worldview(s), 25, 44, 101, 157, 230, 244, 306, 318, 320, 344, 351, 481
Worldwide Evangelisation Crusade (WEC), 326
worship, 17–18, 22–3, 25, 27, 29–30, 40, 42–3, 51, 53–4, 58–60, 63, 66–7, 90, 96–7, 112–14, 116–17, 123–4, 127, 129, 134–5, 137, 148, 157, 161–2, 164, 171, 173, 177, 184–6, 193, 196, 207, 210, 215, 218, 227, 230–1, 233, 239, 243, 249, 259, 269, 271, 275, 278, 290, 293, 301, 314, 317, 336–7, 339–42, 345–6, 366, 370, 381, 386, 397, 409–11, 429–31, 434–5, 459, 469, 474, 481, 483, 486–7
worshippers, 67, 135, 137, 215, 231, 259, 340
Wu, Bishop John B., 85
Wuhan, China, 58
Wujing, Sishu, 376
Wuzong, 20

Xavier, Francis, 133, 204, 353, 375
Xian, 71, 465
Xiao Qun (Little Flock), 383
Xiaomin, Lü, 30, 67, 300
Xie, Moses, 64
Xieng Khouang Province, 169–70
Xin'an, China, 74
Xinjiang, China, 30, 69, 72, 284–5, 426
Xueyuan of Baoding, Bishop Fan, 56

Yamaguchi, Satoko, 422
Yamamuro, Gunpei, 140
Yanaihara, Tadao, 140
Yang, Fenggang, 329
Yangon (Rangoon), Myanmar, 149, 278, 400
Yap (Micronesia), 235
Yasukuni Shrine, 390
Yemen, 130
Yeo, K. K., 377
Yertuntsiin Ezen, 96
Yi-Han, Alexis Kim, 292
Yiguandao, 446
Yihetuan (Boxer) Rebellion, 284
Yinshang house churches, 68
Yizhou, Father Andrew Zhao, 105
yoga, 136
Yogyakarta, Indonesia, 205, 207, 209, 424
Yoido Full Gospel Church, 108, 121, 324, 340, 345, 360, 398, 404
Yokohama, Japan, 135, 273–4
Yongjia County, 23

Yonsei University, 120, 130
Yoshimitsu, Yoshihiko, 141
Young Men's Christian Association (YMCA), 79–80
Young Women's Christian Association (YWCA), 79–80
Young, Brigham, 182
Youngnak Church, 307
youth, 49, 57, 69, 88, 93–4, 97, 135, 152, 160, 164, 177, 179, 183, 201, 220, 231–2, 235–6, 252, 263, 279, 287, 299, 301, 325–6, 359, 403, 410, 426, 448–9, 457, 481–2, 487, 490
Youth With A Mission (YWAM), 97, 179, 299
YouTube, 159–60, 301
YouVersion, 165
Yu-Ping, Cardinal, 105
Yu, Gwan-sun, 121
Yuan, Allen, 64

Yugoslavia, 54, 57
Yunnan Province, 395
Yuttasak, Reverend, 164

Zen Buddhism, 15, 51, 85, 470
Zending, 204
Zhangmeizhichuan, 300
Zhao, Peter, 61
Zhao, Simon, 72
Zhao, Zichen, 378
Zhejiang Province, 20, 23, 64, 271, 329, 427, 473
Zhen Yesu Jiaohui (True Jesus Church), 383
Zhiwen, Ji, 383
Zhongguohua, 45
Zhonghua Jidu Jiaohui, 382
Zoroastrian(s), 20
Zschech, Darlene, 233